Praise for *Bacardi and the Long Fight for Cuba*

"It's hard to imagine that any [Cuban history] is as enjoyable. [Gjelten's] book is as smooth and refreshing as a well-made daiquiri."
—Barry Gewen, *The New York Times*

"Absorbing familial and political history . . . at once a colorful family saga and a carefully researched corrective to caricatures of decadent prerevolutionary Cuba and the fifty-year disaster of Fidel Castro's rule."
—Linda Robinson, *The Washington Post*

"A pistol-packing salsa dance of modern history . . . On one level, this book is the story of a great merchant family and its deeply intertwined relationship with a mysterious Cuban island nation. But it is also a story of the still resonating conflicts between capitalism and communism, nationalism and imperialism, and freedom and tyranny."
—Harry Hurt III, *The New York Times*

"Exhaustively researched, succeeds in painting a vivid portrait of the company's early, scrappy years and its prominent role in the fight against Spanish rule. Gjelten provides a fascinating look at how the company built itself into the multinational giant it has become."
—Randy Kennedy, *The New York Times* Sunday Book Review

"A gem . . . Highly readable, impeccably researched . . . There may not be a better tale than the story of the Bacardi family to convey the broader, messier, and infinitely sadder story of Cuba. Gjelten has managed to capture in a single book almost all that one needs to know of Cuban history. Superb reporting, exquisite storytelling."   —Mirta Ojito, *Columbia Journalism Review*

"With thorough reporting and an eye for rich, often quirky detail, Tom Gjelten traces the story of the Bacardi family, whose product helped shape Cuba's soul until Fidel Castro nationalized its company's facilities in 1960."
—Will Weissert, Associated Press

"An appealingly smooth and colorful history—thorough and open-minded."
—Peter Lewis, *San Francisco Chronicle*

"A thoughtful, thorough piece of reporting. Tom Gjelten subtly and skillfully details the saga of the Bacardi family. You may never look at a mojito or a daiquiri quite the same way." —Peter M. Gianotti, *Newsday*

"A thoroughly researched and lively history of the family-owned drinks business, currently the third largest liquor producer in the world."
—Christopher Silvester, *Spectator Business* (London)

"By the turn of the century, as Gjelten lucidly recounts, the distilling operation that Facundo [Bacardi] had begun in a shed was among the brands most closely identified with Cuba, and the Bacardis became inextricably entangled with the nation's history." —*The New Yorker*

"Gjelten leaves nothing unrecorded in his objective, warts and all, history of an unusual company, illustrating Cuban history without the canonizations by leftist apologists for Fidel and the demonizations by conservative Cuban exiles and their friends." —Ian Williams, *World Policy Journal*

"An engaging portrait of a vibrant though often tragic national trajectory."
—Michael Deibert, *The Miami Herald*

PENGUIN BOOKS

BACARDI AND THE LONG FIGHT FOR CUBA

Tom Gjelten is a veteran correspondent for National Public Radio on international issues and a regular panelist on the PBS program *Washington Week*. His reporting from Bosnia won him George Polk and Robert F. Kennedy awards. He is the author of *Sarajevo Daily: A City and Its Newspaper Under Siege*. He lives in Arlington, Virginia, with his family.

BACARDI

and the

Long Fight for Cuba

THE BIOGRAPHY OF A CAUSE

❧

Tom Gjelten

PENGUIN BOOKS

PENGUIN BOOKS

Published by the Penguin Group

Penguin Group (USA) Inc., 375 Hudson Street, New York, New York 10014, U.S.A. • Penguin Group (Canada), 90 Eglinton Avenue East, Suite 700, Toronto, Ontario, Canada M4P 2Y3 (a division of Pearson Penguin Canada Inc.) • Penguin Books Ltd, 80 Strand, London WC2R 0RL, England • Penguin Ireland, 25 St Stephen's Green, Dublin 2, Ireland (a division of Penguin Books Ltd) • Penguin Group (Australia), 250 Camberwell Road, Camberwell, Victoria 3124, Australia (a division of Pearson Australia Group Pty Ltd) • Penguin Books India Pvt Ltd, 11 Community Centre, Panchsheel Park, New Delhi – 110 017, India • Penguin Group (NZ), 67 Apollo Drive, Rosedale, North Shore 0632, New Zealand (a division of Pearson New Zealand Ltd) • Penguin Books (South Africa) (Pty) Ltd, 24 Sturdee Avenue, Rosebank, Johannesburg 2196, South Africa

Penguin Books Ltd, Registered Offices: 80 Strand, London WC2R 0RL, England

First published in the United States of America by Viking Penguin,
a member of Penguin Group (USA) Inc. 2008
Published in Penguin Books 2009

10

Copyright © Tom Gjelten, 2008
All rights reserved

Photograph credits appear on page 413.

THE LIBRARY OF CONGRESS HAS CATALOGED THE HARDCOVER EDITION AS FOLLOWS:
Gjelten, Tom.
Bacardi and the long fight for Cuba : the biography of a cause / by Tom Gjelten.
p. cm.
Includes bibliographical references and index.
ISBN 978-0-670-01978-6 (hc.)
ISBN 978-0-14-311632-5 (pbk.)
1. Bacardi Corporation (Puerto Rico)—History.   2. Rum industry—Cuba—History.
3. Cuba—History—Autonomy and independence movements.   I. Title.
HD9394.C94B334   2008
338.7'66359097491—dc22   2008015565

Printed in the United States of America

Designed by Carla Bolte • Set in Aldus
Family tree by Jeffrey L. Ward

For Jake, Greta, and Martha

CONTENTS

A NOTE TO THE READER

Cubans follow the Spanish-language custom of using both paternal and maternal surnames. Emilio Bacardi's six children with his first wife, María Lay, were named Bacardi Lay, while his four daughters with Elvira Cape were named Bacardi Cape. In everyday usage Cubans normally drop their mother's name unless it is needed for identification purposes. Facundo Bacardi Lay used his maternal surname to distinguish himself from his cousin Facundo Bacardi Gaillard, his uncle Facundo Bacardi Moreau, or his grandfather Facundo Bacardi Massó. But Fidel Castro Ruz is simply Fidel Castro to most of the world.

I have used Spanish spellings for all names in this book with the notable exception of Bacardi, which in Spanish is accented on the final syllable and spelled Bacardí. The rum brand name, however, has become so anglicized that the accent is dropped in contemporary English usage and among most U.S.-based members of the Bacardi family. For consistency purposes, I use "Bacardi" without the accent throughout the book. I apologize to those family members who maintain the old spelling.

THE BACARDI FAMILY TREE

Magín Bacardi Massó (1802–1886)

Juan Bacardi Massó (1807–1845)

José Bacardi Massó (1823–1907)

Facundo Bacardi Massó (1813–1886) m. Amalia Moreau (1823–1897)

   Emilio Bacardi Moreau (1844–1922) m. (1) María Lay (1852–1885)

      Emilio (Emilito) Bacardi Lay

      Daniel Bacardi Lay

      José Bacardi Lay m. Zenaida Rosell

         Zenaida Bacardi Rosell m. José Argamasilla

            León Argamasilla Bacardi m. Magdalena S. Giro

               Pepín Argamasilla

            José (Tito) Argamasilla Bacardi

            Amaro Argamasilla Bacardi

         Emilio Bacardi Rosell m. Josefina González

            José Bacardi González

      Facundo Bacardi Lay m. Caridad (Cachita) Rosell

         Daniel Bacardi Rosell m. Graciela Bravo

            9 children, incl. Facundo Bacardi Bravo

         Ana María Bacardi Rosell m. Adolfo Comas

           Adolfo Comas Bacardi

           Toten Comas Bacardi

           Lucía Comas Bacardi

           Marlena Comas Bacardi m. Jorge Rodríguez

           Amelia Comas Bacardi m. Robert O'Brien

      María (Mariíta) Bacardi Lay m. Pedro Lay Lombard

         María Emilia Lay Bacardi m. Robert Williams

            3 children, including Elsie Williams

         Ernesto Lay Bacardi

         Eduardo Lay Bacardi

         Pedro Emilio Lay Bacardi

      Carmen Bacardi Lay m. Gustavo Rodríguez

         Clara Rodríguez Bacardi m. Ignacio Carrera-Justiz

           Francisco Carrera-Justiz

           Clara María Carrera-Justiz (del Valle)

         Carmina Rodríguez Bacardi

         Gustavo Rodríguez Bacardi m. Clotilde Gispert

           Gustavo (Gustavín) Rodríguez Gispert

           Gilda Rodríguez Gispert

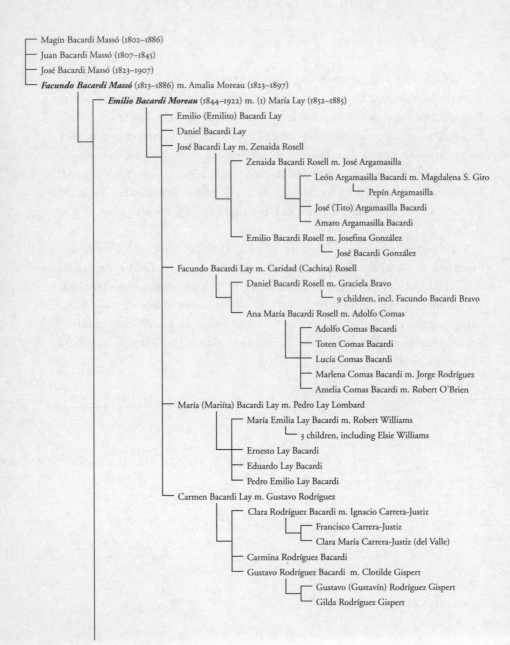

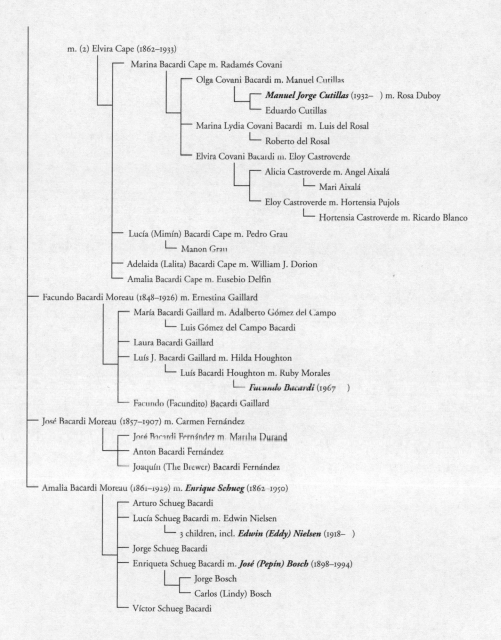

m. (2) Elvira Cape (1862–1933)

Marina Bacardi Cape m. Radamés Covani

Olga Covani Bacardi m. Manuel Cutillas

Manuel Jorge Cutillas (1932–   ) m. Rosa Duboy

Eduardo Cutillas

Marina Lydia Covani Bacardi m. Luis del Rosal

Roberto del Rosal

Elvira Covani Bacardi m. Eloy Castroverde

Alicia Castroverde m. Angel Aixalá

Mari Aixalá

Eloy Castroverde m. Hortensia Pujols

Hortensia Castroverde m. Ricardo Blanco

Lucía (Mimín) Bacardi Cape m. Pedro Grau

Manon Grau

Adelaida (Lalita) Bacardi Cape m. William J. Dorion

Amalia Bacardi Cape m. Eusebio Delfin

Facundo Bacardi Moreau (1848–1926) m. Ernestina Gaillard

María Bacardi Gaillard m. Adalberto Gómez del Campo

Luis Gómez del Campo Bacardi

Laura Bacardi Gaillard

Luís J. Bacardi Gaillard m. Hilda Houghton

Luís Bacardi Houghton m. Ruby Morales

Facundo Bacardi (1967   )

Facundo (Facundito) Bacardi Gaillard

José Bacardi Moreau (1857–1907) m. Carmen Fernández

José Bacardi Fernández m. Martha Durand

Anton Bacardi Fernández

Joaquín (The Brewer) Bacardi Fernández

Amalia Bacardi Moreau (1861–1929) m. ***Enrique Schueg*** (1862–1950)

Arturo Schueg Bacardi

Lucía Schueg Bacardi m. Edwin Nielsen

3 children, incl. ***Edwin (Eddy) Nielsen*** (1918–   )

Jorge Schueg Bacardi

Enriqueta Schueg Bacardi m. ***José (Pepín) Bosch*** (1898–1994)

Jorge Bosch

Carlos (Lindy) Bosch

Víctor Schueg Bacardi

Bacardi chairmen in ***boldface italics***.

BACARDI

and the

Long Fight for Cuba

Preface

A bottle of white Bacardi rum sold in the United States bears a small logo—mysteriously, a bat—and a label that says "Established 1862." Just above the date are the words "PUERTO RICAN RUM." There is no mention of Cuba.

The Bacardi distillery in San Juan is the largest in the world, but the Bacardis are not from Puerto Rico. This family company for nearly a century was Cuban, *cubanísima* in fact—Cuban to the *n*th degree. In the middle of the nineteenth century, Don Facundo Bacardi, the company founder and family patriarch, pioneered Cuban-style rum, lighter and drier than the rough spirit that preceded it. Bacardi rum became the drink of choice on the island just as Cuba was becoming a nation. Bacardi sons and daughters were famous for their patriotism, standing up first against Spanish tyranny and then, in the next century, against the island's homegrown dictators. The family company played another supporting role as Cuba established its cultural identity, becoming the leading corporate patron of Cuban baseball and salsa music. Bacardi was Ernest Hemingway's rum and the rum of the Cuban casino crowd. When Fidel Castro launched his uprising in the mountains outside Santiago de Cuba, their hometown, the Bacardis cheered him on. They did not abandon Castro so much as they were abandoned by him; they left Cuba only after the revolutionary government expropriated their rum business. Nearly fifty years later, the family name is still revered on the island, and the Bacardis are thinking about making rum there again.

Over many tellings, the Cuba story has hardened around a few stale themes—Havana in its debauched heyday or Fidel Castro and his dour revolution—and it has lost much of its vitality and wholeness. This book originated in my search for a new narrative, with new Cuban characters and a plot that does justice to this island that produced the conga line and "Guantanamera" as well as Che Guevara's five-year plans. I have tried to give a nuanced view of the nation's experience over the last century and a half. Cuban history was not preordained. There were choices made and paths not taken, and the men and women who were excluded and then exiled deserve to have their contributions recognized, if only to understand why so many became so angry. The Bacardi saga serves all these purposes.

For Cubans, patriotism began with the effort of poets and intellectuals to define the idea of a distinctly *Cuban* people out of the mix of Europeans, Africans, and natives who inhabited the island. Cuba then needed to free itself from three centuries of harsh Spanish rule and suffocating U.S. attention and become a sovereign, viable, and honorable country. Given the island's cultural mix and plantation-based social structure, this fight necessarily incorporated a struggle for racial equality and economic justice, but it cannot be reduced to a story that ends inevitably with Fidel Castro's socialist revolution. Other threads can guide us, such as that of the Bacardi family in the eastern city of Santiago de Cuba, the cradle of Cuban nationalism.

There was a time when no name in Santiago carried more prestige. Emilio Bacardi, the son of Don Facundo, spent much of his adult life conspiring against Spanish rule and later served as Santiago's first Cuban mayor. Emilio's own son Emilito fought heroically in Cuba's war for independence. But the Bacardis were also remembered in Santiago for their class and character. While they lived in elegant homes, rode in chauffeured carriages, and sent their children to exclusive private schools, they were also known as good Santiago citizens, generous and warmhearted and fair. And they loved to party. The Bacardis probably contributed more than any other local family to Santiago's reputation as a playful, joyous city with a vibrant nightlife. There was no festival in Santiago without Bacardi rum.

In Fidel Castro's revised version of Cuban history, the era before his revolution was characterized mainly by decadence, and the country's elites were corrupt. The Bacardis are barely mentioned, because their record of patriotism and integrity does not match the Castro stereotype. Their family business was widely recognized as among the best-run enterprises in Cuba, and the company management was known for progressive policies and good labor relations. The Bacardi chairman in the 1950s, José "Pepín" Bosch (married to the founder's granddaughter), served for a time as Cuba's finance minister and broke precedent by pursuing wealthy tax cheats. When Castro went to Washington, D.C., shortly after taking power, Bosch was the one Cuban businessman he brought with him. Their break came after Castro embraced socialism; the Bacardi example had inconveniently demonstrated that there actually were capitalists who could play a responsible role in a democratic Cuba.

I do not, however, propose the Bacardis as would-be saviors of Cuba. The Bacardi story appeals to me in part simply because it contains so many critical but unfamiliar elements of the modern Cuban drama. At every stage of the nation's development over the past century and a half, there is some Bacardi angle, some family member who is a key witness or behind-the-scenes player, or some Bacardi-related episode that epitomizes the historic moment. Countless families in eastern Cuba, for example, shared the Bacardis' Catalan and French roots, and by making and selling rum from Cuban molasses, the family pursued an enterprise tied directly to the country's social and economic development. They came of age with the Cuban nation, and the epic tale of their lives and adventures across several generations features classic Cuban themes: revolution, romance, partying, and intrigue.

After Fidel Castro ordered the confiscation of their property and made clear they and others like them were no longer welcome in the new Cuba, the Bacardis left the island, rebuilding their rum enterprise through their operations in Puerto Rico and Mexico. In exile, they took on a new leadership role, this time as organizers and financiers of the anti-Castro opposition. Fidel lost an important ally when he pushed the Bacardis out, and he gained a determined adversary. The Bacardi-Castro conflict came to symbolize the division of the Cuban nation and the rival claims on the country's history. In the first years of the twenty-first century, when the burning Cuban question was what would follow the Castro era, the Bacardis were once again players. Few products are so associated with Cuba as rum, and the family that made Cuban rum famous was anxious to reclaim a piece of that industry, one of the few on the island with promising growth prospects no matter who was in charge.

There is another story buried in this tale, too. Just as Bacardi history helps explain modern Cuba, the company's Cuba connection helps us trace the evolution of this unique family firm. Bacardi Limited entered the twenty-first century as a genuine multinational, headquartered in Bermuda, with a product line that included whiskey, gin, vermouth, vodka, and tequila, as well as rum. It nevertheless remained a private business wholly owned by a single family still feeling its Cuban identity. Its evolution reflects the strengths—and also the risks and challenges—of a closed, dynastic enterprise in an interconnected global economy. The company's sense of heritage helped it survive after the loss of its Cuban headquarters, but there was inevitable tension between the old political values and the new focus on investment returns. On the eve of the post-Castro era, the Bacardi-Cuba connection set up a test that would reveal how the company had changed over the years: If it went back to Cuba—as it said it would—would it prove to be just another big, soulless corporation vying for a piece of the action, or would it return as the family company playing a patriotic role?

The most distinctive element on a bottle of Bacardi rum is the peculiar icon at the top of the label: a black bat inscribed in a red circle. The bat's wings are outstretched, and its head is turned slightly to one side, highlighting its big eyes and pointy ears. No marketing executive today would allow such a creepy image to identify a popular brand. But the Bacardi symbol dates from an era when bats were viewed more tenderly, and the story of its adoption reflects the company's humble Cuban origins. Santiago was a small city full of merchants, slaves, and traders. Don Facundo's homemade rum was occasionally sold in recycled olive oil containers that came with a picture of a bat on the wax seal. As Bacardi rum gained in popularity, some customers in Santiago referred to it as *el ron del murciélago* (the rum of the bat), and the association took hold.

For good reason. The bat was a symbol of good fortune, and it figured prominently in the heraldry of Don Facundo's native Catalonia. As creatures, bats exemplified the ideal of brotherhood, because they lived and flew together; they symbolized self-confidence, because they could fly in the dark without hitting anything; they stood for discretion, because they kept silent; and they represented faithfulness, because they always returned home.

❧

Chapter 1

Santiago de Cuba

Marina Baja Street began in Santiago's harbor area and ran uphill to the town square, where the Spanish governor had his palace. Along the way, it passed through the commercial district, and every day it was filled with oxcarts, men on horseback, and trains of heavily loaded mules. The stench from the waste was strong and the noise constant: the clop-clop-clop of hooves on cobblestones, vendors hawking their produce, dogs barking, mule drivers shouting at their beasts, Spanish sailors being boisterous.

In those years, the 1860s, the brick and stucco building at 32 Marina Baja, two blocks below the square, belonged to the Bacardi family. A fairly elaborate structure for the neighborhood, it was set back from the street by a portico and a row of curbside columns. A series of arched windows ran along the front. Facundo Bacardi, a Catalan merchant, had started a little rum business there and in an adjoining house in 1862 with the help of a French confectioner and experienced *licorista* named Bouteiller. A short time later, they acquired another distillery near the harbor, but they continued to make rum on Marina Baja Street, and the house at number 32 served as their headquarters.

The young, dark-haired man often seen at a desk near an open window was Emilio Bacardi, Don Facundo's eldest son. Usually he was hunched over his books and papers, deep in concentration, his straight hair falling limply across his forehead. Emilio had cut short his formal schooling in order to help his father in the family business, but he remained a man of letters and ideas. In between his work on Bacardi company accounts and rum sales, he stole opportunities to write essays, study Cuban nationalist poetry, and review submissions for an underground newspaper that he and some friends published in defiance of the Spanish authorities' stringent censorship. Emilio was the first Bacardi born in Cuba, and it was his destiny to be the family patriot.

Always a modest man, Emilio explained his political activism as a product of the epoch into which he was born and the Cuban environment in which he was raised. He grew up at a time when Spanish authorities were relying on brute force to maintain their colonial grip on Cuba and claim its bounty. Slavery was degrading Cuban society. Sugar and coffee planters stood in the way of change, but courageous Cubans were calling for democratic freedoms and an end to the slave trade. It was from Emilio Bacardi's generation that the heroes of Cuban history emerged, and he was among the conspirators for the national cause. Though his father's rum eventually brought him great wealth, he drank only on rare social occasions, and he mostly left it to his younger brother to master the art and craft of distilling. He saw his position in his father's rum business first as a cover for clandestine work on behalf of the Cuban independence movement. Who could know whether the slightly disheveled young man behind the desk was writing receipts for rum buyers or passing coded messages to fellow revolutionaries?

In part, he was inspired by the unique heritage of his hometown. By the time of Emilio's birth in 1844, Santiago de Cuba was well into its fourth century. Christopher Columbus, exploring Cuba's coast in 1494, was the first white man to notice a narrow opening in the Caribbean shoreline and sail inland to discover a deep and well-protected bay, with the rugged green slopes of the Sierra Maestra mountains rising up on all sides from the water's edge. Columbus did not establish a settlement there, however, because the area was so thickly populated by Taino Indians. It was not until 1514 that one of Columbus's original conquistadores, Diego Velázquez, finally subjugated the natives. The Taino leader in the area, a chief named Hatuey, put up fierce resistance until he was finally captured by Velázquez and his men and burned alive at the stake. Bartolomé de las Casas, a Spanish priest traveling with Velázquez, reported that a friar tried in vain to convert Hatuey to Christianity in the moments before his execution, telling the chief that if he accepted the faith he would go to heaven and enjoy eternal life, while if he rejected it he would go to hell and suffer eternal torment.

"Tell me," Hatuey allegedly responded, "are there any Christians in this heaven?"

"Yes," the friar answered, "but only the good ones go there."

"Then I'm not interested," Hatuey said. "Even the best are worthless, and I don't want to go any place where I will meet even a single one."

Emilio Bacardi was fascinated by the story of Hatuey, whom he described in an essay as "the first martyr to die for Cuba." (Years later, when the Bacardis moved into beer brewing, they chose "Hatuey" as their brand name, with a likeness of the Taino chief on the bottle label.) Hatuey's heroic defiance of Spanish conquistadores and missionaries, in Emilio's analysis, was the foundation for a tradition of "constant rebellion" in and around Santiago, where the mountains provided a thickly forested sanctuary, first for runaway slaves and later for the Cuban independence fighters known as the *mambises*.

Diego Velázquez founded the city of Santiago in 1514, and as Cuba's governor he immediately declared it the island's capital. The municipal government he established there was the first in the New World, and for years Santiago was the most important city in Spain's territories. Hernán Cortés set off from Santiago in 1518 to conquer Aztec Mexico, having already served as the city's first mayor. Fellow conquistadores Hernando de Soto, Juan Ponce de León, and Francisco Pizarro all came from Santiago as well. In 1553, however, the Spanish governor of Cuba moved his residence to Havana, effectively ending Santiago's reign as capital, and from then on the two cities were rivals.

Havana, anchoring the island on the western end, was as far away from Santiago on the eastern end as Boston, Massachusetts, was from Richmond, Virginia, and the territory between the two cities was rugged and sparsely populated. Santiago developed its own identity, in many ways more attuned to its Caribbean neighbors than to Havana. The city lay just across the water from Jamaica and Haiti, and boat traffic in and out of the harbor was constant. It was to Santiago and its environs that French colonists fled after the 1791 slave uprising and revolution in Haiti, and more arrived a few years later after France lost Louisiana to the United States. Between the Spanish administration, the French influence, and its large population of free blacks, Santiago became the most racially and ethnically mixed city in Cuba.

Walking through town as a young man, Emilio Bacardi heard greetings shouted in African dialects, English, French, and Haitian Creole, as well as in Catalan and Castilian Spanish. The city had only about twenty thousand people, and more than half of them were slaves or former slaves, but there was an abundance of cultural activity, much of it sponsored by transplanted Spaniards—called *peninsulares* to distinguish them from the *criollos* (Creoles) who were born on the island—and by the French planters and merchants who had set down roots there. In Emilio's day, Santiago sustained a Philharmonic Society and a municipal theater that hosted opera and dance companies, comedic productions, chamber orchestras, masquerade balls, even acrobatic shows.

Spain's hold on the city, however, meant the officially sanctioned social life revolved mainly around the affairs of the distant Spanish Crown, the comings and goings of Spanish military officers and their families, and the Catholic Church, which was a strong ally of Madrid. A portrait of Queen Isabella II hung in the local cathedral, and on every notable occasion in her royal life a special Mass would be celebrated and a dance would be held in her honor at the

Philharmonic Society. The Spanish military officers who attended such affairs were viewed as potential husbands for young Santiago women, at least for those girls whose fathers' loyalty was to Madrid. The social dynamic was captured in a sardonic epigram of the day:

> With turkeys and cakes,
> Gifts and trinkets,
> Gil wants to marry his daughters
> To lieutenant colonels.
>
> Don't take this wrong,
> But, oh Gil, they will show you.
> They know the difference between
> The bait and the hook.

Emilio Bacardi, a lifelong collector of local trivia, found the epigram later in an old newspaper and saved it. He was obsessed with his hometown's history, partly because he found it so meaningful, partly because it was so immediate. Almost every notable Santiago event had occurred within walking distance of where he lived and worked. The Marina Baja office was just down the street from the house built for Diego Velázquez in the sixteenth century. The Philharmonic Society was only a few blocks away. And the historical narrative that Emilio observed and recorded was epic: What happened around him in those years was nothing less than the painful and inspiring birth of a nation. Among Spain's colonial territories, Cuba had the reputation of being *siempre fiel*, the "ever-faithful" island, and the dominant position of the *peninsular* Spaniards in mid-nineteenth-century Santiago was evidence of that relationship. But Santiago was far too passionate and vibrant a city to exist contentedly as a colonial outpost. Among the city's native sons was Cuba's first famous poet, José María Heredia, forced into exile as a result of his involvement in an anti-Spanish uprising in 1823. Heredia, who was born in a house around the corner from the cathedral, was one of Emilio Bacardi's Santiago heroes, and he and his friends often assembled secretly to read Heredia's poetry and discuss its significance.

It would take more than romantic nationalist poetry, of course, to liberate Cuba from Spain. By 1830, Cuba had become the single wealthiest colony in the world, almost entirely because of its booming sugar industry. Spain had lost its other New World colonies and was determined to hold on at all costs to Cuba, an essential source of tax revenue for the Crown. More than forty thousand Spanish troops were based on the island, backed by a vast network of paid agents and informers. Wealthy Cuban sugar planters, meanwhile, were firmly allied with Madrid. The sugar industry depended heavily on African slave labor, and the planters were worried that without the protection of Spanish troops they might not be able to keep their slave population under control. Blacks were in the majority in Cuba, and a drive for independence could result in the establishment of a black republic and an end to slavery, just as had happened in Haiti.

Spanish authorities were able to move quickly and ruthlessly to squelch any movement in Cuba deemed potentially subversive. Cubans who dared to challenge the Spanish military regime, regardless of their rank or reputation, were routinely deported, thrown into prison with sentences of hard labor, or even executed. In early 1844, a slave revolt broke out and was met immediately with fierce repression. The Spanish military governor ordered the arrest of thousands of slaves and freed blacks and directed a wave of terror across the island. The year of Emilio Bacardi's birth would go down in Cuban history as "the year of the lash." Blacks suspected of involvement in rebellious activity were tied to a ladder, or *escalera*, and then whipped until they confessed to something. The alleged plot became known as the conspiracy of La Escalera.

All the trends defining Cuba in the middle decades of the nineteenth century came together in Santiago: the flowering of nationalist expression, the oppressive military rule of the Spanish Crown, the cultural sophistication, and the bloody slave revolts. There were also the developments that demonstrated Cuba's impressive economic and industrial progress during those years: the first installation in eastern Cuba of a steam-powered sugar mill, capable of producing 1,300 to 1,500 gallons of sugarcane juice a day, and the construction of a new railroad connecting the mining center of El Cobre, just outside Santiago, to the coastal port of Punta de Sal. By the time the route was inaugurated, Cuba had more railroads than any other Latin American country.

Emilio Bacardi, the dreamer, reformer, and revolutionary, was also a novelist and storyteller, and nothing stirred him more than the tale of his hometown. Late in life, holed up in the library of his beloved Villa Elvira and surrounded by the notebooks and clippings he had been hoarding since his teenage days, Emilio set out to string together all his collected Santiago news tidbits, anecdotes, and official notices in a mammoth work that would come to be considered a classic of historical writing in Cuba. Year by year, month by month, he listed the notable funerals, steamship arrivals, theater openings, political crackdowns, murders, military movements, slave sales, and construction projects of the day. He wrote minimal commentary with this detailed chronology of his hometown, but the events he included in his ten-volume

Crónicas de Santiago de Cuba (Santiago Chronicles) revealed the course of Cuba's national development. "A people's history can be seen in whatever causes a sensation, awakens enthusiasm, jolts sensitivities, provokes protest, and causes hilarity or rage," he wrote. By following the notice of a slave killing in Santiago with a report of the inauguration of a piano and singing academy during the same week, he did not trivialize the importance of the former so much as show how awfully ordinary such things had become. "The deed with all its rawness, the brutally uninhibited telling of fact; here is history," he explained.

Between his *Crónicas* and his term as the city's first Cuban mayor, Emilio was as closely identified with Santiago as anyone during his lifetime. Some Cuban writers have portrayed him as more of a loyal *santiaguero* than a patriotic Cuban, but that misses the point. For Emilio, Santiago was the purest expression of Cuba, and it was the Cuba he experienced personally. He was an indefatigable advocate of Cuban independence, but his perspective was local above all, and he preferred to work where he could make an immediate and practical difference. Though he served Santiago as a thinker and a revolutionary and a politician, he was also an employer and a business leader. Indeed, were it not for the contributions of his father and the rest of his family, Emilio's own impact would have been far more limited. The Bacardis' remarkable story in Cuba was a combination of elements: Emilio exemplified the legendary Bacardi patriotism, Santiago de Cuba provided the setting where it was inspired, and the family's successful rum business gave it power and influence.

Chapter 2

≈⊙≈

Entrepreneur

Facundo Bacardi Massó, Emilio's father, grew up within sight of the harbor in Sitges, near Barcelona, and as a boy he sat on the docks and watched tall ships sail off to the Americas. The cargo holds were loaded with barrels of wine from local vineyards, and waving from the decks were young Catalan men off to seek their fortunes. The old principality of Catalonia, strategically situated at Spain's northeastern tip, had been a center of Mediterranean commerce for centuries, and the Catalans were renowned as merchants. By the early nineteenth century, a Catalan colony was well established in faraway Santiago de Cuba, and Facundo and his brothers heard from acquaintances that Santiago was a boomtown rich with opportunity. Facundo's two older brothers, Magín and Juan, soon headed bravely across the ocean, and at the age of fifteen Facundo followed them, full of energy and ambition.

The Bacardi boys had no trouble finding work among their Catalan contacts. The oldest, Magín, saved enough money within a few years to open a general store, assisted by his brother Juan. They sold everything from hardware to penmanship paper, and in the Spanish tradition of colorful store names that meant nothing, they called their shop simply El Palo Gordo (The Big Stick). When young Facundo arrived, the Bacardi brothers helped get him a job with a business associate and then employed him in their own store as soon as they were able to pay him. A younger Bacardi brother, José, followed the others a few years later. Catalans dominated the Santiago commercial scene at the time and were famous for their work ethic and thrift. As one American visitor to Cuba wrote of the Catalan merchants he met, "They arrive in poverty, begin with a shop six or eight feet square, live on a biscuit, and rise by patience, industry and economy to wealth." The Bacardi brothers, sons of an illiterate bricklayer, fit the mold well.

By 1843, Facundo had saved more than six thousand Cuban gold pesos—equivalent to six thousand dollars—and was ready to establish a business of his own. He was engaged to a twenty-year-old *santiaguera*, Amalia Moreau*, who had been raised by her grandfather on his coffee plantation after her mother and grandmother died from cholera when she was just three years old. She and Facundo were married in August, and three months later Facundo opened a grocery and dry goods business in partnership with an old Sitges acquaintance.

The store, registered on the town books as "Facundo Bacardi y Compañía," was stocked with goods of all kinds: buckets, toys, oil lamps, crockery, knives, jars of preserves, and cans of sardines. From the ceiling hung smoked hams, cooking pots, shovels, and coils of rope. Behind the counter were supplies of dried fish and bags of flour, sugar, and coffee. Santiago shoppers wanted nails and candles and ordinary muslin, but also imported chocolates, linens, and fine china, and Facundo had it all. His clientele came from all social classes. Through his contacts back in Sitges, he provided Catalan wine wholesale to other shop-keepers, but he also tended to the peasant farmer who stopped by looking for a new straw hat or machete. Next would come a pair of Santiago's upper-class women settled comfortably in a *volante*, an elegantly adorned two-wheeled buggy pulled by a single horse. A black slave wearing a bright red waistcoat and a black derby hat sat astride the horse, guiding it, so his mistress needn't bother with the reins. The ladies, wearing long ruffled black gowns and thin satin shoes, waited in the *volantes* while Facundo brought wares out to show them, thus making sure the women did not have to soil their shoes in the dirty street.

Following their wedding, Facundo and Amalia moved into a modest house at 8 Jagüey Street in the heart of Santiago's warehouse district, a few blocks up from the waterfront. The view down the street was of ruts and cobble-stones and horse-drawn wagons and porters struggling under the weight of trunks. The street ended at the harbor side, an area built up with storehouses, customs buildings, shipping offices, and a railroad terminal. Beyond, the dark waters of Santiago's bay were dotted by the masts of moored schooners, with other boats gliding slowly in or out of the harbor. On the far side, the eastern section of the Sierra Maestra rose against the sky. Facundo and Amalia's house, the property of Amalia's godmother, was a one-story dwelling of brick and plas-ter with a small patio off the kitchen. It was mostly indistinguishable from other houses on the street. The roof was flat, and when Facundo climbed up there he could see the bay and the ships at anchor. He often began his day with a few min-utes contemplating the harbor view, just as he had done as a boy back in Sitges.

---

*Amalia's formal name was Lucía Victoria Moreau, but she was known throughout her life as Amalia.

It was in that house that Amalia gave birth to Emilio on June 5, 1844. She cared for the boy largely without the help of her husband, who stayed busy with his commercial activities. Just five days before Emilio was born, Facundo and his partner opened a second store, a retail shop in the mining village of El Cobre, ten miles outside Santiago. Amalia, like most Cuban wives, kept her distance from the businesses. Life on Jagüey Street was hardly luxurious. There was no interior courtyard or garden. The windows in the front parlor opened directly on the street, and the stench from manure was ever present. Not until Emilio himself became mayor of Santiago more than fifty years later was there an organized campaign to persuade residents not to dispose of their garbage simply by throwing it out their front door into the gutter.

A second son, Juan, arrived in 1846, followed by Facundo Jr. in 1848 and a daughter, María, in 1851. Amalia read to the children every day—often in French, the language of her grandfather, who came from Haiti. Emilio, a quiet and reflective boy, learned to read on his own at an early age and also developed a talent for drawing, which he did for hours on end. The young family was largely shielded from the social and political unrest sweeping across Cuba in those years, but Amalia and Facundo were familiar with all the controversies of the day, including slavery, living as they did in downtown Santiago. Town records show that Amalia acquired title to several slaves from her grandfather as part of her dowry, but whether any attended her personally is unclear; it is more likely that they remained on her grandfather's plantation. In August 1851, Amalia sold Rachel, a female slave in her late teens with an infant son named José Dionisio, receiving five hundred dollars for her and her baby. Seven months later, she sold a twelve-year-old girl named Licet for three hundred dollars. It was common in Cuba to hold slaves as an investment, and it is possible that Amalia sold the young women in order to raise capital for her husband's business operations.

Whatever routine characterized the daily life of Facundo and his young family, it all changed on August 20, 1852. The sky that morning was cloudless, the air fresh, and the landscape cleansed by overnight rains. But at 8:36 A.M., with the streets crowded with pedestrians, the daily rhythm was shattered by a horrifying sound like nothing heard before. "It was not a thunderclap like those that normally precede an earthquake," historian Miguel Estorch wrote later in an eyewitness account, "but rather a deep earthly groan." Estorch felt the earth "lift the whole city suddenly up and drop it again, like a child might do with a little toy." People rushed from their houses and into the middle of streets and other open spaces, where they kneeled, raised their hands to the heavens, and cried for mercy. Though it was daylight, rats were scurrying everywhere in search of new hiding places, and frogs were leaping out of the public fountains. The earth shook violently again nine minutes after the first earthquake and four more times over the next four hours, each time causing more damage in the city. The government house, the customs headquarters, and the military hospital were totally ruined; the cathedral and seven other churches were heavily damaged. From the decks of ships anchored in the bay, a gray powdery cloud could be seen hanging over the city, formed by the dust of collapsing buildings.

Only two people were killed during the initial earthquake, but a breakdown of the water and sanitation systems in Santiago produced conditions perfect for the spread of disease. Facundo Bacardi closed his shops and volunteered to help with humanitarian relief in his neighborhood, taking charge of the distribution of soup rations in front of the church of Santo Tomás, not far from his home and his main store. The aftershocks continued for weeks afterward, and many residents abandoned their homes to sleep in sturdier public buildings. For solace, many *santiagueros* turned to their church, but they found little sympathy. The local archbishop, a Spaniard named Antonio María Claret, used the earthquake as an occasion to scold his people for having strayed from the holy path. "God does with us as a mother does with a lazy sleeping child," he explained. "She shakes the child's bed to wake him and get him up. If that fails, she strikes him. The good God does the same with His children who are sleeping in their sins. He has shaken their houses by the earthquakes, but He spared their lives. If this does not awaken them and cause them to rise, He will strike them with cholera and pestilence. God has made this known to me."

Whether sent by God or not, cholera did indeed make an appearance a few weeks later, and within two months a deadly epidemic was sweeping the city. The death toll reached a peak on November 3, when ninety-four people died. At the Santa Ana cemetery, cadavers lay unburied for a day or more for lack of gravediggers. Before it ran its course, the cholera epidemic wiped out a tenth of the city's population. Among the victims were Facundo and Amalia's six-year-old son Juan and their infant daughter María, as well as Amalia's grandfather. Frightened and grief-stricken, Facundo and Amalia decided to take their surviving sons, eight-year-old Emilio and four-year-old Facundo Jr., away from Santiago. In December 1852, they sailed for Spain, where they could stay for a time with Facundo's parents in Sitges.

Facundo, now nearing forty, soon grew restless, however, and after a few months he returned to Cuba with his family—except for Emilio. Facundo and Amalia left him in the custody of a family friend in Barcelona, Daniel Costa, who had promised to oversee the boy's education. Costa was a man of elevated literary and artistic tastes, and Emilio flourished under his personal tutoring. Back in Santiago, meanwhile, Facundo and Amalia went through the most difficult time of their lives, still mourning the loss of their two children and now facing an economic setback. Facundo's shops had been looted while he was away and needed to be restocked. Commercial activity in the city had declined precipitously, as much of the population had fled. Customers to whom Facundo had extended credit were unable to pay bills, and with his own suppliers demanding payment, Facundo was forced to ask his wife for help. Amalia's grandfather had left her ten thousand dollars at his death, and she allowed Facundo to invest it in his business, where it was listed on the books as a loan. He borrowed an additional seventeen thousand dollars from Amalia's wealthy godmother, Clara Astié, a woman who would come to the Bacardis' aid repeatedly.

Santiago's long economic boom appeared to be at an end. Sugar prices were slumping, with the growth in world production outpacing the growth in demand, partly because of the introduction of the sugar beet in Europe. The less efficient Cuban sugar planters, located disproportionately on the eastern end of the island around Santiago, found their profit margins shrinking, and as their fortunes suffered, so did those of the merchants who did business with them. In 1855 the firm Facundo Bacardi y Compañía was declared bankrupt. By liquidating some assets and reorganizing his financing, Facundo was able to safeguard his wife's savings and ultimately repay Clara Astié, but after twenty-five years of hard work, enterprise, and frugality, he faced the prospect of having to start over.

An indistinct family photograph from the 1880s, said to be the only surviving image of Facundo, shows him to have been lean of build, with sharply chiseled features. He is clean-shaven, and his hair is short and combed straight back. A drawing of him commissioned after his death, based on recollections of his appearance, shows him with a stern visage. His eyebrows are narrowed, his mouth is turned down in a frown, and he is perfectly groomed. Even his friends addressed him as *Don* Facundo, with the honorific suggesting respect. Family members would later say they could not recall seeing Facundo in his shirtsleeves, even in the privacy of his own home. His black shoes always lustrous, his shirts perfectly starched, his collars perfectly white, Don Facundo was the embodiment of a sober businessman. Each evening, after returning from a long day of work, he would pace the house, his hands clasped tightly behind his back, his gaze fixed ahead, his thoughts elsewhere. "Facundo, always in that silent place," Amalia often said, knowing better than to interrupt him. It was his daily meditation time, and he would continue pacing until the call for dinner.

A strong will and a shrewd mind were needed to do well in that tumultuous era. Facundo Bacardi never doubted there was money to be made in Cuba, if only he could identify the right opportunity. Selling groceries would not do it, Facundo now realized; he needed to *produce* something. Slowly, an idea took shape. He could make rum.

◆ ◆ ◆

Cuba's rich volcanic soil, tropical climate, regular rainfall, and abundant sunshine made it an ideal island for growing sugarcane. The industry got off to a slow start, but by 1850 Cuba was the number one cane producer in the world. Sugar exports had grown tenfold over the preceding fifty years. Rarely had an industry anywhere expanded so dramatically or produced such quick profits.

Heavily forested and underpopulated, the country was at first better known for its strategically located ports and its ship-repairing industry than for its agricultural production. The sugar industry took off only because of a pair of crucial and nearly simultaneous developments. One was the revolution in Haiti, sparked in 1790 when freed blacks on the island began arguing that they deserved to be treated as French citizens under the terms of the Declaration of the Rights of Man, the document underlying the French Revolution of 1789. Within a year, a full-fledged slave revolt had broken out across Haiti, the eventual consequence of which was the flight of the French plantation owners and the total collapse of the Haitian sugar industry. Cuban planters, previously lagging behind their Haitian rivals, saw their competition disappear. But they still needed to solve their chronic labor shortage. For years, they had been seeking Madrid's permission to import slaves freely, arguing that the unrestricted use of slave labor would boost the sugar economy and bring Cuba previously unimaginable riches. In 1791, just as Haiti was coming apart, the Cuban planters got their wish. The Spanish Crown that year removed all limitations on the slave trade.

Cuba thereby staked its future on the institution of slavery, with profound implications for its economy, for the course of its history, and for its character as a nation. Within a few years, as many as ten thousand enslaved Africans were being shipped to Cuba annually. By the 1850s, there were about four hundred thousand slaves on the island, about 40 percent of Cuba's total population. The vast majority worked on sugar plantations, where production was based as much on brute labor as on technology.

The larger estates employed hundreds of slaves, almost all of them men. Field slaves cut the sugarcane with machetes. Others worked at the "sugar house," a place of overpowering noise and sweet, sticky smells. Slave laborers manually fed the cane stalks into huge, steam-powered iron rollers that squeezed the juice out. Others oversaw the cauldrons where the sugar juice was boiled into syrup or the cooling troughs where the syrup was left to crystallize. The sugar crystals were removed from the syrup by means of a centrifuge, typically a cylinder of wire mesh that spun rapidly inside a drum. The liquid would escape, draining into a catch basin as molasses, with the sugar crystals left caked on the wire mesh. Once dried, the sugar was packed into crates for shipment. The remaining molasses was filtered and collected in huge barrels called hogsheads.

There was a big market for Cuban molasses in New England, where it was used for distilling rum. For nearly a century, rum had been the spirit of choice in the United States. By one estimate, at the time of American independence the average adult male in the thirteen original colonies was drinking between four and five gallons of rum a year. In the beginning, most of the rum came from distilleries in the British West Indies, but the North American demand soon exceeded their capacity. Just as significantly, New England businessmen recognized a moneymaking opportunity. Molasses was relatively cheap and plentiful, and they could make huge profits by importing the molasses and distilling the rum themselves. The combination of African slaves, Cuban molasses, and New England rum gave rise in the early years of the nineteenth century to a variation of the infamous Triangle Trade. New England merchants shipped their rum to West Africa, where it was traded for slaves, who were then taken to Cuba to be put to work on sugar plantations. The slaves were exchanged in Havana or Santiago for Cuban molasses, which was shipped in turn to New England and distilled into rum.

Raw sugar was bringing Cuba so much wealth in the first decades of the nineteenth century that few growers or industrialists bothered to consider whether they could themselves get into the commercial rum business as a sideline to their main sugar operations. To be sure, Cuban sugar farmers had been distilling some form of primitive rum or *aguardiente* (from *agua ardiente*, "burning water," akin to "brandy" in English or *eau-de-vie* in French or *acquavite* in Italian), as long as they had been growing cane. Virtually every sugar mill complex in Cuba had a small distillery attached, even if it was just a simple pot still set up under a tin roof to protect it from the rain. In general, however, the industry was so poorly developed that Cuban rum fetched a mere fraction of the price paid for the better known rums of Jamaica, Barbados, and Martinique. The dean of Cuban sugar historians, Manuel Moreno Fraginals, having reviewed nearly everything that was written about Cuban rum in the early years of the nineteenth century, concluded that even the best versions were considered to have "an unpleasantly musty taste and smell." Within Cuba, locally made rum was often sold straight from the barrel in working-class taverns and neighborhood *pulperías,* open-air stands set up in the door-ways of houses or on public corners, barely a step above a vendor's pushcart. Being respectable merchants, the Bacardi brothers refused to sell Cuban rum in their own shops.

One explanation for the low quality was that Cuba lacked the rum-making heritage of the other "sugar islands," which had benefited by their access to su-perior British and French distilling expertise and technology. Another factor was the puritanical attitude of the Spanish Crown, which for years officially prohib-ited the manufacture of rum in Cuba, citing a need to protect public health and morals. The Spanish authorities finally lifted restrictions on rum production in 1796, but by then Cuba had been left on the sidelines of the rum trade.

As of 1850, basic rum-distilling procedures in Cuba were still at a rudimen-tary level. Molasses was mixed with water and left to ferment in vats. Yeast, either naturally occurring or artificially introduced, converted the sugars in the mix to alcohols. After several days, the fermented "wash," as it was called, was fed into a still or alembic, basically a large copper kettle or pot set over a fire. Once heated, the spirits of the fermented mix would evaporate before the rest of the liquid, because alcohol has a lower boiling point than water. The alcoholic vapor would be piped to a second container where it would cool and condense. A somewhat purer spirit could be produced by running the distillate through the process again. The clear, cold liquid that dripped from the tap at the end was *aguardiente,* rum in its crudest form. It was potent, as much as 85 percent pure alcohol. Towels soaked in *aguardiente* were considered a cure for headaches and thought to speed the healing of wounds. Cubans also washed their hands in *aguardiente* and splashed it on their faces as a cleanser. They just didn't much like the way it tasted.

One problem stemmed from the Cuban molasses itself, which had a rela-tively high sucrose content. In an extrasweet mixture, the yeast consumes the sugar voraciously, producing high levels of alcohol quickly and dramatically raising the temperature of the solution. Either development can kill the yeast and spoil the product. The trouble could be avoided by carefully measuring and adjusting the sugar levels in the wash and by monitoring the heat produced during the fermentation process, but this required expertise, technology, and attention to detail—all lacking in Cuban distilleries. The decision to build the sugar industry on slave labor had resulted in a shortage of skilled and moti-vated workers on the Cuban plantations, and the distilleries were not well tended as a result.

As early as 1816, one business leader in Santiago had argued that more attention should be paid to the rum industry on the island, lamenting that "the molasses with which *aguardiente* is made departs Cuba in immense quantities for the United States, where it is converted into rum at great advantage for that country's industry." He was appealing for a united Cuban front to challenge a tariff system that impeded Cuba's access to the U.S. rum market. Such calls, however, were largely ignored until the 1850s.

The price of molasses had stopped rising by then, in part a consequence of Cuba's abundant output. Rum production in the United States, meanwhile, was declining, as Americans on the lookout for cheap spirits began turning to rye whiskey. New England rum producers were also coming under pressure from the temperance movement, and many decided to close their distillery doors rather than face the protests of activists.

The cutback in U.S. distilling opened an opportunity for Cuban producers. A significant international rum market still beckoned, and no one was better positioned to increase production than the Cubans, who had all the raw material they would ever need. Given the high cost of transporting molasses to market and the relatively low price it was getting at that point, some Cuban growers had actually been feeding their surplus to their pigs or even dumping it in the river. It would make far more sense to turn the molasses into export-quality rum.

• • •

Facundo Bacardi knew he would face competition if he were to get started in the rum business. Having once banned rum production, the Spanish Crown was now offering prizes for the development of a Cuban spirit "able to satisfy the taste of the Court and the elite of the Empire." Between 1851 and 1856, at least a half dozen handbooks on rum making were published in Cuba, summarizing all the available technical information. It was only a matter of time before someone came up with a high-quality product.

At least Facundo was in the right place. Though sugar production was not as advanced in the east of Cuba as in the west, Santiago was Cuba's closest connection to the British and French islands where the best-known rums were made. The French colonists who had come to the Santiago area from Haiti brought with them an appreciation for fine liquors. Santiago was also just a short distance from Jamaica, closer to Kingston than to Havana, and *santiagueros* were probably more familiar with Jamaican rums than they were with those from their own country. One of the first rum producers in Santiago was a Cuban of British ancestry, John Nunes, who opened a small distillery in 1838 near the waterfront on Matadero Street. Nunes knew something about making rum, though in the beginning his operation was as humble as any in the Santiago area. A Bacardi company narrative written many years later included a bit of the Nunes story:

> The alembic installation was poor, rickety, miserable! But Mr. Nunes dabbled a little one day, a little more the next, and he was able to sell his liquor, first in Oriente [province] and afterwards across the whole island. Later he sent small shipments of his product off to American and European markets, though without any label to distinguish it.

By following the example of distillers such as Nunes, Facundo Bacardi could learn some of what he needed to get started in the rum business. But Facundo wanted an alembic of his own, or access to one, so he could begin experimenting with different methods of rum production. One man who could help him was a French Cuban named José León Bouteiller, who had a pot still that he used for making cognac and candies.* Bouteiller rented a house on Marina Baja Street from Clara Astié, Facundo's sometime benefactor and the godmother of his wife Amalia. Through Doña Clara, Facundo established a connection with Bouteiller, and the two men began a friendly collaboration.

When Astié died in 1859, she left her Marina Baja property and the rest of her estate to Amalia and her other godchildren, including fifteen-year-old Emilio Bacardi, who had returned from Spain two years earlier. Bouteiller remained in the Marina Baja house as a Bacardi tenant, and as part of his rental agreement he agreed to share his pot still with Facundo and assist him in rum distillation trials. At last Facundo had the opportunity he had been waiting for. He knew what he wanted to produce: a new Cuban rum that could not only compete with the rums from Jamaica or Martinique but improve on them. Even the best Caribbean rums were strong enough to burn the throat, and many were flavored so heavily that they could be drunk comfortably only when mixed with tea or punch. Facundo wanted to make and sell a rum that would move beyond the old association with buccaneers, rowdy sailors, and working-class taverns and take a place alongside the fine brandies and whiskeys favored by elite drinkers. Cuban rum had that potential, Facundo believed, if he could refine it properly, something no one had yet managed to do.

Bouteiller's alembic was small, and Facundo's plan was for the two of them to work at the Marina Baja location with batches of molasses, distilling just a few

---

*Distillers often made candy as a sideline, because after the fermented wash was boiled to produce the distillate, a semiliquid sugary residue was usually left in the alembic and could be poured into molds to make candy.

jugs of rum at a time, experimenting with yeast strains, varying the sweetness of the water-and-molasses mix, and adjusting the distillation procedure itself. The fermentation of the molasses actually produced a variety of alcohols and other elements, some contributing to rum quality and others detracting from it. Grain alcohol, or ethanol, the most neutral spirit, is almost odorless and flavorless, and in its purest form the ethanol produced in fermenting molasses differs little from that produced in fermenting sugars from potatoes or corn. But fermenting molasses also produced other alcohols, loosely called congeners, with different chemical compositions and therefore distinct flavors. All the alcohols had their own boiling temperatures, so they evaporated at different points during the boiling of the fermented molasses. The lighter alcohols, the first to evaporate, included methanol, which is toxic and therefore undesirable, but along with that came some fragrant compounds called esters, which contributed a fruity aroma to the distillate. The heavier alcohols, the last to evaporate, were loosely called fusel oils, and contained many of the flavors associated with rum. It was those same fusel oils, however, that left drinkers with hangovers and headaches. The key to making good rum was to control the distillation so as to be able to separate the desirable alcohols from the undesirable ones.

An experienced distiller in that era might not have been able to explain exactly what happened chemically during distillation, but he understood enough to discard much of the first condensate to emerge from the still, called the heads, as well as the last portion, called the tails, and to concentrate on the middle portion, called the hearts. The art came in knowing when to make those breaks in order to get the desired flavor and aroma. When the condensate was run through a still a second time, a finer sorting of the elements was possible. Different combinations yielded different flavors, and the distiller could blend the final products to produce a rum pleasing to his taste.

Impurities and undesirable flavors in rum could also be removed through aging. By the late 1600s, rum distillers had already discovered that when rum was stored in barrels for a period of time, while awaiting shipment or during the long passage across the Atlantic, it darkened in color and improved in taste. A distiller writing in 1757 complained of the "stinky flavour" of his spirit and lamented that "the rum must be suffered to lie a long time to mellow before it can be used." Why this worked was not understood, but it was a principle that rum makers would apply in subsequent years. In Cuba, wooden barrels used previously to ship wine were reused for aging the rum. Because the barrels sometimes contained mold from the wine residue, rum makers sterilized them by charring the insides. At some point, they discovered that contact with the charcoal seemed to help mellow the spirit.

After months of experimentation, Facundo Bacardi and José León Bouteiller had improved their rum to the point that they were ready to share it. To test the local market, Facundo sold some of the rum through his brother's general store, using any container available. Though the rum was unidentified, customers knew it was sold by Magín Bacardi and made by his brother Facundo, and around town it became known as *el ron de Bacardi* (Bacardi's rum). Prospects appeared promising, and Facundo and Bouteiller decided they should go into commercial rum production. As it happened, John Nunes, the owner of the "rickety" distillery on Matadero Street, was ready to sell out after twenty-four difficult years. On February 4, 1862, Facundo and Bouteiller purchased the Nunes distillery for three thousand gold pesos.

The facility was little more than a large shed, with wood plank siding, a floor of bare dirt, and a peaked roof made of tin. Wagons and carts were parked alongside in a yard bounded by a wooden picket fence atop a low brick wall. Inside the building was the pot still and several molasses tanks and a tiny walled-off room that could serve as an office or work area. The still consisted of a copper boiler about three feet wide and three feet high, topped by a tall copper stack and a cooling pipe leading to a condensing chamber. Additional pipes coiled from the condenser back toward the boiler for redistillation purposes. The alembic could handle thirty-five barrels of fermented molasses in a single batch, and four batches could be processed each day, a notable improvement over what Facundo and Bouteiller had been able to do in their operation on Marina Baja.

With no money of his own to invest, Facundo turned to his younger brother José for the cash to make the deal. Bouteiller contributed his distilling equipment, which was valued at five hundred pesos and brought the total investment in the new company to $3,500, not counting the Marina Baja property. Facundo contributed only his labor and expertise. His brother José immediately gave Facundo a power of attorney to represent his financial share in the company, however, and Facundo was seen from the beginning as the enterprise head. The preceding years had not been easy for him financially. His family had expanded, first with the birth in 1857 of another son, José, and then four years later with a daughter, named Amalia after her mother. Facundo was now embarking on yet another risky business venture, though he had never before been so hopeful about his prospects. A family friend gave the Bacardis a young coconut palm to commemorate the occasion, and fourteen-year-old Facundo Jr. planted it in front of the distillery.

Later the same month, the Bacardi partners took over another small distillery, also on Marina Baja Street, this one belonging to a Catalan liquor merchant by the name of Manuel Idral. They now had all the distillery equipment and facilities they needed to launch their business. In May 1862, the firm was incorporated under the name "Bacardi, Bouteiller, & Compañía." To maximize revenue, the company made and sold various sweets, from fruit conserves to guava paste to the candies—Caramelos Carbanchell—for which Bouteiller had long been known, along with Bouteiller's cognac and wine made from oranges. But it was the new style of rum that attracted the most attention. "It was a light product, almost transparent," one of Cuba's rum historians would write, "and free of the foul odors that in preceding versions had produced so many headaches. The lines of people waiting to purchase this *aguardiente* were longer every morning, especially after the early months when Don Facundo so cleverly gave away free samples." In the beginning, distribution was limited to the immediate Santiago area, because there were no bottles for the rum— meaning customers had to bring their own containers.

The distillery was just a short distance from the waterfront, and the business quickly became well known as a quality operation among the ship captains who put into the Santiago port. The sailors would buy their rum by the barrel, and on their next stop in Santiago they would return for a refill. Slowly, the reputation of "Bacardi" rum spread across Cuba, and by 1868 it was being sold in Havana. The operation would not be solvent for years to come, and he would not live long enough to be rewarded with great wealth, but Facundo Bacardi Massó, the indefatigable Catalan entrepreneur, had finally found a path to commercial success in Cuba.

Rum experts and Bacardi descendants would debate for decades what secret formula Facundo and Bouteiller developed to produce a rum that was milder and more drinkable than anything previously available. One factor is that they used a quick-fermenting cognac-type yeast rather than the slower yeasts used in making heavier rums. More importance should be given, however, to the system that Don Facundo developed to filter the raw distilled *aguardiente* through charcoal. While vodka makers had been using charcoal filtration for the same purposes since the end of the eighteenth century, Facundo is said to be the first to have done it with rum. Charcoal filtration removed some of the congeners that gave traditional rum its flavor, but because Facundo was deliberately seeking a whiter, nontraditional rum, charcoal served his purposes well.

Another innovation was the use of barrels of American white oak for aging the rum. Aging was one of the most important stages of rum production, but it was also mysterious and controversial, with virtually every rum manufacturer having his own ideas about how it should be done. The wood in the barrel interacted with the rum, imparting its own flavor but also extracting some of the stronger flavors from the rum. Alcohols and oils in the rum were absorbed by the barrel and then lost to the atmosphere through evaporation. American white oak, hard but still relatively porous, turned out to be an ideal wood for the maturation of rum, and within a few decades almost all rum manufacturers were using oak barrels for aging. But the Bacardis were the first.

Perhaps the most important factors contributing to the development of Bacardi rum were nontechnical. "It was the end-product of patient trial and error," one Cuban rum historian wrote, "better filtering here, more ageing there, total attention to details, temperature, ventilation, light and shade, the degree of the cane's ripeness and the quality of the molasses, the right choice of wood for the making of the ageing vats and above all the ability to balance all these factors; or rather, more than ability, the art of using them correctly."

And then there was perhaps the most innovative element of all: Facundo Bacardi was a brilliant marketer. Coming to the rum business from a background in retail sales rather than sugar production, he knew the importance of promotion and publicity. He carefully monitored the rum production, and as evidence of his approval of each batch he personally signed the label on every bottle that came off the production line. His bold signature, "Bacardi M," began with a big *B*, angled sharply up to the right, and ended with a stylized *M* (for Massó) and a dramatic dash back down to the left. It became instantly recognizable. Many rums at the time were sold without labels or other identifying characteristics, but Facundo Bacardi Massó instinctively understood the importance of distinguishing his product. He had taken a cue from the customers who asked for "Bacardi's rum" even before it was bottled under that name. Producing a quality rum was only part of the challenge; he needed to brand it, so that consumers could remember his rum and ask for it. A vigorous defense of the "Bacardi" trademark would forevermore be one of the company's top priorities.

Many consumers in Cuba in 1862 were illiterate, of course, so a memorable rum brand needed an image as well as a name. Facundo and Bouteiller chose the symbol of a bat with outstretched wings. They were apparently inspired in part by the bat image on the gallon containers that were recycled by Magín Bacardi as containers for his brother's homemade rum. Another explanation for the mark's origin, favored in later years by Bacardi publicists, is that Facundo and Bouteiller found a colony of fruit bats living in the Nunes distillery rafters when they bought it. The creatures would have been attracted by the sweet fumes of fermenting molasses. Like the Catalans, the local Taino Indians had regarded the bat as an omen of good fortune, and Doña Amalia allegedly suggested to her husband that the bat would be a fitting symbol for his new Cuban enterprise.

Chapter 3

A Patriot Is Made

As he was nearing fifty and had no money to hire helpers, Facundo Bacardi launched his rum business with the expectation that his sons would be helping him. The oldest, seventeen-year-old Emilio, was big and strong enough for factory jobs, plus he had the intelligence to handle commercial matters and the charm and manners to deal with customers. Don Facundo put him to work immediately.

Emilio would rather have stayed in school. He had inherited far more of his mother's love of literature than of his father's grim determination to succeed in business. His five-year stay in Barcelona away from his parents, from the age of eight to thirteen, had been a richly formative experience, leaving him with a level of maturity and intellectual curiosity far beyond that of other Cuban boys his age. Europe in the 1850s was in the late flowering of romanticism, and the man who educated Emilio, Daniel Costa, admired the leading writers and artists of the day—men like Robert Browning, Victor Hugo, and Eugène Delacroix. While his father back in Cuba was struggling to stave off bankruptcy, young Emilio was exploring the realms of poetry, painting, and even philosophy. When Amalia went to Spain to fetch her boy after Costa's sudden death in 1857, she found a broadly educated young man with a worldly self-assurance.

Back in Cuba, Emilio saw and understood things he hadn't noticed when he lived there as an eight-year-old. He had grown up around slaves, and members of his own family had been slaveholders, but his time in Europe had left Emilio with ideas of his own, and he now thought slavery was wrong. He also realized for the first time how many Cubans felt that Spain's rule over their island was no longer acceptable. Emilio had read history in the company of a learned mentor, and he had lived in Europe in the aftermath of the 1848 nationalist revolutions that reshaped the political landscape there. The opposition of tyranny and freedom now meant something to him; he saw the struggle playing out in his native land and realized that Santiago was sharply divided. Some townspeople still identified themselves as "Spaniards," supported slavery, and defended the joint interests of the Crown, the military, and the church. On the other side were liberals who argued for civil rights, opposed Spanish despotism, held secular values, and favored sovereignty for Cuba, if not full independence. The two views were virtually irreconcilable.

. . .

Upon his return from Barcelona, Emilio's parents enrolled him in the Colegio de San José, a private secondary school in Santiago whose director, Francisco Martínez Betancourt, was a poet and outspoken Cuban intellectual who encouraged his students to think about controversial issues and even arranged Sunday afternoon get-togethers where he and the boys could review what was happening in their country. Almost every night, Emilio went out to meet with classmates somewhere. They assembled in groups of two or three on a corner under the glow of a gas streetlight or in larger groups on the square in front of the cathedral, quietly exchanging stories of the latest acts of anti-Spanish defiance by Cuban patriots and the chilling reprisals that often followed. On Saturdays, Emilio and his friends gathered at a Santiago barbershop, La Flor del Siboney, where the proprietor was an amiable character who pontificated and sang Cuban ballads and appreciated an audience. The young men entertained themselves by reciting and discussing poetry, with all the bravado and seriousness that boys in other times and places showed in talking about sports. It seemed as if everyone in Cuba was a poet, or wanted to be one.

Many of the young men Emilio met at the Colegio de San José or the Siboney barbershop remained lifelong friends. There was Pío Rosado, two years older than Emilio, a tall and skinny lad with a long, straight nose and darting, restless eyes that suggested a bit of wildness, as if he could go out of control at any moment. "All nerves," was the way Emilio described him in a memoir of those days. Rosado tutored young boys in arithmetic, and his combustible energy meant the poor student who crossed him would soon regret it. He later became a rebel commander in the war for Cuban independence, famous for his aggressive, even reckless, actions in combat. José Antonio Godoy, another of Emilio's friends, was a nonstop talker and jokester. He also went on to join the rebel army, and when he was captured one day by Spanish troops, Godoy tricked them into thinking the rebels had kidnapped him. He embraced the commander and thanked him profusely for "rescuing" him. After the war, he became a professional clown.

Their adversaries around town were those young men who felt as strongly about defending Madrid's authority as Emilio and his friends felt about challenging it. Chief among them were the *voluntarios*, members of shadowy volunteer "militia" units recruited by the colonial authorities for the purpose of rooting out emerging proindependence groups in town, by force if necessary. Many of those who signed up were the sons of conservative middle- and upper-class Spanish immigrants in Santiago, including a few Emilio had known as childhood playmates. Other *voluntarios* were simply thugs attracted by the opportunity to wear a uniform, carry a weapon, and bully other Cubans, especially those of color. Emilio and his friends worried that they would be pressured to join the *voluntarios*, and they feared what might happen if they refused to do so.

Mostly, they saw themselves as propagandists. In the early 1860s, they indulged in what Emilio called a *locura de literatura* (literary madhouse), publishing a series of broadsheets to entertain their fellow Cubans and incite them to anti-Spanish action. Their "newspapers" were full of self-important prose, amateurish poetry, and provocative commentary. Emilio, devoting himself to literary pursuits at a time when his father was trying to get him into the family business, published his first essay (titled "El pasaporte") before he turned twenty-one, under the pseudonym Enrique Enríquez. In it, Emilio lamented how colonial authorities made travel impossible for those without political connections or money. No copies of the clandestine newspapers survived, but Emilio kept clippings of his articles, pasting them on the back of the Bacardi, Bouteiller, & Compañía ledger sheets he collected while doing his administrative chores.

Emilio's first experience with direct political activism came in 1865, when he was twenty-one. The authorities in Madrid, in a conciliatory moment, had agreed to set up a joint commission to consider possible revisions in Spain's policies toward Cuba. The Cuban representatives were to be chosen through an election, though the only Cubans entitled to vote were a few dozen male electors selected by the Spanish authorities. In Santiago, the liberals wanted one of the commissioners to be José Antonio Saco, an esteemed Cuban nationalist then exiled in Paris, but they feared the local electors might be intimidated by the Spanish authorities into choosing someone else.

For Emilio Bacardi and his friends, it was the call to action they had long awaited. They spread the word around town for Saco's supporters to mobilize on the Plaza de Armas, in front of the government building where the commission voting was to take place. Pío Rosado, José Antonio Godoy, and Emilio assumed positions at the front to rouse the crowd. They were joined by seventeen-year-old Facundo Jr., who by then was part of Emilio's barbershop circle. One of the pro-Saco electors suggested that at the signal of a beige handkerchief waved from the door of the government building, everyone should shout "*¡Viva Saco!*" The Santiago police repeatedly tried to disperse the crowd, but Emilio and his friends kept bringing the people back together. Again and again, the crowd roared "*¡Viva Saco!*"—loudly enough that the electors meeting inside took notice. Saco was chosen by a wide margin.

The promise of new Spanish policies toward Cuba was soon broken, however. A change of government in Madrid brought hard-liners back to power, the commission's recommended political and economic reforms were summarily rejected, and the Spanish authorities dispatched a new, reactionary captain-general to Cuba. All public meetings on the island were prohibited, and newspapers were once again subject to tight censorship. The crackdown extended even to Cuba's cigar factories, where the colonial authorities ordered an end to the custom of having "lectors" read to the cigar rollers. The practice had made the Cuban cigar workers, many of whom were illiterate, among the most well-versed artisan workers in the world. In Santiago, Emilio and his friends tried to organize a new newspaper, *El Oriente*, but the authorities promptly shut it down.

Discouraged by the political situation, Emilio and his brother Facundo Jr. finally turned their attention to their father's rum business, as he had long wanted them to do.

• • •

With reform forces frustrated, many Cubans concluded that their nation would gain its independence only through a revolutionary war like the ones fought by other Spanish colonies in Latin America fifty years earlier. Before the Cubans moved to armed revolt, however, they would have to deal with the issue of race. The prospect of an empowered black majority on the island had for years kept many white Cubans from pushing for independence, because they figured that without Spanish colonial authority behind them they would lose their privileged place in the country. Now that it appeared there might be no alternative to independence, white liberal Cubans had to face their racial fears squarely. It was unrealistic to think an independent Cuba could keep a large part of its population enslaved. Moreover, it was clear that an independence war could not be won without the active participation of black fighting forces, and Cuban blacks and mulattoes would not support any movement that did not promise an end to slavery. The only revolution with any prospect of success in Cuba would be one whose goals included democracy and racial equality as well as independence.

This would be an ambitious project for a society in which slavery was entrenched and in which blacks and whites did not yet freely mix. Most upper-class Cubans in the 1860s owned slaves. A wealthy Santiago woman would have a female slave attendant to help her dress in the mornings, run errands for her during the day, and even crouch behind her during a theater performance that night. Slaves cooked and cleaned houses and drove the family carriage. Many were well treated, but they remained vulnerable to their masters' whims. The slightest transgression of "slave law," as defined by the slave owner, could bring a severe flogging for even a trusted horseman or a woman's devoted attendant. Male slave owners could take sexual liberties with their female slaves without fear of the legal consequences. José Bacardi Massó, Don Facundo's unmarried brother and business partner, is believed to have fathered two children by slave women, a son named Juan and a daughter named Carmen.* Slaves could under some conditions earn their freedom, but even emancipated slaves had severely restricted rights.

Still, the color lines were not drawn as sharply in Cuba as they were in the Southern United States at the time. Slaves had the legal right to purchase their freedom, and through frugality and enterprise many managed to do so. Freed blacks worked as artisans, shopkeepers, or musicians, often devoting a share of their earnings to guilds that were set up to help those still enslaved. There were numerous social events where Cubans of all colors were well represented, and interracial cooperation in the anti-Spanish cause was evident from the beginning. Antonio Maceo, a politically aware young mulatto in Santiago who had worked as a mule driver, caught the attention of a liberal lawyer in the city who introduced him to a group of white merchants active in anti-Spanish plotting. In 1864 they invited Maceo to join the local Masonic lodge. Like other Masonic lodges around the country, the Santiago temple served as a center of revolutionary planning, due largely to the secrecy around lodge membership and operations. Maceo, the son of a black Dominican woman and a Venezuelan soldier, eventually became a revolutionary hero, known as the Bronze Titan. He commanded white Cuban officers and a large multiracial army, holding a position of authority that would have been unimaginable for a black U.S. soldier at the time.

The first Cuban war for independence began in the fall of 1868 when a plantation owner freed his slaves and invited them to join him in taking up arms

---

*Juan's mother was apparently a slave belonging to Amalia Moreau. In the slavery tradition, she would have taken her owner's surname, so her son's full name was Juan Bacardi Moreau. Upon the death of Emilio Bacardi in 1922, Juan Bacardi wrote Emilio's widow to express his condolences "for the loss of my beloved first cousin." In that letter, he noted that after his own father passed away, his cousin Emilio had acted as "my father . . . and my protector." According to a 1947 company memorandum, José Bacardi Massó also had a daughter named Carmen, born of a slave whom José had purchased.

against the Spanish military. Carlos Manuel de Céspedes, who raised sugar near the eastern town of Yara, was an advocate of democracy and liberal ideas who, like Emilio Bacardi, had been educated in Spain. In the predawn hours of October 10, 1868, Céspedes was meeting at his home with a small group of like-minded growers to discuss plans for an armed revolt when word arrived that the Spanish authorities had learned of their conspiracy and put out an order for their arrest. Knowing they had little chance of escape, Céspedes told his coconspirators it was time to move, and then he summoned his slave overseer, a man named Borrero.

"Ring the bell and call the *fila*, Borrero," he said, meaning the slaves were to be assembled in rank and file, as they were each day when an assignment was to be given. The slaves, both men and women, came stumbling sleepily out of their huts, still weary from the previous day's labor, and lined up obediently in front of their master. Céspedes then addressed them in a booming voice.

"Citizens," he said, "up until now you have been my slaves. From this moment on, you are as free as I am. To win its independence and freedom, Cuba needs every one of its sons. Those of you who want to follow me, follow. Those who want to stay here, stay. Everyone will be equally free."

The declaration became known as the Grito de Yara (the Cry of Yara), and it was repeated across the island as a proclamation of Cuba's independence and an invitation to all Cubans to join in a revolutionary struggle to free their country from Spanish rule. Céspedes appointed himself commander of his little revolutionary army, which at first consisted of just 147 fighters, including his own liberated slaves. But the Grito de Yara drew an immediate response, and by the end of the month Céspedes had twelve thousand men under his command. Many were dressed poorly and armed only with machetes, the long, heavy, curved knives used to cut cane and clear underbrush. But their ranks grew each time they entered a city shouting "¡*Viva Cuba libre! ¡Independencia o muerte!*" (Long live free Cuba! Independence or death!).

◆ ◆ ◆

In Santiago, Emilio and Facundo Jr. joined their friends in cheering the early success of the fledgling rebel army, though they were not personally convinced the time was yet right for an armed revolt, nor were they prepared to answer the call to arms themselves. Others in their La Flor del Siboney circle had no such qualms. Pío Rosado, the high-strung arithmetic teacher who was always ready for adventure, wanted to fight but had no weapon. Clever as a fox, Rosado figured the easiest way to get one was to enlist in the *voluntarios*. As soon as the militia leaders gave him a rifle and a safe conduct pass, he deserted his unit and headed for the hills.

The Bacardi brothers held back partly out of respect for their father, who remained a loyal *peninsular* Spaniard. By the time the independence war broke out, Don Facundo was a respected merchant in Santiago known for his honest dealings and his years of service to the community. With his roots in Catalonia, a semiautonomous and linguistically distinct region of Spain that had long suffered under Madrid's administration, he knew that rule from the *metrópoli* could be arbitrary, but he was totally against the idea of an armed insurrection. Indeed, his response to the independence movement was to join the Círculo Español, a charity and recreation group set up to protect and promote the *peninsular* element in Santiago. Emilio and Facundo Jr. therefore found themselves in a difficult position, committed to the Cuban cause but reluctant to upset their father. Facundo Jr. in particular was troubled. Four years younger than his brother and not having had Emilio's experience living away from his family, Facundo Jr. was less independent of his father than Emilio was. By 1868 he was working at his father's side in the distillery, learning the art and craft of rum making and preparing to follow in his footsteps. Young Facundo was just twenty years old at the time, and the thought of crossing his stern father still unnerved him.

For his part, Emilio feared that an armed struggle would set Cuban against Cuban in a bloody conflict with devastating consequences. The real enemy, he argued, was not so much the government in Madrid as it was the Spanish colonial administration in Cuba. A few months earlier, liberal forces in Spain had managed to remove Isabella II from the throne and install a provisional government that promptly drafted a new constitution establishing universal male suffrage and freedom of the press. In a message to his governors around the island, however, the Spanish captain-general in Havana ordered that repressive policies should be continued, "no matter who is in power on the peninsula." When discussing politics among his friends, Emilio took the position that Cuban nationalists should declare their solidarity with the reformers in Madrid and then work to install a new colonial administration that would honor the constitution enacted back in Spain.

Though he was just twenty-four and had no formal leadership role in the revolutionary movement, Emilio came up with a brazen plan to unseat the colonial governor in Santiago. His idea was to spark a mass uprising in front of the governor's palace at the Plaza de Armas on the night of December 4, 1868. The plaza that night would be full of people assembling for a *retreta*, a musical promenade held two nights a week. Emilio's idea was to disrupt the gathering with a short but fiery speech in which he would urge his fellow townspeople to move en masse on the governor's palace, which faced the plaza. His brother Facundo Jr. and a few close friends agreed to help.

By 8 that night, a crowd had begun to assemble at the plaza. Gas lanterns cast soft halos on the square, illuminating the greenery, the gravel walkway around the plaza perimeter, and the benches alongside. The governor's military band was seated off to one side, playing a variety of operatic selections and Cuban dances. Gentlemen in white twill suits and panama hats strolled leisurely around the plaza, smoking cigars. The ladies came in dresses of delicate muslin or linen, with long folds that swept the ground, and they carried fans, which they fluttered constantly.

Emilio and his brother had been to many *retretas* to watch the girls parade, but on this night they stood nervously on the edge of the plaza, keeping an eye on the Santiago governor, who was watching from his palace balcony. Other conspirators were in position opposite the government building. Emilio had even recruited some guards from the customshouse, and they stood on an adjacent corner, waiting to help lead the uprising. According to the routine of past *retretas,* the military band would stop playing at 10 P.M. and move to the front of the governor's palace, where they would play the "Himno de Riego," a favorite Spanish anthem, and then depart the square in a procession. On this night, the playing of the "Himno" was to be the signal for the uprising. Emilio would make his speech, and his coconspirators, strategically positioned around the plaza, would begin shouting "*¡Libertad!*" and "*¡Viva Cuba libre, unida a España!*" (Freedom! Long live a free Cuba, united with Spain!) Emilio was to urge the crowd to converge on the governor's palace and demand that he resign. Several of the band members had agreed beforehand to stay in place rather than depart the square, and a unit of military engineers and the crew of a visiting war frigate were also supposed to support the action.

Almost nothing, however, went according to plan. The band did not move toward the governor's house as it normally would have. The townspeople began leaving the square before the band began playing the "Himno," unaware of anything out of the ordinary. The frigate crew was nowhere to be seen. Emilio, noticing the crowd in the plaza dispersing, began hollering to get their attention and managed to make a short speech. Facundo Jr. and the other conspirators responded with their "viva"s but to no effect. Those townspeople who had stopped to listen seemed confused by what was happening. Several policemen on the scene, suspecting an effort to incite a disturbance, moved quickly toward the Bacardi brothers, who then turned and fled. One officer managed to grab Facundo Jr. by the arm, but he was able to break loose and run away.

Writing in retrospect, Emilio acknowledged that his plan was nothing but "foolish audacity." It's not easy to arrange spontaneous uprisings beforehand. The townspeople who assembled to watch the *retreta* hardly represented the most rebellious element in Santiago, and Emilio and Facundo and their friends had not thought their plot through very carefully. The Bacardi brothers were fortunate to avoid imprisonment. Both were well known in the city, and given the authorities' well-organized intelligence network, it was inconceivable that the two had not been identified in the square. The prominence of their social position may have saved them. Spanish officials may also have considered the Bacardis' advocacy of reform over revolution and concluded that it was not in the regime's interest to radicalize them and like-minded *reformistas.* At the time, the armed insurgency was heating up in the countryside, and the authorities did not want to fuel it.

Within weeks, combat was taking place in the outskirts of Santiago. On Christmas Eve, Spanish troops and militia members took up positions on street corners around the city, and word spread that the rebels were about to arrive in the city. The heightened security, however, was actually for a meeting between the governor and a rebel emissary. The insurgent representative, accompanied by a Spanish cavalry officer, rode into town on horseback, evidently unconcerned that he could be captured and killed. To the astonishment of old friends, students, and neighbors, it turned out to be none other than Pío Rosado, the former schoolteacher, already a colonel in the revolutionary army barely two months after heading to the mountains. Rosado carried a letter from Carlos Manuel de Céspedes with a complaint that Spanish soldiers were summarily executing captured rebels. Céspedes warned that if the governor did not order an end to the practice, the rebel forces would institute the same policy. The governor rejected the complaint but ordered that Rosado be given safe passage out of the city. When he left the governor's palace, Rosado found that a group of *voluntarios* had cut the stirrups off his saddle. "Idiots," he muttered, and then he leaped deftly onto his horse's back and rode haughtily out of town.

The volunteers were key to the Spanish counterrevolutionary effort, but their fondness for violence sometimes embarrassed even the colonial administration. Any Spanish official who did not take a hard line with the Cuban rebels could find himself in trouble with the *voluntarios,* whose preferred solution to the insurgency was to smash it militarily and terrorize its civilian base. Some of the *voluntario* units could be considered an early Cuban version of the fascist paramilitaries that in later years would make their appearance in Nazi-controlled Europe or the racist white militias that battled native

Algerians or black South Africans. Their recruitment methods were not subtle, as Emilio Bacardi himself discovered. When a group of local *voluntarios* showed up at his family's house to demand his enlistment, Emilio refused to let them in. "If you call yourselves volunteers, what are you doing here?" he said. "I haven't asked for any weapon!" An angry exchange and a shoving match ensued. It ended only when Emilio grabbed a rifle that the quartermaster had brought for him, threw it out the window into the street, and ordered the *voluntarios* out of his family's house.

Competing social and political pressures were putting Emilio in an impossible situation. Now twenty-four, his adolescence and early adulthood had been shaped by conflict. He was torn between his devotion to his own slave-owning family and his personal antislavery views, between his commitment to his father and the enterprise that was his father's life work and his dedication to the struggle for a free Cuba, which was taking more of his time and energy. The tensions in his life appeared again and again, especially as Emilio took on more responsibility in the family and in his father's rum business, where commercial considerations regularly crossed with political realities. His instinct always was to seek compromise solutions, but the Spanish authorities were taking such an intransigent line that any middle ground between the colonial regime and the insurgency was fast disappearing.

A turning point for Emilio came in the spring of 1869. On March 26, Good Friday, a solemn religious procession through downtown Santiago was interrupted when someone suddenly shouted "*¡Viva Cuba libre!*" Police immediately rushed into the crowd in search of the provocateur, causing pandemonium. A young slave named Cornelio Robert, the property of a prominent anti-Spanish activist in Santiago, was arrested and subjected within hours to a court-martial by Spanish military commanders. Mindful of the slave rebellion that had led to France losing Haiti, the Spanish colonial authorities were determined to show no leniency toward suspected black rebels in Cuba. Though no incriminating evidence was presented against him, Robert was immediately found guilty of *infidencia* (unfaithfulness or treason) and executed by firing squad early the next morning. "The Spanish authorities wanted to send a message," the Santiago historian Ernesto Buch López wrote of the episode, "and they were not to be deterred by mere legalities. Their intent was to carry out a series of 'legal murders' that would sow terror in the population." Over the next week, several more alleged rebel sympathizers were arrested and immediately shot. The authorities officially defined the crime of *infidencia* to include providing refuge or intelligence to rebels, expressing subversive or seditious sentiments, spreading propaganda, "and anything else with a political end that disturbs peace and public order or in some way undermines the national integrity."

Disgusted by the bloody crackdown, Emilio Bacardi gave up the *reformista* path and became a revolutionary, devoting himself to underground activities. He was given the assignment of soliciting funds to purchase arms and ammunition for the rebel army, and he served as an intermediary among the fighters in the hills, their supporters in Santiago, and the overseas exiles supporting the revolution. According to Bacardi lore, Emilio himself wanted to join the combatants in the hills, but his comrades argued that he would be more useful in Santiago. It was probably just as dangerous an assignment, given the network of Spanish spies in the city and the consequences of being identified as a supporter of the rebel cause.

Soon it was Don Facundo who was in an awkward position. He did not support revolution, but neither did he endorse the oppressive policies of the colonial administration. When he discovered that some of his *peninsular* compatriots in the Círculo Español were financing *voluntario* death squads, he separated himself from the organization. That action, and his unwillingness to denounce Emilio, soon got Facundo himself in trouble with the authorities. He and his wife were summoned to the palace in Santiago one day to meet with the governor, who heatedly demanded to know why they were allowing their sons to involve themselves with subversives. Don Facundo sullenly refused to answer, but Doña Amalia was not in the least intimidated.

"They are adults, and they are old enough to make their own choices," she said firmly. "It's not for us to direct them."

The governor, infuriated by her impudence, said the Bacardis as a family were proving to be "bad Spaniards," and he ordered Amalia and Facundo to leave the building.

• • •

Variations on the Bacardi family story played out across Cuba, in all the homes where native sons of Cuba joined the independence movement over the objections of Spanish fathers who were loyal to Madrid or even toiled for the colonial administration. In Havana, the teenage son of a Spanish soldier adopted the Cuban revolution as his personal cause.

José Martí, who would become Cuba's greatest national hero, showed such promise in his early academic work that the director of the Havana Municipal School for Boys, a nationalist poet named Rafael María de Mendive, offered to accommodate the lad in his own home when his father was posted outside Havana.

As Daniel Costa and Francisco Martínez Betancourt had done for Emilio Bacardi, encouraging him to think for himself, Mendive did for the young Martí.

He was just fifteen when Carlos Manuel de Céspedes freed his slaves and launched the Cuban revolution, but Martí closely followed what he later called the "glorious and bloody preparation" for that moment. In October 1869, just before the first anniversary of the revolution, Martí was arrested on the basis of an unsent letter found in his house, signed by him and addressed to a fellow student who was preparing to enlist in the Spanish army. In the letter, Martí appeared to encourage the student to reconsider his decision. Though he was barely seventeen years old, Martí was sentenced by the Spanish authorities to six years of hard labor in a prison attached to a stone quarry. For Martí, the back-breaking experience was an education on the suffering of other prisoners, many of whom had been sent to the quarry because of their involvement in revolutionary activities. After several months, Martí's parents were able to get their son's sentence reduced, and he was subsequently allowed to leave Cuba for Spain. Shortly after his arrival in Madrid, Martí published a dramatic account of his experience in prison, *El presidio político en Cuba* (Political prison in Cuba). He was barely eighteen years old. The tract had a major impact among Spanish liberals, largely because of his eloquence in condemning those Spanish authorities who were torturing and killing young Cubans in the name of Spain's "national integrity."

El presidio político en Cuba established Martí's reputation both as a writer and as an advocate for Cuba. He meshed the roles so perfectly that his accomplishments went beyond either literature or politics alone. From Spain, he traveled to Paris, New York, Mexico, and finally back to New York, where he founded the Cuban Revolutionary Party and almost single-handedly rallied the Cuban diaspora to support the cause of independence. He eventually met Emilio Bacardi, and the two became friends and collaborators.

At the time, Emilio was collecting funds for the rebel army, passing messages, and circulating revolutionary literature, even while trying to keep a low profile. Santiago was crawling with Spanish troops and *voluntarios*, ready at any moment to arrest anyone they suspected of being a rebel collaborator. Some people were found to have been "unfaithful" to the state merely on the basis of a report that they had been seen at a rebel location. A week or two later, an announcement would come that the condemned men would be executed. At midnight on the eve of their execution, the prisoners were moved to an execution waiting chamber. Early the following morning, a firing squad consisting of an officer and twenty-five soldiers, mainly drawn from the *voluntario* ranks, would escort the prisoner to the place of execution, which in Santiago was, appropriately, the exterior wall of the municipal slaughterhouse. At 7 A.M. sharp, they would be shot, in full view of anyone walking on the busy street that ran alongside the building. As part of his research for the *Crónicas*, Emilio listed by name all the people executed by the Spanish military or the *voluntarios* in 1869 and 1870 alone. The list went on for twenty-five pages.

Cuba was split into two worlds. In the cities, the Spanish army and the *voluntarios* were in control, while the ill-equipped rebels remained in the countryside, where they dominated. Their top military strategist, General Máximo Gómez, was a master of guerrilla tactics and believed the rebels should weaken the colonial regime by cutting railroads and burning sugar mills. Whenever they destroyed a sugar plantation, the rebels would invite the plantation slaves to join them, explaining that the aim of revolution was the abolition of slavery as well as independence. The rebel army was soon a thoroughly interracial force, including poor white farmers, mulattoes, and free blacks, as well as emancipated slaves. Only about a quarter of the fighters had guns. Most carried machetes, and some former slaves—primarily the Congolese—had only wooden daggers dipped in poison, a technology carried over from Africa. During the earlier civil war in Santo Domingo (later, the Dominican Republic), Spanish troops had pejoratively referred to black fighters as *mambises*, derived from an African word, and during the Cuban independence war, the rebel fighters adopted the name proudly for themselves. The black and mulatto fighters rallied especially behind the twenty-year-old captain Antonio Maceo.

By 1873, however, the revolution was losing force. Many superior officers had been killed in battle or assassinated. The rebel leaders were also demoralized by the lack of support for the Cuban cause in Washington. In October, an American steamer, the *Virginius*, allegedly owned by the Cuban revolutionary committee in New York, was stopped by a Spanish man-of-war in British territorial waters off the coast of Jamaica. Among the ship's passengers were nearly a hundred Cubans who had volunteered to fight in the revolution, plus a shipment of arms and ammunition for the rebel army. The American-British crew managed to throw the war matériel overboard before the ship was seized, but everyone aboard was taken to Santiago to face a court-martial. Within days, fifty-two of the passengers and crew members had been executed on the orders of the Spanish governor in Santiago, General Juan Burriel.

The others would probably have been executed as well but for the intervention of a British naval commander, Sir Lambton Lorraine, who heard about what happened and brought his own frigate into Santiago to confront Burriel. The affair quickly escalated into an international crisis. Lorraine got his superiors' authorization to sink one of the Spanish ships in the harbor if one more British prisoner were shot. That threat forestalled additional executions, at least temporarily, while furious negotiations were conducted. In the end, the Spanish government apologized for the incident, Burriel was relieved of his command, and Sir Lambton Lorraine became a Santiago hero.

The *Virginius* incident had special significance for the Bacardis. The slaughterhouse (*matadero*) was less than a block from the distillery on Matadero Street. Facundo Jr. was working there when the executions occurred and heard the shots. He knew exactly what was happening, having heard firing squads on previous occasions. Clambering over the distillery fence, he looked toward the slaughterhouse and saw a horse-drawn wagon parked by the execution wall. A body had just been thrown in the back, and two legs protruded from the wagon end. It was an image he would never forget.

* * *

In 1874, still in the midst of war, the Bacardi company went through its first reorganization. José Bacardi Massó, who had put up most of the money to buy the Nunes distillery but was minimally involved in its operation, sold his shares to Facundo, his older brother. José León Bouteiller, advancing in age and declining in health, also sold some of his shares. With the help of his wife, Facundo contributed enough capital to establish himself as the senior partner. Bouteiller left a few pesos in the company, and Emilio and Facundo Jr. each contributed 750 pesos from inheritances they had received from their godmother Clara Astié. This gave the company a total capitalization of 6,500 dollar pesos, almost double the initial investment. The new firm was called Bacardi & Compañía, the name under which it would gain worldwide fame.

"Bacardi" was the best-known rum brand on the island, but new competitors were appearing. In 1872 three Spanish businessmen established another rum factory in Santiago. They had experience in making cognac and sherry in Spain and intended to focus on making aged rum, applying some of the same aging and blending procedures long used in sherry production. They sold their premium aged product as Ron Matusalem Extra Viejo (Extra Old Methuselah Rum), named for the Old Testament patriarch who was said to have lived more than nine hundred years.

Facundo Bacardi featured a different rum style. In 1873 his company introduced a new product, Ron Superior Extra Seco (Superior Extra Dry Rum), the lightest and whitest rum ever sold in Cuba. In 1876 the Bacardis sent a sample of Extra Seco to the Centennial International Exposition in Philadelphia, the first major world fair to be held in the United States. Competing against three other Cuban distilleries, as well as several North American and Caribbean rums, Don Facundo's Extra Seco took the top prize in its class. A year later the same label won a gold medal at the Exposición Universal in Madrid.

One development during this period worked to the company's favor. A devastating plague hit the French vineyards in the late 1860s, when the phylloxera pest began infecting the vines. Wine and brandy production dropped almost to zero, and French consumers had to look elsewhere for their spirits. The new rums appearing on the market were an instant hit in France, and in the absence of wine and brandy production, rum imports soared. The Bacardis' international promotion of their rum was paying off. The phylloxera pest spread gradually southward, and soon the wine industry in Catalonia was affected as well. Catalan wine had been one of rum's main competitors in Cuba, and its reduced availability to island drinkers meant a bigger opening for rum.

Satisfied that his company was on solid footing, Don Facundo opted to retire in 1877, leaving the rum business in the hands of his sons. The youngest, twenty-year-old José, worked in sales. Facundo Jr., who had worked closely with his father for years, handled production and became the company's first "Master Blender." Don Facundo, however, named thirty-three-year-old Emilio as president. Being the oldest son mattered in Cuba. A year earlier, Emilio had married María Lay Berlucheau, a *santiaguera* of French descent like Doña Amalia. Around the time Emilio became the company president, María gave birth to a boy, named Emilio after his father but known throughout his life as Emilito.

With his new family and business responsibilities, Emilio was a changed man. No longer the rabble-rouser of his twenties, trying to incite a disturbance in the town square, he had become a respected businessman in a suit and tie and a white straw hat. Still, he did not back off from his work with the independence movement. His higher profile at the family company after Don Facundo's retirement actually gave him an even better cover for underground work. He now had commercial reasons to visit local sugar plantations, where he coincidentally could make contact with rebel representatives. His business dealings took him all around Santiago and even abroad, where he met regularly with rebel supporters and patrons of their cause.

With Emilio at the helm of the family business, the Bacardi name had a dual meaning in Santiago. Bacardi & Compañía was a successful commercial enterprise with international reach. Bacardi rum was above politics, favored by pro-Spanish *voluntarios* and pro-Cuban rebels alike, and did business with whoever wanted to buy rum, wherever there were opportunities, from Havana to Madrid. But the Bacardi sons were Cuban nationalists and independence advocates, and Emilio was an enemy of Spanish authority. This intertwining of nationalist and capitalist identities became a defining characteristic of the family enterprise, and the way Bacardi & Compañía managed the dual roles would distinguish the firm from its competitors for generations to come.

Emilio took over leadership of his father's company just as the Cuban war was entering its final months. Carlos Manuel de Céspedes was killed in 1874 when Spanish troops found him on a farm where he had sought refuge. Antonio Maceo, the brilliant young mulatto general, demonstrated exceptional skill and bravery leading his troops in almost daily combat against superior Spanish forces, but conservative forces renewed old charges that he would rally Cuban blacks against whites and establish a "Negro republic," and his leadership was seriously undercut.

In February 1878, after nearly ten years of war, the "commissioners" of the revolutionary Cuban Republic met with the overall Spanish commander in the village of Zanjón and agreed to end the fighting. The Pacto del Zanjón promised the same political autonomy for Cuba that Puerto Rico then enjoyed, plus emancipation of those slaves who were in the rebel army. It did not, however, meet the revolution's central demands—independence and the abolition of slavery—and Antonio Maceo told the Spanish commander at a meeting in Baraguá that he would not abide by the agreement. Several months later, Maceo himself was forced to accept a truce, but his defiant stand, dubbed the Protest of Baraguá, offered at least a heroic flourish at the end.

The Ten Years' War cost the lives of about fifty thousand Cubans and more than two hundred thousand Spaniards, but it also contributed to the construction of a Cuban nationality that extended across racial lines and to the creation of an ideal for which the Cuban nation had proved willing to fight. José Martí famously described the war as "that wonderful and sudden emergence of a people, apparently servile only a short time before, who made heroic feats a daily event, hunger a banquet, and the extraordinary, a commonplace."

In theory, the Zanjón agreement provided an opening for democratic local government and free elections. A "Liberal" Party, sometimes known as the Autonomist Party, was organized in Cuba to compete politically with the conservative, pro-Spanish forces on the island. Its political program envisioned Cuba remaining a Spanish colony but with political autonomy. Emilio Bacardi was one of the founding members in Santiago, arguing that the political opening afforded by the Zanjón pact should be exploited, regardless of whether it provided all the revolution had sought.

The Liberals soundly defeated the pro-Spain Conservatives in Santiago's first free elections, and Emilio won a seat on the town council. In public office, he displayed a surprisingly moralistic streak given his relatively young age. He cosponsored a measure to crack down on carnival activities in Santiago, for example, by allowing no more than four carnival days per year and barring any public dances or masquerade parades that offended the community's "morals and decency." (This was one part of his legacy that future Bacardis would not always honor.) But Emilio also demonstrated liberal impulses by proposing that the city build low-cost housing units and sell them to workers at discounted prices and by insisting that the right to sell lottery tickets be reserved exclusively for the aged and the handicapped. He showed such interest in schooling issues that he was selected to serve on the local board of education. He became one of the most popular and respected politicians in the city, and his office on Marina Baja Street was filled constantly with people seeking his help or advice.

The flurry of democratic activity in Cuba did not last long. Authorities in Madrid ignored many of the promises made at Zanjón and once again restricted Cubans' rights. Within months, some veterans of the Ten Years' War were arguing that they had to return to combat. In the eastern province of Oriente, former rebel leaders collected their weapons and headed back to the mountains, with hundreds of fighters following them. Emilio argued that taking up arms again would be suicidal, but it was in vain. As soon as he heard that combat had begun again, Emilio headed to the city hall and made arrangements to set up a war hospital there.

The Spanish authorities reacted furiously to the renewed fighting and began detaining anyone they regarded as an opponent, without bothering to make inquiries, gather evidence, or hold trials. The sweep initially targeted Santiago blacks and mulattoes, with more than three hundred arrested immediately and thrown into a dungeon to await deportation, but it was soon broadened. On September 6, 1879, sixty-four-year-old Don Facundo himself was detained at the Matadero facility along with Facundo Jr. They were soon freed, but the police then headed for the Bacardi offices on Marina Baja, where they found Emilio and arrested him.

For more than ten years, Emilio had successfully dodged the authorities while carrying out underground work for the revolution. Ironically, it was only now, when he had disagreed with the decision to take up arms, that he found himself under arrest. "No concrete charges could be brought against him," his daughter Amalia wrote in a biography of her father, "but the colonial authorities knew only too well whom they were taking."

Six others were imprisoned with Emilio: another city councilman, two lawyers, a legal clerk, a journalist, and a twenty-four-year-old municipal employee named Federico Pérez Carbó, who soon became one of Emilio's closest friends. Within a week, they were transferred from the local jail to the Morro, the ancient fortress at the head of Santiago Bay that long had served as a maximum-security prison. The inmates were held incommunicado for more than a month before they were allowed a breath of fresh air or a taste of decent food. Emilio, the inveterate note taker, recorded every development in a tiny diary, from the changes of command to the arrival of new prisoners.

On November 4, Emilio learned he and the others were being sent to Spain. Before leaving, he was allowed just a brief visit from his young wife, María, his firstborn son, Emilito, and his newest son, Daniel. There is no record of their meeting in his diary. He noted only his subsequent arrival in Puerto Rico, the transfer to a second boat, and the departure for Spain. Three days later, at sea, grief overcame him. "It's half past midnight, and from somewhere I can hear the cry of a child," he wrote. "Oh! If only they would bring that child to me, how I would entertain it, how I would kiss that little creature, that child who in this great faraway emptiness reminds my soul of my own Emilio and Daniel. I heard this moan as their cry of farewell, coming all the way from my home! My poor boys! How it seemed I could hear them! How it seemed I heard them say, 'Papa!'"

The resumption of fighting had brought disaster. Hundreds of brave Cuban fighters were killed, including Emilio's longtime chum Pío Rosado, who was caught and executed by a firing squad. A clerk at the field headquarters where he was taken reported that the fearless Rosado was brought before the commanding Spanish officer with his elbows tied behind his back but holding a half-smoked cigar in one hand and showing total contempt for his captors. Within weeks, all resistance to the Spanish troops was gone. The second revolutionary war did not even last one year, and it went down in Cuban history as La Guerra Chiquita (The Little War).

✂⊱⊰✂

Chapter 4

A Time of Transition

Emilio Bacardi was held in Spain for nearly four years, first in a prison in Cádiz, then in a penal colony on the Chafarine Islands off the North African coast, and finally under house arrest in Seville. During the time he was away, Bacardi & Compañía nearly went out of business. Years of war and decades of oppressive Spanish rule and colonial mismanagement had left eastern Cuba drained of resources and energy. The municipal government in Santiago, desperate for revenue, raised taxes, even though the burning of plantations had wrecked the sugar and coffee economies. Many of the shopkeepers who sold Bacardi rum were unable to pay their suppliers, the Bacardis included. In October 1880, the company's debts, largely for the purchase of molasses, barrels, and bottles, totaled more than thirty thousand dollars. Facundo Jr. and his twenty-three-year-old brother José were doing their best to maintain rum production and sales, but with just $260 in cash and about nine thousand dollars' worth of unsold rum, they had no choice but to file for bankruptcy.

One month later, the Bacardis suffered an even more devastating blow. A fire that started in an adjacent warehouse spread to the company offices and distillery on Marina Baja Street, and much of the property burned. Lost in the blaze was the distillery equipment, the barrels of aging rum that were stored there, and all the company records. The property was not insured. The Bacardis still had their distillery on Matadero Street and were able to boost production at that location to some extent, but with the fire on top of the bankruptcy, their company's prospects were as bleak as they had ever been.

They got little sympathy; all of Cuba was suffering. The failure to resolve the conflict with Spain left business and civic leaders exhausted and demoralized. Sugar prices were dropping sharply, in spite of decreased Cuban production. Long-term trends were just as unfavorable. Normal trade and banking activities were distorted by Spain's grip on the island. U.S. timber, mineral, and sugar interests were moving in to take advantage of low land prices and crowding out Cuban capital. Many of the country's most talented and enterprising young men were dead, imprisoned, exiled, or marginalized by the colonial authorities. It was a time for conscientious Cubans, the Bacardis included, to reset aims, review remaining possibilities, and demonstrate resolve.

• • •

Emilio was nearly forty years old when he returned to Santiago, and he came back with the inner calm and strength that the experience of imprisonment can bestow. Many of his fellow Cuban detainees in Spain were poor farmers or workers, and Emilio had shared filthy jail cells with them and endured the same miserable conditions without losing his dignity. He soon earned the other prisoners' respect, and from the beginning he had played a leadership role, intervening with Spanish authorities to secure better rations for the neediest prisoners at a time when they were forced to purchase their own food.

When he was herded onto the prison boat to Spain in November 1879, Emilio left behind a pregnant wife and two small boys. He returned to a three-year-old daughter, named María after her mother, and Emilito and Daniel were now six and five. He was a stranger to all three. Emilio vowed that his family would come first from then on. Within a year of his return, María gave birth to twins, Facundo ("Facundito") and José, thus producing a third consecutive generation of Bacardi boys with those names. Another daughter, Carmen, followed a short time later.

Were it not for the joy of being reunited with his family, Emilio would have had reason to be discouraged. The Marina Baja property was still in ruins, nearly three years after the fire. There was no money to rebuild. In 1881, after the bankruptcy and the fire, Bacardi & Compañía had losses of $9,600, and Emilio's mother had been forced to sell some inherited farmland to help defray outstanding debt. And then there was the political situation. Imprisonment and exile had hardened Emilio's commitment to Cuba's independence, and he was now disgusted by the timid Liberal Party politicians occupying the few government positions still reserved for Cubans.

But Emilio was as energetic as ever, and he promptly set out to help his two brothers with the family business, even walling off a makeshift office in the ruins of the Marina Baja property, the place where he had always preferred to work. It would take several weeks for him to catch up on what he had missed in the rum business during his long absence. His father, Don Facundo, had withdrawn from most daily work but continued to provide strategic guidance and technical advice. Facundo Jr. had continued to experiment with yeast strains and filtration technology and was still trying to improve on his blends. José, the youngest of the Bacardi Moreau sons, was in charge of sales. The two brothers had worked long hours, mortgaged the company properties to the limit, and sold just enough rum to buy more molasses and meet their small payroll.

In 1884 the Bacardis hired a new financial assistant, Henri Schueg, whose grandparents on both sides had been French colonists in Cuba. When he was just a year old, Henri's parents moved the family back to France, leaving their small coffee plantation outside Santiago in the custody of Don Facundo, an old family friend. As a young man, Henri excelled both at learning and in business, and when he finished his schooling he went to work at an import firm in Bordeaux that had trading ties with Cuba. He had picked up Spanish from his parents, and he quickly impressed his superiors with his skills. In 1882, after both his parents died, twenty-year-old Henri headed to Cuba to develop his parents' properties there. After concluding that the family coffee plantation required too much work, he sold it and invested the earnings in a chicken farm. Cuba enchanted him, and "Henri" soon became "Enrique." Though a bicycle accident had left him with a twisted leg, he learned quickly to ride a horse, and for a year he managed the farm himself. The Bacardi brothers, who met him through their father, were impressed by the ease with which the gallant young man made the transition from French businessman to Cuban farmer, and they took an immediate liking to him. After Emilio returned in 1883 and rejoined the family business, he and his brothers invited Enrique to work with them, giving him the assignment of managing the firm's troubled finances.

Enrique Schueg's arrival in 1884 was a lift for the Bacardis just when it was needed most. Because he had been in France throughout the war, he was unaffected by the agonies of that time and brought fresh energy, new ideas, and a joie de vivre into the Bacardis' world. Doña Amalia had raised her children to value their French heritage, and Enrique fit snugly into the family. Though he knew nothing about distilling, he was worldly in his tastes and had ideas about ways to market Bacardi rum outside Cuba.

And then came another blow. In the spring of 1885, Emilio's thirty-three-year-old wife, María, became mysteriously ill. Her condition quickly worsened, and in May she died, leaving Emilio with six children, four of them under the age of five. For the first time in his life, Emilio found himself utterly lost. "It seems like a dream to me," he wrote to his twenty-four-year-old sister Amalia five days after María's death. "But what a long dream it is and so painful!" Unprepared to parent his children alone, he asked Amalia to help him. "María was a saint," he said. "She told me to hug you and say good-bye for her, and she asked that you take her children." Unable to function at home or at work, Emilio withdrew for a time to a country house belonging to María's brother.

She had been his true love, and for half their marriage they had been separated. Her death only underscored how much his imprisonment by the Spanish authorities had cost him personally.

Barely a year later, Don Facundo died at the age of seventy-one, worn down by a lifetime of hard work and still unsure whether his company would prosper or fail. He had few assets to his name beyond his share of the renowned but still struggling rum business and a small farm outside Santiago that he called Los Cocos. With his passing, the first Bacardi era in Cuba came to a close, an era that had begun with a penniless immigrant following his brothers to Cuba to seek his fortune. Don Facundo had envisioned his company as a family firm, but his sons would now have to decide whether they had the interest and commitment to keep it going. Commercial rum producers were popping up all over Cuba, and it would have been easy to find someone ready to buy the business. But each of the brothers had a stake in the enterprise. Facundo Jr. had been doing distillery work since he was a teenager and held all the production secrets in his head. He was as valuable an asset to the firm as the "Bacardi" brand or the physical facilities and equipment. José Bacardi Moreau also considered himself part of the company, though he had moved to Havana to direct rum sales in the capital. Finally there was Emilio, the titular president and now the public face of the Bacardis in Santiago.

Still mourning his wife, Emilio did not hesitate in rededicating himself to the family business. He oversaw another reorganization of Bacardi & Compañía, with the three Bacardi sons getting equal ownership shares. Family cohesion had been a Bacardi strength in Santiago since the day Don Facundo's older brothers helped him get started in the retail world. Hard work can take an entrepreneur only so far without a supportive family behind him. No matter how creative and disciplined he was, Don Facundo would have failed in his business ventures without the money that came from his wife's inheritances. The cooperation of family members helped protect Bacardi company assets again when the firm's semibankrupt status made it vulnerable to creditors. In 1879 the Bacardis had "sold" the distillery on Matadero Street to José Bacardi Massó, Don Facundo's brother and the man who provided the cash to purchase the distillery in the first place. José was barely involved in company operations; the transaction was carried out purely for legal reasons, to shield the distillery from being taken over by a creditor or by the Spanish authorities. The family bonds were reinforced each time the business experienced adversity and gave the Bacardi company a character that made their story notable in business annals. Enrique Schueg, the French-Cuban with impressive business smarts, owed his full incorporation into the Bacardi firm in part to his being adopted by the family. He became a partner only after marrying Amalia Bacardi Moreau, Don Facundo and Doña Amalia's daughter, in 1893.

• • •

The Cuban independence cause was by no means forgotten, but in the aftermath of the unsuccessful Ten Years' War, priorities changed. There were no significant armed uprisings in Cuba against the Spanish presence during the whole of the 1880s. The major Cuban commanders, Máximo Gómez and Antonio Maceo, focused instead on organizing and fund-raising for future efforts, as did José Martí. Though barely thirty, the Cuban writer and organizer was already influential in the exile community, especially in New York, where he settled in 1881. In Martí's judgment, earlier revolutionary efforts had failed largely because of a lack of strategic coordination and civilian oversight. Before any new uprisings could be launched, he argued, the movement needed to be consolidated politically. The notion of "Free Cuba" needed ideological substance. Martí's idea was to bring Cuban émigrés together "in one magnificent democratic enterprise" to draft a political program with broad appeal, because the challenge of achieving independence was not only military, "but a most complicated problem in politics."

The priority Martí gave to popular political education appealed to Cubans like Emilio Bacardi, who always saw intellectual work as a good point of entry into the revolutionary movement. Emilio began to reengage in public activity in Santiago at the urging of his good friend Federico Pérez Carbó, with whom he had been arrested and exiled. Though Federico was eleven years younger, he and Emilio were inseparable companions during their time in Spain. After María's death, the presence of Federico in Santiago reminded Emilio of what he had already endured, and no one stood more closely with him through his bereavement. Gently, Federico brought Emilio back into the political world, initially by cofounding with him the Victor Hugo Freethinker Group in Santiago, with the idea of promoting the liberal ideas associated with the French author.

On the outside, Pérez Carbó was a mild-mannered accountant, but inside he was an adventurous revolutionary, and as a single man with no family responsibilities, he had taken more chances than Emilio had. He had impeccable revolutionary credentials, with a record of engaging in combat and carrying out secret missions for Antonio Maceo. In 1882 he had actually managed to escape from his imprisonment in Spain, traveling secretly to the port of Cádiz and then stowing away on a French steamer bound for New York, where he spent the next fifteen months working with José Martí at various newspapers serving the Cuban exile community. Back in Santiago, Federico joined Emilio Bacardi in opposing the Catholic Church hierarchy on the basis of Victor Hugo's ideas. When a census-taker asked Hugo in 1872 whether he was a Catholic, he famously replied, "No. A Freethinker." For Emilio and Federico, the "Freethinker" commitment to eschew dogma provided an ideological foundation for a democratic and sovereign Cuba, and by promoting their Grupo Libre Pensador Victor Hugo, they were defying the tight colonial alliance of the church and the Spanish Crown.

Emilio's first venture back into the literary world was an essay (under the pseudonym "Arístedes") titled "El matrimonio civil," published in the weekly newspaper *El espíritu del siglo*. Emilio wrote the commentary in response to an edict issued by the archbishop of Santiago in which the church leader denounced as "anti-Christian" a new law that established a civil marriage proceeding in Cuba. The archbishop objected that only the Catholic Church had the authority to join two people in marriage. In the tradition of nineteenth-century liberalism, Emilio saw the church authorities' rejection of civil matrimony as an attack on liberty and religious tolerance. "They would like to impose on us that era when the conscience did not exist, because only the [priest] confessor ruled," he wrote, "when bright ideas were smothered before they could be born, and when terrified men went around mindlessly crossing themselves all day and wondered where their God was."

The burst of energy on Emilio's part after months of depression was due in part to his having met a young Santiago woman, Elvira Cape, who shared his interests and had worked with their mutual friend Pérez Carbó to get him writing again. Elvira was well educated, well traveled, and bilingual in French and Spanish, mainly because her father, who was trained as a physician in his native France, believed his daughters should have the same advantages that young men could have. In July 1887, Emilio married Elvira and moved with her into his parents' former house on Trinidad Baja Street, vacated by Doña Amalia after the death of Don Facundo a year earlier. Just twenty-five at the time of their marriage, Elvira became the mother to Emilio's six young children and filled the void in his life left by the death of María.

• • •

A notable irony of the Bacardi story is that while Emilio and his brothers were supporting the struggle for Cuba's independence from Spain, they were simultaneously courting favor with the Spanish Crown on behalf of their family business. Cuban rum had become popular in Spain, largely due to the number of Spaniards introduced to it while living and working on the island. The

Bacardi brand was a favorite, and Spanish colonial officials regularly sent bottles back to Madrid. To them, it was a Spanish product, because it came from one of Spain's colonies. (The Bacardi rum samples at the Centennial Exhibition in Philadelphia were officially part of Spain's exhibit at the fair and displayed as such.) In 1888 Queen María Cristina—the regent for her two-year-old son, Alfonso XIII—appointed Bacardi & Compañía as a "Purveyor to the Royal Household," a term supposedly bestowed on firms that supplied products to the royal family but which in practice was an honorary designation that entitled a firm to display the royal coat of arms on its product and advertise its connection to the royal family.

While the Bacardi brothers were openly critical of Spanish rule in Cuba, they took their rum business seriously enough to appreciate the commercial advantage a royal "purveyor" distinction gave them, and they did not hesitate in seeking it. They had no qualms about entering their rums in the 1888 Exposición Universal in Barcelona, where they won gold medals, nor had they questioned their father's promotion of Bacardi rum at the exposition in Madrid in 1877, at the very time the Bacardi factory in Santiago was being used as a cover for anti-Spanish organizing.

Indeed, the Bacardi brothers were able to justify the promotion of their rum in Spain on patriotic grounds. For romantic Cuban nationalists, rum—along with tobacco—was a quintessentially Cuban product, incorporating the island's character and experience, from its sun and its soil to its slavery. The Bacardis were eager to underscore this association and prepared their exhibits for the international expositions with the island heritage in mind. For the 1888 Barcelona fair, they constructed a miniature oxcart of the type used on sugar plantations to haul cane from the field to the mill. Bottles and cases of Bacardi rum were displayed on the cart, along with three small oak casks such as those used in the aging warehouse. Before the exhibit was shipped to Barcelona, it was put on public display, and a Santiago newspaper reported that a "huge number" of people went to see it and applauded the presentation.

Madrid may have seen rum from Cuba as a Spanish product, but there was no doubt that many Cubans saw it as a treasure of their own. In later years, Bacardi advertising took this a step further. One popular ad slogan for the rum was *"El Que a Cuba Ha Hecho Famosa"* (The One That Has Made Cuba Famous). Bacardi rum was arguably more "Cuban" than other rums produced on the island. Major competitors, including Camps Hermanos in Santiago (makers of Matusalem rum) and José Arechabala in Cárdenas (makers of Havana Club rum), were run by transplanted *peninsular* Spaniards, while Bacardi & Compañía was now owned and managed entirely by native-born *criollo*

Cubans (and proven patriots), without one peso of foreign capital. The Bacardis were generating Cuban wealth and employing Cuban workers at a time when many *criollo* firms were being displaced by foreign companies. As a Cuban firm making a totally Cuban product and supporting the cause of Cuban freedom, Bacardi & Compañía had reason to see its presence at world fairs and even in the Spanish royal court as a promotion of Cuban national interests.

How long the company would be able to retain its pure Cuban identity was unclear. With foreign investors trolling the island for takeover targets, it was only a matter of time before Bacardi & Compañía attracted someone's interest. In 1889 an English firm offered to buy the rum company outright. The Bacardi brothers patriotically rejected the offer, but in their response they left open the possibility of accepting a foreign capital investment, especially if it could lead to the opening of a new overseas market. "A trifling increase of no more than $2000 in the estimate[d] expenses of production [is all that] would be needed to double the amount of Rum upon which we have based our Estimate," they wrote, in decent but imperfect English. "We might be able to reach markets of such importance as Germany, Russia, and the very England, where the importation would be materially helped by placing at the head of the enterprise a respectable English sindicate [sic]." Though nothing came of the exchange, it showed that the Bacardi partners had expansive commercial ambitions in spite of the setbacks they had endured.

• • •

By November 1889, Emilio Bacardi had fully rejoined the political debate in Cuba. Writing in *El espíritu del siglo*, the newspaper of his Freethinker Group, Emilio turned his wrath on a local campaign to raise $1,500 to buy a velvet cloak to drape over a statue of the Virgin in one of the local churches. "At a time when most of the streets of Santiago are full of mud and puddles of contaminated water," Emilio fumed, "when the *casa de Beneficencia* [poorhouse] is forced to hold a concert to raise money for necessary repairs, when everything around us suggests our community is crying out in hunger and pain, just now, is when a number of people who call themselves Christians, who say they are Catholics, use their spare time going door to door trying to raise 1000 or 1500 pesos to buy the Virgin a new cloak. It seems incredible, but it is true."

Such bold, provocative commentary did not go over well with the Spanish authorities in Santiago. Emilio and his Freethinker friends challenged the colonial power at every opportunity, and the Spanish administration in Santiago was quick to strike back. When *El espíritu* published the text of Article 13 of the Spanish constitution, declaring that every Spaniard "has the right to freely express his ideas and opinions, through speech or through writing... without being subject to previous censorship," the local Spanish authorities confiscated all copies of the newspaper.

The independence movement was heating up again. In Santiago, it initially produced only these small political confrontations over whether Cubans could speak freely or read the books they wanted. Emilio and his Freethinker associates tried to establish a public library, only to be rebuffed by local ecclesiastical authorities who said it might disturb "the tranquility of the Catholic neighbors." But it was a start. Ideological debate was precisely what José Martí had been seeking in his effort to provide the revolutionary movement with a sharper political identity. The next step would be to broaden the critique. The geopolitical situation had evolved since Emilio Bacardi and his associates in Santiago had last conspired, and the work to establish an ideological base for the Cuban independence movement had to involve more than a challenge to the antiliberal positions of the Catholic Church.

In New York, José Martí was focusing increasingly on U.S. imperialist attitudes as a threat to Cuban national interests. The Western Hemisphere had changed since the era when Latin American nations aimed only to free themselves from Spain. The United States was the new ascendant power, and, in Martí's words, the political challenge for the Latin countries was to resist the "powerful and ambitious neighbor" to the north. "Spanish America learned how to save itself from the tyranny of Spain," Martí wrote in December 1889, "and now... the time has come for Spanish America to declare its second independence."

In Cuba's earlier struggle with Spain, some of the most ardent supporters, both in Cuba and in the United States, believed that the island's best interests lay in being annexed as a U.S. state. "Annexationists" had supplied arms to the Cuban rebels and promoted the anti-Spanish cause in the U.S. press. Eager for help from any quarter, Cuban rebel leaders overlooked the question of what ties would be established in the future between the United States and a free Cuba, focused as they were on the immediate struggle. By 1889, however, that issue could no longer be avoided.

Within the United States, Cuban views hardly seemed to matter. Cuba's fate was to be resolved in negotiations between Madrid and Washington. The possibility of purchasing Cuba from Spain, an idea first proposed by Thomas Jefferson, was considered in relation to such issues as the desirability of increased Cuban sugar imports. Opponents of annexation did not base their arguments on what Cubans wanted, but on the burden that Cuba would present to the

United States as a new territory or state. In March 1889, a Philadelphia trade magazine published an article titled "Do We Want Cuba?" that laid out the arguments for and against acquiring the island. Among the disadvantages cited was the "undesirability" of the Cuban people:

> To the faults of the parent [Spanish] race they add effeminacy and a distaste for exertion which amounts really to disease. They are helpless, idle, of defective morals, and unfitted by nature and experience for discharging the obligations of citizenship in a great and free republic. Their lack of manly force and of self-respect is demonstrated by the supineness with which they have so long submitted to Spanish oppression, and even their attempts at rebellion have been so pitifully ineffective that they have risen little above the dignity of farce.

A long excerpt from the article was published approvingly in the *New York Evening Post,* outraging the Cuban community in New York.

As soon as he read it, José Martí wrote a blistering response, in English, published in the *Post* four days later. He did not bother to address the annexation question directly, except to say that "no self-respecting Cuban would like to see his country annexed to a nation where the leaders of opinion share towards him the prejudices excusable only to vulgar jingoism or rampant ignorance." Most offensive to Martí was what he called the "sneer" with which the Philadelphia writer dismissed the Cuban independence fighters. "These city-bred young men and poorly built half-breeds knew in one day how to rise against a cruel government," Martí wrote, "to obey as soldiers, sleep in the mud, eat roots, fight ten years without salary, conquer foes with the branch of a tree, die...a death not to be spoken of without uncovering the head."

In the eight years Martí had lived and worked in New York as a correspondent for Latin American newspapers, his view of the United States had grown more critical. Having lived in Cuba, Mexico, Guatemala, and Spain, he was initially struck by the creativity and energy of a country where "everyone looks like his own master.... Everyone works; everyone reads." In time, however, he was repulsed by what he called "the excessive worship of wealth" in the United States, a tendency, he wrote, which "disillusions people or develops them in a one-sided manner, giving them at once the characteristics of giants and of children." The treatment of blacks and Indians appalled him, as did the influence of money in U.S. politics. By 1889, when Martí responded to the *Post* article, he was focused on what appeared to be the country's intentions "to extend its dominions in America." Still, Martí had to be careful in what he said about the United States, especially when writing for a Cuban audience. He wanted to protect his nation against U.S. encroachment, but he had to remember that tens of thousands of Cubans were moving to the United States every year. "They admire this nation, the greatest ever built by liberty," he acknowledged. His fear was that deeper Cuban ties with the United States would undermine support on the island for total independence.

In 1890 Antonio Maceo, the former rebel commander, was able to visit Cuba, ostensibly to sell some properties there belonging to his mother but actually, he wrote later, to promote "war and the extermination of the colonial system." In Santiago, his hometown, Maceo was greeted as a hero. A dinner party there in July, attended by Emilio Bacardi, concluded with a champagne toast—¡*Por Cuba Libre!*—albeit "in a low voice," Emilio reported, "as the circumstances demanded." During the after-dinner conversation, however, a young man named José Hernández approached Maceo and suggested that it was probably Cuba's fate "to be one more star in the great American constellation."

"Young man," Maceo responded, speaking slowly and softly, "that sounds impossible to me, but in that one situation I might actually be on the side of the Spaniards." Such moments reinforced for Maceo, as for Martí and other revolutionaries, how important it was to carry out grassroots political work before launching a new independence war.

. . .

In Santiago, concern about U.S. hegemony seemed a bit abstract. The acute oppression that Cubans experienced every day was the product of Spain's unrelenting grip on the island, and the battles being fought by Emilio Bacardi and his friend Federico Pérez Carbó were largely with the local colonial authorities.

In October 1892, Cuba marked the four hundredth anniversary of the island's "discovery" by Christopher Columbus. The Victor Hugo Freethinkers and other island liberals, unlike the Spanish authorities, viewed the anniversary with some shame, and its commemoration sparked a vicious debate. Federico Pérez Carbó noted the occasion with a biting commentary in *El espíritu del siglo*, titled "¡Maldición!" (Damn!) He described how the Spanish sailors who arrived in Cuba found "an island crowned by palms," where tribes of gentle Indians lived "without malice, fear, or hate," and he related how the Spanish conquistadores chased the Indians into the jungle, killing many of those they caught. In his version of the Hatuey story, a night breeze stirred the ashes where the Indian chief had been burned, causing them to glow brightly for an instant, and in that moment a voice was heard echoing across the hills: "Damn you!" He went on to say how the slaughter of the Indians was followed in Cuba by the enslavement of blacks, and he told the story of one rebellious slave hung along with eight companions.

> They say that as his body dangled from the rope, still twitching in the throes of death, that echoing voice was heard again: "Damn you!"
>
> Does the curse invoked by those two prisoners hang now over this island?... Evil triumphs over good, crime over justice, shadows eclipse the light... [and] when the sky darkens, and the sea roars, and the burst of wind fells the tree... the traveler hears in those terrible sounds that same voice— "Damn you!"

Not surprisingly, the publication of "¡Maldición!" caused a major stir among pro-Spain elements in Santiago. The town council held a special closed-door session to consider what should be done about Pérez Carbó, who worked as an accountant for the local government. The deputy mayor solemnly reported that his article "has produced a feeling of indignation among all those who love and respect Mother Spain, because far from honoring the great event that is now being commemorated, it tends to place a stain on the Spanish Nation and on the memory of the immortal Christopher Columbus."

In the end, no punitive action was taken. The mayor defused the uproar by suggesting that Pérez Carbó be called before the council to explain the article. Pérez Carbó ignored the summons, and the matter was dropped. The polemic nevertheless served to illustrate lingering questions about Cuba's identity. Was it to be defined by its Spanish colonial origin, as a nation where the Catholic Church and traditional conservative values held sway and where society was dominated by an enterprising white elite? Or did the Cuban story concern the oppression of the colored population—first the Indians and then blacks and mulattoes—and the effort to construct a new, multiracial nation that valued individual freedom and allowed democracy to flourish?

Such issues had been left unresolved in the first war, largely because some independence advocates were white slaveholders who were ambivalent about the role of blacks in the struggle. José Martí and others were convinced that another revolution in Cuba would be definitive only if these social questions were confronted early. The goal of the next Cuban revolution, he wrote, would be "not so much a mere political change as a good, sound, just and equitable social system."

The first independence war had at least represented a start toward this goal, if only because blacks and whites fought side by side throughout that conflict and because one of the war's most heroic and admired figures, Antonio Maceo, was himself a mulatto. By the early 1890s, racial prejudice was still deep in Cuba, but some progress had been made in counteracting it. The official abolition of slavery in 1886 caused less unrest than had been anticipated, because most slaves were simply converted into wage laborers. Many planters, in fact, concluded that it was more costly to buy and maintain slaves and their families than to hire free workers. Whites in Cuba also saw that freed blacks on the island were not organizing en masse to establish a "black republic," as had been widely feared; instead, a process of racial integration was under way. After 1887, Cubans could not be excluded from public employment on the basis of race. Discrimination in theaters, cafés, and bars was outlawed in 1889. After 1893, state schools had to accept black or mulatto children on the same basis as white children.

Among progressive white Cubans, the Bacardis held typical views on racial issues for the time: not without prejudice, but more enlightened than those of most peers. Emilio's second wife, Elvira Cape, grew up in a slave-owning family and had her own slave attendant until the day slavery was abolished.* Emilio often addressed the slavery issue in his own essays and fiction, making clear his opposition to the institution and his support for a multiracial state with equal rights for all. At the same time, he sometimes adopted a paternalistic tone, portraying blacks as malleable and even childlike.

In *Vía crucis*, one of his published novels, Emilio tells the story of a Cuban family whose conflicted ideas about slavery may have matched his own family's mixed feelings. Philosophically, the family opposes the institution, but some slave-owning characters in the book are presented as good-hearted and adored by their slaves. One former slave named Juan joins the rebel army alongside his former owner Pablito to fight together for Cuba's independence. On the battlefield, they are equals, but when Pablito dies in combat and is buried beneath some rocks, the former slave throws himself on the makeshift tomb, weeping. "And he stayed there," Emilio wrote, "like a faithful dog lying on his master's grave." Such literary creations showed that Emilio Bacardi was a prisoner of his own socioeconomic background and life experience. What is also beyond dispute, however, is that he was willing to face imprisonment and even death for the cause of a sweeping social revolution in Cuba that had as a central aim the establishment of racial equality and justice on the island.

By 1892, preparations for another war in Cuba were under way. José Martí

---

*Some Bacardi family members say Elvira was herself a *mulata*, with some black ancestry.

dropped journalism and began organizing a new Cuban Revolutionary Party among exiles in Florida and New York, with the idea that it would provide the framework around which a democratic movement could be built. When he felt the party was ready, Martí traveled to Santo Domingo, where Máximo Gómez was living, and later to Costa Rica to find Antonio Maceo. Both men readily agreed to renew the independence fight. By the fall of 1894, rebel leaders from the previous war had begun quietly assembling in the countryside and stashing weapons.

Santiago had been in a state of revolutionary agitation ever since the visit of Antonio Maceo in 1890. Emilio, Federico Pérez Carbó, and a handful of other *santiagueros* were meeting secretly to make conspiratorial arrangements. Though Emilio remained suspect in the eyes of colonial authorities, his position as a respected and successful Santiago businessman offered him protection. From 1894 until he was arrested again in 1896, Emilio was chief of the revolution's underground network in Santiago and its principal treasurer. Using commercial matters as a pretext, Emilio traveled to New York to see Martí. (Though illness caused Martí to miss his appointment, he sent an apologetic note to Emilio, referring to him as his "dear friend.") When rebel leaders needed to travel outside Cuba, Emilio arranged their transportation. Such activities were kept secret, of course; around the same time, Emilio became a director of the Santiago Chamber of Commerce, representing the chamber's "industry" section.

In 1894 a trade dispute between the United States and Spain, waged over the heads of the Cubans, resulted in Spain's imposition of duties on U.S. products imported into Cuba and steep new U.S. tariffs on Cuban goods sent to the United States. Planters, traders, and merchants who had redirected their commerce away from Spain toward the United States were devastated. To make matters worse, the Spanish authorities were charging Cuba for the cost of the Ten Years' War. Annual interest on the war debt cost the island nearly half its total annual public revenue; another twelve million dollars went to pay the Spanish army in Cuba, leaving only 2.5 million for all other public expenditures, including education. The economic crisis heightened Cubans' anger over their lack of political control and fueled revolutionary sentiment even among many members of the upper classes. By early 1895, it was clear that a new armed revolt was about to begin. In a house just down the street from the Bacardi offices on Marina Baja Street, Emilio met secretly with a handful of other men to set up a commercial trading firm that would have offices in both Santiago and New York and serve as a front for channeling war funds and mes-

sages between the revolution's New York headquarters and the field commanders in eastern Cuba.

On the orders of José Martí, standing by in Florida, the new revolution was
launched on February 24, 1895, beginning with a small uprising directed by
General Guillermo Moncada of Santiago, a Bacardi friend and ally. Antonio
Maceo and a small contingent arrived at the end of March, and Máximo Gómez
came about two weeks later. José Martí himself accompanied the aging general.
After a short sail from Haiti, they came ashore on a rocky beach in Guantánamo province in a driving rainstorm, with Martí taking the forward oar in
the rowboat from their ship. Until that point, Martí had served the revolutionary cause exclusively in a civilian capacity, as organizer, strategist, and pam-
phleteer. Gómez and other military leaders argued that he was more valuable
in that role than as a combatant, but Martí was determined to go to Cuba and
fight alongside other revolutionaries. The Cuban people, he had written, would
view with "a certain disdain and coldness the services of one who preaches the
necessity of dying and does not begin by risking his own life."

Martí had been in ill health much of the preceding year, and with his slight
physique and lack of combat experience he was at a huge disadvantage compared to the other military veterans with whom he was traveling. The humble
soldiers around him, however, deferred to Martí as if to a visiting statesman
and insisted on calling him *Presidente*. Though Gómez and other general officers in his company did their best to keep him away from the front, Martí
was determined to see combat. He finally got a chance on May 19, when Gómez
and the men under his command made contact with a detachment of Spanish
troops. While Gómez was carrying out an encircling move, Martí approached
a young military aide, asked him for a revolver, and insisted that they go to
the front. The two men rode at a full gallop toward the sound of fighting, down
a lane flanked by tall trees, and straight into an ambush. Martí, mounted on a
white horse, was shot in the chest and died instantly.

Martí's martyrdom galvanized Cubans, inspiring an outpouring of volunteers for the revolution. Arguably, however, he could have had an even greater
impact if he had lived. No one else had his vision or leadership quality, and had
he become the first president of a free and independent Cuba—which he surely
would have been—the country might have been spared some of the political
agonies it subsequently suffered.

Chapter 5

❦

Cuba Libre

The Santiago train station was crowded with Sunday travelers and Spanish soldiers. It was Easter, and the day was fair and bright, but on that morning the hubbub was a phenomenon of war. Getting in and out of Santiago had become risky and unpredictable, and the train was by then the safest way to travel. The countryside was effectively under the control of rebel fighters, and there were skirmishes almost every day with Spanish troops. The police had set up checkpoints on all the roads leading out of Santiago in an effort to stop young Cuban men from heading to the mountains to join the rebels, but many were slipping through, some of them by train.

Seventeen-year-old Emilito Bacardi, standing alone on the railway platform, was one of them. He had said his good-byes at home, knowing there would be spies and secret police at the train station. In the six weeks or so since the second war for Cuban independence had begun, Emilito had schemed to join the fight. He and his younger brother Daniel grew up hearing stories about the first war and the role that their father had played in the struggle. Between themselves, they resolved to head to the mountains together as soon as the opportunity arose. Their father had stopped Daniel, who was barely sixteen years old, sickly, and of little use to the rebel army, but Emilito would turn eighteen that summer, and Emilio figured he had no right to stand in his way. From his own experience, however, Emilio knew what mortal danger his son would face as a fighter in the rebel army, and when he and Elvira tearfully embraced their boy that morning, they realized they might never see him again.

Emilito watched some Spanish soldiers in seersucker uniforms and straw hats pace nervously along the platform. He fidgeted with his train ticket, trying his best to look nonchalant. If asked, he would say he was going to see his step-grandmother, Elvira Cape's mother, which in fact was true, because her coffee plantation near the town of La Maya happened to be an assembly point for rebel recruits. He had only a small bag, no weapon except for a little knife made for sharpening pencils, no military training, and little notion of what he could offer the rebel army except his determination to fight for the cause of *Cuba Libre*.

At El Cristo, about seven miles outside Santiago, Emilito got off the train, "borrowed" a horse, and headed to the Cape plantation, known locally as Santo Domingo. A black muleteer by the name of Sixto who worked on the plantation but had ties to the *mambises* put Emilito in touch with a nearby unit. Thanks largely to his father's position and reputation in the revolutionary movement, Emilito was soon given a rifle and his own horse. Within weeks, he was participating in combat actions.

After a few months in the field, he was assigned to General Antonio Maceo himself, the "Bronze Titan." Emilio, an old acquaintance, had written Maceo a letter: "General, my son has gone off to the war, and I would like him to fight under your command." It was hardly a move that would ensure Emilito's safety. Maceo's battlefield exploits were legendary. Those who fought alongside him were inspired by his fearlessness and tended to follow his lead, so going into combat at Maceo's side would be risky. On the other hand, Maceo was certain to take special care of his good friend's son. Upon receiving the letter, Maceo sent immediately for Emilito, had him commissioned as a second lieutenant, and made him an aide-de-camp.

"It was the most emotional moment in my life," Emilito recalled later of his commissioning by Maceo, "finding myself so near to him, shaking his hand, hearing his voice. I had already been part of the forces under his command, and I had been admiring him for a long time, in all the grandeur of his military genius."

This was the ideal of the Cuban revolution: a young white man from a privileged background feeling honored to serve under a dark-skinned commander who was descended from slaves and had once been a mule driver. For a true revolutionary, racism was not just wrong; it was unpatriotic. *Cuba Libre* was to be a land governed by Cubans, for all Cubans.

• • •

Emilio Bacardi wanted to go to the mountains himself to join Maceo and the others he had known and conspired with for years, but he was quickly dissuaded by his wife Elvira and his friends. He was fifty and in no shape for the rigors of guerrilla duty. His eyesight was poor, and he was lost without the thick glasses he wore. He and Elvira now had three young daughters of their own, in addition to Emilio's six children from his marriage to María. There was the family business to manage. His brother-in-law Enrique Schueg was proving to be a huge asset, but the rum company teetered constantly on the edge of insolvency and still required close attention. Finally, Emilio had his underground responsibilities in Santiago, where he was the linchpin of the entire conspiratorial network. No one else had his contacts or knowledge or organizational skills. José Martí might not have been able to resist the call to arms, but Emilio was a much more practical man. It made no sense at all for him to go to the mountains, and he knew it.

In September 1895, five months after Emilito left home, the Bacardi Cape household was shaken again. Emilio's second son, sixteen-year-old Daniel, died from a chronic illness that had plagued him since childhood. Disconsolate, Emilio initially decided to withdraw from all revolutionary work, but in the end he concluded he had to persevere. His role in the underground had become even more important after his close friend and coconspirator Federico Pérez Carbó sneaked out of town to join Maceo, his former commander, leaving Emilio with enormous responsibilities to handle on his own. He dared not dwell long on the loss of Daniel nor on the absence of news from Emilito.

Santiago was more militarized by the day. Spanish soldiers on horseback were on the streets day and night, and uniformed police manned guard posts in each of the public squares. On the outskirts of town, members of the "Civil Guard" patrolled by foot. After 10 P.M., people were not allowed to gather in groups, either outdoors or in homes, not even for a funeral wake. The perimeter was sealed with a series of trenches and barbed-wire fences, which were monitored constantly. Agents reported every development that was slightly unusual, and within the revolutionary movement the need for secrecy was greater than ever. Only a few people beyond his immediate family circle were aware of Emilio's activities. One was his brother-in-law Ramón Martínez, married to Elvira's sister Herminia. Martínez, who knew José Martí from having shared a berth with him on a voyage to Jamaica, was gravely ill and confined to his bed by the time the new revolution broke out, but he told his wife to "do for Cuba's freedom what I cannot." Emilio suggested that Herminia bring Ramón to stay with him and Elvira in his last days. All the visitors coming to the Bacardi house to see Martínez, Emilio figured, would be a cover for the couriers and revolutionary agents who showed up almost every day.

As the rebels' intermediary, Emilio managed the correspondence between them and their outside allies and coordinated arms shipments and rebel supply requests. He oversaw the smuggling of ammunition rounds in bags of beans and rice and even arranged deliveries of dynamite, used by the rebel army to blow up bridges. Avoiding suspicion required constant effort and ingenuity. Emilio signed his correspondence "Phocion," for the Athenian general and statesman known as The Good for his honesty and his commitment to democracy. When he dispatched money or supplies to the rebels in their mountain camps, he sent along half of a newspaper page, keeping the other half. If a different courier returned to make contact, he had to bring the missing half to verify his rebel identity.

. . .

The strengthened ideological foundation of the second independence war meant that it had to be fought with attention to social and political objectives as well as military ones. The new Cuba was to be a nation with more equality and opportunity for its previously marginalized citizens of color, and this would require a realignment of social and economic relations. General Máximo Gómez felt that one of the mistakes of the Ten Years' War had been the reluctance of the revolution's leaders to challenge powerful economic interests, especially in western Cuba. By not taking the war to the sugar heartland, they had compromised the revolution's commitment to the transformation of the country. Gómez also argued that more should be done to disrupt the economy and thereby cut off the revenue Spain needed from Cuba in order to finance the war.

The strategic calculations were complicated, however. How would the commanders deal with the big landowners, for example? The destruction of sugar and coffee plantations would also hurt ordinary Cubans, and the commanders could not agree among themselves on how far to go with economic sabotage. In July 1895, Gómez issued a sweeping order: "The sugar plantations will stop their labors, and whoever shall attempt to grind the crops, notwithstanding this order, will have their cane burned and their buildings demolished." The order also prohibited the transport of industrial, agricultural, and animal products to towns occupied by Spanish troops. But other commanders favored a more lenient approach. Antonio Maceo argued that planters should be allowed to continue grinding cane and producing sugar as long as they paid a war tax to the rebel army and did nothing to hurt the revolutionary cause. Across eastern Cuba, where he was in command, Maceo made several such agreements with planters and mill operators, and the taxes collected under the arrangement became a valuable source of revenue for the revolution.

In Santiago, Emilio Bacardi supported Maceo's position. Emilio himself, in fact, was collecting war taxes from several plantation owners in the Santiago region, beginning with his own mother-in-law on the Santo Domingo plantation. In some months, his collections totaled several hundred dollars, a significant amount for a cash-starved movement. Emilio's opposition to the extreme measures favored by Gómez was also consistent with his family business interests. Bacardí & Compañía would have been shut down by a strict implementation of the ban on sugar production and the prohibition of commerce in Spanish-occupied areas. Without a steady supply of molasses, the Bacardis could not make rum, and if they could not move their product through Havana and other Spanish-controlled cities, they could not continue operations.

Several of the Bacardis' Cuban competitors, in fact, were already closed. Some distilleries were attached to sugar plantations and burned along with other plantation buildings; some distillery owners were targeted as "enemies" of the revolution; some got in trouble with the Spanish. One of the most successful rum producers in eastern Cuba, Brugal, Sobrino, & Compañía, moved operations out of Cuba in the midst of the war and never came back. The owner, Andrés Brugal, was solidly pro-Madrid, but his two sons were rebel sympathizers, and the authorities caught them smuggling machetes out of their father's metalworking shop. Had it not been for Don Andres's friendship with the Spanish commander in Santiago, the two young men probably would have been shot. As it was, the whole Brugal family was forced to move to the Dominican Republic, where their relocated rum company ultimately prospered.

Given the wartime conditions, Bacardí & Compañía was able to maintain operations only through deft political maneuvering, shrewd management, and the good fortune of having a network of buyers and suppliers. Emilio knew which planters were continuing to grind cane—partly because he was dealing with them on behalf of the revolution—and was thus able to secure enough molasses to satisfy the distillery's minimum needs. The factory workforce stayed relatively intact, even when many Santiago men went to join the rebel army. Emilio's underground work earned his company an exemption from the revolution's restriction of economic activity, while to the Spanish authorities the Bacardis' determination to maintain operations suggested faith in the status quo. The risks associated with revolutionary activity, however, were underscored every time that work at the distillery on Matadero Street was interrupted by the sound of gunfire from the slaughterhouse down the street as someone else was lined up against the wall and shot. The death of Daniel, the dangers surrounding Emilio's work, and the fear for Emilito's safety weighed heavily on the family.

Two days after becoming an aide to Antonio Maceo, Emilito and the rest of Maceo's troops—including Federico Pérez Carbó, who had risen to the rank of colonel—embarked on what became known as the "invasion" of western Cuba, a march across the length of the island into the main sugar-growing areas and the fortified defensive positions of the Spanish army. Most of the rebel fighters were on horseback and carried machetes. In close fighting, the rebels used their machetes like swords, waving them above their heads as they charged, screaming, into the Spanish lines. Spanish soldiers who saw arms and heads lopped off with a single machete blow were terrified by the weapon. Time and time again, the rebel army forced the Spanish troops to retreat. By December 1895, Maceo's forces were in Matanzas province, east of Havana. Eighteen-year-old Emilito Bacardi was wounded in close fighting around a Spanish-held fortress, though the wounds were relatively minor and he was able to rejoin Maceo after a short recuperation. A short time later, however, Federico Pérez Carbó was shot in the neck, and his injury was more serious. Maceo left him in the care of a sympathetic sugar mill owner, who eventually got him to Havana and aboard a ship to the United States for medical treatment.

In January 1896, General Arsenio Martínez Campos, the Spanish commander during the Ten Years' War, resigned in frustration just nine months after being called back to lead Spanish troops in Cuba again. He was replaced by General Valeriano Weyler, who was known for his ruthlessness when he served in Cuba during the first independence war. In spite of their stunning advance, however, the Cubans were still significantly short of victory. The Spanish troops remained firmly in control of Havana. Most of their losses were due not to combat but to yellow fever and other tropical diseases to which the Spanish soldiers were especially vulnerable. Overall, the war was largely stalemated. On his first day in command, Weyler issued a proclamation to all Cubans, warning he was taking charge of their island "with the determination that it shall never be given up by me, and that I shall keep it in the possession of Spain.... I shall be generous with the subdued and to all those doing any service to the Spanish cause. But I will not lack the decisiveness and energy to punish, with all the rigor the law allows, those who in any way help the enemy."

Inevitably, Emilio Bacardi again became a target of Spanish suspicions. One day in May 1896, a unit headed personally by Santiago's police chief showed up at Emilio and Elvira's house to carry out a search for anything that might link them to the rebels. Emilio had just written a series of coded letters to Maceo, Pérez Carbó, Emilito, and other rebels, and he was waiting for a courier to pick them up. If they were discovered, it could mean a death sentence for Emilio and prison for the rest of his family. Alerted that the police were headed their way, Emilio and his family scrambled frantically to hide the letters. It was a trusted black servant named Georgina who calmly suggested an idea.

"Don Emilio, give me the letters," she said. "I'll get them out of the house."

Georgina, who had been with the Bacardi family for more than thirty years, was holding Lalita, Emilio and Elvira's baby girl, and Elvira suggested that she put the letters under Lalita's hat when she went out. Emilio's teenage daughter María, seeing there were too many to fit in one place, grabbed a few and tucked them down Georgina's blouse. Just then, the police chief rapped on the front door.

As they began searching, Elvira stood off to the side, her stern expression betraying no trace of the terror she felt inside. Tall and sturdily featured, with long, thick, black hair clipped behind her head, she projected elegance, seriousness, and strength. Turning to the police chief, she pointed to Georgina and said, almost contemptuously, "She's the cook. Is she allowed to go to the market?" The chief hesitated, then nodded, and Georgina left the house with the incriminating letters stuffed in her bosom and under Lalita's hat. She headed straight to the house of Enrique Schueg and Amalia Bacardi and left the letters there for safekeeping.

Though the move probably saved Emilio's life, it did not keep him out of prison. The police claimed they found a letter signed by Tomás Estrada Palma, a longtime Cuban exile who took charge of the revolution's business in New York after the death of Martí. Emilio was hauled off to the Santiago prison, where he was held incommunicado pending further investigation. His imprisonment left thirty-three-year-old Elvira at home with seven children. Under such circumstances, most Cuban wives would have retreated quietly to the privacy of their homes, tending to their children, deferring to other males in their families, and doing nothing that would call attention to themselves or further jeopardize their husbands' position. Elvira Cape, however, was an uncommon woman. Born into wealth and possessing the confidence and poise that good education and international travel conferred on a woman of her era, Elvira saw no reason to take cover behind her family. She shared Emilio's commitment to the struggle for Cuba's freedom, and after he was arrested she resolved to continue his correspondence with the rebels, in spite of the risks to herself and her family.

The arrival of Elvira's first messages left the rebels wondering who had written them. One Cuban officer who chronicled his war experiences wrote that the commanders in his camp were deeply discouraged by the news of Emilio's arrest and wondering how they would survive without him. Shortly thereafter, a messenger arrived with a new package of coded letters. One appeared to be signed "Phocion," the pseudonym Emilio had used. "This surprised us," the commander wrote. "How could Phocion have written us while he was imprisoned in Santiago? Had the Spaniards gotten Bacardi to write that letter to us as part of a trap they were preparing for us?" Once they had carefully decoded the letter, however, the commanders saw that it was signed "Phociona," the feminine counterpart of Phocion. There was no additional clue to the writer's identity, but it contained the same kind of news and instructions that Emilio had been sending.

A portrait of Elvira from this period shows her well dressed, with jeweled earrings dangling from her ears and a long-sleeved black dress with a white lace neckline. But she is unsmiling, and her piercing gaze suggests she is not a woman to be crossed. Like her husband, who disapproved of Santiago's raucous carnival festivities, Elvira was not much of a partygoer. Her sister Herminia later said Elvira did not like to dance, which for a Cuban is almost unthinkable. "She used to say she didn't want any man grabbing her by the waist, smelling her breath, and twirling her like a top," Herminia recalled.

But Elvira was devoted to her husband, and the correspondence between them during Emilio's imprisonment shows they both felt the pain of their separation. After a few weeks, a military judge in Santiago released Emilio from solitary confinement and allowed him and Elvira to exchange written communication. Over the next months, Emilio wrote Elvira a note almost every day, using whatever materials he could scrounge. A brown paper bag, torn in pieces, would give him paper for a dozen or more brief notes. Elvira was Emilio's link to the world, and he often asked her to bring him things: a candle and a box of matches, shoe polish, even some sherbet. ("I'm not dying for it, but if you send some, better to send milk than fruit.") Their anniversary came and went ("9 years? *Hombre*, how outrageous to have it ruined like this!"), but Emilio was always looking ahead. ("I am fine. I hope you are the same. One day more. *Adelante*.") All the notes ended the same way: *Besos y abrazos*. Kisses and hugs.

Emilio's prison notes to Elvira highlight his remarkable powers of discipline and will. Never does he despair. This is a man who is in his second extended imprisonment, and he has no clue when it will end. Months earlier, he has lost a beloved teenage son. His eldest son is somewhere with the Cuban rebel army, wounded once already and in almost constant combat. But every note to Elvira is determinedly upbeat. *Paciencia y paciencia*, he tells her, over and over again.

Notable is the absence of any reference to God or prayer or faith. Emilio is a rationalist, appealing always to logic and reason, a tendency he shows throughout his adult life. He clearly has a sentimental side, especially evident where his children are concerned, about whom he inquires daily. But Emilio Bacardí Moreau is also a proud and stubborn man, and in his prison letters he shows a prickly side of his personality that will come out many times again in his business and political life. When the Spanish prison warden tightens security and puts all the inmates behind an extra set of bars, Emilio is furious and refuses to allow anyone to visit, even his wife. "During visiting hours, I will close my door," he warns Elvira. "Pretend I am on a trip. I swear to you, it would disgust me, more even than this prison itself. It would be to descend to their depths. Remember what I have always said: All we have is our dignity and our honor."

Emilio remained in the Santiago prison for nearly five months. His case in the meantime was turned over to Valeriano Weyler, who was showing no mercy toward anyone suspected of sympathizing with the revolution. (Shortly after taking command in Cuba, Weyler instituted a policy of forcibly moving the rural population into nearby fortified cities, in order to separate the rebels from their civilian supporters.) After considering Emilio's fate for three months, Weyler decided that he should be deported and sent back to the prison in the Chafarine Islands off the African coast. The order to move him came on October 19. Emilio was taken from his cell that night and put aboard a steamship waiting in the Santiago harbor. Elvira had time only to send him a flower, with this note: "Whatever our fate may be, we have planted our path with flowers, and may our children reap the riches of what we have made." Emilio had the note with him that October night as he sat wedged between two police officers in the coach that carried him through the dark and empty streets of his hometown.

The steamer left at 6 A.M. the next day for Havana, slipping out through the fog that hung over Santiago Bay. Emilio and another prisoner were put to work swabbing the deck and then left in handcuffs, propped against the ship's forward hatch. The voyage to Havana took four days. The prisoners were each given an old tin cup, a plate, and a spoon with which to eat their daily meal, though they had no water to wash themselves or their utensils, and each day the sweat and grime and smell was a little thicker. Emilio, ever mindful of his dignity, used his handkerchief to wipe clean his dishes, hands, and face as best he could. He was detained another month in Havana, then put aboard another ship for the voyage to Spain, during which he was tied together below deck with other prisoners, without a glimpse of sky or sea.

Back in Santiago, Elvira found herself increasingly under pressure. The police raided her house several times, suspecting she was carrying on her husband's conspiratorial work. Concluding that her first responsibility was to protect the children in her charge, Elvira chartered a small boat to take her and her family, including Doña Amalia, her seventy-three-year-old mother-in-law, to Jamaica. Before sailing, she passed Emilio's secret codes to Enrique Schueg, making him the rebels' new Santiago agent.

In December 1896, General Antonio Maceo was shot and killed while leading a small reconnaissance team behind Spanish lines in western Cuba. The mission was highly dangerous, and most of Maceo's aides, including Emilito Bacardi, had been forced to stay behind. Killed alongside Maceo was Francisco Gómez, the son of rebel commander Máximo Gómez.

The loss of Maceo shook Cubans almost as deeply as the death of José Martí. Having risen from humble origins under the burden of racial prejudice to lead his country's revolution, Maceo symbolized their nation and its aspiration for independence. His "Protest of Baraguá," when he refused to accept the peace terms at the end of the Ten Years' War, had salvaged the integrity of the cause for which the Cubans had fought and would fight again. Maceo's legendary heroism on the battlefield—he is said to have been wounded in combat twenty-seven times—and his military genius inspired the rebel army and frustrated his Spanish adversaries. Máximo Gómez, having lost his own son as well as his top general, struggled to contain himself but resolved to keep fighting. In a letter to Maceo's widow, María Cabrales—exiled in Jamaica along with Elvira Cape and many other Cuban women—Gómez wrote, "Weep, weep, María, for you and for me both, since for this unhappy old man, the privilege of relieving his innermost grief by letting go a flood of tears is not possible." On December 28, 1896, Gómez announced Maceo's death in a general order: "Now the country mourns the loss of one of its most mighty defenders, Cuba the most glorious of its sons, and the army, the first of its generals."

Two days later, Emilio Bacardi arrived for the second time in his life on the Chafarine Islands after more than a month of being shuttled from one awful Spanish prison to another and being marched, handcuffed, in his filthy clothes through the streets of Málaga. Another prison detention lay ahead, but on that day his thoughts were characteristically patriotic:

Morocco in front of me, Spain to one side, lost in the haze.... And over there, across the immense Ocean, bluer and bluer the more it looks toward the sky, Cuba; yearning and battling for her freedom...with the flames of her fires edging the clouds with red and highlighting the colors of her flag, falling at times, but never defeated!

Chapter 6

The Colossus Intervenes

The Republican Party delegates who gathered in St. Louis, Missouri, for their national convention in June 1896 were reminded every day of the fighting in faraway Cuba: Hanging prominently from the pine rafters in the convention hall was a big Cuban flag. No one objected to its placement. Cuba's struggle against Spain was one of those easy-to-embrace causes that had broad popular support at the time and almost no opposition. An adjacent banner said "Republicanism Is Prosperity."

Whether the convention delegates paid much heed to the issue was questionable. The convention chairman, Charles Fairbanks of Indiana, declared in his opening address that the Cubans' independence fight "enlists the ardent sympathy of the Republican Party," but the line was buried deep in his speech, and the only people in the cavernous convention hall who could hear him were the newspaper reporters seated in the front row. The paramount issue at the convention was whether the United States should use silver as well as gold coinage. The silverites lost. The delegates nominated a "sound money" man, William McKinley, to be the Republican presidential candidate. The party platform approved at the convention did say the U.S. government "should actively use its influence and good offices to restore peace and give independence to [Cuba]," but it was just one plank among many. The platform also called attention to the massacres in Armenia, declared that Hawaii belonged to the United States, backed the construction of a canal across Central America, demanded tougher immigration controls, and called for better pensions for Civil War veterans.

The Cuba plank was noteworthy largely because it suggested a possible Republican challenge to the policy of President Grover Cleveland, who was interpreting American neutrality laws as requiring the interdiction of arms shipments to Cuba from U.S. territory and the prosecution of any U.S. citizen found to be assisting the independence struggle. In Spain, outraged parliamentarians censured the Republicans for having endorsed the Cuban independence cause; Cuban-Americans were thrilled. When McKinley went on to defeat the

Democratic presidential candidate, William Jennings Bryan, Cuban rebel leaders hoped for a major policy change in Washington. They had been urging the U.S. Congress to recognize their revolutionary movement as a "belligerent" party, which would have put it on the same legal basis as the Spanish colonial authority and made it easier to acquire weapons.

Among the Cubans closely following the American political developments was Elvira Cape in Kingston, Jamaica, where she was managing a large household of children and other Bacardi family members, along with her sister Herminia and other exiled Cuban friends. Elvira had a U.S. connection through her old friend Federico Pérez Carbó, who had gone to the States to recover from the gunshot wound he suffered in combat. After McKinley was elected, Elvira wrote to Pérez Carbó to ask whether he thought the new administration might bring a turn in Cuba's fortune.

U.S. Cuba policy at the time was one of Pérez Carbó's chief concerns. Tomás Estrada Palma, the "chief delegate" of the exiles' revolutionary committee, or junta, in New York, had made Pérez Carbó deputy chief of the "Expeditions Department," which organized the smuggling of arms and volunteer fighters to Cuba. He worked out of the junta's headquarters in a dingy building at 120 Front Street in lower Manhattan, just off Wall Street. José Martí had lived and worked there, in a cramped room on the fourth floor at the end of a dark corridor, and the building subsequently had become the center of Cuban exile activity in the city. Among the volunteers who manned the Front Street offices and prepared propaganda flyers, the mood was upbeat, but Pérez Carbó did not share their optimism. Cuba, he noticed, was barely mentioned during the presidential campaign. Already a grizzled and grumpy old-timer at forty-one, Pérez Carbó had endured a long imprisonment in Spain, he had combat experience in both revolutionary wars in Cuba, and he knew the struggle for independence would be long and hard. U.S. Navy ships were halting more than half of his arms shipments to Cuba, and by the end of 1896 their interference had made him bitter. His response to Elvira Cape's query about the meaning of McKinley's election could not have been more harsh.

"You're thinking about McKinley? Well, dear friend, let me dispel your illusions," Pérez Carbó wrote. "Expect nothing, absolutely nothing, from these people." After winning the election, Pérez Carbó explained, McKinley had backed away from any commitment to support Cuban independence, as had some of Cuba's alleged friends in the U.S. Senate.

Haven't you seen how the clamor [for Cuba] in the press and the Congress
has suddenly disappeared? This should give you an idea of how much these

men are capable of doing for Cuba in her desperate fight for freedom. Fire and blood! That's our salvation.

In the months that followed, the McKinley administration proved to be just as opposed to granting the Cuban rebels belligerency status and just as determined to deny them arms and ammunition as the Cleveland administration had been. "There are spies all around us," Pérez Carbó wrote to Elvira in May 1897, "watching every move we make." Some Cubans suspected U.S. investors in Cuba had managed to convince the new administration that if a state of belligerency were recognized in Cuba, the Spanish government could no longer be held responsible for the protection of U.S. properties there. Others believed the United States was simply waiting for an opportunity to take Cuba for itself. José Martí had warned that the "Colossus of the North" could eventually be as great a threat to Cuban independence as Spain had been. Antonio Maceo, his fellow rebel leader, had agreed. "I don't expect anything of the Americans," General Maceo wrote to Pérez Carbó in July 1896, a month after the Republican convention in St. Louis. "We must stand on our own efforts. It is better to rise or fall without their aid than to contract debts of gratitude with such a powerful neighbor."

Those debts were eventually incurred, however. Cubans soon had to rethink their patriotic struggle in a new geopolitical context, facing U.S. prejudice and arrogance rather than Spanish tyranny.

◆ ◆ ◆

Pérez Carbó's complaint about the diminishing U.S. "clamor" over Cuba notwithstanding, 1897 brought a surge of sympathetic reporting from the island. In some of the first examples of what would later be called human rights journalism, American correspondents described in detail the murderous reality of General Valeriano Weyler's "reconcentration" of Cuban civilians in tightly confined areas, with the disease and starvation it inevitably produced. The rebels' cause remained broadly popular in the United States, and newspaper publishers such as William Hearst and Joseph Pulitzer saw a great opportunity to boost circulation: Compelling stories about barefoot Cuban rebels holding out year after year against the vastly superior Spanish army made for good reading. U.S. newspapers were soon expending considerable resources in their Cuba coverage.

For journalistic effect, the U.S. correspondents routinely exaggerated the heroism of the rebels, the innocence of the Cuban victims, especially women, and the cruelty of "The Butcher" Weyler and other Spanish commanders.

Accurate reporting in 1897 would have shown both sides to be suffering and in trouble militarily. After the death of Antonio Maceo, rebel forces were not able to continue his offensive in western Cuba, and across much of the country they were reduced to hit-and-run guerrilla actions and defensive operations. But the situation of the Spanish troops was no better. An insurrection in the Philippines had forced Spain to fight a two-front war, and Spanish forces in Cuba were overextended, exhausted, and undersupplied. A Santiago writer described what he called the "grave" situation in his city in April 1897:

> The Spanish army has not been paid for seven months. The troops in the streets are poorly dressed and undernourished. The hospital is full of wounded and sick soldiers. Military barracks have been turned into infirmaries, because every day there are more patients in need of attention. The local economy is in crisis. People are working in exchange for food, without getting paid. The poor people who wait outside the military gates, hoping for scraps from the soldiers' rations, are out of luck. There are no scraps.

Spanish authorities, determined to combat the insurgency, resorted to desperate measures. In May, police raided the house of Emilio's brother-in-law Enrique Schueg, who was still functioning as the rebels' underground agent in Santiago. They found no incriminating papers but imprisoned him anyway. He was released only after the French foreign minister, a friend of Schueg's, interceded on his behalf with the government in Madrid.

A key turning point in the war came in August 1897, when Spanish prime minister Antonio Cánovas was assassinated by an Italian anarchist. His replacement, Práxedes Sagasta, was an advocate of home rule for Cuba, and within months Spanish authorities on the island began pursuing negotiations. Valeriano Weyler resigned his command and returned to Spain. ("The monster fell!" Federico Pérez Carbó rejoiced in a note to Elvira.) The new Spanish government prepared another constitution for Cuba, granting it political autonomy, and almost all Cuban political prisoners were freed, including Emilio Bacardí.

Rather than bringing peace to Cuba, however, the reforms had the opposite effect. Cuban rebel leaders, sensing victory was near, vowed to fight to the end. Conservative elements in Cuba were equally stubborn in their rejection of any reform that did not leave the island as Spanish territory, and in January 1898 they staged violent demonstrations in downtown Havana. The fiery U.S. consul general, General Fitzhugh Lee (a Confederate Army veteran and nephew of General Robert E. Lee) reported that the Spanish authorities were in danger of losing control in the capital, and he suggested that a warship be sent to Havana to demonstrate America's determination to defend its interests there. President William McKinley promptly dispatched the USS *Maine*, a heavily armored cruiser.

From then, events unfolded quickly. A mysterious explosion aboard the *Maine* three weeks later caused the ship to sink in the harbor with the loss of more than 260 American sailors. U.S. newspapers accused Spain of blowing the ship up deliberately, a judgment tacitly supported by a U.S. Navy Court of Inquiry. (Investigations years later indicated the explosion was an accident.) With all public information pointing to Spanish culpability, a prowar fever swept the United States, and though Spanish diplomats worked feverishly to avoid a confrontation, the McKinley administration prepared for military action. The intervention in Cuba would not be justified on the basis of human rights concerns nor by the justice of the Cubans' yearning for independence. With American lives having been lost, U.S. honor was now at stake. The new war cry was "Remember the *Maine*! To hell with Spain!"

. . .

In December, Emilio Bacardi Moreau was reunited with his exiled family in Kingston, Jamaica. Exile had taken a toll. Four months before he was released from prison, his seventy-four-year-old mother had died in Kingston, attended by her daughter Amalia and her daughter-in-law Elvira. Amalia Moreau had known achievement and disappointment in her life. She had seen her husband's rum enterprise attain promising commercial success, but the war that separated her from her son and grandson was far from settled. Born into wealth and once a slave owner herself, Doña Amalia had embraced the idea of a new Cuba, and she took pride in her family's idealism, patriotism, and sophistication.

Emilio's own faith in the nobility of the Cuban cause had sustained him during his imprisonments and the separations from his family. Not being religiously devout, he held sacred the idea of *Cuba Libre*—a free and sovereign nation ruled by the Cuban *people*, white, black, and mulatto, and representing the dreams of the generations that preceded them. In an essay he wrote for a little hand-produced prison newspaper on the two-year anniversary of the 1895 independence war, Emilio used frankly spiritual language in honoring the thousands of Cubans who had died in the national struggle:

> We are not going to disturb the calm of those who have fallen, either by noisily praising them or by loudly lamenting their loss. The disciples of Jesus

considered themselves at home wherever they met as brothers....We are imitating them today, as we gather on these African rocks under a splendid sun like the one shining on our own beloved land. We are celebrating fraternal love, and in the sanctuary of our hearts we recall the memories of so many heroes: Peace in heaven for the black Aponte* and peace in heaven for the white Martí.

By the third anniversary of the war in February 1898, Emilio was in Jamaica. By then his nation's fate lay in the hands of foreign powers. The epic battle that had inspired him through long, dark times seemed a little smaller, swallowed up in a confrontation between Washington and Madrid. On his return from imprisonment in the Chafarines, Emilio had followed Elvira's example and written to Federico Pérez Carbó in New York for an assessment of the McKinley administration's thinking on Cuba. In his response, Federico sounded as discouraged by the American attitude as he had been in his letters to Elvira. "[They say], 'The time has not yet arrived to do something,'" he wrote. "And when will that time come? It's obvious: when the two powers agree on it. Then the Yankees will take the chestnut [i.e., Cuba] from the fire and eat it for themselves."

◆ ◆ ◆

Cuban concerns about Yankee designs were well founded. The closer the United States moved to war with Spain over Cuba, the less Cuba's own interests were taken into consideration. The prointervention arguments put forward by the McKinley administration and its political allies revolved almost entirely around U.S. strategic concerns. With a canal about to be built across the Central American isthmus, it would be important to control the maritime approaches and project sea power in the Caribbean. Given Cuba's key location, U.S. naval bases would be needed on the island. Theodore Roosevelt, though serving only as an assistant secretary of the navy, had already emerged as a forceful advocate of U.S. territorial expansion, and he was eager to go to war.

Despite the broad public support for Cuban independence, the McKinley administration paid little heed to that aim. One familiar objection, echoing Madrid's long-standing prejudice, was that an independent Cuba would be ungovernable because of its large black population. There were also tactical reasons for opposing Cuban independence. One top U.S. diplomat argued that if

---

*José Antonio Aponte, a Havana wood-carver of African descent who, inspired by Moses, resolved in 1812 to lead Cuban blacks "out of bondage" and was hanged for his conspiracy.

the United States went to war in Cuba as an ally of a provisional Cuban government, it would be far more restricted in the way it could subsequently operate there than if it were to go there alone and claim the island "transiently ours by conquest." When President McKinley asked Congress in April for authorization to go to war, there was no mention of Cuba's independence or of the "Cuban Republic" set up by Cuban leaders as their provisional government.

Not surprisingly, McKinley's request drew an immediate protest from Cuban rebel leaders and their allies. "We will oppose any intervention which does not have for its expressed and declared object the independence of Cuba," the rebels' representative in Washington, Gonzalo de Quesada, warned. Such arguments swayed Cuba's friends in the U.S. Congress, and ultimately a compromise was reached—or so it seemed. The Joint Resolution that empowered the president to use military force in Cuba included what came to be known as the Teller Amendment, affirming that the United States had no intention to occupy Cuba "except for the pacification thereof" and vowing "to leave the government and control of the island to its people" once that goal was met. Fatefully, however, the Teller Amendment left the occupation timeline and the definition of "pacification" all too vague.

The resolution was followed by an ultimatum to Spain and then a declaration of war against Spain in the Philippines as well as Cuba. In the opening engagement, U.S. naval forces destroyed the Spanish fleet in the Battle of Manila Bay, and in June American troops went ashore on the southeastern coast of Cuba. Among them were the "Rough Riders," the diverse, all-volunteer unit of frontiersmen, farmers, college professors, and Ivy League adventurers, commanded by Army colonel Leonard Wood and by Theodore Roosevelt himself.

Despite the Cuban rebels' impressive three-year record of fighting a much better-armed and better-equipped Spanish foe to a standstill, U.S. military commanders treated them with utter contempt and issued strict instructions not to work with them unless absolutely necessary. The campaign was limited to eastern Cuba, with no attention paid to Cuban forces in central or western Cuba (where Emilito Bacardi was fighting). The only Cuban commander with whom U.S. officers met was General Calixto García, who directed rebel forces in the area around Santiago. García, a veteran of the first revolutionary war, was given the assignment of securing the area around Daiquirí where U.S. troops were to come ashore and then blocking Spanish reinforcements from engaging the Americans. García's soldiers carried out the operation perfectly, and the U.S. Army was able to land fifteen thousand troops in a twenty-four-hour period without a hostile shot being fired. "Landing at

Daiquirí unopposed," Major General William R. Shafter, the commanding U.S. general, announced triumphantly in a cable. He made no mention of the Cubans' role.

The Cuban campaign was immortalized by Secretary of State John Hay's characterization of it as a "splendid little war," a phrase resounding with the U.S. imperialist aspirations of the era. The highlight was a bloody battle on July 1, when the Rough Riders and other units led a charge against entrenched Spanish positions on San Juan Hill on the outskirts of Santiago. The battle earned Roosevelt and Wood lasting fame, but it was costly: 214 U.S. soldiers were killed and more than 1,300 injured, meaning a loss of about 10 percent of the total U.S. force engaged that day. Roosevelt reported that his forces took the hill only "at a heavy cost" and acknowledged that "the Spaniards fight very hard." After the San Juan Hill battle, however, the remaining Spanish defenses proved weak. U.S. army and naval forces soon had Santiago surrounded and under siege, by land and by sea.

* * *

Among those stranded in the city were Emilio Bacardi's brother Facundo and his brother-in-law Enrique Schueg, both of whom were determined to keep their rum business operating. The sound of cannon fire echoed over the city constantly, and wayward shells from U.S. ships occasionally landed within the city itself. Deafening explosions shook nearby buildings and sent shrapnel flying in all directions. All shops were closed, and the market was empty, with all available supplies taken for the Spanish troops. The townspeople were terrified, hungry, and falling sick from contaminated water. With the local police and military mobilized to defend the city perimeter, downtown Santiago descended into lawlessness. Facundo knew he had enemies among the pro-Spain element in town, because of his well-known sympathy for the rebel cause. Enrique, too, was suspect, having been arrested once already and escaping a long imprisonment, or worse, only because of high level intervention.

The two men soberly reviewed their options. If the distillery, bottling factory, and barrels of aging rum were left unguarded, the facilities would no doubt be looted or burned. But if they both died in the siege, there would be no one to attend to their families and manage the enterprise after the war. They decided that one should stay and one should leave. As a French citizen, Enrique had freedom of movement, and on July 2, he departed Santiago with other French residents in a convoy arranged by the French consul. Facundo, whose family was with Elvira in Jamaica, heroically stayed behind.

Early the next morning, the six Spanish ships remaining in the bay made a dash for the open sea, hoping to break the naval blockade. The American ships waiting outside closed on them immediately and within four hours destroyed every ship, with a great loss of Spanish life. The destruction of the Spanish fleet sealed the fate of the Spanish forces in Cuba. The Spanish commanding officer in Santiago, General José Toral, nevertheless refused to capitulate. On July 4, Schueg returned to Santiago at the request of the French consul to meet with Toral and arrange the evacuation of the rest of the French colony in the city, including all those who were sick or injured or who had been unable to leave the city previously. He managed to find a number of mule wagons, loaded them with as many people as he could fit, and led them out of the city to the village of Caney, by then under American control. The refugee settlement soon swelled to more than fifteen thousand people. A Cuban resident described the stream of people arriving in "liberated" Caney each day from Spanish-ruled Santiago:

> Men and women loaded down with trunks and bundles; children wailing hysterically; old people, weakened by the march, dragging their tired legs; the sick and handicapped carried on stretchers or on someone's shoulders.
>
> The crowd, squeezed tightly together, crossed the front line silently, filing past the Spanish trenches. And when they were finally behind the Cuban and American lines, that great multitude erupted in unison with one loud roar: *¡Viva Cuba Libre!*

They camped in the open under makeshift tents made from bed sheets and branches. A drenching rain fell every afternoon, turning the scene into a muddied, mosquito-infested mess. Clean water was nowhere to be found, and mangoes were all there was to eat.

The population remaining in Santiago by then consisted of Spaniards and their local allies, people defending their property, men of combat age who were forced to stay, residents who were too ill to be moved, and the fearless and foolish. Not surprisingly, Facundo Bacardi Moreau found that his rum was in great demand. Had he wanted to barter, he could have traded a bottle for fresh bread or a box or two of cookies stamped "USA" and smuggled in from behind the American line. A bit of Bacardi rum mixed in a glass of contaminated local water was thought to kill the germs and improve the taste. Facundo and his most loyal employees took turns guarding the distillery and aging warehouse, with extra vigilance during the nighttime hours. For two more weeks, they hung on in Santiago with the rest of the residents, until General Toral finally capitulated to General Shafter and the siege was lifted.

The surrender ceremony was held near San Juan Hill just outside Santiago on

Sunday morning, July 17, under a ceiba tree known thereafter as the Tree of Peace. General Toral, who was waiting with his officers under the tree, raised his hat as General Shafter approached, and the rotund American saluted in return. Toral handed over the Spanish flag, Shafter reciprocated with a sword, and a Spanish bugler sounded a call. No Cuban representative was allowed to be present.

. . .

A large share of the hostility U.S. officers showed toward the Cuban rebels amounted to simple racism. The American units were mostly white, while the Cuban forces were mostly black. "To be brief and emphatic," a U.S. Army surgeon from New York told a reporter, "they are nothing more or less than a lot of half-breed Cuban niggers." It was inconceivable to many American officers, coming from a society that was still racially segregated, that black Cubans could be militarily competent or prepared to share political responsibility for their nation. General S. B. M. Young, a division commander, dismissed the Cuban rebels as "degenerates" and scoffed at the notion that Cuba could be independent. "They are no more capable of self-government," he said, "than the savages of Africa."

The crude American racism on display in Cuba contrasted sharply with the efforts of the Cuban rebel leadership to lay the foundation for a free society based on tolerance. Cuba in 1898 was decades ahead of the United States in ending racial discrimination, and the military and civilian leaders of the independence struggle were outraged by the sneering attitude of senior U.S. commanders. General Calixto García wrote to General Shafter personally to say how offended he was by Shafter's order to bar Cuban troops from Santiago on the grounds that they were likely to engage in looting there or carry out revenge attacks against the remaining Spaniards there. "Allow me, sir, to protest against even the shadow of such an idea," García fumed. "We are not savages, ignoring the rules of civilized warfare. We are a poor, ragged army as ragged and poor as was the army of your forefathers in their noble war for independence, but like the heroes of Saratoga and Yorktown, we respect our cause too deeply to disgrace it with barbarism and cowardice."

Civilian leaders were similarly upset by the Americans' disdain for Cuban capabilities. The head of the San Carlos Club, the center of elite society in Santiago, called a public meeting to draw up a petition to President McKinley in Washington, declaring that "all [the undersigned] desire a government of our own, as compensation for the sufferings and heroism of our army, and the definite establishment of the Cuban Republic, with Cuban authorities." The petition, however, was ignored. Months after the defeat of the Spanish forces,

General Shafter said he considered all Cuban territory occupied by the U.S. Army to be "part of the Union" until declared otherwise. His navy counterpart, Admiral William Sampson, was even more dismissive of the Cuban complaints. "It does not make any difference whether Cubans prove amenable to the sovereignty of the [occupation] government or not," he said. "We are there. We intend to rule, and that is all there is to it."

A peace protocol with Spain was signed on August 12 in Washington, and the terms were confirmed in December 1898 with the Treaty of Paris, an accord from which the Cuban party was once again excluded. Though it had started in 1895, the conflict would be recorded in history as The War of 1898, and though the Cubans had done far more of the fighting and dying, it was called the Spanish-*American* War.

• • •

In Jamaica, a hundred miles across the water, Emilio Bacardi got his news about the situation in Santiago from the local newspapers. They were all published in English, but he did not miss the comments by U.S. commanders belittling the contributions of the Cuban people. After spending seventeen months in Spanish prisons for the Cuban cause (not counting his earlier detention) and with a son wounded three times in combat against Spanish forces, Emilio was infuriated. He was just as angered by the Americans' arbitrary imposition of authority in Cuba and the dismissal of any governing role for Cubans. When he read of a U.S. edict warning Santiago residents that they would be arrested and forced to do hard labor for thirty days if they did not immediately report the death of someone in their household, Emilio fired off a stinging response: "The obligation of those in authority is to be at the service of those who suffer. It is not for those who suffer to be at the disposition of those who command."

Emilio and his family returned to Santiago in August 1898. The American flag by then was flying over the city hall, and the town was ruled by a U.S. military governor, Brigadier General Leonard Wood, promoted to brigadier rank for his role in the Battle of San Juan Hill. No sooner had Emilio moved back into his house on Marina Baja Street than old friends began stopping by to air their complaints about the new U.S. administration. After writing his "open letter," however, Emilio had calmed down. Cuba was finally free of Spain's suffocating colonial grip. The United States, though temporarily occupying the country, had pledged under the Teller Amendment to abandon Cuban territory at some point and recognize the country's independence. In the meantime, there was much work to do. Emilio immediately went to see his brother Facundo and Enrique Schueg to review the condition of Bacardi & Compañía. Miraculously, the factory had survived the war intact, and while at times rum production had slowed to a trickle, it had never stopped completely. Emilio was still the president of the firm, though once again it had operated without him a long time, and after his return he left it largely in his brother's hands, concentrating instead on the reconstruction of his hometown.

The beneficial side of the U.S. military occupation of Santiago soon became clear. For all their domineering ways, their insensitivity, and even their racism, the Americans were unmatched in their capacity for getting things done, and quickly. The U.S. Army was precisely what Santiago needed at that moment. No one, in fact, better personified the U.S. military's talents, as well as its narrow-mindedness, than Leonard Wood himself, Santiago's appointed governor. A native New Englander, Wood grew up with Yankee values of hard work, frugality, athleticism, and patriotism. He was trained as a physician at Harvard only after failing to gain an appointment to West Point, and shortly after graduation he signed up for a career in the army. He was sent to the western frontier during the final years of the Indian Wars and so distinguished himself in the pursuit of the Apache chief Geronimo that he was awarded a Medal of Honor for his role.

Assigned later to the White House, he served as an attending physician to Grover Cleveland and William McKinley but yearned for another battlefield assignment. While in Washington, he met Theodore Roosevelt, with whom he shared a passion for strenuous outdoor activity. Both had high-level political connections and used them without hesitation to secure their command positions with the Rough Riders in Cuba. With a rigid, barrel-chested physique and short, dark hair combed straight back, Wood could intimidate with a single glance, and he needed no weapon to convey authority, only the riding crop he carried everywhere. He took on the mission of administering Santiago with characteristic efficiency and determination.

Emilio Bacardi had not seen Santiago at its worst. Leonard Wood had. Having been neglected and besieged, the city of fifty thousand was without food and sanitation, and two hundred people were dying from starvation or disease each day. In an account he wrote later, Wood described his first trip into the city on July 20:

> Long lines of wan, yellow, ghastly looking individuals dragged themselves wearily up and down the filthy streets, avoiding the dead animals and heaps of decomposing refuse, or sank wearily in some friendly shade, seeking to recover strength in sleep. Frightful odors poured out of the abandoned houses, speaking more strongly than words of the dead within. The very air seemed laden

with death.... Men could not bury the dead fast enough, and they were burned in great heaps of eighty or ninety piled high on gratings of railroad iron and mixed with grass and sticks. Over all were turned thousands of gallons of kerosene and the whole frightful heap reduced to ashes. It was the only thing to be done, for the dead threatened the living, and a plague was at hand.

As governor of Santiago, Wood immediately took charge of feeding the hungry and caring for the sick as well as burying the dead. He had no tolerance for laziness; men who resisted a street-sweeping assignment could face a public horsewhipping. He was Santiago's virtual dictator in those first weeks, but he impressed many who came into contact with him. On the job at the break of dawn, he would ride through the streets personally supervising the cleanup efforts, getting off his horse occasionally to show a workman it was easier to sweep downhill than up or move his cart toward a pile of trash rather than carry the trash to the cart. At night, he would stay at his desk working after everyone else had left. "The passion for 'the job' had taken possession of him," his biographer Herman Hagedorn wrote. "For the first time since the Geronimo days, he had found an undertaking commensurate with his powers." While representing Yankee energy and efficiency at their best, however, Leonard Wood also exhibited the imperiousness and condescension that would ultimately sour U.S.-Cuban relations. Even while helping Cubans, he belittled their readiness to assume responsibility. "With one or two exceptions," he wrote to his wife, "not a Cuban has come forward to do anything for his people."

In September, Emilio Bacardi and other prominent proindependence *santi-agueros* assembled to discuss what position they should take with respect to the U.S. military occupation, given its positive and negative aspects. Emilio argued that they should cooperate, offer assistance, and trust the United States to comply with the commitment it had made to Cuban independence. With his steady manner, his enormous prestige in the community, and his idealistic vision, Emilio was bound to come to Leonard Wood's attention, and he soon did—for his reputation and also for his family's rum. In November, a group of Santiago citizens who had been advising Wood suggested it was time they have one of their own as their mayor, and they asked him to appoint Emilio Bacardi. Wood agreed, concluding he was one of the most talented men available.

"If that man is as good at being mayor as he is at making rum, there's no one better," Wood said. On the other hand, he told an aide, "I don't know what my puritanical friends in Massachusetts will think when they learn I have selected Mr. Bacardi."

Chapter 7

A Public Servant
in a Misgoverned Land

Havana's Prado, the wide and shady boulevard leading from the city's central park down to the harbor, became a tent city when the U.S. Army set up camp in Cuba's capital at the end of 1898. Space was tight, and soldiers had to pitch their tents snug against each other. They drove their stakes into the patches of dirt around the trees that lined the broad sidewalks and strung laundry lines between the lampposts. On the balconies of the mansions that flanked the boulevard, Cuban women with fluttering fans and Cuban men in white straw hats stood watching the activity below with amazement and a little horror. On New Year's Day 1899, with the formal transfer of sovereignty, the Spanish flag that flew over the old fortress at the harbor entrance came down, and the Stars and Stripes went up in its place. The Cuban flag was nowhere to be seen.

Police patrolling duties in the capital were taken over by the U.S. Army's Eighth and Tenth Infantries. The U.S. military governor of Cuba moved into the Havana palace previously occupied by the Spanish captain-general, though not until American soldiers hauled more than thirty wagonloads of trash out of it. Nearly four centuries of Spanish dominion over Cuba were being quickly undone by an American military administration determined to teach Cubans to speak English, enact U.S. laws, adopt American management practices, buy made-in-the-U.S.A. products, and turn their attention from bullfighting to baseball (something they were anxious to do anyway). U.S. commanders and their superiors in Washington felt free to reshape the country, literally, as they saw fit. Not only were Cuba's educational and tax systems changed; even the maps were redrawn. The Isle of Pines, just off the southern coast, had been part of Cuba as long as Spain had ruled, but the U.S. government—without notifying the Cubans—claimed the island for itself under the Treaty of Paris. In the spring of 1901, as U.S. military commanders pressured Cuban lawmakers to give the United States a standing right to intervene in their country, the territory became a bargaining chip. "The Isle of Pines I think we can afford to drop if necessary," General Leonard Wood suggested in a letter to U.S.

secretary of war Elihu Root, noting that the island didn't have a good harbor. Having first thought they were on the winning side in the war, Cubans learned they had to negotiate with the United States just to keep their country intact.

The U.S. occupation disoriented Cubans, confusing them about who their enemy was and what progress meant. They despaired when American politicians and military commanders openly boasted that the U.S. flag would never come down in Havana, but at the same time they marveled at how their island was so quickly transformed. During the occupation years, the United States paid and supervised crews to clean and repair Cuban streets, build new highways and bridges, install water and sewer systems, and lay telegraph lines linking towns from one end of the island to the other. Cuban patriots faced a difficult choice: Support the occupation, even as it diminished their nation's sovereignty, or oppose it, even as it took their country into the twentieth century as fast as it could be taken. For decades, the fight for freedom had simply meant a military struggle against the Spanish army. But the achievement of full Cuban independence was now a political challenge, and in the new era the nation needed leaders with common sense and sound judgment more than it needed men who were good with guns and machetes.

The U.S. military presence was first felt in Santiago, and as the new mayor, Emilio Bacardi was among the first Cubans to consider the advantages and disadvantages of the American occupation. As long as he lived, Emilio was never accused of halfheartedness in his advocacy of a free and independent Cuba. Years later, the Santiago veterans of the "Liberation Army" made him their honorary president, even though he had never held a weapon. But Emilio was a forward thinker and believed in modernization, and he identified those principles above all with the United States. He wrote later that his favorite phrase in American English was "Go ahead," because it suggested a sense of "absolute freedom" that in any other language lost the element of directness it had when an American said it. When Leonard Wood came charging into Santiago in 1898 with an energy like no one there had seen before, Emilio was immediately drawn to him. The challenge would be to work with him in the reconstruction of Santiago despite Wood's lack of support for the independence cause to which Emilio had dedicated his life.

As Santiago's mayor, Emilio Bacardi represented the native *criollo* leadership Cuba desperately needed in its postcolonial period but mostly lacked. The issues he faced in his own dealings with the Americans mirrored his country's experience with the occupation, and the wisdom he demonstrated as mayor and later as a senator in Havana earned him a place among Cuba's esteemed sons. Within the Bacardi family, Emilio set an example of civic responsibility that later generations could follow as they also struggled to define what their Cuban nationality required of them during difficult times.

• • •

On his first day as mayor, Emilio Bacardi called local reporters to the Santiago city hall and laid out his goals: "To promote the material development of the population, to provide employment to those who need it most, and to attend to all local needs, to the maximum extent possible. If I do not meet these goals," he said, "it will not be for a lack of trying but rather for a lack of competence on my part, and I will correct that by dutifully giving up the position I accept today." It was a typically straightforward declaration for a man who always gave priority to local action and sought immediate results. His predecessor as mayor was a U.S. Army major named McLeary, and on the day McLeary stepped down, Emilio persuaded the U.S. soldiers serving with him in the municipal government to abandon their positions as well, so their jobs could go to unemployed Cuban war veterans. With that one move, Emilio not only met a pressing community need but also signaled his loyalty to the Liberation Army, an institution U.S. commanders were determined to discredit. He further underscored his political leanings with his first mayoral appointment, choosing his close friend Federico Pérez Carbó, the accountant-turned-revolutionary, to serve as city clerk. Federico had just come home after almost two years in the United States arranging arms deliveries for the Cuban rebels, and his presence in the government would remind Leonard Wood and the other U.S. authorities that Santiago remained a *ciudad héroe*, as it had been in one insurrection after another.

Emilio made no major political decision or budgetary commitment, however, without checking first with General Wood, who as the U.S. military governor was the supreme authority in the Santiago district, and he encouraged the city residents to support Wood, no matter their feelings about how the war had ended. On the night he took office, he stood on the city hall balcony, bareheaded, facing a huge, cheering crowd in the square below. The gathering might have become riotous, given the population's frustration over not yet having gotten a government they could call their own, but Emilio was determined to keep his people's patriotic energy in check. He invited a U.S. Army officer and a Cuban rebel general to join him on the balcony, placing one on each side of him. "We have three parties represented here," Emilio told the crowd in his booming voice: "the intervening government, in the form of the U.S. Army; the Cuban Army, to whom we owe our freedom; and the Cuban people, whom I represent as mayor. It is on the partnership of these three entities that our future will depend during these critical times."

Emilio was not naive. He knew the depth of the American military's prejudice against Cubans, especially those of color, and he realized that U.S. commanders doubted the country was genuinely capable of governing itself. His goal as mayor was to prove them wrong, at least in Santiago, where he could personally demonstrate effective Cuban leadership. With no city council to assist him, Emilio convened an *asamblea de vecinos* (assembly of neighbors) as his advisory body, in order to address local issues and projects with "public value."

At the time, U.S. and Cuban political leaders still had serious disagreements. The U.S. government had refused to recognize the "Republic in Arms," which the civilian leaders of the revolution, including Emilio, viewed as an authentic Cuban government that could be institutionalized as soon as Spain relinquished sovereignty. The "Republic" gave rise to a Cuban Constitutional Assembly that began provisional work shortly after the war. General Calixto García, the former Cuban army commander in the Santiago area, proposed free elections with suffrage extended to every Cuban male over the age of twenty-one, a reform that had long been part of the revolution's political program. But U.S. officials ignored the Assembly and refused to consider its recommendations. When the Assembly sent a commission, including General García, to Washington in November 1898 to discuss the situation in Cuba, President McKinley and other U.S. officials agreed to meet with the delegates only as individuals and only to discuss one subject: the dissolution of the rebel army. Frustrated and angered by the hostile reception given his group, Calixto García fell ill while in Washington and died there.

Cuban leaders had been hoping to keep their army intact as a symbol of their nation. While the new Constitutional Assembly struggled to achieve some small measure of sovereignty, the existing Liberation Army units remained encamped around the country, awaiting word on their disposition. Emilito Bacardi Lay, having risen to the rank of lieutenant colonel at the age of just twenty-one, was in charge of a unit in Consolación del Sur, in the province of Pinar del Río at the western end of Cuba. Weary and restless and bothered by conflicts with fellow officers and soldiers, Emilito wrote to his father in December 1898 to complain. As Santiago's new mayor, adjusting to the reality of the U.S. military occupation, Emilio could only counsel patience. "I am surrounded by the same difficulties you face," he wrote, "and I resolve them by forcing myself to be strictly impartial.... As for your own matters, determine what's best for you, but you must put the public interest, the interest of the Nation, above all else."

A photo taken during Emilio's initial months as mayor shows him and Leonard Wood, the military governor, during a review of Santiago street-cleaning operations. The two men are seated on a park bench along a walkway near the bay. Wood is in his Rough Rider uniform, pressing slightly forward, intense as ever. Emilio, in a gray suit and vest and loosely knotted bow tie, leans back confidently, one arm resting on the back of the bench. He wears a white straw boater hat with a dark ribbon around the flat crown, as he does in almost all photos from that time, and he appears altogether relaxed, as if he were watching a parade.

Mayor Bacardi and General Wood were able to work together harmoniously on behalf of many causes in Santiago, from clean streets to public education. Barely a third of the school-age children in large cities such as Santiago were enrolled, and a much smaller proportion in rural areas. Within months of taking charge, Wood and Emilio had together opened twenty-five new kindergartens in the city of Santiago, and they were organizing new teacher training schools, one for men and one for women. After he discovered that three hundred girls in one school were sharing a single instructor, Emilio ordered the provincial school board to hire additional staff. When the board balked, Wood intervened on Emilio's behalf, and the teachers were hired.

The two men even developed a friendship of sorts, complicated by their political relationship but still genuine. They continued to correspond for many years after Wood left Cuba. For a time, each served the other's purposes. Emilio praised Wood's initiatives, such as his efforts to fight yellow fever and reconstruct the water and sewer system, and as mayor he always showed Wood the respect and deference a general officer expects. Wood was generous in return. Early in his term, Emilio decided Santiago needed a municipal museum for a display of relics from the city's heroic history, beginning with the early colonial period and extending through the days of slavery and the independence struggles. Rather than bypass Leonard Wood on the project, which he probably could have done, Emilio went to him first with the proposal. As a result, he won the governor's support, plus a two-hundred-dollar monthly appropriation, enabling him to establish Cuba's first city museum in February 1899.

One reason the mayor and the general got along well, of course, was that they focused on street cleaning, school reform, and municipal policing rather than on such divisive issues as voting rights and the limits of Cuban sovereignty. General Wood knew Emilio felt strongly that Cuba deserved its political independence, and as long as Emilio was the mayor, Wood chose his words carefully on the subject, at least in public. In an article he wrote for the magazine *North American Review,* published in May 1899, Wood said some form of civil government should be established in Cuba "as soon as possible," and he cited the local authorities in the Santiago area as exemplary. "The claim that the Cubans are not capable of governing themselves," he wrote, "has thus far not been substantiated in this Province." He suggested that Santiago could be a model for the establishment of good government in the rest of the country. But then he added, "When I say that the civil government should be established as soon as possible, I do not wish to be understood as recommending its immediate establishment in all its branches, but rather its gradual establishment, commencing at the bottom and ending at the top."

That caveat hinted at the major disagreements that lay between Wood and proindependence Cubans. In Wood's view, the establishment of democracy in Cuba not only had to be a gradual process, it had to be controlled by the Americans. In a July 1899 letter to President McKinley, Wood characterized his own attitude toward the people of Santiago as one "almost of paternalism":

> I tell them frankly that this is a military occupation, that all appointments have to be approved by the military commander, but that they must look upon the military commander, not as an arbitrary individual, but as a friend, who will use his authority, not for the purpose of oppression, but to get the best men into office.

Though Wood did not say so publicly at the time, he thought Cuba should be annexed to the United States, and he was convinced it eventually would be. The man in the U.S. government who probably knew him best, Theodore Roosevelt (by then the governor of New York), summarized Wood's private views in a July 1899 letter to Senator Henry Cabot Lodge of Massachusetts, a mutual friend:

> Wood believes that we should not promise or give the Cubans independence: that we should govern them justly and equitably, giving them all possible opportunity for civil and military advancement and that *in two or three years they will insist upon being part of us.* [emphasis added]

In supporting Emilio Bacardi and other *santiagueros* with whom he had a good relationship, Wood believed they might be drawn closer to the United States, and his commitment to improving Santiago schools reflected his interest in promoting a pro-U.S. outlook in Cuban youth. "Without exception, all [Cubans] desire—I might say demand—American teachers," he wrote in the spring of 1899, generalizing wildly. "They are anxious to learn English; they are anxious to become Americanized."

· · ·

Given his principled idealism—which sometimes came out as stubbornness— it was probably inevitable that Emilio Bacardi would become frustrated as mayor. After just eight months in office, he resigned abruptly in July 1899. A turf battle had erupted between Emilio and General Demetrio Castillo, a former Cuban army commander whom Wood had appointed as the civil governor of Oriente province, to which Santiago belonged. Both men had strong opinions, and neither fully trusted the other. Emilio wrote Wood a letter detailing each of his disagreements with Castillo, "so that you can judge for yourself the justice of my reasons." Their dispute concerned which government— Bacardi's municipal or Castillo's provincial—had the authority to supervise school examinations and regulate store hours and public dancing.

Wood was occupied with another dangerous yellow fever epidemic in Santiago at the time and probably found Emilio's complaints to be relatively petty. The problems that led to his resignation, however, raised substantive questions about the U.S. occupation. With so few governing positions open to Cubans, so little authority invested in them, and no clear delineations of responsibility, conflicts like the one between Emilio and General Castillo were inevitable. Emilio Bacardi was a proud and ambitious man and had good reason not to want to continue working, in his words, "as no more than a simple administrative agent of a civil governor [i.e., Castillo] who has the power to overturn everything the mayor decrees." Leonard Wood, as the U.S. military governor for eastern Cuba, had not devolved much responsibility to the Cubans whom he appointed nor put much effort into building new political institutions.

Wood in fact was dead set against full Cuban independence, as were most senior American officials who dealt with Cuba. The U.S. government could hardly ignore its commitment under the Teller Amendment to surrender jurisdiction over the island, but Wood and others argued the amendment would be irrelevant if Cubans chose voluntarily to join the United States. To be sure, a clear majority of Cubans favored independence, but if voting were restricted so as to exclude a sufficient number of proindependence Cubans, that fact should not matter. "The *property-holding* Cubans favor annexation to the

United States," Wood told a *New York Times* reporter in June 1899, "because they realize we can give them a stable government."

In December 1899, Leonard Wood was appointed the U.S. military governor for all of Cuba, replacing General John Brooke. He went to work immediately on ways to limit voting in Cuba to those most likely to favor annexation. His partner was Elihu Root, the new secretary of war. Within weeks, the two men had prepared a limited suffrage plan they believed would accomplish their objectives. By binding U.S. decree, the right to vote would be extended only to those males who were literate, had at least $250 in property, or had served in the Cuban rebel army. Disenfranchising the poorest and least educated voters, in Root's words, would exclude only the "ignorant and incompetent," and Wood agreed. "Giving the vote to this element," Wood wrote, "means a second edition of Haiti and Santo Domingo [the Dominican Republic] in the near future." The element Cuba had in common with those two countries was its largely illiterate black population. Wood was far too sophisticated to resort to overt racial slurs in making his arguments, but Herman Hagedorn, Wood's biographer, made clear the general's view: "The possibility of negro dominance lay like a thunderhead on the horizon."

The restricted suffrage plan was a masterpiece of hypocrisy. In his *North American Review* article, Wood had written that Cuba needed "a liberal and just government of the people, for the people, and by the people," but the immediate consequence of his new plan was to bar about half the voting-age males from participating in an upcoming municipal election or in a subsequent election to choose delegates to write a Cuban constitution. Telegrams poured in to Wood's office from outraged citizens and their local governments. The local administration in Santiago accused Wood and Root of trying "to block the will or desire of each and every Cuban, precisely at this historic moment when the constitution of municipal governments will be the cornerstone for building the country." In a letter to Root, Wood acknowledged there was still "some talk of universal suffrage"* but insisted that the "best people" agreed with the limitations he had decreed.

Wood had overestimated the Cubans' desire to join the United States, however. Even with the "ignorant and incompetent" citizens barred from voting, the June 1900 municipal elections brought sweeping victories for the political parties that supported Cuba's independence and opposed annexation. The pro-U.S. Democratic Union Party found so little support among the electorate that it barely bothered to compete. In an official report to Washington, Wood

---

*The term "universal suffrage" at the turn of the century in Cuba and most other countries was generally taken to refer only to males.

lamented that the results were a victory for "the extreme and revolutionary element" in Cuba. The political significance of the elections was nonetheless clear: Like it or not, the United States had to prepare for Cuba becoming independent, regardless of whether the island's fledgling government institutions, political parties, and leadership class were ready for the challenge.

Faced with the prospect of losing control over Cuba, War Secretary Root— a successful lawyer before joining the McKinley administration—proposed that the United States force Cubans to grant a formal U.S. right to intervene on their territory at any time in order to maintain "stable government" there. At Root's urging, Senator Orville Platt of Connecticut introduced legislation in early 1901 stipulating that the United States could not end its military occupation of Cuba until the drafters of the country's new constitution inserted a provision explicitly guaranteeing the intervention right. When the U.S. Congress passed the Platt Amendment in March, Cubans erupted in protest over what they saw as nothing less than U.S. government blackmail. In Havana, demonstrators assembled outside Wood's residence carrying torches. In Santiago, former rebels warned at public rallies that yet another revolution might be necessary, this one directed against the United States. But Wood held firm, reiterating that the U.S. Army would not withdraw from Cuba until the Platt provision was included in the Cuban constitution. Elihu Root warned that if the Cubans continued, in his words, "to exhibit ingratitude and entire lack of appreciation of the expenditure of blood and treasure of the United States to secure their freedom from Spain, the public sentiment of this country will be more unfavorable to them."

◆ ◆ ◆

By a one-vote margin, fifteen to fourteen, delegates to the Cuban Constitutional Convention agreed in May 1901 to include the Platt Amendment language in the country's new constitution, having narrowly concluded that limited independence was better than continued U.S. military occupation. The Santiago delegation, headed by a local politician named Antonio Bravo Correoso, nevertheless voted unanimously against the Platt provision, viewing it as a betrayal of the U.S. promise to recognize Cuba's sovereignty. Emilio Bacardi was one of Bravo Correoso's closest allies, and when a political rally was held in Santiago to congratulate him and the other local delegates for their principled stand against the Platt language, Emilio was among the featured speakers.

Less than two years after resigning his appointment as Santiago's mayor, he was now campaigning for a follow-up term, this time as the first Cuban to be freely elected to the mayoral post. In the intervening time, Emilio had gained a better sense of the seriousness of the political challenge facing his country. His opposition to including the U.S.-mandated Platt provision in his country's constitution showed he was still a Cuban nationalist, but standing squarely for independence was no longer enough; more than anything, his country needed responsible governmental leadership. Spain had left Cuba with no political culture from which representative government could easily spring, and the U.S. military administration on the island seemed more determined to belittle the country's nascent democratic institutions than to nurture them. Cuba consequently had a large share of scoundrels in public life.

In the fall of 1900, Leonard Wood's Cuban secretary and personal interpreter, Alejandro Gonzales, had written to Emilio to warn him against aligning automatically with any Cuban politician who parroted an *independentista* line, referring specifically to some of the constitutional convention delegates:

> They exploit your good faith and lead you to believe they are as patriotic as you are, when I know that they take nothing into account beyond their personal well-being. You who are honorable believe that everyone else is. I have served as an interpreter for many, and I know what I am talking about. . . . Don't defend them.

In fact, Emilio needed no such reminders. As mayor and then as a private citizen, he regularly confronted politicians who had been heroes during the independence wars. Demetrio Castillo and Tomás Padró, two of his biggest political enemies in Santiago, were both former rebel generals. Padró, whom Wood had chosen to replace Emilio as Santiago's mayor, fired municipal employees who refused to join his political party and shut down a newspaper that criticized him.

In the 1901 mayoral election, Emilio ran more as a reformer than as a fervent patriot, taking "Morality and Justice" as his campaign slogan. At the age of fifty-seven, he presented himself as the candidate who would restore order and transparency to city government after the shabby performance of the Padró administration. He won with a 61 percent majority, though only after enduring a nasty campaign. Padró, himself the subject of a misconduct investigation, had spread unsubstantiated allegations that some of the money Emilio had raised for the Liberation Army had gone into his own pocket.

Emilio, a man easily offended, was outraged by such attacks. Before taking office, he wrote to Leonard Wood in Havana, asking "Have you confidence in me?" Having been undercut in his authority during his first term as mayor,

Emilio was seeking assurances that the U.S. military administration would not appoint one of his political enemies as civil governor of his province (and thus his own superior), a situation Emilio warned would be "impossible" for him. His sensitivity to criticism was underscored a few months later when he prepared a draft of his will, with the charges and countercharges of the campaign still fresh. Emilio concluded his testament with a short declaration "for my children, so that they may never be ashamed of their father."

> All the evil things said against me are the calumnies of wretched and miserable men. I have been honorable all my life, perhaps too honest, if that is possible, and I have never stolen one cent from anyone;...moreover, the most exalted of all those who defamed me and [still] defame me, from the first to last, owe favors to Emilio Bacardi; if I am to be punished for anything I have done in this life, it will be for my one sin: having loved to a fault my nation and all those who have suffered for it.

Though his self-righteousness may have been annoying at times, Emilio Bacardi was indeed an honorable man, and his personal integrity was above question. He was infuriated by those Cubans whose patriotism struck him as self-serving, precisely because he took his own so seriously. His proudest moment in his second term as mayor was his inauguration of the Fiesta de la Bandera (Festival of the Flag), a New Year's Eve ceremony that became a Santiago tradition. At the stroke of midnight on December 31, 1901, as the cathedral bells rang twelve times over an assembled multitude in the main plaza, Emilio hoisted a huge Cuban flag, twenty-five feet long, over the town hall. Cuba was not yet independent, and Emilio had to get the U.S. military's permission for the ceremony. Local citizens raised the funds to pay a local tailor to sew the giant banner, the biggest anyone had ever seen. It rippled gently in the night breeze, a red triangle on the hoist side containing a single white star with blue and white stripes adjacent, barely lit against the heavens. The town band played the national anthem. With the last note, whistles, cheers, and shouts of "*¡Viva Cuba Libre! ¡Viva!*" echoed across the square. The people of Santiago had never before seen a Cuban flag flying over their own city hall.

· · ·

The Cuban flag was not raised over the old fortress in Havana until May 20, 1902, when the United States surrendered jurisdiction over Cuba and recognized its conditional independence. Leonard Wood and the rest of the U.S. military government sailed back to the United States, finally leaving the Cubans to govern themselves, nearly four years after the end of the war with Spain. The new president was Tomás Estrada Palma, elected five months earlier after his only opponent, former general Bartolomé Masó, withdrew from the presidential race in protest over the appointment of an election commission stacked against him. Estrada Palma had spent more than twenty years in New York and favored continued ties with the United States. U.S. officials made no secret of their preference for him over Masó, an outspoken opponent of the Platt Amendment.

In Santiago, Emilio Bacardi was on his way to an exemplary five-year term as mayor. During that period, he opened municipal employment opportunities to women for the first time, giving preference to those whose husbands had been killed in the war, and he improved health care for the poor. Recognizing that the opening of the Panama Canal would mean increased ship traffic, he allocated city funds to deepen the harbor and improve the port infrastructure. He cracked down on illegal cockfighting, moved aggressively against prostitution, and took action against town employees found guilty of malfeasance. He fought to get Havana to allocate more money to Santiago for sanitation services, shamelessly warning that a failure to do so might prompt another U.S. intervention, given that the Platt Amendment obliged the Cubans to keep their cities clean. Finally, a week did not pass when Emilio did not speak at some war anniversary gathering, attend a veteran's funeral, visit a widow, or find some other way to pay tribute to the independence struggle that had consumed so much of his own life.

At the same time, Emilio maintained his personal relationships with powerful Americans, beginning with Leonard Wood. He was friendly as well with Theodore Roosevelt, Wood's ally and fellow adventurer. When Roosevelt was elected president in November 1904, Emilio sent him a succinct telegram:

ROOSEVELT. PRESIDENT. WASHINGTON.
SANTIAGO ONCE CONGRATULATED A VICTORIOUS "ROUGH RIDER."
TODAY, A PRESIDENT-ELECT.
BACARDI. MAYOR.

In the spring of 1906, when Roosevelt's twenty-two-year-old daughter, Alice, went to Santiago for a visit, Roosevelt asked Emilio to attend to her. He and Elvira, who were described by a Santiago chronicler as "personal friends" of Roosevelt, feted Alice so warmly during her stay that she left Santiago "enchanted."

Emilio by then was the most popular public figure in Santiago, virtually without political opponents. Friends and allies suggested he run for provincial governor. Instead, ready at last to focus on national issues, he chose the Senate. Cuban politics had grown dirtier by the year, with electoral fraud practiced on all sides and widespread graft within the government itself. Emilio was affiliated with the Moderate Party, which supported the reelection of Tomás Estrada Palma as president. For Emilio, the most serious problem in Cuba was corruption, and although Estrada Palma was a weak president, he was widely viewed as an honest man. Other members of Estrada Palma's government, however, were less principled. In the fall of 1905, Interior Secretary Fernando Freire de Andrade began dismissing government employees, even schoolmasters, who favored the opposition Liberal Party and their presidential candidate José Miguel Gómez. The campaign turned violent, with repeated clashes between the opposing groups, and the candidates and their supporters took to carrying weapons wherever they went.

In September, Gómez came to Santiago on a presidential campaign visit. Emilio did not support the Gómez candidacy, but he was worried about the possibility of a violent confrontation and rode his horse four miles out of town to meet the Gómez party on its way in. After greeting the candidate, Emilio accompanied him and his entourage all the way into the city, having ordered the Santiago police force to salute the Cuban flags the group was carrying. As a result, the rally in Santiago occurred without any incidents. But Emilio's civic spirit was the exception rather than the rule in Cuba in those days. Barely a week later, a Gómez campaign event in the city of Santa Clara ended in a bloody brawl, with a leading Liberal politician and the police chief both killed. The Liberals withdrew their candidates in all major races, saying it was clear that their ruling party opponents would resort to violence if necessary to defeat them.

• • •

Emilio's term in the Senate was his first exposure to national politics, but he arrived in Havana as a star, due partly to the national fame of Bacardi rum and partly to Emilio's highly regarded record as Santiago mayor. Within days of taking his seat in April 1906, he was engaging in floor debates on a variety of issues, generally taking progressive positions. He argued that anarchist labor agitators should not be covered by Cuba's extradition treaty with Spain, because they were not common criminals but defenders of socialist ideas. "It would be a travesty," Emilio said, "for a country like Cuba, having achieved freedom thanks to the unbreakable idealism of its sons, now to deport men who fight for other ideas, wrongly or not, to Spain, where they will be condemned to the worst punishment." He introduced legislation to provide a form of workmen's compensation insurance, not yet existent in Cuba, and he told his fellow senators that if they could appropriate money for a new Senate building they should be able to provide housing for flood victims. Emilio Bacardi was clearly headed for a position of major national leadership.

His country, however, was fast slipping back into crisis. The opposition Liberals, concluding they had been forcibly excluded from political life, decided to seize power by force. Armed struggle had produced a whole generation of Cuban heroes, and the Liberal Party ranks included many former rebel army officers and fighters. By August 1906, the party leadership had mobilized a militia force of about twenty-four thousand disgruntled men, many of them black, and they were marching toward Havana. The insurrection was by no means suicidal. The United States, as the occupying authority, had successfully dismantled the old Cuban army and barred the creation of a new one, so the government in Havana had few troops to defend itself. President Estrada Palma warned the Liberals that if they did not back down he was prepared to ask the U.S. military to return to Cuba and reoccupy the island.

Emilio saw his country descending into chaos yet again, to his enormous frustration. He could not comprehend the shortsightedness of Cuban politicians—on the Liberal side for threatening the security of the nation itself in order to gain political power, and on the side of the ruling government party for having refused to bring the Liberals into the political process. Most alarming by far was President Tomás Estrada Palma's threat to request U.S. military intervention. Another American occupation of the island would wipe out the whole structure of self-government the Cubans were trying to erect and destroy their fragile new sense of national purpose. Emilio resolved to do whatever he could by himself to avert a final showdown. "For winners and losers alike, the consequences will be the loss of our independence," he warned in a public message. On September 8, when he realized neither side was compromising and his fellow senators were doing nothing on their own, Emilio sent an urgent telegram to the Senate president, Ricardo Dolz:

IT ASTONISHES ME THAT IN THESE GRAVE MOMENTS THERE IS SO MUCH INDIFFERENCE, NOT CALLING CONGRESS INTO EXTRAORDINARY SESSION.

Dolz replied:

I DON'T HAVE AUTHORITY TO CONVENE CONGRESS IN EXTRAORDINARY SESSION.

Within hours, Emilio sent another:

I EXPECTED THAT ANSWER. BUT UNDER THE CURRENT CIRCUM-
STANCES, WHEN ALL CUBANS NEED TO COME TOGETHER, CONGRES-
SIONAL AND PARTY LEADERS WILL SHARE THE RESPONSIBILITY FOR
NOT HAVING CONVENED CONGRESS. TO SAY A MATTER OF SUCH IM-
PORTANCE IS THE DOMAIN OF THE EXECUTIVE BRANCH SHOWS INDIF-
FERENCE.

But Emilio was almost alone among his colleagues in recognizing the threat
to Cuba's nationhood. His efforts to get the Senate to intervene and forestall
a U.S. intervention went nowhere. Estrada Palma asked President Theodore
Roosevelt to send two ships to Cuba, and he followed that request by asking
that two thousand to three thousand U.S. troops be sent "with the greatest
secrecy and rapidity." Roosevelt chose instead to dispatch Secretary of War
William Howard Taft to mediate between the opposing sides. The Liberal
revolutionaries agreed to lay down their arms if new elections were called.
Estrada Palma and his vice president would themselves stay in office until a
new government could be formed. But Estrada Palma rejected the compromise.
He was determined to provoke a U.S. intervention by any means necessary,
believing it would save him. On September 25, he said he and his vice president
were resigning, fully aware the move would leave Cuba without any functioning government and thus force the United States to take charge.

Emilio Bacardí was furious; at the Liberals, at Estrada Palma, and—to an
extent he had not expressed before—at the United States, for having put Cuba
in this situation. "My increasingly firm idea," he wrote to Elvira on September
27, "is that the American [side] is playing with the two parties. They will get
a president to their liking...and then they will come." A day later, he was even
more discouraged, writing to Elvira that he and a handful of other senators
were pursuing a futile effort to get their chamber to reject Estrada Palma's
resignation. "The die is cast," he wrote. "What we're doing is a waste of time."
Estrada left office the next day with the rest of his government. William Howard Taft took official control of Cuba on behalf of the United States, establishing
the second U.S. occupation of the country in less than ten years. Emilio left
Havana, never to return to national politics.

• • •

The collapse of the Cuban Republic was a greater personal blow to Emilio
Bacardí than it was to other Cuban patriots. A free and independent Cuban

nation had been his sacred cause, the ideal that inspired and sustained him through exile and imprisonment. It would have been easier if he had carried a weapon during the independence war and fought on a battlefield, like his son Emilito and all the former generals who were now making a name in politics. In their *Cuba Libre* experience, they had worried about their ammunition supplies and food for their soldiers, with less time or reason to idealize their struggle. To the extent they were subsequently disillusioned, it was less painful than what Emilio felt.

He simmered for months, trying to understand what had happened and why. In February 1907, Leonard Wood wrote from the Philippines, where he was again a colonial administrator, asking for news about Cuba. Emilio wrote back to say that the sugar mills were grinding cane and the countryside was quiet but that there was much uncertainty about the country's future. He laid much of the blame for his country's suffering on Tomás Estrada Palma.

Cuba needs to be governed by someone who knows the country and its people, and this has perhaps been President Estrada Palma's major failing. His long stay in the United States made him forget his own kind, and when he tried to govern them, he didn't know them at all.

As Emilio knew well, Estrada Palma had been Wood's personal choice to take over the Cuban presidency, precisely because of his loyalty to the United States, so the letter amounted to a rare rebuke of the U.S. general.

Emilio's anger at what had happened to his country boiled over one day in April 1908. Charles Magoon, sent by Theodore Roosevelt to administer Cuba after the 1906 intervention, had ordered all the provincial governors and their legislative councils to resign as part of the preparation for new elections. The idea that democratically chosen Cuban officials could be ousted by an occupying foreign power infuriated Emilio, and he promptly wrote a commentary for a local newspaper:

To my people:
    We have taken another step backwards.... We have ratified our own incompetence. [We hear:] Governors and Councils, Stop Working!!! And this is not a cry to eliminate this useless cog in the gear of our state; that would be a sign of progress. No. What is sought is that we proclaim before the whole world that it is better to bow down before a foreigner than to obey a brother. And to stay bowed down, because we have no faith in ourselves and no civic consciousness. We believe it is only under the yoke of someone dominating us that we will not be a hindrance to civilization.

After years of admiring America, Emilio was coming to the conclusion that the United States—by its sheer size, its expansionist impulse, and its instinctive tendency to flex its muscles and dominate its neighbors—inevitably presented a danger to smaller, weaker neighbors. It was not that the United States was especially aggressive; its behavior was typical of all the big colonial powers of the day. In his commentary, Emilio cited the anti-imperialist views of Guglielmo Ferrero, an Italian historian and socialist of that era. "Never—not in the past nor today—has any nation governed another people with a spirit of justice," he quoted Ferrero as saying. "It is not to stop them from falling that it extends a hand, but rather to push them all the faster toward the bottom of the abyss." The United States had extended a hand to Cuba in 1898 but doomed its development. Emilio returned to the theme in a December 1908 letter to Carlos García, the son of Calixto García, the Cuban general spurned by U.S. commanders. In the letter, Emilio referred to "the American enemy, wise and astute, that for many years has been entangling us in the meshes of a preconceived plan."

He was making a rhetorical point. Emilio's admiration for the United States was undiminished, as was his affection for Americans, even those whom he held responsible for Cuba's troubles. His March 1907 letter to Leonard Wood ended with an invitation to visit Cuba the following fall. Even in his anti-imperialist newspaper commentary, Emilio described the American nation as "a big, generous, and honest people," and he and Elvira sent their daughters to be schooled in the United States. With other Cuban nationalists, however, he had drawn a lesson from the intervention experience: Small countries like Cuba need to keep their distance from large countries like the United States if they want their independence preserved, just as José Martí had forewarned.

In the years that followed, Emilio worked on his ten-volume *Crónicas de Santiago de Cuba.* His hometown seemed to him a purer representation of the Cuban nation whose development as a whole had been so tragic. He briefly returned to political life in 1916, though only to be on the Santiago city council. On this occasion, he ran on the Liberal ticket. When a young writer asked why he had switched parties, Emilio said his party identity had become irrelevant. "My only affiliation is *santiaguero*," he said. Even that engagement proved disappointing, however. After the first council meeting was marked by partisan disagreements, Emilio announced his immediate resignation. He devoted the rest of his life to writing and to the Bacardi rum business.

Chapter 8

~✸◕✸~

The One That Made Cuba Famous

In the first decade of the twentieth century, *"Cuba Libre"* went from being a cause to being a cocktail. As patriots, the Bacardis were disappointed that the dream of a genuinely free Cuba had mostly fizzled. As rum makers, they could not have imagined more promising business opportunities than what they soon saw, due to the popularity of new rum-based drinks such as the Cuba libre. The U.S. soldiers, businessmen, and tourists who came to patronize bars and nightclubs from Havana to Santiago found that light Cuban rum mixed well with everything, giving rise to an era of libation. American companies supplied the ice machines and the Coca-Cola, and drinking history was made.

The Bacardi story of the first Cuba libre comes from Fausto Rodríguez, who worked in his teenage years as a messenger for General Leonard Wood when Wood was military governor. He went on to become the Bacardi advertising chief in New York City, which raises questions about his impartiality, but he did tell a good tale. By his recollection, there was a barman named Barrio who presided at one of the many turn-of-the-century establishments in Havana that catered to U.S. military personnel. Eager to please his American customers, Barrio sent in a supply of Coca-Cola. One day, on a whim, the Cuban bartender decided to mix some Bacardi rum with Coke and offer the drink to his patrons. They liked it, so Barrio refilled the glasses and made a toast: *"¡Por Cuba Libre!"* To Free Cuba!

"¡Cuba Libre!" the soldiers answered, holding their glasses high, and the rum-and-Coke cocktail got its proper name.

The daiquiri was another postwar innovation. The iron mines near Daiquirí, like most of the mines in eastern Cuba, were owned by U.S. corporations. The U.S. personnel who managed the mines received a gallon of Bacardi rum each month as part of their pay allotment and were always looking for creative ways to drink it. Jennings Cox, the general manager, is credited with the idea of mixing the rum with lime juice, raw sugar, and crushed ice and shaking it vigorously. The drink caught on among the other mine workers, and within a few years it was the most popular cocktail in Cuba.

Sensing the moment had come for a big marketing push, the Bacardi partners promoted their product wherever they could, both at home and abroad. Enrique Schueg sent Bacardi rum samples to every international exhibition or fair: Paris 1900, Buffalo 1901, Charleston 1902, St. Louis 1904. For the Pan-American Exposition in Buffalo, Schueg had an elaborate pavilion built, featuring fourteen-foot columns of mahogany and other exotic Cuban woods. The centerpiece was a huge replica of a Bacardi rum bottle, complete with a painted label and crowned by a bat, the symbol of the firm, along with a bundle of sugarcane. It might have been ugly, but it made a statement: The Bacardis had arrived. Their rum beat out eleven Cuban competitors in Buffalo to win a gold medal. At the St. Louis World's Fair, the Bacardis won a grand prize.

In Santiago, the Bacardi name was soon associated with progress and celebration. Mayor Emilio Bacardi negotiated the first contract to bring electric lights to Santiago, and the big moments of modernization in the years that followed often had some Bacardi connection. So it was on the day in 1911 when the first airplane appeared in Santiago, flown by an intrepid American named James Ward. The historic event took place on San Juan Hill, before a crowd of wide-eyed townspeople. A few local men had to give Ward a push to get him started, but then he zoomed off toward the mountains, circled back toward the city, and landed on the same field where he had taken off. He was greeted at planeside by a Bacardi & Compañía agent who on behalf of the company and the city of Santiago presented Ward with a complimentary bottle of Bacardi Elixir, a raisin-flavored rum drink the company had just introduced. In the nineteenth century, civic involvement for a Cuban company like Bacardi meant supporting the independence movement. In the twentieth century, it could mean promoting air shows or sponsoring professional baseball teams, as Bacardi also did.

As the reputation of its rum spread, the company increased production, bringing molasses to the distillery in railroad tank cars. No longer was their company a rustic operation with a few dozen workers and old-fashioned technology, hovering constantly on the verge of bankruptcy. It had become a modern firm and was set to outlive those who were present at its birth. Bacardi & Compañía had established its own identity, separate from the lives of its founders, and its own corporate interests to be defended. It was still a family firm, but in the new century, under different conditions, the way this private Cuban enterprise could serve its nation would inevitably change.

A big part of the Bacardi success story was the company's extraordinary good fortune in having three gifted business partners in the same family, with talents that complemented each other perfectly. Facundo Bacardi Moreau, Emilio's brother, had the deepest history with the company, having worked at the distillery almost from the day it opened and directing it during the years Emilio was imprisoned. Facundo mastered every aspect of the rum-making operation, from the distillation to the charcoal filtration to the aging and the blending. No technical problem was beyond his understanding, and it was hard to imagine the distillery, the factory, or even the bottling plant operating smoothly without the benefit of his expertise.

Unlike Emilio and Enrique, who arrived at the Bacardi offices in a carriage—in later years, by automobile—the unpretentious Facundo walked to work, generally going straight to the factory on Matadero Street. He was quiet in demeanor, steady in times of crisis, and the workers considered him the most approachable of the partners. A tidy dresser like his father, Facundo in later years showed up at the factory in a white shirt and a vest, with a watch on a gold chain tucked in the vest pocket. He kept his white beard neatly trimmed, though his long, thick mustache drooped at the corners of his mouth. Like Emilio, Facundo married a *santiaguera* of French descent (though born in Uruguay), Ernestina Gaillard, with whom he had two daughters, Laura and María, and two sons, Luis and "Facundito," both of whom would go on to play roles in the business.

A friend and admirer of both Emilio and Facundo wrote later that the brothers had "the same sentimentality" but "totally distinct personalities."

> Emilio was the man of action, almost harsh in the way he imposed his will on those around him, having such confidence in the respect and authority he had earned that he seemed to delight in taking command. Facundo, meanwhile, was soft, almost mystical in his generosity, never calling attention to his many acts of charity.
>
> Had both brothers been dedicated to religion, Facundo would have been the ascetic in the cave on the side of a steep cliff, deep in prayer, while Emilio would have been the one who went down into the city with a crucifix in hand and the sword of Christ under his robe.

Emilio, the crusading Bacardi, served as the company president, even while taking little interest in the technical aspects of rum production. He also considered himself poor with numbers, that being the domain of his brother-in-law Enrique. Emilio was the public face of the firm, at a time when its image and reputation were still being established. In the postwar years, with the memories of struggle still fresh and the dream of a free Cuba not yet realized, national pride was still a powerful sentiment, and with Emilio as its head, Bacardí & Compañía could be represented as the most genuinely *Cuban* of the island's rum companies. Cubans were regularly reminded that Bacardí rum was served in the bars and nightclubs of Madrid, Paris, and New York. It was *"El Que a Cuba Ha Hecho Famosa"* (The One That Has Made Cuba Famous), and no one could represent the rum more prestigiously than Emilio Bacardí, the esteemed patriot.

Apart from his public relations responsibilities, Emilio represented Bacardí in dealings with the governing authorities. During some of the hottest periods of the Cuban insurgency, Emilio was negotiating simultaneously with the rebel high command, big landowners, and the colonial Spanish administration just to keep the family rum business operating. When the Cuban state was reorganized under the U.S. military occupation, the company's political relations were again important, and with his experience and connections as Santiago mayor, Emilio was well suited to handle that responsibility. His reputation as a troubleshooter was such that other companies also sought his services, and on one occasion in 1901 it even got him in a bit of trouble. Emilio had arranged a payment of three thousand dollars to a New York lawyer who was working to secure a tariff reduction that would benefit a company in which Emilio had an interest. When reports of the transaction caught the attention of War Secretary Elihu Root, Leonard Wood felt compelled to intervene in Emilio's defense. "He is an honest man in every way," Wood wrote to Root, "but he is addicted to the business methods of former times in all that pertains to obtaining concessions from the government." The notion that a businessman might pay a lawyer to obtain "concessions from the government," of course, did not exactly prove to be an idea without a future. Emilio Bacardí foresaw the role lobbyists would play in a business world where taxes and government regulations affect the bottom line, and their services became as important to Bacardí as to other firms.

Much of the credit for the success of Bacardí & Compañía in the early years of the twentieth century, however, went to Emilio's brother-in-law Enrique Schueg, who showed business acumen from his earliest days at the company in the 1880s. It was Enrique, with his commercial training in France, who realized that in order to prosper in the postwar period the company needed to grow dramatically, and he pushed for expansion at every opportunity. He negotiated the opening in 1910 of a factory in Barcelona, Spain, where "Bacardí" rum would be produced using Spanish raw material under a license with a Spanish distiller by the name of Francisco Alegre. Spain was the company's most important overseas market, and with a Barcelona operation it could eliminate shipping costs and bypass custom duties, thus allowing the company to sell rum in Spain at lower prices.

Export promotion was always a Schueg priority. Another early sales target was the U.S. territory of Puerto Rico. With extraordinary foresight, Schueg sensed that the island could be a key point of entry into the all-important U.S. market. In 1909 he sent one of his top salesmen, M. I. Estrada, to Puerto Rico to promote Bacardi sales there. Estrada's letters back to Santiago described the painstaking work involved in building a market in another country from the ground up. "The other day I made a little trip to the island of Vieques," he wrote in February 1910. "I sold several cases there, and it's a good place for business, but what work it is to go there! I got terribly seasick on the way over, then nearly crippled myself riding a horse around the island." He asked for metal advertising signs, because the cardboard signs he had were ruined in the rain or got pulled down by boys. Estrada complained that customers didn't pay on time, that they refilled his empty bottles with cheaper rum and sold it as Bacardi, and that some merchants told him they wouldn't sell a foreign rum that competed with the country's own producers. He fretted about missing his family and having to work out of a hotel room in San Juan. But Schueg kept Estrada there for months on end, and Puerto Rico ultimately became Bacardi's most important base outside Cuba.

◆ ◆ ◆

In 1911 the Bacardis retired the old pot still the company had used for nearly fifty years, replacing it with the latest version of a modern "Coffey" still, which processed larger quantities of fermented molasses far more efficiently. The decommissioning of Don Facundo's ancient still was a poignant moment for his sons Emilio and Facundo Jr., and they had it set aside as a reminder of the company's humble origins. The brothers had grown up with the old alembic in the Matadero Street distillery, and they would forever associate rum making with its creaky pipes and hissing tubes and with the heavy, pungent smell of the simmering molasses wash in its pot.

The new still was invented by an Irishman named Aeneas Coffey and first used by Irish whiskey makers. The fermented wash was processed through a column, with the alcoholic vapors escaping through a series of ports near the top. It worked continuously. Facundo Bacardi Moreau wanted one as soon as he heard about it, recognizing a technology that would help him produce the more refined rums that were his father's specialty. The company ordered its first Coffey still after Enrique Schueg saw one demonstrated at an international exhibition in Paris in 1889. The Bacardis were the first rum makers in Cuba to use a Coffey still, and they were so pleased by the purity and lightness of the rum it produced that they eventually discontinued the use of pot stills altogether.

Each of the Bacardis' rum-making innovations, from charcoal filtration to aging in oak barrels to the use of double-distilling Coffey stills, moved them closer to their goal of developing a spirit that could reach a market not previously associated with rum. When Don Facundo went into the business in the 1860s, relatively few upper-class consumers had any interest in rum. Though flavorful and appealing to hearty drinkers, it was far too heavy to be taken in sophisticated company. By the early 1900s, rum had a whole new status as a light spirit that could be enjoyed by all drinkers, including women, and the Bacardi company could claim a large share of the credit for its transformation.

These were the early years of the age of cocktails, when consumers were beginning to choose spirits that enhanced other flavors rather than overwhelmed them, and Bacardi rum was well positioned to take advantage. Many competitors at the time were focused on the production of sipping rums or more highly aged *añejo* products. Bacardi also produced an *añejo* rum, but from the beginning Don Facundo had concentrated on the production of light rums, and the company soon had the dominant share of that developing market. Bacardi got another boost during World War I, when the fighting in Europe hampered shipments of wine, whiskey, and cognac across the Atlantic and caused North American drinkers to consider alternatives, such as Cuban rum.

The Bacardis' innovative filtering technology removed impurities, and their rum was consequently less toxic than other distilled spirits in its effect on the body. For years, the company actually claimed that drinking Bacardi rum was good for one's health. The pitch got its start in 1892, when the physician to the royal court in Madrid prescribed Bacardi rum for the boy king Alfonso XIII, who was so sickened with a high fever that his life was thought to be in danger. The doctor decided an alcoholic stimulant might help him, and from the royal liquor storehouse he selected a bottle of Bacardi rum. According to company lore, the boy took a drink and promptly went to sleep, and when he awoke his fever was gone. The physician wrote the Bacardis a note, thanking them "for making a product that has saved His Majesty's life." Needless to say, the royal letter was featured often in Bacardi publicity from then on.

In later years, the health claims got bolder, allegedly based on medical grounds. An ad from about 1910 declared that Bacardi rum was "highly recommended for home use in cases of pulmonary consumption and debility," on the grounds that it could "enrich the blood." A British physician touted the "chemical and physiological merits of rum" in a report to the British West Indies Committee, and as late as 1934 a Cuban doctor published a book entitled *El ron Bacardi en terapéutica y dietética* (Bacardi Rum in Therapeutics and Dietetics). The good health argument was less well received in the United States, where the American Medical Association passed a resolution in 1917— on the eve of Prohibition—declaring that there was no research to support the argument that alcohol had medicinal properties. Consumers believed what they wanted to believe, however, and in the United States as well as in Cuba there were always doctors ready to say rum was good for you.

• • •

As his company matured, Emilio Bacardi Moreau was able to devote more time to private pursuits. He invested his money wisely, including the inheritance from his godmother Clara Astié, and he became a wealthy man. He built a luxurious mansion outside Santiago on farm property that had once belonged to his parents, calling it Villa Elvira in honor of his wife. In 1912, at the age of sixty-eight, he took Elvira on a long overseas trip, heading first to New York and then to Paris, Jerusalem, and Egypt, an epic journey he described in his book *Hacia tierras viejas* (Toward Old Lands). Everywhere he and Elvira went, they collected items for the Bacardi museum in Santiago, gathering desert sand, fragrant herbs, and antiquities. What the slightly eccentric Cuban couple really wanted to bring back, however, was a genuine Egyptian mummy. Emilio went from one dealer in Egypt to another until he finally found an antiquarian in Luxor who had a mummy in his house and was willing to sell it. Emilio immediately cabled the Santiago museum director, José Bofill, with the good news. "It's a young woman," he wrote. "She was pretty, and she's well preserved." On the mummy's arrival at the Santiago port, the Cuban customs authorities had no idea how to tax it. Some suggested assessing the mummy as a work of art; others said it should be considered "dried meat."

Even by the loose standards of their day, Emilio Bacardi and Elvira Cape were unconventional Cubans. Classic freethinkers, they spurned the church and raised their children with heightened social and political awareness. Both were adherents of "theosophy," a spiritualist movement that contained elements of Hinduism and Buddhism and promoted universal brotherhood and humanitarianism. Determined to stimulate creative thinking in their children, they sent two of their daughters, Mimín and Lalita, to the progressive Raja Yoga School in Point Loma, California, where the guiding principle was "to reduce the purely mechanical work of the memory to an absolute minimum and devote the time to the development and training of the inner senses, faculties, and latent capacities." When Mimín showed an interest in drawing and sculpture, Emilio and Elvira arranged for her to study in Paris and later in New York, where she became active in the woman suffrage movement. Years later, Mimín's daughter wrote that Emilio "taught her and molded her from the time she was little to have a wider vision of the world than the one prevailing at the time."

Religious dogma in particular bothered Emilio. He did consider himself a Christian in the broadest sense of the term, and in Palestine he was moved to walk where Jesus had walked, but his commentary on the Palestine visit in *Hacia tierras viejas* suggested that he doubted Jesus' divinity. "The church that is said to be yours is further and further away from you," Emilio wrote, "as far as he must be who distorts you by calling you God." The hostility Emilio felt toward organized religion, however, was rooted less in theology than in his view of the church as a political institution. Palestine to him was the place where there arose "a doctrine of peace and brotherhood between all peoples, in the name of which its presumed interpreters and guardians never tired of spilling blood and imposing [their faith] by force, rather than through the persuasion and love made holy by the martyrdom of their founder."

In Cuba, Emilio saw the Catholic Church as an arm of the repressive colonial power. One of his angriest antichurch outbursts came in August 1910, when he wrote to the mayor of Bayamo to protest his decision to involve the local church in a memorial ceremony honoring Francisco Aguilera, a hero of the first independence war who fought alongside his fellow sugar planter Carlos Manuel de Céspedes. "Remember that this Catholic church, from Rome down to the parish priests here on the island, never did anything but condemn the freedom fighters," Emilio raged.

> Remember they were more implacable than the army itself; remember that they never recommended clemency; remember how they slandered Céspedes and Aguilera; remember that they didn't offer prayers for them when they fell in battle; remember that they never spoke out against the death penalty and even encouraged it to the end.

In that same letter to the Bayamo mayor, however, Emilio wrote that some who reject "the official cult" still have a religion of their own "in their internal temple." He was presumably referring to himself. For Emilio, the issue was always freedom, from the arbitrary exercise of authority and from constraints on individual expression and thought.

· · ·

By 1919, with rum production and sales growing from month to month, the Bacardi partners decided it was time to reorganize their firm as a stock corporation, to be known as the Compañía Ron Bacardi, S.A. (Bacardi Rum Company, Inc.). They declared it to be worth an astounding $3.7 million, about two thirds of which ($2.43 million) was their estimate of the value of the Bacardi name and all their trademarks, including their bat symbol and their various rum brands. Such a high valuation of intangible assets as a proportion of total capital was virtually unprecedented at the time. The Bacardi partners had not considered intellectual property in earlier valuations, and their assignment of such a high dollar figure to their trademarks was an indication of how vigorously they intended to defend them.

Emilio Bacardi Moreau kept his position as company president, though at the age of seventy-five he had mostly retired from business affairs and spent most of his time in his spacious library at Villa Elvira, writing novels and essays, reading, and corresponding with friends and family. Facundo Bacardi Moreau and Enrique Schueg were the first and second vice presidents of the new company. At the incorporation, each of the three partners took about a third of the shares in the new corporation, making them instant millionaires on paper. They later set aside some of their own stock to provide a 10 percent share for the heirs of José Bacardi Moreau, the third Bacardi brother, who had died twelve years earlier (after selling his share of the business to his brothers and to Enrique Schueg). Five other company officers each received shares worth ten thousand dollars, including Facundo Bacardi Lay, one of Emilio's sons from his marriage to María Lay, Pedro Lay Lombard, a cousin of Elvira's who had married Emilio's oldest daughter María, and Alberto Acha, a Bacardi executive known later for being the grandfather of Desi Arnaz Jr. of *I Love Lucy* fame.

The family business was surging ahead on a wave of rising revenue. Four years earlier, the company had expanded its distillery and factory on Matadero Street. The old building had become a decrepit fire hazard. The wood siding was half rotten, the roof leaked, and it was far too small for the company's production needs. The new building was erected carefully around the coconut palm that fourteen-year-old Facundo Bacardi Jr. had planted in front of the distillery in 1862 and that had subsequently become a symbol of the company's survival. Another expansion was carried out in 1922 with the construction of an entirely new distillery, just down the street from the original site. The Bacardis' rum-making enterprise by then comprised more than a dozen buildings, including a boiler house, an aging warehouse holding hundreds of barrels, a bottling plant, an ice factory, a laboratory, and a carpentry shop. The Bacardis employed several hundred workers, and the demand for their rum was still growing.

The new distillery was inaugurated on February 4, 1922, the sixtieth anniversary of the company's founding. The facility was capable of processing seventy-five thousand liters of molasses per day, and its opening was an occasion for ostentatious celebration. According to the local newspaper, a crowd of fifteen thousand townspeople turned out for the festivities, including "an uncountable number of automobiles carrying distinguished families." The inauguration was made official with the raising of the Cuban flag over the distillery by Enriqueta Schueg, the twenty-five-year-old daughter of Amalia Bacardi Moreau and Enrique Schueg, and Marcos Martínez, a retired Bacardi employee who had worked at the distillery in its earliest days. Enriqueta wore an enormous straw hat to keep the bright sun off her face, and she carried a bouquet of flowers under her arm. The elderly Martínez was dressed in his finest gray suit. Emilio stood between them, holding his white straw boater hat in his hands. His thick hair, brushed straight back over his head, was pure white, like his mustache and beard. His wire-rimmed spectacles sat low on his nose. He looked a bit fatigued.

It was his last major public event. Emilio Bacardi Moreau died on August 28, 1922, at the age of seventy-eight. Suffering from a heart ailment, he was bedridden in the month before his death but still reading and receiving company at Villa Elvira. On the last afternoon of his life, he discussed sectarian violence in Ireland with a visitor, saying he thought the root of the problems there was religious fanaticism and intolerance. A couple of hours later, his heart stopped.

The mayor of Santiago ordered the suspension of all public events for two days, as the city mourned the death of its favorite son. The funeral procession, which began at Villa Elvira, brought the biggest outpouring of people ever seen in the city for such an occasion. The parade was led by the city's public servants, with one observer noting how "the khaki uniforms of soldiers mixed with the blue uniforms of the police, the gray uniforms of the firemen, and the white uniforms of the municipal band, followed by the fancy suits of the dignitaries." As the ornate, horse-drawn carriage containing Don Emilio's body rolled by, ordinary citizens joined in the march, and by the time the cortege reached the main plaza it was ten blocks long. The casket was set down in front of the town hall, and as the band played the Cuban national anthem, the huge flag that flew over the town hall was slowly lowered, falling finally on Don Emilio's casket.

With the exception of Don Facundo, the patriarch and company founder, no one looms larger than Emilio in the Bacardi story. Though his name is mentioned in few Cuban history books, Emilio Bacardi Moreau was a rare example of enlightened and responsible civic leadership in Cuba at a time when such men were in short supply. One of his mourners described him as "the ultimate *criollo*," the ultimate homegrown Cuban, "rooted in the deepest layer of the Cuban subsoil." His friend Federico Pérez Carbó, who was imprisoned in Spain with him, served with him in the Santiago government, and stayed close to him as long as they both lived, described Emilio in a eulogy as "a great rebel, above all. Political tyranny, social inequality, human pride, ignorance, misery, vice; he condemned them all." But Emilio Bacardi was not ashamed to be a capitalist, and he believed that businessmen should be leaders in their community. He advocated policies to foster economic development, and he volunteered to serve on the Santiago Chamber of Commerce. Fernando Ortiz, one of Cuba's greatest twentieth-century intellectuals, wrote that Emilio Bacardi was "a man of business without being greedy, an idealist without being utopian, generous without being showy, and Cuban, always Cuban."

Chapter 9

❧❦❧

The Next Generation

On the morning of January 17, 1920, Americans woke up in a dry country. Liquor sellers boarded up their shops, and saloon keepers hung signs on their doors advising their customers to go home. The short story writer and lyricist Ring Lardner spoke for millions of drinking citizens:

> Goodbye forever to my old friend Booze.
> Doggone, I've got the Prohibition Blues.

A lot of people apparently favored Prohibition: The Eighteenth Amendment was approved by large margins in both houses of Congress and eventually ratified by legislatures in forty-six of the forty-eight states. But there were also many who had no intention of abstaining. Enforcement was weak enough that "speakeasy" houses flourished wherever alcohol was still in demand. For every legal bar or saloon that closed, five underground establishments opened, where a doorman would welcome anyone who knew the password.

People who were ready for a real adventure could always head to Cuba. Train-and-steamer packages brought thirsty Americans from all over the country to the welcoming Caribbean island, where they could drink and carouse and gamble without interference. Between 1916 and 1928, the annual number of U.S. tourists visiting Cuba doubled, from forty-four thousand to ninety thousand. Bartenders who lost their jobs in the United States moved to Havana and found ready work, as the city's café and club scene was refashioned to accommodate visiting Americans. Some U.S. bar owners crated up their tables, chairs, signs, and mirrors and relocated their entire operations to Cuba, where they reopened under their old names, offering familiar food and drinks. The island was easily reachable from the United States and had a fabulous winter climate.

In Cuba, visitors were not troubled by nosy, judgmental neighbors or by moralizing authorities. When Americans got stumbling drunk in Cuba, the regular police would look the other way. If intervention was required, special tourist police would escort the offending visitor back to his hotel, or perhaps to the police station to sober up, but almost never would he be charged. There were outlets for virtually every indulgence, from racetracks to brothels to opium dens. And it was not just its libertine atmosphere that made Cuba so popular. The whole tropical setting was carefree and seductive, and women as well as men found Cuba irresistible: the luxuriant warmth and fragrant nights, the sea breezes, the light, exotic cocktails, the soft music that seemed to flow from everywhere, the graceful, sensuous dancing, the beautiful bodies and elegant clothes.

The favored Havana watering hole was Sloppy Joe's, an enormous bar that was packed from noon till midnight and never closed its doors. The place catered to Americans fleeing Prohibition, and its advertising motto was "Out Where the Wet Begins." There was also the Sevilla (owned by the former barman at the Biltmore in New York), the Inglaterra Bar and Patio (popular after a night at the opera), and the Plaza. To accommodate American tastes, all the bars offered whiskey, but in Cuba one was supposed to drink rum, and drinking rum in Cuba meant drinking Bacardi. The noted travel writer Basil Woon reported that the cocktails most in demand in 1920s Havana were the daiquiri, the presidente, and the Mary Pickford. All three featured Bacardi rum. The presidente, half Bacardi and half French vermouth with a dash of either curaçao or grenadine, was "the aristocrat of cocktails," Woon reported, "the one preferred by the better class of Cubans." The Mary Pickford was two thirds pineapple juice and one third Bacardi with a dash of grenadine. No one made it better than Constantino, the barman at La Floridita, where Woon watched him prepare six at a time:

> The drink is shaken by throwing it from one shaker and catching it in another, the liquid forming a half-circle in the air. This juggling feat having been performed several times, Constantino empties the glasses of ice, puts them in a row on the bar, and with one motion fills them all. Each glass is filled exactly to the brim and *not a drop is left over.*

Bacardi executives recognized the commercial opportunity that Prohibition presented, and their advertising staff designed campaigns accordingly. One ad showed a Caribbean map, with Florida colored a dry red and Cuba a lush green. A big Bacardi bat with outstretched wings carried an Uncle Sam figure, empty cocktail glass in hand, across the straits to the island, where a young man in a palm tree waited to offer him a drink of Bacardi. The ad was captioned "Flying from the Desert." Another ad, in art deco style, showed a woman dressed in flapper style with a tight felt hat and a feather boa around her shoulders, sitting saucily on a bar stool and holding a cocktail glass. The caption: "Cuba is great. There is a reason. Bacardi." Pan American Airways began operating flights to Cuba from Miami to take advantage of the Prohibition-driven tourism, advertising jointly with Bacardi. "Fly with us to Havana," the airline said, "and you can bathe in Bacardi rum two hours from now." A Bacardi agent was on hand in the Havana airport with free drinks for all arriving passengers.

The Cuba travel boom gave Bacardi a huge boost, with tens of thousands of cases of rum sold to the bars and clubs that served American customers in Cuba. The growing international reputation of Bacardi rum, meanwhile, helped export sales, which by 1924 had surpassed a half million liters of rum per year and were still rising, even with Prohibition in effect. Some studies even suggested that overall alcohol consumption may have slightly risen during Prohibition, due perhaps to the "forbidden fruit" effect. With U.S. distillers forced to shut down, however, foreign suppliers and moonshiners had the U.S. market all to themselves. The result was a jump in (illegal) imports of alcohol across the Canadian border or by sea from the Bahamas. U.S. drinkers who previously consumed only American bourbon or whiskey had to settle for moonshine or buy the foreign-made spirits that were smuggled into the country—Scotch or Canadian whiskey or perhaps Cuban rum. Prohibition actually lifted the Scotch whiskey industry out of a depression, and it similarly worked for the benefit of Bacardi.

In 1924 the company began construction of an opulent new art deco office building in Havana, with ornamental details designed by the famed illustrator Maxfield Parrish. The richly decorated black and gold building, with a facade adorned by bronze bats and inlaid glazed panels marked with images of nymphs, promptly became a city landmark. At the top of the central tower was a huge statue of the Bacardi bat with outstretched wings, presiding majestically over the Havana skyline. The Edificio Bacardi became a regular stop for American tourists, who were treated to free drinks in an ornate bar on the mezzanine level. Needing only a fraction of the office space for its own Havana headquarters, the company rented out most of the building, and its architectural grandeur served mainly to showcase the Bacardi name and presence in the nation's capital. Cuba was in a new phase of its history, and the Bacardi Rum Company was changing with it, with different leadership and an evolving corporate mission. By 1925, it was said to be the largest industrial enterprise on the island.

Following the death of Emilio, the company directors chose Enrique Schueg as their new president, passing over Facundo Bacardi Moreau, the founder's second son. It was a momentous decision, suggesting that the directors valued business expertise over Bacardi blood. Amalia Bacardi Cape, Emilio and Elvira's daughter, wrote in her family memoir that the choice of Schueg "could not have been more just." Don Enrique, she pointed out, was "the commercial brains of the enterprise, although Don Emilio had ennobled it with his great personal prestige and Don Facundo [the son] with his famed mastery of rum manufacturing." Amalia, of course, was writing as Emilio's daughter. Whether Facundo's children viewed Schueg's promotion the same way is another question. It was not in Facundo's character to complain over the decision, but he did leave Santiago shortly after Schueg was chosen as president and from then on spent much of his time at his summer home in Allenhurst, New Jersey, until he died in 1926.

One of the most significant aspects of Schueg's selection as Bacardi president was the way the decision was made. The time when anyone could exercise authority in the company merely through the force of his personality had passed. Corporate decisions after the death of Emilio were made by shareholder vote. His 30 percent share in the company passed to Elvira and to his children and when combined with Schueg's constituted a clear majority. For voting purposes, the Emilio bloc was represented on the board of directors by Emilio's son Facundo Bacardi Lay* and by Emilio's son-in-law Pedro Lay Lombard. A new governance structure was in place. Compañía Ron Bacardi, S.A., was no longer a partnership of individuals; it had become a family-run corporation. Emilio Bacardi was gone, but his wife and children collectively retained his voice in company management. When Facundo Bacardi Moreau died four years later, his heirs were similarly represented on the corporate board as a single group and voted accordingly. This pattern of family bloc representation and voting characterized—and complicated—Bacardi management decision making for decades to come.

As company president, Enrique Schueg had to respect the positions of the Emilio and Facundo family branches, just as he had deferred to Emilio and Facundo themselves when they were his partners. He was indeed the ideal executive for the management challenge, with the business training and aptitude to handle his corporate responsibilities. Like Emilio, Enrique was well read,

---

*Facundo Bacardi Lay's twin brother, José Bacardi Lay, died of influenza in 1918. Six years later, Facundo also died prematurely, of pneumonia.

though more attuned to French literature than to Cuban. Every year he made a voyage to Paris and returned with a trunk full of books, which kept him busy until his next trip. Though he had been a coconspirator with Emilio and others during Cuba's war for independence, he was even more deeply a French patriot. He made sure his five children with Amalia Bacardi Moreau all spoke French (his Spanish had a heavy French accent), and he insisted they maintain French citizenship as well as Cuban. When his oldest son, Arturo, volunteered to join the French army at the beginning of World War I, Enrique was immensely proud. An expert horseman, Arturo became an officer in a French cavalry unit and rode into battle wearing a shiny gold helmet with a silver tassel. His experience ended tragically; like many French soldiers, Arturo became ill with influenza during the war and died in Flanders in 1917.

Whereas his brother-in-law Emilio could be temperamental and given to polemics, Enrique kept his political opinions mostly to himself, focusing on business affairs instead. Unlike Facundo, however, he was neither shy nor retiring. When faced with a business problem, he approached it creatively and then acted decisively. He spent little time on the distillery or factory floor, working instead at his wooden rolltop desk in the offices on Marina Baja Street. He was never seen without a tie, and with his round spectacles and serious expression he looked every bit the sober accountant he was trained to be. The childhood bicycle accident that left him with one leg a couple of inches shorter than the other caused him to limp, but he compensated for the disability by wearing a boot with a special cork bottom, and he even managed to play a decent game of tennis.

Other members of the family brought a more freewheeling aspect to the Bacardi image in Cuba. The three sons of José Bacardi Moreau, José Jr. ("Pepe"), Antón, and Joaquín, having been given a 10 percent share of Bacardi stock shortly after the 1919 incorporation, were the first of their generation to be fully vested with a portion of the family fortune and among the first to start spending it. Their mother, Carmen Fernández, died in 1910, three years after the death of their father, so the family's share was all theirs. Pepe Bacardi, a debonair and handsome young man with dark, wavy hair, was the oldest of the three and set the pace for his brothers. His marriage in 1922 to a nineteen-year-old Santiago beauty named Martha Durand lasted only a few weeks before his young wife announced she could not put up with his carousing. Their very public and colorful breakup produced a high-society scandal and provided a glimpse of the social lives of the Cuban upper class in the 1920s.

Martha Durand was herself from a distinguished French-Cuban family in Santiago, well educated and multilingual, having traveled often to Paris and

New York with her mother and father. She grew up socializing with Bacardis of her age, including Amalia Bacardi Cape, Emilio's daughter, and Enriqueta Schueg, the daughter of Amalia Bacardi Moreau and Enrique Schueg. Martha and Pepe's wedding was described by one local newspaper as "the loveliest and most sumptuous that Santiago has ever known." Making the nightclub rounds in Havana on their honeymoon, the young Cuban couple exemplified glamour and wealth: the former national beauty queen in a bejeweled satin frock, carrying an ivory and gold fan and escorted by her new husband, the handsome Bacardi heir, in a dinner jacket cut especially for him by an English tailor in Havana.

Martha later claimed that Pepe's philandering doomed their marriage from the start. She laid out her whole melodramatic story in an exposé titled "My Mad Romance with Bacardi, the Rich Rum King, Conqueror of Women," a titillating (and suitably embellished) tale that ran in ten weekly installments in Sunday newspapers across the United States in December 1923 and January 1924. She claimed in her story to have gone into the marriage with misgivings. "There was a great deal of talk in Santiago," she wrote, "about Pepe Bacardi and about his young cousins, the new generation of Bacardis who in no way resemble the stiff-spined old men who made the Bacardi name really great. I heard enough to make me know that Pepe was leading a wild, gay life and that he had a decided predilection for pretty girls and for his own rum."

Martha went ahead with the wedding anyway, but to be safe she had Pepe Bacardi sign a prenuptial agreement in which he promised not to contest a divorce request on her part and to pay child support if she were left with children to raise. The agreement was witnessed by Martha's friend (and Pepe's cousin) Enriqueta Schueg and by Enriqueta's new husband, José "Pepín" Bosch, another wealthy young man from Santiago with a reputation as a partyer, but who as a Bacardi son-in-law was destined to play a big role in the family business in the coming decades.

Martha Durand's description of her honeymoon provided her U.S. readers, four years into Prohibition, with a tantalizing peek into the Havana of the early 1920s. She described visits to posh private dinner clubs where young women in various exotic costumes, or nothing at all, paraded before the patrons. But her marriage soon crumbled. Martha said it was finished the night Pepe Bacardi dragged her out of bed and insisted she come downstairs and entertain him and his drunken friends. Pepe initially refused her request for a divorce, however, saying it would bring dishonor on his family. When Martha asked him for money, he told her to get it from Enrique Schueg, the Bacardi president, or Pedro Lay Lombard, the general manager, but they said she would get nothing until she returned the new automobile Pepe had given her as a wedding gift. "At last I realized that I was engaged in a war," she wrote, "that I was really being persecuted by the whole Bacardi family, which had constituted itself a sort of 'general staff' in this campaign against one poor, lone, defenseless girl."

The Bacardis were indeed loyal to each other, and Martha Durand was not the last Bacardi spouse to feel like an outcast after a marital breakup. But they were also generous and good-hearted, and when young Bacardis partied, they made many friends. Basil Woon reported during his travels in Cuba that the Bacardis were "famous throughout the island for their charity and benevolence." In Santiago he was entertained by "Facundito" Bacardi, the fun-loving son of Facundo Bacardi Moreau and a party companion of his cousin Pepe. After his father retired from the rum business, Facundito became a Bacardi vice president, but he still found time to entertain friends in Santiago and Havana. When he died tragically a few years later, the *New York Times* reported that the charismatic Facundito was "one of the most popular men in Cuba."

. . .

The younger Bacardis, like those who came before them, believed in the Cuban cause, but it was not so clear anymore what that meant. They grew up in an age of more prosperity but less idealism, a time when Cuba was officially free but politically flawed. The elections that came every four years were regularly marred by charges of fraud, and they were mostly inconsequential. There were no real ideological differences between the parties, and political rivalries were driven mainly by competition for the power to dispense sinecures and handouts. After the restoration of Cuban sovereignty in 1909, direct U.S. interference in Cuban affairs diminished, though the U.S. role continued to be controversial. The 1903 Reciprocity Treaty gave Cuban sugar preferential treatment in the American market, reduced duties on American imports to Cuba, and encouraged further American investment on the island. The deal brought the country short-term prosperity but at the expense of making the economy excessively dependent on the sugar sector and on U.S. trade and investment, thus harming long-term development prospects. Cuba boomed when sugar prices soared in the immediate aftermath of World War I, but when prices turned sharply down in the early 1920s, banks failed across the country.

The country's unsteady economic performance compounded the disappointment Cubans were feeling over their political circumstances, and by the mid-1920s many were wondering what had been achieved by the establishment of the Cuban Republic in 1902. In the spring of 1924, Emilio Roig de Leuchsen-ring, an influential Havana lawyer and intellectual associated with the *Cuba Contemporánea* journal, gave a speech titled "The Very-Much-Alive Colony: Cuba Twenty Two Years after the Republic." His tone was discouraging:

> We have seen the emergence of the same vices and defects that the men who carried out the Revolution proposed to extinguish: Fierce hatreds, egotism, an eagerness for enrichment, a lack of love for the nation, a lack of respect for the law, the abuse of power by those who govern, and the awful passivity of those who obey. We have changed flags and governments, but in the end the difference between the Republic of today and the Colony of yesterday is hardly perceptible.

The obstacle to a free and sovereign Cuba was no longer some imperial power or outside enemy. The Cubans had to establish a foundation of national pride on which to build their country themselves. In 1925 Roig de Leuchsen-ring directed a group of Cuban writers, intellectuals, industrialists, and histo-rians in the compilation of a lavishly printed, nine-hundred-page book they called *El libro de Cuba* (The Book of Cuba). Their goal was to emphasize their country's unrealized potential:

> If we have taken our place among the most hardworking and productive peo-ples on the planet despite all the difficulties of the colonial period and the careless mistakes made during our short life as a free republic, what can stop us in the future—with course corrections, good judgment, and experience—from achieving the highest level of prosperity, progress, and wealth?

Compañía Ron Bacardi, S.A.,* was one of the Cuban firms asked to submit a report for the massive book. No native company could claim to have made a more notable contribution to the national product. The enterprise was entirely Cuban-owned, still without one cent of foreign capital. The major raw ingredient—molasses—was a Cuban commodity, and it was Cuban talent and expertise that kept the business going. "This trademark and this enterprise," the Bacardi directors wrote, "constitute without a doubt the industrial entity that has given and will give the most prestige and benefit to the country, for being wholly native and totally linked to this land, both spiritually and eco-

---

*Hereafter, I will generally refer to the firm as the Bacardi Rum Company (or just Bacardi Rum), ex-cept when the context makes the legal Cuban name, Compañía Ron Bacardi, S.A., more appropriate.

nomically." Unlike the sugar barons, the Bacardis manufactured a finished industrial product, making use of technology, skilled labor, and their secret distilling, aging, and blending procedures. Because a large percentage of its sales were overseas, the firm's performance was at least partly independent of the swings in the national economy. The Bacardi directors declared that their company's aim was "to serve Cuba," and argued that its growth over the preceding years had been a triumph for the whole Cuban nation:

> The facts showed daily that industrial excellence can be achieved in Cuba just the same as in Manchester, Lyon, or Chicago.... *Casa Bacardi* [the House of Bacardi] was no longer just the creator of the third national product [after sugar and tobacco]: It also constituted the best and most powerful Cuban industry, perhaps the biggest in all Latin America, and it was, above all, another positive force for the Cuban nation, a genuine [source of] pride for the lone star Republic.

In 1927 the Bacardi role in the Cuban economy expanded in a new direction with the opening of a brewery in Santiago. None of the Bacardis knew anything about beer, and they faced stiff competition from other Cuban manufacturers, one of which had purchased the entire facilities of a U.S. brewing company several years earlier. Enrique Schueg nonetheless believed there was an unexploited market for premium beer in Cuba. He had persuaded his partners back in 1920 to acquire the defunct Santiago Brewing Company, and over the next few years he upgraded the facility, investing in new tanks, drilling a well to improve the water supply, and hiring German brewmasters to oversee the operation. In another reflection of the family's Cuban nationalism, the Bacardis called their beer "Hatuey," after the Indian resistance hero whose martyrdom had inspired generations of Cuban patriots.

◆ ◆ ◆

The bigger the Bacardi company grew, of course, the more complex its challenges became. Prohibition helped the company prosper, but it also brought risks. The Bacardis broke no law by selling their rum to whoever wanted to buy it, but they knew that much of their product was ending up in the hands of criminal groups. The company had a solid reputation for integrity, and it could not afford to see it jeopardized by shady business connections, so Bacardi sales agents maintained as much distance as possible from their clients. When large quantities were sold, the deals were often managed by third parties, and the identities of the buyers were not revealed. In many cases, Bacardi agents had no way of knowing where their rum was going after it left Cuba. A listed destination of "Shanghai" on a shipping label suggested the rum would be moved just offshore or to a nearby port, where it would then be transferred to another boat. Facundito Bacardi was fond of telling visitors, with a wink and a grin, that boatloads of his family's rum went to Shanghai because "there are more drinkers in Shanghai than anywhere on earth."

U.S. Department of Commerce figures suggested that about a third of the liquor smuggled into the United States in 1924 entered via "Rum Row,"* the area off the eastern seaboard of the United States just beyond the line marking international waters. Ships loaded with thousands of cases of liquor would wait just outside the limit while small, fast boats would come out to purchase the liquor and sneak it back to shore. With liquor distribution in the hands of organized crime syndicates, the U.S. business was outside government regulation, and false labeling and product tampering became rampant. The problem was if anything greater for Bacardi. American drinkers were generally less familiar with rum than with their favorite whiskey and less likely to distinguish between the genuine Bacardi product and an imitation, especially because rum was usually drunk in a cocktail. The Bacardis had been dealing with false labeling ever since they first registered their trademarks, and company executives were especially sensitive to the problem. Facundito Bacardi, the son of the family's original rum master, was so outraged to find fake Bacardi rum at an upscale Manhattan speakeasy that he denounced the establishment in public, and New York newspapers took note of his protest.

The Bacardis also faced problems with their own government in Havana. President Gerardo Machado, elected more or less honestly in 1924, soon set a new standard for corruption, buying the votes of congressmen by giving them lucrative lottery collectorships and using vast public works projects to build up a network of officials and businessmen who were indebted to him. As one of Cuba's most important private firms, Bacardi Rum needed to remain on harmonious terms with the government if possible, but Machado's demands on the company increased steadily. In 1928 his tax department decided to challenge the company's calculations of how much rum evaporated during the aging process, a loss the company claimed as an expense against its income. Machado's inspectors said the loss was exaggerated and declared that Bacardi owed an additional $75,000 in business taxes. When the company protested, the government ordered the firm to shut down all operations. The Bacardis

---

*Illegal liquor was referred to generically as "rum," and the shipowners and liquor traffickers were known as rum runners, even though most of the liquor smuggled from Rum Row was whiskey.

were already paying more than a half million dollars to the government each year, and Enrique Schueg drew the line at what he considered an unjust assessment. Machado lifted the order a few days later pending an "investigation" of the technical issue, but not before the chief of secret police personally warned Schueg that he could be arrested for conspiring against the government.

The days had passed when Bacardi could advance its corporate interests simply by highlighting its patriotism and charity. The changing commercial and political realities in Cuba underscored the need for new strategic thinking. Enrique Schueg, one of the sharpest business executives on the island, had already persuaded the Bacardi directors to diversify into beer production; next he argued that the company's interests would be well served by expanding internationally. The Machado experience showed that even the most progressive and responsible companies in Cuba were vulnerable to government meddling, especially during periods of heightened corruption in ruling circles. An investment outside Cuba made good political sense. Schueg saw opportunities in Mexico, a country with an abundant sugar supply. U.S. citizens, deprived of liquor at home, were streaming across the Mexican border in search of cheap booze, and Schueg wanted to meet that demand with locally produced Bacardi rum. In 1929 he established a distribution subsidiary in Mexico and contracted for the construction of a new rum blending facility and a bottling plant there. With the exception of the 1910 licensing of a Bacardi franchise in Barcelona, it was the company's first overseas expansion; unlike the Spanish operation, rum production in Mexico would be overseen and controlled by the Bacardis themselves.

Economic and political developments complicated the new investments but also vindicated them. The U.S. stock market crash in the fall of 1929 was followed by a dramatic decline in travel to Cuba. The subsequent falloff in Bacardi rum sales diminished the company's revenue just as it needed capital to finance its new ventures. The Hatuey beer business, however, appeared promising, and the Bacardis concluded they had acted wisely in diversifying. The decision to start investing outside Cuba was also validated by the deepening problems on the island. In 1930 the U.S Congress passed the Smoot-Hawley Tariff Act, raising the tariff on Cuban sugar to two cents a pound and effectively slamming the door on Cuban producers. Combined with the fall in world sugar prices, the effect on the sugar-dependent Cuban economy was disastrous. Desperate for new tax revenue, President Machado took aim for the second time in three years at the Bacardi coffers. His Economic Emergency Bill proposed various new taxes, including one on rum sales and exports. Machado by then was devoting a substantial portion of his budget to the army and police, and public monies were being diverted through graft. Enrique Schueg was furious.

The Mexico investment, however, gave the company new leverage with the Machado administration. Schueg publicly warned that the Bacardis were prepared to move their entire rum operation out of Cuba if the new taxes were enacted. The jobs of two thousand Cuban workers would be jeopardized if Bacardi left, so the threat had to be taken seriously, and in early 1931 the Cuban House of Representatives voted to drop the rum tax proposal. The Bacardis had prevailed over the Machado administration, but Enrique Schueg had learned again how important it was for his company to maintain independence from the Cuban government.

The new Bacardi rum factory opened in Mexico in May 1931, under the direction of Pepe Bacardi, Martha Durand's ex-husband. Though he lacked the training and experience to be a successful businessman, Pepe had persuaded his uncle Enrique to let him be the first Bacardi to direct a rum production operation outside Cuba. Schueg joined him in Mexico for the inauguration of the new factory in 1931, as did Pedro Lay Lombard, the company's general manager. Pepe Bacardi dressed for the event in a white linen suit with white shoes and swung a high-fashion walking cane. With big round spectacles and an ear-to-ear grin, he looked like a merry prankster at his own party.

◆ ◆ ◆

President Gerardo Machado proved to be a murderous tyrant, outlawing all political parties outside his direct control and ruthlessly eliminating his most determined opponents. The U.S. government did not seem to care, delighted that Machado favored, in his own words, the "closest possible cooperation" with Washington. It was a mistake the United States had made before and would make again: overestimating the benefit of having a loyal ally in Havana while underestimating the cost of supporting governments that stunted the country's political development. At the very time Machado was ordering the assassination of labor activists and student protest leaders, President Calvin Coolidge was reassuring him that the United States would not object if he ignored the Cuban constitution and stayed in office beyond his term.

By 1931, three years after Machado was supposed to have given up the presidency, Cuba was ready for another revolution. A new generational conflict had emerged: Young Cuban activists, all born after the independence war of 1895–98, felt that many of the war veterans serving in government had betrayed the cause of the revolution by plundering state resources and corrupting public life. These young Cubans revived the names of José Martí and Antonio Maceo and portrayed themselves as the true heirs of the original revolutionary movement, the promise of which had long since been abandoned in Cuba.

Their goal was the overthrow of the Machado regime and the installation in its place of a democratic government committed to the social and economic goals that had inspired Cuba's independence struggle.

Among those who got caught up in the new movement was José "Pepín" Bosch, the Pepe Bacardi friend who in 1922 had married Enrique Schueg's daughter, Enriqueta. Bosch had become a wealthy young man managing a sugar mill for his father at the height of the sugar boom, and after his marriage to Enriqueta, he went to work for the National City Bank in Havana. He and Enriqueta had two young sons, Jorge and Carlos, and a comfortable upper-class life, but Bosch was passionate in his hatred for the Machado regime. When he heard that a friend, Carlos Hevia, was planning to take part in an armed insurrection against the government in August 1931, Bosch agreed to help.

The plan was for Hevia and an associate named Emilio Laurent to land with a group of volunteers on the northeast coast of Cuba and lead an attack on the nearby town of Gibara. Bosch's assignment was to arrange the funding. Short and prematurely balding at the age of thirty-three, he looked far more like a banker than a revolutionary. He had no military experience and knew nothing about armed struggle, but he was a self-confident young businessman and had gained a reputation for toughness and shrewd judgment in his banking work. At great risk to his own life and to the welfare of his young family, Bosch helped find a boat for the expedition and assisted in the purchase of arms and ammunition.

The rebellion failed utterly. Though the expeditionaries captured the Gibara police station, telephone exchange, and city hall, neither the townspeople nor local army units joined the uprising, and it soon collapsed. Machado sent an elite military unit to Gibara, blocked the harbor to keep the rebels from escaping by sea, and bombed the city from the air. Many of the fighters were caught and killed. Pepín Bosch, his life now in danger, fled to the United States with his wife Enriqueta and their two young sons.

For the Bacardi family in Santiago, Gibara was just the first in a quick series of crises. In February 1932, an earthquake struck Santiago, the worst since 1852. More than half the buildings in the city were destroyed or seriously damaged, including the Bacardis' Hatuey brewery, their administrative offices, and a rum storage warehouse. Four months after that, Facundito Bacardi, the high-living bachelor son of Facundo Bacardi Moreau, was gravely injured in a bizarre accidental shooting. He had stopped in the Club San Carlos, the Bacardis' favorite drinking spot in Santiago, and was enjoying himself with friends when a policeman approached him to borrow some money, offering his service revolver as collateral. As Facundito tried to wave it away, he accidentally knocked the gun to the floor and it discharged, sending a round into his abdomen. Facundito clung to life in a Santiago hospital for six days and then died. Yet another tragedy befell the family in May 1933, when Pepe Bacardi became ill in Mexico with pneumonia and quickly succumbed to the disease. Six young men of a single Bacardi generation had died young,[*] leaving some to wonder whether the family was cursed.

Cuba, meanwhile, was sliding into a deep political crisis. The anti-Machado struggle of a few years earlier had slowly evolved into a full-scale revolution, with the goal of overthrowing the entire political and economic system in Cuba. Led originally by radicalized university students and faculty, the movement gained the support of workers and their leaders. After Machado's police opened fire on a public rally outside the presidential palace and killed about twenty demonstrators, workers across the country walked off the job. With chaos spreading, Machado resigned the presidency and left Cuba on August 12, 1933, for the Bahamas. He was replaced by Carlos Manuel de Céspedes Jr., a colorless diplomat known mainly for being the son of the sugar planter who sparked Cuba's 1868 independence war.

The collapse of the Machado government brought no break in the violence, however. Mobs of revenge-seeking Cubans hunted down hated members of Machado's security forces, in some cases dragging them into the street and killing them. The houses of senior Machado allies were burned and their offices ransacked.[†] Workers and their unions, meanwhile, took advantage of the chaos to demand sweeping labor reforms. Cuba was caught up in a revolutionary fervor.

* * *

The Bacardis had supported previous Cuban revolutions, but the events of 1933 presented a new political challenge. Earlier that year, Bacardi workers had organized as the Sindicato de Obreros y Empleados de la Empresa Bacardi (Union of Bacardi Workers and Employees) and affiliated with the Communist-led Confederación Nacional Obrera de Cuba (CNOC), National Labor Confederation of Cuba. On August 15, three days after Machado fled Cuba, the Bacardi workers went on strike in order "to demand our rights." Though the union raised issues related to wages and working conditions, the action was more a

---

[*]Daniel Bacardi Lay (1895); Arturo Schueg (1917); José Bacardi Lay (1918); Facundo Bacardi Lay (1924); Facundito Bacardi Gaillard (1932); José "Pepe" Bacardi Fernández (1933).

[†]Among those targeted was the pro-Machado mayor of Santiago, Desiderio Arnaz, whose father-in-law, Alberto Acha, was a Bacardi executive. Arnaz was imprisoned, but Acha was able to intervene to secure his son-in-law's release. Arnaz, his wife Dolores, and his sixteen-year-old son, Desi Jr., then left Cuba for the United States, where Desi Jr. found television fame as the husband of Lucille Ball.

reflection of the general mood of labor militancy in Cuba than of dissatisfaction at the rum company. For years, Bacardi had been a progressive if somewhat paternalistic employer, providing benefits to its workers far beyond those required under Cuban law, including retirement and sick pay, an eight-hour workday, housing loans, and profit sharing. The Bacardi workers had seen no need to organize a union, much less go on strike. The new Bacardi union leadership, however, was more ideological in its orientation, reflecting its Communist affiliation. A flyer distributed by the Santiago labor federation to which the Bacardi union belonged explained that workers in the city "have seen the importance of a 'single front' of the exploited and the oppressed against the exploiters and the oppressors."

The news that the Bacardi workers had gone on strike reached Enrique Schueg by cablegram in Havana. He angrily wired the company's general manager, Pedro Lay, warning that he would not accept any "union imposition." Lay, however, believed an accommodation was possible, and he informed the union leaders that Schueg had agreed to return early from Havana "for the purpose of studying and dealing with the issues raised...on August 15." He asked the union representatives to meet with Schueg as soon as he arrived, and a fairly routine negotiation ensued. Schueg, having calmed down, presented a point-by-point counteroffer to the union's demands and made a written plea for labor-management harmony—for Cuba's sake.

"In this critical hour," he said, "when the Nation rises vigorously after being eclipsed by a despotic and horrible governmental regime, we believe that all members of this industry...should put aside an attitude of intransigence and violence." He told the Bacardi workers that "the desire for insane profits has never been part of our approach," and he attributed the disruption of fraternal labor-management relations to "error" on both sides. Nine days later, they reached an accord. The Bacardi management agreed to recognize the CNOC-linked union, the union moderated its wage demands, and a new labor contract was signed. "The Bacardi Company reconsidered and went back to its roots," the union leaders announced, "finding there the productive force of those workers and directors who made it worthy, within Cuban industry, of being first in the Universe."

Other labor conflicts in the country were not resolved so amicably. Sugar workers seized control of sugar mills and called for socialist revolution. They were joined by tobacco workers in western Cuba, dockworkers in Havana, and coffee workers in eastern Cuba. The unrest even spread to Cuban military bases. In early September, a thirty-two-year-old army clerk named Fulgencio Batista and some of his fellow soldiers took control of Camp Columbia outside Havana in order to press their demands for better pay and housing. The students and labor leaders who were behind the larger movement recognized a political opportunity and joined forces with the dissident soldiers in a "coalition of convenience," and what had started as a simple episode of military insubordination turned into a full-fledged military coup. Carlos Manuel de Céspedes Jr. was deposed as president and replaced by Ramón Grau San Martín, a university professor allied with the students and their revolutionary allies. Grau announced that his government would abrogate the Platt Amendment, enact woman suffrage, and mandate such labor reforms as a minimum wage, an eight-hour day, and binding arbitration.

The U.S. ambassador to Cuba, Sumner Welles, warned his State Department superiors that some members of Grau's team were "frankly Communistic." At Welles's urging, Washington chose not to recognize the new government, concluding that Grau's quasi-socialist agenda and nationalist ideas represented a threat to U.S. economic and political interests in Cuba. The Grau government had actually taken steps to curb Communist influence in the country's trade union leadership, even while following a generally prolabor program and opposing the role of foreign capital in the Cuban economy. Nationalism and non-Marxist socialism were the guiding ideologies. Welles, however, was uncomfortable with the revolutionary passion that infused the new Cuban government and began working behind the scenes to undermine Grau, in a manner reminiscent of the efforts of Leonard Wood thirty years earlier to block the movement for Cuban independence and universal male suffrage.

Welles chose to work with the army sergeant Fulgencio Batista, who in the aftermath of the military coup had managed to get himself appointed commander-in-chief of the Cuban armed forces. Believing that Batista could bring order and stability to Cuba, Welles openly encouraged him to conspire against Grau, and in January 1934 Batista informed Grau that the army was against him. He first arranged for Grau to be replaced by his agriculture secretary, Carlos Hevia, Pepín Bosch's coconspirator in the Gibara attempt, but two days later Batista installed former president Carlos Mendieta (also a Gibara conspirator) in office. Within a week, the United States officially recognized the Mendieta government, having refused to do so with the Grau government through its four-month term. Mendieta was followed over the next five years by three other puppet presidents, all of them beholden to Batista.

The student and worker groups who had opposed Machado and then aligned with Ramón Grau went back into the opposition. Antonio Guiteras, Grau's interior minister and the man who had drafted his ambitious social and economic reform program, attempted to organize an armed insurrection but was hunted down and killed by pro-Batista security forces. Other Grau supporters formed a new political party, the Partido Revolucionario Cubano (Auténtico), the "authentic" reincarnation of José Martí's Cuban Revolutionary Party. Historians later viewed the abortive 1933 struggle as an "unfinished" or "frustrated" revolution that presaged Fidel Castro's own revolutionary movement in the 1950s. One measure of the popularity of Grau's reform program is that the Batista-backed governments that followed him eventually adopted many of his prolabor and nationalist proposals. The Platt Amendment was abrogated, Cuban economic and commercial interests were given preference over foreign ones, and social welfare spending rose. Washington did not object, because Batista's military kept the country under tight control and was supportive of U.S. security interests. The Cuban students and workers who had spearheaded the revolutionary movement were disillusioned, however, and their pent-up anger fueled another insurrection two decades later.

• • •

The struggle of 1933 differed from the Cuban revolutions of the nineteenth century in that the adversaries were divided more by social class than by nationality. It was mostly a fight over how to distribute wealth and organize Cuban society. For the Bacardi family business, the old commitment to the Cuban national cause was becoming more complicated. What did it mean in 1933, when the Bacardi unions were under Communist leadership and the company was a private capitalist enterprise?

And yet the parties reached an accord. When the union representing Bacardi office workers drew up its founding statutes, it offered remarkably complimentary words for the company management, even while affirming its own Marxist ideology:

> Although we know the capitalist class is always antagonistic in its relations with the proletariat, ... we recognize that the Bacardi Rum Company of Santiago de Cuba, *making an exception to the rule*, has always maintained the most cordial and friendly relations with its employees, to whom it has been most considerate, in spite of their being undefended and without protection by virtue of not having a union. [emphasis added]

The union's words went to the core of the Bacardi ideal. From the company's earliest days, the Bacardis wanted their enterprise to be "an exception to the rule" that private firms serve only their pecuniary interests and not those of their community or nation. But rules are rules, and exceptions don't last forever. The Bacardi leadership was to be tested again and again.

Chapter 10

The Empire Builder

Cubans might not have been able to live without their rum, but Bacardi boss Enrique Schueg should have known that Mexicans were tequila drinkers; the national plant was maguey, not sugarcane. Businessmen with a taste for imported spirits preferred brandy or Scotch. Mexican women generally didn't drink, and sales to visiting Americans did not materialize the way Schueg had expected. The new Bacardi rum factory in Mexico City generated sales of only about forty thousand dollars in 1931, not nearly enough to justify the company's investment. And 1932 was no better.

After the sudden death of Pepe Bacardi in May 1933, Schueg sent Pepe's Harvard-educated brother Joaquín to Mexico to assess the company operation. Prohibition was likely to be lifted in the United States before the end of the year, meaning U.S. citizens would have no more need to go south of the border to purchase liquor. Seeing little prospect of a turnaround, Joaquín recommended that the company cut its losses and close the Mexico facility. Reluctantly, Schueg agreed, deeply disappointed that his first major rum production venture outside Cuba had failed.

On an impulse, he asked José "Pepín" Bosch, his daughter Enriqueta's husband, to take charge of shutting down the Mexican operation. After the failure of the 1931 Gibara uprising, Bosch had been a marked man in Cuba, and he had moved with Enriqueta and their two young boys to Boston, where Enriqueta's sister Lucía lived and where the young family would be beyond the reach of President Machado's murderous thugs. Schueg visited his daughters and their husbands during a trip to the United States in 1933 and found Bosch with little to occupy his time. It occurred to him that his son-in-law's business and banking experience and his strong backbone made him ideal for the Mexico assignment. "You're not doing anything," Schueg told him. "Why don't you go to Mexico and help us sell off the business?"

Bosch was a proud and stubborn man, and since his 1922 marriage to Enriqueta he had refused all job offers from his Bacardi in-laws. The assignment

126

to oversee the Bacardi liquidation in Mexico, however, appealed to him in a way previous opportunities had not: Here was a chance to work independently in a new setting, using his own instincts and business judgment in a position of major responsibility. He immediately agreed to go, beginning a career with Bacardi that would span more than four decades and establish him as a pivotal figure in the company's development and in Cuba's modern business history.

. . .

Pepín Bosch acquired his self-confidence and enterprising vision partly from his father, who immigrated to Cuba from Spain at the age of thirteen and worked his way up through a series of jobs to become one of the leading businessmen in Santiago. José Bosch Sr. was president of the Chamber of Commerce, a founder of the local hospital, an original partner in the electric and streetcar utilities in Santiago, and a major real estate developer. Young Pepín attended the best schools in Cuba, and his father sent him to the United States to attend prep school and college. After getting his high school diploma at the age of fifteen, Bosch enrolled at Lehigh University in Pennsylvania, but he dropped out before the end of his first year. "I was a bum student," he said later; "too much money and too much good time." He worked for the next two years at low-paying, undemanding jobs in New York until his father grew tired of sending him an allowance and called him home to help in the family sugar business. In Cuba, Bosch promptly showed he had inherited his father's business skills, and within three years he had saved a small fortune from his share of the sugar profits. The money only reinforced his determination to be independent, however, and he resolved from then on to chart his own career path.

Bosch had never been afraid to express maverick views, and in accepting the Bacardi Mexico assignment at the age of thirty-six, he told his father-in-law he would like to draw his own conclusions about what should be done there. At the National City Bank in Havana, he had worked in the collections department, deciding which business loans to cancel and which to extend, and the job gave him valuable experience assessing a company's business prospects. In Mexico he decided it was premature to give up on the rum-making operation. Noticing that Mexicans drank a lot of Coca-Cola, Bosch proposed a bigger emphasis on the promotion of Bacardi-and-Coke cocktails. He also figured that Mexicans, with their rich handicrafts tradition, would be more inclined to buy rum in wicker-covered jugs, the way it was often sold in Cuba. Schueg was intrigued by his son-in-law's suggestions and approved a bigger Mexico advertising budget. By December 1934, Bosch had turned the operation entirely around, doubling rum sales and paying off the Mexico debts.

Delighted by his son-in-law's performance, Schueg offered him another, even more challenging, assignment. While Bosch was in Mexico, Prohibition had been repealed. The vast U.S. liquor market was once again open to Bacardi and other producers, a commercial opportunity like no other. In the months preceding Repeal, industry analysts had predicted that U.S. drinkers would consume two hundred million gallons a year when they could buy liquor freely again. With the domestic supply depleted after fourteen dry years, imported spirits would have a huge share of the liquor business. If Bacardi were to break into the top rank of global spirits producers, it would need to establish a big U.S. presence. U.S. sales in the first year after Repeal, however, had fallen a bit short of expectations, and by the end of 1934, Schueg was looking for ideas to invigorate the American marketing. After seeing how he turned around the Bacardi operation in Mexico, Enrique Schueg figured Bosch could help the company even more by taking charge of the U.S. business, and Bosch agreed to give it a try.

The U.S. liquor business had become highly complicated. In order to address the overly aggressive alcohol marketing that had spurred the Prohibition movement, the U.S. Congress conditioned the relegalization of the alcohol trade on its stringent regulation. The industry was put generally under the control of state governments (leaving individual states free to remain "dry" if they so wished), though with guidelines established under the Federal Alcohol Administration Act. A three-tier distribution system was established: Distilling companies and other alcohol manufacturers could sell their products only to wholesale distributors, who then sold to retail outlets. State authorities enforced strict separation between each tier, thus ensuring that alcohol sales could be closely monitored and efficiently taxed. For Bacardi and other foreign liquor companies, there was an additional complication: They could sell only to a wholesaler with an importing license.

Competition among the importers for the Bacardi contract had been intense. As many as forty thousand cases of Bacardi rum made their way annually into the United States during the Prohibition period, more even than in the years when the trade was legal, and the widespread sale of fake "Bacardi" only made the brand more famous. "For the plump hand of the House of Bacardi there have been many suitors in the past six months," *Time* magazine reported in the fall of 1933. "At one time or another nearly every U.S. liquorman has pleaded for the exclusive right to market Cuba's rum after Repeal." Enrique Schueg himself traveled to New York in October 1933 to select a sales partner. In the end, he chose an importing subsidiary of the Schenley Distillers Corporation, a Pennsylvania-based house with deep roots in the whiskey business.

Schenley also landed importing deals for French champagne, wines, and vermouth, Spanish ports and sherries, Italian Chianti, and Dubonnet, making it one of the major importers in the post-Prohibition period. Under the arrangement, Bacardi would sell its rum to the Schenley subsidiary, which would see to its distribution in bars, package stores, and other retail outlets across the country. Schueg sealed the deal with Schenley president Harold Jacobi, and as the papers were signed before a crowd of reporters, Jacobi ordered that a bottle of Bacardi be brought out for display. As it was passed around, Schueg noticed to his amusement that the "Bacardi" was a bootleg product with a counterfeit label.

Some liquor importers, in their eagerness to land the Bacardi rum contract, had boasted they could guarantee sales of up to a half million cases per year, a figure no Bacardi executive considered credible. Schenley contracted to import just one hundred thousand cases for 1934 and of that managed to sell only eighty thousand. Economically squeezed by the Depression, Americans had cut back sharply on their liquor consumption. By the time Bosch showed up in New York in early 1935, sales were still stagnant. He went to work at the Bacardi office in the Chrysler Building alongside William J. Dorion, another Bacardi son-in-law whom Schueg had previously appointed as the company representative in the United States. Dorion, who had married Emilio Bacardi's daughter Adelaida ("Lalita"), continued to manage some U.S. affairs for the company, but Bosch was the new man in charge.

His first contribution was to promote the cocktails that had made Bacardi famous a decade earlier among U.S. tourists in Cuba. A former American bartender at Sloppy Joe's in Havana, Jack Doyle, was put to work mixing daiquiris and Cuba libres at the Schenley company bar in Manhattan, while traveling salesmen were given portable bars, so they could teach bartenders around the country how to make proper Bacardi cocktails. Enrique Schueg, however, was interested in more than his son-in-law's clever marketing ideas. For the venerable industrialist, the significance of Pepín Bosch's achievement in Mexico was that it demonstrated what he had long argued: that Bacardi rum could be produced successfully outside Cuba. The white-haired, bespectacled man who deserved most of the credit for Bacardi's growth over the previous three decades still saw expansion as the key to the company's future. The company would be better positioned to compete internationally if its production were not restricted to Cuba. Mexico had been a test case. Schueg now wanted Pepín Bosch to explore the possibility of producing Bacardi rum on U.S. territory, for sale in the States. In 1934 the U.S. import duty on Cuban rum had been lowered from $4 to $2.50 a gallon (compared to a duty of $5 a gallon on other imported spirits), but even the lowered tariff left Bacardi rum at a disadvantage in comparison to spirits produced domestically. With a factory in the United States, Bacardi could compete with U.S.-made bourbon and gin. Even before he sent Pepín Bosch to New York, Schueg had laid the legal groundwork for a U.S.-based facility, establishing the Bacardi Corporation of America in Philadelphia.

The concept was bold. Throughout Bacardi history, the company's Cuban character had been key to its identity. The Bacardis had sold their rum as "the one that made Cuba famous," and in the chapter they had prepared ten years earlier for *El libro de Cuba,* they had boasted that their rum was "totally linked to this land." Rums made outside Cuba would never be as good as theirs, they wrote, "because they don't have available the best raw materials in existence, which are precisely the syrups of Cuban sugarcane." Now the company was challenging its own argument by moving to produce rum outside the Cuban homeland. The new Bacardi marketing strategy was to emphasize the rum's uniqueness and to highlight the "secret formula" behind its manufacture, not its Cuban origins, as the basis for its appeal. Other firms made rum, but only the Bacardi Rum Company made "Bacardi," a distilled spirit whose taste and character put it in a category all its own. Consumers associated "rum" with the Caribbean, but "Bacardi" could be made anywhere, as long as it bore the family name and was distilled and blended according to Don Facundo's formula. The reimaging would make business history. Makers of premium Scotch whiskey never considered manufacturing their products outside Scotland, and it was unthinkable for Rémy Martin or Courvoisier to produce cognac outside France.

Half the battle was already won. A 1935 article in the *New York Times* cited "Bacardi" as an example of a proper noun that had entered the English language as a generic term, much as "Kleenex" and "Band-Aid" did later. With such a strong brand identity and clear differentiation from its competitors, it shouldn't matter where the rum was actually manufactured. To benefit from that advantage, however, the company had to be able to defend its proprietary rights to the Bacardi name. Within two years of Repeal, Bacardi distributors found that New York bartenders weren't always using Bacardi rum when they prepared a "Bacardi cocktail" (basically a daiquiri). At the direction of Pepín Bosch, by then a vice president of the Bacardi's U.S. subsidiary, company lawyers sued the Barbizon Plaza Hotel in Manhattan, alleging that its barmen were misrepresenting drinks as Bacardi cocktails when they were not actually made with Bacardi rum. Enrique Schueg himself came to testify, and the company called barmen who agreed that a genuine Bacardi cocktail had to be made with Bacardi rum. (Other bartenders, called by the defendants, said they saw no reason not to use any rum available in mixing a Bacardi cocktail.) After a defeat in the lower court, the company won on appeal, and New York bartenders were enjoined from using non-Bacardi rum when filling an order for "Bacardi" cocktails. The company considered the case so important that it ran an ad campaign advising drinkers of the court's finding: "It isn't a Bacardi Cocktail unless it's made with Bacardi!"

As the trademark case moved through the courts, Pepín Bosch was surveying possible U.S. sites for a Bacardi factory. Soon after arriving in the United States, he rejected his father-in-law's idea of basing an operation in Pennsylvania, given the state's high liquor taxes. Bosch briefly considered Louisiana and Florida, but he soon decided the best place to set up a distillery was in the U.S. territory of Puerto Rico. The eastern Caribbean island had a rum-making tradition as old as Cuba's, and some of Bacardi's fiercest competitors were Puerto Rican, as sales representative M. I. Estrada had learned years earlier when he traveled the island on horseback. Because the island was considered part of the United States for trade purposes, Puerto Rican rum was not subject to any import duty. The island produced sugar in abundance, and low prevailing wages kept labor costs down. Bosch visited Puerto Rico in February 1936 and assured the territorial officials that tax revenues from a Bacardi operation could easily bring the island treasury a million dollars a year. Within weeks, the Bacardi Corporation of America—Bacardi's U.S. subsidiary—was given a license by the Puerto Rican territorial authorities to establish a rum-making facility on the island, and Bacardi technicians were soon setting up a distillery in an abandoned factory in Old San Juan.

Pepín Bosch had not given enough attention to the political mood in Puerto Rico, however. Many Puerto Ricans in 1936 were angered by the extent to which the U.S. government still ruled their island, and they were sensitive to the idea of any "foreign" company setting up operations in their territory. Like Cuba, Puerto Rico had been ruled by Spain until the 1898 war, after which the United States took over. Unlike the Cubans, however, the Puerto Ricans were not able to win their independence, and the island effectively became a U.S. colony, with even less autonomy than it had enjoyed under Spanish rule. It had a legislature, but the resident U.S. governor could—and often did—veto the laws it passed. Puerto Rican representatives repeatedly petitioned the U.S. Congress for more self-rule, but were rebuffed year after year. By the mid-1930s, a minority group on the island was promoting violent revolution as the only way to achieve independence. In February 1936, the same month Pepín Bosch came to scout industrial sites, the island's U.S. police chief was assassinated by two Puerto Rican militants.

Members of Congress in Washington promptly drew up legislation to thwart further Puerto Rican moves toward independence, threatening an immediate cutoff of all economic aid, an imposition of tariffs on Puerto Rican products, and a withdrawal of U.S. citizenship offers if independence proposals were advanced. The U.S. proposal, however, only had the effect of further fueling the independence movement in Puerto Rico, so that by the time the Bacardis were ready to begin operations there, the island was in a state of nationalist uproar. Puerto Rican rum companies joined forces with proindependence Puerto Rican legislators to draft a law that would ban the production of any rum under a trademark not in use on the island as of February 1, 1936. The provision, aimed squarely at Bacardi, was passed with an explanation that its purpose was to protect the island's native rum industry "from all competition by foreign capital."

Bacardi lawyers immediately challenged the Puerto Rican law on constitutional grounds, saying the Puerto Rican government had no right to tell the Cuban company it could not use its trademark. At the same time, Pepín Bosch launched a publicity campaign aimed at showing Puerto Ricans what Bacardi could contribute to the island. Most Puerto Rican factories at the time were paying male workers about two dollars a day, and women often earned only half that amount. Bosch promised that Bacardi could double those wages. "I shall consider my life a failure," he told the local press, "if Puerto Rico does not come to feel proud that Bacardi has been established on this island." He pointed out that Bacardi was committed to sending ten thousand cases a month to the United States from its Puerto Rico facility, more than any local company could deliver. He also claimed there were thirty-six U.S. states anxious to accommodate the company and pocket its tax payments if Puerto Rico declined. In the end, Bacardi lawyers managed to get a temporary injunction against the enforcement of the trademark ban, and in January 1937 the company was able to initiate production in Puerto Rico. The case went all the way to the U.S. Supreme Court, however, before the anti-Bacardi law was finally overturned and the legality of the company's Puerto Rico operation officially established.

• • •

On February 4, 1937, the Bacardi Rum Company celebrated the seventy-fifth anniversary of its founding in Santiago de Cuba, with parties and fireworks. The tin-roofed, dirt-floored distillery on Matadero Street where Don Facundo began his business in February 1862 had evolved over the years into a multi-million-dollar facility employing 1,200 workers, though the entrance was still marked by the spindly coconut palm planted by fourteen-year-old Facundo Jr. shortly after the distillery opened.

By tradition, the Bacardi daughters personally delivered cash contributions each February 4 to needy institutions around Santiago in commemoration of the company's founding. For the seventy-fifth anniversary, the recipients included the local poorhouse, the old people's home, a children's hospital, a clothing distribution center, an institute for the blind, the Masonic lodge, kindergartens, secondary schools, and a horticultural center, among many other institutions. In addition, the company made cash gifts to independence war veterans who were confined to local hospitals. The contributions cost the Bacardis only a few thousand dollars, but by recognizing the work of local institutions the company managed to highlight its image as a socially conscious corporate citizen in the humanitarian tradition of Emilio Bacardi.

Pepín Bosch knew the Bacardis' progressive record was one of the company's selling points in Cuba, and it was a reputation he wanted to see established as well for the new Bacardi operation in Puerto Rico. To commemorate the company's seventy-fifth anniversary, Bosch took out full-page ads in all Puerto Rican newspapers summarizing the principles that guided Bacardi wherever it operated. The company promised "to elevate the moral level" of the spirits industry in Puerto Rico, barring pictures of women in its advertising so that no one could accuse it of using sex to sell liquor. Bacardi also said that, to avoid encouraging youth liquor consumption, it would not air radio commercials during daytime, and it resolved to keep good relations with its Puerto Rican workers, striving always for their "social betterment."

But this was the 1930s, a time when corporate promises to be good to workers were greeted everywhere with skepticism. The gap between the rich and the poor widened during the Depression years, and from San Juan to Detroit, London, and Santiago de Cuba, union militancy increased sharply along with the appeal of socialism and the influence of Communist political parties. The Bacardi corporation faced the same worker pressures as did other capitalist enterprises, its progressive reputation notwithstanding. Years passed before Bacardi was entirely welcome in Puerto Rico, and in Cuba the company was repeatedly torn between its urges to be a competitive private business and a generous employer at the same time.

Cuba's behind-the-scenes strongman and political manipulator, Fulgencio Batista made a tactical decision during this period to ally with the Cuban Communist Party and allow it to regain control of the trade union movement. The Confederación de Trabajadores de Cuba (CTC), the Confederation of Workers of Cuba, a new central labor federation linked to the Communist Party, became so favored by the Ministry of Labor that it basically functioned as a government union. Emboldened by their powers, labor groups across Cuba made new demands on employers, and the internationally famous Bacardi Rum Company was an irresistible target. For the owners, it was a no-win situation, because the Bacardi union now saw labor-management conflict as a natural and unavoidable fact of industrial life. Even a minor grievance could lead to a major confrontation. This happened, for example, when the company decided in 1939 to start packaging rums in cardboard boxes rather than in wooden cases, a switch that brought the dismissal of "more than 200 workers," according to the union.

The company quickly responded to the union claim, saying that the only people affected by the change were the ten full-time and six temporary workers who had been assembling the wooden crates and that all had been reassigned to other jobs on the basis of seniority. The management said customers preferred the cardboard boxes because they were light and easy to handle, and it pointed out that competing manufacturers had made the same change without union opposition. The issue was soon dropped, but the labor-management tensions continued. Union leaders labeled the Bacardi bosses "semi-imperialist" and "anti-Cuban." That last charge struck a nerve, and frustrated Bacardi executives complained to the Labor Ministry that the company deserved more respect, "not only because of the patriotic accomplishments of its founders but also because of its record of freely and generously pioneering the very social reforms now in favor across the nation." Their objections went unheeded.

Part of the Bacardis' problem was that they were challenging a government with relatively broad popular support. In 1940 Fulgencio Batista decided to step out of uniform and run for president himself, as a civilian. A constituent assembly had just drafted a new constitution for Cuba, replacing the 1901 document that was written during the U.S. occupation and included the hated Platt Amendment provision. The new document mandated a single four-year presidential term and introduced civil liberty guarantees and extensive social welfare provisions. It would be recalled by Cubans for generations to come as a model of progressive political thought. Many of the previously legislated labor rights were made permanent, with workers being entitled to paid vacations, fair wages, and union representation. Though few Cubans considered him a genuine democrat, Batista managed to associate himself with the reforms, and in an election widely seen as the freest Cuba had ever held, he defeated his old rival Ramón Grau San Martín, the candidate of the Auténtico party.

The Bacardi labor troubles returned in April 1943, when several hundred distillery and brewery workers staged an impromptu sit-down strike to back up their demand for an unscheduled wage increase. The company management claimed the strike violated both the union contract and existing labor legislation and appealed to the government, but the Labor Ministry refused to order a halt to the job action, and Batista personally ordered Bacardi to meet the union demands. Tensions rose sharply when an appeals court sided with the company management and suspended Batista's presidential decree. The Communist-controlled CTC leadership, by then directing the Bacardi union, immediately fired off a letter to Batista warning that his acceptance of the appeals court ruling would "legalize the Fascist resistance of the [Bacardi] company." In a major escalation of the dispute, the labor federation called on Batista to show his support for the Bacardi union "through the seizure of the company."

Batista may have seen the Bacardis as political enemies, due to their known sympathy for his *auténtico* opponents. He may have wanted to shore up relations with his Communist allies in the union movement, or perhaps he genuinely believed the Bacardi workers were being treated unjustly. For whatever reason, he went along with the CTC request and in October 1943 sent government agents to Santiago, escorted by provincial and national police troops, to take over the Bacardi distillery. Management officials were ordered to step aside. The Cuban Supreme Court ordered an end to the seizure just one day later, but the damage had already been done. With his "intervention" in the Bacardi business, Fulgencio Batista had alarmed the entire business community in Cuba and earned the Bacardis' lasting enmity. They would never trust him again.

The adverse reaction from the business community undoubtedly bothered Batista. Though he depended on the Communists politically, it was an alliance of convenience, made easier by the Allies' wartime pact with the Soviet Union, and he did not want to associate so closely with the Communists as to jeopardize his relationship with the United States. Within a year, Batista was moderating his antiemployer stance. At the same time, some Bacardi executives and family members began to wonder whether the company had been a bit intransigent in dealing with its union workforce. The company's legal position had been strong, but that did not address the merits of the wage increase demand. Some Bacardi workers, in fact, were paid less than workers in comparable jobs at other companies, in part because the Bacardi union had moderated wage demands in years when the company was struggling. The events leading to the government's seizure of the factory were an embarrassment for a company that had always been considered a pillar of the community and a generous employer. That reputation was central to the Bacardi identity, and it would now have to be renewed.

Whether by coincidence or not, the labor troubles at Bacardi came at a time when the company's leadership was in transition. The estimable Enrique Schueg turned eighty-one in 1943, having already outlived his wife, Amalia Bacardi Moreau, by fourteen years. Always the debonair Frenchman, Schueg was still an honored guest at Santiago parties, banquets, and receptions, regaling friends and strangers alike with his ageless charm and wit. A dinner held in his honor at Santiago's Rancho Club in January 1944 attracted 1,200 guests, a number never seen in eastern Cuba for such an occasion. By then, however, Don Enrique was paying less heed to the day-to-day operations of his company than he had in the past. With the outbreak of World War II, his attention had turned back to his beloved French homeland, now under Nazi occupation, and he organized a solidarity committee in Cuba to support the French Resistance. He was in the final years of his life. As president and managing director of the company, Schueg was unchallenged, but who would succeed him?

A major concern was the state of labor-management relations. The point man in all union dealings during this time was José Espín, who served as the company's chief accountant and as Enrique Schueg's executive assistant (owing largely to the fact that he was fluent in French). Not being a family member, even by marriage, Espín had virtually no chance of ascending to the top executive post in the company, but he still had leadership ambitions. As Bacardi sons and sons-in-law positioned themselves to succeed Enrique Schueg as chief executive, Espín aligned himself with Luis J. Bacardi Gaillard, the company's deputy managing director and the surviving son of Facundo Bacardi Moreau. Luis controlled 30 percent of the company stock as the representative of his family branch on the company board, so he was a significant force, especially when allied with Schueg's top assistant. Among the Bacardi sons, he seemed a logical choice to succeed Enrique Schueg. But Luis and Espín had both been singled out by union leaders as difficult to deal with, and they were held partly responsible for the deterioration of labor relations. Within the family, moreover, Luis was seen as a bit reserved and lacking in dynamism and entrepreneurial vision. By the early 1940s, his prospects were fading.

The rising Bacardi star was Pepín Bosch, who had performed so impressively in Mexico, New York, and Puerto Rico. Loyal though Schueg was to his assistant José Espín and respectful though he was of Luis J. Bacardi's family clout, it was to his son-in-law that he increasingly turned for advice. Bosch personally knew many of the prominent players in Cuban politics, including two former Cuban presidents, Carlos Hevia and Carlos Mendieta, coconspirators during the Gibara uprising. Luis J. Bacardi and José Espín were known to be resentful of the attention Bosch was suddenly getting, even though he showed little interest in any leadership rivalry and did not openly campaign for an executive position. When Espín and Luis blocked action on Bosch's business recommendations, he simply resigned rather than argue with them and did not return to the company until Schueg and other family members pleaded with him to do so.

Schueg liked to use his son-in-law as his ace troubleshooter, which meant Bosch was always on the move, shuttling between Santiago, Havana, New York, Puerto Rico, and Mexico. In the midst of the 1943 labor crisis, Schueg asked Bosch to come to Santiago and take charge of union dealings. As a fresh face and personality in the management, Bosch was able in the following months to turn union relations in a more positive direction. In early 1944, the Cuban supreme court ruled definitively that the Batista government could not unilaterally order the Bacardi management to raise wages, but the ruling had little practical effect. With Schueg's support, Bosch was already initiating meetings with union leaders, and he soon arranged wage and benefit increases that in some cases actually went beyond what Batista had decreed. Whereas company officials had previously fired employees who violated contract obligations, Bosch only suspended them temporarily. He introduced a bonus system for Bacardi workers, including a monthly bottle of rum.

Some of the Bosch moves were paternalistic, including individual assistance to employees with pressing medical or family needs, but they succeeded in putting the Bacardi management on better terms with the workforce. At the same time, Batista and his Communist labor allies made a strategic political decision to defuse tensions with Cuban employers generally. There would be more labor-management conflict at the Bacardi company, but the era of constant confrontation had finally passed.

◆ ◆ ◆

In November 1944, Enrique Schueg installed Pepín Bosch as the company's deputy managing director, replacing Luis J. Bacardi. No one seriously challenged the decision. For fifty years, Enrique Schueg's business instincts had brought the Bacardis wealth, and family members knew to defer to his judgment. Luis retained his position as first vice president of the company, but it was clear he had lost out in the leadership struggle, and he generally withdrew from company business affairs. In the coming years, he showed up at the plush corporate offices at the Edificio Bacardi in Old Havana for a couple of hours each morning, but only to linger in the reception area and receive friends who stopped by for a visit. José Espín, his ally and associate back in Santiago, was demoted to the purchasing department and never again played a major leadership role in the company. Though Pepín Bosch officially had to answer to his father-in-law, he was now the company's chief executive for all practical purposes.

Bosch had turned around the failing Mexican operation, defended the company's position in the U.S. market, and fought back a stubborn anti-Bacardi drive in Puerto Rico. Bacardi rum sales from the overseas facilities he oversaw were bringing the company more than five million dollars a year in revenue. Now he was back in Cuba, and his next challenge was to deal with the fifty or so Bacardi family members—his wife's relatives—who between them held almost all the stock in the company he was set to manage. They were a diverse group. Some had only a few shares, some had many. Some were industrious and eager to be involved in company operations, some only wanted to be sure their dividend check arrived on time. None held a controlling interest. Bosch was closest to those family members with actual business responsibilities, such as his brother-in-law Víctor Schueg. Brilliant but temperamental and an excessive drinker, Víctor had known he would not make an ideal company manager, and during the Bacardi leadership struggle he had thrown his considerable family clout behind Bosch.

Bosch also leaned heavily on Daniel Bacardi, the youngest family member in a position of responsibility at the company. Daniel was the son of Facundo Bacardi Lay, one of Emilio's twin sons from his first marriage. Just thirteen when his father died suddenly in 1924, Daniel started work in the Bacardi factory as an errand boy. Like other Bacardi children, he was sent to the United States to be educated and learn English, but Daniel was not the most diligent of students. His law schooling in Havana was cut short when President Machado closed the university in the face of political unrest, and he did not return after it reopened. Within the Bacardi family, Daniel was known as a fun-loving young man who liked to tear around town on his motorcycle, terrifying his mother but making friends everywhere he went. He got his first official job in the Bacardi factory in 1935, while still in his early twenties; to his older relatives he would always be known as Danielito. An eager and enthusiastic apprentice, he learned the secret Bacardi filtration techniques and blending formulas, and by the time Pepín Bosch took over the company, Daniel was a rum "master blender" in the tradition of his great-uncle, Facundo Bacardi Moreau. Away from work, he carried on the Bacardi partying tradition as a warmhearted, woman-chasing carouser. But each morning found him somewhere in the distillery or on the factory floor, a short and cheerful figure in a white guayabera shirt and black horn-rimmed glasses, sampling products, grilling the workers about their procedures, or solving the latest technical problems.

Another key figure was Joaquín "The Brewer" Bacardi, the sober, Harvard-educated son of José Bacardi Moreau who had been the technical director of the Hatuey brewery virtually since it opened. The company's union troubles had been acute in the brewery, and the quiet, sometimes taciturn, Joaquín had not been especially adept in labor relations. He was highly competent and hardworking, however, and Pepín Bosch held him in high regard. Joaquín's brother Anton, on the other hand, had barely worked a day in his life and promoted the family business largely by buying Bacardi rum drinks for himself and his friends.

While most of the stock-owning family members had little to do with day-to-day operations at the company, that did not mean they could be ignored or their concerns brushed aside. Among the most important shareholders were the eight daughters of Emilio and Facundo Bacardi Moreau, all of whom had inherited sizable holdings.* None played a significant role in the company, but they were far more independent than most Cuban women of their era and followed the development of the family business carefully. Having grown up with the company when it was run informally, they were comfortable calling on company officials or employees for personal favors or assistance. Some of their husbands were influential players behind the scenes.

The most colorful family member was undoubtedly "Emilito" Bacardi, Emilio's firstborn son and the bearer of his father's revolutionary mantle as a decorated veteran of the independence war. In the early 1930s, he resided in Paris as a representative of his family's company but without significant work obligations. His four years fighting under Antonio Maceo and other independence heroes constituted the high point of his life, and he never tired of telling his war stories. After his time in Paris, Emilito settled in Havana, where he took it upon himself to make sure the family's rum products were up to his standards and those of his friends. When his investigation displeased him on one occasion in December 1943, he immediately notified his nephew Daniel, in a letter typed on Bacardi letterhead.

"Dear Danielito," he wrote. "With genuine sincerity, I must warn you that the public consumer of *añejo* [Bacardi's aged rum product] is beginning to complain about its bad quality, and based on what I have tasted myself, I must say the complaints are justified." Emilito said he had been unhappy with the *añejo* he was served at his favorite social club one day and promptly purchased a bottle directly from the inventory at the corporate office in Havana. "I opened it myself," he told Daniel, "and found that its flavor was most disagreeable."

---

*Emilio's wife, Elvira Cape, died in 1933. Facundo Jr.'s wife, Ernestina Gaillard, died in 1949.

Daniel Bacardi, barely thirty at the time, responded tactfully to his sixty-six-year-old celebrity uncle, challenging his assertions ever so gently. Daniel said he was sure the complaints Emilito had heard were "part of an attack against our product by the competition." He noted that the criticism of the *añejo* rum came "just as a new campaign began against our Carta Blanca label here in Santiago, and it is reminiscent of what you describe." He suggested the campaign was instigated by "subversive" elements and assured Emilito that nothing had changed in the way the company made its aged rum. "All I can imagine," Daniel concluded, "is that between the bad bottle you were given in the club and all the propaganda against us, you may have been predisposed to be critical and momentarily lost your taste for it."

• • •

Bacardi executives knew they had to be sensitive to the concerns of family members. Pepín Bosch maintained that tradition, realizing that the environment of intimacy in a company like Bacardi was a corporate strength. But Bosch also believed that a firm the size of Bacardi Rum had to be efficiently managed if it was to compete and grow. He established an atmosphere of openness by setting up his own desk in the middle of the administrative area of the company offices, with no doors or walls between him and his associates, and he made it clear to family members that they were welcome at all times. He assured them they could call Bacardi staff for help with their special needs, no matter how trivial. At the same time, however, he promoted discipline in the company management by having the office staff keep a careful record of all "personal" transactions, and at the end of the year, each Bacardi family member was presented with a detailed account statement, down to the penny, with a debit for each postage stamp taken, each cash advance on a dividend, each bottle of *añejo* delivered to their home, each gift parcel sent out to a family friend.

The policy was typical of Pepín Bosch's management style, which involved flattery and intimidation at the same time. Exceedingly polite and charitable, he managed also to convey such seriousness of purpose and strength of conviction that his "suggestions" were taken without question as commands. He was by no means a physically imposing man, being rather short and almost bald, with blue eyes that twinkled behind his wire-rimmed glasses when he spoke. His voice was soft, even squeaky, and people sometimes had to strain to catch what he was saying. But there was not a trace of self-doubt or weakness in his manner, and his friendliness stopped short of genuine warmth, so that his subordinates were never entirely certain they had satisfied him, no matter how hard they tried. His lawyer and aide, Guillermo Mármol, who for many years worked as closely with Bosch as anyone in the company, recalled years after Bosch's death that he could not remember ever calling his boss anything but "Señor Bosch."

When Bosch wanted to communicate his management philosophy to someone, he gave them a copy of *A Message to García*, an inspirational tract written in 1899 by Elbert Hubbard based on an incident that is said to have happened during the Spanish-American War in Cuba. A young American army lieutenant named Rowan was supposedly dispatched to deliver a message from President McKinley to General Calixto García, the Cuban rebel commander, whose whereabouts were unknown. Against all odds, Lieutenant Rowan did exactly what he had been instructed to do, tracking García down in the Cuban jungle and delivering the message. The business world, Hubbard argued, was in great need of men like Rowan, the dutiful soldier who, "when given a letter for García, quietly takes the missive, without asking any idiotic questions, and with no lurking intention...of doing aught else but deliver it." Hubbard's essay neatly summarized an idealized work ethic for the industrial age, and millions of copies were sold. Pepín Bosch ordered leather-bound copies by the dozen and distributed them widely to his employees, smiling broadly but making clear that he, too, did not appreciate "idiotic questions" or excuses for unfinished assignments. Having been so forewarned, Bacardi employees thought twice before approaching Bosch to ask a favor or make a complaint.

In company matters, Bosch shared his father-in-law's strategic commitment to international expansion. Having succeeded in setting up distilleries outside Cuba, Schueg and Bosch took their ideas a step further in 1944 by establishing a Bacardi importing subsidiary in the United States, Bacardi Imports, Inc., thereby cutting out Schenley Distillers. The subsidiary would buy Bacardi rum from Puerto Rico and Cuba and sell it at a markup to U.S. distributors, just as Schenley had done.

The elimination of Schenley as the importing middleman seemed to make great economic sense, but in practice it was another gutsy Bacardi move. For an import company to have only one brand in its portfolio was unheard of. Bringing liquor into the country involved paperwork, promotion, advertising, and office expenses. The importing companies with a wide assortment of products could spread their overhead costs across a much bigger business operation. The Bacardis were relatively small-time players, and in the tightly organized and highly competitive U.S. liquor market, the big importers moved instinctively to crush them. Schenley Distillers, furious that Bacardi had canceled its importing deal, immediately purchased Carioca Rum Co., another Puerto

Rico–based firm. A decade earlier, *Fortune* magazine had dismissed Carioca as "an American imitation of Cuban rum," but with its acquisition of the brand, Schenley was prepared to mount a challenge for the dominant position in the U.S. rum market.

Bacardi, however, had the notable advantage of brand familiarity. In the first year of its operation, Bacardi Imports earned more than a half million dollars for its parent company above and beyond what the royalty payments from Schenley would have brought. Pepín Bosch reported the results in a memorandum to Enrique Schueg in October 1945. "It would be my suggestion that we continue on the path we laid out a year ago and that has given us such good results," he wrote. Bosch also noted that Schenley had paid four million dollars for the Carioca company and that the Bacardi facility in Puerto Rico was three times bigger. "It's reasonable to think," Bosch concluded, "that the Puerto Rico operation could be sold for more than twelve million dollars, so the stockholders ought to be very happy with this empire you have created with such little economic pain."

It was about the last good news Enrique Schueg and the Bacardis would get for a while. Within a year, Schueg suffered a major stroke, leaving him mentally weakened and unable to continue working. At about the same time, Bosch himself had a devastating accident, when an engine fire caused his yacht to blow up in the Santiago marina just as he and Joaquín Bacardi were preparing to set out on a fishing expedition. The yacht captain was killed, and Joaquín and Bosch were injured—Joaquín from swallowing toxic water, Bosch with a smashed leg. He would never walk normally again. Bosch had barely been released from the hospital when a warehouse fire in Santiago caused hundreds of thousands of dollars in damages to facilities, aging stock, and equipment. As a final blow, Bacardi's U.S. business prospects dimmed in 1946. During World War II, U.S. rum sales had boomed as a result of a reduction in European whiskey shipments and a rationing of U.S. whiskey production, but whiskey stocks were replenished when the war was over, and many consumers who had switched to rum went back to drinking whiskey. By the end of 1946, U.S. liquor dealers had about three million cases of unsold rum in their inventories.

After analyzing the rum surplus, Pepín Bosch and the president of Bacardi Imports, Bartolo Estrada, decided to halt all new Bacardi shipments to the United States, opting to meet the rum demand instead through a redistribution of existing inventories. Over the next year, Bacardi Imports bought up excess rum stock from dealers who were oversupplied and shipped it to dealers who needed more. The effort cost the company a half million dollars, but it restored good relations in its distribution network. By 1948, Bacardi rum sales in the United States were on the upswing again, and the company had re-established its position there as the favored rum brand.

Most of the Bacardi rum sold in the United States by then came from the company's facilities in Puerto Rico, with the exception of the premium and aged Bacardi rums, which were still produced in Cuba. The Puerto Rico operation accounted for an even larger share of the business after Cuba lost its preferential tariff status under the new General Agreement on Tariffs and Trade (GATT), negotiated in 1948. The new agreement committed the signatory nations, including the United States and Cuba, to reduce tariff differentials in order to promote freer world trade, and the preferential arrangement for Cuban rum was dropped. The preference had meant Cuban rum entered the United States with a fifty-cent-per-gallon advantage over rums from other Caribbean producers, and after the preference was eliminated, Jamaica overtook Cuba as the top foreign rum supplier, behind Puerto Rico.

The decline of their U.S.-Cuba rum trade disappointed the Bacardis, at least from the standpoint of family and national pride. Company advertising in the early 1940s had declared that the Bacardi factory in Santiago made "The World's Finest Rum," while the Bacardi products made in Puerto Rico carried a far more modest claim: "Puerto Rico's Finest...at a Popular Price." By the end of the 1940s, however, the company had so much invested in its Puerto Rican facilities that a drop in rum shipments from Cuba was of little commercial consequence. Pepín Bosch and Enrique Schueg had years earlier settled on Puerto Rico as their point of entry to the U.S. market, and the Bacardi Rum Company had been steadily expanding its Puerto Rico facilities.

Bacardi's Puerto Rico operation was also boosted during this period as the result of a new million-dollar advertising campaign launched by the Puerto Rican government on behalf of all rums from Puerto Rico. Under the terms of the 1900 Foraker Act, which defined Puerto Rico's relations with the U.S. mainland, all excise taxes collected on rum (and other products) made in Puerto Rico and sold in the United States were returned to the Puerto Rican government. The rum boom in the U.S. market during World War II had brought a cash bonanza to Puerto Rico, and in the postwar years the island's territorial government was so anxious to see a continuation of U.S. rum sales that it was willing to underwrite a huge promotional effort on behalf of all rums produced in Puerto Rico. The free advertising helped Bacardi more than any other company, though it came with a condition that struck at the heart of the Bacardis' long attachment to Cuba. From that time on, the label of almost every bottle of Bacardi sold in the United States carried the words "PUERTO RICAN RUM."

Chapter 11

❧❦❧

Cuba Corrupted

Charles "Lucky" Luciano, the Mafia's Boss of Bosses, visited Havana in 1946 and felt immediately at home: Here was a city with gambling casinos, racetracks, brothels, cocaine parlors, and—best of all—palm trees. "When I got to the hotel room the bellhop opened up the curtains on them big windows, and I looked out," he said later. "Every place you looked there was palm trees, and it made me feel like I was back in Miami. I realized for the first time in over ten years that there was no handcuffs on me, and nobody was breathing over my shoulder."

Luciano had been arrested more than a decade earlier in New York on pandering charges and deported early in 1946 to his native Sicily. From there he quietly made his way to Cuba, a country whose government did not interfere with criminal business interests. His longtime associate Meyer Lansky, the legendary Mafia financier, had been involved in gambling operations in Havana since 1938, thanks to deals he cut with Fulgencio Batista. The gambling business slowed during the war years, but by 1946 U.S. tourists were again flocking to the island, the casinos and racetracks were producing huge profits, and the authorities looked the other way when organized crime bosses came to town. Havana was an ideal place for the Mafia leaders to assemble for one of their rare summits. There was much for them to discuss. The burgeoning Caribbean drug trade, the gambling business, and the emergent Las Vegas empire all raised questions about how territory and interests should be divided among the big crime families. Luciano still considered himself the supreme leader of the U.S. Mafia and was looking for ways to reassert his control. He sent word to Meyer Lansky to organize a gathering of the chieftains in the Cuban capital.

The meeting was held in December 1946 at the Hotel Nacional, a grand and luxurious property set majestically on a bluff overlooking Havana harbor. The hotel entrance was at the end of a long, palm-lined driveway ideal for Mafia captains fond of ostentatious arrivals. Lansky's friends in the Cuban government made all the necessary arrangements for maximum convenience and security. National Airlines, the U.S. air carrier, was authorized by the government to begin direct daily service to Havana from Newark, New Jersey, and the flights coincidentally began the week before the meeting was held. Virtually every top mafioso in the United States showed up, including Vito Genovese, Joe "Bananas" Bonanno, Frank Costello, Santo Trafficante Jr., and dozens more. The "delegates" took over the top four floors of the Nacional and the hotel mezzanine, while other guests, police, and Cuban government officials were kept away. For five days, the capos feasted on Cuban specialties, including roast breast of flamingo, black beans, marinated pork, tortoise stew, oysters, and grilled swordfish, washing it down with Bacardi rum and Hatuey beer and relaxing afterward with top-quality Cuban cigars. Frank Sinatra was flown in for entertainment. The impunity with which the group was able to assemble in Havana was illustrated by the fact that not a single Cuban newspaper dared take note of the gathering.

The Cuban president whose administration hosted the unprecedented meeting was none other than Ramón Grau San Martín, the former university professor who just thirteen years earlier had symbolized the hopes of a generation of idealistic young Cuban revolutionaries. Grau, the founder of the "Authentic" Cuban Revolutionary Party, had defeated Carlos Saladrigas, Batista's officially designated successor, in the 1944 election. In his campaign, Grau had nostalgically recalled the reformist promise represented by the administration over which he had presided for four months in 1933, and voters swept him into office with high expectations of honest government under conditions of peace and prosperity. His inauguration was celebrated across the country with ringing church bells and artillery salvos echoing through the hills.

To Cuba's lasting misfortune, however, Grau failed his nation miserably. His most prominent followers, the student "revolutionaries" of 1933, had been on the political sidelines for more than a decade, but instead of seeing a chance finally to put their country on the road to stability and good government, many took their return to power as an opportunity to settle old scores and grab their own share of the public wealth, emulating the worst practices of those they had opposed a decade earlier. The government payroll soon doubled in size, presenting new opportunities for selling jobs. Underpaid government officials and judges demanded payoffs in return for their public "services." Public works contracts were often given to the builders offering the biggest kickbacks, while criminals with high political connections or pockets full of bribe money were free to act with impunity. Grau's accommodation of the 1946 Mafia summit was just one example of how he deepened Cuba's corruption.

For Meyer Lansky and other Mafia figures on the island, the transition from Batista to Grau had gone so smoothly as to suggest that Batista had secretly favored Grau. "Lansky and Batista had him strictly in their pockets," Luciano himself said of Grau many years later.

The Bacardi Rum Company could not stay out of the reach of crooked public officials in the Grau administration any more than it could avoid *batistiano* labor leaders in the preceding years. Government auditors, health inspectors, and tax collectors routinely visited factories around the country, and generally they found something to criticize or condemn—unless some private accommodation could be made. Finance Ministry inspectors showed up at the Bacardi plant in Santiago one day in 1947 carrying the old, yellowed files on the company's calculation of distillate losses to evaporation, the same papers the Gerardo Machado administration had produced nearly two decades earlier in an effort to pry more taxes out of the Bacardi firm. To the company's astonishment, the inspectors were threatening to revive the challenge against the company's loss claim.

Pepín Bosch was furious. While some businessmen would simply have bribed the inspectors to drop the challenge (which was what they expected), Bosch fought it. The government was in the hands of his former *auténtico* comrades, and now they were demanding payoffs from old friends. Still recovering from his boat accident and burdened with bills from the fire that had damaged Bacardi facilities earlier that year, Bosch flew to Havana to confront the Grau administration. He went to see the Grau cabinet member he knew best, Prime Minister Carlos Prío, with whom he had once collaborated in anti-Machado activities. Prío was one of the student leaders closest to Grau during the events of 1933, and he and Bosch were both good friends of the longtime *auténtico* activist Carlos Hevia, one of Bosch's chief coconspirators in the Gibara uprising. Prío apologized to Bosch for the finance inspectors' actions and arranged to have the matter dropped, though not without advising Bosch that he was doing him a favor and that he might some day ask that it be returned.

· · ·

Cuba was becoming a criminal state. For decades, political conflict on the island had been associated with violence, and during the Grau presidency the pattern became even more deadly. Struggles for power and influence within the Cuban Congress or the trade union movement were routinely resolved through gun battles or even duels. Nowhere was the violence more pronounced than at the University of Havana. The campus was by tradition off-limits to police and soldiers, and as a result it had long been a haven for antigovernment militants. Weapons and ammunitions could be freely stockpiled there, and student leadership positions often went to those individuals with the best-armed and most intimidating supporters.

Among the activists seeking to establish a university power base during this period was a brash young law student named Fidel Castro. He had grown up on a farm in the countryside of eastern Cuba and lacked the cultural sophistication of fellow students from Havana's upper class; some of his close friends teased him by calling him *guajiro* (country boy). Though he had plenty of money thanks to his father, a wealthy landowner, Castro's clothes were poorly matched and not always well laundered. He showed little interest in parties, did not dance or listen to music, and appeared to be incapable of flirting with girls. But his bold nature showed in the self-important way he carried himself on campus, dressed in a pinstriped jacket and gaudy tie, an eager student politico ready at any moment to pontificate on some subject and persuade others of the correctness of his position. Tall and solidly built, with a long, sloping nose and high forehead, the nineteen-year-old Castro projected self-confidence and authority. His fellow students were either drawn to him as a natural leader or put off by his know-it-all attitude and his tendency to monopolize conversations.

Far from being deterred by the thuggish aspect of the campus political scene, Castro sensed it was a world in which his physical courage and leadership abilities would stand out. Within weeks of arriving on campus, he was campaigning for election to the Federación Estudiantil Universitaria (FEU), the University Student Federation. What he stood for politically at the time is a mystery. "I arrived at the university as a political illiterate," Castro himself told an interviewer many years later. It was an important acknowledgment, hinting that his legendary activism originated less in his political ideas than in some need for a stage on which to perform. "I never went to classes," he boasted later. "Where I hung out was in the park—there were some benches there—talking to people. Various people gathered around me, and I explained things to them." He made his big public speaking debut at a rally in November 1946, in the fall of his second year at law school, urging his fellow students to rise up against the Grau administration.

He was soon going everywhere with a loaded pistol stuck in his belt, just like other young aspiring politicians at the university. At the time, political activities on the campus were dominated by two armed gangs, the Movimiento Socialista Revolucionario (MSR), the Revolutionary Socialist Movement, and its archrival, the Unión Insurreccional Revolucionaria (UIR), the Revolutionary Insurrectional Union. In his first year, Castro largely steered clear of the gangs, but according to several friends, he soon decided it was in his interest to find a place for himself in their world, and he began acting like a typical campus gangster, primarily but not exclusively in UIR circles. Castro later claimed he armed himself only after a pro-Grau hit man warned him to abandon his activism or face the consequences. "That was when my own armed struggle began," Castro said. "A friend got me a fifteen-shot Browning. I decided if I was to give up my life, it would be at a cost."

Several of his university colleagues later claimed that Castro himself attempted to assassinate a fellow student activist named Lionel Gómez, seeing him as a rival and hoping to impress a gangster figure whose political support Castro wanted. According to an eyewitness, Castro spotted Gómez walking near the university sports stadium one day in December 1946, around the time the Mafia capos were meeting at the Hotel Nacional, a few blocks away. The eyewitness, who was with him at the time, said Castro hid behind a stone wall and shot Gómez in the back without warning, seriously injuring him. Gómez eventually recovered, and Castro was never charged with the shooting, but the incident left him with the reputation of being a campus pistolero.

As an activist, Castro focused on grand issues, such as imperialism, rather than on student rights or other immediate concerns. He was active in a campus committee to support the independence movement in Puerto Rico, and he headed the local Dominican Pro-Democracy Committee, which worked for the overthrow of Rafael Trujillo, the dictator of the Dominican Republic. Quiet political work, such as community organizing, held little interest for Castro; he preferred leading rallies and demonstrations and making fiery speeches in front of big crowds. He enjoyed getting in the middle of melees and was unafraid of physical confrontation, even at the risk of getting killed.

In 1947 Castro joined an expedition to the Dominican Republic to lead an anti-Trujillo uprising, only to see the Cuban authorities, urged by the U.S. government, intervene to end it. A year later, he helped organize an "anti-imperialist" students' congress in Colombia to coincide with a meeting of Western Hemisphere foreign ministers. While he was in Bogotá, a popular Colombian politician, Jorge Eliécer Gaitán, was assassinated, and the capital erupted in riots. Castro jumped eagerly into the action, grabbing a gun from a police arsenal, stealing a uniform to give him cover, and then engaging in a gun battle while leading an effort to take over a police station. He was soon arrested, but Cuban diplomats were able to get him out of the country. The experience in Bogotá stayed with Castro, however. He had seen and felt what it was like to be a revolutionary, if only for a few days, and he would never forget the thrill.

Cubans were growing weary of the secret deal making and gangsterism that characterized political life in their country. In 1947, progressive elements within Grau's Auténtico party, led by his former student follower Eduardo Chibás Jr. of Santiago, broke away to form the Partido del Pueblo Cubano (Ortodoxo), the Party of the Cuban People. Chibás added "Ortodoxo" to the party name in order to emphasize its "orthodox" adherence to the original Cuban revolution and the principles of José Martí, just as Grau had added "Auténtico" to his own party label. In his weekly Sunday evening radio broadcast, "Eddy" Chibás attacked his old allies in the Grau administration and preached constantly of the need to guard against graft. In the 1948 presidential elections, he ran against Auténtico candidate Carlos Prío, Grau's former prime minister. Using a broom as his campaign symbol, Chibás promised to sweep house and end corruption. The *ortodoxos* were especially popular among the university students, and Fidel Castro—recognizing a promising politician when he saw one—soon emerged as Chibás's leader on campus, appearing at his side whenever possible.

Prío nevertheless won the election handily (and fairly), after agreeing that corruption was indeed a problem and promising the Cuban people he would implement a reformist program. Just forty-five years old at the time of his election and as charming as he was handsome, Prío would be remembered in Cuba as *"el presidente cordial."* He had many flaws, including a love of luxury and an eagerness to get rich, but even his critics regarded him always as a gentleman. As one historian wrote, "It was difficult to dislike Prío and difficult to take him quite seriously." Once he became president, Prío blamed Cuba's suffering on his predecessor, Grau, who by then was facing prosecution for embezzlement.

Prío had not been long in office, however, before he faced serious challenges of his own. The problem of political violence had persisted, even though Prío had attempted to buy off the leading gangsters with jobs for them and their followers. Chibás continued to hammer Prío in radio broadcasts, describing his government as "a scandalous bacchanalia of crimes, robberies and mismanagement." To divert attention from his problems, Prío wanted to announce a massive new public works program, but he didn't have the money in the state treasury to carry it out, and Cuba was having trouble getting external loans. His only hope was to recruit a sharp and respected finance minister, and he knew it would have to be someone from outside his immediate political circle.

Fortunately, he was still on good terms with one of the best-known and most highly regarded business executives in all Cuba: Pepín Bosch of the

Bacardi Rum Company. If Prío could persuade Bosch to join his administration, it would signal his presidential commitment to reform, shore up his support with the business community, improve Cuba's image with external lenders, and link his government with a prestigious private enterprise. In spite of its well-publicized labor troubles and the criticism it had taken from some Communist commentators, Bacardi was still one of Cuba's most esteemed native companies, and as its chief executive, Bosch was carrying on the tradition of progressive leadership for which the family had long been known. His contribution to the struggle against the Machado dictatorship had demonstrated his patriotism, and his successful management of Bacardi's international expansion showed his skill as a businessman. President Carlos Prío saw Bosch as the man who could save his administration, and in the fall of 1949 Prío asked him to come to Havana and serve Cuba as his finance minister. As the supervisor of government contracts and the collector of taxes and custom duties, the Finance Ministry had long epitomized the problem of corruption in the Cuban state bureaucracy.

But Bosch rejected Prío's job offer. "I told him I was running Bacardi and had a factory in Puerto Rico and various others to oversee," he recalled years later. "I told him it was impossible. I said I just couldn't do it." Enrique Schueg, though officially still the company president, had drifted into senility, and Bosch's corporate leadership was indispensable. The company had just two years earlier opened a new Hatuey brewery in El Cotorro, outside Havana. Business in Mexico was booming, with the factory there producing rum for export to Canada as well as for the Mexican market. Work was continuing on new Bacardi facilities in Puerto Rico. With the reports of new gangster attacks in Havana, continuing labor unrest, and the escalating rhetoric of Eddy Chibás and his followers, Bosch considered the offer of a position in President Prío's cabinet about as appealing as a jail term.

President Prío was nevertheless persistent, telephoning Bosch repeatedly. Presidents of Cuba were accustomed to being pestered for cabinet positions, not having to do the pestering themselves. Finally, Prío summoned Bosch to his office in the presidential palace. There would be no more pleading. Standing tall behind his desk, he looked down squarely at the balding Bosch, five years his senior. "I am the president of Cuba," Prío said, "and you are a Cuban, and I am now ordering you to take over the Ministry of Finance." Bosch finally gave in but told Prío that his Bacardi responsibilities meant he could make only a short-term commitment. His appointment was nonetheless greeted with enthusiasm, with the *Havana Post* noting that "the naming of the dynamic boss of Bacardi to handle the nation's purse strings is a sign that the Prío government is going all out to make a good record for itself."

In after-dinner remarks at a Rotary Club banquet shortly before leaving for his new job, Bosch said he was going to Havana with "no political ambitions whatsoever." He said he would work for "whatever is best for the country, not acting to enrich the rich or abandon the poor but trying in every way to raise the economic level of all Cubans and especially of those who for lack of opportunity have not been able to gain a good living." Though he was not a party activist, Bosch still identified with the *auténticos* and their left-of-center social welfare platform. At the same time, he made clear to his fellow businessmen that he considered himself one of them and that as finance minister he would pursue probusiness policies.

Bosch moved into his office on the seventh floor of the Finance Ministry in downtown Havana on January 9, 1950, to great acclaim. So many friends, family members, and business associates showed up for Bosch's swearing-in ceremony that even the hallway outside the minister's office was packed with people. Bosch arrived with his twenty-four-year-old son Jorge, Santiago mayor Luis Casero, and his wife's cousin Emilito Bacardi, the family's celebrity war veteran from the previous century. At seventy-three, white-haired and a bit grizzled in appearance, "Colonel" Bacardi was still loath to let pass an opportunity to mention his exploits in the independence war, even when it was someone else's occasion. "I was an aide to Maceo and made the western march with him," the colonel reminded the Bosch crowd, before adding that he was "happy to see Bosch in such a high place of honor."

The reluctance with which Bosch had accepted the ministry job turned out to be a factor he could use to advantage. Because he was already wealthy, he was able to turn down the minister's salary ($595 monthly), as well as the offer of a government car, thus sending a clear signal that his services were not for sale. Because he came into office without political debts to pay and because he had no further political ambitions, he was free to ignore the patronage demands that plagued other government ministers. Bosch genuinely wanted to return to Santiago and his Bacardi responsibilities as soon as he could, which motivated him to reform Finance Ministry operations as quickly as possible. "I'm a working businessman, and I like to speak more with actions than with words," he said. His objectives were threefold: to secure financing for Prío's planned two-hundred-million-dollar public works program, to eliminate the fiscal deficit, and to put a halt to corrupt practices in his ministry. Reassured by Bosch's appointment, officers at the World Bank in Washington within a few weeks approved loans to cover the public works program.

Bosch's other challenges would not be met so easily. As one newspaper columnist noted later, "Dodging taxes, next to night baseball, was the most popular and highly skilled sport in Cuba," with Cuban businessmen routinely colluding with crooked treasury inspectors to evade their obligations. Bosch resolved to end that practice. "Everyone will pay," he insisted, "without exception or privilege." On the day he took office, Bosch put his tax collectors on notice that he would monitor their work, and he shocked his subordinates by working eighteen or nineteen hours a day himself. Within three months, tax receipts were running at an unprecedented rate of one million dollars a day or more, and the Finance Ministry was on target to produce a six-million-dollar surplus in the state budget by the end of the fiscal year. The previous year had ended with an eighteen-million-dollar deficit. Prío was delighted, happily acknowledging that some of his own family members were found to have tax delinquencies.

Bosch, however, faced an uphill struggle. The custom of using government spending for political purposes was deeply rooted in Cuba, having been established in the Spanish colonial administration, and Bosch's reform efforts soon ran into fierce opposition from Cuban politicians. Congressmen repeatedly called him before investigating committees to harass him, in one case questioning him until three in the morning. Though Bosch theoretically had the support of President Prío, he often found himself politically isolated. The only Bacardi colleague he brought with him to the Finance Ministry was his personal secretary, the twenty-nine-year-old lawyer Guillermo Mármol. Most of the deputies who worked with Bosch in the ministry were allied with prominent Cuban politicians, and Bosch was not convinced of their loyalty to him. Though there was less gangsterism surrounding government dealings than there had been in the 1940s, it had not entirely disappeared.

In September 1950, one of Bosch's top deputies, Tulio Paniagua, was shot and killed in his law office. Paniagua had taken a leave of absence from his ministry post in order to work with the president of the Cuban Senate, Miguel Suárez Fernández, his political patron. Though there was no evidence the assassination was related to Paniagua's position at the Finance Ministry, the murder underscored for Bosch the seriousness of having political enemies in Cuba. When *Carteles* magazine subsequently reported that Bosch aspired to be Cuba's next president, he marched into the magazine offices and demanded a retraction. "I don't want to be president," he said. "What I want to do is go back to Oriente [province] and attend to my business. I'm tired of this."

Enrique Schueg had died in August at the age of eighty-eight. In his final months, Schueg was largely incapacitated as a result of the stroke he had suffered earlier, but his death was still a Bacardi turning point. He was born the same year the rum company was founded, in 1862, and went to work for the

Bacardis at a time when Don Facundo himself was still alive and nominally in charge. After helping Emilio and Facundo Jr. manage the company through the critical wartime years and into the twentieth century, Enrique Schueg steered the company almost single-handedly into the modern era. He was the key link between the small family firm and the big corporation it subsequently became; without his business vision, the company would not have prospered as it did. *Santiagueros* knew Schueg as the man who saved many French-Cuban citizens during the city siege in 1898 and as the patriarch whose charity and patronage supported the city for decades. His funeral was a huge event, reminiscent of that of his brother-in-law Emilio twenty-eight years earlier. Santiago's church, civic, political, and military leaders walked behind the casket in a procession to the town square, along with trucks loaded with floral displays. Hundreds of Bacardi workers, given the day off, joined in the procession. At the head of the parade were Don Enrique's sons Víctor and Jorge and his son-in-law Pepín Bosch, who was also there as Schueg's successor as Bacardi chief and as a representative of President Prío and the Prío cabinet.

Seven months later, shortly after the Bacardi directors formally elected him the new company president, Bosch resigned as finance minister. He had held the ministry job for fourteen months and managed in that time to turn the budget deficit into a fifteen-million-dollar surplus. He gave ill health as his official reason for quitting, though *Time* magazine speculated that Bosch "realized that as the 1952 presidential campaign drew nearer, pressure would grow to finance the government campaign out of the Treasury, as it was financed more or less in 1948." The magazine quoted a Havana newspaper's commentary on his departure: "Bosch took office to the profound disgust of the politicians, and leaves accompanied by their broad smiles as they wait outside the ministry doors to assault the Treasury he guarded."

In the twelve months after Bosch left Havana and returned to Bacardi, Cuba was shocked by a series of events from which it would not recover. Eddy Chibás, having grown ever more strident in his denunciations of corruption and the Prío government, made a final effort to get Cubans' attention with a frenzied radio broadcast on August 5, 1951. "Sweep away the thieves in the government!" he screamed into the microphone. "People of Cuba, arise and walk! People of Cuba, wake up! This is my last call!" He then shot himself in the stomach. Ten days later, he died. His successor as the leader of the Orthodox Party, Roberto Agramonte, became a favored candidate to win the June 1952 presidential election, with the support of a strong segment of the Cuban Left, including the lawyer-activist Fidel Castro, who was himself running for a congressional seat on the Orthodox ticket. The *auténticos*, still struggling to overcome their reputation for corruption, nominated Pepín Bosch's old friend Carlos Hevia, who had been president in 1934 for seventy-two hours. Hevia had remained close to Bosch and was running the Bacardis' new Cotorro brewery outside Havana at the time he was nominated. The third presidential candidate—and least likely to win—was Fulgencio Batista, who had returned to politics in 1948 as a senator.

Faced with the prospect of losing the election, Batista staged a coup d'état three months before the scheduled vote, overthrowing the Prío government with the help of the Cuban army. Democracy in Cuba was finished.

Chapter 12

❦

Cha-Cha-Chá

Cuba entered 1952 on a wave of prosperity, thanks to booming sugar production and a resurgence of tourism. Foreigners came for the marlin fishing, the horse racing, the beaches, and glitzy nightclubs like the Sans Souci and the Tropicana. The Tropicana had a new glass-walled Arcos de Cristal performance space, built around palm trees with openings in the ceiling for the fronds. In the adjacent outdoor Bajo las Estrellas cabaret, guests dined and danced the rumba under a starry sky to the spirited salsa strains of top Cuban orchestras. Lavishly produced Afro-Cuban floor shows featured thunderous *batá* drumming, chanting choruses, and showgirls in skimpy, feathered costumes. Cubans boasted the best tobacco and rum in the world, the most beautiful women, and the hottest music—and, unlike the foreign tourists, they enjoyed such pleasures all year long. The Bacardi Rum Company summed up the prevailing national spirit with an advertising slogan introduced in the late 1940s—"*¡Qué Suerte Tiene el Cubano!*" (How Lucky the Cuban Is!)*

Fulgencio Batista's coup early on March 10 took the country entirely by surprise. Shortly before 2 A.M., Batista pulled up to the main gate of the Cuban army headquarters at Camp Columbia in a car driven by a uniformed army officer. A sympathetic sentry waved them through, and minutes later Batista had the army chief of staff out of bed and under arrest. Army regiments outside the capital surrendered soon after. Cubans woke up that morning to military music on their radios and learned, to their astonishment, that Carlos Prío had been pushed out of the presidency, that Batista was once again their ruler, and that there would be no election in June.

The coup provoked virtually no public protest. A group of students, responding to rumors of Batista's return, came to the presidential palace at dawn

---

The slogan "¡Qué Suerte Tiene el Cubano!*" caught on to such an extent that it became something of a national motto, appearing as the caption for a magazine spread on Cuban women and being used as a line in TV shows and popular songs. A 1999 dictionary of "Cubanisms" included the slogan among its entries, one of the more unheralded Bacardi contributions to Cuban culture.

to ask Prío for weapons and ammunition to defend his government, but Prío did not respond, fearing the students would be slaughtered. After a short-lived attempt to find a military unit somewhere willing to back him, Prío gave up and took refuge in the Mexican Embassy. Eusebio Mujal, the head of the Cuban Workers' Federation, called for a general strike, but his order went unheeded, and within twenty-four hours he made his own peace with Batista. After a few days, Prío left Cuba for Mexico and later Miami.

The resignation with which most Cubans accepted Batista's coup was partly due to their disgust with Prío, who had failed to inspire public trust or end the corruption that had prevailed for so long. But their passivity also reflected a national sense of embarrassment. Many Cubans regarded themselves as politically superior to their Latin American neighbors. Only Argentina, Chile, and Costa Rica had a higher literacy rate. In May, the nation was to mark the fiftieth anniversary of the founding of the Cuban Republic. Their 1940 constitution was considered exemplary, and many Cubans were ashamed that the weakness of their political system had now been exposed before the whole world. Writing three months after the coup, the columnist and historian Herminio Portell Vilá lamented, "The foreign visitor departs from our country thinking that the gloss of civilization has not penetrated very deeply."

The 1950s would be seen simultaneously as Cuba's best and worst years. The country's irresistible sensual pleasures were on full display, but it also became clear that the overripe fruit was due to burst. The good life would succumb to ills that had gone untreated for too long. There were Cubans skilled enough to lead their country through those difficult years, and there were Cuban enterprises, such as Bacardi, with the outlook and the resources to help. But they were too few in number or too weak to make a lasting difference, and the Cuba that entered the 1950s did not make it to the decade's end.

* * *

Most of Cuba's big sugar barons and bankers welcomed Batista back to power, appreciating his firm hand, but not the Bacardis and especially not Pepín Bosch. With his military coup, Batista had overthrown the president under whom Bosch had dutifully served and blocked the possible presidential election of Bosch's old *auténtico* ally Carlos Hevia. In the years that followed, few, if any, Cuban businessmen opposed the Batista dictatorship more vigorously than Pepín Bosch or worked harder for the restoration of democratic rule on the island.

As an old Cuban firm, Bacardi had an established reputation for patriotism and integrity, and Bosch and other company executives had worked hard over the years to promote that corporate image. Bacardi rum was advertised as *"Sano, Sabroso, y Cubano"*—Healthy, Flavorful, and Cuban. On the eightieth anniversary of the day in 1868 when sugar planter Carlos Manuel de Céspedes freed his slaves and launched the Cuban independence struggle, a Bacardi advertisement showed a pair of black hands thrust skyward with broken chains on the wrists and Céspedes's famous words to his slaves: "From this moment, you are as free as I am." For the country's jubilee celebration in May 1952, the company hung an enormous Cuban flag down the entire six-story front of its Havana headquarters. A new edition of *El libro de Cuba* was prepared that year, and Bacardi executives were once again invited to submit a corporate profile, just as they had done for the 1925 edition. Titled "Bacardi, the Great Cuban Industry," it described the extension of the company's international operations as "an expansion that no comparable industry in Cuba has carried out" and highlighted the family's "parade of contributions to the fatherland" over four generations. Just one industrial enterprise in Cuba was larger—Textilera Ariguanabo, S.A., a textile manufacturing business—and it was owned by a U.S. family.

By producing Cuba's most popular rum and beer brands, Bacardi was intimately associated with national celebration. By the 1950s, the company had become the island's leading corporate patron of Cuban culture. Emilio Bacardi and his wife Elvira Cape had set the precedent with their establishment of the Museo Bacardi, the Biblioteca Elvira Cape, and the Academia de Bellas Artes, all in Santiago. In the 1940s, the Premio Bacardi (Bacardi Prize) was established to reward the best book on the independence war hero Antonio Maceo. In Havana, the wood-paneled mezzanine bar in the art deco Edificio Bacardi was one of the city's leading intellectual salons, with lectures, readings, and literary discussions featuring such prominent Cuban poets and writers as Nicolás Guillén and Alejo Carpentier. The Cuban ballerina Alicia Alonso got her start thanks to Bacardi sponsorship of her dance company, Ballet Alicia Alonso, which after 1959 became the National Ballet of Cuba.

Nothing stirred Cuban passions more than dance music and baseball, and Bacardi was linked with both. The rum company had sponsored baseball in Cuba since the 1880s, when it fielded a Santiago team in the summer league. By the twentieth century, the Casa Bacardi team—with players recruited from the factory workforce—was a semipro organization. The Bacardi-baseball connection was a natural one: Fans in Cuba at even the most dilapidated parks watched their games with a glass of Bacardi rum or a Hatuey beer in hand. The scoreboard at the main stadium in Havana carried huge ads for Bacardi and Hatuey, and when baseball games were first telecast across the island in the early 1950s, Hatuey was the commercial sponsor. Cutaway shots showed Manolo Ortega, a popular newscaster and sports announcer, sitting in a broadcast booth with a big red Hatuey sign behind him and a can of Hatuey beer at his elbow. The most popular Cuban player of the 1940s and early 1950s, Roberto Ortiz, went to work for Bacardi as soon as he retired from baseball, officially as a salesman but unofficially as a public relations representative.

Bacardi support for Cuban musicians was just as prominent. In the 1940s and 50s, Cubans heard most of their music on the radio, and no program was more popular than the "Bacardi Hour," carried on the CMQ station and showcasing the top Cuban musicians of the day. Bacardi also sponsored a musical program on Radio Progreso, featuring the famed Sonora Matancera orchestra and lead singer Celia Cruz, who within a few years gained international renown as the "Queen of Salsa." Each Christmas, the company sponsored an islandwide music broadcast featuring a "danceable program" that ran until 4 A.M. and was meant to ensure "that our inimitable Cuban music is present at every social gathering," along with Bacardi rum, of course. During commercial breaks, the announcer encouraged the radio listeners to "head to the bar and ask for a Cuba libre for yourself and for your companion!" When Cuban partygoers drank Bacardi, they could even feel they were honoring their homeland:

> Friends, Bacardi is more Cuban, purer, and better tasting than any foreign liquor. It is made for the hot Cuban climate, and for that reason it's healthier. . . . So toast with Bacardi! Made in Cuba to delight the universe!

With such advertising campaigns, Bacardi was promoting the very rum-and-rumba lifestyle that Fidel Castro and other revolutionaries would later condemn as decadent. In the Bacardi view, however, there was no contradiction between Cuban patriotism and Cuban playfulness. The idea was not to encourage escapism and self-indulgence, but to make Cubans feel good about themselves and proud of their nation, even while dancing the night away.

The Bacardis had a democratic style in their own socializing. In Santiago, a city known across Cuba for its wild celebrations, Bacardi men (and sometimes women) had a well-established party reputation. At the private San Carlos Club downtown or the Hotel Venus across the plaza, they were known for their generosity at the bar. If the only way to keep an establishment open another half hour after closing time was to tip the barman and buy another round for the entire house, there was almost always a Bacardi ready to pay. No family member was more beloved than Daniel Bacardi, Emilio's gregarious grandson, who by the early 1950s was in charge of company operations in Santiago. Daniel was the public face of the Bacardi family, and he took the responsibility seriously, regularly visiting all the major nightclubs, bars, restaurants, and other social venues, always promoting Bacardi products and the company image. Though a wealthy man, he had friends from all social backgrounds and was widely admired for his down-to-earth demeanor and joyful approach to life and work. Family members were fond of telling the story of Daniel coming home at dawn one morning after an all-night outing and finding his wife, Graciela, already up and waiting for him at the door, none too happy about the hour. "This is not the time to be coming home," she said.

"You're right," Daniel said. "It's time to go to work." Without entering the house, he turned and headed for the Bacardi office. Daniel was famous for his ability to hold his liquor. A younger Bacardi worker in Santiago recalled years later that Daniel could finish off an entire fifth of white Carta Blanca rum in a single nighttime drinking session with a few friends and still show up early the next morning at the factory or the distillery—clear-headed, steady on his feet, and totally in charge.

The Bacardis' patronage of revelry in Santiago peaked each year in July during the annual carnival celebrations, the most exuberant in all Cuba. City business effectively came to a halt during the three-day carnival, as throngs of people filled the narrow streets to drink and dance. The highlight of the weekend was the annual parade of *comparsas*, neighborhood bands that competed against each other as part of the local celebrations. Each *comparsa* featured a dozen or more residents in outlandish costumes, playing conga drums or trumpets, ringing bells, shaking maracas, even banging frying pans in harmony with the driving conga rhythm. Those who didn't play instruments danced in a line behind the others, in the traditional Santiago carnival routine that gave rise to the original "conga line." Suckling pigs were roasted on street corners, and vendors moved among the carnival-goers selling beer and rum. The Bacardi management customarily distributed bonuses of up to one hundred dollars to its employees in the days immediately preceding the carnival, and the Bacardi workers were among the biggest carnival celebrants, making sure the company rum flowed freely. The partying was continuous—morning, noon, and night.

By the 1950s, the Santiago carnival had essentially become a Bacardi event, so closely was it identified with the hometown firm. Bacardi Rum helped decorate the entire city with lanterns and banners, offering a prize for the best-adorned neighborhood, and it sponsored the annual "Carnival Queen" election. Anyone with a label from one of various Santiago products, including Hatuey beer and Bacardi rum, was entitled to a vote for the prettiest and most regal candidate.

• • •

People from across Cuba traveled to Santiago each July for the carnival festivities, so no one paid much notice to a caravan of fifteen automobiles, packed with young men, heading out from Havana on July 24, 1953. Only a few of the men knew where exactly they were going. The others understood only that they were to take part in a "revolutionary" military operation under the direction of the man who was riding up ahead in the rented 1952 blue Buick sedan, Fidel Castro.

The young Orthodox Party firebrand had been one of the few Cuban politicians energized by Batista's coup. Always an improviser, Castro saw opportunity in the interruption of the democratic process, concluding that Batista's dictatorial rule could provoke a violent uprising in Cuba and that he could lead it. It was an idea that appealed to him far more than conventional electioneering ever had. After the coup, Castro immediately went underground to begin planning something spectacular, and he was finally ready to carry it out. The plan was to lead an assault on the Moncada barracks in Santiago, an old Cuban army installation named for independence war hero Guillermo Moncada. Castro personally recruited and equipped about 160 men for the operation, most of them young factory workers or farmhands with little military training or political ideology apart from their opposition to the Batista regime—and their enthusiasm for a social revolution.

Castro figured he and his men could seize the barracks by surprise and gain access to its arsenal, which would permit him and his ragtag fighters to equip themselves for further guerrilla operations. He had chosen carnival weekend for the operation, thinking the nightlong festivities in Santiago would enable him to slip his fighters into town unnoticed. The assault was planned for 5:15 A.M. on Sunday, July 26, when many of the soldiers and their officers would be weary, maybe even drunk, after a long night of celebrating. The plan, however, was naive and the execution amateurish. Castro was not yet much of a military commander, and his men were armed only with an assortment of ancient army carbines, an old machine gun, and small-caliber hunting rifles and shotguns. The inexperienced fighters got separated in the confusion of the assault, lost all element of surprise, and were thoroughly routed within a half hour. Fidel Castro and his twenty-one-year-old brother, Raúl, managed to escape and flee to the mountains nearby, but nearly half his force was either killed during the operation or captured and later executed.

The Moncada barracks were located not far from the center of Santiago, and the gunfire early that Sunday morning was heard across much of the downtown area. The sun was barely up, and many late-night partyers were still making their way home when the fighting erupted. A group of Bacardi people—employees and family members, including Jorge Bosch, the twenty-eight-year-old son of Pepín Bosch—had been out all night and then attended early morning Mass at a church on Plaza Dolores near the center of the city. As they were leaving the church, the group heard gunshots coming from the Moncada fort, barely half a mile away, and they jumped in a car to investigate. Nearing the military complex, they saw a car speed past, filled with men in uniform, heading toward the mountains. Castro's men had worn homemade army uniforms to disguise themselves, and Bosch and his friends later realized they had seen some of the *moncadistas* fleeing the city.

Word of the attack spread quickly. *Santiagueros* prided themselves on their revolutionary heritage, and ever since Batista's coup sixteen months earlier, there had been periodic talk in the city of a new armed insurrection against the government. As in Havana, the political stirrings were concentrated in the local university. One of the students who had taken part in demonstrations to protest the Batista coup was Vilma Espín, the twenty-two-year-old daughter of Bacardi executive José Espín. As a well-brought-up girl in a conservative, upper-class Cuban family, she had refrained from carnival partying on Saturday night and was sound asleep when the gunfire began at the Moncada, a few blocks from the Espíns' house. "We could hear and feel the shots clearly," she recalled in an interview years later, "and I immediately jumped out of bed and ran through the house yelling happily, 'They're attacking the Moncada! They're attacking the Moncada!'" José Espín, the French-speaking accountant who had served as Enrique Schueg's executive assistant and Bacardi labor negotiator, did not share his daughter's political leanings. He was alarmed by her enthusiasm over the Moncada assault and worried that she might even have been involved somehow. She was not, but she admitted later that she viewed an armed insurrection at the time "as some kind of romantic thing, like with the *mambises* [the nineteenth-century independence fighters], without knowing what it was."

Pepín Bosch and his wife, Enriqueta, lived on a hilltop outside the city overlooking Santiago Bay and only heard about the Moncada attack when friends started calling Sunday morning. There was a rumor that it was part of a larger organized revolt against the Batista regime directed by former president Carlos Prío, who was said to be coming to Santiago to take command. Bosch immediately got in his car and drove to the Santiago airport to await Prío's arrival.

Though opposed in principle to an armed insurrection against the government, he remained loyal to the president he had served as finance minister. "If this was something Prío was doing, that was another matter," Bosch later explained. "I could understand Prío. I knew him as a talented man and a good Cuban." Bosch waited at the airport for several hours before finally realizing that the report of Prío's involvement was incorrect. The notion had not been without reason. After going into exile in Miami following Batista's coup, Prío had repeatedly expressed support for a violent overthrow of the man who had deposed him, going so far as to secretly raise funds for weapons to be smuggled to Cuba. In June, he had signed an agreement in Montreal with other Cuban leaders, pledging to oppose Batista's regime and work for the creation of a new provisional government. Among the other signers was Carlos Hevia, the Bacardi brewery executive and Pepín Bosch friend who had been Prío's designated candidate in the aborted 1952 presidential election. The anti-Batista movement by 1953 was already broad and serious.

The Moncada operation, however, was entirely the brainchild of Fidel Castro, as Batista's police soon figured out. His brother Raúl was caught as he made his way on foot to his parents' farm. Three days later, Fidel himself was found hiding in a farmhouse and brought to the Santiago city jail. Unshaven, in the same dirty, short-sleeved white sports shirt and dark slacks he had worn for six days, Fidel was surly and defiant throughout his interrogation, boasting that the people of eastern Cuba would have supported an uprising if only it had gone according to plan.

• • •

Those who knew Fidel Castro personally were not surprised by the news of his ill-fated operation. Like most of Fidel's ideas, the plan was daring and audacious, and it put him squarely in command of the action, which was where he demanded to be if he was to be involved at all. For Juan Grau, a young chemical engineer working for Pepín Bosch at the Bacardi distillery, the Moncada story fit with everything he had associated with Castro since they were fellow students at the Jesuit-run Dolores school for boys in Santiago. Grau had befriended Castro at the school, and Fidel often stayed with "Juanito" and his family on weekends. After Dolores, both boys moved on to the elite Belén school in Havana. Grau knew Castro could be powerfully persuasive, even irresistible, and also that he was hugely reckless and egotistical.

One of Grau's most enduring recollections stemmed from an expedition he and Castro took in 1943 when they were both members of a Belén mountaineering club. Castro, who was seventeen years old at the time, told a school priest that he and a younger friend intended to ascend a 2,300-foot peak in western Cuba called Pan de Guajaibón. The priest worried that the expedition was too dangerous for the boys to undertake on their own, and he asked Juan Grau to go see his friend Fidel and talk him out of it. When they got together, however, Fidel did most of the talking, persuading Grau and another friend that they should come along on the trek.

The expedition was a near disaster. Fidel had not brought maps along, and the boys got lost on the mountainside as soon as they started out. After three days of hiking through the rugged range, they were still short of the summit. That night, they camped under the trees, preparing for their final climb the next day. They had consumed nearly all their supplies, save for a single can of condensed milk and some bread. In the middle of the night, Grau woke up and saw Fidel standing above him, guzzling the can of milk.

"Fidel, what the hell are you doing?" he said. "You can't drink the milk like that!"

"Yes I can."

"But Fidel," Grau said, "in the morning we can go to some farmer's house and get some coffee and put the milk in the coffee and make it last longer."

"I'm drinking it this way," Fidel said. When Grau continued to object, Fidel snarled at him, "You can eat shit." (*Es que tú eres un comemierda.*) Grau immediately jumped up out of his sleeping bag and charged after Fidel.

"Don't you call me a *comemierda* [shit eater]," he said, taking a swing at Fidel. The other two boys, awakened by the ruckus, got up and separated Grau and Fidel, and the fight was over. Two days later, the four boys arrived back at Belén. They were welcomed as heroes, but Grau never forgot what had happened on the mountainside. When he heard it was Fidel who was behind the Moncada attack, Grau told his wife it brought back memories of his mountain-climbing adventure. "Fidel is *loco*," he said, "just like always." But Grau said it with a grudging respect, seeing his old friend as a man with undeniable courage and leadership talent.

Castro also had superb political instincts, as he showed in the aftermath of the Moncada attack. He was responsible for an operation that resulted in the deaths of half of the young men who had entrusted their lives to him, and yet Castro found a way to turn the debacle to his favor and build a reputation on it. He was helped by the brutality of Batista's commander in Santiago, Colonel Alberto del Río Chaviano, whose men executed many of the rebels they captured. Del Río Chaviano invented false stories of rebel atrocities and had the murdered prisoners' bodies arranged so as to suggest they died in combat. When photographs emerged to show they had been killed in cold blood, the sympathy of many Cubans swung to the side of the *moncadistas*, and Castro was widely seen as a hero, especially among Cuban youth.

His trial was held in Santiago in September 1953, with Castro acting as his own attorney. Knowing he was certain to be convicted, he used his courtroom time to argue that Batista deserved to be overthrown. His lengthy oration was not recorded, but Castro later recalled his oral argument, quoting himself as saying, "I do not fear prison, as I do not fear the fury of the miserable tyrant who took the lives of my comrades. Condemn me. It does not matter. History will absolve me."*

After the Moncada attack and the bloody response by the police and army, the middle class in Santiago turned thoroughly against Batista. The city had always been associated with uprisings, and the Moncada attack fit squarely into that heroic tradition. One of the first rebels to be killed, Renato Guitart, was friends with Pepín Bosch's son Carlos. Guitart's father, who worked at the customs office in the harbor, was a man of only modest means but had many friends in the city, including Pepín Bosch. Though Bosch did not approve of the violent methods Castro advocated, he was horrified by the response of the local authorities and quietly arranged to cover funeral costs for several of the young men killed in the Moncada operation.

Castro was sentenced to fifteen years in prison and sent with his brother Raúl and other rebels to a penitentiary on the Isle of Pines, where they spent twenty-two months before being released under a general amnesty. In the meantime, the movement against the Batista regime gathered strength. In the months following Fidel Castro's trial and imprisonment, more anti-Batista conspiracies were planned. In December 1953, Carlos Prío was arrested in Florida on charges of having violated the U.S. Neutrality Act by sending arms and ammunition to Cuba. His main agent on the island was Aureliano Sánchez Arango, who had served him as education minister and later as foreign minister.

The Bacardi clan hated Batista and, like other Cuba liberals of the time, sympathized broadly with the efforts to overthrow his government. Pepín Bosch remained loyal to Prío and friendly with Aureliano Sánchez Arango, with whom he had served in the Prío cabinet. He was not yet convinced of the wisdom of armed insurrection, but he was willing to help in an emergency.

---

*Castro was apparently inspired by the words of Adolf Hitler, on trial for his role in the failed Beer Hall Putsch in Munich in 1923: "You may find us guilty a thousand times over, but the goddess of the eternal court of History will...tear to tatters...the sentence of this court. For she will acquit us." Thanks in part to the lengthy speeches Hitler made in his own defense, his popularity actually increased during the Munich trial. Castro carefully studied Hitler's life and may have been seeking to replicate his courtroom success.

On one occasion, when Sánchez Arango needed to get off the island in a hurry, Bosch paid the expenses. Such activities could be dangerous. After almost every sabotage action, Batista's police rounded up suspects, and being known as a prominent Prío supporter was enough to get one detained.

To the extent Bacardi family members wondered about their own vulnerability, they learned a terrifying lesson one day in February 1954. Daniel Bacardi's chauffeur, Guillermo Rodríguez, picked up Daniel's eight-year-old son Facundito that morning to take him to school. About an hour later, Rodríguez returned, telling Daniel's wife Graciela that someone had stopped his car, forced him at knifepoint to drive to a site out of town, and then abducted Facundito. In fact, Rodríguez himself had taken Facundito to a spot on the main highway outside Santiago and left him with an accomplice named Manuel Echevarría. Upon hearing the chauffeur's terrifying story, Graciela sent him to the Bacardi distillery to find Daniel, who told Rodríguez to go with him to the Moncada barracks so they could report the kidnapping to the army command. When Rodríguez protested vigorously that the move would jeopardize Facundito's safety, Daniel grew suspicious and asked the police to question Rodríguez himself.

Before long, the news of the kidnapping had spread throughout Santiago. A huge crowd of sympathizers gathered around the Bacardi home in the fashionable Vista Alegre suburb, and hundreds of volunteers, some of them armed, headed to the countryside, determined to track down the kidnappers. More people gathered around the Moncada. Pepín Bosch made arrangements to pay the ransom, but he also called the U.S. consul in Santiago, who contacted the commander of the U.S. naval base at Guantánamo Bay to request a helicopter, which was shortly provided. The Bacardi family definitely had clout. Helicopters were a rare sight in the Cuban countryside in those years, and the noisy approach of the navy aircraft alarmed Echevarría, the accomplice. Emerging from under a bridge where he had been hiding, Echevarría grabbed Facundito and started walking hurriedly down the highway. The two were quickly spotted by a Cuban army patrol.

Facundito was returned to his parents unharmed, but the story was not over. When the soldiers showed up at the Moncada with Echevarría in custody, a crowd of angry townspeople attacked him. Only the intervention of the soldiers saved him from being lynched on the spot. The Bacardi chauffeur, already in custody, was not so fortunate. Colonel del Río Chaviano, the army commander responsible for the execution of the *moncadista* prisoners just a few months earlier, promptly reported that Rodríguez had been shot "while trying to escape." Bacardi family members learned later that he had been tortured and killed while in police custody. The relief they felt at the return of Facundito and their appreciation for the outpouring of sympathy from their fellow *santi-agueros* were tempered by their disgust with the conduct of the police command and by the reminder that Cuba had become a violent and dangerous country.

• • •

On the Isle of Pines, Fidel Castro used his prison time to read history, write letters to friends and allies, and plan the national insurrection he had long envisioned. One of his major projects was to reconstruct the oration he had delivered extemporaneously during his trial in Santiago, an elaborated version of which he wrote as an essay titled "History Will Absolve Me." Though it had limited circulation at first, the tract was read widely in the coming years and taken as the definitive statement of Castro's program.

No document better illustrates the brilliance of his political thinking. On the one hand, he was careful to remain within the ideological parameters of conventional left-wing Latin populism. The movement Castro saw himself representing encompassed anybody with a grievance, including "Cubans without work...farm laborers who live in miserable shacks...industrial workers and laborers whose retirement funds have been embezzled...small farmers who live and die working land that is not theirs...teachers and professors who are so badly treated...small businessmen weighed down by debts...[and] young professional people who finish school anxious to work and full of hope, only to find themselves at a dead end." Castro's perspective, moreover, was reformist rather than revolutionary. He said he was committed to the restoration of Cuba's 1940 Constitution and wanted to see his country return to the time when Cuba had a president, a Congress, and courts, when there were political parties, public debates, and free elections.

On the other hand, no Cuban who read "La historia me absolverá" could have doubted that Castro stood for sweeping social and political change. Under the program he proposed, agricultural land would have been transferred to the tenant farmers who worked it, and workers in industrial enterprises would have been given the right to share in 30 percent of their firms' profits. It was as if Castro was determined to lay out the most radical political program conceivable that could still attract popular support. In that regard, he was largely successful. Among those who ultimately endorsed Castro's progressive analysis and vision for Cuba, at least in principle, were the Bacardis.

By the time he was released from prison under a general amnesty in May 1955, Castro was seen as a noble and charismatic figure, and he reentered public life in dramatic fashion. A crowd gathered on the docks to await the boat that ferried him and his fellow *moncadista* prisoners from the Isle of Pines, and, as always, Fidel rose to the occasion.

"Do you plan to stay in Cuba?" a reporter asked, as Castro stepped off the boat, dressed in a baggy, double-breasted suit with an open-collared white shirt.

"Yes, I plan to stay in Cuba and fight the government in the open," Castro answered, "pointing out its mistakes, denouncing its faults, exposing gangsters, profiteers, and thieves." He had grown a mustache in prison, but his appearance was otherwise unchanged by nearly two years behind bars. He had been kept in a good-sized private cell, with his own toilet facilities and a hot plate on which he could cook.

"Will you remain in the Orthodox Party?"

"We will struggle to unite the whole country under the flag of Chibás's revolutionary movement."

"Would you accept a solution through elections?"

"We are for a democratic solution. The only party here opposed to peaceful solutions is the regime. The only way out of the Cuban situation, as far as I can see, is immediate general elections."

By his own later admission, however, Castro was moderating his public positions in order to broaden his appeal and disguise his more extreme intentions. In 1965 he told a visitor that when he filed to run as a parliamentary candidate in the 1952 elections, it was with the intent of "using the parliament as a point of departure from which I might establish a revolutionary platform and motivate the masses in its favor.... Already then I believed I had to do it in a revolutionary way." From the time he began organizing his followers politically, there is no sign that Castro ever considered himself accountable to anyone but himself. Behind the indisputable brilliance of his strategic analysis were early signs of the narcissism and megalomania that would later characterize his rule. While still in prison, Castro ordered one of his collaborators, Melba Hernández, to organize a rally in support of him and the other imprisoned rebels. His written instructions to her were chilling for what they foreshadowed: "Show much guile and smiles to everyone. We will have time later on to trample underfoot all the cockroaches."

Castro's declaration upon leaving prison that he would pursue "a democratic solution" proved hollow. Within days of his release from prison, he was telling his followers that he intended to build a new revolutionary organization called the Movimiento 26 de Julio, the M-26-7, in commemoration of the Moncada attack on that day. It would take time, however, and he figured it would be unsafe to do it in Cuba. In July 1955, Castro left for Mexico, just two months after promising to stay on the island and work "in the open."

Chapter 13

꧁꧂

A Brief Golden Age

After a day of writing and maybe some fishing, Ernest "Papa" Hemingway liked to stop in Old Havana for a few drinks at his favorite bar, El Floridita, on Calle Montserrat. The saloon had a feeling of worn but cozy grandeur, with a magnificent mahogany bar and red velvet curtains, a place where the food was cheap but good and the drinking was serious. Hemingway always went directly to a stool on the far left side of the bar, in what the regulars called "Papa's corner." Hemingway brought the Floridita a certain fame as a bar where visitors might see or even have a drink with the celebrity writer, who on most days was gracious to those who came up to shake his hand.

Hemingway had seen and written about war up close, and his fondness for bullfighting, big game hunting, and beautiful women enhanced his reputation as a hairy-chested adventurer. At the Floridita, he always drank daiquiris, a cocktail often chosen by women, though he favored a double-rum version. In Hemingway's heyday, Constantino "Constante" Ribalaigua was still presiding over El Floridita, as he had been in the 1920s when the British writer Basil Woon was impressed by his cocktail talents. Constante's special "Papa Doble" daiquiri was so dear to Hemingway's heart that it made an appearance in his novel *Islands in the Stream:* "He had drunk double frozen daiquiris, the great ones that Constante made, that had no taste of alcohol and felt, as you drank them, the way downhill glacier skiing feels running through powder snow...."

Arguably, Hemingway did more than anyone else to popularize the daiquiri, and by so doing he also promoted Bacardi rum. Much of Hemingway's writing was inspired by his years living and drinking in Cuba, and in his novels he mentioned Bacardi products by name. In August 1956, about a year and a half after Hemingway won the Nobel Prize in Literature, the Bacardi Rum Company hosted a reception for him and his wife, Mary, at its Hatuey brewery, not far from the Hemingways' home. He had been offered parties at exclusive private clubs, but he agreed only to the event at the brewery, because he knew

168

he could bring his fisherman friends, even if they came barefoot and in shorts—as they did.

The event was held in the brewery garden, with abundant supplies of Bacardi rum and ice-cold Hatuey beer, served with roast suckling pig, tamales, boiled yucca, fried bananas, and rice with red beans. A wooden stage was erected at one end of the garden, with a banner across the back reading, "Bacardi Rum Welcomes the Author of *The Old Man and the Sea*," which was Hemingway's most recently published novel. The master of ceremonies was Fernando Campoamor, a famous Havana journalist who specialized in coverage of the social scene and was one of Hemingway's regular drinking buddies. The guest of honor seemed a bit uncomfortable under the crush of attention. "I am gratified and moved by this undeserved honor," he said, speaking in heavily accented but fluent Spanish. Hemingway had brought along the Nobel gold medal, and he held it in his hands. A year earlier, he had said the prize belonged to Cuba, because his work was created there. "I have always been of the belief that writers should write and not speak," Hemingway said, looking at Campoamor. "I am donating this Nobel Prize medal to the Virgin of Charity [*Nuestra Señora de la Caridad del Cobre*], the patron saint of this country I love so much." And then he handed the medal to Campoamor. The Virgin of Charity represents the spiritual soul of Cuba, and no act could have endeared Hemingway more to the Cuban people. "Cuba loves you like a mother loves her son," Campoamor said. The medal was taken to the shrine of the Virgin of Charity in Cobre, the small mining town outside Santiago, where it would remain.

· · ·

It was the summer of 1956, and Cuba was in a magical era, or so it seemed. With Hemingway as one of the attractions, Havana was a compulsory stop for jet-setters and movie stars. At the Finca Vigía (or sometimes at El Floridita), Hemingway and his wife entertained Marlene Dietrich, Jean-Paul Sartre, the Duke and Duchess of Windsor, Gary Cooper, Spencer Tracy, Errol Flynn, Barbara Stanwyck, and Ava Gardner. Havana nightclubs in those days were featuring the best American and foreign entertainers, with Nat King Cole at the Tropicana, Tony Bennett at the Sans Souci, Maurice Chevalier at the Montmartre, and Frank Sinatra at the Hotel Nacional. Jazz musicians like Cab Calloway, Woody Herman, Tommy Dorsey, Sarah Vaughan, and Benny Goodman appeared regularly at hotel bars and clubs. For a rum company like Bacardi, Cuba in the mid-1950s appeared to be an ideal place and time to be doing business.

Cubans themselves, however, were growing increasingly uncomfortable in their country. The good times came at a cost. Havana nightclub owners could afford to hire classy entertainment only because they were making so much money in their casinos. Havana had become the Las Vegas of the Caribbean, and the high living depended, in the end, on gambling profits. It was actually worse than Las Vegas, in fact, because the country was in the hands of a profoundly corrupt dictator, Fulgencio Batista, who had essentially sold Cuba to the American Mafia. Batista put Meyer Lansky on salary as his "gambling adviser," even though Lansky had been identified as one of the six top gangsters in the United States. At Lansky's urging, Batista had changed the gambling laws in 1955 to allow the sale of a gaming license to anyone investing a million dollars in a new hotel, no questions asked. Lansky had the high-end Montmartre casino, and he was building the new Riviera Hotel. His brother Jake ran the casino at the Hotel Nacional. Gambling at the Sans Souci was overseen by Santo Trafficante Jr., the Tampa-based mobster. Most of the financial arrangements surrounding the gambling activities in Havana were under the table; the official price for a gaming license was twenty-five thousand dollars, but the secret payoff to Batista and his friends could be ten times that amount. The casino owners also had to be sure the construction contracts went to Batista's friends and relatives. The police responsible for overseeing the casinos had to be paid, as did the government bureaucrats and legislators who made sure the rules got bent when necessary. The rule of law had become virtually meaningless; protection could be purchased.

Along with gambling came more marijuana and opium bars, heroin trafficking, brothels, and pornography. The Shanghai Theater in the Chinatown section of Old Havana featured live sex shows that outdid even the most sordid X-rated clubs in the United States. Many of the women who found work there came from towns and villages in the Cuban countryside, which remained largely untouched by the wealth on display in Havana. Cuba had become a nation of stunning contrasts: 87 percent of urban housing units had electricity, but only 9 percent of rural homes; only 15 percent of the rural population had running water, as opposed to 80 percent of city residents. While the country as a whole still had the fourth-highest literacy rate in Latin America, nearly half the people in the countryside could not read or write. Poverty and unemployment in the rural areas drove desperate residents to Havana and contributed to the growing crime and prostitution in the capital.

Ordinary Cubans were disgusted by all the crooked politicians and their mobster allies and yearned for a government of which they could once again be proud. Some Cubans took heart in an effort by an esteemed independence war veteran, Cosme de la Torriente, to unite the opposition behind a demand that Batista hold free elections. Fidel Castro refused to support the initiative, however, and from exile in Mexico he issued a declaration denouncing the "cowardice" of those who were willing to negotiate with Batista, including his former Orthodox Party colleagues. Castro's own M-26-7 organization, however, was by then just one segment of the anti-Batista movement. University student groups were in the forefront, and they were repeatedly targeted by Batista's brutal police, both in Havana and in Santiago.

Among the *santiagueros* rallying behind the anti-Batista struggle was Vilma Espín, the daughter of Bacardi executive José Espín, the former labor negotiator and assistant to Enrique Schueg. Very smart and very pretty, with delicate features, dark eyes, and a lissome figure, Vilma was a well-bred, upper-class Santiago girl with a rebellious streak, as had been seen when she jumped for joy over the Moncada assault. At the University of the Oriente in Santiago, she had majored in chemical engineering, one of the first women to do so. One of her instructors was the young Bacardi engineer Juan Grau, Fidel Castro's old friend, by then working at the Bacardi distillery as well as teaching part time. The two knew each other already—Grau's father associated with Vilma's father—and they became good friends at the university. After failing to persuade her to come work with him at Bacardi, Grau urged Vilma to continue her engineering studies at the Massachusetts Institute of Technology, where he had gone to school, and he even called the director of admissions and secured her acceptance.

José Espín also pressed his daughter to go to MIT. Still, she resisted. After her university graduation in 1954, she took a job in a laboratory at a sugar refinery near Santiago but continued to get together with friends and former students who shared her political interests. One day a colleague slipped her a copy of Fidel Castro's "History Will Absolve Me" while she was working on a lab analysis. "I couldn't put it down," she recalled in a 1985 interview with Castro biographer Tad Szulc. She immediately threw herself into clandestine work in Santiago in association with one of her old chemistry professors, a Spanish Communist.

Her father was displeased by her increasingly radical views. "He started insisting all the more that I go to MIT," Vilma said. "He knew what I was getting involved in, and he wanted me out of there." José Espín, after all, was an executive at a big capitalist firm, and he had spent much of his professional life at Bacardi battling leftist labor leaders. Finally, in late 1955, she gave in to her father's urging and headed to Boston for graduate studies.

She lasted only a few months. Having marched in demonstrations and participated in secret revolutionary activities back in Cuba, Vilma felt totally out of place among her apathetic MIT classmates and decided to end her studies and return. On the way home, she stopped in Mexico, having arranged through friends to meet Fidel Castro and his brother Raúl. The two met her at the Mexico City airport, and she spent three days with them, heading back to Cuba with a bundle of letters from Fidel to his followers.

Vilma returned to Santiago ready to be a revolutionary. While most colleagues in her old Bacardi world shared her antipathy for the Batista regime, some were a bit uncomfortable with her militancy and self-righteousness. Juan Grau noticed that she had developed a new hostility toward the United States during her stay in Massachusetts. "She had been somewhat anti-American before she left," Grau said, "probably under the influence of that professor from Spain. I had thought going to MIT would change her attitude, but it seemed to make it worse."

In fact, resentment of the United States seemed to be growing in Cuba, in tandem with the broadening anti-Batista sentiment. A U.S. proposal to dig a canal across the island so as to facilitate trade with South America outraged Cubans of all political persuasions. Some Cubans even blamed Americans for the increased crime and vice in their country. They pointed out that Americans introduced racetrack betting to Cuba and opened the first casinos, ran the best-known bars, patronized the brothels and sex shows, and were generally the biggest drunkards.

Cubans active in the movement against Batista also resented the way that the United States was propping him up. The U.S. government had recognized Batista as Cuba's president just seventeen days after he took power in 1952 through unconstitutional means. In contrast, the United States never recognized Ramón Grau San Martín's 1933 government, though he was freely elected and held office for four months. Whereas Grau had been seen as unfriendly to U.S. business and security interests, Batista catered to Washington. With U.S. funding, he created a special intelligence unit called the Bureau for the Repression of Communist Activities. Vice President Richard Nixon came to Havana to toast the Batista regime's "competence and stability" at a black-tie reception in February 1955, and CIA director Allen Dulles came a short time later. The U.S. ambassador to Cuba at the time, Arthur Gardner, was so friendly to Batista that it embarrassed the dictator, who knew the issue of U.S. interference in Cuban affairs was a sensitive one. "I'm glad Ambassador Gardner approves of my government," Batista once said, "but I wish he wouldn't talk about it so much."

The Bacardis' interwoven political views, business interests, and cultural heritage meant their relationship with the United States in the 1950s was a bit complicated. Because of their deep French and Spanish roots, some Bacardis felt closer to Europe than to North America. But many Bacardi sons and daughters were sent to the United States for schooling, and some settled there. More Bacardi rum was sold in the United States than anywhere else, and the company had an important subsidiary—Bacardi Imports—headquartered there. Most of the Bacardis were Cuban nationalists, however, and by the middle to late 1950s, family members sometimes found that they and their U.S. friends were on opposite sides politically. When the CIA and the FBI helped Fulgencio Batista track his domestic opponents, the Bacardis may have been among those monitored. While the U.S. government shipped arms, ammunition, airplanes, and artillery to Batista's military forces, some of the Bacardis were funneling cash to Batista's rebel enemies. In Cuba the Bacardis advocated generous social welfare policies, agrarian reform, and trade union rights; in the United States such positions could have marked them as left-wingers.

In truth, the Bacardis stood in the center of the political spectrum in Cuba, but they represented something in short supply: enlightened business leadership. The Bacardi directors saw a social and political role for private enterprises in Cuba, and they were able to articulate it better than any other Cuban firm. One such statement came in a newspaper ad the company took out in February 1954, on the occasion of its ninety-second anniversary. Under the words "With a Head Held High," the ad showed a smiling young Cuban man making a toast, with pictures of Bacardi workers and factory installations and the following commentary:

> In the early days of our company, when Cuba was crying out for a valiant contribution from her sons, the managers and workers of this very Cuban company answered, Here we are! Later, when the young Republic needed an economic push from its domestic industries, the Bacardi Rum Company cooperated enthusiastically, creating jobs that sustained hundreds and hundreds of Cuban families.
>
> Today, upon celebrating 92 years of unending labor and thanks to the Cuban people's demand for our products, the Bacardi Rum Company has become one of the biggest industrial enterprises in the world, able through its tax payments to contribute to the funds needed to plan, construct, and educate the nation.

The Bacardi Rum Company also believes it has contributed to the glorification of its homeland on the international scene. Because of its unsurpassed quality, Bacardi has established itself around the world, becoming a prestigious ambassador. It is with genuine pride that we hear the name of our country joined with that of our company on the lips of men in all languages and latitudes. The natural product of our sugarcane and our climate has become the chosen drink of all continents!

For all these reasons, we stand today before the Cuban people with our head held high.

Bacardi. Healthful, Delicious, and Cuban.

The ad made no reference to the current Cuban government, to Batista, or to those who opposed him. The message was simple, expressed in the platitudinous language of the 1950s. Nevertheless, it reflected a coherent idea: that a private firm plays a useful and even patriotic role in a nation by providing employment and economic stimulus and by identifying with its homeland and the national cause. A healthy state needs a strong economic foundation, and that foundation is built in part through successful private enterprise. This core tenet of liberal democratic capitalism was buttressed in the Bacardi case by the company's civic record. Whether it was the legacy of Emilio Bacardi or the result of being entirely owned by a single Cuban family, the Bacardi Rum Company had earned the right to say it contributed to the national good simply by being a responsible and well-managed private business.

Cuba's misfortune was that there were not more successful companies. A World Bank team that visited the island in 1950 concluded that too many private employers were "static" or "defensive" in their business approach, seeking immediate profits rather than investing for the long term. Bacardi was an exception. Under the leadership of Enrique Schueg and Pepín Bosch, the company had aggressively developed export markets and plowed profits into new ventures. The move into beer production had been especially foresighted. The Hatuey breweries in Santiago and Havana provided a steady flow of cash and made possible the financing of further expansion at a time when the capital market in Cuba was thin at best.

In part, the company was motivated by the need to stay ahead of its Cuban competitors. Rum production in general was a bright spot in the Cuban economy. Don Facundo and his successors had not been the only businessmen to recognize the good sense of building an enterprise around a raw material Cuba possessed in abundance, molasses, adding value through the application of technology and skilled labor. While the World Bank team had harsh criticism

Santiago de Cuba in the nineteenth century, when goods were transported to and from the harbor by mule train.

Emilio Bacardi at about the age of thirty, a time when he was deeply involved in revolutionary activity in Santiago.

The tin-roofed Bacardi rum distillery on Matadero Street in Santiago. The palm tree in the front yard was planted by Facundo Bacardi Jr. shortly after the distillery was opened in 1862.

Don Facundo Bacardi, the family patriarch, standing in the rear, with his son Facundo Jr. on his left and his wife, Amalia Moreau, and their daughter Amalia on his right, alongside Georgina, the family servant. Emilio Bacardi and his wife, María Lay, are seated with five of their six children, in early 1885.

Antonio Maceo, the "Bronze Titan,"
commander of Cuban rebel fighters
during two independence struggles.

José Martí, the apostle of Cuban
independence, in Jamaica, 1892.

The Agramonte Regiment of the Cuban rebel army, during the second independence war.

Officers of the Cuban rebel army, a racially diverse force.

Colonel Emilio "Emilito" Bacardi
as a young rebel army officer.

Teddy Roosevelt and his Rough Riders atop San Juan Heights, Santiago, July 1898.

Emilio Bacardi as mayor of Santiago, at work in his city hall office.

Gen. Leonard Wood and Emilio Bacardi, reviewing street cleaning operations in Santiago. Wood is seated on the left. Emilio is in the white straw boater hat.

Santiago, before and after Leonard Wood's cleanup and reconstruction campaign.

Leonard Wood, the U.S. military governor of Santiago and later all Cuba. Mayor Emilio Bacardi respected Wood's practical achievements, but like other Cuban nationalists he was dismayed by Wood's efforts to thwart Cuban independence.

Emilio Bacardi Moreau—rum company president, mayor, senator, author.

Elvira Cape, Emilio Bacardi's second wife and fellow revolutionary conspirator.

Emilio, Elvira, and their daughter Amalia playing chess.

Emilio and Elvira on a trip to Egypt, 1912. They purchased a mummy while in Egypt and sent it back to Santiago for display at the Bacardi Museum.

Mimín Bacardi Cape, with her bust of José Martí, one of many sculptures she made.

Emilio Bacardi and Elvira Cape, with their children (with spouses) and grandchildren at Villa Elvira.

Facundo Bacardi Moreau (Facundo Jr.) on a trip to Europe. He was the first master rum blender in the Bacardi firm, having learned the art of rum making at his father's side.

Emilio (holding his hat) at the inauguration of a new Bacardi distillery, 1922. At right is Enriqueta Schueg, daughter of Amalia Bacardi Moreau and Enrique Schueg. It would be one of Emilio's final public appearances.

Three Cuban gentlemen: left to right, José "Pepe" Bacardi, Facundo "Facundito" Bacardi Gaillard, and Pedro Lay. Pepe Bacardi was sent to Mexico to oversee the Bacardi expansion there. Facundito Bacardi was generous with his money and made friends across Cuba. Pedro married one of Emilio Bacardi's daughters and rose to a senior management position in the company.

A group of Bacardi employees and sales agents in the 1920s. The sign in the background features the slogan "The One That Has Made Cuba Famous" alongside the Bacardi bat. The bottle of Bacardi rum on the map of Cuba sits at the location of Santiago, the Bacardi hometown, on the island's eastern end.

An ad for Bacardi during Prohibition days, when tourists were encouraged to fly from the "dry" United States to "wet" Cuba, where Bacardi rum would be available in abundance.

Advertising aimed at U.S. tourists in the 1920s and 1930s promoted the Bacardi association with Cuba, a favored vacation destination.

for the management of most Cuban industries, the island's rum companies were a notable exception. "After detailed investigation," the team reported, "the Mission is happy to report that it can suggest no improvement in production of Cuban rum."

The domestic market in Cuba was split between *rones superiores*, premium rums, and *rones corrientes*, or common rums, which were cheap and produced for mass consumption. There were dozens of brands in the *corriente* category, but the Bacardi directors worried mainly about their premium competitors. Two were serious rivals: Matusalem, made in Santiago by the Álvarez Camp company, and Havana Club, made in Cárdenas by the Arechabala company. Matusalem, named for the Old Testament patriarch Methuselah, specialized in aged rums, with its top product a fifteen-year-old sipping rum. Havana Club, like Bacardi, produced lighter rums. The companies tried to keep their operations, and especially their best wholesale prices, secret from each other. When a Bacardi executive got hold of a Havana Club invoice that showed the Arechabala company was beating Bacardi prices, he complained to his Bacardi colleagues that the Arechabalas were "discrediting" their own rum brands by pricing them too low. For its part, Matusalem was found to be undercutting Bacardi prices at the bars on the U.S. naval base at Guantánamo. When Bosch heard of the Matusalem discount, he arranged to have Bacardi rum sold on the base by the barrel. "With a little good fortune, we'll soon have that competitor eliminated," Bosch assured the sales agent who had alerted him to the problem.

He was one tough businessman. "Pepín Bosch never misses an opportunity to strike a blow against a competitor, be it a high one or a low one," observed the weekly Havana magazine *Gente* in May 1956. His calculating and occasionally ruthless style made Bosch stand out among Cuban businessmen, most of whom fit a more easygoing Latin style that emphasized personal relations and friendships over strategic maneuvering. The traditional way of doing business in Cuba, criticized as old-fashioned by the World Bank experts, involved much backroom dealing and favor trading, habits that Pepín Bosch disdained. Indeed, he operated at the other extreme, discouraging friends and family members from expecting automatic Bacardi employment.

There were few Cuban businessmen in his day who were less Cuban in personality and style. In Havana, Bosch was almost always dressed in a dark suit. He was slightly more relaxed in his native Santiago and usually wore white linen there, though not without a bow tie. Unlike Daniel Bacardi, Bosch did not frequent the bars and clubs in Santiago and seemed uncomfortable with back slapping and banter. He may have thought it put him at a disadvantage as a rum merchant, however, because one day he asked Daniel and José Argamasilla, the Bacardi public relations chief, to take him out.

"You know everybody in town," Bosch said. "Show me around." In Daniel and Argamasilla, after all, he had the perfect guides. The two men were at home in virtually every Santiago establishment, from the classiest to those known for cheap drinks and loose women. They kept Bosch entertained and drinking for hours and did not send him home until about four o'clock the next morning, by which time he was quite drunk. The outing was so unusual that Daniel and Argamasilla could not imagine what Bosch would say the next time they saw him. Knowing how serious he was about his Bacardi business, they figured that Bosch would show up for work as usual when the Bacardi offices opened at 7 A.M. and that they should be there when he arrived.

The layout of the Bacardi office area was open, with no cubicles or walls separating one desk from another. Bosch's desk was on the main floor, in a central location so he could keep an eye on almost everyone in the company. Daniel sat nearby. José Argamasilla was on the mezzanine level, overlooking the open area below. On the morning following their Santiago bar adventure, Daniel and José arrived at opening time and went straight to their desks, waiting nervously for Bosch to come through the door. To their surprise, he had not shown up by 8 A.M. After nine o'clock, they began to wonder if he was all right. Finally, about 10 A.M., Bosch came in, heading straight to his desk without a word to anyone. After a few minutes, he wrote something on a piece of paper and motioned to his secretary, saying, "Take this to Daniel." The note said, "*¡Tú me jodiste, cabrón!*" (You fucked me up, you bastard!)

The story of his one outing with Daniel Bacardi and José Argamasilla became legendary within the family, precisely because it was so out of character for Bosch. If anything, the baby-faced man was seen as a bit prudish. He was devoted to his wife, Enriqueta Schueg, to his fishing boat, and to his car, a yellow Buick convertible with red leather seats. His quiet but precise management style allowed him to get the most out of the people who worked for him, though sometimes only by scaring the wits out of them. A superb judge of talent, he often identified promising young employees in the company and then gave them assignments that other managers (and often the employees themselves) would have considered beyond their expertise. The employees would be thrilled that Bosch had the confidence in their abilities to trust them with such a large responsibility, but they were also unnerved by the realization that if they failed to meet his expectations, they would probably not get another chance. He was continually testing his subordinates to see how they measured up. Shortly after he went to work for Bacardi in 1950 as a chemical engineer, Juan Grau got a call from Bosch, who was then in Havana serving as finance minister under Carlos Prío. Bosch had authorized Grau's hiring but had not spoken to him since he joined the company.

"Juan, could you come see me here in Havana?" Bosch asked, in his soft little voice that sounded even squeakier over the long distance phone line.

"Of course, Mr. Bosch," Grau quickly answered. "Should I bring anything?"

"No," Bosch said, "just meet me at the side entrance to the Finance Ministry tomorrow at 7 A.M." Grau immediately booked a flight for the six-hundred-mile trip to the other end of the island. He was at the Ministry door the next morning when Bosch pulled up in his chauffeured car, and Bosch led him upstairs to his office. Grau, who was just twenty-three years old at the time, was trembling with fear. Bosch was not only the Bacardi boss; he was Cuba's minister of finance. What could he possibly want with a lowly chemical engineer?

When Bosch was settled behind his desk, he turned to Grau with his famous twinkling smile and piercing eyes. "Juan, what are nitrites in the water?"

Grau figured the question was just a way for Bosch to start a conversation. "You know, Mr. Bosch, nitrites are..." He found himself stammering. "They come from the deterioration of organic matter. They indicate contamination in the water."

"OK, Juan," Bosch said. "Thank you very much." He smiled at Grau but said nothing else. The young man sat there, frozen, not knowing what else to say or do and without a clue what was coming next. In fact, the session was over. "You can go now," Bosch said finally. It had been a test, no more. Had Grau not been able to tell Bosch what nitrites were, he could well have been out of a job.

The anxiety Grau experienced when he faced Bosch as a young engineer never quite disappeared. In Bosch's view, employees should be prepared to do their job, whatever the assignment, without asking questions or making excuses. He usually left his employees alone once he gave them an assignment, but even so, he earned only the grudging respect of his subordinates, without much affection for him personally. He was an authoritarian corporate leader who did not tolerate anyone second-guessing his decisions, and he sometimes offended experienced Bacardi managers who had confidence in their own judgment. "I felt it my whole life," Grau said, decades later. "He would say, 'Would you like to be the manager of this thing?' But with that very same little voice he could just as easily say, 'You know, I don't think you can work for this company any more.' And those eyes, they would look straight through you."

As an employer, Pepín Bosch was despised by some Bacardi workers, admired by others. He made regular rounds of the Bacardi facilities, taking careful note of jobs well done but also scolding anyone whose performance did not meet his standards. Whether such evaluations mattered for much was debatable; there was little job turnover in the Bacardi company. Union contracts and labor law made it difficult to fire a worker for any but the most egregious offense, and relatively few workers left the company on their own, so advancement opportunities were limited. A position at Bacardi—whether in the distillery, the rum factory, the Hatuey brewery, or the administrative offices—was seen in Santiago as providing better-than-average wages and benefits and good job security. Once young Santiago men or women got a foot in the door at the Bacardi Rum Company, they generally stayed and often did all they could to get family members hired there as well.

Pepín Hernández, for example, went to work for the Bacardis in 1954 at the age of nineteen, following in the steps of his father, a foreman in the Hatuey beer-bottling facility. The job was only a temporary position, but his father was determined that Pepín get off to a good start with the company. "He was a big believer in the Bacardis," Hernández recalled in a 2002 interview in Santiago. Hernández was by then serving as director of the Museum of Rum after working forty years in the Cuban rum industry, first for the Bacardi company and then for its socialist successors. He recalled that Joaquín Bacardi, the Harvard-educated master brewer at Hatuey, befriended his father, taking him fishing on his yacht, and Bosch himself on more than one occasion told the elder Hernández how highly he regarded his job performance. "My father said that when Bosch believed in someone, he always gave him the opportunity to develop himself," the son recalled.

That was also the experience of Raimundo Cobo, who worked at the Bacardi company for nearly twenty years when it was still under family ownership. Cobo had been a part-time worker in the company foundry until Pepín Bosch came by the metal shop one day and asked him to make a bronze cast. Bosch returned a few days later and was so pleased by Cobo's work that he immediately secured a full-time position for him. Interviewed in Santiago at the age of eighty-six, long since retired, Cobo recalled Pepín Bosch as *afectuoso y respetuoso,* a friendly and respectful employer. He worked for the Bacardis in an era when personal attention and two free cases of beer and a bottle of rum *añejo* at Christmastime helped ensure employee loyalty, before socialism made workers suspicious about bosses' intentions.

For Pepín Hernández, a gentle and scholarly man who made the study of

Bacardi history his avocation, fishing trips and Christmas gift packages were evidence of an attitude of "paternalism" on the Bacardis' part toward their workers. Hernández readily acknowledged that the company paid well and respected worker rights, but he also insisted that the Bacardi executives in the end were, like other capitalists, mainly interested in "money and commerce." Like other Bacardi employees, he recalled the "cold and steely" side of Pepín Bosch and the autocratic ways that did not always go over well with workers who were confident enough in their character and position to demand that they be treated with dignity.

One such worker was a tall black man named Pablo Rivas Betancourt, employed at the rum company as a distiller. Pepín Hernández, who worked at his side as a young man, remembered Rivas as "a gentleman with nineteenth-century manners" who put a high premium on honor and chivalry and did not hesitate to challenge another man to a duel if he felt his courage and character were questioned. A cultured man, he read poetry and carried himself with elegance. "At the distillery he was just Pablo," Hernández said, "coming to work in scruffy pants, a T-shirt, and a baseball hat. But around town, he was Don Pablo Rivas Betancourt, dressed in a panama hat, a fine linen guayabera, and perfectly pressed cotton drill trousers." Hernández recalled one night at the Bacardi distillery when he was in his early twenties, working as a watchman, and Rivas was the distiller on duty. Pepín Bosch unexpectedly showed up that night for one of his surprise inspections. At their stations on the second floor, Hernández and other Bacardi workers could always tell when it was Bosch who was coming to see them, because after his 1946 boating accident he walked with a limp, and dragging himself up the distillery stairs was a slow and arduous task.

Hearing Bosch approach, Hernández rapped a key on one of the distillery columns, the signal to alert his colleagues that the boss was coming. Most of the workers scrambled to look busy, but Rivas, sitting on a stool with his back against the distilling tank, did not move a muscle. When he saw Rivas, Bosch came over to him and in a slightly sarcastic tone of voice said, "Be careful you don't fall asleep."

Rivas did not appreciate the comment. He raised the brim of his hat and stared hard back at Bosch. "So, that's the 'Good evening' you have," he said, "for a worker who's doing a hard night shift for you, so you can get rich?" Without answering, Bosch turned and walked away as briskly as he could. On his way to the stairs, he asked another distillery worker, "What's his name, the guy in the hat?" Before his colleague could respond, Rivas answered Bosch himself, loudly, making sure the boss heard him. "Pablo Rivas Betancourt!"

The encounter made a lasting impression on Hernández and the other workers who witnessed it, though it said at least as much about one proud distillery worker and his insistence on being treated respectfully as it did about Pepín Bosch and his imperial manner; there were no repercussions. For the most part, surviving Bacardi workers in Santiago remember the family and its company fondly. The working atmosphere was fairly relaxed, and Bacardi employees earned fringe benefits that other Cuban employers did not offer. The company took out life insurance policies for its workers, for example, and Pepín Hernández recalled that when his father died young, it was the payout from the Bacardi policy that allowed his mother to keep the house where they had been living. In the fall of 1954, Bosch offered Bacardi workers an opportunity to buy shares in a new mining company he was creating, Minera Occidental Bosch, S.A., that was to dig for copper in an area of western Cuba. The company failed, and Bosch's major investors lost their money, but Bosch personally reimbursed each Bacardi worker for the amount of his or her loss, out of his own pocket.

Bosch could be a tyrant, but he always valued good labor relations and took pride in the fact that the company was never again crippled by a strike after he took charge. Guillermo Mármol, whose legal work for Bacardi focused on collective bargaining issues, recalled a brewery administrator in Havana who once settled a labor dispute at the plant by setting up a "yellow" procompany union and signing an agreement with the illegitimate union "leadership." Bosch was furious when he heard of the arrangement, telling Mármol it was certain to come back at some point and haunt the company. He ordered Mármol to tear up the agreement with the yellow union and draft a new, more generous collective bargaining contract proposal, one that could be ratified by representatives of the Confederación de Trabajadores de Cuba (CTC), the leading union group in the country.

By 1955, Bosch was overseeing the construction of new distilleries in Puerto Rico and Mexico, and he had his eye on Brazil, having visited there a year earlier with his wife to explore business opportunities. The major challenge in expanding rum production overseas was finding a way to maintain the quality that had been achieved back in Santiago. Some aspects of rum making could not be easily replicated. A key to the character of Bacardi's Cuba rums lay in the process by which the distillate was aged in oak barrels in the aging warehouse, or *nave*. The Bacardis' aging facility in Santiago was called the Nave Don Pancho, after Francisco "Don Pancho" Savigne, the man who was in charge of the facility during the 1920s and 1930s (and a first cousin of Emilio's wife, Elvira Cape). The *caldos*, as the aging distillates were called, constituted the Bacardis' single most important physical asset in Cuba, because they could be mixed to produce rums of different average ages. The aging process itself was mysterious and dictated by time-honored traditions, with many myths developing around it. There was a railroad station across from the warehouse, and one local explanation for the quality of aged Bacardi rum was that the *caldos* were gently shaken every time a train rolled by.

Much of the knowledge that went into rum distilling and blending came only through long experience. The "master blenders" in the family, such as Daniel Bacardi, had it, but so did some veteran Bacardi workers who had labored most of their lives in the distillery or the factory. For many years, the production chief at the Santiago rum factory was Alfonso Matamoros, whose older brother Miguel was a famous composer of traditional Cuban music and the founder of the Trio Matamoros. The Matamoros boys were black and grew up poor in Santiago. Miguel had worked as a driver for Facundito Bacardi, the fun-loving son of Facundo Bacardi Moreau, and often sang at Bacardi parties. When his brother Alfonso needed a job, Miguel asked Facundito if he would hire him. Alfonso went to work for the Bacardi company as a young man and advanced to the top position at the factory, where the rums were blended.

No Bacardi facility was more secret. The factory was kept locked around the clock, and no one was allowed to enter unless authorized by Daniel Bacardi. Alfonso Matamoros was the only person with a key. One day in the late 1950s, a young Bacardi engineer in his early twenties—Manuel Jorge Cutillas, a grandson of Emilio's daughter Marina—needed to get into the factory to make some technical check. Alfonso Matamoros, about thirty years older and in no doubt about his authority, insisted on escorting Cutillas, not caring in the least that he was a Bacardi family member. At one point, Cutillas climbed on top of a vat where the rums were mixing and was overwhelmed by the sweet smell. He asked Matamoros what was going on in the vat.

"I don't know," Matamoros said, scowling.

"What do you mean, you don't know?" Cutillas demanded. "You run the place!" In fact, Matamoros was one of a tiny handful of people outside of Daniel and other family members who had some idea of the "secret formula" by which Bacardi rums were produced. But he wasn't about to say anything to this upstart engineer, no matter who he was. "I don't know," Matamoros repeated. "Just do what you have to do." He would answer no more of Cutillas's questions.

With the production of Bacardi rum so dependent on tradition-bound methods, it was a constant struggle for the company to reproduce its success in different climes with new facilities and personnel. The Bacardi rum produced in Puerto Rico was close in taste to that produced in Cuba, but for some reason the Mexican version was quite different. One possible explanation was that the Mexican rum was distilled in a leased facility, not built according to Bacardi specifications. The company therefore bought a sugar hacienda called La Galarza, about eighty miles southeast of Mexico City, with the idea of building a new Bacardi distillery there from the ground up. The owner sold Bacardi the hacienda with the idea that he could supply the distillery with molasses from his sugar crop. The property dated to the seventeenth century, and Bosch gave orders to preserve the chapel and the crumbling colonial ruins that came with it. His plan was to turn the facility into a picturesque but modern distillery with bountiful gardens, a walled orchard, and a lovely old house where guests could be accommodated. In 1955 he dispatched Juan Grau to supervise the distillery's construction.

The blueprints Grau prepared were based on the distilling facilities in Santiago, and he expected the Mexico distillery to function just as the Santiago distillery did. Daniel Bacardi, the family rum expert, came to inspect the first product. Rather than taste it, he opened the tap on a barrel and let some rum trickle into his palms, then rubbed his hands together and sniffed them. It was the best way to sample the rum's essence. As Grau waited expectantly at his side, Daniel's brow furrowed. He splashed some more on his hands and held them to his nose again.

"Well?" Grau finally asked.

"No," Daniel answered. "No. No. This is not good."

"Well, no, it's not exactly the same," Grau admitted. He had been hoping Daniel would at least find the rum acceptable.

"No." Daniel was shaking his head. "No, no, this is not the same at all."

"Tell me how it's different," Grau said.

"That's for you to figure out."

Daniel returned to Cuba to report the bad news to Pepín Bosch, and Bosch promptly summoned Grau back to the island for another chilling conversation. "Juan, did I put any restrictions on you in Mexico?" he asked in the intimidating little voice Grau had come to know all too well.

"No, Mr. Bosch," Grau answered, "you gave me a free hand."

"Then why didn't you give me the product I wanted? What are you going to do about it?" It was vintage Bosch, mercilessly holding a subordinate accountable for what had been a disappointing outcome.

"Mr. Bosch, all I know to do is what I was taught to do at MIT, which is to start over from the beginning and take it step by step," Grau said. He decided he would need a special small-scale distilling unit to serve as a pilot plant, so that he could carry out a series of test distillations, changing one variable at a time. The unit he acquired was no more than six feet wide and twelve feet tall, including a fermentation tank, a molasses-heating unit, a centrifuge, and a small distillation column about a foot wide. For his test runs, Grau asked Pepín Bosch to send two barrels of Cuban molasses to Mexico in his private plane.

It proved to be the key. Rum made in Mexico with Cuban molasses was almost identical to the rum made in Cuba. The next challenge would be to isolate the distinguishing characteristics of Mexican molasses and then adjust the fermentation and distilling procedures to correct for the differences, so that a "Cuban" rum could be produced from Mexican molasses. Grau was a brilliant engineer and after eight months of experimentation, he achieved his objective. It was a turning point in Bacardi distilling history. From then on, Cuban-style Bacardi rum could be produced from almost any molasses, as long as the correct technical procedures were followed. It would taste the same whether produced in Mexico or Brazil or the Bahamas or Puerto Rico.

Consistent quality was one key to the company's commercial success in the coming years; another was that Bacardi remained a private, family-owned business. Management experts have long debated the relative merits of family ownership, but Pepín Bosch and other Bacardi executives learned early how to turn it to their advantage. Bosch had the confidence of his Bacardi in-laws, and that fact gave him more leeway in directing the company than other chief executives might have had. For a businessman who liked to make quick decisions, such flexibility was important.

His authoritarian management style notwithstanding, Bosch maintained an atmosphere of openness and intimacy in the administrative offices in Santiago. In the mid-fifties, the Bacardi firm was still headquartered in the brick building on Marina Baja Street, renamed Aguilera Street, where the French *licorista* José León Bouteiller had begun his rum distillation trials with Don Facundo himself nearly a century earlier. In the spring of 1954, an architectural firm assessed the firm's office space and reported that it was overcrowded and inefficiently organized. It was time for a new headquarters, and Pepín Bosch and his Bacardi family directors decided they would settle for nothing less than world-class.

They purchased a large piece of land alongside the main highway leading out of Santiago and hired Ludwig Mies van der Rohe, the famed German-American architect, to plan a modern industrial landmark. His commission was to design an architectural showpiece befitting Bacardi's international reputation but also reflecting the familial atmosphere to which the firm had long been accustomed. The final Mies design featured an open space, 130 feet square and 18 feet high, with glass sides and a roof of reinforced concrete that extended outward about 20 feet in each direction, supported by eight concrete columns. The design was considered so unique and important that the sketches were later included in architectural history books. The building itself was never constructed. Events in Cuba intervened.

Chapter 14

❦

Rising Up

Juan Grau, the Bacardi engineering whiz, was driving from Mexico City to the new rum distillery at La Galarza one day in September 1956 when he and the Bacardi lawyer riding with him decided to stop for a bite at a roadside taco eatery. There were dozens of taquerias along the highway, and the one they chose in the little town of Río Frío was no different from the others. Shortly after the two men sat down at the counter, the door opened and more patrons walked in. Glancing over his shoulder, Grau saw several men with full beards and dusty clothes, but paid them little heed as they grabbed chairs and settled noisily down at the only two tables in the establishment.

Suddenly, the tallest of the newcomers jumped up and shouted, "Juanito Grau!" Turning around, Grau saw it was Fidel Castro, his Santiago school chum and fellow mountain climber.

"Fidel, what the hell are you doing here?" Grau said, rising to embrace his old friend. He had not seen Castro in years, though from the newspapers Grau knew he was exiled with some of his followers in Mexico. There were rumors about a new revolutionary uprising in Cuba.

"We're coming from Veracruz," Castro said cryptically. In fact, he had just presided over a meeting there of his rebel volunteers, several of whom were now returning with him to the Mexican capital. The insurrection Castro would lead in Cuba was less than three months away, and he was on the lookout for a boat he could use to ferry his little guerrilla force back to the island. Among the bearded men with Castro in the café that day—unfamiliar to Grau, of course—was the Argentine adventurer Ernesto "Che" Guevara, already one of Castro's close collaborators. Leaning close to Grau, Fidel whispered, "I'm going to call you. This is important, what we're doing." Grau nodded and gave him his telephone number, though privately he was thinking that a call from Fidel was likely to bring nothing but trouble.

Even in those early days, Castro was seen by many Cubans as a man capable of leading a national insurrection. Grau had a wife and two small daughters to support, but he might still have been tempted to go along if Fidel had made a serious effort to recruit him. "I really don't know what I would have done," Grau said later. "I mean, I hope I would have had enough sense not to go with him, but it could have been a dangerous moment. He might actually have convinced me, you know?"

Castro had already worked his powers of persuasion on a Cuban-born military officer from Spain named Alberto Bayo, who had been a guerrilla warfare expert on the Republican side during the Spanish civil war. Castro looked him up in 1955 to seek his help in training his rebel volunteers to fight in Cuba. The sixty-five-year-old army general had retired from military service by then and was running a small furniture factory in Mexico City. Recounting their meeting later, Bayo said he told Castro he would help train his rebel army but could only afford to give him three hours a day. "No, General Bayo," Castro responded, "we want you the entire day. You must give up all your other occupations and devote yourself fully to our training. Why would you want a furniture factory if inside a short time you could come with us and be victorious together in Cuba?" Bayo wrote that he was so "intoxicated" by Castro's enthusiasm and confidence that he promised on the spot to sell his business and devote himself to training the Cuban rebels, few of whom knew anything about military operations.

Such stories became legendary over the course of the Cuban revolution. Fidel Castro came to power more through the force of his personality and his awesome ability to inspire or intimidate than through his skills as a military leader. In operational planning, he was consistently sloppy, disorganized, and reckless, but he made up for it through sheer audacity, irresistible energy, and political cunning. Cubans came to see him as a man who genuinely believed in the need to build a more just and humane society in Cuba and whose strength of conviction and character meant he would not be corrupted as easily as his predecessors had been. If he insisted on having total charge of the revolution, it was understandable. In time, it was believed, he would be forced to compromise and share power with others. His drive and enthusiasm were contagious, and Cubans of all backgrounds and social classes—including the Bacardis of Santiago—rallied behind him. In "History Will Absolve Me," Castro had challenged his countrymen to "fight for it with everything you have," and the people of Cuba soon proved they were willing to do just that, without knowing for sure whom they were following or what would come next.

Fidel Castro's revolutionary uprising got off to a feeble start. The boat he finally purchased for the expedition, an aging diesel-powered yacht named the *Granma*, was meant to carry no more than twenty-five people, but Castro squeezed eighty-two aboard, plus two antitank guns, ninety rifles, three machine guns, forty automatic pistols, and several boxes of ammunition and supplies. His plan was to land with his guerrilla fighters on the southern coast of Oriente province in the darkness, just as his followers in Santiago were launching an anti-Batista rebellion in the city.

The coordinator of the 26th of July Movement in Santiago was a twenty-one-year-old schoolteacher named Frank País. In many ways, he was Fidel Castro's polar opposite: modest where Castro was self-aggrandizing, deliberative where Castro was impulsive, and pragmatic and organized where Castro was bold and careless. The son of a Baptist minister, he carried a Bible with him at all times and taught in a private Baptist academy. His sincerity and seriousness impressed all those who knew him. By the time Fidel and his guerrilla force set off from Mexico on the *Granma* in late November 1956, País had built up an extensive underground network in Santiago, working closely with Vilma Espín and other M-26-7 collaborators.

Just before leaving Mexico, Fidel sent País a coded message saying he expected to reach Cuba with his guerrilla fighters on November 30 and that País should plan on launching his uprising that same day as a diversion. País followed the instructions precisely, leading a force of about three hundred volunteers in early-morning raids on the Santiago police headquarters, the customs office, and a coast guard station. The next day, País staged more raids, and for a few hours all public activity in the city was again brought to a halt.

The *Granma*, however, was still at sea. The overcrowded yacht could not move nearly as fast as Castro thought it would. Weather conditions were terrible, and only three of the men aboard the boat had any idea how to navigate and steer. By the time the *Granma* finally did touch land on the morning of December 2, it was on a sandbar more than a mile from the point where the guerrilla band was supposed to rendezvous with fellow rebel fighters. The men had to wade ashore in daylight, leaving most of their weapons, ammunition, and supplies behind. The Cuban military, having squelched the Santiago uprising, was by this time on full alert and quickly located the *Granma* fighters making their way haphazardly through the jungle.

On December 5, government troops found most of the rebels camped in a sugarcane field and attacked. Under fire from all directions, the rebels fled in a panic, leaving most of their remaining equipment behind. Many were killed; others were captured and executed. Of the eighty-two rebels who had come ashore, only twenty-two escaped to regroup in the nearby mountains. Among the survivors were Fidel, his brother Raúl, and Che Guevara. It had been a repeat of the Moncada debacle, and once again Castro refused to take personal responsibility for what had happened. Though the *Granma* landing disaster was due largely to his own bad judgment and reckless planning, Castro chose to lash out at his men for losing their weapons in the chaotic aftermath. "The one and only hope of survival that you had, in the event of a head-on encounter with the army, was your guns," he raged. "To abandon them was both criminal and stupid."

For the next two months, the Castro brothers, Che Guevara, and their surviving followers stayed hidden while government troops combed the mountains for them. In Santiago, Frank País and his fellow M-26-7 volunteers went underground again to await further developments. For all that most Cubans knew, Fidel Castro and his 26th of July Movement had been obliterated. Public attention turned instead to other insurgent anti-Batista groups, such as the Student Revolutionary Directorate, the university-based movement that was carrying out acts of sabotage in Havana. Former president Carlos Prío, Pepín Bosch's old boss, was still funding an insurrection group of his own.

Fidel Castro, however, had the advantage of imagination. He and his followers were underequipped, isolated in remote reaches of the Sierra Maestra, and constantly on the run, but Castro understood that propaganda and public perception were what mattered. He decided that he needed to be visited and interviewed in the Sierra Maestra by a credible foreign journalist, someone who would then report that Fidel Castro and his followers had survived the crossing from Mexico and were engaged in revolutionary operations.

The contacts were to be made by Felipe Pazos, a distinguished economist who had been the first president of Cuba's central bank during the time Pepín Bosch was finance minister but who then resigned in protest over Fulgencio Batista's military takeover. He later became a prominent M-26-7 supporter, partly through the influence of his son Javier, a university student and one of the movement's top collaborators in Havana. Pazos had stayed close to Pepín Bosch, and when Bosch formed his Minera Occidental venture in 1954, he asked Pazos to be the company president, giving him an office in the Bacardi building in Havana. Having served with the International Monetary Fund in Washington, Pazos spoke English and knew many U.S. journalists, and his M-26-7 colleagues in Havana figured he would be the best person to arrange an interview with Fidel Castro in the Sierra Maestra.

Pazos promptly set up a meeting in his Bacardi office with the resident *New York Times* correspondent in Havana, Ruby Hart Phillips. Realizing a visit to the Sierra would jeopardize her own status in Cuba, she suggested that the Castro interview be given to Herbert Matthews, a veteran *Times* reporter and editorial writer who had been to Cuba several times. Matthews quickly flew to Havana and then headed to eastern Cuba, posing as an American tourist. He was accompanied by Javier Pazos, who spoke English from his school days in Washington and served as interpreter. In Manzanillo, the men switched to a jeep and drove into the mountains as far as they could, then proceeded on foot in the darkness to the rendezvous point, using birdcalls to make contact with a scout who led them to the site where the interview would take place. Castro arrived at daybreak.

Matthews and Castro spoke for hours, as rebels paced back and forth around them. Che Guevara later reported that Castro had told him and the others to "look sharp, like soldiers," which under the circumstances wasn't easy. "I looked at myself," Guevara wrote, "then at the others; shoes falling apart, tied together with wire; we were covered with filth. But we put on an act; we filed off in step with me in the lead." Indeed, the deception went beyond Che's little act. Raúl Castro at one point brought over a random fighter and had him announce, "*Comandante*, the liaison from Column number two has arrived," to which Fidel responded, "Wait until I'm finished." Castro told Matthews the Batista forces were organized "in columns of 200; we in groups of ten to forty, and we are winning." It was all a ruse to fool the visiting journalist, and it worked. Castro at that point commanded only a couple of dozen men, all of whom were present during the interview.

Matthews's first article, published on February 24, began: "Fidel Castro, the rebel leader of Cuba's youth, is alive and fighting hard and successfully in the rugged, almost impenetrable fastnesses of the Sierra Maestra, at the southern tip of the island." Matthews said Castro's political program "amounts to a new deal for Cuba, radical, democratic, and therefore anti-Communist." As for Fidel himself: "It was easy to see that his men adored him," Matthews wrote, "and also to see why he has caught the imagination of the youth of Cuba all over the island." The front page stories had precisely the effect Castro hoped they would have; he became an instant celebrity in the United States and a hero in Cuba.

On March 13, the Student Revolutionary Directorate launched an attack on Batista's presidential palace in Havana, intending to kill him. Batista had been tipped off, however, and was barricaded on the top floor, accessible only by a locked elevator. The student attackers were repelled by the palace guard, and at least thirty-five were killed. The Directorate was essentially wiped out, and Fidel Castro—greatly strengthened by the *New York Times* publicity—was left as the leader of the anti-Batista struggle.

Batista responded to the assassination attempt against him with the bloodiest repression Cubans had ever experienced. A cruel and lazy tyrant, he whiled away his time playing canasta and watching horror films, and he put sadists in charge of the police. After the palace assault, Cuban jails were filled to capacity. Police interrogators tortured and killed prisoners with impunity, tearing out fingernails, breaking bones, shattering internal organs, and leaving victims with disfigured faces. The more humble a prisoner's origin, the more likely he was to be killed, and many prisoners were never seen or heard from again.

Like the repressive Spanish authorities who had used *voluntario* death squads against proindependence activists in Cuba nearly a century earlier, the Batista regime armed paramilitary groups and encouraged them to pursue suspected rebels. Among the most notorious were Los Tigres, a small army of thugs in Santiago directed by Rolando Masferrer, an ex-Communist who had led an especially violent campus gangster group at the University of Havana when Fidel Castro was there in the 1940s. A decade later, Masferrer was a pro-Batista senator and newspaper publisher dedicated to tracking down and eliminating regime opponents, often demanding extortion money from those he intimidated. A burly, scowling man with thick, hairy arms and a mustache, Masferrer habitually dressed in a cowboy hat and sunglasses and took a retinue of heavily armed bodyguards with him wherever he went. Masferrer regarded Santiago, the city of revolutionary heroes and Bacardi rum, as his personal domain.

Among those his men killed was a young Bacardi worker named Eladio Fontán, a member of the M-26-7 underground in Santiago. A group of Tigres pursued Fontán and cornered him in a dry-cleaning establishment. The Bacardi management had a bronze plaque made in the company foundry and mounted at the site where he died:

> TO ELADIO MANUEL FONTÁN,
> WHOSE LIFE WAS A CONSTANT BLAZE OF IDEALS.
> YOU WILL LIVE FOREVER IN OUR HEARTS.
> YOUR BACARDI COMRADES.

• • •

In the wake of the attack against him, Fulgencio Batista began demanding public demonstrations of loyalty from anyone who depended on government largesse or favors—public employees, landowners, pro-Batista union leaders, businessmen, and bankers. Workers who failed to take part in scheduled demonstrations could be fired. A succession of industrial leaders, fearful of alienating the regime, called on Batista to offer their sympathy and pledge their allegiance.

As president of the largest wholly Cuban-owned industrial enterprise, Pepín Bosch was among those under intense pressure. Bosch later said he was warned that unless he declared his support for Batista, his life could be in danger. Bosch stood fast, however, refusing even to offer perfunctory tribute to Batista. By then, he was convinced Batista would never give up power voluntarily. Though he had not approved of the 1953 Moncada assault, Bosch told his assistant Guillermo Mármol that he "applauded" the Santiago uprising in November 1956. In the preceding weeks, he had become increasingly outspoken against Batista's abrogation of the Cuban constitution. In October, he hosted a luncheon at the Hatuey brewery in Havana for editors and reporters visiting from across the Western Hemisphere for the annual assembly of the Inter-American Press Association. Batista's repressive rule and the prospect of revolution in Cuba were the main subject of discussion, and in his remarks to the journalists, Bosch referred obliquely to the situation in his country. "Almost all of us here," he told the group, "have known democratic freedom, and it is difficult for us to accept... that unconstitutional rule could prevail. Democracy and freedom must triumph, and we should all join together in a noble effort to bring this about."

Shortly after the attack on the presidential palace in March, Bosch received a letter from Rolando Masferrer's office, informing him that the senator was organizing a "National Anti-Communist Congress" in Havana in support of Batista's policies "against the agents of Russia." Attached to the letter was a blank donation form, which Bosch was to fill out with the amount he wished to pledge in support of the rally. "We will collect the funds for this event from friends of the cause," the letter stated, "among whom we include you." To ignore such an appeal under the prevailing circumstances in Cuba was a risky move, but Bosch was as courageous as he was stubborn. He passed the letter on to his secretary, with a brief instruction scrawled across the top: "Return—regretting not being able to cooperate."

Bosch was apparently unmoved by Batista's charge that Fidel Castro was a Communist. He once wrote in an unpublished commentary that there was "little difference" between Communism and military dictatorships in their attitudes toward national business. While no capitalist entrepreneur could ever support Communism, he wrote, neither should he support military dictatorships:

These dictatorships have two economic phases. At the beginning, the dictators and their henchmen limit themselves to government monies. Embezzlement and the misdirection of public works funding is enough to satisfy their desire for enrichment. [But] in the second phase, those funds are no longer enough, and they move to appropriate national businesses for their own use. The examples we have seen of this are infinite.

Bosch may have been thinking of Gerardo Machado, who as Cuba's dictator in the 1920s tried to force Bacardi president Enrique Schueg—Bosch's father-in-law—to give him equity in the company. He may have been thinking of Batista himself, who had briefly taken control of Bacardi in 1943. Given the deepening corruption of his regime, his coziness with organized crime figures, and his willingness to ignore legal and constitutional constraints, there would be little to stop Batista if he wanted to move against Bacardi again. Any businessman who wanted to remain independent, Bosch concluded, should be wary of dictators of any stripe. "There is just one system we should all support," he wrote. "Democracy."

Bosch clearly had probusiness views, but he considered himself socially and politically progressive. He was also a Cuban nationalist, and on several occasions he made known his concern about the extent to which U.S. capital had left little room in Cuba for the development of native entrepreneurship. By the spring of 1957, he had concluded that the best hope for reestablishing democracy and constitutional rule in Cuba lay with Fidel Castro and his 26th of July Movement. Castro was calling for sweeping social and economic reforms, but his program did not go significantly beyond what other politicians across the hemisphere had proposed, including Luis Muñoz Marín, the governor of Puerto Rico, whom Bosch greatly admired. He was also reassured by such M-26-7 supporters as his friend and business associate Felipe Pazos, who was among the most respected economists in all Latin America and a man known for his commitment to fighting poverty.

Pazos was at work on Minera Occidental business in his office in the Bacardi building one day when he looked up from his desk and saw a police lieutenant standing in front of him. The officer had a description of the Pazos family car, including the tag number, and politely asked Pazos if he was the owner. "Yes, sir," Pazos said.

"Have you loaned it to anyone recently?" the officer asked. A few days earlier, Javier had taken the car to ferry weapons to his M-26-7 contacts in the mountains of eastern Cuba. When Pazos refused to answer, the officer informed him that the car had been found loaded with weapons apparently destined for the Sierra Maestra. Pazos hoped this meant that his son had not himself been caught. "If you don't tell me whom you loaned it to, I'll have to detain you," the officer said.

"Lieutenant, if that's your obligation," Pazos answered. He was taken to the police headquarters, where a similar interrogation occurred, this time by the police commandant. Again, Pazos refused to cooperate. He had figured that Batista's police would not want to arrest him, because linking a famous economist and former National Bank president to Fidel Castro at that point would only have added to Castro's prestige. Pazos was soon released, though inwardly he was shaking with fear and thinking that from that point on he would have to watch his moves very carefully. So would Pepín Bosch, who just a few weeks earlier had given Pazos two thousand dollars for the purchase of arms and ammunition.

• • •

On a steamy Saturday evening in June 1957, fifteen local civic and business leaders gathered for a quiet dinner at the El Caney Country Club just outside Santiago. With sporadic shootings taking place around town almost every night, no one was anxious to venture out after dark, and the men had the private club entirely to themselves. About two weeks earlier, the bodies of four Santiago youths had been found hanging from trees, having been tortured, stabbed, and then shot. In response, thirty-one church, civic, professional, and social organizations had issued a statement demanding that Batista end "the reign of terror" in the city. M-26-7 guerrillas, meanwhile, had been staging daring ambushes of their own. The men at the country club had gathered to discuss the worsening situation in Santiago with a visiting U.S. journalist, Jules Dubois of the *Chicago Tribune*.

Among the dinner organizers were Daniel Bacardi and Pepín Bosch. Daniel that year was president of the Chamber of Commerce, following the example of his grandfather Emilio, who directed the Santiago Chamber of Commerce in 1894, another year of crisis for the city. The distinguished *santiagueros* at the country club also included the presidents of the Rotary and Lions Clubs, the priest who led the local Catholic Youth Movement, the president of the University of Oriente, and the heads of the Santiago medical and bar associations. Another guest was Manuel Urrutia, a local judge who had just given legitimacy to the insurrection by issuing an opinion that a hundred young Santiago men being held on "rebellion" charges were acting "within their constitutional rights" when they took up arms against the Batista regime, "in view of the usurpation and illegal retention of power by Batista and his followers."

Dubois, a veteran Latin America correspondent, had flown to Santiago from Havana the night before in order to report on the spreading rebellion against the Batista dictatorship. He was met at the airport by Pepín Bosch, whom he had known for years. As they rode into town through darkened city streets, Bosch turned to Dubois and said, "It is fortunate you came tonight." He told Dubois that a Batista soldier had been killed that morning, presumably by M-26-7 guerrillas, and that as an important U.S. journalist, his presence in Santiago that night might keep the police and army from engaging in more reprisal killings.

As the group sat down for dinner in the otherwise empty dining room, Dubois noticed an extra place at the head of the table. A card marked "Reserved" was conspicuously propped on the plate. A prominent local coffee exporter by the name of Fernando Ojeda stood up to offer a toast to Dubois. "One of our compatriots had planned to attend this dinner in your honor tonight," Ojeda announced, gesturing to the vacant chair, "but he sent his regrets that he could not make it. We can understand that, and we accept his excuses, because he is engaged in an important mission for Cuba. *His name is Fidel Castro.*" Dubois was stunned. The men around the table constituted the upper crust of Santiago's business, professional, and cultural leadership, and here they were offering a formal tribute to the bearded revolutionary of the Sierra Maestra.

Two days after the country club dinner, having confirmed his impressions about the depth of middle- and upper-class support in Santiago for the revolution, Dubois filed his *Tribune* report. "The wealthiest and most prominent men of Santiago," he wrote, "most of whom never have been involved in politics before, are backing the rebel, Fidel Castro, as a symbol of resistance against Batista." Bacardi president Pepín Bosch was clearly out front. While many businessmen and professional people were supporting the 26th of July Movement in private, Bosch was one of the few willing to do so publicly, and Dubois asked him to explain why Castro had so many people behind him in Santiago. "We have a fervent desire for freedom, justice, and democracy," Bosch said, according to Dubois. "I don't conceive that I can continue to live the way we have to live here. This is why every one of us is making every effort to do our duty for our country."

· · ·

A key to the broad support for Fidel Castro's movement in Santiago was the work of Frank País, the young Baptist schoolteacher. País had organized an independent "civic resistance" network in the city of mostly middle- and upper-class residents who were not yet ready to join the 26th of July Movement themselves but wanted somehow to support it. Among the collaborators in the Resistencia Cívica were some high-profile businessmen. Teofilo Babún and his two brothers, owners of a major timber and shipping firm in Santiago, used their business as a cover to transport arms, ammunition, and radio equipment to Fidel's fighters in the Sierra Maestra. Bacardi rival Gerardo Abascal, the head of the Álvarez Camp rum company in Santiago, smuggled rifles in the trunk of his car. Lily Ferreiro, who owned and managed the ultramodern supermarket in fashionable Vista Alegre, allowed the rebel underground to use her home as a meeting place. The owner of Tube Light, a Santiago firm that sold electrical and neon signs, supplied the rebels with wire to detonate land mines.

The Resistencia "treasurers" in Santiago were Enrique Canto, who owned a department store, and José Antonio Roca, a dentist. Daniel Bacardi and Víctor Schueg (the son of Enrique Schueg and Amalia Bacardi Moreau) were among Roca's regular patients, and they regularly brought along some cash for Fidel's fighters when they came for a dental exam. Roca later recalled that Víctor on one occasion alone gave him an envelope containing ten thousand-dollar bills. Pepín Bosch, who generally funneled his contributions through Enrique Canto, contributed even more. In interviews with a U.S. diplomat in Mexico City in 1960 and with the *New York Times* in 1963, Bosch acknowledged giving Castro $38,500 of his own money (a contribution that in 2008 dollars would be at least $275,000), and family members said he probably gave more than that. Like other wealthy Cubans who supported Castro, Bosch later regretted having helped him and was reluctant to discuss it. Nor was Castro anxious to admit how much help his movement accepted from the very businessmen whose properties he later confiscated. The result, in the words of a U.S. diplomat based in Cuba, was "a mutually convenient conspiracy of silence" on the extent to which the Cuban bourgeoisie financed Castro's rise to power, but it was significant.

One of Bosch's most important roles in the anti-Batista struggle was to promote contacts between the 26th of July Movement and the U.S. government. Bosch was friends with the U.S. vice-consul in Santiago, Bill Patterson, and he knew that Patterson was an undercover CIA field operative. Though the United States was still officially behind Batista, the political turmoil in Cuba was of serious concern, and the Santiago consulate was an important base for gathering intelligence on Fidel Castro and his movement. Bosch personally introduced Patterson to Vilma Espín and Frank País, in order to give the two M-26-7 activists an opportunity to persuade the United States that their movement was worthy of support. Bosch also helped arrange a secret meeting between the M-26-7 leaders and a group of U.S. officials from Washington, including CIA Inspector General Lyman Kirkpatrick, who made a fact-finding visit to Santiago in the spring of 1957. Vilma Espín assured the U.S. delegation that Castro and his followers were only working for "what you Americans have: clean politics and a clean police system." The M-26-7 representatives, meanwhile, took note of U.S. concerns about their movement. Frank País wrote to Fidel Castro afterward that "financial sectors" in the United States feared that the 26th of July Movement, if it defeated Batista, might be too unstable to govern Cuba effectively.

Shortly after the meeting with the U.S. visitors, País arranged for two of the more moderate M-26-7 sympathizers—the economist Felipe Pazos and Raúl Chibás, the brother of the late Orthodox politician Eddy Chibás—to be taken to the Sierra Maestra for a meeting with Fidel Castro to review the 26th of July Movement's political goals. Though the initiative caught Castro somewhat by surprise, he spent several days with the two men, and Pazos later claimed that Castro suggested that Pazos could be president of a provisional M-26-7 government. The conversations produced what came to be known as the Sierra Manifesto, laying out a political program the movement supposedly intended to implement. The document called for a democratic government in Cuba, with an absolute guarantee of press freedom and open elections in all labor unions. In the economic sphere, the manifesto proposed an agrarian reform program, increased industrialization, and a halt to gambling. There was no mention of nationalizing industries or collectivizing landholdings.

Frank País was pleased by the Sierra Manifesto and by Castro's apparent acceptance of the principles that underlay it. The relationship between the two men had always been a bit charged. País was one of the few M-26-7 leaders who dared to challenge Castro's judgment. In 1956 he had actually traveled to Mexico to argue (unsuccessfully) that the time was not yet right for an uprising in eastern Cuba. Castro respected País's organizational abilities, and he depended heavily on the steady flow of weaponry, supplies, and volunteers that País oversaw. But Castro was never comfortable with M-26-7 activity outside his direct control or influence, and he had limited patience for País's Baptist religiosity or his constant harping on the need for "democracy" in the anti-Batista movement. Many historians later guessed that a collision between the men was inevitable, but the truth will never be known. On July 30, 1957, shortly after returning from the Sierra meeting with Pazos and Chibás, Frank País was shot dead on a Santiago street by a police assassin. He was only twenty-two years old.

• • •

Batista's men in Santiago knew how important Frank País was to the 26th of July Movement, and with his killing they sent the local population an intimidating message. His body was deliberately left in the street for all to see, lying in a puddle of blood. As word of his killing spread, all of Santiago erupted in outrage. On the day País was buried, the entire city was shut down. Virtually every store was shuttered and every business closed, including the Bacardi Rum Company. As head of the local Chamber of Commerce, Daniel Bacardi championed the general strike. For five days, shopkeepers refused to open their doors and workers stayed off the job. The action was entirely spontaneous. Strikes were illegal in Cuba at the time, and by staying home the Santiago workers defied their own union leadership, which was still allied with Batista.

The regime prohibited the Havana media from reporting news of the Santiago strike, for fear it would spread to the capital. The authorities were furious at the civic and business leaders in Santiago for supporting the strike and did all they could to force them to back down. Pepín Bosch was in Mexico at the time of the País assassination, and the Santiago rum and beer operations were in the hands of Daniel Bacardi, who found himself under intense pressure to order his workers back on the job. He nevertheless refused, and on the third day of the work stoppage police arrested Pepín Bosch's son Carlos and detained him in the Moncada barracks, thinking it would give them leverage with the Bacardi management.

Though he had once given an M-26-7 fund-raiser two hundred dollars to buy pistols for the Sierra guerrillas, thirty-year-old Carlos had been barely involved in anti-Batista activities. Known to his friends and family as "Lindy" from the day he was presented to Charles Lindbergh as an infant, the young Bosch was devoted mainly to sailing, an activity he had shared with his friend Renato Guitart, one of the young men killed in the Moncada attack. Though he was not physically mistreated during his detention in the Moncada barracks, the experience opened Lindy's eyes to the reality of Batista's repression. The barracks that summer was crawling with paid thugs, employed by the military police to terrorize or assassinate regime opponents. While Lindy was being held at the barracks, one group was called out on a special "mission" in town. When they returned to the barracks later that night, Lindy overheard one of the thugs gloating that he had "got one."

The situation in Santiago was as tense as it had been since the uprising in November 1956, with heavily armed soldiers patrolling the streets. The regime authorities had already warned striking workers that they would be fired if they did not return to work immediately, though the threat was empty in those cases where the employer backed the strike. Around the time Lindy Bosch was taken away, soldiers arrived at Daniel Bacardi's house in the upper-class neighborhood of Vista Alegre and remained there for several hours, saying they would not leave until he signed a document telling workers to return to their jobs. Instead, he and other commercial leaders issued a statement saying they neither supported nor opposed the general strike. "We cannot stimulate tensions that would result in brotherly hatred," it said. Once it became clear the strike was not spreading to other parts of Cuba, the Santiago workers gradually began returning to their jobs.

Bosch and his wife Enriqueta were unaware of the developments in Santiago, because an earthquake in Mexico had severed telephone communications. His aide Guillermo Mármol finally had to fly there and personally deliver the news about their son's imprisonment, tracking them down at La Galarza distillery. On August 6, three days after he had been detained, Lindy Bosch was released from custody, just as his parents were returning to Santiago. Enraged by his arrest, they had immediately flown back to Cuba. Upon landing in Santiago, Bosch headed straight to the Moncada barracks to demand an explanation from the commander. The officer claimed he was ready to turn against Batista and had ordered Lindy detained in order to force Bosch to return to Santiago to direct an uprising. Bosch knew that his sympathy for the 26th of July Movement was public knowledge, and he suspected that the army commander was trying to trap him into making a declaration that would justify his arrest. He ignored the commander's suggestion, walked out of the barracks, and made preparations to leave Cuba for the duration of the revolution.

The experience convinced Bosch that he had to find a way to keep his company out of Batista's grasp. He figured that Batista was looking to punish him for supporting Fidel Castro's movement and seeking some opportunity to seize at least partial control of the Bacardi company. The solution Bosch devised to protect the family holdings was ingenious. He organized a new company, Bacardi International Limited (BIL), legally separate from Compañía Ron Bacardi, S.A., but owned by the same shareholders. The new company, to be based in the Bahamas, would hold the exclusive rights to manufacture and distribute Bacardi rum outside Cuba, except for the United States and Mexico. Given the political uncertainties on the island at the time, the move made great sense, and Bosch had no trouble persuading the Bacardi directors to approve the creation of the new unit. Fulgencio Batista might try to impose new taxes or come up with some other way to punish the Bacardis or pressure them, but the most valuable segment of the company's commercial business would be safe.

At the time, the most successful Bacardi operations were the ones outside Cuba. The new distillery at La Galarza in Mexico was open and impressing everyone who visited it. "In all Mexico I have not seen a cleaner and more highly performing installation than what exists at La Galarza, and I doubt one exists outside the country either," gushed a prominent Mexican businessman after touring the new plant. "That installation breathes efficiency and good management." Planning was under way for a new distilling operation in Brazil, and the new plant in Puerto Rico was nearing completion. Pepín Bosch's friend Luis Muñoz Marín, the Puerto Rican governor, inaugurated the facility in January 1958, christening it the "Cathedral of Rum." It was the largest rum factory in the world.

. . .

It would be a while before they realized it, but the key question as early as 1958 was not so much whether the Bacardis wanted a revolution in Cuba as whether the revolution wanted them. Like many other Cubans, the Bacardis assumed that the Sierra Manifesto and other such declarations summarized what the 26th of July Movement actually stood for politically. They did not fully understand that there were competing revolutionary factions and that the views of Felipe Pazos and other moderates in the urban underground were not necessarily shared by the more radical rebel fighters in the mountains, Che Guevara among them.

Guevara, the freelance Argentine revolutionary, had been in Guatemala when the CIA arranged the ouster of the elected president, Jacobo Arbenz, after he alienated the United Fruit Company with his attempt to carry out a modest program of land reform. For Guevara, the Guatemala experience showed that the United States would not tolerate a democratically elected left-wing government in Latin America, and he argued that only a genuinely Marxist-Leninist revolutionary state aligned with the Soviet Union could survive U.S. opposition. In his private diary, Guevara referred to M-26-7 sympathizers Felipe Pazos and Raúl Chibás as "cavemen" and showed nothing but scorn for the "bourgeois" ideas they espoused during their visit with Fidel Castro in the Sierra. Castro at the time was being extraordinarily careful with his public statements. The one question visiting journalists always asked him was whether he was a Communist, and he always answered no. But Guevara could not help himself. In December 1957, he got into an extraordinary (and significant) behind-the-scenes disagreement with René Ramos Latour, who had replaced Frank País as the underground leader in Santiago. From his mountain camp, Guevara wrote Ramos Latour a scathing letter, accusing him of trying to move the revolutionary movement "toward the Right." He then blurted out his own pro-Soviet views. "I belong to those who believe that the solution of the world's problems lies behind the so-called Iron Curtain."

Ramos Latour wasted no time in responding, emphasizing that he and his ideological allies advocated a strong but independent Latin America, "an America that can stand up proudly to the United States, Russia, China, or any other power that tries to undermine its economic and political independence. On the other hand, those with your ideological background think the solution to our evils is to free ourselves from the noxious 'Yankee' domination by means of a no less noxious 'Soviet' domination." Explicitly at stake in the exchange was the future character of the revolutionary movement, and Fidel Castro was to be the arbiter.

The factional dispute was next reflected in a disagreement over revolutionary strategy and tactics. The urban wing proposed a nationwide general strike, while the mountain wing favored the expansion of guerrilla military operations. It was a decisive debate. If the general strike went according to plan and brought an end to the Batista regime, workers, businessmen, professionals, and all others who participated could legitimately share a claim of the credit. On the other hand, if Batista were defeated through military action, the guerrilla leadership in the mountains would be in a stronger position to dictate the makeup of a new government. In the end, Fidel Castro endorsed the strike, though somewhat halfheartedly and only after much hesitation.

The call was issued on the morning of April 9, 1958, with M-26-7 operatives interrupting radio broadcasts to advise the Cuban people to stay away from work. Within hours, many cities in the interior of Cuba were effectively shut down, most notably Santiago. At the Bacardi facilities, more than 1,200 workers walked off the job at midday, supported in their action by Daniel Bacardi himself. In Havana, however, the strike failed. Only a few businesses were affected, and the M-26-7 saboteurs who attempted to disrupt utilities and communications were quickly neutralized by Batista's police.

Once it appeared that the strike was unlikely to succeed, Vilma Espín called on workers in Santiago to return to their jobs, breaking from René Ramos Latour and allying herself with the M-26-7 hardliners in the mountains. A few weeks later, Fidel Castro convened a meeting in the Sierra Maestra to discuss the apparent failure of the strike. There would be no more internal debates. At that meeting, Castro officially designated himself the commander-in-chief of the entire revolutionary movement. The M-26-7 leaders who had pushed for the strike, including Ramos Latour, were repudiated and reassigned to other positions in the movement, clearly subordinate to the mountain command. Ramos Latour, who had dared to challenge Che Guevara's acceptance of "Soviet domination," was put in charge of a frontline combat unit. He was killed in action a few months later.

Batista sensed an opportunity in the failure of the general strike and ordered a massive military offensive, sending more than ten thousand troops into the Sierra Maestra. The government campaign was dubbed Plan FF for *"Fin de Fidel,"* and the mission was precisely to bring about the "End of Fidel" and his rebel force. In the meantime, however, there had been an important change of circumstances: The U.S. government had come to the conclusion that Batista was unlikely to survive politically and cut off all arms shipments to his regime. By midsummer, the government offensive was collapsing. The Cuban army was not well trained or equipped for guerrilla warfare and was unable to make major progress against Castro's rebels, who limited themselves to hit-and-run attacks. Peasants were also battling Batista forces in the Escambray mountains, and Raúl Castro took a rebel column and opened still another front in the Sierra Cristal mountain range. Vilma Espín joined him, and the two began a wartime romance. Fidel Castro dispatched Che Guevara with a column of fighters toward Las Villas province, and he sent Camilo Cienfuegos, another top *comandante*, toward the west. Government forces were hit by desertions and defections, while new recruits flowed steadily into the rebel ranks.

Dozens of Bacardi workers volunteered for rebel army duty, having been assured by Daniel Bacardi (acting as company chief in the absence of Pepín Bosch) that their jobs would be waiting for them when they returned. Bacardi women, including Daniel's sister Ana María, knit caps and stockings for the rebels, who were fighting in the chilly reaches of the Sierra Maestra. The M-26-7 leaders recognized the Bacardi enterprise as an ally and issued orders to spare its facilities from damage. The company had just that year opened a brand-new distillery in Santiago, and it was untouched. Rebels in the Santa Clara area deliberately left a nearby bridge intact so as not to impede shipments from Bacardi's Hatuey brewery in Manacas. The brewery manager, Augusto "Polo" Miranda, had rebel contacts and kept them informed of his shipping schedule.

Inevitably, however, the rebels' military activity affected commerce as a whole. By the fall of 1958, transportation and communications in the area around Santiago had been severely disrupted. Several zones were under rebel control, and traffic on the main roads was blocked. In Santiago itself, the police and Rolando Masferrer's private militia engaged the rebels in running gun battles somewhere almost every night. Manuel Jorge Cutillas, the young Bacardi engineer, was working long hours as the manager of the new distillery in Santiago, and he often chose to sleep in the plant rather than risk his life driving home through the darkened and dangerous city streets.

Before long, electricity was cut off in Santiago, and Bacardi managers had to cut back production. A shortage of glass forced a suspension of work at the bottling plant, and the Bacardi rum factory was closed for the first time in anyone's memory. With all roads in and out of Santiago blocked and train transportation halted, the only way Bacardi managers could get their product out of the city was by boat, via Havana, just as in the previous century. In the first three weeks of December, about forty thousand cases of Bacardi rum were shipped by sea to Havana, all for distribution elsewhere within Cuba.

Conditions in the capital had remained relatively normal, and the Bacardi staff there did not initially realize how bad the situation in Santiago had become. On November 4, the company's Santiago-based sales chief, José Bou, described conditions in the city in an epistle he titled, "Letter from a *santiaguero* to a Havana Friend." He addressed it to his Bacardi colleague Juan Prado, the sales manager in Havana, though it could have gone to just about anyone in the capital who was clueless about what was happening at the other end of the island.

"Dear Juanito," he began. "You in Havana are completely detached from reality. It's like Havana is Cuba, and the rest of the island is 'Korea.'" Bou said there were no groceries in the Santiago stores, no milk for the children, and no drinkable water, except for what could be bought from vendors. And then there was the violence.

What would you all say if, seated by your windows, you had to contemplate a panorama of airplanes surrounding the city and strafing the suburbs? What would you say if you saw your city militarily occupied, if you saw tanks and armored cars patrolling the streets, and truckloads of soldiers with their machine guns pointed in every direction, threatening even the most peaceful citizens? What would you say to your children, who, upon seeing these vehicles, ran away screaming and crying and hating anyone in uniform?

A courtly gentleman with grown children, Bou's main concerns had been to see his family doing well and Bacardi sales growing. He was no follower of Fidel Castro and did not consider himself political, but with the brutality he had seen from the Batista security forces, Bou was becoming increasingly upset.

We feel so oppressed and badly treated that the moment will come when, no matter how old we may be, there will be nothing left for us to do but take up arms...against those inhuman and beastly ones who feel not a drop of pity when they kill in cold blood....I would rather die heroically than continue under the bloody boots of these men who have no soul.

Bou's letter indicated why the revolution was able to triumph in Cuba. He and others in Santiago had come to hate the Batista regime so much that they were willing to support virtually any rebellious movement that could bring about its downfall, no matter what questions were raised about the rebels at the time. Manuel Jorge Cutillas, the young distiller, recalled later how he and his Bacardi relatives and colleagues would climb to the top of the Hatuey brewery for a better view of the fighting outside the city. From there, they could see a huge black and red M-26-7 flag flying in the nearby hills. Batista's airplanes swooped down and strafed the area, and puffs of smoke rose from the trees. But Cutillas and his colleagues then heard the rebels on the ground firing back, and they cheered wildly, "Get 'em! Get 'em!"

◆ ◆ ◆

By the fall of 1958, the CIA had concluded that Batista was opposed by at least 80 percent of the Cuban people. Even his most stalwart defenders in the U.S. government were coming to the conclusion that he would have to go, though they were not anxious to see his regime replaced by a government dominated by the worrisome Fidel Castro. The CIA and the FBI were reporting that Castro himself was not necessarily a Communist but that he was surrounded by several people who were, including his brother Raúl and Che Guevara. In a last-ditch effort to find an alternative, a group of U.S. government officials and businessmen proposed that Batista step aside voluntarily in favor of a caretaker government dominated by anti-Batista military officers and respected civic leaders, most notably Pepín Bosch of Bacardi. Batista, however, refused to consider the initiative.

It probably would not have worked in any case. Fidel Castro had said on more than one occasion that he and his followers would not be satisfied with a military coup that removed Batista from power, and by December 1958 his movement was essentially unstoppable. The U.S. ambassador soon advised Batista that the United States no longer believed he was effectively in control of Cuba, and Batista began making plans to flee. At 2:40 A.M. on January 1, 1959, he left Cuba on an airplane with his family and a few friends. Fidel Castro got the news while eating breakfast at his headquarters in the sugar mill town of Central América outside Santiago. Fearing that senior dissident military officers might attempt to install a new government on their own and thus block his revolution, Castro ordered rebel units to move immediately on Santiago, so that he could declare himself in charge.

Castro encountered no resistance, and he was in Santiago by the end of the day. He and his small army of fighters and sympathizers arrived in a two-mile long caravan of trucks and jeeps, snaking slowly through streets crowded with wildly cheering throngs. All along the way, people hung out windows and crowded onto balconies, screaming in joy as the caravan passed.

"*¡Viva Fidel! ¡Viva la revolución! ¡Viva! ¡Viva!*"

Fidel stood in his jeep, waving and shaking the hands of people who rushed up to him. It was midnight on New Year's Day before he arrived at Céspedes Park, the main plaza between the cathedral and the town hall, the spot where Mayor Emilio Bacardi had first raised the Cuban flag exactly fifty-seven years earlier. Emilio's great-grandson Manuel Jorge Cutillas and other Bacardi family members were wedged onto the balcony of the Club San Carlos, overlooking the plaza, which was packed with thousands of delirious Castro supporters. Daniel Bacardi and other town leaders waited for Castro at the town hall, in a second-floor conference room. Castro moved around the room shaking hands, then stepped out onto a balcony overlooking the plaza and faced the roaring crowd, his hands raised high in triumph.

Among those greeting him was the Santiago commander of the National Police, Colonel Bonifacio Haza, who had surrendered his police units to the rebel army. After a few minutes, Castro went back to the conference room to review the latest news on army movements, while various Santiago civic leaders took turns offering prayers and making speeches to the people in the plaza. At about 2:15 A.M., Castro himself returned to the balcony. To thunderous applause, he announced that Santiago, "the strongest bulwark of the revolution," was to serve as Cuba's new capital. It was one of many promises that Castro would soon break.

Chapter 15

Giving Fidel a Chance

Fidel Castro was a genius in the exercise of power. Within a few hours of arriving in Santiago, he had designated a new president for Cuba—the anti-Batista judge Manuel Urrutia—and declared that "the full authority of the Republic" was vested in him. The significance of the act, however, was precisely the opposite of what Castro said it was: He had taken for himself the right to choose the country's chief executive, and he had made sure that no one dared to challenge his decision. Similarly, Castro told the crowd in Santiago that he had no political ambitions, only to turn his immediate attention to the reinforcement of his personal position among the Cuban people.

A lesser politician under the circumstances would have rushed to Havana to lead the national cheerleading over Batista's ouster; Castro chose instead to make a slow overland trip from Santiago to the capital, leading a caravan of trucks, armored cars, and other vehicles up the country's main east-west highway. The six-day journey enabled him to present himself dramatically to the population, town by town. Standing in his open jeep, waving to people along the road, followed by his scraggly rebel entourage, Castro over the course of those six days became the embodiment of the Cuban revolution. At every opportunity, he stopped to make speeches about the prospect of social and economic justice for Cubans of all classes. Each day, the crowds were bigger and more enthusiastic, with new rebel "recruits" joining the procession after every stop. Throngs of people waited for hours along the way, holding signs that said, "¡Gracias, Fidel!" Almost every scene and rousing speech was broadcast on Cuban radio and television, and Castro's deliberate lag in reaching Havana served only to make the people there all the more excited to see him. The weekly magazine *Bohemia* prepared a special one-million-copy "Freedom Edition," with a painting of Castro on the cover, captioned "Honor and Glory to the National Hero."

Castro's route took him through the Havana suburb of El Cotorro, where the Bacardi company had one of its Hatuey breweries. As a family firm identified with Cuban patriots and untainted by any association with Batista, Bacardi Rum was eager to show its support for the country's new leader, and the management and workers arranged a welcoming luncheon for Castro at the Cotorro brewery, just as the company had done for Ernest Hemingway in 1956. Another sumptuous feast was prepared, and the brewery workers hoisted a hand-painted banner on the brewery fence, welcoming Castro with the same message he saw in every city he passed. "*¡Bienvenido, Fidel! ¡Gracias!*"

The luncheon was to be Castro's last stop before his grand entrance to Havana. By early afternoon, the highway in front of the brewery was clogged with traffic and onlookers. The motorcade now included busloads of rebel volunteers, open trucks crowded with hitchhiking revolutionaries, and Sherman tanks driven awkwardly by young guerrillas still unfamiliar with the controls. Fidel himself had switched that morning to a new British helicopter his men had found at an army base five days earlier in Holguín. He landed at a field just south of El Cotorro, then made his way to the brewery in a jeep, with his driver weaving around the stalled traffic and even pulling onto the sidewalk, yelling to the frenzied crowd to stay back. Just as Castro approached the brewery, a messenger arrived with the news that his nine-year-old son Fidelito was waiting for him at a Shell gas station down the road. The boy's mother, Mirta Diaz-Balart, whom Fidel had married and divorced years earlier, had arranged for Fidelito to be taken to the United States while Fidel was preparing his revolution, and Fidel had not seen him for more than two years. The brewery siren was already wailing to signal the guest of honor's arrival, but upon hearing that his son was nearby, Fidel told his driver to go straight to the gas station. Aides who had been waiting at the brewery rushed off to catch up with him.

The Bacardi employees and family members were disappointed that Fidel had not bothered to stop to see them, but they were still caught up in the excitement of the moment. Some followed Fidel downtown, while others watched him on television. Fifty-seven-year-old Joaquín Bacardi, the sole surviving son of Emilio's younger brother José, had been among those waiting to greet Fidel in El Cotorro. The Harvard-educated and Denmark-trained brewer had a reputation for being sparse with words, but on the day Fidel and his men entered Havana, he was overcome with emotion. "It is the most marvelous thing that I have ever seen or expected to see in my life," he told reporter Jules Dubois. "Cuba is now free, and I hope it will remain so for many years."

A day earlier, the Bacardi company had published an ad in Havana newspapers addressed to Cuba's liberators: "Thank you to the people of Cuba and to the Cuban Revolution. Because of your efforts and sacrifice, once again it's possible to say, 'How lucky the Cuban is!'" In the preceding months of violence, *¡Qué suerte tiene el cubano!* had seemed a bit inappropriate as a Bacardi ad slogan. The Bacardi and Hatuey names had nevertheless remained prominent over that time in baseball stadiums, in magazine and newspaper advertisements, and on radio and television. The nightly newscast on the leading television network in Cuba, CMQ, was sponsored by Hatuey beer, and this was in the era when commercial sponsorship meant a company effectively owned a program. Manolo Ortega, the same broadcaster who announced Hatuey-sponsored baseball games, read the news each night and then concluded his program by raising a glass of Hatuey to the camera and toasting his viewers. It was via Manolo Ortega and his nightly "Hatuey Newsreel" that many Cubans first saw and heard Castro making revolutionary speeches.

* * *

Some questions about Fidel Castro's rule had been raised immediately after his arrival in Santiago, when he began ordering the execution by firing squad of *batistiano* policemen, informers, and other regime collaborators. Capital punishment was prohibited in Cuba under the very 1940 Constitution that Castro had promised to uphold, but he justified the killings on the basis of a rebel "criminal code" he and his followers had drafted a year earlier in their mountain camp. The condemned men were offered only the barest excuse of a legal proceeding before they were lined up and shot.

The mass executions (seventy in a single day in Santiago alone) bothered some of Castro's own supporters, including some Bacardis. Their rum factory was just down the street from the slaughterhouse wall where hundreds of Cuban independence sympathizers, including the *Virginius* crew, had been shot in the previous century by Spanish troops. Manuel Jorge Cutillas, the young Bacardi engineer and great-grandson of Emilio, was staying with his parents in their house in the Vista Alegre neighborhood one night when he and his wife Rosa were awoken by gunfire; it continued so long that they never got back to sleep. The next day, Cutillas learned that a mass execution had taken place that night on nearby San Juan Hill, under the direction of Raúl Castro, Fidel's brother. The next night, the firing squads resumed their work. To his astonishment, Cutillas learned that among those executed was Colonel Bonifacio Haza, the former Santiago police commander who had personally surrendered his forces to Castro and stood alongside him on the balcony on January 1. The executions made Manuel wonder about the character of the new revolutionary regime.

Those doubts, however, were not shared by Manuel's parents, his grandfather Radamés Covani, or his grandmother Marina Bacardi, Emilio's daughter, all of whom remained enthusiastic supporters of Fidel Castro and his new government. The majority of Cubans, in fact, seemed to accept the executions as a necessary step. Some of those shot were known torturers or assassins, and many Cubans figured they got what they deserved. For Castro, the executions served an additional purpose by demonstrating that he would not hesitate to use maximum force against those he judged to be mortal foes of the revolution. When the killings prompted an international outcry, Castro responded defiantly, calling on Cubans to show their solidarity at a mass rally outside the presidential palace on January 21. At least a half million people responded. "We will show them that public opinion is behind us, and that we are doing the right thing!" Castro declared. Many in the crowd carried banners that said, *¡Que Sigan Fusilamientos!* (May Firing Squads Continue!) Cubans were ready for big change in their country, and most saw Fidel Castro as the man who could make it happen.

Among those willing to give Castro the benefit of the doubt was Bacardi chairman Pepín Bosch, who returned from exile in Mexico on January 5, full of optimism about the future of his country. Having opposed Batista for so long, Bosch was thrilled that he was finally gone. "The triumph of the revolution makes me extremely happy," Bosch told a reporter upon his arrival at the Havana airport. "Although it may not have appeared so, it had the support of almost all the Cuban people. The men who directed it are well intentioned, and they will have success in the difficult tasks that await them in reordering the national life." Reminded that he had once been mentioned as a possible presidential candidate, Bosch dismissed the idea. "This is the hour of the youth," he said, "and we can expect nothing less than great days ahead for Cuba." Privately, Bosch told friends and Bacardi associates that the mass executions and Castro's bellicosity left him uncomfortable, but, for the moment at least, he was willing to look past such concerns.

Santiago, the Cuban city that had suffered most in the previous two years, quickly returned to normal. Traffic began moving again, and the stores reopened. The Bacardi rum plant, having shut down in November, resumed operations. Before long, the city was back to its old partying ways, and young people who for months had been hiding from the police were out in the streets again. Barely three weeks after the fall of the Batista regime, Santiago hosted the biggest social event of the new era: Vilma Espín and Raúl Castro, the revolution's First Couple, got married in a civil ceremony at the Rancho Club, a fashionable restaurant and motel founded and co-owned by Pepín Bosch.

José Espín, the longtime Bacardi executive and stockholder, arranged a huge wedding reception for his daughter and her new husband, adorning the venue with hundreds of fresh flowers and supplying forty cases of champagne. Virtually the entire Bacardi clan was in attendance, including Emilio Bacardi's ninety-four-year-old sister-in-law, Herminia Cape, the younger sister of his wife Elvira Cape. Emilio and Elvira's daughter Marina Bacardi and her husband Radamés were also there, along with Marina's grandson Manuel Jorge Cutillas, who came despite his personal misgivings about the Castro brothers. Hundreds of Santiago residents showed up, as did many of Raúl's fellow revolutionaries, with the exception of his brother Fidel, who was in Venezuela on his first overseas trip since taking power. Raúl arrived in his guerrilla uniform, black beret, and M-26-7 armband, packing his .45 pistol. Though twenty-seven years old, he still had trouble growing a full beard, and, perhaps to compensate, he had let his hair grow especially long, tying it back in a ponytail that Vilma's girlfriends found amusing.

The wedding was a high point of the Bacardi-Castro relationship: a daughter of Santiago's elite, deeply rooted in the Bacardi circle, united with Fidel's own brother, the man Fidel would designate as his heir and successor. The Bacardis and the Castros at that point shared not only their upper-class roots in Oriente province but their commitment to a new Cuba.

The man who could carry the partnership forward on the Bacardi side, Pepín Bosch, went to Havana two weeks after returning to Cuba and pledged his support for the new government. On January 22, the day after the big proexecution rally at the presidential palace, Bosch paid a visit to Castro's new minister of finance, a U.S.-educated economist named Rufo López-Fresquet. Bosch brought with him a check for $450,000, the amount the Bacardi company expected to owe in taxes later that year. Batista and his cronies had depleted the Cuban state treasury before they fled the island, and Bosch was making his company's tax payment several months ahead of its due date in order to help the government pay its bills. Other Cuban businessmen were also paying their taxes in advance, but the Bacardi payment was the biggest to that point. López-Fresquet's deputy drafted a receipt on the spot, thanking the company "for the cooperation you are lending to the Government of the Revolution."

Fidel Castro and his team had already made clear they intended to implement sweeping economic and political changes in Cuba, but the country's most prominent businessman was not alarmed. Back in Santiago after his meeting with López-Fresquet, Pepín Bosch dictated a series of letters to friends expressing nothing but enthusiasm for the new government. "It pleases me to inform you that things in Cuba are very good," he wrote to a friend in Tampa. "I can tell you with all sincerity that the people are very happy and that if we stay on this path I foresee an excellent future for Cuba." He also shared his views on Fidel Castro's administration with his friend Luis Muñoz Marín, the governor of Puerto Rico. As a politician who considered himself a socialist in his youth, Muñoz Marín had taken great interest in Fidel Castro and his revolution and was making it known to his Cuban friends that he would help in any way he could. His comment to reporters on the mass executions was that it amounted to "a bad thing happening in the midst of a great thing." In his letter to Muñoz Marín, Bosch expressed cautious hope that Fidel Castro would be an effective leader for Cuba. "To judge Dr. Castro's capacity for governing is difficult," Bosch observed, "because he has no history as such. But I have always said that a man who has known how to do what he has done and has known how to maintain discipline among a number of more or less great men necessarily has to have superior qualities, and it can be expected that he will have success."

The winter 1959 issue of *Bacardi Gráfico*, the company's quarterly magazine, opened with a feature article titled "Crusade of Freedom," celebrating the triumph of the revolution, with a full-page picture of Fidel Castro atop a tank holding a Cuban flag. "The people of Cuba found in Fidel Castro the exceptional figure they needed in their hour of distress," the photo caption read. "At a time when most people doubted, he knew how to maintain faith and revive spirits." The short editorial that ran opposite the picture left no doubt that Fidel and his revolution were admired within the Bacardi family:

> The first of January of 1959 brought a climate of freedom back to Cuba. In the Sierra Maestra and the Sierra Cristal, Fidel and Raúl Castro created a rebel army. The army was not defeated, and with the help of almost the entire Cuban population, a military and economic situation was created such that the dictatorship had to collapse.... Today we Cubans are happy. We have faith in our nation, and we hope that our country can be organized for the benefit of all and not just for the few, as it has been until now.

The company magazine devoted two pages to profiles of Bacardi workers who had joined the revolution, and more such profiles were promised for the next issue. "We congratulate Dr. Fidel Castro and the people of Cuba," the article concluded, "for this glorious victory that brings us so much happiness."

Pepín Bosch himself approved every word that went into *Bacardi Gráfico*, and there is no reason to think the published tributes to Castro and his revolution were anything but sincere. The new government included men Bosch had known and respected for years, beginning with Manuel Urrutia, the Santiago judge who had been with Bosch at the country club dinner in June 1957.

The prime minister was José Miró Cardona, formerly the head of the Cuban Bar Association. Felipe Pazos, whom Bosch had installed as president of Minera Occidental, was once again in charge of Cuba's central bank. Finance Minister Rufo López-Fresquet was another highly regarded economist, generally considered probusiness, as was his vice minister, Antonio Jorge. The new foreign minister, Roberto Agramonte, had been the Ortodoxo candidate in the 1952 presidential election and would probably have won that year were it not for Batista's coup.

With his outspoken support for Castro's revolutionary government, Pepín Bosch was daring to challenge the more conservative views of many people in Washington. The outgoing U.S. ambassador to Cuba, Earl Smith, opposed the U.S. decision to extend diplomatic recognition to the new regime, because—according to his later testimony—he feared Castro was a Marxist whose succession to power "would not be in the best interests of the United States." Members of Congress were also quick to criticize Castro's conduct. In mid-January 1959, Republican senator Homer Capehart of Indiana said the firing squad executions "create the spectacle of a bearded monster stalking through Cuba," while Democratic representative Wayne Hays of Ohio asked State Department officials what they planned to do "to calm down Fidel Castro before he depopulates Cuba."

Bosch was clearly aware of such negative comments and did his best to spread the word that the developments in Cuba were no cause for worry. "The situation in Cuba is very sound," he assured a Bacardi colleague in Nassau on January 23, referring to the uproar over the summary executions by firing squads. "While it is true that the prosecution of the murderers does create an international worry, internally it seems that the majority of the people are in favor of the procedure which is being followed." In a January 27 letter to Alberto Parreño, the president of the Cuban Chamber of Commerce in New York, Bosch was determined to defend his country from those who were criticizing it abroad. "Now it's your turn to help," he told Parreño. "Maybe you could invite some pre-eminent person from Cuba to one of your lunches, to present the Cubans' side of the story. *Herbert Matthews would do it well.*" (emphasis added) Bosch at the time was well aware that Matthews had written adulatory stories in the *New York Times* about Castro and his triumph and that he was being harshly criticized for them by Ambassador Smith and his allies in Congress.

One U.S. politician whose views on Cuba matters aligned with Bosch's own was Charles O. Porter, a liberal Democrat from Oregon who had been one of the leading congressional critics of U.S. arms shipments to Fulgencio Batista and who, after the rebels' victory, became one of Fidel Castro's strongest supporters in Washington. Porter visited Santiago in February 1959 and spoke at a banquet offered in his honor by local civic leaders, including Daniel Bacardi and Pepín Bosch. "Fidel Castro," Porter said, "has done more than any other Cuban to move the consciences and the emotions of Americans and to remind your friends to the north of the historic and profound ties of friendship that unite Cuba with the United States." Porter said the U.S. criticism of the summary trials and speedy executions in Cuba showed that Americans "did not comprehend how the indignation that was bottled up in a morally sensitive and oppressed people had to find some outlet, nor that the public judgments against known assassins was, in effect, a safety valve for a nation demanding retribution." He praised Castro's proposals for land reform, for reducing unemployment, and for reorganizing the Cuban military. At the same time, Porter was a cold warrior, and he warned his Santiago audience to "be careful with the Communists, who will try to make you believe that they speak as Cubans devoted to Cuba." He suggested that Cubans should reach out to the United States for assistance and court constructive U.S. investment.

Pepín Bosch was so pleased by Porter's analysis of the Cuba situation that he had the complete text of his remarks translated and published in the Bacardi magazine. Like Porter, Bosch was prepared to believe that Castro could be good for Cuba, as long as he could be moderated. Bosch knew that radicalizing influences were at work in the country, and he recognized that Castro slipped easily into anti-U.S. rhetoric. But criticism of U.S. foreign policy was standard fare for a populist politician in Latin America. Bosch himself had not forgotten how in 1950 Wall Street bankers and their allies in Washington had opposed the National Bank of Cuba, for fear its creation would weaken the position of U.S. banks in Cuba. As a result of that experience, Bosch had concluded that Washington was sometimes more concerned about protecting U.S. investments in Cuba than about promoting Cuba's own economic and political development. He was allied with Felipe Pazos and others on Castro's team who wished the United States were more helpful. Among them was Finance Minister Rufo López-Fresquet, who in early February scolded a *Wall Street Journal* reporter in Havana for grilling him about the firing squads. "You Americans!" López-Fresquet said, shaking a finger at his visitor. "Instead of criticizing the executions, you ought to be doing everything you can to support our new government. We've just had the only non-Communist revolution of the 20th century!"

The new authorities in Havana did indeed seem committed to bringing about sweeping social, political, and economic change in Cuba without veering in the direction of totalitarian Communism or alienating the United States. The question was whether it would be possible to maintain such a careful course. The inclination of reformers, including *auténtico* veterans such as Pepín Bosch and his friends, was to back the new government and urge the United States to do the same, while simultaneously pressing Fidel Castro and other revolutionary leaders to avoid sharp turns. Former President Ramón Grau San Martín, the founder of the Auténtico Party, went so far as to suggest that the United States give the Guantánamo naval base back to Cuba, a measure that would have helped satisfy the nationalist demands being made in the heat of the revolutionary moment. The U.S. government, wary of Fidel Castro and his intentions, refused to consider the idea.

Conflict between the United States and the new Cuban regime was probably inevitable, notwithstanding the hopes of Cuban liberals for harmonious relations. Cuban nationalism for more than fifty years had been fueled by resentment of the U.S. domination of the country, and even a moderate revolutionary government was likely to challenge U.S. interests and provoke a negative reaction from Washington. Fidel Castro, moreover, appeared set from the beginning on having a combative relationship with the United States. After taking power, he refused for weeks to have a serious conversation with the new U.S. ambassador, and he seemed to go out of his way to pick fights with Washington. Those who knew Castro best could not have been surprised. He felt most comfortable operating in an atmosphere of confrontation, and the hegemonic power ninety miles to his north was his ideal adversary. In June 1958, while still in the Sierra Maestra, he had written to his aide Celia Sánchez that "the Americans are going to pay dearly for what they're doing. When this war is over, I'll start a longer and bigger war of my own: the war I'm going to fight against them. I realize that will be my true destiny."

It also became apparent that Bosch and other liberals were overestimating their influence in the new Cuba. As a former finance minister, respected businessman, and possible presidential contender, Bosch had been one of the country's opinion leaders, and in early 1959 he had little reason to think his views no longer mattered. When Bosch objected to an item on the nightly "Hatuey Newsreel" on CMQ-TV, he could expect as the program's sponsor that any changes he requested would be made. Thus, on January 27, displeased that the program producers were using film of firing squads at work, he sent a one-line note to the CMQ owner, Abel Mestre, a longtime business associate.

My dear Abel,

I beg you not to show any executions in the Hatuey newscast.

Yours affectionately,

José M. Bosch

Bosch apparently did not realize that Mestre and other broadcast outlet owners now had to answer to Fidel Castro and his associates, and not just to commercial sponsors, if they wanted to stay in business. What Fidel wanted broadcast would be broadcast.

Two weeks later, Bosch got another lesson in how Cuba was changing. Friends in Puerto Rico alerted him that unnamed Cuban emissaries were inserting themselves into the longstanding debate over Puerto Rico's proper status with respect to the United States. On February 9, Bosch wrote to Cuban prime minister José Miró Cardona, an old acquaintance, to advise him of the developments. "It seems that some member of the [Cuban] government declared that Puerto Rico was a colony that had the right to be independent," Bosch said. "You know well that the situation in Puerto Rico is the product of the free will of the people of that island, and a declaration by Cubans about its status could be used in such a way as to hurt our friends. Your efforts to avoid such frictions will be much appreciated."

Bosch was assuming that Miró Cardona controlled his own administration. But the "prime minister" had no such power. Even without a formal political office, Fidel Castro was the supreme authority in Cuba, and his government cabinet was fast becoming irrelevant. On February 13, four days after Bosch wrote to him about the Puerto Rico comments, José Miró Cardona resigned as prime minister, saying Castro held all the power in Cuba as the "chief of the revolution" and should therefore take the office for himself in order to avoid confusion over who was in charge. President Manuel Urrutia promptly appointed Castro to Miró Cardona's old position. "Now the Government, the revolution and the people will take the same path," declared the newspaper *Revolución*, the official organ of the July 26th Movement. *New York Times* correspondent Ruby Hart Phillips put it more simply, saying the appointment of Castro showed he was to be regarded by Cubans from then on not just as the head of the government, "but as the very government itself."

What this meant in practice became clear almost immediately. In early March 1959, a military tribunal in Santiago unexpectedly acquitted forty-three airmen from Batista's air force who had been charged with mass murder in connection with the bombing of civilians in three eastern provinces during the anti-Batista struggle. Defense attorneys had argued that the air crews were innocent of the charges against them because they had dropped their bombs on unpopulated places and falsified their mission reports to their commanders. Castro, however, was outraged by the verdict and demanded that a new trial be held. His word being law, another military court was hastily organized, and although no new evidence was presented, the airmen were convicted and sentenced to long prison terms. "Revolutionary justice is based not on legal precepts, but on moral conviction," Castro explained, in a sweeping declaration that shocked even some of his own supporters. He was saying that whether the pilots had actually bombed civilians was not even relevant. "Since the airmen belonged to the air force of... Batista," Castro said, "they are criminals and must be punished."

Even after this brazen demonstration of his authoritarian rule, Castro remained popular. The Cuban revolution held out the promise of long overdue social and economic changes, and Castro was still seen by many Cubans as a force for good, no matter his excesses.

• • •

Pepín Bosch was working in his Havana office one day in April 1959 when he received a call from Celia Sánchez, Fidel's aide and confidant. Castro had accepted an invitation to speak before the American Society of Newspaper Editors later that month in Washington, and Sánchez was helping him arrange his trip. "Dr. Castro asked me to call you," Sánchez said. "He would like you to accompany him to the United States."

Bosch's admiration for the "Maximum Leader" had diminished with Castro's creeping usurpation of state authority, his increasingly hostile attitude toward the United States, and his continued use of firing squads (at least 475 executions as of April 11). Bosch was keeping an open mind—Bacardi was still the commercial sponsor of Castro's regular appearances on CMQ-TV's *Meet the Press* program—but he was worried by the signs of a developing dictatorship in Cuba. He told Sánchez to thank Castro for the invitation but explain that he was buried under work obligations as a result of having been in exile for the previous two years.

Later that day, Bosch's telephone rang again. This time it was Castro himself. "Señor Bosch," Fidel said politely, bringing the full force of his persuasive power down on the Bacardi president. "You cannot refuse me. It is your obligation to come with me to Washington." Bosch then agreed to go. "I had to give him the benefit of the doubt," he explained later. "I wasn't sure whether I was right or wrong."

Bosch had never met or spoken with Castro, and the U.S. trip taught him much about Castro's ideas and style. Fidel arrived two hours late for the flight to Miami, keeping Bosch and the rest of his entourage waiting at the airport. Bosch noticed immediately that he was the only businessman in the group. Castro apparently saw him as someone whose presence in the official delegation would send a message that the new Cuban government would be respectful of the business community and willing to work with those capitalists who genuinely wanted the best for their country. Bosch would have felt more comfortable, however, if he had had some company. Castro showed up looking as if he had just come down from the mountains, poorly groomed and wearing a worn and wrinkled uniform, with a pistol on his belt. His appointment secretary sat next to him on the flight out of Havana, cleaning Castro's fingernails. Bosch took a seat alongside Ernesto Betancourt, a bright young economist who had been the July 26th Movement's official representative in Washington and then the managing director of the Cuban Bank of Foreign Trade. Finance Minister Rufo López-Fresquet and Bosch's friend Felipe Pazos, the central bank president, were also on the trip. Neither Raúl Castro nor Che Guevara came along.

On the flight to Washington, Castro moved up and down the aisle, chatting with members of the delegation. When he came to Pepín Bosch, Castro squatted on the floor next to him, like a pupil facing his teacher. It was the first encounter of these two brilliant personalities, each utterly confident in his own judgment but uncertain of the other. "Señor Bosch," Castro said, "Tell me what do you think we can do for the economy in Cuba." The unkempt guerrilla leader was showing as much deference as he could manage before the short, bald businessman in the natty three-piece suit. Bosch, who was old enough to be Fidel's father, looked down at him with his famously icy smile.

"Well, consider our resources," he said, in his soft, high-pitched voice. "We have iron, we have nickel, we have manganese, we have cobalt, and we have the Hanabanilla," a large hydroelectric plant then under construction in Las Villas province. Bosch had long been a proponent of hydroelectric power in Cuba, and he had worked hard in the previous years to promote the dam-building project on the Hanabanilla River. "So we could certainly make steel, and we could even become a high quality producer."

It was clearly an idea that appealed to Castro, who had argued often in favor of ending Cuba's dependence on sugar production. His eyes widened. "Do you think we can produce more than the United States?" he asked.

Bosch was stunned by the question, for its obvious naïveté and for what it revealed about Castro's U.S. obsession. "Of course not, Fidel!" he said. "Whatever are you talking about?"

But Castro was not finished. "Why don't you help me?" he said. As Cuba's most respected businessman, Bosch had enormous influence with his fellow industrialists. Labor leaders saw him as an employer who treated his workers fairly and negotiated in good faith with the unions who represented them. Castro was anxious to establish a business-labor coalition in support of his revolutionary project. After taking power, he had mandated wage increases for workers in many industries, but he had also prohibited strikes and work slowdowns, saying that labor and management needed to work together on behalf of his revolution. "You could help me," he said again to Bosch.

In the coming years, Bosch related many times the story of his exchange with Castro on the flight to Washington, always recalling that he told Castro he could not help him. "We capitalists are not afraid of labor," he quoted himself as saying, "but we are afraid of the combination of labor and government. With your system, you are dominating labor, like Batista did. You want to control labor, and you want to control private enterprise. You can't get help that way. If you want me to help you, you'll have to allow elections and give the workers their freedom. Then you'll see how the country can develop." Bosch claimed that when he uttered the word "freedom," Castro took off "like an arrow," and that they spoke no more during the remainder of the trip. Ernesto Betancourt, who was seated next to Bosch and overheard the entire conversation, recalled it later as Bosch described it.

In a breach of protocol, Castro had not consulted the State Department before applying for his visa to the United States. President Eisenhower snubbed him, leaving town to play golf. Acting Secretary of State Christian Herter, however, hosted a luncheon for Castro and a few dozen invited guests. In remarks at the luncheon, Castro declared that he favored democracy, not Communism, that he would hold free elections, and that he was open to U.S. investment. Pepín Bosch sat in the audience, doubting Castro's honesty. After his unpleasant conversation on the plane, he decided he did not want to continue on the Castro trip and told other delegation members he was ill and wanted to return to Cuba. First, however, he went to New York to visit the offices of Bacardi Imports, where according to Bosch's subsequent accounts he advised his old friend Bartolo Estrada, the company president, that he foresaw problems for Cuba and for Bacardi as long as Castro was in charge.

The tall, bearded rebel leader in rumpled fatigues made a mostly favorable impression wherever he went on his U.S. tour, particularly among the college students he met in New York, Harvard, and Princeton. Passionate and untamed, Fidel electrified his audiences with his eloquence in describing the changes in store for Cuba. The country would not settle for "theoretical democracy," he said, but was determined instead to establish "real democracy," with the right to work, to read, and to write, as well as the right to speak and organize. For those who feared Cuba was turning toward radicalism, he said that private property would be protected and that the only nationalizations he foresaw were those of public utility companies. In what appeared to be a criticism of Communism and capitalism alike, Castro advocated a sociopolitical model "that does not forget the rights of man, [that wants] no bread without freedom, no freedom without bread, no dictatorship of one man, one class, one caste."

Pepín Bosch by then had concluded that Castro would say anything that suited his immediate political purposes, though he was careful not to make that charge in public. In comments to Cuban reporters following his meetings in Washington, Bosch said he remained confident that U.S. investors would come to Cuba, and he gave Castro credit for inspiring them. "In all candor," he told the *Diario de la Marina* newspaper, "it can be said that Dr. Fidel Castro has known how to capture the imagination and the sympathy of the people and the authorities in this capital. His public presentations have been well received, and we should be satisfied and convinced that this visit will serve to tighten the ties of friendship between the two nations." Fidel Castro's public works minister, Manolo Ray, had asked Bosch to serve as the unpaid director of the Hanabanilla hydroelectric project, and shortly after his return from Washington he accompanied Ray on an inspection tour. To Bosch's delight, Castro's government had increased the budget for the three-year-old project by 50 percent, making its completion a top priority, and Bosch's review of the dam operation generated considerable press attention.

Castro's reform program for Cuba, meanwhile, remained broadly popular. In March the government mandated rent and utility rate reductions, providing an immediate benefit to the urban proletariat. Racial discrimination was abolished, and dozens of hotels, restaurants, nightclubs, and beach resorts were opened for the first time to black Cubans. In May the government announced a new agrarian reform law, under which no person or corporation would be allowed to own more than 995 acres (though exceptions were made for the best cattle ranches and most efficient sugar and rice plantations). Landholdings in excess of that figure were to be expropriated and turned over to landless families, with the former owners compensated in state bonds. A few wealthy Cubans and right-wing commentators grumbled that the new law appeared to be a step in the direction of socialism, but the consensus in favor of the reform was remarkable. The leading conservative newspaper in Cuba, the *Diario de la Marina* in Havana, endorsed the land redistribution scheme and published a series of articles, complete with photographs, highlighting the wretched conditions under which many farmworkers were living. The Bacardi Rum Company showed its support for the program by donating five tractors to the agrarian reform institute, acting jointly with the Bacardi unions.

At the Ministry of Finance, Rufo López-Fresquet and his team of young, idealistic economists were crafting a new tax code. The law that emerged from their deliberations in the spring of 1959 favored Cuban firms over foreign companies, manufacturing industries over sugar, and small businesses over large ones. The code was progressive, with the heaviest taxes imposed on old landowning families and inheritances. In the interests of more balanced economic development, the provinces were advantaged over Havana. Personal income tax rates were increased (though they remained moderate by U.S. standards), with heavier penalties for tax evasion. López-Fresquet said the tax code was written both to redistribute existing wealth and to provide incentives for the creation of new wealth, a philosophical approach consistent with what Pepín Bosch himself advocated when he was finance minister a decade earlier.

By the summer of 1959, Cuba was showing that a major social and economic transformation could be achieved in a country without destroying private enterprise. The change was not painless for the moneyed class; in the first six months after Castro took power, a significant shift of wealth took place in Cuba, with real wages rising by about 15 percent and the incomes of landlords and businessmen declining by a similar amount. Progressive firms like the Bacardi Rum Company cooperated nevertheless. Antonio Jorge, the chief economist under López-Fresquet, would later recall those months as a time of great potential for Cuba. "You had entrepreneurs willing to divest themselves of a sizable portion of their assets and donate them to a revolutionary government in order to promote the economic development of the nation and cultivate solidarity," he said in an interview in 2004 in Miami, where he was a Cuban exile teaching economic history. "All the classes were ready to cooperate and make a success of the Cuban revolution. What a historic opportunity for the country! And it was wasted."

· · ·

In the dramatic period after Fidel Castro's triumphant rise to power, the new governing authorities repeatedly singled out Compañía Ron Bacardi, S.A., as a Cuban firm that could serve as an example of what it meant for a capitalist enterprise to be a revolutionary partner. One of the company's most important assignments was to be a corporate sponsor of the new government's propaganda operation. On February 13, the vice president of the CMQ radio and television network, Arturo Chabau, informed the Bacardi marketing team that Fidel Castro wanted CMQ to broadcast a new daily dramatic series called *Pathways of Freedom,* which would relate the detailed story of the Cuban revolution, from its origins in the Sierra Maestra to the collapse of the Batista regime. Chabau said Bacardi would be the "ideal" commercial sponsor for the TV series "precisely because of the theme and because of how much the company was affected by the overthrown regime. Indeed, it would be hard to find another company in Cuba with more right to sponsor the program."

A few months later, the Bacardi Rum Company was asked to support an even more ambitious project. Fidel Castro asked the country's poor farmers and farmworkers—the *guajiro* population—to come to Havana on July 26 for a massive rally in support of the revolution and its agrarian reform plans. Housing for the visitors would need to be arranged, and the rally organizing committee asked Bacardi executives to use their print, radio, and television advertising slots to encourage Havana citizens to accommodate people who needed a place to stay. The organizers even enclosed a script they wanted the company to use in its radio and television announcements, and they made clear they anticipated the company's compliance with their request. "Given the extraordinary cooperation you have given to all the [26th of July] Movement initiatives," the organizers wrote, "and given the singular importance of this first July 26th [celebration] in liberated Cuba, we expect your rapid, thorough, and decisive collaboration."

The decision whether to support Fidel Castro's revolutionary program or resist it carried huge and inescapable consequences. There could be no case-by-case collaboration; the revolution demanded total loyalty. The practical significance of that reality for Bacardi business operations had gradually become apparent, beginning just a few weeks after Castro's triumph. The Bacardi unions immediately presented the company management with a new list of demands, asking for a reduction of the work week from forty-eight to forty hours with no cut in pay. In the past, the management could have negotiated with the union leadership on issues like that, but now it would have to consider what the "revolutionary" position would be.

The all-or-nothing mentality put Cuban liberals in a precarious position. One of the first to complain was a courageous man named Luis Aguilar who wrote a political column in Havana's *Prensa Libre* newspaper. As early as March 1959, Aguilar fretted about the "excessive facility with which the term 'counterrevolutionary' is flung in every direction, as if it were not quite possible to make a distinction between a poisonous censure and a criticism or dissent which is honest and sincere." Writing three months later, he described the dilemma facing liberal dissidents in more anguished terms.

> On one side, like a torrent of energy, the Revolution displays its accomplishments and its programs, its dream of justice and its will to heal, and this invigorating force makes the soul thrill with love for Cuba and gives rise to a loyal devotion to duty.
>
> On the other side, there appear the inevitable negative aspects of every movement, the excesses,...and one feels the temptation to raise his voice humbly and serenely to warn, advise, or dissent. Ah! But one is immediately reminded that to point out a mistake of the Revolution means to cooperate with the somber legion of enemies who inside and outside of Cuba are planning a sinister revenge.

Aguilar, a Santiago native close to the Bacardi family, was expressing publicly what many Bacardis were feeling privately. Despite their concerns about Fidel Castro and his dictatorial governing style, despite their displeasure over the summary executions and the increasingly harsh anti-American rhetoric, the Bacardis for the most part kept quiet, not wanting to be portrayed as enemies of the revolution. In July the company agreed to use its advertising to promote the *guajiro* rally in Havana, precisely as it had been asked to do. "Embrace for history," read one newspaper ad taken out by the company:

> On this July 26th of freedom and happiness, the Cubans of the capital open their arms in a fraternal embrace of their brothers from the countryside. Hatuey and Bacardi enthusiastically support this embrace of our history by our present. May this bringing together of our people assure a future of happiness for the nation.

◆ ◆ ◆

Fidel Castro played a cynical game with many Cuban employers, tacitly encouraging them to believe that a collaborative attitude on their part would make it less likely that the revolutionary government would move toward socialism. He once joked with an interviewer about all the bankers and businessmen who had come to see him in the first days after his triumph, eager to show they were ready to cooperate with the revolution. "I said to myself, 'Let them think as they please. The more they believe they can count on us, the more they will be surprised,'" Castro recalled.

By the summer of 1959, while still emphatically denying he was a Communist, Castro had begun to attack those who were raising alarms about Communist influence in his government. When President Manuel Urrutia told a television interviewer in mid-July that "the Communists are inflicting terrible harm on Cuba," Castro reacted furiously. In a carefully staged move, he announced he was resigning his position as prime minister, and he blasted Urrutia mercilessly in a four-hour televised speech, saying he was fabricating a Communist threat in Cuba in order to invite the United States to intervene against the revolution. Castro, who just six months earlier had promised to "surrender" his authority to Urrutia, now claimed that the president was frustrating genuine revolutionaries with his refusal to support their initiatives.

The dramatic resignation speech was pure political theater; Castro had no intention of giving up power. Upon hearing his denunciation of Urrutia, thousands of angry Cubans descended on the presidential palace, just as Castro knew they would, demanding Urrutia's ouster. Within hours, the president had submitted his resignation and taken refuge in a friend's house, fearful of arrest or even execution. But Castro was not yet satisfied. Whether he would himself continue in power, he said, was a decision for the "Cuban people," by which he meant those who would appear at the big rally on July 26. It was only then, to the crowd's roaring approval, that Castro announced he would accept "the will of the people" and remain prime minister. "This is real democracy!" he shouted, waving his arms. As with the proexecution rally six months earlier, Castro had shown that he did not need elections to consolidate power; he could strengthen his position and destroy his enemies by mobilizing crowds. It was a practice Castro shared with dictators everywhere.

To many observers, however, the mass demonstrations in Cuba were qualitatively different from the fascist rallies seen in Franco's Spain, Mussolini's Italy, or Hitler's Germany. In Cuba, they were happy, partying affairs where mothers brought their babies and people laughed and sang, including a paean to Castro, "With Fidel, with Fidel, always with Fidel," sung to the tune of "Jingle Bells." Castro was unquestionably a tyrant, determined to eliminate all dissent and impose absolute rule, but he and his allies were also making efforts to curb corruption and improve the lives of ordinary people. The Havana municipal administration, for example, built thirty-eight new school complexes in 1959 for the same amount of money that had been paid out in bribes a year earlier.

Even those Cubans who were upset by Castro's authoritarianism and leftist ideas retained some faith that the trends would not last. An article on the "sputtering" Cuban economy published in the *Wall Street Journal* in July 1959 cited "a school of thought...that maintains that if the economy gets into grave trouble, Mr. Castro will adopt more moderate economic policies in an effort to prevent total collapse." Within the Bacardi family, no one saw any reason for panic. As worrisome as the political situation may have been, business prospects were bright. Pepín Bosch told a television interviewer that Hatuey beer was enjoying its best sales since 1952.

. . .

In March 1959, a director of the Seagram liquor empire, Noah Torno, visited Bosch at the Bacardi offices in Havana, hoping to interest him in a business consolidation. As Bosch explained later in a letter to Daniel Bacardi in Santiago, Torno came with various ideas for a Bacardi-Seagram collaboration in the rum business, suggesting that Seagram purchase 30 percent of the Bacardi rum interests in Puerto Rico. When Bosch told him no portion of the Bacardi operation in Puerto Rico was for sale, Torno suggested the two companies jointly purchase the Merino rum company in Brazil, or the Serralles distillery in Puerto Rico. Each time, Bosch said no. "I told him we work exclusively for our Bacardi shareholders," Bosch wrote Daniel. "We finished on friendly terms, though he kept repeating his desire for a merger with us that would give us control of three quarters of all rum sales in the world. But I explained that we didn't want to join with any other company and that our shareholders didn't want to sell any portion of their stock." After their meeting, Bosch escorted his Seagram suitor to the nearby Floridita bar and treated him to a Hemingway daiquiri, prepared with white Bacardi rum. "He said our product was a wonder," Bosch wrote Daniel. "I then gave him a glass of 73 [the Bacardi premium aged rum] to taste, and he told me it was the best rum he had ever tasted. We parted as good friends."

Noah Torno had come to Cuba as a personal representative of Seagram patriarch Sam Bronfman, the brilliant but ruthless liquor baron who had become rich during Prohibition selling whiskey through Meyer Lansky's syndicate. Bronfman sent Torno to meet with Pepín Bosch because he knew a successful business operation when he saw one, and he wanted a piece of it.

Before long, so did Fidel Castro.

Chapter 16

❧❧❧

The Year Cuba Changed

In March 1960, about fifteen months after Fidel Castro took command of Cuba, Pepín Bosch brought Bacardi rum distributors and their wives together for a three-day convention at a resort on the Isle of Pines, the former pirate hideout said to have been the inspiration for Robert Louis Stevenson's *Treasure Island*. A week later, Bosch and his wife Enriqueta hosted Hatuey beer distributors at a beachfront hotel in Cienfuegos, on Cuba's southern coast. Both events were lavish affairs. The salesmen gamely met each day to work out marketing strategies for the coming months, but the conventions were meant more for relaxation and recreation than for serious work. At lunchtime, Bosch circulated cheerfully among his guests, a glass of beer in hand, dressed casually in a short-sleeved sport shirt, offering congratulations for notable sales achievements. At sixty-two, he had barely any hair left and his waist had thickened considerably, but he still carried himself with great confidence, and he was determined to project good humor and optimism. He arranged boat rides and fishing excursions for the sales agents and their wives, and at evening banquets he applauded as couples rose to dance the *cha-cha-chá* before a live orchestra.

They were vintage Bacardi gatherings, celebrating the good life and the carefree Cuban spirit with which the company had long been associated. But the prevailing mood was one of nostalgia. The new Cuba was a more austere place. Fidel Castro and his comrade Che Guevara were promoting a new revolutionary morality, and drinking and dancing were frowned upon. The Isles of Pines resort where the Bacardi sales agents gathered was just a few miles from a prison where a famous dissident *comandante* named Huber Matos was being held in a dark and dirty cell.

On the night before the Hatuey convention opened in Cienfuegos, government agents took over the CMQ television network. The network owner, Abel Mestre, had gone on air that afternoon and denounced Fidel Castro for his dictatorial rule. Pepín Bosch had known Mestre, a fellow *santiaguero*, for years and helped him buy his broadcasting operation, and the government's confiscation of Mestre's network hung heavily over Bosch as he gathered with his Hatuey distributors in Cienfuegos. At the conclusion of the convention, his wife Enriqueta insisted that an impromptu Mass be held in one of the hotel meeting rooms, presided over by a local priest. The meeting ended on a quiet note. Given the hostility the revolutionary authorities were showing toward all "bourgeois" activity in Cuba, no one knew whether there would be any more such company celebrations.

• • •

The term "revolution" was tossed around freely in Cuba. In the previous hundred years, there were at least three or four, and almost every major political party in Cuba from the time of José Martí onward found a way to call itself *revolucionario*, whether of the "authentic" or "orthodox" variety. In January 1959, most Cubans assumed that Fidel Castro's "revolution" was the one he had just led against Batista. But that was only the start. "The revolution is beginning now," Fidel said on that New Year night when he addressed the people of Santiago from the town hall balcony. The words might have been lost in the euphoria of the moment, but Castro meant just what he said. The real Cuban Revolution—a social, political, and economic refashioning of the country into a rigid socialist state—came only in 1959 and 1960. Castro advised Cubans at the outset that it would be "a harsh...undertaking, particularly in the initial phases," and indeed it was. It required the dismantling of a capitalist economic system, the uprooting and displacement of an entire social class, and the replacement of "bourgeois" political institutions and free media with a new structure of state control and one-party rule.

Castro needed time to set the revolution in motion, which was one reason for his installation of respected moderates in the first post-Batista government. What only a tiny number of Cubans realized at the time was that key policy decisions during those early months were not being made inside the government at all but by a parallel task force meeting secretly in a beach house a half hour's drive from downtown Havana. In addition to Fidel Castro, the group consisted of his brother Raúl, Che Guevara, Vilma Espín, and a handful of others, most of them committed Marxist-Leninists. The group allowed the appointed cabinet ministers to proceed with their moderate reform program, unaware that more radical plans were afoot. Finance Minister Rufo López-Fresquet, in his book *My Fourteen Months with Castro*, recalled being so overjoyed when Fidel signed the tax reform law in May 1959 that he spontaneously hugged him, only to notice that Fidel was laughing. "Maybe when the time comes to apply the law," Castro said with a grin, "there won't be any tax-payers."

By the end of 1959, twelve of the twenty-one cabinet ministers Castro had chosen in January were gone, having resigned or been forced out. At the central bank, Pepín Bosch's friend Felipe Pazos had been replaced by Che Guevara, who knew nothing about economics and looked to the Soviet bloc for political inspiration. There could have been no more dramatic or symbolic ministerial shift. Guevara seemed to take delight in ridiculing the business leaders with whom he met. When asked on one occasion about the future role of private enterprise in Cuba, Guevara said there were plenty of sidewalk curbs that needed to be painted. The government, he predicted, would control the "important" industries, but private manufacturers would still be allowed to make such items as women's handbags. Cuban businessmen weren't sure of Guevara's seriousness or whether he spoke for Castro, but a sign of the government's intentions came in December 1959, with the confiscation of Textilera Ariguanabo, the big textile manufacturing firm owned by the Hedges family of New York. The Bacardi Rum Company was left as the largest industrial firm still in private hands.

Desperate to shield their enterprises from government intervention, the Cuban National Association of Manufacturers came up with a plan to impress the authorities. They would back a law that would set aside a share of company profits in Cuba to establish a fund to support the country's industrial development. In early 1960, a delegation went to see Finance Minister Rufo López-Fresquet with their idea. By then convinced that Fidel Castro and Che Guevara had no interest in protecting private Cuban companies, López-Fresquet told the businessmen not to waste their time.

A turning point in the perception of Castro's plans for Cuba had come the previous autumn, when he ordered the arrest of Huber Matos, a rebel army commander serving as military governor of Camagüey province. Matos had summoned up the courage to complain personally to Castro about growing Communist influence; after Castro ignored his protest, Matos resigned, saying he feared he would become "an obstacle to the revolution" if he remained in his position of command. At the time, Castro and his allies were still consolidating their power, and he knew that any allegation that his government was turning toward Communism could do serious damage. He promptly ordered Matos arrested, denouncing him as an agent of reactionary forces and accusing him of trying to ingratiate himself with the United States. At another of his massive outdoor rallies a few days later, Castro made a series of unsubstantiated allegations against Matos and then turned to the crowd and asked what should be done with him. "¡*Al paredón!*" the crowd answered. "To the wall!" Put on trial two months later, Matos was allowed to call no witnesses in his own defense. Raúl Castro suggested he should "die on his knees."

Matos calmly denied each charge presented against him but refused to ask for mercy and insisted he remained loyal to the revolution for which he had fought. "If this court believes that in order for the revolution to triumph and Cuba to progress, you must condemn me to the firing squad, I shall accept that decision," he said. "And if you do, I invite the judges to witness my execution to show you that a commander from the Sierra Maestra knows how to die, shouting with his last breath: 'Long live the Cuban revolution!'"

Matos was not executed, but Castro had him sentenced to twenty years in the same Isle of Pines prison where he had been sent after his own Moncada conviction. Whereas Castro had been held in a comfortable room with books and cooking facilities, however, Matos was confined to a tiny, unlit cell, beaten, denied medical attention, and forced to sleep in his underwear on a stone floor. Castro had been released after only twenty-two months, but he kept Huber Matos in prison for every minute of his sentence, not releasing him until October 21, 1979, twenty years to the day after his arrest. Central bank president Felipe Pazos left the Castro government in response to the Matos affair, as did Manolo Ray, the public works minister (and codirector with Pepín Bosch of the Hanabanilla hydroelectric project).

• • •

The ministers who were pushed aside in 1959—Miró Cardona, Urrutia, Pazos, Ray—were the very ones whose appointments had once given Pepín Bosch confidence in Castro's government. Bosch was nevertheless careful to avoid making any provocative statements that might aggravate his own relations with the authorities, or those of his company. His New Year's message to Bacardi workers, executives, and shareholders in January 1960 offered only a poignant hint of uncertainty about the company's place in Cuba from then on:

> The ninety-eighth year in the life of this company is now beginning. Long years of joy and sadness have passed by. In all times, members of this organization have contributed their best and most sincere efforts to the Nation, in order that freedom, democracy, and human rights might be a reality in our country. We must always make such sacrifices and take such risks for our country without expecting anything in return.
>
> No one can predict the future; we will know it only as it unfolds. But with hopes of the best for all, I send you this greeting of happiness and joy.

By springtime, Bosch suspected that the Castro government was preparing to move against Bacardi Rum. Among the warning signs was a union accusation that the company was engaging in "counterrevolutionary" behavior by investing in Brazil rather than in Cuba. Workers at the Hatuey brewery in Manacas denounced the plant manager, Augusto "Polo" Miranda, as a "capitalist enemy." Such charges caught Bosch's attention, because one method the authorities used to take over the management of a firm was to declare it had an "insoluble" problem with its unions, at which point the Ministry of Labor would intervene. A detailed questionnaire arrived from the National Institute of Agrarian Reform (INRA), the government agency that was expropriating farms, businesses, and other private property in Cuba. The INRA wanted to know what products Bacardi made at each of its facilities and in what quantities, plus how many workers were employed and on which shifts. In April 1960, the top Bacardi executive in the United States, Bartolo Estrada, asked his lawyers to determine whether a seizure of the company's Cuban headquarters would affect the legal standing of its U.S. subsidiary, Bacardi Imports, within the United States. The answer was no.

A more serious question was the security of the Bacardi trademarks. Pepín Bosch had concluded that the creation of Bacardi International Limited (BIL) in 1957 did not provide adequate protection of the company's intellectual property. Though BIL now held exclusive rights to sell Bacardi products outside Cuba, the Bacardi trademarks themselves officially remained the property of Compañía Ron Bacardi, S.A., in Santiago. If the Cuban company were nationalized, the trademarks could be in jeopardy. Though it would be a tricky process, the legal ownership of the marks somehow had to be shifted outside the country. As a first step, Bosch needed to get the original certificates out of the country. Fearing they would be seized by airport inspectors if he attempted to carry them out himself, Bosch mailed the certificates to New York, one by one.

The revolutionary authorities were meanwhile shutting down the remaining semi-independent media in Cuba. After the *Diario de la Marina*, the oldest of Havana's newspapers, was "occupied" by workers in May, the courageous Santiago columnist Luis Aguilar dared to criticize the move in his column in *Prensa Libre*. "Now the time of unanimity is arriving in Cuba," he wrote, "a solid and impenetrable totalitarian unanimity.... There will be no disagreeing voices, no possibility of criticism, no public refutations." Such commentaries often appeared in the newspaper with a critical postscript criticizing the writer, inserted by the printers' union or by some journalist willing to do the bidding of the revolutionary authorities. In a note appended to Aguilar's column, an anonymous writer pointed out that for anyone who objected to "totalitarian unanimity," there was always prison, exile...or the wall. After its publication, a mob confronted Aguilar in the streets with shouts of "*¡Al paredón!*" Chastened, he left Cuba with his wife and children.

The authorities justified the suppression of independent media voices by saying they needed to protect the Cuban revolution from its enemies. They cited the policies and actions of the U.S. government, which had indeed concluded that Fidel Castro's revolutionary regime had to be brought to an end. In March 1960, President Eisenhower issued a secret presidential order to the CIA to begin recruiting Cuban exiles who would be willing to return to the island and direct a guerrilla campaign against the Castro government. In June, U.S. oil companies announced they would not refine the Soviet crude oil that began arriving that month, prompting a new wave of anti-U.S. sentiment. In retaliation, the Cuban government nationalized $850 million of U.S. oil company assets on the island.

Among the firms affected by the measure was an oil exploration company named Trans-Cuba, which Pepín Bosch had cofounded a few years earlier with the assistance of some U.S. investors. In the course of investigating Trans-Cuba assets, Cuban officials learned the firm had $1.8 million in a New York bank. They succeeded in getting the Trans-Cuba treasurer to write a check for the balance, payable to the Cuban government, but Bosch had included in the by-laws a requirement that the company president had to cosign all checks. A Cuban navy officer soon showed up at Bosch's office with the check and a personal message from Fidel. "He praised me for my patriotism and my love of Cuba," Bosch recalled later, "and then he asked me to sign the check."

Until that moment, Bosch had managed to stay out of trouble. Even after he abandoned the Castro delegation in Washington, Bosch said later, Fidel treated him with "utmost respect." But now Castro had Bosch cornered. If he refused to sign the check, he could be arrested. Bosch told the navy officer he would have to consult with his shareholders before signing the check. Realizing there was no way out of his predicament, he began preparations to leave Cuba, fearing the navy officer would return. When his request for an "exit permit" didn't receive prompt attention, Bosch went to the Interior Ministry to demand it. Told the minister was not there, Bosch said, "O.K., I'll wait for him," and took a seat in the reception area. When the minister, whom Bosch knew, finally arrived four hours later, he had no option but to approve the permit on the spot. Before leaving the country, Bosch stopped to say good-bye to his lawyer and aide Guillermo Mármol at the Bacardi building in downtown Havana. "We're next," Bosch warned. "We'll be right behind the oil companies."

Bosch then headed to the airport with his wife Enriqueta, destined for Miami.

It had been less than four months since the two of them had entertained Bacardi and Hatuey sales agents at Cuban beach resorts. For the second time in three years, a Cuban dictator had forced Bosch into exile. Like other Cubans who were leaving, he believed the Castro government would not survive and that he could soon return and pick up where he had left off, just as he had done after the collapse of the Batista regime a year and a half earlier. Fidel Castro was not Fulgencio Batista, however, and Pepín Bosch never set foot in Cuba again.

• • •

Some of the Cubans most angered by Fidel Castro's radical turn were those who, like Pepín Bosch, had once supported him and even defended him against his critics. Feeling personally betrayed, they resolved to work for his overthrow. By the summer of 1960, Manolo Ray and Rufo López-Fresquet, Castro's former public works and finance ministers, had both gone underground to conspire against the regime. For López-Fresquet, the last straw had been Castro's decision to sign a trade pact with the Soviet Union. David Salvador, the head of Cuba's main trade union organization, had also gone underground. Salvador had been an outspoken *fidelista* throughout 1959, committing Cuban labor to the revolutionary cause, but he broke with Castro after realizing that he would not allow Cuban workers to be independently represented. The three men formed an underground opposition group, the Movimiento Revolucionario del Pueblo (MRP), the Revolutionary Movement of the People, advocating a continuation of the Cuban revolution and its key reforms but without Castro as its head, *fidelismo sin Fidel.*

No anti-Castro resistance effort was making headway, however. Fidel was far more adept at countering his foes than Batista had been—and far more popular. The rent and utility rate reductions, the expansion of health and education opportunities, and his firm nationalist stance earned Castro support among the Cuban people. For all his excesses, he was still calling for Cuba to move dramatically ahead for the benefit of those most in need, and his revolutionary movement still captivated members of the poor and working classes in particular, who did not remember life being so great when the 1940 Constitution was still in effect.

Cubans were becoming more polarized by the day in their views of Fidel Castro and what he was doing to their country. Tensions were even developing within the Bacardi family. The Bacardi name had been linked to every revolution Cuba had experienced, and some family members felt that to turn against this one would be to betray their heritage. Herminia Cape, who had conspired with her brother-in-law Emilio Bacardi during the 1895 revolution, remained a fervent *fidelista*. Daniel Bacardi recognized that Castro was becoming a dictator, but he argued that the objectionable actions of the revolutionary government should be seen in a historical context and that its social and economic reforms were producing a more ethical nation. "The tyrant Batista and his rogues left our poor country impoverished," he wrote to a friend in November 1959. "Thank goodness that the suffering of the people in that infernal time has purified the soul and the ideals of the Cuban, who now is good and wants this country to be for everyone and not just for a few." Even after moderates began deserting Castro's government, Daniel struggled to remain loyal, telling other family members that the progressive Bacardi record in Cuba meant the company would not be touched by the revolutionary authorities.

With Pepín Bosch's departure in July 1960, Daniel became the top Bacardi executive in Cuba. Their contrasting views of Castro and his intentions put him and Bosch at cross-purposes: Daniel tried his best to keep the company on cooperative terms with the Castro government even as Bosch began discreetly supporting efforts to undermine it. Whether Daniel knew it or not, other family members and Bacardi people, including Daniel's first cousin Emilio Bacardi Rosell, whose father was a twin brother of Daniel's father, had already begun to work secretly with opposition groups. The only Bacardi of his generation named after his celebrated grandfather, Emilio got involved in anti-Castro underground work in Santiago with his wife Josefina; the two of them later escaped arrest only by climbing a fence at the U.S. Guantánamo naval base and taking refuge there. Augusto "Polo" Miranda, the manager of the Hatuey brewery in Manacas, and Rino Puig, the sales manager for Hatuey beer in Santiago, were also collaborating with the resistance movement. Miranda, having supported the 26th of July rebels during the anti-Batista uprising, switched sides and joined the anti-Castro opposition in 1960 after his brewery workers denounced him as a capitalist. Puig, who had lived in Spain in childhood, told his Bacardi colleagues that Fidel reminded him of the Nazi, Fascist, and Communist leaders who had ruined Europe.

Puig was an energetic and athletic man who had competed along with his brother in the 1948 Olympics in London as a member of the Cuban rowing team, and he was prepared to do whatever he could to oppose the Castro government. He kept his contacts with the anti-Castro underground secret, but his opposition views soon resulted in a tense confrontation with Daniel Bacardi at the El Cotorro brewery outside Havana. Daniel had taken charge of the company, and when Puig saw him at a business meeting at the brewery, he asked to speak to Daniel privately.

"Daniel," Puig said quietly, staring him hard in the eyes. "You know we're fucked, don't you?"

"What are you talking about, Rino?"

"This is Communism, Daniel."

Daniel's face reddened. For months, he had been having these arguments with others in his family and in the company. The harsh antibusiness rhetoric from Che Guevara and others, the elimination of independent voices, and the expanding alliance with the Soviet bloc had made his position no easier, but he was determined not to waver. Daniel had seen how the landless plantation workers, the laborers, and the marginalized black Cubans for the first time in their lives felt they had a government that cared about their interests. He knew that young people were volunteering to go into remote mountain areas to teach illiterate peasants how to read, and he had seen teams of medical workers for the first time carrying out mass vaccinations and other public health campaigns. Of all the Bacardis, Daniel was the most beloved in his community, the one with friends in every corner of the city, famous for his warmth and generosity. "Rino," he said, his voice rising, "this is not Communism. *This is the Revolution.*"

Rino—a full head taller than Daniel, nearly twenty years younger, and strong as a horse—did not flinch. "I swear to you, Daniel. They're going to take all this away. We've got haciendas, we've got enormous businesses, and it's all lost. I promise you."

"Rino," Daniel responded, his eyes flashing, "it was at your mother's house that I met my wife, and I have great admiration for you. But if anyone else were talking like this to me, I would pick up the phone and have him arrested!"

"Daniel!" Puig shouted back. "They're going to fuck you completely!"

"If they take me, they take me! We can't let imperialism defeat us!"

The conversation was over. Daniel Bacardi was in an impossible situation, and he knew it. With Bosch gone, he was now the head of Cuba's largest private industrial enterprise, and the company was a tempting takeover target, no matter his personal loyalty. Che Guevara was already saying the Cuban revolution was guided by Marxist principles, and that as the official in charge of the economy he wanted all strategic industries in the hands of the state.

Daniel simply could not bring himself to believe that Bacardi Rum, nearly a century old and arguably the Cuban company most closely identified with the national soul, would be taken away from the Bacardi family. He began to recognize the political reality, however, when an official from the local labor department showed up at the rum-bottling plant in Santiago on September 30, 1960, and ordered a fifteen-minute halt in operations. The official said he was acting at the request of the bottling workers' union, though he could not tell Daniel what labor complaint prompted the action. Daniel immediately wrote an angry letter to the labor office, asking how he could respond to the workers' complaint if he didn't even know what it was.

. . .

Manuel Jorge Cutillas overslept a few minutes on the morning of October 14, just enough to miss the top of the 6 A.M. newscast on the clock radio by his bed. The first thing he heard was the announcer reading a list of Cuban firms: "...Compañía Azucarera Yatefas, Compañía Azucarera Fidelidad, S.A., Azucarera Oriental San Ramón, S.A...." It was a group of sugar mills. The announcer then started with a new list, what he called *Grupo B:* "Compañía Destiladora San Nicolás, S.A., José Arechabala, S.A...." At the mention of the latter, Cutillas sat up quickly, wide awake. Arechabala made Havana Club rum, the chief Bacardi rival in Cuba. Cutillas instantly suspected what was coming: "Compañía Ron Bacardi, S.A., Cervecería Modelo, S.A., Cervecería Central, S.A...."

"Oh my God," he said quietly to his wife. "It's happening." The Bacardi rum and beer business in Cuba, founded by Don Facundo in 1862 and maintained by four succeeding Bacardi generations, had become the property of the Cuban government. A few hours earlier, Fidel Castro had signed a decree ordering the nationalization of the Cuban and U.S. banks on the island, plus 382 private companies, of which all but twenty were entirely Cuban owned. In addition to the Bacardi Rum Company and its affiliated Hatuey breweries, the Castro government seized thirteen department stores, sixty-one textile factories, 105 sugar mills, sixteen rice mills, thirteen grocery suppliers, nineteen construction firms, four paint factories, and eleven movie houses, as well as more than a hundred other private companies.

The government justified the nationalizations by saying that Cuba's private entrepreneurs followed "a policy contrary to the interests of the Revolution" by taking profits in cash rather than reinvesting them, by borrowing money rather than risking their own operating capital, and by abandoning their firms and thus their workers. The Bacardi firm was guilty of none of these things. What was "contrary to the interests of the Revolution" was merely that the company was continuing to exist as a capitalist firm. The nationalization law made clear that socialism was to be the official guiding ideology in Cuba. The country's economic development, the government declared, "can only be achieved through economic planning...and national control of all basic industries," just as Che Guevara had argued for months.*

Cutillas, the fourth-generation Bacardi son, dressed quickly and rushed to the distillery on Matadero Street, half expecting to find it surrounded by armed troops. Though just twenty-eight years old, he was already one of the key figures in the family business. His grandfather Radamés Covani was second vice president, his father, Manuel Cutillas Sr., was administrator of the Hatuey brewery, and Manuel Jorge himself was the top chemical engineer at the distillery. He showed up at the plant itching for a fight, but to his astonishment he found everything operating normally. The guard posted at the entrance was the same man who was there every morning, and the workers were going on with their jobs as if nothing had changed. Everyone had heard about the nationalization decree, but no government agent had arrived to take charge.

Despite what they had done to prepare for the nationalization, the revolutionary authorities had not bothered to determine where the Bacardi Rum Company was actually headquartered. Instead of going to the main company office on Aguilera Street in Santiago, the Cuban military officers in charge of the expropriation had headed that morning to the Bacardi building in downtown Havana, where the company had only a sales office. The most senior company employee they could find there was Juan Prado, the thirty-year-old sales manager. Prado, cheerful and engaging, was a born salesman and a rising star within the company. Impressed by his early performance, Pepín Bosch had put him in charge of the Havana region at the age of twenty-six. Nothing Prado had previously encountered, however, prepared him to deal with the sudden appearance in his office of two Cuban marines and several armed *milicianos*. The senior officer clutched a copy of the Bacardi expropriation order, a one-page mimeographed document with several misspellings and ungrammatical phrases.

"You need to take the paper to Santiago," Prado said. "That's the company headquarters." But the marines said their orders were to come to the Bacardi building in Havana and get the keys to the office. Not knowing what else to

---

*Enrique Oltuski, who served as a vice-minister under Che Guevara, said in a 2005 interview in Havana that Bacardi was nationalized "in spite of the fact that the owners had a positive historical role. It was a general rule. The nationalization of Bacardi was not against the enterprise, nor against that family. It was part of a national measure. Many North American enterprises took a very radical position against the Revolution, but the nationalization of Bacardi came [only] after we declared socialism, when we were against the big companies."

say, Prado asked the senior revolutionary officer for a receipt. "I have to have something to show my boss," he said awkwardly. The officer scribbled something on a piece of paper, and Prado handed him the keys.

The two men had met previously around town, and the officer did his best to be friendly with Prado. "You don't owe Bacardi anything," he said. "You're not family. This will be a people's company from now on. It'll be a big opportunity for you. Why don't you stay with us?" Prado acknowledged the offer, but said nothing. Anxious to consult with Daniel Bacardi and other executives over the next steps but reluctant to talk on the phone, he immediately booked a seat on an afternoon flight to Santiago. To his unpleasant surprise, the two marines were on the same flight, having belatedly realized they should have gone to Santiago in the first place.

In the meantime, several dozen armed *milicianos* had shown up at the company facilities in Santiago and established a perimeter around the property. As he left the distillery that afternoon, Manuel Jorge Cutillas was stopped at the front gate by one of the *milicianos* and asked to open his trunk. Cutillas was furious, but the *milicianos* all had guns, and with clenched teeth he went along with the request. When Juan Prado arrived from Havana, he told Daniel that he had been invited to stay with the company and asked him whether that would be helpful. "I can't tell you to do that," Daniel said. He was still trying to grasp what had happened and didn't know what to say.

Early the next morning, Daniel sat down at a table in the company offices with two representatives of the state conglomerate into which the rum and beer companies were to be absorbed, a lawyer from the "industrialization" office of the National Institute of Agrarian Reform, and the man designated by the revolutionary government to be the new administrator of the Bacardi enterprise, a mild-mannered accountant by the name of Andres Yebra. Three Bacardi union leaders were also there. Daniel represented the company, assisted by the treasurer, Orfilio Peláez, and three executives who had married granddaughters of Emilio Bacardi: Manuel Cutillas Sr., from the Hatuey brewery, José Argamasilla Sr., the public relations chief, and deputy manager Luis del Rosal. At 8:40 A.M. on October 15, 1960—designated by the revolutionary government as "the Year of Agrarian Reform"—Daniel Bacardi and the other company executives affixed their signatures to an *acta de entrega*, delivering the ninety-eight-year-old Bacardi enterprise to the Cuban state. The expropriation covered every physical asset the company held in Cuba, from the distillery and bottling plants to the warehouse where thousands of barrels of Bacardi rum were aging to the company's administrative offices on Aguilera Street to the three Hatuey breweries to the Edificio Bacardi in downtown

Havana. Accountants estimated that the seized properties had a total value at the time of about $76 million. The Cuban enterprise founded by Facundo Bacardi Massó, kept alive by his sons Emilio and Facundo Jr., and developed by his son-in-law Enrique Schueg and his granddaughter's husband Pepín Bosch, had been taken away from the Bacardi family.

Among the first people Daniel called after signing over the company's Cuban assets was Rino Puig, the Hatuey sales manager with whom he had clashed so fiercely at the brewery in El Cotorro. Reaching him at home, Daniel tried his best to be cheerful. "Rino, how are you? Feeling screwed? I'm calling you to say you were right and I was wrong." Even so, Daniel didn't want to admit that all was lost. "You'll see, Rino," he promised. "They're going to have to give it all back to us." Rino only grunted.

Castro's confiscation of the family rum business was a blow to the Bacardi soul, with family members feeling they had lost the foundation of their identity. Many had no idea what to do or where to go. Some of the nonfamily employees who had spent their lives with the company were just as grief-stricken. Juan Prado, another who had defended the revolution against its critics, had no other job prospects, but he was close to the Bacardi family and would not consider staying at the company under conditions of state ownership. After two days in Santiago, Prado flew back to Havana, and early the next morning he went to his office to collect his belongings. Arriving early, he was surprised to hear voices coming from the manager's office. He recognized one of the speakers as Gustavo Rodríguez Bacardi, the fifty-two-year-old son of Carmen Bacardi—Emilio's youngest daughter by his first wife María—and a minor executive in the export department. When Gustavo emerged from the manager's office, Prado noticed that he was accompanied by men dressed in olive green M-26-7 uniforms.

"Prado," Gustavo said airily, "what are you doing here so early?"

"I came here to resign," Prado said. "What about you?"

"They just reconfirmed me," Gustavo said. "I'm staying on." Prado was stunned. Even as a nonfamily member, he was so angered by the Bacardi nationalization that he wanted nothing to do with it.

The new managers recognized Prado's talents, however, and tried repeatedly to get him to stay, even offering him the management of the nationalized Coca-Cola subsidiary in Havana as an alternative. Prado said he would consider the offer and make up his mind within the next week or two. It was only a stall for time to manage his affairs. Within a month, Prado had left Cuba with his wife and two small children. In the aftermath of the confiscation, a stream of senior Bacardi managers and family members went into exile. Of those who stayed on the island, many did so in the hope (and expectation) that the United States would soon intervene in Cuba and bring an end to Castro's rule.

Within days of the seizure of the brewery at El Cotorro, Hatuey sales manager Rino Puig was devoting all his time and efforts to the resistance. On October 22, accompanied by two comrades in arms, Puig went to a house where he had been told an arms cache had been left for him and his fellow rebels. When he knocked, a man came to the door and asked his name.

"Rino," he answered.

"We've been looking for you," the man said. "You're the head of the counterrevolution in this area." Armed men immediately emerged from the house to arrest him and the two men with him. Puig was taken away to prison and quickly convicted of counterrevolutionary conspiracy. He was spared execution only because he was unarmed at the time of his arrest and the authorities had no proof against him. Puig was sentenced to fifteen years in prison, however, and because he refused to acknowledge his guilt, he served his entire term and was released only in October 1975.

◆ ◆ ◆

Anyone in the extended Bacardi community who remained loyal to Fidel Castro after October 1960 was siding with a government that had imprisoned Rino Puig and seized the family business. Among those who nevertheless did so was Manolo Ortega, the Bacardi television announcer, who went on to become the chief broadcaster of the Cuban revolution, exhorting his compatriots to help out with the sugarcane harvest and follow Fidel. Another was Raúl Gutiérrez, who designed and produced most of the Bacardi advertising campaigns and was a close friend of many Bacardi executives. José Espín, who had faithfully served Enrique Schueg and Luis J. Bacardi and had once been in line to become the company manager, also sided with the Castro government, though in his case it was mostly a matter of loyalty to his daughter Vilma, Fidel's sister-in-law and the most powerful woman in revolutionary Cuba.

The old radical Herminia Cape continued to applaud Castro, though at ninety-five she had moments of confusion, and some of those who cared for her doubted she was genuinely a *fidelista*. The most important family members still supporting the revolution were Gustavo Rodríguez Bacardi and his two children, Gilda and Gustavín. By staying with the government even after the Bacardi confiscation, Rodríguez earned the wrath of his seventy-six-year-old mother, Carmen Bacardi, who saw him as betraying the life work of her father Emilio. Even worse for her was the day her grandson Gustavín, just twenty-one years old, showed up at her door in the uniform of a *miliciano* and informed her he had been appointed as the agent responsible for taking over the Royal Bank of Canada, where she had her money on deposit. The idea that her own grandson would be complicit in the seizure of her life savings so upset Carmen that she ordered Gustavín out of her house and said she never wanted to see him again. She left Cuba for Puerto Rico shortly thereafter and had no more contact with Gustavín, who went on to become a state security agent for the Castro regime, serving in a variety of overseas posts.

In Fidel Castro's Cuba, loyalty to the revolutionary state took precedence over all other allegiances. Political trustworthiness was also the paramount consideration in the selection of personnel to manage the state and the economy, even if it meant putting people in positions for which they lacked the most rudimentary skills. Nationalization resulted in a spectacular downgrading of management competence across Cuba in 1960 and 1961, with bus drivers or typists taking charge of factories and farm laborers assigned to manage cattle ranches and orange groves. The Bacardi family's Hatuey brewery in Manacas was put under the control of a pro-Castro militant whose previous job had been as a handyman at a nearby motel.

Bacardi engineer Manuel Jorge Cutillas had seen the consequences of this political approach to enterprise management several months before his own company was nationalized. The Cuban authorities expropriated U.S.-owned mining operations in Cuba in the summer of 1960, and shortly thereafter an official at the Ministry of Mines called Cutillas to ask him to provide some technical advice to the newly appointed manager of a nearby manganese mine. "We're having some problems with the ore processing at that mine," the official told Cutillas. "Would you be willing to help us?" Cutillas, who had a part-time job teaching chemical engineering at the local university, agreed to do what he could, and the new mine manager came to see him. "The American engineers all left when we took over the mine," the man said, "and we don't have anyone who really knows what to do."

Cutillas said he didn't know what process the American engineers had been using with their ore. "There are hundreds of possibilities," he said, "and they probably had a proprietary, patented process of their own."

"Well, can you tell me something at least?" the mine manager said. "I think they were using some acids or something." When the man said his previous job had been as a surveyor's helper, Cutillas told him there was nothing he could do to help him.

At Compañía Ron Bacardi, S.A., the nationalization changes took a few weeks to play out. Many of the technical people and some of the managers remained on the job while considering their next move. Andres Yebra, the new company administrator, was more practical than many of the other new enterprise managers around the country and asked all Bacardi employees to stay. Even Daniel Bacardi, though excluded from all management decision making, encouraged personnel to remain on the job. "Don't worry," he told them. "We'll solve this. Something will happen. Fidel will see he made a mistake, and they'll change this back, I promise."

One Bacardi worker who stayed for a time was a Cuban of British ancestry named Richard Gardner, a supervisor at the Hatuey brewery in Santiago. Shortly after nationalization, Gardner had a confrontation at the brewery with a union leader who wanted him to assign two workers to a machine that only needed one. "This place belongs to us now," the union leader said. Gardner said no.

"Whether this place belongs to the Bacardis or to the government, what's right is right," he said, "and that machine only needs one worker." Gardner expected to be dismissed, but to his amazement, Yebra supported him. After two more senior Hatuey brewers left Cuba, Yebra made Gardner the master brewer and begged him to stay, even though he knew Gardner was no fan of the revolution.

It was a revealing moment. Fidel Castro and other revolutionary leaders were of two minds about professionals like Gardner. On the one hand, they recognized that the country needed technical and professional expertise in order to keep Cuba working. Anyone wishing to leave Cuba needed a *permiso de salida* —an exit permit—from a military intelligence unit, and for those Cubans with essential skills, it could be nearly impossible to get. On the other hand, professional Cubans were considered politically unreliable, with a "bourgeois" and individualist mentality, and they often found themselves ridiculed and insulted.

Manuel Jorge Cutillas decided he wanted to leave Cuba, but his passport identified him as an engineer and therefore presented special problems. His second son had been born with a heart defect, and he and his wife were desperate to get the boy to a specialist in the United States. They applied for restricted exit permits for the specific purpose of taking their boy out of the country for medical treatment. When Cutillas went to pick the permits up in Havana, however, he noticed that his own had not been signed. The army captain in charge, it seemed, had a few questions.

"Where do you work, Señor Cutillas, and why do you want to leave Cuba?" he asked. Hoping to conceal his Bacardi identity, Cutillas said he was teaching chemical engineering at the University of the Oriente in Santiago and that he and his wife wanted to take their son to the United States to see a heart specialist. "O.K.," the captain said, "but you'll have to bring a letter from the university rector giving his permission." Cutillas silently cursed. The university rector had only recently been appointed, and he was an ardent Santiago *fidelista*. Keeping a brave face, however, Cutillas told the captain he would return to Santiago and get the letter. "Well, in the meantime," the captain said, "give me your passport." Cutillas had no choice but to hand it over.

Cutillas's wife, Rosa, was waiting outside in a car, packed and ready to go to the airport with their two sons. As he approached the car, Rosa could see by the look on Manuel Jorge's face that he did not have the permit. "This guy," he told her, "just proved beyond any doubt that we have to leave Cuba. You can't live in a country where something like this happens." Rosa decided to hold off on leaving Cuba until she saw whether Manuel Jorge would get his permit. A few days later, however, the Cutillas boy died of his heart ailment. Now desperate to leave Cuba, Manuel Jorge sent his wife and surviving son on to Miami, then made contact with the anti-Castro underground in hopes of finding a way to flee the island secretly. It would be a risky move; anyone caught leaving Cuba "illegally" could be imprisoned or worse. Cutillas eventually managed to leave on an aging cargo boat with a half dozen other disgruntled Cubans, taking nothing with him but the clothes on his back. After six terrifying days at sea, the group finally made it to Miami.

Daniel Bacardi considered his prospects for a few weeks, but after a tearful encounter with Víctor Schueg, his longtime ally and close friend, he decided to join the exodus. Feeling betrayed by his old allies in the government and estranged from those family members with whom he had argued often about Fidel, Daniel and his wife Graciela and their children headed to Madrid rather than Miami. He remained in seclusion there for several months before reuniting with Pepín Bosch and rejoining the rum business. His sister, Ana María Bacardi, married to a physician named Adolfo Comas, left Cuba at about the same time. Her husband had been pressing her to leave for weeks, and they had sent their two draft-age sons to Florida at a time when it was still possible to do so. Ana María, however, was devoted to her brother Daniel, and she had followed his lead on Fidel, defending him almost to the end. By the time she was ready to leave, the act of getting a U.S. visa required running a gauntlet of Cuban hostility. Her teenage daughters Amelia and Marlena had to stand in line at the U.S. embassy in Havana all night long, enduring the taunts of the *fidelistas* who had been sent there to harass Cubans headed for the United States.

When Cubans did get permission to leave the island, they could take only what they could fit in a suitcase or two. They had to prepare an inventory of their household goods, valuables, and Cuban bank accounts and leave all such assets behind. The Comas Bacardi family gave their house key to their neighbor, telling her she could have whatever she wanted of their art, antiques, and furniture. Travelers could bring only the jewelry they were wearing, and some women showed up at the airport looking like ornamented Christmas trees, with one earring dangling from the end of another. Even so, the inspectors often confiscated anything that appeared to be of value. Pepín Bosch's son Carlos and his wife left with their infant son, who was clutching a silver drinking cup. The customs guard took one look at the cup and snatched it away.

• • •

Within a few weeks of the government's seizure of the Bacardi properties, virtually all the top management and technical staff were gone from the company, but operations at the rum factory and the breweries continued. The government said the enterprise would be known as the Compañía Ron Bacardi (Nacionalizada), as if the change of ownership warranted only a parenthetical note. The company was so closely identified with the Bacardi name that changing it seemed unthinkable. After Richard Gardner and the other brewers left, the government brought in technical advisors from Czechoslovakia to keep the breweries operating. The rum factory was more critical, but along with the physical facilities the revolutionary government had taken possession of thousands of barrels of aging rum, and those reserves were enough to keep production going for years to come.

The new management also had the services of two veteran rum workers in Alfonso Matamoros and Mariano Lavigne, who between them had nearly sixty years of Bacardi experience. Lavigne started at the company as a thirteen-year-old errand boy and subsequently rose to a position of confidence. When Pepe Bacardi was sent to Mexico in the early 1930s, Lavigne went along. Alfonso Matamoros had worked alongside Daniel Bacardi for more than twenty years. Neither man had much formal education or professional training, but through practical experience they had learned almost everything there was to know about rum making, and they were among the select few inside or outside the family who could replicate at least a portion of the Bacardi "secret formula."

Given their experience and skills, both men could have gotten jobs at one of the Bacardi distilleries outside Cuba. A few months after leaving Santiago, in fact, Daniel Bacardi wrote to both Matamoros and Lavigne from Spain, saying they could count on his help if they wanted it. The first letters were intercepted by authorities and never delivered. Lavigne was able to retrieve a third letter from the rum factory only after a colleague told him about it. In the letter, Daniel made veiled suggestions that Lavigne and Matamoros leave Cuba under the pretext of going on holiday to Mexico and Puerto Rico. "I imagine by this point you all deserve a rest," Daniel wrote. He gave Lavigne the name of a doctor in Santiago who could help make arrangements for the trip, and he offered to pay the airfare and all other expenses for Lavigne and his family. Daniel wrote as if his own separation from Cuba were temporary ("Any day now I intend to return and go back to work"), and he was careful not to suggest that he was asking Lavigne to abandon Cuba, saying the "vacation" would enable him to go back to work "with a better spirit." But thousands of Cubans had already fled the island at that point, and Lavigne well understood what Daniel was suggesting.

His offer to help Matamoros and Lavigne get out of Cuba may have been an indication of how much the two Bacardi veterans meant to Daniel personally and how much he missed the camaraderie of the rum factory, but he also wanted to keep the revolutionary state from taking advantage of the men's rum-making experience and knowledge. The Cuban authorities understood that as well, which is probably why Daniel's letters were intercepted. In the end, either man would have had great difficulty securing an exit permit, even to take a "vacation."

Furthermore, while the Bacardis and their upper-class friends were leaving the island en masse, exile was less imaginable for Cubans like Matamoros and Lavigne, who were anchored to the island in a way that more worldly people were not. The Bacardis had family members outside Cuba to help them get reestablished, and some of them even had overseas bank accounts that the Cuban government could not touch, but Matamoros and Lavigne were both of humble origin. When the revolution tore Cuba along class lines, Alfonso Matamoros and Mariano Lavigne found themselves on the side that generally stayed put. Lavigne put Daniel's letter carefully away in the cabinet where he kept all his Bacardi things, and it stayed there as long as he lived. More than forty years later, Lavigne's daughter Felicita was still guarding the letter and wondering how her life would have been different had her father taken his family out of Cuba when Daniel invited him to do so. "He stayed here for family reasons," she said. "It had nothing to do with politics."

Most of the thousands of Cubans who went into exile in 1960 and early 1961 were convinced they would soon return to the island, that Fidel could not last: His more pragmatic government partners would unseat him, or there would be a popular uprising against him, like the one that overthrew Fulgencio Batista. Indeed, the same methods Fidel and his allies had used in their revolution were now being turned against them. The peasants in the Escambray Mountains, an independent group even during the anti-Batista struggle, took up arms again, this time in opposition to the government's heavy hand.

Castro had taken a lesson from Batista's hapless efforts at counterinsurgency, however, and he responded to the Escambray guerrillas with more force and ruthlessness than Batista had dared employ. With the guidance of Soviet counterinsurgency experts, Castro sent thousands of army troops into the mountains to pursue the guerrillas. Captured Escambray insurgents were often executed on the spot, and in a move reminiscent of the Spanish army's "reconcentration" strategy during the independence war, Castro ordered the relocation of entire villages where the guerrillas enjoyed mass support. The villagers were moved en masse to western Cuba, where they could be closely monitored. Castro's successful suppression of the resistance fighters discouraged the U.S. government, which had settled on the Escambray guerrillas as the spearhead for a broader anti-Castro resistance movement. The CIA resolved instead to organize an exile army that would carry out a full-scale invasion of Cuba the following spring.

The result was the disastrous Bay of Pigs invasion in April 1961. The new U.S. president, John F. Kennedy, fearing that the operation would be seen as a U.S. military intervention, barred the use of U.S. air bases and ordered that all military training take place outside U.S. territory. At nearly the last minute, he moved the invasion site from Trinidad, on Cuba's southern coast, to the "less spectacular" Bay of Pigs location. He also canceled a series of air strikes that were to have destroyed Castro's air force. As a consequence, the force was vulnerable to air attack. Fidel Castro's troops quickly surrounded the invading army, capturing nearly 1,200 of the approximately 1,300 exiles who managed to make it to shore.

Among the exile fighters was Manolo Puig, the older brother (and Olympic rowing partner) of Rino Puig, the Hatuey sales manager arrested in Havana the previous October. Deeply shaken by Rino's imprisonment, Manolo volunteered to join a reconnaissance unit that went in ahead of the main invading force. They were promptly discovered, however, and Manolo was brought before a firing squad and shot. Rino Puig, in the Isle of Pines prison, got the news several days later, with a report that Manolo was unflinching to the end. For the remaining fourteen and a half years of his own imprisonment, Rino clung to the idea of his brother's courage in the face of death and later credited his own survival to the inspiration he drew from that thought.

· · ·

The Bay of Pigs disaster was a turning point—for Cuba, for the United States, for Fidel Castro, for Cuban exiles, and for the anti-Castro movement, which never recovered from the defeat. Castro described the attack as a "Yankee-sponsored invasion" and portrayed its failure as "the first imperialist defeat in America." In a May Day speech, he declared for the first time that Cuba was a socialist nation and need not bother with elections. His Bay of Pigs victory boosted Castro's popularity on the island and so demoralized the opposition forces that they were never again able to mount a serious challenge to Castro's rule. In December 1961, secure in power, Castro announced that Cuba would follow "a Marxist-Leninist program adjusted to the precise objective conditions of our country."

Had he been a Communist all along? The question remains unanswered, largely because Castro himself made contradictory declarations. During his rise to power and for about two years afterward, Castro insisted he was not a Communist and even offered cogent criticisms of Communist systems. As late as the summer of 1960, he insisted that the Cuban revolution had to steer "between capitalism, which starves people to death, and Communism, which resolves the economic problems, *but suppresses freedoms, the freedoms which are so dear to man.*" (emphasis added) Such rhetoric earned Castro the support of progressive but non-Communist Cubans like Daniel Bacardi.

On later occasions, however, Castro said he had always been in the Communist camp. In a 2003 interview with the French writer Ignacio Ramonet, Castro said he was already "a convinced Marxist-Leninist" at the time of the Batista coup in 1952, using the writings of Marx and Lenin as a political "compass." His younger brother Raúl aligned himself earlier with the Communists, but in that 2003 interview, Fidel disputed the notion that Raúl was more of a Communist than he was. "Raúl was on the left, but really it was I who introduced Marxist-Leninist ideas to him," Castro said. Many historians, however, took such arguments as revisionist boasting, meant to show how he had fooled people into thinking he was someone other than who he really was.

During his rise to power, Castro was probably too much of an individualist to have been a good Communist. There were aspects of Marxism-Leninism that undoubtedly appealed to him, however, such as its hierarchical conception of political power and its rejection of pluralist approaches. Carlos Franqui, a prominent M-26-7 member and journalist who was himself a Communist Party member, once quoted Castro as saying the lesson he took from reading Joseph Stalin's *The Fundamentals of Leninism* was that "a revolution must have only one leader if it is to remain whole and not be defeated." Nothing characterized Fidel's rule more consistently than his refusal to share power with anyone.

Castro's own interest in ideology was always more opportunistic than dogmatic. By following a Marxist-Leninist path, Castro set himself on a collision course with the United States and tore his own country apart, driving a half million Cubans—about 6 percent of the population—into exile by 1970. But for Castro and his allies, that was just fine. They intended from the beginning to have an adversarial relationship with the United States and also to turn Cuban society upside down. "I measure the depth of the social transformation," Che Guevara once told Egyptian President Gamal Nasser, "by the number of people who are affected by it and feel they have no place in the new society."

There could be no room for private wealth or enterprise in Cuba, because it would compete with the power and authority of Fidel's revolutionary state. There could be no room for aspirations apart from the promise of the revolution. Those Cubans who had their own ideas and dreams had to be pushed out, even if they were fair-minded and generous patriots. Fidel said those who abandoned his Cuba were *gusanos* (worms), and when Cubans spit on people standing in line for a U.S. visa, it was because he encouraged them to do so. "What do the ones who left signify?" he asked in a 1962 speech to medical students. "It is the same thing as squeezing a boil. Those who have left are the pus, the pus that was expelled when the Cuban revolution squeezed the society. How good the body feels when pus is eliminated!"

Chapter 17

Exile

Twice each day, a white Pan American DC-7B propliner landed in Miami with a full load of grim-faced Cubans who had boarded an hour earlier in Havana. A few of the passengers whooped for joy or shouted, "*¡América!*" or "*¡Viva libertad!*" as they stepped off the plane in Florida, but most descended silently onto the tarmac, and some were quietly weeping. The agonizing wait for an exit permit, the surrender of their homes and all their possessions, the prospect of a long, perhaps permanent, separation from family and friends who stayed behind, and the pain of having to flee their native land had made their final days in Cuba emotionally devastating. Then came the indignities and terror at the airport, where sneering customs inspectors rummaged through their luggage for something to confiscate and poked in their pants and down their blouses in one final, deliberately humiliating routine. After all, they were only worms, bound for the *gusanera* that Miami had become.

Pepín Bosch had his son Jorge make arrangements for some Bacardi people who arrived with no place to stay or family members to help them. At thirty-five, Jorge had been a brewer in Santiago, a vice president of the Mexican subsidiary, and his father's representative in overseeing the Puerto Rico operation, so he knew almost everyone in the company at the middle management level or above. He rented several apartments in a part of Miami that was becoming known as Little Havana. If people were able to call ahead to say they were coming on a particular flight, Jorge would be at the airport to meet them and set them up in one of the company apartments, having already stocked it with groceries. Most also needed cash assistance, because the Cuban authorities allowed people leaving the island to take no more than five U.S. dollars with them. For those who showed up unexpectedly in Miami, having been delayed at the last minute in Havana because of a document some airport official didn't find correctly prepared, some order from a higher authority, or simply the arbitrariness of an inspector, there was always a phone number to call upon arrival; Jorge or someone else would rush to the airport. After helping more than a dozen arriving Bacardi families, he recognized a pattern: The newcomers would be in a semiterrified state for a day or two, numb from exhaustion and anxiety and unable to talk easily about what they had gone through. He would leave them alone—"to decompress," he explained—and return a day later to check on them, at which time their stories would come pouring out.

Such assistance put Bacardi people—employees and family members alike— in a privileged category compared to other Cubans who showed up in Miami penniless and helpless. From 1960 through October 1962, when the Cuban missile crisis brought an end to commercial air traffic to and from Havana, an average of about 170 Cuban refugees arrived *per day* in the United States, the vast majority of them landing in Miami. Although U.S. visas were required, there was no quota for Cubans, and virtually all qualified for refugee status. Local and federal immigration and welfare agencies were overwhelmed by the demand for their services, and many Cuban newcomers were forced to fend for themselves and restart their lives from scratch. The extended Bacardi clan, however, had a support system underneath them from start to finish. At the instruction of Pepín Bosch, lawyer Guillermo Mármol postponed his own departure from Cuba in order to help Bacardi employees and family members get exit permits and reservations on one of the Pan Am flights, which were generally booked six months in advance. Once they made it to Miami, employees who wanted to continue working with Bacardi were put on "salary," at least temporarily, and Pepín Bosch tried to find them work—if not in Miami, then in Puerto Rico, Mexico, or Brazil.

The survival and reorganization of the Bacardi rum company following its displacement from Cuba would amount to one of the more notable tales in business history. For a century, the Bacardi family had personally nurtured the business, guiding it through difficult days and imbuing it with a cohesiveness and internal strength that were the envy of other firms. In exile, the roles were reversed: It was the company that supported the Bacardi family, nonblood members included. This dynamic relationship of family and firm provided the foundation for the Bacardi success in the years that followed, just as it had in the past. The family members and Bacardi employees who came out of Cuba together provided the skills, experience, and personal commitment that enabled the business to prosper beyond what anyone could have foreseen in 1960, and in turn the firm offered them a foundation for their new lives.

But was Bacardi still a Cuban company? Torn from its roots in Santiago, no longer sponsoring Cuban baseball games or patronizing Cuban culture and excluded from the civic and political life of the island, Bacardi in exile would be a name without a homeland. The corporate headquarters was moved to the

Bahamas and then to Bermuda. The family members dispersed across three continents, from Panama to Florida and Spain. Those who remained in south Florida became part of a new Cuban exile community that included former Batista allies, sugar magnates, and the old Havana aristocracy, as well as all those ordinary Cubans who had simply decided they could not live under Castro's dictatorial rule. The Bacardis, most of them, remained Cuban nationalists and continued to think of their business as a patriotic enterprise, but now those terms meant something different from what they had meant on the island. After 1960, the fight for Cuba was redefined as a battle against Fidel Castro and the regime he put in power. It was waged from a distance, and it was motivated in part by revenge. Castro had seized the Bacardi rum business in Cuba in the name of the Cuban revolution, and the Bacardi family and those who had built and managed the business were determined not to let him get away with it.

◆ ◆ ◆

The revolutionary authorities might have renamed it Compañía Ron Bacardi (Nacionalizada), but they did not make clear what exactly they were nationalizing. The buildings and equipment and inventory were now the property of the Cuban state, but what else? Under the nationalization order, the government claimed the Bacardi company in Santiago and "its subsidiary, affiliated, and related enterprises," but the one-page document signed by Daniel Bacardi and other company executives was a lawyer's nightmare. No terms were defined and no provisions made clear. The one relevant sentence simply declared that the company had been nationalized pursuant to the law passed a day earlier, and it named a new administrator for the firm. The authorities did not say what they understood Compañía Ron Bacardi, S.A., to comprise, and for a firm with as complex an organization as Pepín Bosch created, that was a fatal mistake.

The Santiago company was the original Bacardi firm, but it had spawned four other companies, each with a separate structure and legal identity. Though they were owned by the same shareholders who owned Compañía Ron Bacardi, S.A., they were not subsidiaries and were therefore beyond the reach of the authorities in Havana. The Bacardi operations in Mexico and Puerto Rico were independently run. So was New York–based Bacardi Imports, which had the exclusive right to import and sell Bacardi rum in the United States. Finally, Pepín Bosch in 1957 had organized Bacardi International Limited (BIL) in the Bahamas with the rights to manufacture and sell Bacardi rum everywhere outside Cuba with the exception of the United States (including Puerto Rico) and Mexico. At the time he established the company, Bosch had been worried that Fulgencio Batista might make a move against Bacardi assets in Cuba, but as it turned out, Bacardi International provided a shield against Fidel Castro instead. The nationalized rum company in Cuba would not be able to sell "Bacardi" rum overseas without facing a strong legal challenge from Bacardi International. Even in the preglobalization era, Bosch recognized the benefits of a transnational, globally organized enterprise.

Bosch was not done, however. While BIL had the right to manufacture and market Bacardi overseas, the actual ownership of the Bacardi trademarks might have been contested by the Cuban government. Almost immediately after the nationalization of Bacardi operations in Cuba, Bosch had his lawyers reconstitute Compañía Ron Bacardi, S.A., in New York as a firm with the same organization and shareholders as were behind the Cuban company. The new company promptly claimed ownership of the various Bacardi trademarks, arguing that as the intellectual assets of the Santiago company, they had not been nationalized by the Cuban government and remained the property of the original owners. Their claim was reinforced by the fact that the Cuban authorities had neglected to mention trademarks or other intangible Bacardi assets in their nationalization order. Pepín Bosch—at the recommendation of his New York lawyers—had already mailed the original trademark certificates out of Cuba, and they were safely in the custody of the new company in New York.

Bosch and his fellow Bacardi officers were set to do battle with the Castro regime on all fronts. On October 17, just three days after the Santiago nationalization, Bacardi Imports president Bartolo Estrada wrote an open letter to "all importers and dealers in alcoholic beverages in the United States," advising them that his company would take legal action against any "person, firm or corporation" in the United States that attempted on its own to import so-called Bacardi rum from Cuba. Major U.S. liquor dealers, having well-established contacts with the old family management, would have been highly unlikely to do business with the new, nationalized operation in Communist Cuba, but the Bacardis were taking no chances. The sharply worded announcement sent a message that the firm intended to take an aggressive approach in defense of its interests. Indeed, the fight over Bacardi assets moved almost immediately to the courts. The first case involved an account the Santiago company had in the Bank of Nova Scotia, one of just two private banks (the other being the Royal Bank of Canada) still doing business in Cuba. When the Cuban authorities attempted to access the funds in the old Bacardi company account—which was held in a New York branch—the reconstituted Compañía Ron

Bacardi S.A., sued the Canadian bank and the nationalized "Bacardi" company in U.S. district court and won. The court said the United States had made clear with prior actions that it had a "national policy" against recognizing the Cuban government's confiscation of property, including bank accounts, outside Cuba.

That court decision was on U.S. territory, however, where the Castro government had little standing. If the Bacardi rum company was going to survive as a player in the international market, it would need to defend its exclusive use of the "Bacardi" brand around the world and establish once and for all that the newly nationalized, government-owned rum company in Santiago had no right to sell a product it called "Bacardi" rum, even if it was made by the same workers who had been making Bacardi rum for years, by the same old methods with the same old ingredients, at the site of the Santiago factory that Don Facundo had opened a century earlier. To make that case, Pepín Bosch and the Bacardi family needed good lawyers, but also a good salesman.

• • •

Juan Prado arranged to leave Havana three days ahead of his wife and their two small children, half expecting the authorities at the airport to block his departure. He made it to Miami, however, and Pepín Bosch himself was there to meet him. Bosch had big plans for his young sales manager. He booked Prado in a hotel room and gave him a few hundred dollars to buy a used car and rent a cheap house where he could get his family situated. Then he laid out the assignment.

"We have to reestablish our international sales," Bosch said. He feared that liquor importers outside the United States were less aware of what had happened to the Bacardis in Cuba and therefore might be more inclined to continue buying rum from the nationalized enterprise in Santiago. "I need you to go visit our distributors in Europe and tell them that our factory in Cuba has been confiscated by the government, but that we can still supply them from our other plants," he told Prado. "Your job is to go on the road for us, wherever you need to go. *Camine el mundo.*" Prado was barely thirty years old, without a penny to his name, and he had a young wife who would have to find her own way in an unfamiliar city with two children under the age of two. He had been to London once as a tourist, but that was the extent of his overseas travel. And here he was, being asked by Pepín Bosch to go off on his own and rebuild his company's global sales network, to "walk the world" for Bacardi.

On December 7, barely two weeks after arriving from Havana, Prado left for London. He brought only a handwritten list of Bacardi distributors. All the files on rum sales had been left behind in Cuba, and Prado had no idea who had outstanding orders, nor for how many cases. His first meeting, at the Hedges & Butler spirits firm in London, did not go well, and Prado left thinking that the distributor was likely to stick with the Santiago product, no matter who made it. He moved on to Amsterdam, discouraged. Bosch had put him on a tight expense limit, and he was spending his nights alone in a shabby hotel room or walking the streets. His first Amsterdam meeting, however, cheered him up considerably. Rather than make a sales pitch, Prado just told his personal story about fleeing from Fidel Castro's island prison. It worked like a charm. "You just got out of Cuba?" the Dutch distributor said, his eyes widening. "Wow! Tell me about it." Within fifteen minutes, the distributor was sold. "Of course I'll stick with the Bacardi family," he said. "How could I not?"

It was only the first morning of his first day in Amsterdam, and Prado had nothing else to do. When the distributor said he generally moved only about two hundred cases of rum per year—about what Prado sold to a single bar back in Havana—it occurred to Prado that he had more to achieve in Europe than just getting distributors to reconfirm prior Bacardi orders. "Look," he told the distributor. "I've got three days here, and I can't be a tourist. Would you mind if I went out with one of your salesmen?"

The distributor immediately set him up with an English speaker, and Prado spent the next two days with him visiting liquor wholesalers. "This is Mr. Prado," the salesman would say. "He works for Bacardi, and he's just come from Cuba." It was all the opening Prado needed. He related whatever he could remember about Castro as a university student, about the time when as a Procter & Gamble salesman he had sold Fidel's father five hundred candles for his company store, and about the day the militiamen came to take possession of the Bacardi office in downtown Havana. "I told twenty stories that were true and at least ten that were not," Prado recalled later, "and by the end of the day we had orders for another twenty cases."

Prado's schedule had him visiting two European countries per week until he had covered most of the continent. In each country, he had the same experience, quickly persuading the distributor to stay with the Bacardi family and its reorganized network and then asking whether he could accompany a sales agent on his rounds. Prado had been a salesman all his life, and his warm, appealing manner suited him perfectly for the calling. At each stop, promoting his product personally, Prado managed to boost Bacardi orders.

On December 23, Prado arrived in Hamburg. The country was shutting down for Christmas Eve celebrations, and the local distributor was stunned when Prado called for an appointment. "You realize it's Christmas, don't you?" he said. The distributor told Prado he would have invited him to spend the holiday with his German family had they not all been going out of town. As a consolation for not meeting him, he sent a bottle of Bacardi *añejo* over to Prado at his hotel.

The next day, Prado ate lunch alone in the hotel restaurant, which was packed with holiday diners. The restaurant closed after lunch, however, and the hotel soon emptied of all the guests except for Prado and an airline crew. Hours later, when he asked at the reception desk where he might find dinner, the clerk said he was out of luck. Every restaurant in the city was closed for Christmas Eve. Prado returned to his room, finished off the courtesy basket of crackers the hotel had left on his dresser and drank half the bottle of *añejo*. Soon he was shivering. With the hotel nearly empty, the management had lowered the heat, and his room was becoming inhospitable. So Prado took off walking.

The streets of Hamburg were cold and empty, but every house Prado passed was ablaze with light, and people inside were noisily celebrating. The contrast with his own sharp loneliness could not have been more painful. Three months' worth of anxiety and loss swept over him, and tears ran down his cheeks. Here he was, walking strange streets in a city in Germany, late on Christmas Eve, separated from his wife and little children, and exiled from his beloved Cuba. The brightly lit German houses all around him and the half bottle of rum he had drunk on a nearly empty stomach pushed him over the brink into a sadness he had not until then allowed himself to feel. He could not stop weeping.

◆ ◆ ◆

Prado returned from his trip convinced that the European market for Bacardi rum was not being exploited to the limits of its potential, and he wrote Bosch a letter to that effect. Years passed, however, before his recommendations were acted on. Bosch's goal in sending Prado to Europe had been less to promote Bacardi sales than to defend the Bacardi brand. He wanted to block Fidel Castro from establishing any presence on the continent with his socialist version of "Bacardi" rum. If a single European distributor switched orders from the Bacardi family's product to the "Bacardi" rum being shipped from the nationalized plant in Santiago, Bosch feared, it would raise the question of which was the real thing.

As expected, the trademark dispute escalated quickly into a legal confrontation. Bacardi company lawyers found the Cuban authorities attempting to export rum under the "Bacardi" label to at least five countries, and each time they took them to court. When Bacardi executives learned that a shipment of "Bacardi" rum from Cuba had arrived in the Dutch Antillean colony of Aruba, they alerted the local customs authorities, advising them that the manufacturer did not have a legal right to export rum under that name. The local courts agreed, and the entire rum shipment was thrown overboard. The Bacardi lawyers sued the Cuban government for trademark infringement even in Israel, where the costs of litigation far exceeded the value of the commerce. The final and most decisive court battle was in the United Kingdom, where it was the agents for the Cuban government who actually initiated the litigation, demanding that the rights to the Bacardi trademark be transferred to the nationalized company in Santiago. The case ended with the Cuban government agreeing to withdraw the suit and stop using the trademark, in exchange for the Bacardi company agreeing to pay all its own court costs, which were substantial.

It was only with the settlement of the British case in March 1968 that the Bacardi trademark was finally secure. Bacardi executives later said they had never been entirely confident that courts around the world would recognize their proprietary rights to the trademark. Intangible assets cannot be confiscated as easily as distilleries, but if the Cuban government had explicitly decreed in October 1960 that it was claiming the Bacardi trademarks, courts in some countries might have looked more favorably on the Cuban position. Enrique Oltuski, a vice minister of industry under Fidel Castro during the period when the trademark battles were being fought, said years later that his government had simply been out-lawyered by the Bacardi company. "That was a product of our inexperience," he said in a 2004 interview. "We were all very young, and in those first years we were entirely caught up in all the problems we had. We just didn't think to register the Bacardi trademark, so we lost it. We had the factory that produced the real Bacardi rum, but we couldn't keep the name." Part of their problem was their Marxist preconceptions; in the Marxist view, it's the "physical means of production," not the intangible assets, that accounts for the value of an enterprise.

Pepín Bosch took personal pleasure in his victory over Fidel Castro's regime in the trademark battle, and he spoke of it often in the years that followed. On at least one front, he and his company had taken on the double-crossing dictator and beat him. With its trademarks protected, the company would survive confiscation. Thanks to the business vision of Enrique Schueg, who had decided that the firm's future lay in international expansion, and to the skill with which his son-in-law Pepín Bosch had turned that vision into reality, Bacardi in 1960 was in a position to prosper even without its operations in Cuba. In August the company inaugurated a second distillery in Mexico. The two operations plus the plant in Puerto Rico were by that point producing three times as much rum as was the original plant in Santiago, so the company's overall capacity remained largely intact in spite of the nationalization. Moreover, Bacardi had in Pepín Bosch a classic enterprise leader—one who moved boldly, managed risk, and responded creatively to business setbacks.

The company's move to Brazil was a good illustration. Bosch saw as early as 1952 that with the country's abundant sugar crop, it would be a good place to make rum. In the coming years, he visited often to determine the best location for a distillery and to assess the potential Bacardi market. Believing that Brazilians would appreciate a quality rum as well as their beloved *cachaça* spirit, Bosch convinced his Bacardi stockholders to approve the investment. The site he chose for a new distillery was Recife, at Brazil's easternmost tip, a city where tax breaks for industrial development were available. Juan Grau, the engineer who had directed new Bacardi distillery projects in Mexico, Santiago, and Puerto Rico, was dispatched to oversee design and construction of the facility.

Grau arrived in Recife with his wife and children in February 1960. The company's future in Cuba was uncertain at the time, but Bosch insisted that Grau move full speed ahead regardless. Eight months later, Grau heard that all the Bacardi assets in Cuba had been seized by the government, and he called his boss to offer his sympathy. "Oh, it was to be expected," Bosch said.

"So what should we do here?" Grau wondered.

"What, are you having some technical problems or something?" Bosch asked.

"No," Grau said, "but how can we go ahead here, considering all you've lost in Cuba?"

"Look, Juan," Bosch said, "that's my problem. I'll worry about the money. You worry about getting that distillery finished."

In fact, there was reason to be concerned about Bacardi's financial condition in the aftermath of the Cuba confiscation. Beyond the loss of the rum facilities, equipment, and aging reserves, Bacardi had lost its Hatuey beer business, the company's most important source of financing. Because beer did not need to be aged or transported long distances, the breweries generated immediate cash income, and that revenue helped underwrite the company's expansion. The confiscation of the old distillery on Matadero Street in Santiago was an emotional blow to the Bacardis, but from a financial perspective the loss of the beer operation was far more painful. In order to move ahead with his expansion plans in Brazil and beyond, Pepín Bosch had to turn to his banker, George S. Moore, the chairman of National City Bank (later named Citibank) and an acquaintance from Bosch's own days at the bank thirty years earlier. Bosch had gone to National City for help in financing the second Mexico expansion, but at that time he had assets in Cuba to offer as collateral. Now Bosch needed more money, and he had lost a chunk of his collateral. Moore extended Bosch credit regardless. In the early 1960s, relationships still mattered in banking, and Moore trusted Bosch as a businessman.

The Brazil move, however, was appearing increasingly risky. Almost from the beginning, it was plagued with problems. Bosch thought he had an agreement with the local government for the waste molasses slops to be piped into a nearby river, but the authorities objected when they realized how much discharge would be produced. Grau had to arrange for the slops to be taken on a barge and dumped at sea. (Later he persuaded the authorities that the slops, all organic, could be sluiced into the nearby sugarcane fields as fertilizer.) The distillery was built and put into production in record time, but then a second, more serious, problem emerged: The rum wasn't selling. Bosch had chosen the Recife site for its proximity to the sugar-producing areas and in order to take advantage of the tax breaks Bacardi was offered there, but the rum would have to be sold in the more heavily populated south, near São Paulo and Rio de Janeiro. Realizing he was facing a marketing challenge, Pepín Bosch called for Juan Prado, who had just finished his swing through Europe. Prado spent two years in Brazil, but even he—considered by his colleagues to be the best liquor salesman in the world—was unable to build a strong Bacardi rum market in the country. The Brazilians' preference for beer and *cachaça* and the relatively remote location of the Recife distillery, two thousand miles from Rio over unimproved roads, presented overwhelming odds.

But Pepín Bosch was a smart businessman. Realizing there would never be enough Bacardi rum sold in Brazil to justify the investment there, he decided to use the Recife facility to supply rum for other markets. The quality of the rum produced there was technically as good as that from any other Bacardi factory. Leasing stainless steel tankers, Bosch shipped the rum to other distribution points and bottling plants in an arrangement that proved profitable. Yet again, he had produced success from a potential business failure.

· · ·

The Bacardis' devotion to their history was symbolized over the years by their attention to the skinny coconut palm that stood alone in front of the main factory in Santiago. Don Facundo's fourteen-year-old son Facundo Jr. planted it the day the distillery opened in 1862 or shortly thereafter, and in the following decades *el coco* became a hallowed and untouchable symbol of the family enterprise. Each time the building was renovated, enlarged, or rebuilt, the construction had to take place around the palm, so that by the 1950s the spindly tree, leaning hard to the right, appeared to be in a cage, trapped behind a modern facade and a huge BACARDI sign. A bronze plaque mounted on the side of the building next to the coconut palm read:

> Ever since the foundation of Bacardi in the year of 1862, the factory has existed in this same place, though the building has twice been reconstructed. The coconut palm planted here when the enterprise was founded has been jealously guarded through all these times.

The coconut palm died, however, right around the time Fidel Castro's regime took the factory away from the Bacardi family. The *coco* legend was that the rum company would survive as long as the palm lived, or so it was claimed in subsequent Bacardi publicity. "In the year that the Bacardi family members were uprooted from their Cuban homeland," the company claimed, "the palm, as if in protest, withered and died." *Santiagueros* less invested in Bacardi lore say the palm was well on its way to dying before Fidel came to power and that the notion of its survival being linked to the survival of the family company was mostly concocted after the tree had already died. In any case, the story made for a nice symbolic narrative, and it certainly fit the reality: that Fidel Castro was responsible for effectively ending Bacardi life in Cuba.

February 4, 1962, was the one hundredth birthday of the Bacardi business. Past anniversaries had been celebrated with fireworks, charity events, and the company's renowned sailing regatta. But the centennial passed almost without notice. Family members were scattered across several continents, some of them with little to their name, and they had little prospect of returning to Cuba any time soon.

The new priority was to survive and show Fidel Castro that the company still existed as a vibrant private enterprise. The goal was met through the defense of the trademark and a reorganization of the corporate structure. The reconstituted Compañía Ron Bacardi, S.A., transplanted from Santiago to New York, moved again to Nassau, where it became Bacardi & Company, Ltd. As the successor to the original firm, it held the Bacardi trademarks and provided strategic guidance for the other Bacardi companies. Pepín Bosch was chairman.

Daniel Bacardi, having recovered from the humiliation of Castro's betrayal, returned from Spain to serve as president.

The loss of their properties in Cuba prompted Bosch and his shareholders to expand even more aggressively. In September 1961, a month before the first bottle of Bacardi rum came off the production line in Brazil and just a year after the inauguration of the new distillery in Tultitlán, Mexico, the company announced its intention to build a four-million-dollar distillery and bottling plant in the Bahamas. Rum produced there could be exported to British Commonwealth nations on the same tax-free basis that Puerto Rico provided with respect to the U.S. market. Its opening in January 1965 meant that Bacardi rum was being distilled in five plants in four countries. Just four years after the expropriation of his company and his personal assets in Cuba, Pepín Bosch was commuting between homes in Mexico, Brazil, and Miami and presiding over a growing and prosperous company. The time had come to gloat. "Fidel Castro took away $70 million from us, and we don't even feel it," Bosch told a reporter.

Another distillery opened thereafter in Canada, followed a few years later by new facilities in Martinique, Panama, and Spain. With so many Bacardi distilleries, thousands of miles apart, the challenge was quality control. Uniformity of taste had always been a hallmark of Bacardi rum manufacturing. The company took great pride in being able to guarantee that a bottle of white Bacardi rum opened in Germany or Brazil would be indistinguishable from one opened in New York or Mexico City. Consumers liked knowing what they were going to get. Gone, however, were the days when Daniel Bacardi would check the rum by splashing some on his hands and sniffing his palms. Technical evaluation was now favored, led by the analytical methods developed by Juan Grau. He had determined, for example, that what made Bacardi rum in Mexico different from the Puerto Rican or Cuban versions was the high sulfite content of Mexican molasses. Grau then developed a procedure for purifying the molasses before the fermentation began and thereby neutralizing the offending flavor. His methodology was explained in a technical manual used in every Bacardi production facility around the world. Chemical engineers at each location monitored the production to make sure the rum met the company's technical standards. A quality-control laboratory was established at Bacardi & Company in Nassau, and each month every Bacardi distillery sent rum samples to be analyzed by the laboratory technicians and rum experts.

From the early 1960s to the late 1970s, Bacardi reported the greatest growth spurt in the history of any liquor company. The company sold 1.7 million twelve-bottle rum cases worldwide in 1960, the year its Cuban operations were nationalized. By 1976, annual global sales had surpassed ten million cases, for an average yearly increase during that time of 12.5 percent. Juan Prado, reflecting on the company's development in the years after Cuba, suggested that the confiscation of its Cuban properties actually gave Bacardi a boost. "A lot of people think Bacardi should thank Castro for what he did," he said, "because we never would have achieved what we did if we had stayed in Cuba." The big change, Prado argues, was that the loss of its Cuban operations pushed Bacardi out of the beer business and forced it to focus all its efforts on rum. Outside Cuba, Hatuey beer was virtually unknown and would have faced competition far beyond anything Bacardi rum had to deal with. Moreover, the high costs involved in brewery construction and freight made an investment in a new beer business prohibitively expensive. Without its Hatuey subsidiaries, the Bacardi company had no choice but to expand its rum production internationally if it was to survive. It expanded, and it prospered.

• • •

Exile meant a division of Bacardi history into "before" and "after" periods. As a private business in the heroic city of Santiago, owned entirely by a Cuban family closely associated with the city's revolutionary heritage, Bacardi Rum was the quintessentially Cuban company. That changed when the family and the senior management and technical personnel took the company and the Bacardi name abroad—to the Bahamas, Miami, Bermuda, Puerto Rico, Mexico, Brazil, and beyond. The transition from small, locally oriented Cuban firm to global corporation, already under way in 1960, was dramatically accelerated. In the 1970s, marketing research in Puerto Rico suggested that the lingering image of Bacardi rum as a Cuban product was actually hindering sales, apparently because the Cuban exiles who had settled there had a reputation among the local population for arrogant and elitist attitudes. In response, the company revised its marketing in order to associate Bacardi more with Puerto Rican traditions, even sponsoring an annual arts-and-crafts fair at its distillery site outside San Juan, to showcase Puerto Rican artisans.

The experience of exile, however, did not end the Bacardi-Cuba connection so much as it made it more private. On the inside, Bacardi remained Cuban. The company continued to be entirely family owned, and the Bacardis themselves remained keenly aware of their Cuban heritage, as did the Bacardi employees who left Cuba with the family and stayed with the company. In exile, the Bacardis' ties to the company and to each other as an extended family became a way of holding on to their Cuban identity. Manuel Jorge Cutillas, the company engineer and great-grandson of Emilio Bacardi, saw the significance of the bond years later when he became chairman of the Bacardi board of directors. "Because of Bacardi, we as a family were not as negatively affected by exile as many Cuban families were," he said. "We had Bacardi, it became our country. We were able to keep a little piece of Cuba within ourselves."

The Bacardis' personal dependence on the business during the early exile years, for their income as well as their identity, reinforced the company's familial character even as it was becoming more international in its orientation and operation. In 1963, Bosch shifted the headquarters of Bacardi Imports, the U.S. company, from New York to Miami. The move coincided with the arrival of hundreds of thousands of Cubans in south Florida and gave Bacardi a U.S. home in the heart of the Cuban-American community. Though Bacardi Imports was but one of several Bacardi companies, its location in Miami allowed it to serve as the hub of the Bacardi diaspora. Family members were scattered in many countries, but more settled in Miami than anywhere else. The city had always been a business and commercial center for Latin America as a whole, and the influx of a new Cuban population made it all the more so.

For his new Miami offices, Bosch commissioned the design of a flashy new eight-story tower. Two sides of the resulting building were covered by blue and white ceramic tiles that formed floral images, designed by a Brazilian artist from Recife named Francisco Brennand. Each of the twenty-eight thousand six-inch-square tiles was hand-painted in Brennand's studio before being fired and glazed. The office building itself was erected on four columns with an open plaza below, so that it appeared to float in midair. The tower took up only a small fraction of the Biscayne Boulevard site, leaving most of the land for gardens. The color, vitality, and playfulness of the Bacardi building evoked a whimsical and carefree Latin spirit.

Bacardi's public image, however, was another matter. In spite of its own heritage and its location in the U.S. city with the second-largest Cuban population outside Havana, there was no mention of Cuba in any company marketing. Beginning in the 1960s, the main advertising theme was Bacardi's "mixability." It went with soda. An especially long-running ad campaign featured the Bacardi bat logo or another Bacardi symbol alongside various soft drink brands, with the caption "Bacardi. The Mixable One." One ad showed a wooden Bacardi crate filled with Coke, 7UP, Pepsi, Fresca, Schweppes Tonic, Canada Dry Ginger Ale, and Squirt, along with two bottles of Bacardi, and was titled simply, "A Bacardi party to go."

In 1965 Bacardi advertising executives negotiated a joint marketing agreement with Coca-Cola, premised on the promotion of Bacardi-and-Coke cocktails. For Coca-Cola, whose advertising had always emphasized wholesome themes, it was a bold move. One of the first products was an advertisement in *Life* magazine in May 1966 that purported to explain the origin of the rum-and-Coke craze. The ad featured a notarized affidavit signed by Fausto Rodrí-guez, the Bacardi ad executive who had long claimed to have been present the first time Bacardi rum was drunk with Coca-Cola. In his affidavit, Rodríguez swore that he was employed as a messenger by the U.S. Army Signal Corps.

I became friendly with a Mr. _____, who worked in the office of the Chief Signal Officer. One afternoon, in August 1900, I went with him to the _____ Bar, and he drank Bacardi rum and Coca-Cola. I just drank Coca-Cola, being only 14 years old. On that occasion, there was a group of soldiers at the bar, and one of them asked Mr. _____ what he was drinking. He told them it was Bacardi and Coca-Cola and suggested they try it, which they did.

The soldiers liked it. They ordered another round and toasted Mr. _____ as the inventor of a great drink.

The drink has remained popular to the present time.

It was, of course, the famous "Cuba libre," but in the *Life* ad it became a "Rum & Coke." The words "Cuba" and "Havana" were nowhere to be seen in the "affidavit." Cuba in 1965 was associated with revolution and counterrevolution, Fidel Castro and Communism, a failed U.S. invasion, and a nuclear missile crisis. Controversy and strong partisan feelings do not go well with advertising campaigns, and in public presentations there was no sign that Bacardi was still connected to its island home.

The unfortunate truth was that "Cuba" no longer meant what it once had. There was no single Cuban nation, no simple notion of a Cuban patriotism. Cuba was torn in two. One part was still on the island and living with Fidel Castro if not genuinely supporting him, the other part outside. Bacardi, as a family and a company, had ended up on the side in exile. Under the circumstances, a different kind of Cuban patriotism emerged: angrier, less liberal, more negative. Fidel Castro had so usurped the rhetoric of social justice and national sovereignty, even claiming Cuba's independence heroes in the name of his revolution, that he left little room for idealism. Now there was just one issue: Cubans stood either with Fidel Castro or against him.

Chapter 18

Counterrevolution

When Pepín Bosch and his wife, Enriqueta, arrived in Miami in July 1960, they found the city's restless exile community already abuzz with anti-Castro intrigues. Ex-*batistiano* army officers were alternately plotting and quarreling with supporters of ex-president Carlos Prío, while disaffected *fidelistas* huddled with CIA agents to discuss weapons shipments and invasion scenarios. The U.S. government was hoping that Cubans themselves would rise up and overthrow the Castro regime, and toward that end the CIA had assembled the Frente Revolucionario Democrático (FRD), the Democratic Revolutionary Front, an unwieldy group that was supposed to bring the disparate and squabbling exile factions together in support of an exile invasion force.

Back in Cuba, Daniel Bacardi and others were still clinging to their faith in Fidel Castro, but from the moment he left the island, Pepín Bosch was ready to support the CIA-led conspiracies. U.S. government agents immediately solicited his help. In September 1960, Bosch visited Richard Cushing, a political officer at the U.S. Embassy in Mexico. Cushing wanted a situation report from Cuba, where he had served for five years during the Batista era, and he sought Bosch's advice on how the Castro regime could be undermined and who could lead a resistance movement. Bosch had strong opinions and was not shy about sharing them. According to an embassy cable on the Cushing meeting, Bosch had "little good to say" about the directors of the Frente Revolucionario Democrático in Miami, though he praised Eduardo Martín Elena, an ex-Cuban army colonel who had been chosen by the FRD directorate to supervise the military training of the exile force that was to go back to Cuba. As commander of the Cuban army garrison in Matanzas in 1952, Martín Elena had taken a courageous stand against the Batista coup and thereby earned Bosch's admiration. "Bosch is so impressed with [Martín] Elena as a leader," Cushing reported, "that, although almost sixty and slightly crippled, Bosch would willingly be part of any invasion force that Elena might muster."

Bosch was actually sixty-two. He had his hands full with Bacardi affairs, and his boast that he was ready to volunteer for a Cuba invasion force should have been ignored. Over the next several years, however, Bosch would indeed devote much of his own time and money to the cause of fighting Fidel Castro. In addition to sponsoring propaganda campaigns aimed at turning U.S. public opinion against Castro, Bosch financed commando actions and sabotage operations inside Cuba. His politics had changed dramatically. In Cuba, Bosch's activism had been forward-looking and idealistic, but in exile he was more rancorous, his sense of civic duty now channeled into an angry determination to bring Castro down, by any means necessary.

◆ ◆ ◆

Outside Miami, many Americans were still fascinated by Fidel Castro and his revolution. An aura of romance and adventure had always surrounded Cuba in the U.S. imagination, and the charismatic bearded president provided colorful material as he rode around the Cuban countryside in an open jeep, orated passionately for hours before adoring crowds, and smoked cigars and discussed imperialism late into the night with visiting celebrities and world leaders. Foreign journalists were charmed by what CBS News correspondent Robert Taber, writing in 1961, called the "human quality" of the Cuban revolution, evident at the *fidelista* rallies:

> One sees a ferocious-looking *rebelde* with a magpie's nest of a beard, carrying a submachine gun and armed with a tremendous revolver as well. From the pocket of his shirt protrudes a huge harmonica. His companion, equally hairy and ferocious, is eating an ice-cream on a stick, and grinning cheerfully, while Fidel, with the same good humor, lectures an old man in the crowd who complains that he has not yet been given a cow.

The American sociologist C. Wright Mills toured Cuba in the summer of 1960 and returned to write an adulatory book about the revolution titled *Listen, Yankee.* Written in a popular, accessible style, with Mills taking on the voice of the Cubans with whom he had traveled, the book sold four hundred thousand copies within the first few months of its publication.

To Fidel Castro's U.S. supporters, the anger and noise coming from the exile community in south Florida mainly reflected the bitterness of people who had lost their privileged class position in Cuba and refused to support the social and economic transformation there. Herbert Matthews, the *New York Times* correspondent who had interviewed Castro in the Sierra Maestra four years earlier, was still defending him in February 1961, even after Pepín Bosch and other old Cuban friends had turned against the revolution. In an interview on WBAI radio, a public radio station in New York City, Matthews praised Castro's government for its social and economic reforms, scoffed at the charges that he was a Communist, and chided the U.S. government and the exile community for their hostility to the revolutionary regime. A few weeks later, Corliss Lamont, a wealthy New York socialist whose father was J. P. Morgan's business partner, wrote a letter to the *New York Times* criticizing those who labeled the Cuban government "Communist" solely on the basis of its deep reforms in agriculture and industry and its commercial agreements with the Soviet Union and Communist China.

Pepín Bosch was dismayed by the continuing enthusiasm for Fidel Castro among leading U.S. journalists and intellectuals. Just two years earlier, he had promoted Herbert Matthews as someone who could explain "the Cuban side" of the Castro story, but that was before Fidel turned sharply to the left. After hearing of his comments on WBAI, Bosch wrote Matthews a personal letter, imploring him to reconsider his rosy assessments of Castro's revolution. "To Fidel, you are the equivalent of an army division," Bosch said, "so winning you away will be quite a victory."

During the anti-Batista struggle, Bosch had been a key source and pro-Castro spokesman for many U.S. journalists, including Robert Taber of CBS, Jay Mallin of *Time*, Jules Dubois of the *Chicago Tribune*, and Ruby Hart Phillips and Homer Bigart of the *New York Times*, as well as Herbert Matthews. In exile, it occurred to Bosch that he could use his contacts and influence in the U.S. media to get across his new message—that Fidel Castro had betrayed those who believed in the promise of his revolution and that he was installing a Communist dictatorship in Cuba. About a week after writing to Matthews, Bosch submitted a lengthy letter to the *New York Times*, saying he wanted "to clarify some misconceptions" about "the so-called Cuban Revolution." Rather than have his commentary edited to fit in the "letters" column on the editorial page, Bosch took out a paid advertisement in the name of Bacardi and ran his entire letter in the allotted space under the Bacardi corporate logo. Addressing the *Times* editor, he complained about pro-Castro comments made by "your" Herbert Matthews and also about the Lamont letter:

> It is my opinion that neither Mr. Matthews nor Mr. Lamont knows what is really going on in Cuba—or does not wish to know. For Mr. Castro, in the name of Communism, has led my people into poverty, disease, slavery, and the loss of that gaiety and happiness that have always marked the character of the Cuban people. Castro could very easily have given his country freedom

and justice, and the opportunity for the pursuit of happiness. He could have offered his people a better education in a free society; and he could even have doubled the national income in a few short years. Instead of this, he has destroyed our national wealth and practically everything of material and spiritual value in my country.

By the time Bosch published his open letter, the peasants' rebellion in the Escambray Mountains and the underground resistance movements in Havana had all been crushed. The CIA-organized exile army was left as the only hope for overthrowing the Castro regime. Bosch was kept apprised of the invasion planning by Polo Miranda, the former Hatuey brewery manager in Manacas. Miranda had turned against Castro while still in Cuba, going from cooperating with the M-26-7 guerrillas to buying and smuggling arms for the anti-Castro rebels in the Escambray mountains. A report filed by CIA agent Bernard Barker in June 1960 had judged him a "superior" candidate for CIA assignments. Though he fled Cuba before taking any CIA work, Miranda went on to take part in various Agency-supported capers, and in Miami his Bacardi job was mainly to serve as Bosch's intermediary with the exile groups working against Castro.

The organization of the exile army was problematic, largely due to CIA heavy-handedness. Some popular exile leaders were barred from the effort because they were seen as leaning too far to the left. Pepín Bosch's favorite commander, Colonel Eduardo Martín Elena, quit after the American agents in charge of organizing the army barred him from contact with the Cuban troops he was supposed to be leading. By early 1961, however, exiles who wanted to fight Fidel Castro effectively had no alternative but to sign up for the CIA force preparing to invade Cuba. Among the volunteers were three young men from the Bacardi clan. Two were great-grandsons of Emilio Bacardi Moreau: José Bacardi, the son of Emilio Bacardi Rosell, and Roberto del Rosal, whose grandmother was Marina Bacardi Cape. The third was Polo Miranda's nephew, a former law student named Jorge Mas Canosa, a brash young man who would later become the dominating political figure in the Cuban exile community.

The three men, about twenty-one years old when they joined the exile invasion force, had known each other back in Santiago and managed to get assigned together. They were part of a group that was to land in Oriente province with the aim of creating a diversion from the main force due to come ashore at the Bay of Pigs. After arriving at their destination, the Bacardi boys spent two nights huddled with their comrades in a boat off the Cuban coast, waiting for the signal to move ashore. The order to disembark came on the second night, and the young men nervously prepared to move, heavy packs on their backs and rifles in hand. The operation was aborted at the last minute, however, when the commander got word that government soldiers had spotted the boat and were prepared to massacre the group as soon as it touched shore. The Bacardi cousins and their friend Jorge never managed to set foot on Cuban soil.

◆ ◆ ◆

With the attempt to foment an anti-Castro uprising, Cuban history was repeating itself. In the first place, those Cubans who took up arms to oppose the Castro regime were carrying on a long-standing insurrectionist tradition on the island. In the nineteenth century, Cuban rebels fought three wars against their Spanish rulers, and there were at least five more armed uprisings in the first half of the twentieth century. A readiness to resort to violence in pursuit of political aims was part of the national culture in Cuba. Second, the anti-Castro movement was characterized by petty internal rivalries, in a pattern reminiscent of the way Cuba's political parties had fragmented in previous decades and made dictatorships possible. Finally, the opposition was tainted by its close association with the U.S. government, another long-standing issue in Cuba's uneven political development. Nationalists on the island had long railed against the "Platt mentality" of those Cubans who looked to the United States for political guidance, in a manner reminiscent of those Cuban legislators who supported the 1901 amendment that gave the United States a formal right to intervene in Cuban affairs.

Infighting among the exile leaders and their dependence on U.S. assistance played straight into Fidel Castro's hands, allowing him to portray those who opposed him as ineffectual lackeys of U.S. imperialism. Castro, in fact, almost seemed to welcome efforts to overthrow his government. "A revolution that was not attacked," he wrote in a 1961 essay, "would in the first place not be a true revolution." It was only when Castro saw a genuine *counter*revolution emerging, led by those he considered his enemies, that he could be sure he was transforming Cuba in the way he wanted. Any political outcome not opposed by Cuban capitalists, by the island's upper class, and by the U.S. government would not have satisfied him. "A revolution that does not have an enemy in front of it," he wrote, "runs the risk of lulling itself to sleep."*

---

*Castro's eagerness to see a counterrevolution develop in Cuba came straight from his reading of Karl Marx. Writing about the 1848 "February revolution" in France, Marx observed that it advanced not through its own achievements, "but on the contrary by the creation of a powerful, united counter-revolution...in combat with whom the party of overthrow ripened into a really revolutionary party." Castro was convinced that the same dynamic held in Cuba.

For their part, Pepín Bosch and other exiles working against the Castro regime did not necessarily object to the "counterrevolutionary" label. To the extent anti-Americanism and state socialism defined the Cuban revolution, they were indeed determined to counter it. In dedicating themselves to that goal, they acted in pursuit of their own interests and principles as Cubans and not on the orders of the U.S. government. The big question was whether they were capable of challenging Castro without U.S. assistance. Most concluded they could not.

* * *

President John F. Kennedy inherited the "Castro problem" from the Eisenhower administration, but he was no less determined to overthrow the Marxist regime than his predecessor had been and perhaps more so. It was an assignment he gave mostly to his brother, Attorney General Robert F. Kennedy. After the Bay of Pigs fiasco in April 1961, the attorney general directed the CIA to design a new anti-Castro plan. The result was "Operation Mongoose," a covert action program largely focused on sabotage operations with the goal of disrupting the Cuban economy and thereby weakening the Castro regime. The program was to be implemented in tandem with an embargo on all trade with Cuba, initiated in February 1962.

Over the next nine months, more than fifty million dollars were spent on some of the most outrageous and bizarre initiatives in the history of U.S. foreign policy. The planned actions under Operation Mongoose ranged from attempts to induce Cuban crop failures to the staging of "provocations" that could then be used as pretexts for U.S. military action. In the "psychological" operations category, Mongoose planners contemplated a massive airdrop of toilet paper, then in short supply in Cuba, with the idea that the Cuban people would cheer the United States for coming to their rescue. CIA officials also made contacts with organized crime figures to arrange Castro's assassination. One CIA agent went so far as to deliver poison pills to a Mafia figure in Miami, who in turn was supposed to pass them to a contact in Cuba. Few of the schemes got past the planning stage, and Operation Mongoose was significant mostly for providing Fidel Castro with facts and anecdotes to back up his repeated claims that the United States was out to get him and that the deep economic problems in Cuba were the consequence of U.S. sabotage efforts.

Years later, Kennedy aide Arthur Schlesinger dismissed the idea of Operation Mongoose as "silly and stupid," but it was called off only when the "Castro problem" was superseded by something far more dangerous: the threat of nuclear war. In October 1962, after U.S. spy planes discovered nuclear missile sites in Cuba, the United States and the Soviet Union stood at the brink for nearly two weeks, with Fidel Castro urging Soviet premier Nikita Khrushchev not to back down.* In the letter that resolved the missile crisis, President Kennedy assured Khrushchev that in exchange for the removal of the missiles, the United States would not invade the island. Such assurance did not theoretically prohibit covert sabotage operations, but having narrowly avoided a confrontation with the Soviet Union, the Kennedy administration thought it wise to put an end to all CIA-sponsored activities inside Cuba, at least temporarily. If operatives were caught in Cuba, the Soviets might have been able to justify their missile deployment as a reasonable measure to protect their Cuban ally against U.S. subversion and attack.

After a few months, the Kennedy administration reactivated its covert anti-Castro program, albeit this time intending only "to obstruct or slow down the pacification of the population and the consolidation and stabilization of the Castro Communist regime." The new program would only support "autonomous Cuban exile groups and individuals." There would be no more CIA-managed operations with fully controlled agents. It was time to give the Cuban exiles relatively free rein to do what they wanted to do.

• • •

Shortly after arriving in Miami, Pepín Bosch agreed to the CIA's request that he join the Frente Revolucionario Democrático, later rechristened as the Consejo Revolucionario Cubano (Cuban Revolutionary Council), but he was never impressed by the directorate's work, and he skipped a lot of meetings. In the first two years after he left Cuba, Bacardi business took almost all his time. He and his lawyers were battling in courts around the world to defend the family's ownership of the "Bacardi" rum brand. He was overseeing the construction and operation of new production facilities in Brazil and Mexico and the relocation of the corporate headquarters to the Bahamas. He was helping family members and veteran employees resettle outside Cuba and finding jobs for those who needed income. The operation in Brazil occupied so much of Bosch's attention, in fact, that he acquired Brazilian citizenship, a step he never bothered to take in the United States.

---

*In a letter to Khrushchev on October 26, Castro appeared to suggest that if the United States were to send U.S. ground troops into Cuba, the Soviet Union should respond with a nuclear strike on the U.S. homeland. "I tell you this because I believe that the imperialists' aggressiveness is extremely dangerous," Castro wrote, "and if they actually carry out the brutal act of invading Cuba, that would be the moment to eliminate such danger forever through an act of legitimate defense, however terrible the solution would be."

With so many of the exile leaders quarreling among themselves, Bosch gained prestige by staying above the fray, becoming known in south Florida mainly as a benefactor of the Cuban exile cause and as the chairman of Bacardi. The company enjoyed a place of honor among exiled Cubans, not only because of its history but also because it survived Fidel Castro's confiscation and emerged even stronger for the experience. In late 1961, when Fidel Castro was demanding an "indemnity" payment in exchange for the release of the 1,200 Bay of Pigs prisoners, Bosch offered to donate up to one hundred thousand dollars in Bacardi money to a private fund in order to purchase the prisoners' freedom. "Bacardi cannot turn its back on the patriots who were taken prisoner at the Bay of Pigs for defending the Cuban cause," he declared.

By the end of 1962, Bosch was ready to take a more active and personal part in the anti-Castro struggle. The resolution of the missile crisis in October had brought an end to U.S. government–sponsored sabotage activities, but Bosch remained convinced that Castro could be overthrown only through the use of force. In his single most brazen and reckless act as an exile leader, Bosch secretly decided to finance and organize a military action of his own in Cuba. His thirty-six-year-old son, Carlos, learned about the plan only incidentally. At the time, Carlos was trying to start an air cargo service in Miami, having purchased on old DC-4 transport plane and hired pilots to haul freight to and from the Caribbean and South America. To his frustration, however, the U.S. government repeatedly denied him permission to initiate the operation. When he told his father about his problems with the aviation authorities, Pepín nodded knowingly.

"Hmmm," he said, "maybe it's because of the plane I'm keeping in Costa Rica." Carlos had no idea what his father was talking about, and he was flabbergasted when he found out: Bosch had a plan to bomb oil refineries in Cuba from the air. Such a mission, he reasoned, could be carried out with a minimum risk of civilian casualties. Power plants that depended on oil for fuel would have to be shut down, cutting off the flow of electricity across the island. Daily activities would come to a standstill, and the stage would be set for an uprising. Without informing anyone, including his CIA contacts, Bosch discreetly purchased a Douglas B-26 bomber, using an insurance company as his purchasing agent, and had it flown to Costa Rica, whose government at the time was accommodating of Cuban exile plotting against the Castro regime. The next step was to hire a pilot willing to fly the bombing mission. It should not have been difficult. B-26 aircraft, known as Invaders, had been extensively used during both World War II and the Korean War, and Cuban exile pilots had flown them on a series of bombing runs two days prior to the Bay of Pigs invasion.

On March 1, 1963, an unidentified person (not Bosch) approached a Cuban exile pilot named Gaston Bernal and offered to pay him to carry out the refinery mission. He was not told who was putting up the money. Bernal was working with the CIA-organized Consejo Revolucionario Cubano at the time, and he immediately informed the Consejo military chief, who in turn relayed the information to the CIA. According to a CIA report, Bernal was told that the bombing mission should take place during the last two weeks of March, though the exact date and target were to be left to Bernal's discretion. The mission was to be carried out with the help of officials in Costa Rica, who had promised to provide accommodation for the pilot, and with the Nicaraguan air force, which was to provide a crew that would install twelve rocket mounts on the aircraft and supports for six 260-pound bombs. When the mission was completed, Bernal was told, the anonymous sponsor would assure a safe return to his home base. Such assurances were apparently not enough to convince Bernal, however. The CIA report noted that Bernal rejected the offer, saying he considered the mission "suicidal."

The CIA quickly determined that Pepín Bosch was behind the refinery bombing plan. (It was no wonder that his son Carlos was blocked from starting an air freight business out of south Florida; U.S. authorities may have wanted to be sure it was not tied to his father's bombing plans.) Agency officials, however, did not immediately intervene to halt Bosch's operation from going forward. If carried out successfully, it would have been a good example of the "autonomous" exile activities the Kennedy administration had decided to allow, if not patronize. At a White House discussion of the new covert program, the participants had specifically concluded that "refineries and power plants seem to be particularly good targets." In the end, however, Bosch's bombing idea never materialized. Neither a volunteer pilot nor the necessary munitions could be found, and after Costa Rican officials began getting nervous about the mission, Bosch gave up his idea and surrendered his B-26 Invader to the local authorities.*

The notion of a respected Cuban businessman privately purchasing an attack aircraft and organizing a bombing raid on an oil refinery in his native land would subsequently strike some observers as outrageous, but in the context of the broad opposition to Fidel Castro in 1963, Pepín Bosch's activism was seen as responsible behavior. Many other patriotic and progressive Cuban exile

---

*Bosch's B-26 Invader was later delivered to the Honduran air force. Years later, by then painted black and orange and nicknamed Versatile Lady, the aircraft was put on display at the History and Traditions Museum at Lackland Air Force Base in Texas.

leaders, including former presidents Carlos Prío and Manuel Urrutia and former members of Castro's own government, were undertaking similar projects or at least supporting them. By 1963, "counterrevolutionary" activities were viewed approvingly within U.S. anti-Communist liberal and intellectual circles, where Bosch was personally well connected.

Even as he plotted the bombing mission, Bosch was providing the bulk of the funding for the establishment of a "Citizens' Committee for a Free Cuba" in Washington, D.C., an organization founded in April 1963 with the objective of initiating "a nationwide discussion on the problem of Cuba, the threat its Communist regime poses to the Americas, and the measures that must be taken to put an end to it." The committee members included such leading public figures as the playwright, journalist, and diplomat Clare Boothe Luce, professors Sidney Hook and Hans Morgenthau, Admiral Arleigh Burke, lawyer (and Kennedy family friend) William vanden Heuvel, the physicist Edward Teller, and Jay Lovestone, a top official of the AFL-CIO labor federation. Within months of its organization, the group was advocating "aid to the Cuban freedom fighters" and lobbying—according to the notes of its secretary—on behalf of "the forces inside the [Kennedy] Administration who wish it to adopt an active liberationist policy" with respect to Cuba.

With its high-profile membership, the "Free Cuba" committee soon caught the attention of members of the U.S. Congress. Some administration officials were not pleased, however, by what they saw as an effort to inflame what was already a sensitive internal government debate over Cuba policy. The committee's weekly newsletter, compiled largely from exile accounts, often included unsubstantiated allegations about what was going on inside Cuba. The State Department's Miami-based liaison with the exile community, John Crimmins, told a congressional committee he was "frankly disappointed" by the newsletter contents. "I have found that it repeats essentially what I would call the usual kind of report from exile sources," Crimmins said. "There have been factual errors."

In his congressional testimony, Crimmins revealed that Pepín Bosch was the committee's key backer, identifying him as "one of the principal figures in the [Cuban] exile community from the standpoint of financial substance and influence." In the next few years, in fact, FBI agents and CIA officers saw Bosch's name come up again and again in their exile activity reports. The Bacardi chairman was one of the few exiles to come out of Cuba with money in the bank, and he was willing to spend large sums on the anti-Castro cause. CIA officials warned the White House in April 1963 that the new policy of supporting "autonomous" exile operations inevitably meant that "acts will be

Parque Céspedes, or the Plaza de Armas, the town square in Santiago, as it appeared in the 1920s. Emilio Bacardi and his brother Facundo attempted to provoke an anti-Spanish uprising here in 1868. The three-story building at the left is the Club San Carlos, the favored Bacardi drinking location for many years. Family members gathered on the club balcony to watch Fidel Castro speak triumphantly upon his arrival in Santiago on January 1, 1959.

Emilito Bacardi with his sisters, about 1930. To his right are María (center) and Carmen, daughters of Emilio Bacardi and María Lay. In front are Emilito's half sisters, the daughters of Emilio and Elvira Cape. From left to right: Marina, Lucía ("Mimín"), Adelaida ("Lalita"), and Amalia.

Bacardi advertising in the 1930s and 1940s.

Inside the Bacardi factory in Santiago about 1930. Bacardi rum was bottled and sold in wooden crates, visible at right, or in wicker-covered jugs, shown stacked on the mezzanine.

Bacardi administrative offices in the 1930s. The company management favored open space to facilitate communication.

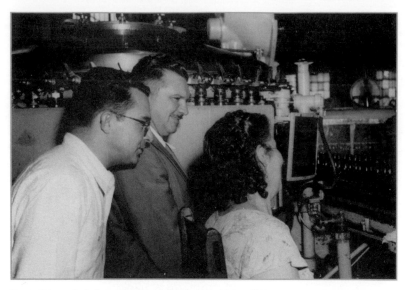

Daniel Bacardi, left, with Labor Minister José Morell-Romero in 1950, on a visit to the Bacardi factory in Santiago.

Enrique Schueg, son-in-law of Don Facundo Bacardi, the company founder. Schueg presided over the Bacardi Rum Company during its years of key growth and international expansion, from 1922 to 1950. He is seated before the company's original pot still.

The art-deco Bacardi building in downtown Havana in 1952, the fiftieth anniversary of Cuban independence.

Bacardi president José "Pepín" Bosch, the son-in-law of Enrique Schueg, speaking at a convention of Bacardi sales agents in 1953. Seated to his left is Olga Covani Bacardi, granddaughter of Emilio Bacardi and mother of future Bacardi chairman Manuel Jorge Cutillas.

Bacardi president Pepín Bosch (center) at a dinner in Santiago, speaking to Cuban president Carlos Prío, under whom he served as finance minister. On Bosch's left is Luis Casero, mayor of Santiago and a fellow minister in Prío's cabinet.

Ernest Hemingway (center) was feted by Bacardi in 1956 in honor of his Nobel prize. To his right is Fernando Campoamor, noted Havana columnist and Hemingway drinking pal.

Juan Grau, a Bacardi chemical engineer (and classmate of Fidel Castro) who pioneered the analysis and evaluation techniques behind Bacardi quality control procedures.

Pepín Bosch, during a rare moment of relaxation.

The Bacardi factory in Santiago as it appeared in the 1950s. The factory was built on the site of the original distillery on Matadero Street, and the coconut palm is the same tree planted at the site by Facundo Bacardi Moreau in 1862.

The Bacardi administrative offices on Aguilera Street (formerly Marina Baja) in the 1950s. This was the first Bacardi facility in Santiago, and it was where Emilio Bacardi worked for his father as a young man in the 1860s.

Cubans and foreigners alike were entertained at the world-renowned Tropicana Night Club during Havana's golden age in the 1950s. Fidel Castro kept the Tropicana open to show that the revolution still honored Cuba's salsa heritage.

Fulgencio Batista, the former army clerk who dominated Cuban politics in the 1930s, was elected president in 1940, and returned to power through a military coup in 1952. The Bacardis of Santiago were among his most outspoken opponents.

Bacardi executive José Espín is served by his daughter Vilma, as her lover and revolutionary comrade Raúl Castro stands at her side. Fidel Castro is at the end of the table, his head bowed.

Raúl Castro and Vilma Espín at their wedding in Santiago in January 1959. The lavish affair was attended by dozens of Bacardi family members and friends.

Fidel Castro, Raúl Castro, and Che Guevara in Havana in 1963. Che Guevara was killed in Bolivia in 1967. Raúl Castro formally succeeded his ailing brother Fidel as Cuba's president in February 2008.

Fidel Castro, accompanied by local Communist Party and government officials, speaking to workers at the old Bacardi rum aging house in 1963. It was his one and only visit to the former Bacardi facilities in Santiago.

Fidel Castro with Gilberto Cala, a worker at the former Bacardi factory, in 1963. Castro asked Cala to suggest a new brand name for the rum previously produced there under the "Bacardi" label.

Bacardi boss Pepín Bosch directed the highly successful reorganization of Bacardi operations outside Cuba after the company's facilities were confiscated by the Castro government in 1960.

Eighty-nine-year-old "Emilito" Bacardi with other family members at the annual company anniversary dinner in 1966. The company had survived the loss of its Cuban properties, and family members were prospering with the spectacular growth of Bacardi rum sales across the world.

President Ronald Reagan honors Jorge Mas Canosa, who rose from humble beginnings to a position of power, wealth, and influence in the Cuban exile community. He began his political career at the side of Pepín Bosch, and Mas Canosa's Cuban American National Foundation received generous Bacardi support.

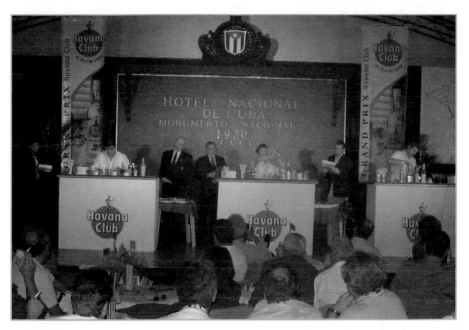

A rum cocktail competition at Havana's Hotel Nacional in 2004, featuring bartenders from around the world. The event was sponsored by Havana Club International, a French-Cuban joint venture. Havana Club, originally produced by the Arechabala family in Cuba, became the government's top export brand after Fidel Castro came to power and took over the company.

The distilling columns installed in the 1950s by the Bacardi Rum Company at their distillery in Santiago are still in use today.

The Bacardis' old rum aging warehouse in Santiago, as it appears today. Horse-drawn taxis are still a familiar sight in Santiago. The slogan on the side of the warehouse says, "Santiago de Cuba—Rebellious Yesterday, Welcoming Today, Heroic Forever."

performed which are not in conformity with current U.S. policy." As a well-known freelancer, Pepín Bosch was one of those whose moves the CIA felt needed to be monitored. Ideologically, the Bacardi boss remained loyal to the progressive political vision for which the Bacardi family and firm had long been known in Cuba, but Bosch was now consumed by his determination to see Fidel Castro removed from power, and that obsession on occasion took him to the edge of illegal activity.

In November 1963, the United States was deeply shaken by the assassination of John F. Kennedy. His killing shattered the spirit of optimism he had inspired and left the nation traumatized. Rumors of a Cuba connection abounded. Fidel Castro was said to have ordered Kennedy killed in retaliation for the plots the Kennedy administration had initiated against him. Another theory focused on Cuban exiles, outraged by Kennedy's last-minute abandonment of the Bay of Pigs operation and his subsequent agreement after the missile crisis to halt all invasion planning. In any case, Americans were in no mood to hear about more shadowy plots. Pepín Bosch and other Cuban exile leaders found their conspiratorial activities coming under even closer scrutiny.

In May 1964, one of the CIA's Cuban informants alerted the Agency to an exile plan to pay the Mafia $150,000 to have Fidel Castro, Raúl Castro, and Che Guevara assassinated. Pepín Bosch was identified as a possible sponsor. The informant, who worked for Cuban shipping magnate (and Bosch acquaintance) Teofilo Babún, formerly of Santiago, reported that Babún had been approached by a fellow shipping executive named Byron Cameron, and that Cameron had hinted that he was in touch with people who could arrange the assassinations. Babún allegedly agreed to help raise money for the hits, and in April he sent one of his employees to the Cuban industrialist deemed most likely to contribute funds for the operation—Pepín Bosch. A second exile informant allegedly privy to the plotting reported that Bosch agreed to put up fifty thousand dollars on his own. The informant said Bosch "believes that a quick change for the better in the Cuban situation can be brought about only by the physical elimination of Fidel Castro and that his elimination is well worth $150,000." The CIA report on the plot said Bosch "hoped he could get the balance of the money from the United States government or from other sources."

The prominent mention of Pepín Bosch in the alleged assassination plot was an attention grabber, and the subsequent report shot straight to the top of the CIA bureaucracy. A memorandum on the findings, signed by deputy CIA director Richard Helms, was sent in June to the White House, the State Department, the Defense Intelligence Agency, and Attorney General Robert Kennedy.

White House aide Gordon Chase forwarded a copy of the memorandum to his boss, McGeorge Bundy, President Lyndon Johnson's national security adviser, with a sensational subject line: "a plot to assassinate Castro which would involve U.S. elements of the Mafia and which would be financed by Pepín Bosch." Within a week, the State Department told its Miami officer, John Crimmins, to put a stop to the plot, and Robert Kennedy ordered the FBI to investigate Bosch and anyone else involved in the affair. If the plot proceeded under Bosch's sponsorship, he could possibly be exposed to conspiracy charges.

In July, FBI agents went to see Bosch at the Bacardi offices in Miami, advising him that he was not required to make any statements, that anything he said could be held against him in court, and that he was entitled to consult an attorney before speaking with them. Bosch said he needed no such legal protections, and he volunteered what he knew of the assassination plot. Two Cuban exiles had come to see him, he said, with a story that the Mafia was willing to arrange the Castro brothers' assassination. Bosch told the FBI agents that he would not have assisted in any murder or assassination plot "under any circumstances," but he also said he told the two Cubans who visited him that he would "consider" their request for funds. He did so, Bosch explained, in order to buy him time to report the assassination plot to the CIA, which he said he promptly did.

The Agency station chief in Miami, Ted Shackley, was by then a close associate of Pepín Bosch, having been one of those who encouraged Bosch to take part in the CIA-directed Consejo Revolucionario Cubano. For his part, Shackley confirmed that Bosch came to see him about the Castro assassination plan, though he did not quite recall Bosch being especially horrified by it. Indeed, Shackley remembered Bosch suggesting that the CIA help finance the proposed Mafia hit, as the original exile informants had also reported. No evidence was ever produced, however, to indicate that Bosch gave the Mafia offer any additional thought.

Pepín Bosch had long been a maverick operator, but by 1964 he was reconsidering his old ways, and the alleged assassination scheme did not fit with his latest thinking about how Castro should be opposed. The failure of his plan to bomb Cuban oil refineries a year earlier had taught Bosch an important lesson: Individual ventures would not work. If Cuban exiles were to have any chance of overthrowing Castro, they would have to unite. The only operation with any prospect of success, Bosch concluded, would be one undertaken on behalf of the entire anti-Castro opposition.

It would not be easy. The Consejo Revolucionario Cubano had effectively fallen apart after its leaders claimed the U.S. government had reneged on a promise to support a second invasion of Cuba. To replace it, Bosch proposed the designation of a civilian leadership, democratically chosen by the exiles themselves, which would then supervise all military operations deemed necessary for Cuba's "liberation." His idea was to convene an assembly of several dozen exile leaders who would then nominate five people to serve as representatives of the whole Cuban population outside Cuba. The exile community, identified through a census, would then vote in a certified postal referendum on whether to endorse or reject the proposed slate. If approved, the nominated exile representatives would be constituted as a directorate authorized to supervise military actions and deal with the U.S. administration and foreign governments on behalf of the entire Cuban exile population. Bosch would personally underwrite the referendum project with a fifty-thousand-dollar contribution.

The Bacardi boss first presented his plan in November 1963 during a packed press conference in a banquet room at the Everglades Hotel in downtown Miami. Standing behind a table, flanked by his twenty-member "referendum committee," the bald, bespectacled businessman could have been addressing a Rotary Club luncheon. Now sixty-five, his voice had grown even softer, though his gaze was still steady and penetrating, and his slightly imperious manner was as evident as ever. He spoke slowly and seriously, choosing his words carefully. "This new organism," he whispered into the microphone, "will demonstrate our unbreakable will and our dream of reestablishing the freedoms that were snuffed out by the Red tyranny." A reporter asked whether Bosch himself might serve as an exile representative. He smiled slightly and took out a cigarette. "I won't," he said, pausing to light the cigarette. "For one thing, I'm the one pushing the idea. For another, I'm getting too old to manage a hectic schedule."

Four months later, Bosch convened his assembly, consisting of sixty Cuban men and a single woman, all chosen by Bosch's referendum committee. After a nine-hour meeting at the new Bacardi headquarters on Biscayne Boulevard in downtown Miami, the assembly chose five men to be constituted as the Representación Cubana del Exilio (RECE), Cuban Representation in Exile, and act on behalf of the Cuban diaspora. The military chief would be thirty-one-year-old Erneido Oliva, a black Cuban and professional soldier who had been second in command during the Bay of Pigs invasion. The other nominated representatives included a former labor lawyer, a union leader, and an accountant. The fifth representative, selected only after another nominee dropped out, was twenty-four-year-old Jorge Mas Canosa, the handsome and energetic nephew of Pepín Bosch's assistant Polo Miranda. Mas was just a Miami milkman at the time, but after his experience in the Bay of Pigs invasion, he had received eight months of U.S. Army training at Fort Benning in Georgia, and he was anxious to take part in some exile military activities. A year earlier, Bosch had asked Mas to help with some of the arrangements for the B-26 bombing mission out of Costa Rica.

Bosch's "referendum committee" had collected the names and addresses of about seventy-five thousand Cuban exiles across the world, and all were sent ballots. After two months, about forty-two thousand had been returned. The results resembled those of Fidel Castro's elections: 40,905 ballots were marked in favor of the proposed exile representatives, with just 979 against. Critics of the process were quick to speak up. Some members of the defunct Consejo Revolucionario Cubano called it a "pseudo-referendum," because the exile voters were given no choice other than "to approve or reject the authority of Sr. Bosch." The right-wing exile newspaper *Patria*, identified with pro-Batista elements, ridiculed the referendum outcome and raised the sensitive issue of Bosch's past fund-raising work on behalf of Fidel Castro. "Pepín Bosch's referendum showed that with his money, or with that of the Bacardi firm, he could do just as he felt like doing and make a fool of the exiles," *Patria* commented. "Now we have one more exile organization of which Pepín Bosch will be the treasurer, just like he was the 26th of July treasurer." The RECE directors nevertheless moved swiftly to demonstrate their seriousness, holding press conferences in Miami and Washington, D.C., and emphasizing their willingness to work on behalf of all exiles, no matter their politics. The RECE leaders appealed to the Organization of American States (OAS) for military aid and said they would organize commando raids inside Cuba as soon as they were able to finance them.

With his bankrolling of RECE on top of his other activities, Pepín Bosch had become as closely identified with the Cuban counterrevolution as any single exile leader, and he had done so while simultaneously running his rum company. "What extra time there is, I help Cuba," he told *Miami Herald* reporter Don Bohning in August 1964. "I am one of the few Cubans who has a prosperous enterprise. It is my feeling that we have an obligation to our country. When a man's country is at war, everyone is obligated to do what he can. If I were a younger man and not a cripple, I would take a more active part." The leg injury he had suffered in his 1946 boating accident was causing Bosch ever more pain and slowing his gait considerably. Bohning was impressed by Bosch's humble manner, and in his account of the interview he noted that Bosch appeared to be "neither a millionaire nor a revolutionary but perhaps a retired gentleman likely to be found in Bayfront Park feeding the pigeons."

As a directorate that was to act on behalf of the entire Cuban exile community, RECE proved to be a bust. It did serve, however, as a launching pad for two of the most important and controversial figures to emerge from the Cuban exile world, Jorge Mas Canosa and Luis Posada Carriles. One went on to become the most powerful single player in the Cuban-American community, with contacts and clout that were the envy of every lobbyist in Washington. The other became notorious as a violent anti-Castro saboteur, regarded by the United States and other governments as a criminal terrorist and by Fidel Castro himself as a mortal enemy.

The RECE story was supposed to unfold differently. In August 1964, the RECE directors boldly announced they were organizing a "Cuban Liberation Force" that was to return to the island and fight to free Cuba from Fidel Castro's rule, as soon as the funding and logistical support could be arranged. Two of the five RECE directors—the military chief, Erneido Oliva, and the "foreign relations" chief, Ernesto Freyre (the former Havana labor lawyer)—left shortly thereafter on a tour of Latin American countries in search of military aid and a place to organize RECE combat operations. They headed first to Brazil, hoping that Pepín Bosch's contacts with the new military government there might prove useful, but they came away with little to show for their efforts beyond the Brazilian generals' sympathy and moral support. In Panama they asked President Marco Robles if volunteer RECE pilots could use local airstrips for training purposes. Robles said he would have to "think it over." In Nicaragua the Cuban exiles met with former president Luis Somoza but were unable to see his brother Anastasio, the strongman general best positioned to make things happen. In Costa Rica, according to a CIA report, Oliva and Freyre saw no one in a position of authority and "were refused any cooperation of the Costa Rican government." The two men returned to Miami without a single commitment.

Pepín Bosch, who had agreed to lead a RECE fund-raising drive within the Cuban exile community, fared no better. Discouraged by the poor response to his appeal, he began cutting back on his own financial support for RECE activities. Bosch continued to allow his aide Polo Miranda to serve as the RECE office manager while drawing a Bacardi company paycheck, but he was unwilling to bankroll the entire RECE organization to the extent he had during the period of its formation. Frustrated by the difficulties they were encountering, RECE directors Oliva and Freyre went to Washington to seek U.S. government support. For President Lyndon Johnson and his administration, the top U.S. foreign policy concern was the situation in Vietnam, not the Castro threat in

Cuba. Oliva and Freyre secured only a one-time contribution of twenty-one thousand dollars from the CIA, with a commitment from the Agency to secretly provide eight hundred dollars a month to keep the RECE office open.* The CIA funds fell far short, however, of what RECE would need to organize a new exile army or sustain guerrilla operations inside Cuba. In March 1965, the directors announced they could not carry out "the projected military effort" and offered to refund all exile contributions.

RECE did, however, play an important function as the foundation for the remarkable political career of its youngest director, Jorge Mas Canosa, the former student activist and Bay of Pigs volunteer who worked during the day as a milkman. Mas Canosa owed his RECE position largely to his uncle, Polo Miranda, who managed the organization for Pepín Bosch, but he quickly emerged as a fiery RECE spokesman on his own, showing up at public rallies to denounce Fidel Castro and appearing regularly as a commentator on Spanish-language radio stations. With his tinted horn-rimmed glasses, open-collared shirts, and full head of wavy black hair, the brash young Mas was a refreshing contrast to the older Cuban men in business suits and pencil-thin mustaches who dominated the south Florida exile elite at the time.

Between his U.S. Army training and Bay of Pigs experience, Mas had just enough military preparation to make him yearn for more action. His organization might not have been able to raise the funds for a full-scale invasion of Cuba, but Mas would settle for an occasional commando operation or act of sabotage. In May 1965, two months after RECE announced it was abandoning the "military effort," Mas arranged for an RECE operative to throw two homemade bombs into the Mexican-Russian Cultural Relations Institute, a pro-Soviet organization in Mexico City. According to a subsequent FBI report, Mas boasted that his RECE agent had managed to travel to Mexico and back to Miami without being bothered by U.S. authorities, even though his actions were "common knowledge" in the exile community. Anxious to plan more missions, Mas sought assistance from Luis Posada Carriles, a fellow Bay of Pigs veteran whom he had met when they were both at Fort Benning in Georgia. Posada had trained as a demolitions expert, and Mas wanted to use him for special sabotage missions. Unbeknownst to Mas, however, Posada had secretly signed on with the CIA and was keeping the Agency informed of all RECE projects. When he reported in June 1965 that Mas had given him five

---

*No one besides Freyre and Oliva was supposed to be aware of the CIA funding, which, according to a CIA memorandum, was processed "through a cover mechanism and therefore could not be traceable to the Agency."

thousand dollars to blow up a Cuban ship anchored in the port of Veracruz, Mexico, Posada's CIA handlers ordered him to "disengage" immediately.

According to one of Posada's CIA reports, Pepín Bosch in mid-1966 was channeling as much as five thousand dollars a month to RECE from various sources, including Bacardi. By then, however, Bosch had no interest in little sabotage missions. His new priority was public relations. He asked Mas to take charge of the monthly RECE newsletter, with the idea of making it an important news and opinion outlet for the exile community. Mas was a born propagandist, and the assignment suited him perfectly.

He needed to earn some money to support his growing family, however. Working through his RECE connections, Mas secured a position at a Puerto Rico–based telecommunications construction firm. In 1971 he borrowed fifty thousand dollars from a friendly Cuban exile banker and purchased the firm's Florida branch. Building again on his extensive contacts in the exile community, Mas began securing lucrative contracts, and his company was soon bringing in a million dollars a year.

Mas was meanwhile continuing to promote his uncompromising anti-Castro message through the pages of the RECE newsletter. Along with most other exile activists, he had finally concluded that Castro's well-defended regime was unlikely to be overthrown by military attacks from outside Cuba, and he turned his attention instead to political action. Forswearing violence, Mas became an ace lobbyist on behalf of the anti-Castro cause. His first target was U.S. Senator Richard Stone, a Florida Democrat whose candidacy Mas had vigorously backed. At Mas's personal urging, Stone persuaded more than a dozen other senators to join him in cautioning the Ford administration against any relaxation of the Cuba trade embargo.

It was the opening engagement of what Mas would later call "La Batalla de Washington." In 1981, at the urging of senior officials in the new Reagan administration, Mas founded the Cuban American National Foundation (CANF), largely building on the old RECE framework and sustained by the same base of exile support, Bacardi money included. By the time he reached fifty, the former milkman and exile firebrand who owed his career to Pepín Bosch and Bacardi was one of the most powerful and influential lobbyists on the U.S. political scene. He had turned the old "Platt mentality" of Cuban politicians on its head. Like them, he saw the route to change in Havana as going through Washington, but Jorge Mas Canosa never deferred to members of Congress or cabinet secretaries. Instead, he mobilized his fund-raising network and his political machine to convince Washington politicians that they should serve *his* interests. "We have used the Americans," he said in an interview shortly before his death in 1997, "but we have never left the initiative for Cuban issues in the Americans' hands. That's what happened with the Consejo Revolucionario and the Bay of Pigs."

Mas's old RECE cohort Luis Posada Carriles, meanwhile, headed in the opposite direction. While Mas presented himself as a responsible businessman and lobbyist, Posada—whom the CIA had once regarded as less of a "warrior" than Mas—vigorously and openly embraced armed struggle as the proper way to oppose the Castro regime. Unlike Mas, Posada had never been comfortable in public work; undercover activity and bomb making were his specialties. After leaving RECE, Posada moved to Venezuela, where he became a senior official in the state intelligence service, responsible for tracking down Cuban intelligence agents in the country. While he was in that position, the CIA reestablished contact with Posada, though the nature of his relationship with the Agency was a secret. He became associated with Orlando Bosch (no relation to Pepín), another Cuban exile leader who had once been close to RECE and who in later years also turned to increasingly violent methods. The two men were subsequently linked to two of the most serious terrorist acts of their time, the assassination of former Chilean diplomat Orlando Letelier and his U.S. research associate in downtown Washington in September 1976 and the mid-air bombing of a Cubana civilian airliner two weeks later, killing seventy-three people.

· · ·

Though he and the Bacardi corporation were fiercely criticized later for having sponsored a "dirty war" against Castro's Cuba, Pepín Bosch did not promote terrorist acts.* During the period when he helped to finance armed action against the Castro regime, Bosch backed only those operations that had a relatively low risk of causing human casualties, such as bombing oil refineries or sinking ships while they were anchored in port. Bosch insisted that he never approved an assassination attempt against Fidel Castro. Jorge Mas Canosa may have been involved in planning one such mission, but only marginally, and no RECE operation during the "military" phase of its history was any dirtier than the violent actions carried out by Fidel Castro's own July 26th Movement during the anti-Batista struggle. The 1960s were a time of "liberation" wars and "revolutionary" commando actions on both the left and the right.

---

*When the violently anti-Castro militant Orlando Bosch requested a two-hundred-thousand-dollar contribution from Bacardi in February 1975, Pepín Bosch sent a representative to inquire what he was planning with the money, and he had an associate report the request to the FBI.

Still, there was something sad about the counterrevolutionary activism of Pepín Bosch and his Bacardi and RECE associates. Born of a love for Cuba and a pride in their own role in its history, their patriotism was narrowed and made more spiteful as a consequence of exile. Pepín Bosch was determined to show the world there was more to Cuba than Fidel Castro's revolutionary makeover of the island and to fight to free Cuba from Fidel's grasp. This man of moderate politics and classic liberal views would no doubt have preferred to spend the rest of his active years promoting hydroelectric power, native industry, labor-management harmony, and generous welfare legislation,* but instead he found himself bankrolling bombing missions and paramilitary operations.

Like other Cuban exiles, Pepín Bosch developed a permanent enmity toward Fidel Castro and a deep hatred of Communism. Fidel was the man who destroyed the idea of Cuba that had inspired Bosch and who effectively denied Bosch any role in Cuba other than to be a cheerleader for Fidel's own revolutionary ideas. The Communist ideology Fidel implanted in Cuba was being promoted at the time from Southeast Asia to Africa, and Bosch later supported anti-Communist movements in those lands almost as fervently as he did the anti-Castro struggle in Cuba. His political activism became more ideological and less practical.

One of the few occasions when he offered his opinion on an issue unrelated to Cuba or Communism was in August 1984, in the midst of a presidential campaign, when Bosch weighed in on the debate over supply-side economics between President Ronald Reagan and his challenger, Walter Mondale. In a commentary for *Diario Las Américas* titled "Memories of an Ex-Finance Minister," Bosch warned that budget deficits resulting from insufficient tax revenue would in time erode savings and pensions and disproportionately hurt "workers, the poor, and middle class families." President Reagan at the time was a hero to Bosch and other Cuban exiles for his firm anti-Communist stance, but Bosch did not hesitate to criticize Reagan's tax cut policies for unduly favoring the upper-income class. "It seems to me," Bosch wrote, "that Mr. Reagan should impose on the rich the same sacrifices he is obliging the rest of the society to suffer. So far, this government has not caused me any sacrifice whatsoever. . . . To me, this doesn't seem right."

---

*Bosch always denied having had higher political ambitions in Cuba, but many of his closest associates suspected he would have jumped at a serious and realistic opportunity to be Cuba's president. In a 1984 interview on the U.S. government's Radio Martí, Bosch told the program host, a former Cuban politician named José Ignacio Rasco, that the presidential "shoe" would not have fit him, but he did not deny having a political calling. "You cannot be a merchant, an industrialist, or a banker and not be a politician," Bosch said.

Chapter 19

※♋❀

Socialist Rum

By the time Fidel Castro showed up at the construction site of the new Santiago power plant that steamy July afternoon, he had already visited a nearby dam-building project and eaten lunch with road crews at work on a highway linking Santiago with agricultural areas to the west. He spent hours at each location, cajoling the workers to be more diligent and dedicate themselves more earnestly to their revolutionary assignments. Unable or unwilling to offer a material reward, Castro relied on moral suasion to boost the workers' productivity. He and Che Guevara and their followers were trying to build socialism in Cuba, and the project could succeed only if workers focused on the needs of their nation and not just on their individual circumstances.

"Are you satisfied with your production?" Castro asked the Santiago power workers. "It seems to me it has been a little weak." About eight hundred workers were gathered under a burning sun for an impromptu meeting with the *comandante* himself. Castro was dressed in his rumpled fatigues, a beret on his head and a pistol on his belt, surrounded by an entourage of government officials and local Communist Party bureaucrats. He told the workers they were "honorable, fighting, and strong people," but the more he talked, the more obvious it became that Fidel was not happy with the progress on the new power plant. He jabbed the air with a long, thin finger as he spoke, sweat beading on his forehead.

"If the working class does not construct its own economy, who do you think is going to come and do it for them?" he asked. "The people want housing. Everybody is asking for a house. Do you think the houses are going to build themselves? Do you think the bourgeoisie are going to come back and build houses for you, if they didn't do it before? All they left behind for you were tenements and slums!" Many of his meetings with Cuban workers went like this, with Fidel alternately teasing and scolding. He told the power plant workers that they weren't doing as well as the highway crews he had met with earlier. "They show a real spirit for work," he said. "They face their tasks as soldiers would when they have to seize a trench."

Castro rarely made a speech without some reference to war or combat. It was July 1963, just nine months after the Kennedy-Khrushchev missile confrontation. Cubans had not realized at the time how close the world was to nuclear war, but they had been told that a massive U.S. attack on the island was imminent, and Castro warned them repeatedly afterward that Cuban counterrevolutionaries in Miami were plotting another invasion. The Cuban revolution, he emphasized, was still in a life-or-death struggle. "We must take this fight to every part of the country," Castro told the workers, his voice rising. "That is the task ahead for all of us: work. If a man is milking three cows, he must be told to milk twenty. Farm work is hard. Cutting sugarcane is hard. This work you're doing here is hard. But it's necessary to spend all these hours under the sun." With the Santiago carnival days coming later that month, the workers' discipline would soon be tested. "Then we will really see how absenteeism goes," Fidel said, "because you Santiago people are known for carousing."

His mention of the carnival apparently reminded him of the Santiago rum company that for such a long time had been associated with the July celebrations. "Next, I'm going to the Bacardi factory," he told the power plant workers, "to check out the quality of the production there." Though the Bacardis themselves had been gone from Cuba for nearly three years, the facility on Matadero Street still bore their name, and the rum produced there still carried a Bacardi label.

The lives of Cuban workers, however, had changed under socialism. The high labor standards established by Cuban unions in prior years were voided, with workers regularly asked to stay on the job for ten hours or longer without overtime pay. Food was rationed. Each person was limited, among other staples, to a quarter pound of butter, a pound and a half of beans, and just five eggs per month. Many consumer goods, especially those coming from outside Cuba, could no longer be found, and store shelves were often empty. Standing in line for an hour or more— to pick up food rations, buy shoes, or wait for a bus—was a daily routine. Since February 1962, the economic problems had been aggravated by the U.S. trade embargo, which denied the country U.S.-built supplies and replacement parts. Castro often highlighted the costly effects of the embargo in his meetings with workers, while emphasizing the benefits the revolution had brought. He reminded the Santiago power workers, for example, that their health care was now assured, that their wives now had maternity benefits, and that new hospitals and schools were being built around the country.

The old Bacardi company, like other formerly private enterprises, was now a component of a large, state-run industrial conglomerate. Two years earlier, Castro had declared that Cuba was to follow the Marxist-Leninist model of development. Che Guevara took over the Ministry of Industry in February 1961 and promptly announced that the Cuban economy would be guided by a highly centralized planning process. The Cuban engineers, technicians, and professional managers and administrators who had gone into exile were replaced by advisers from the Soviet bloc countries or by Communist Party functionaries. The workers still belonged to unions, but the principle of representation had been reversed: The role of the union leadership was to pass down to the workers the quotas and other production goals dictated by government officials, rather than to represent the workers before the higher authorities, as unions normally would.

The early results from the country's experience with socialist economic management were not encouraging. In spite of Soviet and other Communist bloc aid worth more than five hundred million dollars in 1962 and 1963 (on a per-capita basis, about twenty times the value of U.S. aid to Latin American countries), Cuba's economic output was declining, especially in those industries affected by a shortage of technical and management expertise. Che Guevara himself was upset by widespread signs of incompetence and mismanagement. Why was it, he asked his associates, that so many shoes produced after the revolution in Cuban factories lost their heels with just one day's wear? And why did the Coca-Cola coming out of the newly nationalized factory in Havana taste so vile?

* * *

The meeting with the Santiago power workers went on longer than Fidel's schedulers expected, leaving no time that day for a visit to the old Bacardi factory downtown. The *comandante* was determined to talk to some rum workers, however, and he and his entourage arrived at the factory gate early the next morning, a Saturday. The factory was closed, so no one was on hand to receive Fidel except for the two laborers whose turn it was to sit by the front gate as security guards. They paid no heed when two unmarked sedans pulled up. When one of the car doors opened and Fidel Castro himself climbed out, the guards nearly fell out of their chairs.

"*Compañeros*," Castro said, pointing to the closed factory gate, "how do I get in?"

One of the guards, a skinny black man in a tattered white shirt and baseball cap, jumped to his feet and stammered, "Well, *comandante*, I'm afraid I have to say there's no way, because I don't have a key."

"How about I kick the damn door down?" Castro suggested with a wink at the guard, a man named Gilberto Cala.

"That's fine, *comandante*," Cala said, suitably deferential. "Or we can go in down there where they're building a bar." He pointed down the street to an entrance to the rum-bottling plant, where carpenters were at work on a little refreshment area. "I think it's open down there." By the time they reached the door, a crowd had begun to gather. Cala, who had worked in the maintenance department at the rum plant since 1946, took Fidel in and showed him the bottling operation. His coworker had run off to find one of the factory supervisors, and Cala found himself all alone with the *comandante*, single-handedly representing the enterprise. "This is where we bottle the *añejo*," he said, with all the pride and authority of a factory executive.

"How about we try some?" Fidel said. Cala grabbed an empty bottle, filled it with the golden *añejo* rum from one of the tanks that fed the bottling line, and passed it to the *comandante*. Fidel handed the bottle to his personal physician, René Vallejo, who accompanied him everywhere. After several assassination plots, Castro did not drink or taste anything without Vallejo's clearance. Vallejo took a drink and passed the bottle on to the others in his group, and when nobody toppled over dead, Fidel himself took a sip. Within minutes, the bottle was empty.

Word had gone out that Fidel was at the factory, and a crowd of workers soon showed up to greet him. But Castro was enjoying the company of Gilberto Cala and directed all his questions to the wiry maintenance man. "You know, *compañero*," Fidel said, looking at Cala, "we're going to have to come up with a new name for this rum. They say we can't call it 'Ron Bacardi' anymore. What do you think we should call it?"

Cala, basking in Fidel's attention, was momentarily taken aback by the question, but then his eyes brightened. "How about we call it 'Ron Patria o Muerte'?" he suggested, eager to show he was familiar with the *comandante*'s favorite slogan. Only in Cuba would a worker suggest producing something called Fatherland or Death Rum.

"I don't think so," Castro said, chuckling. Looking around the facility, Castro asked which rum the enterprise was bottling in preparation for the carnival days, which were just over a week away. Cala explained that the carnival rum, a cheaper white variety, was in another warehouse. "Let's go there," Castro said. "And where's this guy Matamoros? I want to see him."

Alfonso Matamoros, the veteran rum blender who had worked for years alongside Víctor Schueg and Daniel Bacardi, was recognized as one of the heroes of the revolutionary Cuban rum industry. Like his colleague Mariano Lavigne, he had passed up the opportunity to follow the Bacardi family into exile, and his rum-making expertise was key to the survival of the enterprise after nationalization. Fidel had heard that Matamoros had proved his loyalty to the revolution by showing up at the Bacardi factory on the night of the Bay of Pigs invasion in April 1961, armed with a .44-caliber revolver and ready to defend the facility against any returning exiles who might attempt to reclaim it. The story might or might not have been true, but Fidel wanted to meet the rum hero in any case.

Alfonso Matamoros could not be located that Saturday morning, however, and Castro had to settle for being guided around the facility by Reynaldo Hermida, one of the foremen at the aging warehouse. Gilberto Cala tagged along, not wanting to miss out on the experience of a lifetime. When another guard stopped Cala at the entrance to the warehouse to ask where he was going, Cala responded, "I'm the one who received Fidel," and the guard let him pass.

At the warehouse, Castro interrogated Cala and Hermida and other rum workers, asking how many cases they were setting aside for the carnival celebrations, whether production techniques had changed since the factory was nationalized, and what steps they were taking to maintain rum quality. Hermida said the company veterans like Matamoros and Lavigne knew the Bacardi rum production secrets and were keeping the quality as high as ever. He showed Fidel some of the fifty thousand barrels the enterprise had inherited when the government nationalized the Bacardis' rum operation in Santiago. Fidel, stroking his beard, listened intently. While he could talk for hours about construction or agriculture or even medicine, he knew next to nothing about rum making.

"What's important," he said finally, "is that you do whatever you can to maintain and even improve the production here. Our rums are one of the key things we can export, and this industry is vital to our nation." After that, Castro left. He told the rum workers he wanted to return and talk some more when he was back in Santiago on another occasion, but after his July 1963 visit, Castro did not visit the old Bacardi factory again.

Gilberto Cala followed him out of the warehouse, still not believing he had actually been able to meet the *comandante* and guide him around the factory. Shaking his head incredulously, he turned to Gabriel Molina, a reporter from the *Noticias de Hoy* newspaper who was accompanying Castro, and whispered, "¡Pero mira como vine a conocer yo al hombrín, compay!" (See, brother, how I got to meet the Man!) Molina quoted Cala in his story about the factory visit, describing the Bacardi worker as "a prototypical *santiaguero*" and calling his comment on meeting Fidel "somewhat disrespectful, but so spontaneous as to be excusable."

As Fidel left the factory, he was mobbed by well-wishers in the working-class Santiago neighborhood. Castro and his entourage could barely reach their cars, and it took a half hour for them to inch their way through the crowd and proceed down the street. Now in his fifth year in power, the charismatic Fidel Castro clearly remained a popular leader—at least in Santiago, the cradle of Cuban revolutions. The affection many Cubans felt for him, however, did not translate into ideological support for Marxism-Leninism, nor did it mean that Cuban workers would be inspired to toil and produce on behalf of the revolution, no matter how hard Fidel exhorted them to do so.

• • •

In 1964 the Cuban government finally gave up trying to export any rum under a "Bacardi" label, having been blocked from using the brand in one country after another. Their Marxist focus on the rum workers and their physical facilities as constituting the essence of the Bacardi enterprise had blinded the revolutionary leaders to the importance of the intangible trademark. Some of the rum bottled for the domestic market would still be sold as "Bacardi," at least for a while, but the premium product made in the old Bacardi factory in Santiago would now be known as Caney rum, using the Taino Indian name for a chief's lodge. The label change did little to boost overseas rum sales, however. The nationalized company had lost virtually all the overseas orders that the Bacardi family filled from its Santiago facility, and until those orders could be replaced with sales to the Soviet bloc countries or to Western buyers interested in the new Caney product, the nationalized company's export earnings would be negligible.

The Santiago rum factory was now part of the Empresa Consolidada de Licores y Vinos (ECONLIVI), Consolidated Enterprise of Liquors and Wines, a huge government conglomerate in which were included all the previously private liquor and wine companies across the entire island. ECONLIVI was in turn part of the massive Ministry of Industry, presided over by Che Guevara himself, employing more than 150,000 people and comprising nearly three hundred formerly independent companies. The organization of Cuba's industries under Guevara's version of socialism was highly centralized and hierarchical, with individual enterprise directors having little or no freedom to make their own commercial or strategic decisions. The problems of rigidly top-down management were further aggravated by a high turnover of the administrative staff. The nationalized Bacardi company in Santiago went through four directors in its first three years under state ownership, and none of the four had a business management background, not to mention liquor industry experience.

The company also had to get by without its top professional and engineering staff, almost all of whom had left after nationalization. The distillery laboratory was virtually shut down, and the science-based quality control work that had been overseen by top Bacardi engineers such as Juan Grau and Manuel Jorge Cutillas ground to a halt. Finally, the U.S.-imposed trade embargo and the revolutionary government's unwillingness to spend precious hard-currency reserves on imported items meant that the rum and beer operations in Santiago soon faced shortages of such items as labels and bottle caps. The enterprise began using corks to seal the bottles, but before long a glass shortage meant bottles themselves were hard to come by. A shortage of chemicals and spare parts adversely affected water treatment procedures in the rum distillery, raising the danger of contamination. The rum enterprise that had operated so efficiently under Bacardi family ownership lurched from one crisis to another in the first years after nationalization.

Whether the quality of the rum produced in the old facility was immediately affected, however, was a matter of some dispute. In Miami, Pepín Bosch and other members of the Bacardi family claimed that any rum coming from their factory after the Communists took it over was an inferior product. In mid-1964, the Canadian ambassador in Havana wrote to Bosch to request six cases of family-produced Bacardi rum, and to Bosch the reason was obvious. "Fidel makes bad rum," he explained to a *Miami Herald* reporter. For Bosch, any assessment of the quality of Cuban rum after 1960 was inseparable from the broader question of Castro's rule.

In Santiago, however, veteran Bacardi workers—including some who had been loyal to the family for years—were offended by such sweeping criticism. Mariano Lavigne, who had gone to work for the Bacardis in 1918, was especially indignant. For at least three years after nationalization, he claimed, virtually all the rum bottled in Santiago was drawn from the reserves the government had confiscated from the family company in October 1960, meaning it was essentially the same product the Bacardis had sold. "If [Cuban] Bacardi is bad now, it always was," Lavigne told a Cuban reporter in December 1963. He said the practice of drawing down the reserves would continue through the end of 1964, while the company was being reorganized.

The quality of socialist Coca-Cola had deteriorated rapidly, but rum production was different. The industry had deep social and cultural roots in Cuba, and many veteran rum workers on the island saw themselves as custodians of a national heritage that superseded ideology or political loyalties. Regardless of whether the workers saw themselves as committed *fidelistas*, many were motivated (at least in the beginning) by the pride they took in manufacturing a genuinely Cuban product, a sentiment not shared by Cuban workers in other industries, with the notable exception of cigar making. Finally, there was an aspect of artisanship in rum manufacturing that was learned through experience, not in engineering schools, and among the Bacardi workers who stayed on the job after the factory was expropriated, there was enough practical knowledge to ensure some continuity in traditional Bacardi rum-making procedures.

The Don Pancho aging warehouse, a windowless building where barrels of rum were stacked from floor to ceiling, looked and smelled the same as it had in the days when Emilio and Facundo Bacardi Moreau ran the company. The warehouse foreman, Francisco Ayala, installed by Pepín Bosch in 1959, was only the second man to hold the position since "Don Pancho" himself had died in 1940. Humberto Corona, the factory production chief, had held the same position under the Bacardis, and the cantankerous Alfonso Matamoros was still blending rums. Matamoros was as strict about the rum factory during the socialist era as he had been when it was family owned, and he resented interference from Communist bureaucrats just as he had resented Bacardi family members who showed up at the factory thinking that access to it was their birthright.

It was Mariano Lavigne, however, who played the most essential role in keeping the former Bacardi enterprise operating. No one knew it better. Lavigne had gone to work in the Santiago factory at the age of thirteen in order to help support his mother after his father died. In the beginning, he washed bottles, glued labels, swept floors, and helped the carpenters build barrels and casks. Everyone at the factory knew him as Marianito, a diminutive nickname that would stay with him his whole life. Knowing his mother depended on the meager wages he brought home, the lad put in long hours and soon impressed the company management with his diligence and his seriousness. Gradually he was given more responsibilities, and as a quick learner he began picking up the basics of rum making and increasingly gained the confidence of Bacardi family members. "They pampered me," Lavigne said later of the Bacardis. "I was almost like an adopted son." Facundo Bacardi Moreau, the son of the company's founder and its first master rum blender, was in his final years in the family business when Lavigne went to work for the Bacardis, and the young man had the opportunity to watch the master at work and absorb some of his knowledge. Though he had no formal technical training, Lavigne learned the organoleptic method of assessing rum quality, judging it by its taste, its odor, and even the way it felt on one's hands.

Lavigne spent many years working at the Bacardi facilities in Mexico, and his familiarity with Bacardi rum-making techniques was such that a Mexican competitor once tried to lure him away, saying that with Lavigne's experience and expertise they could put Bacardi out of business in Mexico. Lavigne claimed later that he rejected the offer out of hand, believing that to go to work for Bacardi's Mexican rival would be "an act of treason" to Cuba and to the family that had brought him along since his childhood. "Somebody told me, 'you're an idiot,'" Lavigne said, "to which I responded, 'I may be an idiot, but I'll never be a traitor.'"

Lavigne's ties to the family were broken, however, when the Bacardis went into exile following the confiscation of their properties in Cuba. By agreeing to serve the nationalized enterprise, Lavigne distinguished between his loyalty to the Bacardis and his loyalty to Cuba, and the choice he made put him and the Bacardi family on opposite sides of an unbridgeable divide. He would not forget his long association with the family, however, and in the privacy of his Santiago home, Lavigne filled a china closet with Bacardi mementos: drink glasses etched with the Bacardi logo, Bacardi swizzle sticks, photographs of himself with Daniel Bacardi, Pepín Bosch, and other family members, plus every Christmas card and letter he and his wife received from old Bacardi friends.

He was never much of a revolutionary, and Lavigne's one encounter with Che Guevara almost turned into a disaster. As minister of industry, Guevara visited the nationalized Bacardi factory in 1964, one of many such stops he made around Cuba. While Lavigne was passionate about his rum, Guevara cared only about the fate of the Cuban revolution. From the outset, he made clear that what interested him about the former Bacardi operation in Santiago was how it would contribute to the strengthening of the revolutionary Cuban state, not whether the legendary quality or unique character of Cuban rum could be maintained.

"So where do you make this rat poison?" Che asked Lavigne in their first meeting. Che came dressed in his olive green fatigues and beret, his black hair curling over his ears, a cigar in his shirt pocket. He was conducting business in his typically brusque, informal fashion, as if he were still a guerrilla leader in the midst of a revolution. Lavigne, like many Cuban men of his generation, prided himself on his appearance and came to work each day dressed neatly in a sports shirt or a guayabera. He was visibly annoyed by Guevara's impertinence.

"We don't make rat poison here," Lavigne answered curtly. "We make the best rum in Cuba." He then took Guevara on a tour of the distillery, describing how ethanol alcohol was made through the process of fermentation, boiling, and evaporation, and how the distillates were then processed, aged, and blended to produce rum. Lavigne showed Guevara the factory and the aging warehouse and explained that the rum being bottled that day had actually been produced years earlier. Guevara followed Lavigne's explanations carefully, but he had come with an idea of his own. Some of the "extra dry" rum produced in the factory was being sold in pharmacies for use by diabetics. Guevara proposed that the production for this purpose could be expanded if the rum were not left so long to age, because the water loss from evaporation would be less. Lavigne dismissed the suggestion out of hand, saying rum produced under his supervision would not be consumed before it was properly aged.

In his later retelling of the visit, Lavigne said Che in the end was impressed by his commitment to quality in the rum production process. "He put his arm around my shoulders and slapped me on the back," Lavigne said, "and he went away convinced that this was not some barnyard operation to make rat poison but an enterprise that earned our rum gold medals at international fairs." Lavigne's daughter Felicita, in an interview many years after his death, said her father's troubles with Che Guevara were not so easily resolved, however. She said Guevara pressured Lavigne to set down in writing the Bacardi rum formula. Lavigne resisted, she said, fearing Guevara would commercialize it, but in the end agreed to write a letter outlining what he understood to be the formula. Guevara's office, however, somehow lost the letter and asked him to write the formula down again. This time, according to his daughter, Lavigne refused. Whatever happened between him and Che Guevara, Lavigne apparently did nothing to get himself in serious trouble with the revolutionary authorities. Under his supervision, Caney rum in 1966 earned a gold medal at the Leipzig Trade Fair in East Germany (competing mostly against products from socialist countries), and a year later Lavigne was sent to Montreal, Canada, to promote Caney rum in Cuba's pavilion at the Expo 67 world fair.

In part because of the discipline shown by veteran rum workers like Mariano Lavigne and the skills they acquired during the years when Bacardi rum was the pride of Cuba, the Caney rum factory in Santiago was one of the more successful state-owned enterprises in the country during the early years of the revolution. It made a product for which there was significant demand, and it brought the state much-needed revenue. The enterprise still had major problems and deficiencies, but it proved to be a partial exception to the rule in revolutionary Cuba, where socialist management in case after case brought disastrous results.

Fidel Castro's determination to implement Communism was an experiment doomed to failure. Cuba was an underdeveloped country with an undiversified economy built almost entirely around sugar production and a professional and technical class depleted by emigration, conditions that made the adoption of socialism even more difficult than it otherwise would have been. Moreover, the Cuban leadership opted for an extreme version, disregarding lessons Soviet bloc countries had learned through their own experience.

For ideological reasons, Castro opposed all private enterprise, being determined to put economic activity entirely in the hands of the state. After the nationalization of the largest firms in Cuba, medium-sized companies were expropriated, and in 1968 even family-owned shops and microbusinesses were taken over. The authorities suppressed the operation of free-market forces in favor of centralized economic planning, with the smallest business decisions left to bureaucrats. Most importantly, Castro refused to link wages to proven work skills or performance, thinking that Cubans could be motivated by their solidarity with the revolution rather than by a desire for their own economic betterment. He insisted on maintaining control over the system, involving himself regularly in minor management and investment decisions, which was not exactly helpful to the cause of speed and efficiency. His arbitrary exercise of authority and his rejection of contrary opinions meant there were none of the checks and balances that can restrain bad decision making in democratic systems.

The flaws in Castro's thinking soon became apparent. As it turned out, Cuban workers were not inclined to work harder for the simple sake of the revolution, despite the propaganda urging them to do so. The government generously raised workers' wages at the start of the revolution, but with the reduction in imports and no increased production, there were fewer goods for Cubans to buy. Money lost its purchasing value, and the government was forced to introduce rationing. Many workers showed up at their jobs only long enough to collect their ration coupons. After that, their labor brought no material reward, and they saw no reason to continue working. Absenteeism soared.

Rather than recognizing that moral incentives were not working as they had intended, Fidel Castro and Che Guevara responded by making loafing a crime. A labor regulation issued at Guevara's direction in 1964 set severe sanctions for workers who failed to produce in line with the norms established for their positions or did not put in the minimum required hours on the job. Other laws gave the state the power to transfer workers from one place to another, to set the wages they were to receive, and to dictate what jobs they should perform. All workers were required to carry an identity card, and beginning in 1969 their names were registered in a "labor history file" that included their employment history and work evaluations, as well as detailed personal information.

Many Cubans who had initially been enthusiastic supporters of the revolution turned increasingly cynical as its economic failures became more obvious and promises proved hollow. In 1961 Che Guevara announced a four-year economic plan premised on wildly optimistic annual growth rates of 15 percent, saying the plan would make Cuba self-sufficient in food and agricultural raw material. A year later, Fidel Castro promised that "what is scarce today will abound tomorrow." When such goals proved unrealistic, Cuban leaders simply made new promises. In 1964 Castro told the Cuban people that within ten years "our production of milk will exceed that of Holland, and our production of cheese will exceed that of France." Instead, Cuba's economy stagnated. By 1970, with the labor force fully employed, the country was still producing less than it had in 1958, when 31 percent of Cuban workers were jobless.

The problems and inefficiencies that plagued Cuba were characteristic of centrally directed socialist systems. With the economy guided by government "planners," such basic decisions as what products should be made and at what prices they should be sold were made by government bureaucrats sitting in an office somewhere rather than determined by supply and demand pressures in the marketplace. For such a process to be even modestly effective, the government's economic planners needed timely and accurate information from enterprise managers, suppliers, and customers, but such information was slow in coming and often erroneous. Production supervisors had to estimate their supply and raw material needs weeks or months in advance and send in their requests to the government ministry of which they were a part. When they misjudged their needs, they ended up with too many hammers and not enough nails, or they had to barter with other enterprise directors for what they needed. Lacking bank credits and the freedom to do their own purchasing, enterprise managers sometimes had to halt production because of the shortage of a critical item.

The situation with prices was even more chaotic. At Castro's personal direction, government planners were supposed to set the price of a commodity or service in line with its "social function," i.e., its perceived value to society, rather than the cost of its production. The cost method, Castro said, "reeks too much of capitalism." With prices set independently of market factors, there was no way to encourage the increased production of goods in short supply or to decrease production of goods for which there was an excess. Prices often remained unchanged all year long, when they normally would have fluctuated according to seasonal factors. Similarly, uniform pricing meant there was no reason to pay attention to quality. If hastily made cigars fetched the same price as those that were carefully made, why would a cigar enterprise put any effort into making them better? An enterprise's profitability, in fact, became irrelevant, because all expenses were covered out of the central state budget, and all revenues were forwarded to the state treasury. Efficiently run enterprises could not be distinguished from inefficient ones, and no one—from the top administrators to the workers on the plant floor—had any real interest in seeing that an enterprise actually made money. The important objective was to turn out as many units—pairs of shoes, bags of cement, or cases of rum—as the national economic plan established, and even that goal was often missed.

The centralization of economic decision making in Castro's Cuba meant that workers, supervisors, and even enterprise managers learned to shift responsibility ever upward, so that even mundane decisions were often left to higher officials. Cubans were so worried about getting into trouble that they were reluctant to take the initiative, even when decisiveness was needed, and a culture of passivity developed within Cuban firms.

To anyone familiar with the efforts to establish state socialism in Eastern Europe or the Soviet Union, none of the problems that emerged in Cuba came as much of a surprise. Sympathetic foreign visitors urged the Cuban leadership to learn from mistakes made in the Soviet bloc. K. S. Karol, a Polish-born political scientist who had lived for many years in the Soviet Union, visited Cuba four times in the 1960s "in a spirit of solidarity" and met several times with Che Guevara and Fidel Castro. "I have seen the havoc caused by false ideas of how to build socialism," Karol later wrote. He urged Guevara to develop a way to identify and reward the best-performing state enterprises. But Karol, like other friendly critics, was generally rebuffed. Guevara, he said, "smelled a revisionist rat" in the proposed reforms.

René Dumont, a left-wing French agronomist who was invited to Cuba several times to consult on development issues, was astonished at how fiercely the Cubans resisted giving more autonomy to the state-run enterprises. "The failure of the non-autonomous production unit is no longer even a matter of discussion in the Soviet Union," he pointed out. Dumont condemned the U.S. trade embargo on Cuba as "morally indefensible," but he thought the Cuban authorities were too quick to cite the embargo "to justify the privations imposed on the population." The Havana port, he pointed out, was consistently full of ships. The Cuban officials with whom he met, Dumont said, were eager to blame their country's economic problems on its condition of underdevelopment. "This makes it possible," he noted, "to cover up incompetence, inertia, paralysis of individual initiative, conformism, gigantism, waste, and disorganization."

• • •

After his six-month stint promoting Caney rum at the Montreal Expo in 1967, Mariano Lavigne was sent on a similar mission to the Soviet Union and Eastern Europe. His job was to sell Russians and Eastern Europeans on the virtues of tropical Cuban rum cocktails. It was a challenge. Cuba had done little trade with the Soviet bloc prior to Castro coming to power, and though the Slavs were heavy drinkers, they generally preferred their vodka, slivovitz brandy, and beer. If rum was drunk at all, Lavigne discovered, it was mostly in the wintertime, in small quantities, mixed with tea or with hot water and sugar as a rum toddy. He and his delegation went first to Moscow, then to Leipzig for the annual trade fair, and on to Berlin, Budapest, and Prague. Lavigne played the role of a flamboyant Latin bartender, bringing Cuban color and energy to the dreary nightclubs and run-down bars of the rapidly aging Soviet bloc.

While in Czechoslovakia, Lavigne invented a new rum cocktail he called the High Tatras, after the mountain range along the border with Poland. He had gone sightseeing there, admiring the snow-covered pine trees he saw high on the mountain slopes. Back in Prague, he devised a drink with equal parts rum and slivovitz, garnished with an orange slice and a piece of pineapple; it was a concoction meant to represent the cocktails of both countries. But he was missing a slightly bitter taste to contrast with the sweetness of the fruit. Inspired by his trip to the High Tatras, Lavigne fetched a tiny pine sprig, washed it, and sprinkled it with powdered sugar. Perched on the edge of the drink, the sprig evoked the snowy Polish woods. Lavigne's High Tatras cocktail proved an instant hit in the bars where he served it, though to Lavigne's horror, the Czechoslovaks actually ate the little sugary pine sprigs. "I thought they were going to kill me," he said later.

From Czechoslovakia, Lavigne moved on to Bulgaria, where he spent four months as the guest host of a massive, Soviet-style lounge at the Golden Sands resort on the Black Sea. During the time he was there, the lounge was renamed the Caney Bar and remodeled to promote the Cuban rum of that name. The ceiling was covered with Vietnamese grasses to resemble a Cuban thatched roof, and the lounge was decorated with various trinkets and articles to suggest the African and indigenous features of faraway Cuba. Colored lights were hung from fake calabash trees. "The clients all wanted to buy the stuff and take it home with them," Lavigne said after returning to Cuba. "I think they thought it was genuine. We put up some masks and wooden swords one day, and the next day they were all gone."

Lavigne traveled through Eastern Europe in much the same way that Bacardi rum salesman Juan Prado had moved through Western Europe a few years earlier. Both men found themselves alone in distant lands, promoting a product to which they were deeply attached, but under somewhat disturbing circumstances. Prado was keenly aware of his separation not only from his family but from his native Cuba, a country he could not be sure he would ever see again. Lavigne knew he would return to Cuba, but his trip through the Soviet bloc brought home the reality that his country had now become part of a new and alien world, far removed from the easygoing life Cubans had known before Fidel.

◆ ◆ ◆

In 1969 Fidel Castro committed the whole country to a massive—many would say foolish—effort to achieve a ten-million-ton sugar harvest in 1970. The record sugar harvest up to that point had been 7.3 million tons in 1952. A ten-million-ton harvest would bring Cuba an abundance of income at a time when it was financially strained, and Castro presented the target as if it were a sports record to be achieved, saying it involved "the engagement of the nation's honor." He made it known that the whole population should contribute, and civil servants, teachers, students, and factory workers all went to "volunteer" in the cane fields. The harvest nonetheless fell about 1.5 million tons short of the target, despite the fact that about half of the 1969 sugarcane crop was left uncut so it could be counted toward the 1970 total. So many resources were redirected from the rest of the economy to the sugar sector that the country's labor minister, Jorge Risquet, said the total cost of harvesting the sugar crop may have been three times what the crop was actually worth on the world market.

At his Moncada anniversary commemoration on July 26, 1970, Fidel Castro took responsibility for the failure to achieve the ten-million-ton target, and for the first time he acknowledged that he and other Cuban leaders had made errors in their management of the Cuban economy. "Learning to build the economy is much more difficult for revolutionaries than we imagined [it would be]," he said, "and the problems are much more complex." Not only had sugar production fallen short of the goal; so had the production of milk, fertilizer, cement, paper, tires, batteries, shoes, textiles, soap, and even bread. Castro said he and other Cuban leaders had been too idealistic in their thinking about how to develop socialism and would now have to be more pragmatic.

Still, his move toward economic reform was slow, and when it came, it was often haphazard. Some managers found they were suddenly being held accountable for the profitability of their enterprises, even though they did not yet have the authority to set realistic prices for their products, to allocate workers to those areas where they were most needed, or to organize industrial operations in an efficient manner. Part of the problem was Castro himself. His commitment to economic reform was uncertain, and he did not establish an atmosphere in which alternative approaches could be freely explored. The French agronomist René Dumont identified the problem: "The man who opposes Castro's ideas is quickly rejected, and as a result when Castro sets forth a mistaken proposition nobody dares oppose him if he wants to hold on to his job."

. . .

The former Bacardi factory in Santiago had a special assignment as part of the 1970 ten-million-ton campaign: to supply 40 percent of the rum that was to be distributed across the country at the celebrations due to be held at the conclusion of the sugar harvest. Interviewed about the assignment in April 1970, Mariano Lavigne told a reporter for the newspaper *Juventud Rebelde* that the enterprise would do its part. "We have some difficulties with the bottling right now," he said, "but if necessary we will just roll the barrels out into the street and let the people get their drinks straight from the tap."

What was perhaps most noteworthy about the rum quota assigned to the Santiago factory, however, was that it was only 40 percent of the total that was to be set aside across the nation. In the decade since the Bacardi enterprise had been taken over by the state, the authorities had gradually deemphasized the Santiago operation relative to other rum-producing facilities in Cuba. The bruising fight with the Bacardi corporation and the loss of the trademark had apparently chastened Castro and his team. In the following years, the state authorities directed only minimal investment toward the former Bacardi properties, choosing instead to concentrate on the Bacardis' former rival, José Arechabala, S.A., which had produced Havana Club rum in Cárdenas, just east of Havana. Unlike the Bacardis, the Arechabalas had not expanded their firm outside Cuba, and when they left the island after the confiscation of their family properties, they could not keep their rum business going. Sensing perhaps that the Arechabalas were less likely to challenge them, the Cuban authorities chose to develop their new rum industry largely on the Arechabala infrastructure in

Cárdenas rather than at the old Bacardi site in Santiago. By 1970, the Cuban government was building a new distillery near the old Arechabala facility. Even more importantly, the Cuban economic authorities chose to use "Havana Club" as their export brand for state-owned rum factories across the island. By 1973, even the quality rum produced at the Bacardis' old factory in Santiago was being sold overseas under a "Havana Club" label, though the rum produced there for domestic consumption was still sold as "Caney" rum. When "Havana Club" rum from revolutionary Cuba turned up for sale in Canada, Mexico, and some Western European countries, the Arechabala heirs did not immediately object, and the Cuban authorities moved cautiously ahead.

The rum business was proving to be one of the brighter spots in an otherwise underperforming Cuban economy. In 1972 *New York Times* correspondent Herbert Matthews returned to Cuba and visited the old Bacardi factory in Santiago, a place he knew from his earlier friendship with Pepín Bosch. Matthews sampled the product and wrote that in his opinion the managers had learned from the problems they had encountered shortly after the enterprise was expropriated by the Cuban state. "As a rum drinker," Matthews concluded, "I would say the quality is as good as it was." His judgment no doubt irritated Pepín Bosch, but their friendship had deteriorated years earlier anyway.

What Matthews did not discover on that quick visit to the old Bacardi factory, however, was how often the veteran workers there had tangled with state authorities over their rum production goals. The efforts by Mariano Lavigne and others to promote Cuban rum exports to the socialist bloc were apparently successful, because within a few years the demand in those countries for the product was high. State authorities repeatedly pressured the management of the rum enterprise to boost production. At the old Bacardi factory, however, they faced stiff resistance from Lavigne himself and from Humberto Corona, the production chief. Both men courageously stood up to government officials who wanted them to cut the rum-aging process short and dilute the aged rum to make it stretch further, just as Che Guevara had urged years earlier. Corona, who had learned his craft under the Bacardis, argued that changing either the aging process or the rum-blending formulas would damage the quality. When Cuban journalist Leonardo Padura interviewed former Bacardi workers in Santiago in 1988, they told him that Corona's "unending zeal" in the late 1960s and the 1970s blocked what would have been "the definitive ruin" of Santiago's rum-making heritage:

> With all his might, Corona opposed the triumphalist plan to double rum production. Although laudable on the surface, that idea would have brought the

premature depletion of the old rums. Humberto Corona refused to allow even the production of one liter of rum beyond what the formula established, and he thereby saved the future of the rum industry in Santiago.

One by one, however, the old-timers from the Bacardi era retired or passed from the scene. Mariano Lavigne died in 1977, having worked nearly sixty years in the rum business. He remained active until the end and was buried as a Cuban hero, with an elaborate funeral procession that began at the door of the old Bacardi factory, where hundreds of rum workers paid him homage, and ended at the Santa Ifigenia cemetery under a canopy of branches and flowers. His old Bacardi colleague Alfonso Matamoros had long since retired, having chafed at the increasing regimentation of the rum-making operation. Gone were the days when he was trusted with a key to the rum factory and had the freedom to come and go as he pleased. The new system was bureaucratic and controlling, and Matamoros was just one more rum worker expected to follow the regulations imposed by the Ministry of Industry.

Under socialist administration, the entire rum-making procedure was defined as a series of component steps, which were then spelled out in great detail and set down as a series of work standards. Production practices that were informal in the era of Bacardi family management were formalized and listed in a handbook, as if the manufacture of rum could be so regularized that no special expertise was necessary. The technical norms to be followed in washing corks and gluing labels were described in almost as much detail as were the guidelines for aging the *aguardiente* or filtering the base rums, with as little as possible left to human judgment. The idea of judging a rum blend by its smell or feel on one's hands, as done by Daniel Bacardi or Mariano Lavigne, gave way to the procedure specified in the handbook: "When the blending and adjustment of a certain type of rum is to be carried out, first request from the corresponding aging warehouse the desired quantities according to the indicated date...." The old factory on Matadero Street was now part of Administrative Unit 1, a subdivision of the Santiago Beverage Combine, which in turn was under the Provincial Directorate of Beverage and Liquor Enterprises. *Santiagueros*, however, never called it anything but the Bacardi factory.

Chapter 20

❧❦❧

Family Business

The old man showed up at the Bacardi building in Miami just before noon, smartly dressed in a white linen suit of the type long favored by Cuban gentlemen. Even at ninety, bald and leaning on a cane, he carried himself with a slight swagger. Peering over his horn-rimmed glasses, the man spotted his great-nephew, José Argamasilla Bacardi, and ordered him to have a drink with him in the company bar.

"*Tío*, it's too early!" Argamasilla would say. "I have to work!"

"Come on, just sit down. Don't worry about it."

Emilito Bacardi Lay, the oldest son of Emilio Bacardi Moreau and María Lay, was never one to worry much about working. He had shown great courage and patriotism at the age of seventeen when he left home to join the Cuban *mambí* rebels who were fighting for Cuba's freedom from Spain, but in the years that followed, "Colonel" Bacardi served the family rum business mostly by sharing old war stories with company clients. A rainy day would revive aches from long-ago combat injuries. "Ohhh," he groaned, "that's the *machetazo* they gave me at Calimete," and for the hundredth time he told of the day he was bloodied by a Spanish bayonet. He told the stories at the Bacardi bar in Havana and later in Miami, where he lived with his second wife, Zoila, in a high-rise building overlooking Biscayne Bay. In exile, the stories sometimes took on a twist, with the colonel launching into a tirade against Fidel Castro, the Bacardis' new enemy. "If only the *mambises* could come back to life waving their machetes," he said, "Fidel would soon see how we could fight." Bacardi boss Pepín Bosch, married to Emilito's cousin Enriqueta, would spot him in the company bar and bring some visitor over to meet him. Emilito would invariably pretend to be annoyed, but he loved the attention.

After an hour or so at the Bacardi building, Emilito—as he had been called since he was a boy—usually went off to have lunch with his half sister Marina. His other half sisters—the sculptress Mimín, Adelaida (Lalita), and Amalia, the youngest—were living by then in the Bahamas, New York, and Madrid. Emilito's two full sisters, Carmen and Mariíta, had settled in Puerto Rico and Pennsylvania respectively.

As grandchildren of Facundo Bacardi Massó, the company founder, and his wife Amalia Moreau, Emilito and his sisters were part of the third Bacardi generation. So were his cousins Luis, Laura, and María Bacardi, the son and daughters of Don Emilio's brother Facundo Jr., as well as Joaquín "The Brewer" Bacardi, the sole surviving son of Emilio's brother José. Then came the Schuegs—Lucía, Jorge, Víctor, and Enriqueta—the children of Emilio's sister Amalia and his business partner Enrique Schueg. All these Bacardis had grown up with their grandfather's company in Cuba, and they or their children, nieces, and nephews now owned almost all the stock. They were the Bacardis whom Pepín Bosch and other company executives had to serve.

By the 1960s, the Bacardi business comprised five companies with operations from the Bahamas to Brazil, but it remained a family enterprise, bound together by personal relationships among relatives. Pepín Bosch's success as the top Bacardi executive was in large part the result of his positioning of the firm internationally and his clever arrangement of commercial relations between the Bacardi companies, but it was also due to his understanding of the Bacardi family and his careful management of family relations over the previous twenty-plus years. He did not necessarily admire all his wife's relatives, and he could be autocratic in dealing with them, but not for a moment did he lose sight of the reality that he was directing a family business as well as a modern industrial operation.

In turn, the Bacardis themselves were dependent—both financially and emotionally—on the family rum company. While they had all been wealthy in Cuba, they had given up their bank accounts and their possessions when they left. Some had savings outside Cuba, but others did not and looked to Pepín Bosch to find them a job, even if it was in a distant country. For many, the quarterly dividend checks from their Bacardi stock were an important income source, at least in the beginning. Under the circumstances, the family business was run in a way that distinguished it from companies where the stockholders' only common interest was to see growth in the share price. Recognizing the family's strained financial situation, Pepín Bosch decided the various Bacardi companies should distribute as much as half their net earnings as dividends. It was a debatable move in light of the loss of the Cuba assets and, more seriously, the revenue from the Hatuey breweries. A firm with the demonstrated growth potential, the expansion plans, and the new capitalization requirements that Bacardi had in the early 1960s would logically have chosen to retain a higher percentage of its earnings for investment purposes, but Pepín Bosch needed to give priority to Bacardi family needs.

Similarly, the firm's continued association with Cuba and the exile cause—through its patronage of the anti-Castro RECE operation, for example—did not make obvious sense in terms of Bacardi business strategy, only in the context of its family identity and character. The Bacardi-Cuba tie was never mentioned in company advertising, and with each passing year fewer people outside of the Cuban exile community were even aware of the connection. Within the family, however, it was unquestioned, at least in the early years. Zenaida Bacardi, one of Don Emilio's granddaughters, praised Pepín Bosch's direction of the Bacardi family enterprise in a 1974 essay addressed to Don Emilio, more than fifty years after his death. "You have a successor who follows your path," she wrote, "one who sees in your factories *not just a means of making a profit but a way to raise high the name of Cuba* [emphasis added]."

Those lines were written nearly fourteen years after the confiscation of the Bacardi properties in Cuba. The question was, How long would the family history and nationalist political agenda continue to matter in the Bacardi enterprise, given business and competitive pressures? Each successive Bacardi generation was likely to feel less Cuban and more American. Some family members did not trust their relatives or harbored suspicions about their motives or plans, and all the normal family jealousies inevitably arose. Once the Bacardis realized that they would not be returning to Cuba any time soon and that their century-old rum company would have to compete in a global marketplace, they had to clarify their corporate identity. What exactly did it mean for them to be a family business? Should Bacardi be any different from its rival liquor firms?

* * *

Pepín Bosch was just the third man to lead Bacardi after the firm's 1919 incorporation, following Emilio Bacardi and Enrique Schueg. He held on to his leadership position for more than thirty years in spite of his intimidating personal manner, because he gave family members what they wanted—steadily growing dividend checks—and because he was virtually irreplaceable. The interconnected structure of the various Bacardi companies, as devised by Bosch and his lawyers, was so complicated and unusual that no one but Bosch could really claim to understand it. Though they shared the same stockholders, each of the five Bacardi companies had its own president, directors, and board chairman, and officially they were independent entities. The closest thing to a holding company in the Bacardi organization was an informal group of seven key family members who met periodically under Bosch's leadership to discuss business developments and make key strategic decisions for the Bacardi empire as a whole.

Bosch had presided over the parent company in Cuba, and in exile family members continued to defer to his leadership, giving him leeway to set Bacardi policies as he saw fit. In 1962 Bosch arranged for the sale of 10 percent of the equity in the Bacardi Corporation, the family's Puerto Rico–based operation, to the public. The limited offering in one of the five Bacardi companies left the business still family owned for all practical purposes, but for the first time it created a market for Bacardi shares and thus established a valuation for at least part of the Bacardi empire. Family members would have a better sense of what their shares were worth and could even sell a few of them if they felt compelled to do so. The public offering also meant that the Puerto Rico company, which produced all the Bacardi rum sold in the United States, would have to issue regular financial reports. The figures that came out showed a booming business. Yearly net rum sales for the Puerto Rico company increased 56 percent from 1962 to 1965 and another 215 percent over the next ten years. By 1974, based on the market price of its publicly traded shares, Bacardi Corporation alone was worth as much as $330 million. The value of the Bacardi business empire as a whole could not be determined because the remaining companies were still privately owned, but Bacardi family members had gotten the message Pepín Bosch hoped they would get: They were doing well under his stewardship. When Bosch chose to install his son Jorge as president of Bacardi Corporation in San Juan, there was no protest, nor was there when he sent his second son, Carlos, to Bermuda to run Bacardi International.

For his part, Bosch let it be known that he expected the family's automatic support. Not one for false modesty, Bosch told all who would listen that he believed the Bacardis should be grateful to him for what he achieved on their behalf. "I made every one of them millionaires," he boasted to a Miami friend. "When they came here, they were *con una mano adelante, otra atrás*," an expression meaning "with one hand in front, the other in back" and suggesting they were essentially naked, with nothing to their name.

The unraveling of the family business ties began only after the death of Bosch's wife, Enriqueta Schueg, in October 1975 after a long struggle with cancer. As the daughter of Amalia Bacardi Moreau and Enrique Schueg, Enriqueta had been at the center of family and business affairs for more than fifty years. It was she who had hoisted the Cuban flag over the new Bacardi distillery in Santiago in February 1922, standing alongside her ailing, white-haired uncle Emilio, and it was to her, not to her prickly husband, that the Bacardis turned when there was family trouble. A warm and gentle woman, she tended to the extended Bacardi family with the same care and patience that she gave to her beloved Bacardi gardens in Santiago, Havana, and Puerto Rico. After her death, family members said things about each other that they would not have dared say when she was alive, and no one emerged who could play the same unifying and conciliating role.

Pepín Bosch was devastated by his wife's death. She had been his *compañera* for fifty-two years, and he depended on her to help him in all the family negotiations, for which he had little patience. Bosch was now seventy-seven, and with Enriqueta gone he decided it was finally time to turn responsibility for the Bacardi empire over to someone else. Though his two sons each had executive experience, neither had shown much interest in the top position, and neither had the proven leadership or management skills to run a business operation as large as Bacardi had become. Bosch decided he needed to hire a professional chief executive who could work, at least in the beginning, under his direct supervision. Accustomed to acting on his own, and becoming more willful with each passing year, Bosch did not bother to inform key family shareholders before moving to recruit his replacement. It was a big mistake.

Decision making at Bacardi had always been shaped by the voting of shares in family blocs, according to lines of descent. The three Bacardi partners at the time of the company's 1919 incorporation—the brothers Emilio and Facundo Bacardi and their brother-in-law Enrique Schueg—had each taken 30 percent of the shares, with 10 percent going to the heirs of their late brother José. A half century later, the Bacardis were still voting their shares in those same four blocs. Pepín Bosch was able to count on the votes of the Schueg bloc, and the descendants of Emilio and José Bacardi had usually supported him,* giving him effective control within the company. After the death of Enriqueta Schueg, however, the old loyalties began to shift, most notably when the news of Bosch's hiring plans emerged. First to defect was Enriqueta's nephew Edwin "Eddy" Nielsen, the son of her sister Lucía. Nielsen was president of Bacardi Imports, the company with the exclusive right to sell Bacardi rum in the United States. He was considered a star executive in the family, and when Nielsen signaled that Pepín Bosch could no longer be sure of all the Schueg votes, others in the family began to switch as well.

---

*Alliances within and between the Bacardi family branches were sometimes based on trustee relationships. Some large amounts of stock inherited by younger family members were held for them in trust by others in the family, giving the trustees power within the company beyond what their own stockholdings would have provided.

Nielsen had never opposed Bosch on a key issue, but after consulting with other family members, he told Bosch that bringing in an outsider was not a good idea. Nielsen said the prevailing family view was that if Bosch wanted to turn executive responsibilities over to someone else, the job should go to a family member or someone close to the family. Bosch reacted angrily. In his view, the Bacardis were questioning his judgment of what was best for the family business, after all he had done over the years to make them wealthy. Enriqueta was no longer there to calm him down, and in a fit of pique Bosch announced he was quitting. "I'm looking now for a new job," he told the *New York Times*.

That impetuous response was entirely in keeping with Bosch's nature. His strong convictions and unwavering self-confidence served him well when he was standing up against Cuban dictators or leading his company boldly through its darkest days, but Bosch could certainly be obstinate. Once offended, he did not forget. Within weeks of announcing his resignation from Bacardi in the spring of 1976, he was gone. His departure was another big turning point for the company, less dramatic than its separation from Cuba but momentous nonetheless.

Over the years, Bosch had personally acquired enough stock in the five Bacardi companies to give him about a 2 or 3 percent equity share. His wife, Enriqueta, as one of Enrique Schueg's four children, inherited a quarter of Schueg's original 30 percent share, and by prior arrangement with Pepín she left all her stock to their two sons, Jorge and Carlos. In 1977, however, Bosch and his sons sold their entire stake to the Canadian liquor company Hiram Walker, putting a portion of the Bacardi business in the hands of a rival for the first time ever. Bosch and his sons were joined by a few other family members who had been seeking an opportunity to sell part of their own holdings, and the total sale involved about 12 percent of all the shares in the Bacardi companies. Bosch had been willing in theory to sell the stock back to the Bacardi family, but the sincerity of his offer was disputed. Some Bacardis later complained that Bosch had given the family only a few days to suggest a price and that he had not seriously pursued a deal with them. Hiram Walker paid only $45 million for the entire Bosch/Schueg chunk, a price that valued the Bacardi interests as a whole at about $375 million. A year earlier, Bosch himself had estimated the Bacardi assets to be worth about $700 million. Not only had outsiders acquired a piece of Bacardi; they had gotten it at a bargain price.

• • •

Business school professors who study family-owned enterprises cite the issue of leadership succession as the biggest challenge such companies face. As long as the founders are in charge, family businesses tend to outperform others.

Most such firms, however, do not survive the transition to a second generation of family owners, and still more fail during the third generation. Typically, the company founders do not want to step down and let go of their life work, no matter their age. Their children or designated successors, meanwhile, may be ambivalent about taking over and do so reluctantly.

By the time Pepín Bosch retired, the fourth Bacardi generation was well represented in the company, and it appeared the firm might be an exception to the rule that family companies have limited longevity. Don Facundo's sons guided the business through long years when it was continually on the verge of bankruptcy. Emilio Bacardi, after taking over from his father, was replaced by his brother-in-law Enrique Schueg, who in turn passed the reins to his own son-in-law, Pepín Bosch. Each of the successions had gone smoothly. But Bosch, having managed Bacardi's rebirth outside Cuba, was almost a second founder of the company, and his departure was jarring. As the *New York Times* observed, Bosch ran the firm "by sheer strength of intellect and business acumen, operating virtually without secretarial help or close aides, and traveling constantly despite his age." In the mold of other brilliant family businessmen, Bosch refused to retire at a normal age, apparently unwilling to trust his own sons—or any other family members—to carry on without him.

The Bacardi enterprise demonstrated both the benefits and the dangers of family-owned companies. For years, the Bacardis had been an example of how family stockholders take a longer-term view than investors who buy into a company looking for a quick profit. They had shown that a chief executive with family ties to his stockholders is likely to enjoy a level of autonomy that other executives could only dream of. And they had shown that being free from the quarterly scrutiny of financial analysts means that families with their own companies can use them to pursue social or political objectives. Had Bacardi been publicly owned, the stockholders would surely have been less likely to support a corporate aim to "raise high the name of Cuba."

On the other hand, a family-owned company like Bacardi had to be on guard against the perils of nepotism, especially given the Latin tradition of taking care of one's relatives. Pepín Bosch and his predecessors had to worry that by keeping their enterprises private they were denying themselves access to the capital funds that were available in public equity markets. In addition, familial loyalties (or jealousies) could get in the way of clear-eyed strategic decision making. A focus on social and political missions can lead a family company to invest in peripheral, even self-indulgent, activities that have nothing to do with bottom-line needs. With the retirement of Pepín Bosch, the Bacardis found themselves facing all these issues and more. They hung over the family business for the next fifteen years, and the strain of dealing with them brought the business close to a breaking point.

◆ ◆ ◆

Pepín Bosch was not formally replaced in 1976 as the Bacardi boss, because his authority did not derive from any particular executive position. To the extent he had a successor as the overall leader of the family business operation, it was Eddy Nielsen, the Bacardi executive around whom the family had rallied when Bosch first announced his intention to step down. Nielsen's only official post, however, was at Bacardi Imports, where he had presided since 1971. Even after assuming the new family leadership role, Nielsen kept his old job title and his same corner office in the Bacardi building on Biscayne Boulevard.

At Bacardi Imports, Nielsen had proven to be an exceptional corporate manager. As a grandson of Amalia Bacardi and Enrique Schueg, he had deep family roots, and Spanish was his mother tongue. He was rarely seen in anything but a conservative business suit, however, and upon meeting him few people guessed that he was Cuban. Born in Massachusetts to Lucía Schueg and Edwin Nielsen Sr., a Norwegian immigrant physician, Nielsen had been schooled in the United States and spent four years in the U.S. Army before heading to Cuba to take a position with the family company. After Castro's revolution, Pepín Bosch sent Nielsen to Mexico to serve as assistant manager of the Bacardi operation there. He was of the same generation as Daniel Bacardi, who had been second in command of the Santiago operation, but as a U.S. citizen and fluent English speaker, Nielsen was better positioned to direct the company's multinational operations, and by 1975 he was recognized as the senior executive within the family after Bosch. For his part, Daniel had toiled most of his Bacardi work life in the shadow of Pepín Bosch and shown little interest in the political maneuvering that would be needed to secure the top leadership position. (Nor did he control enough shares to give him the leverage he would need to run the company.)

At a family meeting, Eddy Nielsen received the support of the other Schueg shareholders and the descendants of Facundo Bacardi Moreau, as well as the tacit support of the Emilio and José Bacardi branches, and he became the de facto chairman. His goal was to bring more order and openness to Bacardi corporate planning and policy making. The increasingly complex business environment, in Nielsen's opinion, demanded a more institutionalized organization than what Bosch's informal family council provided. He organized a new Bacardi entity, mysteriously named International Trademark Consultants

(INTRAC), with the sole function of overseeing the five Bacardi companies. The executive secretary was Guillermo Mármol, Pepín Bosch's longtime lawyer and confidante and someone who understood as well as anyone how Bosch had managed the Bacardi companies' intertwined activities. Like Bosch's family council, the INTRAC board had seven members, with two representatives from each of the three main Bacardi family branches, and one from the smaller group of shareholders descended from José Bacardi Moreau. Nielsen was the board president. His closest colleague was Manuel Jorge Cutillas, the distilling engineer from Santiago and grandson of Emilio and Elvira's daughter Marina. Though just forty-four, Cutillas had held top positions with Bacardi Mexico, Bacardi & Company in Nassau, and Bacardi International in Bermuda. He had one of the family's sharpest managerial minds, and the *New York Times* had already identified him as a possible successor to Pepín Bosch.

The organization of INTRAC came at a critical time in the evolution of the Bacardi business. Each of the companies in the rum empire had significantly grown, and their relations were becoming complex. The largest, Bacardi Corporation of Puerto Rico, had the biggest rum distillery in the world, selling most of its production to Miami-based Bacardi Imports, the exclusive U.S. supplier. Mexico was the province of Grupo Bacardi de Mexico, S.A., which had its own distilleries at La Galarza and Tultitlán. Bacardi International in Bermuda owned distilleries in Canada, Brazil, Spain, and Martinique and oversaw rum sales everywhere but in Mexico and the United States. Nassau-based Bacardi & Company owned the rights to the Bacardi trademark, meaning other Bacardi companies had to pay it for using the mark. One of the thorny issues was how to establish what prices and fees the companies should charge each other. Family members didn't necessarily own shares in the same proportions across all the Bacardi companies, so they were always watchful to see that one company was not favored over another in the allocation of expenses and profits.

In the first few years, Nielsen was generally successful in his efforts to keep family members happy and the business thriving. From 1976 to 1979, total Bacardi sales in the United States leaped an astounding 70 percent. Consumers during those years switched en masse from whiskeys to the "white" spirits, rum and vodka. The trend was especially pronounced in the African-American community, where rum and Coke became the drink of choice. Among the partying crowd, the daiquiri and piña colada cocktails became hugely popular. By 1980, Bacardi rum was the single most popular liquor brand in the United States, outpacing the previous top seller, Seagram's 7 Crown whiskey. By 1983, about two thirds of all rum sold in the world carried a Bacardi label.

But the dramatic growth in Bacardi income presented the family business with a new strategic challenge: The companies found themselves with more cash than they knew how to handle. In the past, excess revenue had been reinvested in new rum production facilities, but Bacardi executives decided they did not need more industrial capacity. Alternatively, the family rum business could acquire additional liquor brands. Bacardi was unusual among major liquor manufacturers in being a one-brand company, and that put it at a major disadvantage in competing for distribution clout against those companies that owned a portfolio. By 1983, however, liquor sales in general had begun to level out, particularly in the United States, where there was a move toward moderation in drinking and increased interest in health and fitness. Under the circumstances, it did not seem to be a good time to invest in other liquor companies. It was a time for major business decisions.

Eddy Nielsen and his Nassau ally, Manuel Jorge Cutillas, argued that the family should consider moving outside the spirits sector together. Within the space of a few months, they persuaded Bacardi directors to purchase Lloyd's Electronics, a New Jersey–based importer of cheap audio equipment, telephones, and clock radios, and also to set up a new company called Bacardi Capital. Financial services was a booming sector, and Nielsen and Cutillas were convinced that a diversification in that direction would be a profitable move for the Bacardi family. Bacardi Capital was organized with the idea that it could serve the Bacardi family by investing in the financial markets.

Not all the family members were convinced that it made sense for Bacardi to expand outside the business it knew best. One skeptic was Daniel Bacardi. Having grown up around the factory in Santiago and overseen its operations for many years, Daniel had a deep sentimental attachment to the rum industry. At seventy, he still considered himself a Cuban patriot and loyal *santiaguero*. He was proud that over the previous century his family had become synonymous with rum making, and he believed it should stick to that enterprise. If there was excess cash beyond what was needed to sustain and build the rum enterprise, Daniel argued, it would be better to return the money to the stockholders and let them invest it as they pleased. His counsel proved prescient. Lacking the knowledge and experience needed to develop a sound business strategy in either the electronics or financial services field, the Bacardis failed miserably in both areas. By the time Bacardi Corporation divested itself of Lloyd's in 1985, the venture had lost close to thirty million dollars, and with its disastrous attempt to play the bond market, Bacardi Capital cost its investors more than fifty million before it, too, was shut down. There would be no more attempts to diversify outside the spirits industry.

There remained the problem, however, of Bacardi's competitive disadvantage as a one-brand liquor business. Under laws enacted after Prohibition, liquor manufacturers or importers in most states were required to sell their products in the United States through independent distributors. A company with a portfolio of liquor brands had more leverage with a distributor, because it could provide him with a variety of products in a single commercial relationship and pressure him to carry the whole package. If Bacardi were to survive and prosper in the consolidating spirits industry, it would need to build strategic alliances with other liquor companies, if not pursue formal partnerships.

The association with the Canadian liquor company Hiram Walker that sprung from the Pepín Bosch stock sale provided a starting point. In the summer of 1985, Eddy Nielsen and Manuel Jorge Cutillas discussed a possible strengthening of the tie between the two companies through a stock swap. In addition to the 12 percent share of Bacardi stock that Hiram Walker already owned from its purchase of the Bosch bloc, the Canadian company could pick up another 10 percent or so, increasing its Bacardi position to more than 20 percent. In return, the Bacardis would take a minority stake in Hiram Walker. Depending on the valuation of the Bacardi shares transferred to Hiram Walker, the Bacardi investors would have to pay additional cash for the Hiram Walker shares. The deal would allow both liquor concerns to strengthen their distribution networks by linking their product lines, a promising move given the early indications of a consolidation trend in the spirits industry.

But it would have also put as much as a quarter of the family rum business in nonfamily, non-Cuban hands, and that news sent the family into an uproar. To the older Bacardis, the idea of selling off another sizable portion of the patrimony was unthinkable. No one was more upset than eighty-six-year-old Amalia Bacardi Cape, the youngest daughter of Emilio and Elvira. Amalia was the family guardian of her father's memory, and for her the Bacardi firm existed in part to uphold his legacy. She mobilized relatives to make telephone calls and write letters, and they soon turned a majority of the family shareholders against the proposed stock swap, effectively killing the Hiram Walker deal before it was even negotiated. In 1987, Bacardi repurchased the stock that Pepín Bosch and his sons had sold Hiram Walker a decade earlier, thus ending any relationship with the Canadian company.

The family disagreements that erupted around the Hiram Walker deal lingered, however. Behind the dispute was a Bacardi identity crisis, years in the making. This was a company that had always belonged to a single Cuban family with a deep sense of national heritage. By the 1980s, however, it was also a transnational liquor firm struggling to compete with larger and more diversified companies. The family directors needed to resolve what those two facts meant for the firm's evolution. To the Bacardis, there was no more powerful symbol of their Cuban roots than the company that bore their name; on the other hand, they wanted their company to grow and prosper, and that necessarily meant change. But how much and in which direction? The answers were no longer obvious.

• • •

The ties between the stockholders and the management in a stable family company are likely to be unusually trusting, but those same relations become acrimonious when the family members are squabbling. The arguments over diversification and the Hiram Walker stock swap eroded the good feeling that had existed previously between the Bacardis and their corporate leadership. Some family members, notably Daniel Bacardi, began to question the judgment of Eddy Nielsen and Manuel Jorge Cutillas. Daniel soon emerged as the leader of a "dissident" minority group within the family that wanted to limit management prerogatives. Debate escalated into confrontation, shattering friendships and straining family relations, and the tensions lingered for years.

The dispute divided the Bacardi family along old lines of wealth and status. A key issue was how earnings should be split between reinvestment and dividends. In the first years after the family left Cuba, Pepín Bosch had instructed Bacardi executives to maintain dividends at about 50 percent of earnings, but the proportion had subsequently declined, to the dismay of the smaller shareholders. Because dividends are taxed at a higher rate than capital gains, stockholders who did not need extra income preferred to see their shares grow in value, while the less wealthy family members favored bigger quarterly checks. Daniel Bacardi's dissidents were largely united by their concern that the Bacardi management could not be trusted to act on such sensitive questions in the best interests of all family members.

The conflicts within the family prompted the dissident group in 1986 to oppose a management move to reprivatize the Puerto Rico–based Bacardi Corporation, 10 percent of whose stock had been publicly traded since 1962. Daniel Bacardi and his followers opposed the buyback because privatization would have freed the company from Securities and Exchange Commission (SEC) reporting requirements. From the management's point of view, SEC regulations hindered the company's freedom of action. But the dissidents feared that another merger plan might be pursued behind closed doors, so they opposed any move that would enable the management to operate with greater secrecy. The disagreement led to litigation and was not resolved until 1992.

With comity eroding, other family conflicts were exposed, including a division between those family members who were employed by Bacardi and those who were only stockholders. As with other intrafamily squabbles, this one arose along lines of descent; Emilio Bacardi had more children and grandchildren than did his brothers, Facundo and José, or his sister, Amalia, so stockholdings in his branch were dispersed among many more heirs. Being less wealthy on average, Emilio's descendants were more likely to look for a job within the company. Generally they got one, and some relatives who did not work for the company complained that the tradition of Bacardi employment had gone too far. In the increasingly competitive business environment, they argued, the widespread employment of Bacardi family members (or their spouses) was a drain on company resources.

To the working Bacardis, such criticism rankled. The Bacardi heritage in Cuba, they pointed out, was established at a time when the family was still close to its humble origins and not associated with the sugar barons, coffee planters, rich merchants, and other Cuban elites known for laziness and self-indulgent lifestyles. The family members who continued to toil for the company, it could be argued, were closer to the Bacardi working tradition than those who lived off their dividends.

One Bacardi who caused the family some embarrassment in that regard was Luís Gómez del Campo Bacardi, a grandson of Facundo Bacardi Moreau and one of the family's biggest individual shareholders. In 1993 Gómez del Campo became involved in a nasty high-society divorce in Switzerland, with soap opera overtones reminiscent of the Martha Durand–Pepe Bacardi divorce nearly seventy years earlier. He had served on the Bacardi board off and on since the prerevolution days back in Cuba but had worked for the company only briefly. In 1993 a British newspaper ran a profile of Gómez del Campo in the midst of his divorce proceedings in Geneva, reporting that he was worth about three hundred million dollars, had yearly dividend income of seven million dollars, owned a fifteen-million-dollar home in Monte Carlo, and had purchased a royal title in Britain, enabling him to be called the Lord of the Manor of Bayfield Hall cum Coston. "A picture is emerging of the lifestyle of one of the world's wealthiest men," the paper reported, "bearing one of the world's most famous names. It is a life beyond the comprehension of most people, funded by the dividends of the Bacardi liquor empire and hardly touched by the tax authorities."

The media loved such stories, and messy Bacardi divorces produced rich material. But on occasion those stories also highlighted the enduring family bonds. Martha Durand discovered the importance of Bacardi blood loyalties when she divorced Pepe Bacardi, and she was not the last to learn that lesson. Ricardo Blanco, a Santiago-born Cuban who married Marina Bacardi's great-granddaughter, had a similar experience sixty years later. Blanco worked for Bacardi for five years in the mid-1980s, until his divorce soured relations with his in-laws and ended his ties to their company.

"No one knows about the Bacardi family," Blanco said in an interview, "but they're a very closed family. They don't want anybody from the outside to be more than them." Blanco said the only way for him to flourish in the company was to embrace the Bacardi family identity. "They did not acknowledge me as Ricardo Blanco. I was Ricardo Blanco *Bacardi*. You had to change your name and abide by their cult.... If you had an idea, they didn't even give you a chance to explain, because they're a hundred years old, and they know everything there is to know."

But this "cult" aspect of the Bacardi family enterprise was not always experienced negatively by outsiders. Some veteran nonfamily employees, like the distilling engineers Juan Grau and Richard Gardner and the marketing genius Juan Prado, came to have quasi-family status. Reflecting on his long Bacardi career in a 2004 interview, Grau said the company had such a tight family culture that senior employees—family and nonfamily alike—may have felt an even deeper sense of shared kinship than did actual Bacardi family members who were connected to it only by being a shareholder. "Bacardi has a culture that you have to sit within the company to experience," he said. "Even though it's a family culture, you can't be a part of it just by being in the family."

Richard Gardner, whose forty-plus years with the company took him from Cuba to Brazil to Nassau, noted later that he and other nonfamily employees felt a loyalty to the company from their earliest days. "When the company in Cuba was confiscated, many of us who were not family members stayed with it," he said, "even though we could have obtained much more lucrative jobs with other organizations. Bacardi was not in a position to be able to pay good salaries at the time, but having made one feel a part of the family worked in their favor."

• • •

The ongoing intrafamily conflict at Bacardi obscured what was in fact a remarkable business success story. By increasing worldwide rum sales from 1.7 million cases in 1960 to over 22 million cases in 1989, the company achieved a rate of growth that no other liquor firm could match, and it came in spite of bad investments, management mistakes, and shareholder squabbling. Beverage industry analyst Tom Pirko, who probably knew the company as well as any outsider, remarked in 1990 that the Bacardi management and shareholders had blown a chance to put even more distance between themselves and their competitors. "One can't fault their success," he said, "but one can fault that they haven't been more successful."

The key elements in the Bacardi business formula were quality control, brand promotion, and strategic marketing. If there was one guiding principle for production, it was that every bottle of Bacardi rum should taste exactly the same, no matter where in the world it was distilled or purchased. It should be slightly sweet but barely noticeable. Pepín Bosch established a quality control laboratory at Bacardi & Company in Nassau, the operation that owned the trademark, and every Bacardi distillery sent monthly samples of its rum production there to be evaluated. Bosch initially gave the quality control responsibility to Daniel Bacardi, who had been tasting rum at the distillery in Santiago for more than twenty-five years, but engineers Manuel Jorge Cutillas and Richard Gardner were in charge of the scientific analysis. No rum, no matter where it was distilled, could carry the Bacardi trademark unless it had been tested and approved by the quality control experts.*

The Bacardis' defense of their trademarks was legendary, dating from the time they protested the forgery of Don Facundo's signature on bottles that were not produced in his distillery. After the Bacardis lost their properties in Cuba and went into exile, the company executives began producing a highly detailed "Trademark Guide," including specifications for the use of the company's famous bat logo. The name "Bacardi," the guidebook explained, had to be used as an adjective followed by "rum," and not as a noun, such as "a drink of Bacardi," for fear it would come to be seen as a generic term for rum in general.

It was not that Bacardi was above making cheap rum. Back in Cuba, the company had made a variety of "common" rums, though they did not carry the Bacardi label. In Puerto Rico, Bacardi Corporation introduced a new rum

---

*The one "Bacardi" facility that consistently presented problems in this regard was the distillery in Barcelona, Spain, which Enrique Schueg had licensed to Francisco Alegre in 1910. Unlike other Bacardi operations, the Barcelona distillery functioned independently, and Alegre's distillation and manufacturing techniques were not under Santiago's control. The Bacardi tasters in Cuba considered the Spanish "Bacardi" undrinkable, and Pepín Bosch did all he could to cancel the license. Schueg had made a long-term agreement with Alegre and his family, however, and Bosch was not able to secure the closure of the Barcelona plant until 1975.

in 1966 after sales managers realized that the cheaper Ronrico brand was out-selling Bacardi rum in the bars. Rather than lower his price to compete with Ronrico, Pepín Bosch ordered up a new rum, Ron Castillo, that would sell for even less. By straddling Ronrico in the market—putting a cheaper rum below while keeping Bacardi Silver Label above—the company was able to squeeze it from both sides and win the competition.

Such strategic marketing moves were a Bacardi strength. The company's great growth in the United States came when it concentrated on one product, white rum, and targeted a particular audience: young men and women. Silver Label Bacardi rum was so gentle on the tongue that it could, in liquor market-ing terms, "alcoholize" a Coke without significantly altering the taste. The marketing research director for Bacardi Imports in 1987, Paul Nelson, told a reporter that a large portion of the Bacardi U.S. market was "the naïve seg-ment," by which he meant women, "particularly younger females who don't like the taste of alcohol but want to participate socially." Back in Cuba, Bacardi had been well known for its highly aged *añejo*, a sipping rum, but there was little demand for *añejo* in the United States, and the company didn't promote it. Rum connoisseurs, as well as distillers who produced more sophisticated rums, tended to ridicule the blandness of Bacardi white rum, but there could be little disputing the fact that Bacardi knew its market and pursued it success-fully and profitably.

In business circles, "Bacardi" by 1990 had become first and foremost a brand, one of the dozen or so most valued in the commercial world. Next, the word represented a successful global spirits company. Only after that did it name a family, and at that a somewhat dysfunctional one, stressed by the ex-perience of exile and the divisive effects of wealth.

◆ ◆ ◆

In 1992 the internal management dispute that had divided the Bacardi family for several years was settled under a comprehensive "peace accord" between Daniel Bacardi's dissident shareholder group and the top management. The agreement covered such controversial issues as the portion of net after-tax earnings that the company should return as dividends (half). For the dissidents, it also brought more clarity of control and ownership and a restriction of man-agement prerogatives. The historic element, however, was an agreement by both sides that the five Bacardi companies should be acquired by a new entity—Bacardi Limited—which would serve as a holding company, with a single chairman and one board of directors, headquartered in Bermuda. The family business would once again be wholly private. The original rationales for the creation of independent companies—to protect the family business from confiscation and shield it from taxation—were no longer operative. No government was in a position to move against the Bacardi assets, and the taxation authorities in the various countries had become so sophisticated that there was no longer much to be gained through creative headquartering.

The push to create Bacardi Limited was directed by Manuel Jorge Cutillas, who served at the time as the INTRAC chairman and therefore the family business chief. Cutillas argued persuasively that there was a wave of consolidation in the spirits industry and that it would be hard for Bacardi to participate if the business continued to exist as five separate entities. If another liquor brand became available, which of the five Bacardi companies would buy it? The creation of Bacardi Limited solved that problem. The "peace accord" also gave management a green light to diversify as long as any deal was put to a stockholder vote.

Indeed, within months of the agreement, Bacardi Limited made the first major acquisition in the history of the firm, purchasing Martini & Rossi, a spirits company known primarily for its vermouth. Like Bacardi, Martini & Rossi was an old family company (founded in 1863), and it had played a role in its native city of Turin, Italy, not unlike the Bacardi role in Santiago.

In acquiring Martini & Rossi, Bacardi took on a company bigger than itself, with greater gross sales (though lower profits). The move cost Bacardi $2.1 billion, and for the first time in the firm's history the management had to turn to investment bankers for financing assistance. Risky as the move was, it made strategic sense. Recent years had seen a wave of consolidation in the spirits industry, and more mergers and acquisitions were on the horizon. If Bacardi were to compete, it would need more brands in its portfolio. Martini & Rossi was a good fit, being strong in parts of Europe where Bacardi was weak, notably in the former Soviet bloc countries, an important new market. In subsequent years, the company acquired more high-profile brands, beginning with Dewar's whiskey and Bombay Sapphire gin in 1998.

After 130 years, Bacardi was finally moving beyond its exclusive association with rum, and the new products diminished the company's Cuban character. It seemed as if an era had passed. That sense grew still sharper with the death in February 1994 of Pepín Bosch after a brief but debilitating illness at the age of ninety-five. Bosch was the Bacardi executive who had saved the company after it was uprooted from its native soil, while tying the family name to the Cuban cause more tightly than anyone since Emilio Bacardi, his wife's uncle. By the time of his death, nearly two decades had passed since he had left the company, and in his final years neither Bosch nor his two sons bothered to stay in touch with their Bacardi relatives. For years, he had imagined that he would take the rum business back to his beloved Cuba someday, but Bosch died in Miami.

Ironically, the Bacardi management was just then beginning to turn the company's attention back to Cuba, and in a big way.

Chapter 21

Havana Club

Premium tickets for the floor show at the Tropicana in downtown Havana
bought patrons a seat at one of the tables around the edge of the circular stage,
just a few feet from the dancers in sequined pink bikinis and feathered head-
dresses. Red and white spotlights swept wildly across the floor as the conga
drummers pounded out a driving rhythm and the *corista* girls kicked their
legs high. Around the room, waiters in tuxedo jackets scurried from table to
table with fresh bottles of rum and Cuban beer. Cigar smoke drifted overhead.
More than two decades had passed since Fidel Castro imposed his strict moral
values on Cuban society, but the Tropicana in the 1980s was still one of Havana's hottest nightspots.

Cuban cultural life under Communism involved a curious mix of pre-Castro
licentiousness and postrevolution austerity. Castro closed all the casinos and
most of the nightclubs that had made Cuba such a favored vacation spot in
earlier decades, but the Tropicana survived, and its famous floor show was preserved as a kind of souvenir spectacle, reflecting the island's Afro-Cuban flam-
boyance. In theory, the other clubs were shut down not because of a
revolutionary objection to eroticism and extravagance per se, but because of
their association with gambling, drug trafficking, prostitution, and the Mafia.
By keeping the Tropicana open as a national treasure, the authorities could
show that the revolution did not require a wholesale rejection of Cuban salsa
music, rumba dancing, *batá* drumming, or rum-fueled celebrations. Communism did not have to look the same in every country; Fidel Castro presided over
a sexy Cuban variant.

The new Tropicana was a bit different from the old one, of course. Castro's
rule on cultural activity in Cuba was, "Within the revolution, everything;
against the revolution, nothing," and the nightclub had been purged of all the
"counterrevolutionary" elements. Photographs of some salsa stars of the past
still hung on the wall, but there was no trace of Celia Cruz nor of any of the
other notable Tropicana performers who had rejected Castroism and gone into

exile. The clientele had also changed. The audience included some Canadians and Europeans and a few Americans, but most of the patrons were from the Soviet bloc: East German tourists, Czechoslovak and Bulgarian trade officials, and hordes of Russian advisers. The Cubans called the Russians *bolos,* joking that their white skin and big, round bottoms made them look like bowling pins. Unaccustomed to the tropics, the Russian visitors often seemed out of place in a Havana nightclub, not realizing that guayabera shirts were meant to be worn outside their pants and proving themselves utterly unable to keep up with a Cuban dance rhythm. They quickly learned to appreciate quality Cuban cigars, however, and at the Tropicana they consumed enormous quantities of Cuban rum—in daiquiris or mojitos, with cola or on the rocks—just as patrons in the old days had done.

Before Castro, however, it would have been Bacardi rum; now the Tropicana served only Havana Club, the rum that had previously been made by the Arechabala family of Cárdenas. Within a few years of taking control of all private enterprise on the island, the Cuban government decided to make Havana Club its premier rum. In 1977 Fidel Castro personally inaugurated a new Havana Club distillery in Santa Cruz del Norte, about fifty miles west of the Arechabalas' old plant in Cárdenas. The Havana Club bottle was redesigned to feature an image of La Giraldilla, a seventeenth-century bronze female figure that sat atop the oldest fortress in Havana and served as a symbol of the city. The new label identified the product as "pure Cuban rum, founded in 1878." There was no mention of the Arechabalas as the founders, and few of the visitors who drank Havana Club rum had any sense of the brand's history prior to the revolution. No matter. While Bacardi had been the iconic spirit of the old Cuba, Havana Club was the rum of Castro's Cuba, served at every hotel bar, restaurant, and nightclub on the island.

* * *

The Cuban revolutionary authorities began promoting "Havana Club" only after seeing that the Arechabala family would not block them from using the rum brand. The Arechabalas' assets on the island were confiscated on the same day in 1960 that the Bacardi properties were seized, but unlike the Bacardis the Arechabalas made no effort to salvage their rum business by reorganizing it outside of Cuba. None of them had ever planned and built a rum distillery in a foreign country from the ground up, as the Bacardis had done several times already, and the Arechabalas had no commercial or industrial base in exile from which they could continue operating. When their business in Cuba was nationalized, they basically surrendered.

José Miguel Arechabala, the production manager at the Havana Club rum factory before the revolution, left for the United States, where he took a job with the American Sugar Refining Company in Philadelphia. During a court proceeding years later, he told a lawyer that his family did not attempt to maintain its rum business because it couldn't afford to. "Who's going to give you the money?" he said. "I don't want to make a fool of myself going to the bank and asking for the money." His brother Ramón Arechabala, the Havana Club sales manager in Cuba, stayed on the island until he was forced out in early 1964. For the next twenty years, he bounced from job to job in south Florida, working mainly in auto repair and auto sales. Most of the other Arechabalas settled in Spain, where the family had a long-established residency. Without a figure like Pepín Bosch around whom they could rally in exile, the Arechabalas drifted apart. Unlike the Bacardis, they did not become active in the anti-Castro movement, in spite of their anger over their losses. The Arechabalas had backed Fulgencio Batista to the end and therefore did not share the Bacardis' sense of having been personally betrayed by a revolutionary movement they had once supported.

Some of the Arechabalas' former rivals at Bacardi were a bit surprised they didn't put up more of a fight to defend their claim to the family rum trademark. Juan Prado, the ace Bacardi salesman, had always coveted the "Havana Club" brand. As a marketing man, Prado believed a product's value in the marketplace could derive as much from the appeal of its brand name as from its intrinsic quality. "Bacardi" sounded good in any language and was easy to remember. "Havana Club" likewise had a nice ring to it. English-language product names are recognizable everywhere, and this one was especially clear and lyrical. "Havana Club" also connoted the lively night scene for which Cuba had long been known. It was a product name worth fighting for, Prado believed, and when he saw that the Arechabalas were apparently ready to give up the brand, Prado suggested that Bacardi buy the rights to it. If the Arechabalas were not going to contest the Cuban government's use of the brand, maybe Bacardi could.

In 1973 Prado helped arrange for Ramón Arechabala to fly to Nassau to meet with Orfilio Peláez, the Bacardi executive designated by Pepín Bosch to handle Cuba-related issues. The two men discussed the prospect of a joint Bacardi-Arechabala effort to reclaim the Havana Club trademark. No accord was reached, however. Peláez said he needed to check on the status of the brand at the U.S. Patent and Trademark Office (USPTO), and the Arechabalas did not follow up. Other pressing commercial concerns soon intervened, and the idea of a joint Havana Club initiative was dropped.

Most products manufactured in Cuba after Fidel Castro's revolution were not of export quality, but there was a moderate international demand for Havana Club rum. Perhaps it was its Tropicana cachet, as the rum associated with the vibrant Havana nightlife, or maybe it was as smooth as its promoters claimed it was. Veteran rum workers in Santiago or Cárdenas knew the basics of distilling, aging, and blending, notwithstanding their lack of technical expertise and their ignorance of basic business management principles. The quality was undoubtedly inconsistent, but for every bad bottle there was at least one decent bottle. A *Washington Post* travel writer in 1978 reported that Havana Club rum was "good enough to drink any time of the day or night." A rum reviewer for *Playboy* magazine wrote in 1983 that the Havana Club rums from Cuba that he tasted were "quite muted, with a shade more taste and character than the Puerto Rican ones."

In 1973 the Cuban authorities began exporting Havana Club to Canada, where a bottle could bring six dollars or more. In 1978 the president of Pepsi-Cola's Wine and Spirits International subsidiary, Norman Heller, put his company in position to bring Havana Club to U.S. drinkers. President Jimmy Carter was moving toward the restoration of commercial relations with Cuba, and Heller hoped to be first in line to import Castro's rum. In a letter to the president of the Cuban government's export agency, Cubaexport, Heller said he and his fellow Pepsi executives were "very much interested in importing and selling Havana Club Rum in the U.S. market and are hopeful that we will be able to do so in the not too distant future." In Europe the rum was distributed by Cinzano, the Italian vermouth manufacturer. By the early 1980s, Havana Club had been introduced in Spain, France, Germany, Italy, Sweden, and even in Britain, where it was served to customers at Trader Vic's bar in the London Hilton.

None of the Western markets ever accounted for a significant part of the Cuban rum trade, however. Fidel Castro, the only Cuban whose judgment mattered, believed Cuba's future lay with the socialist East, not the capitalist West, and he cared more about satisfying the trade requirements of his Soviet bloc partners than about establishing new commercial relationships with Western companies. Between 1975 and 1984, the Soviet bloc took over 90 percent of Cuba's rum exports.

In return for its rum—as well as its tobacco, sugar, citrus products, and nickel—the socialist bloc gave Cuba virtually everything it needed. The Soviet Union shipped about thirteen million tons of oil each year to Cuba, about three million tons more than what the island needed. By selling the surplus on the world market, Fidel Castro's government earned more than $500 million a year in much-needed hard currency. Socialist countries also financed and built steel mills, oil refineries, fertilizer factories, and nickel plants in Cuba and provided the island with most of its manufactured goods and half its food supply. The trade was on highly favorable terms, and Cubans were able to enjoy a relatively good standard of living.

And then came the great shock: The whole socialist system suddenly unraveled, and Cuba was left on its own. In the late 1980s, Soviet premier Mikhail Gorbachev cast Marxist-Leninist orthodoxy aside and embraced free-market principles. When Fidel Castro defiantly refused to follow his example, Gorbachev insisted that Soviet aid to the island be restructured as loans rather than grants. But that was only the beginning. Encouraged by Gorbachev's reforms, citizens across Eastern Europe rose up in the summer and fall of 1989, toppling Communist regimes from Berlin to Bucharest and decisively repudiating the very ideology that was the basis of Fidel Castro's rule. Within months, new democratic governments took power across the region and began canceling the subsidized trade arrangements upon which Cuba depended. With the dissolution of the Soviet Union at the end of 1991, all its aid to Cuba—both military and economic—was eliminated. Russia and other former socialist countries continued to trade with Cuba, but only on the basis of international market prices.

For the Cuban economy, the effect was staggering. In 1989 Cuba received about six billion dollars in aid and subsidies from socialist allies; in 1992 it received zero. The effects of the U.S. trade embargo became a far more serious concern. Seeing an opportunity to undermine Castro's rule, the U.S. government in 1992 made the embargo even tighter. A fall in the market price of sugar, Cuba's main commodity export, made the situation still worse. Cuban economists estimate that the country's total output during the 1989–92 period shrank by at least 40 percent. With oil supplies cut in half, the industrial sector operated at only half its capacity. Factories were open only during daylight hours, and many closed during the months of July and August, with the workers being sent to the countryside to do agricultural work. Oxen replaced tractors in the fields.

Many observers predicted the Castro government would collapse under the strain, as surely and suddenly as the socialist governments of Eastern Europe had fallen. Castro himself seemed to welcome the crisis, just as he had embraced earlier life-or-death moments in his revolution—at the gates of the Moncada, in the Sierra Maestra mountains, at the Bay of Pigs, or during the nuclear showdown in October 1962. He would either survive or go down in glory, taking his revolution with him; the prospect of a final suicidal stand actually seemed to excite him. Faced with the collapse of the Soviet bloc, Castro replaced his old "fatherland or death" exhortation with a new one: "*socialism or death*." His speech before a meeting of the Communist Youth in April 1992 was pure bravado: "True revolutionaries never surrender, never sell out, never betray. That is for cowards, traitors and opportunists. None of us want that trash that [capitalists] are offering us. We prefer any sacrifice, any fate, to the humiliation that capitalism entails."

In reality, Castro knew he had no practical choice but to compromise if his regime were to survive. Within a year of that 1992 speech, he was grudgingly moving to allow reforms he had spurned just a few years earlier. Cubans would for the first time be allowed to hold hard currency, including U.S. dollars, and spend them in stores previously reserved for diplomats, tourists, and foreign businessmen. The reform made it possible for Cubans to receive cash remittances from their relatives in exile, providing the Cuban economy with a boost in foreign currency earnings. Castro also agreed to tolerate self-employment in Cuba, in areas ranging from shoe shining to handicrafts, and he allowed farmers' markets to reopen. But such reforms were not enough. Abandoned by his old socialist allies, Castro realized he would have to integrate Cuba with the West if his revolution were to survive. He would have to do business with capitalists.

The Cuban government in 1982 had authorized foreign investment on the island, as long as it was carried out through joint ventures with the Cuban state. The conditions were restrictive, however, limiting the foreign partner to a minority stake, and Castro did not bother to promote the few investment opportunities that did exist. He made no secret of his distaste for foreign capital, and the Cuban government offered minimal legal protection for those Western businesses willing to invest on the island. As of 1988, the only joint venture on the island was the Sol Palmeras Hotel at Varadero Beach, partly owned by Sol Meliá, a Spanish hotel company.

The Varadero venture was a logical starting point, however. Cuban officials knew that tourism, once scorned by Castro, held enormous potential for the island, and in 1990 the government loosened the labor regulations for tourism ventures, giving managers in those enterprises more leeway in firing and hiring decisions. Several more hotel developments soon followed. In 1992, three months after denouncing the "trash" that capitalism brought, Castro approved new terms for foreign investment in Cuba, allowing foreign partners in joint ventures to hold up to 50 percent of the shares and permitting them to repatriate all profits. "Capital and capitalism are not the same," he told a group of visiting businessmen and potential investors. "Capitalists will not be the own-ers of our country. The country will continue to be socialist." Foreign investors heard what they wanted to hear and ignored the rest. By 1993, the number of joint ventures in Cuba had risen to more than a hundred. Many were in tour-ism, but there was considerable foreign interest in other promising sectors of the Cuban economy, including nickel, tobacco, telecommunications...and rum.

. . .

When the Soviet bloc collapsed, so did Cuba's rum trade. Commercial rela-tions in the socialist world consisted largely of barter deals, and Cuba had been sending large quantities of rum to its allies in direct exchange for other prod-ucts. No attention was paid to marketing, and there were almost no commer-cial distribution networks of the type that existed in Western countries. Among the socialist allies, rum was treated as just another commodity, like sugar or oil. When the big government-to-government trade deals were suspended, most of Cuba's rum went unsold. In 1986 Cubaexport had shipped more than a half million cases of Havana Club to the Soviet Union and Eastern Europe. In 1992, with Cuba's trade relations reshaped by free-market forces, the agency managed to move only four hundred cases across the same region. About 175,000 cases were sold in the rest of the world that year, but it was the lowest Havana Club export volume in more than a decade.

The global changes affected the Cuban rum business more than the coun-try's sugar, citrus, or nickel industries, because those products were relatively undifferentiated and could be sold in quantity at prevailing world prices. Rum, on the other hand, had to be marketed. Consumers cared about brands and color and quality; they had to be convinced to buy Havana Club in particular rather than another spirit. Cuban state enterprises, moreover, had less experi-ence in brand promotion and advertising than did their Western commercial counterparts and were therefore not well positioned to compete, especially in those countries where Cuban products were not well known. If the Havana Club rum operation were to do well under the changed geopolitical circum-stances, it would need a foreign partner with marketing expertise.

There was immediate interest among Western companies. After Commu-nism's collapse, potential investors figured it was only a matter of time before Cuba would also make the transition to capitalism. Foreign firms were anxious to get an early foothold on the island, and the Cuban rum business held great promise. The tourism boom was bringing hundreds of thousands of foreign visitors to the island each year, and the number was rising sharply. Just as U.S. visitors to Cuba during the early part of the century had become fans of Bacardi rum, tourists in the 1990s were likely to go home hooked on Havana Club. Seagram's, the Canadian liquor giant, and Britain's International Distillers & Vintners (IDV) both began maneuvering to get a piece of the Cuban rum business.

The most eager suitor, however, was Pernod Ricard, the French company best known at the time for its anise spirits. The Pernod Ricard president and chief executive, Thierry Jacquillat, saw the possibility of a joint rum venture as a way to move Cuba toward a market economy. "The idea was that the Communists had failed," he said later. "I thought the Cuban people should get assistance from other countries than Russia. I thought it would be a good idea for them to work with European companies." In the fall of 1992, Jacquillat sent the Pernod Ricard director for Spain, Michel Bord, to Havana to inquire about the possibility of a joint French-Cuban venture to develop the Havana Club brand in Europe and beyond.

To Jacquillat's dismay, Bord came back from Havana with a pessimistic report. The Cubans, it seemed, had such strong emotional and cultural ties to their rum that they did not want to share it with a foreign capitalist partner. Selling oil exploration rights or access to Cuba's nickel deposits or beaches was one thing; rum was apparently something else. Bord told Jacquillat the Cubans with whom he met told him Havana Club was a "national jewel," and he predicted it would be "tough" to negotiate co-ownership of the brand with them. Jacquillat, however, was determined to pursue a deal. In Spain and a few other Western markets, Havana Club rum was already emerging as a top-performing brand. With more professional marketing and the Pernod Ricard distribution network, the brand clearly had growth potential.

The key official on the Cuban side was Luis Perdomo, a veteran Cuban bureaucrat who had gone from directing the state flour company to taking charge of rum production at the Empresa Bebidas y Licores (Beverage and Liquor Enterprise). Perdomo was a loyal member of the Cuban Communist Party, but he was also a savvy businessman, and he was not going to negotiate joint ownership of the Havana Club brand at anything below a steep price. In September 1993, he and other Cuban officials reached a tentative agreement with Pernod Ricard representatives on a joint venture: The Cubans would produce Havana Club rum, and Pernod Ricard would market it.

◆ ◆ ◆

Bacardi executives followed all these developments closely. Havana Club was by no means a serious competitor, but the Bacardis still resented that it was marketed as the "genuine" Cuban rum. Bacardi was now a multinational company with no overt connection to Cuba, but since the early 1960s the Bacardis had been determined to return to Cuba and reestablish operations there. At this key moment in Cuban history, they were not inclined to stand aside and let Fidel Castro and his foreign capitalist friends claim the heralded Cuban rum business for themselves.

Thirty years earlier, the Bacardis and the U.S. government had supported attempts to overthrow Fidel Castro by force. But it now appeared the Castro regime might collapse under its own weight, fatally weakened by the same maladies that had undermined Communist governments in the Soviet Union and Eastern Europe: inefficiency, corruption, mismanagement, and popular alienation. Around the world, the socialist model was proving to be unsustainable, and the suspense in Cuba lay mostly in the uncertainty of *how* the end would come, what would be preserved, and who would emerge in control of national jewels like the rum and tobacco industries.

The Bacardis had hoped there would be a sharp, clean break from the Castro era and a quick transition to democracy and a free-market economy. What was shaping up instead was a gradual and negotiated change. The Eastern Europe experience demonstrated that the end of Communist rule did not necessarily mean the end of power and privilege for the *nomenklatura* elite who had been on top during the years of dictatorship. Negotiated transitions to democracy were likely to leave many of the old elites in control of the very resources and institutions they had dominated previously. With the privatization of state-owned enterprises, the former managers of those enterprises could emerge with a big share of the profits, because they knew the assets of the enterprise and had all the important contacts. Too often, in Russia and elsewhere, the transition had not been from Communism to democracy and free markets, but from Communism to cronyism and more corruption. The battle looming might not be with Fidel Castro so much as with those other actors, including foreign corporations, who were positioning themselves to move in after Fidel was gone.

In October 1993, Bacardi chairman Manuel Jorge Cutillas wrote an open letter to liquor executives around the world cautioning them about investment deals with the Cuban government and warning that such actions could get them in legal trouble with his own company, which had not abandoned its claim to the Cuban assets it had lost more than thirty years earlier. "Bacardi has reason to believe that its properties are among those being offered by the Castro regime to prospective purchasers," Cutillas wrote.

It is Bacardi's position, supported by expert legal advice, that its confiscated assets continue to be its lawful property, and that no one who accepts a purported conveyance of any such property from the Castro regime will acquire good title under either Cuban or international law. Once the rule of law and representative government are restored in Cuba, Bacardi intends to take every appropriate step both to recover its properties and also to seek appropriate compensation from those who have acquired from the present regime, exploited and misused those properties during the period when Bacardi was deprived of their possession.

Thierry Jacquillat of Pernod Ricard was among those to receive the Bacardi letter, but he dismissed the warning as irrelevant. Pernod Ricard did not contemplate the purchase of any physical properties in Cuba and was not seeking any former Bacardi assets.

The contract that Pernod Ricard signed with the Cuban government created a joint venture company, Havana Club International, co-owned by Pernod Ricard and a new Cuban company, Corporación CubaRon, S.A. Legally, CubaRon was an independent private Cuban corporation, with individual shareholders, but in reality it was simply a spin-off of the rum-producing unit of the Bebidas y Licores state enterprise under the Ministry of Food. The capital came from the Cuban state, the profits went to the state, and the individual "shareholders" were Cuban government officials. Under the terms of the joint venture agreement, CubaRon was to produce and bottle Havana Club rum and then sell it to the joint venture. Pernod Ricard, as the French partner, would provide the marketing expertise and distribution network. Thierry Jacquillat flew to Havana for the signing ceremony, accompanied by Patrick Ricard, the chairman of the Pernod Ricard board. Fidel Castro hosted the men for dinner after giving his blessing to the enterprise.

The thirty-six-page joint venture agreement committed the Cuban authorities to "follow the usage of the market economy" in operating their rum business, something they had virtually no experience in doing. A "non-compete" clause obligated the Cuban government not to promote any of its other rum brands in export markets where Havana Club was sold. The agreement was drawn up under the close attention of Pernod Ricard lawyers, who knew their company could face litigation over the deal. One provision required the Cuban side to guarantee there was "no claim in or out of court against the owner of the [Havana Club] trademark...and that it is not aware of any reasons or circumstances that may cause a claim of this nature." The Arechabalas had last registered the mark in 1953 for a period of twenty years. Because the registration had since expired, Pernod Ricard was satisfied that the family had abandoned its claim to the mark.

Neither side divulged the price Pernod Ricard paid for its half of the Havana Club operation, though *Forbes* magazine reported it was fifty million dollars.

◆ ◆ ◆

Juan Prado, the veteran Bacardi rum salesman, felt some envy when he heard Pernod Ricard had completed the Havana Club deal. The fact that Pernod Ricard had been willing to work hard and spend a lot of money to get half of the "rights" to the rum trademark vindicated his earlier judgment that the Havana Club brand was a valuable asset. On the other hand, Prado was angry that Pernod Ricard had agreed to do business with Fidel Castro, a dictator responsible for driving a million Cubans into exile and imprisoning or executing thousands more. Prado had chosen Pernod Ricard to distribute Bacardi rum in France,* and along the way he had become friends with Thierry Jacquillat, the chief executive. When news of the deal with the Cuban government appeared in the press, Prado wrote to Jacquillat to chastise him:

December 3, 1993

> Dear Thierry,
> Because I am retiring at the end of the year and will be consulting for Bacardi in the area of Cuba issues, I have perhaps been more sensitive to the news of your agreement to distribute Havana Club worldwide. I must confess I was surprised.
>
> In case you are not aware, the Arechabalas are an honorable family whom I have known since I was a child, were illegally expatriated [sic] of all their properties in Cuba and obviously believe they own the brand.
>
> Please accept my apologies for commenting on your commercial decisions, but I felt our friendship has been sufficiently long standing to allow me to express my opinions.
>
> Regards,
>
> Juan Prado

Prado sent copies of the letter to his Bacardi boss, Manuel Jorge Cutillas, to

---

*After the 1992 acquisition of Martini & Rossi, which had an excellent distribution system in France, Bacardi cut its ties with Pernod Ricard. Prado and other Bacardi executives realized that one of the reasons the French firm pursued Havana Club was to replace Bacardi in its own distribution network, and their annoyance with Pernod Ricard was somewhat moderated by that understanding.

Patrick Ricard, and to Ramón Arechabala in Miami, the former Havana Club sales manager with whom Bacardi executives had discussed a deal twenty years earlier in Nassau. The 1973 talks had gone nowhere, but the news of the Havana Club deal made the Arechabalas players in the Cuba drama once again.

Eleven days after hearing from Juan Prado, Ramón himself sent a letter to Patrick Ricard, saying he and other members of his family were "concerned" that Pernod Ricard had agreed to market the Cuban government's rum under the Arechabalas' old label. More than thirty years had passed since the Arechabala family had given up their rum business, but Ramón said he and his relatives still intended to take steps "to recover possession of our property and also to seek appropriate compensation from those who have exploited and misused those properties when we were deprived of their possession," language that appeared to be lifted almost word for word from the letter Manuel Jorge Cutillas had sent out six weeks earlier. Pernod Ricard executives interpreted the Arechabala letter, with its echo of the Cutillas warning, as an indication that Bacardi might join forces with the former Arechabala shareholders and take Pernod Ricard to court. Thierry Jacquillat said later that he took the Bacardi message to be: "Cuba is ours; don't touch it."

There was little Bacardi could do to stop Pernod Ricard from becoming the lead Cuban rum distributor in Europe and elsewhere, but the company directors were determined to try. If the Arechabalas would sell Bacardi their historic "rights" to the Havana Club trademark, the Bacardis could take the lead in opposing Pernod Ricard's use of it. Thierry Jacquillat may not have been far off when he characterized the Bacardi viewpoint as "Cuba is ours." For nearly a century, it had been. The Bacardis' ties to their homeland had been broken only when they lost their business and were compelled to leave the island. The idea that a European company like Pernod Ricard could now claim to represent "genuine" Cuban rum was simply unacceptable to the Bacardi old-timers.

In early 1994, Manuel Jorge Cutillas flew to Spain to discuss a possible purchase of the Arechabalas' claim to the Havana Club trademark. When he arrived in Madrid, Cutillas found out that Bacardi was not the only company with that idea. A Pernod Ricard lawyer had offered the Arechabalas one hundred thousand dollars in exchange for abandoning any Havana Club claim they might have. The family had rejected the offer outright, but it was talking with another company, International Distillers & Vintners, the same British company that just a few months earlier had been negotiating with the Cuban government for a piece of the Havana Club business. Having lost out to Pernod Ricard, IDV was proposing a joint venture with the Arechabalas to redevelop the "Havana Club" trademark outside Cuba. After a few months, however,

IDV suddenly lost interest. The Arechabalas' door was finally open to Bacardi.

. . .

The new Havana Club operation in Cuba got off to a promising start. With Pernod Ricard's informal assistance, the Cubans strengthened their quality control procedures and upgraded their bottling operation, with a higher grade of glass and better bottle caps. Efficiency concerns did not figure very highly in the Cubans' approach to business, but this factor may actually have worked in favor of higher-quality products. Even their young rums were aged for three years in old barrels, a practice that more profit-oriented enterprises would have been less likely to follow, given that it made it more difficult to achieve high-volume, low-cost production. As a result, the Cubans' "white" rum product was slightly yellow, like white wine. The Cubans had never highlighted this difference, but the Pernod Ricard team immediately recognized it as an advantage. A clear white product would have been harder to differentiate from the much-better-known Bacardi brand, but a straw-colored rum could be presented as distinctively Cuban, more highly aged, slightly more flavorful, and marketable at a premium price. The new advertising strategy for Havana Club rum in European markets featured a heavy emphasis on its age and its Cuban origin. Every bottle carried a bright red banner with the phrase *"El Ron de Cuba"* (The Rum of Cuba).

To the Cuba-born Bacardis who remembered their own company's old advertising on the island, the slogan grated. To younger Bacardi executives who focused more on marketing, the French-Cuban venture was worrisome for the commercial challenge it presented. Six months after the establishment of Havana Club International, the Bacardi distributor in Spain sent a memorandum to his company headquarters advising that Havana Club already had "a high image level" in the country and that he and his sales agents were seeing "steady growth in HC brand awareness." The Pernod Ricard strategy in Spain was to tie the rum marketing to the promotion of Cuban tourism; any bar owner who could move a hundred cases of Havana Club was offered a free trip for two people to Cuba. "When the bar owners come back from Cuba," the distributor reported, "they are the best public relations for the brand, and they recommend it as the authentic rum." Havana Club International was flying Cuban bartenders to Spain and sending them on tours around the country, demonstrating how to make genuine mojitos, daiquiris, and Cuba libres, thus spurring new demand for Cuban rum. The Madrid agent warned that the French-Cuban brand would soon present "a real threat" to Bacardi commercial interests in Spain.

The report on Havana Club's success in Spain raised two concerns for Bacardi marketing strategists. The first was the likelihood that demand for the Cuban rum would spread throughout the European market, as more Europeans visited the island as tourists. The second concern was even more sobering. With Fidel Castro appearing to be losing his grip on Cuba, the possibility of major political changes there seemed greater than it had been in many years. President Bill Clinton was considering a diplomatic opening to Cuba. An end to the U.S. trade embargo was a real possibility, meaning that genuine made-in-Cuba rum might soon become available again for sale in the United States. As things now stood, that rum would be Havana Club, marketed and distributed by one of Bacardi's top corporate rivals.

For more than thirty years, Bacardi advertising in the United States had made no mention of the rum's origins in Cuba. The island was associated with Communism and revolution, and few Americans visited. But the prospect of the island's opening sparked a sudden surge of interest in all things Cuban. For the first time, Bacardi executives began exploring the possibility of developing and introducing a new Cuba-themed rum of their own, to be promoted with reference to Bacardi's own Cuban heritage.

But it would take more than another product and a new marketing campaign to address the Havana Club threat. Bacardi needed to challenge Pernod Ricard directly, on political or even legal grounds. After all, Havana Club's entrance into the U.S. rum market presented more than just commercial issues; behind it was a European company partnering with the Castro regime, just as Cuba was changing. The joint venture raised the possibility that the post-Castro scene could be dominated by foreign corporate interests in collusion with the Communist elite, to the exclusion of exiles and other marginalized parties.

The Bacardis' political activism on Cuba issues until then had been largely private, prompted by the family's own sense of betrayal by Fidel Castro, but their political and commercial interests were now coinciding. It was time to go to Washington as Bacardi Limited, the corporate heavyweight, rather than as individual Bacardi family members. The company prepared to join the Arechabalas in arguing that it was unfair of Pernod Ricard to "purchase" co-ownership of the old family trademark from a dictator who had confiscated it without compensation years earlier. If the argument was successful, the French company might be thwarted in its attempt to bring Havana Club rum to the U.S. market. But there was more at stake than a commercial rivalry. Cuban rum was indeed a "national jewel," and the maneuvering for control of the industry in the post-Castro years was a fight for the future of Cuba itself.

Chapter 22

❧❧❧

Rum Politics

The Biltmore Hotel in Coral Gables was built around the same time as the Hotel Nacional in Havana, in the same grand Mediterranean revival style, with a towering orange belfry, sprawling grounds, and a driveway lined by palm trees. The hotel is in the heart of the Coral Gables residential area, where the wealthiest Cuban exiles in south Florida live in verdant splendor, surrounded by tropical gardens and exotic banyan trees. With its vaulted ceilings and Moorish colonnades, the Biltmore is the favored local venue for gatherings of the exile elite, perhaps because it is reminiscent of the glamour and beauty of Old Havana.

It was at the Biltmore, on a hot and humid Monday in April 1995, that about 150 prominent members of Miami's Cuban-American community gathered in a chandeliered ballroom for a $500-a-plate luncheon in honor of Republican Senator Jesse Helms of North Carolina. Helms was one of the most vociferous foes of Fidel Castro in the U.S. Congress, and he had come to Miami for the anniversary of the 1961 Bay of Pigs invasion, an occasion that each year prompted noisy demonstrations in the streets of Little Havana. He was introduced at the Biltmore that day by Jorge Mas Canosa, the head of the Cuban American National Foundation (CANF), and by Rodolfo Ruiz, the president and chief executive of Bacardi-Martini, the U.S. subsidiary formerly called Bacardi Imports.

The luncheon cohosts represented an alliance born more than thirty years earlier. Jorge Mas Canosa had gotten his start in exile politics as a director of Representación Cubana del Exilio (RECE), the exile action group founded by Bacardi boss Pepín Bosch, and the political firebrand had risen to prominence in the Cuban-American community as editor of the Bacardi-funded RECE newsletter. By 1995, Mas was himself a political kingmaker and multimillionaire businessman, having long since traded his milkman uniforms for expensively tailored double-breasted suits, but when he needed help sponsoring a CANF fund-raiser for Jesse Helms, it was to Bacardi that he quietly turned. Bacardi family money had underwritten CANF activities for years. Rodolfo Ruiz was not a family member, but, like other key Bacardi executives, he was a Cuba native, and when it came to Cuban matters he shared the Bacardi ethos. In his introductory remarks at the Biltmore luncheon, Ruiz praised Helms's commitment to the cause of freedom for the Cuban nation. Ruiz had come to the United States alone at the age of twelve, one of the approximately fourteen thousand children whose parents sent them unaccompanied out of Cuba under the U.S. government program known as Operation Peter Pan, and he was as committed to the anti-Castro struggle as anyone in the room.

The luncheon at the Biltmore netted about fifty-six thousand dollars for Helms's reelection campaign war chest, according to Federal Election Commission records. Among the Bacardi people in attendance, besides Ruiz, were the Bay of Pigs veteran José Bacardi, Juan Prado, the veteran salesman who had been assigned to coordinate Bacardi company planning on Cuba-related issues, Jorge Rodríguez, a Bacardi public relations executive married to Daniel Bacardi's niece, and several guests who came at the company's invitation. The fund-raiser was not a big event, and it was hardly the first time individual Bacardi family members or executives had rallied behind a Washington politician who was willing to speak out against Fidel Castro. The Bacardi participation in the Helms luncheon was noteworthy, however, because it coincided with an important new development: The company itself was staking out a position in the U.S.-Cuba policy debate. While it had previously made known its determination to reclaim its confiscated properties on the island, Bacardi as a corporate entity had largely steered clear of Washington politics around the Cuba issue. That was now changing.

A year earlier, Bacardi took a lead role in organizing the U.S.-Cuba Business Council, a corporate group established to focus on U.S.-Cuba trade and investment issues in advance of the expected transition to the post-Castro era. About a dozen U.S. companies, from Chiquita Brands and Amstar (a sugar company) to the Coopers & Lybrand accounting firm, also joined the Council, but Bacardi was the instigator, and Bacardi CEO Manuel Jorge Cutillas was the first chairman. At the time, many U.S. companies were eager to invest in Cuba, but the Council recommended that the U.S. government move slowly in restoring trade with the island. The Council's founding mission statement, issued over Cutillas's name, said it would argue that the rule of law and respect for private property rights should be seen "as necessary conditions for U.S. commercial activity and economic development in Cuba."

An even clearer sign of the new Bacardi outspokenness around Cuba questions came in October 1994, when Miami-based Bacardi-Martini fired its public relations firm, Burson-Marsteller, after two of the PR agency's vice presidents criticized the Cuba trade embargo in a public forum. As soon as news of their comments reached Rodolfo Ruiz at Bacardi headquarters in Miami, he canceled the firm's multimillion-dollar contract. At the time, the Clinton administration was weighing a relaxation of the trade sanctions. "It is exactly because of the increasing pressures on the Administration to change the embargo that we came out strongly," Ruiz told a reporter. He said Bacardi-Martini was ending its relationship with Burson-Marsteller in order "to make the [U.S.] government aware that to lift the embargo is the last thing that should be considered." Such unambiguous political pronouncements were virtually unprecedented for the company. Bacardi support for exile causes had generally been low profile. The funding of the tiny RECE operation, for example, amounted only to a few thousand dollars a month, largely for office expenses and one or two salaries, and few people outside Cuban exile circles even knew about it.

Ironically, the new Bacardi corporate interest in the U.S. government's Cuba policy came just as the company's own Cuban character had been diluted as a result of the Martini & Rossi acquisition. Bacardi Limited had become a big, multibrand global corporation, and each year the shareholders paid more attention to dividend returns and stock value and less to the old Bacardi mission "to raise high the name of Cuba" and reclaim their Cuban heritage. To be sure, family members were enraged when they discovered that some of the "Havana Club" rum marketed internationally by Pernod Ricard had been produced at the old Bacardi factory on Matadero Street in Santiago. But by 1994 the company's involvement in U.S.-Cuba policy discussions was driven less by revanchist exile passions than by concerns about the commercial threat that a Cuban rum backed by Pernod Ricard would present in the U.S. market. More broadly, Bacardi worried that the French company (and other Western partners) could prolong the life of the Castro regime by providing it with badly needed capital and professional expertise. Given its own history on the island, Bacardi would be able to return to Cuba only after Castro was gone, so any action by Pernod Ricard or any other firm that postponed the regime's definitive collapse was injurious to Bacardi interests. Family passions aside, the company had a clear strategic interest in supporting U.S. policies that would bring a clean end to the Castro era, as opposed to a gradual or negotiated transition.

In February 1995, two months before his visit to Miami, Jesse Helms had introduced new sanctions legislation that targeted foreign companies investing in Cuba. Republican congressman Dan Burton of Indiana sponsored companion legislation in the House, and their proposal became known as the Helms-Burton bill. One of the bill's novel features was that it took up the cause of Cuban-Americans whose properties had been confiscated by the Castro regime. The original U.S. trade embargo against Cuba had been prompted by Castro's seizure of the property of U.S. citizens and companies, but the interests of Cubans who had suffered losses were not taken into consideration. Helms-Burton changed that, by offering Cuban-Americans the opportunity to sue, in U.S. courts, any foreign firm that was making use of their confiscated assets in Cuba. That provision, Title III of the bill, was largely the work of Daniel Fisk, the staff director of the Senate Foreign Relations Committee (which Helms chaired) and Ignacio Sánchez, a young Cuban-American lawyer from Miami. Bacardi was not originally a prime mover behind the Helms-Burton legislation, but the bill soon caught the attention of company lawyers. Title III offered a weapon Bacardi could potentially use against any firm that touched former Bacardi properties in Cuba, including Pernod Ricard. The legislation would not apply to a non-U.S. firm like Bacardi Limited, the parent company in Bermuda, but its Miami-based subsidiary, Bacardi-Martini, in theory could initiate a lawsuit. The company was soon tagged as the leading corporate backer of the Helms-Burton legislation, and critics took to calling it the Bacardi Claims Act.

The old Bacardi-Cuba dynamic was entering a new, more controversial phase. For the first time in thirty years, the company's Cuba agenda was tied to specific pieces of U.S. legislation and to particular members of Congress. Commercial, moral, and political considerations regarding Cuba were blended together, exposing the company to charges that it was exploiting anti-Castro sentiment in part to advance its own business interests. The focus of the new Bacardi activism was Washington, not Havana. While Pepín Bosch had attempted to subvert Castro's rule through action on Cuban soil, the Bacardi battle over the developing Cuban rum business would be fought in the U.S. courts, in the U.S. Congress, and in federal agency offices. Over the next few years, Bacardi would acquire a reputation in Washington for aggressive lobbying, just as the corrupting effect of special-interest money on the political process was becoming a major reform issue.

The family and its corporate directors had earned considerable respect over the years for their remarkable business success and their progressive outlook. Now it was time to draw on some of that goodwill. To meet the new Bacardi goals on Cuba, the company joined the ranks of firms jostling for position and influence on Capitol Hill, unseemly though the exercise inevitably would be.

The Helms-Burton law, enacted in March 1996, proved to be of little use to Bacardi in the company's effort to challenge Pernod Ricard's investment in the Cuban rum industry. Presidents Bill Clinton and George W. Bush both waived application of the Title III civil lawsuit provision, meaning Bacardi and other Cuban-American interests were not authorized to initiate court fights against foreign firms "trafficking" in their former assets. It would have been an uphill fight for Bacardi in any case. After the first year or two of its operations in Cuba, Pernod Ricard had generally been careful to avoid contact with any former Bacardi properties. The party with the best case against Pernod Ricard was the Arechabala family, which saw its rum brand adopted by the French-Cuban joint venture and used around the world. But most of the Arechabalas lived in Spain, not the United States. They had abandoned the rum business and did not have the resources to go up against Pernod Ricard and the Cuban government. If there was to be a battle over Havana Club, the Bacardis would have to wage it on the Arechabalas' behalf.

Thus began the "rum war" of the 1990s. It would be a highly technical, at times arcane, struggle involving trademark and property law, international treaties, and the U.S. embargo. For all its complexity, however, the underlying questions in the dispute were fairly straightforward: When could Cuban rum be sold in the United States, by what company, and under what label? Though it came at a time when Fidel Castro was still in vigorous health, it was arguably the first big fight about post-Castro Cuba. Among the parties represented were the key players in Cuba's future—exile interests, foreign capital, and the U.S. and Cuban governments—and the battle foreshadowed legal and political issues that were certain to come up again and again.

The Bacardi legal strategy was to acquire the Arechabalas' claim to the Havana Club trademark and then defend it in the U.S. courts as if it were a Bacardi brand. The U.S. Patent and Trademark Office had given the Havana Club trademark to the Cuban government in 1976, but Bacardi lawyers would argue that the reassignment was invalid because the trademark had been illegally confiscated. The Havana Club brand therefore had remained the property of the Arechabalas, meaning that Bacardi had the right to buy the brand and use it. If Bacardi won, Pernod Ricard and its Cuban partner would not be able to export rum to the United States under the Havana Club label, even after the embargo was lifted, barring a settlement.

One problem with this strategy was that the Cubans generally did all they could to avoid being drawn into any U.S. litigation. Because of the trade embargo, no Havana Club rum was being sold in the United States, so there was nothing to contest. Somehow, Bacardi lawyers had to provoke a fight. In the fall of 1995, the company shipped sixteen cases of rum bearing a hastily prepared "Havana Club" label from the Nassau distillery to a company warehouse in Jacksonville, Florida. It was a bold act. The Arechabalas had not yet formally agreed to sell Bacardi their trademark rights, though the two sides were in negotiation. The token shipment was meant purely to demonstrate the company's "intent to use" the Havana Club trademark and—more importantly— to goad its French-Cuban adversary into a fight. But it worked. In December 1996, Pernod Ricard and its Cuban partner sued Bacardi in a New York federal district court, charging that the Bacardi version of "Havana Club" rum represented a trademark infringement. The stage was set for an epic legal confrontation.

In April 1997, Bacardi officially acquired the Arechabalas' claim to the Havana Club trademark and the family's former properties in Cuba for a mere $1.25 million. By comparison, Bacardi had paid more than two *billion* dollars for the Martini & Rossi brand five years earlier. Still, Bacardi gave the Arechabalas more than ten times what Pernod Ricard had offered. In truth, the Arechabalas were in no position to demand a higher price, because it was far from clear that any court would recognize their claim, given that they had not produced their rum for more than thirty years, that they had allowed their trademark registration in the United States (and other countries) to lapse, and that a Cuban government agency in the meantime had registered the Havana Club trademark as its own, following all required legal procedures.

For two years, the opposing sides filed a series of claims and counterclaims. The presiding federal judge, Shira Scheindlin, dismissed some of the claims but decided the issues were difficult enough to warrant a bench trial. Both sides immediately launched civil discovery efforts, taking depositions and gathering documents to buttress their respective cases. Some Bacardi family members wondered what the company might be getting itself into. Bacardi had grown over the years by investing in new distilling facilities around the world, by developing successful marketing campaigns, and more recently by beginning to build a diversified brand portfolio. The management was now proposing that the company spend millions of dollars on litigation in order to take control of a trademark already in use by a key rival. To some board members, it looked like "investing in a lawsuit."

The initiative happened to coincide with a leadership change at the company. In March 1997, Bacardi chairman Manuel Jorge Cutillas relinquished his chief executive position, with the management responsibilities going to his executive vice president, George Reid, the lawyer who had helped resolve the intrafamily legal dispute five years earlier and then directed the company's reorganization. Reid relished the idea of a new courtroom battle with Fidel Castro's lawyers, although in his private presentations to the Bacardi board, he was careful to sell the Havana Club litigation strictly as a business proposition. The stakes were only growing higher. In the first four years of the French-Cuban joint venture, Havana Club sales doubled. By 1997, they were generating at least $60 million yearly, even without a presence in the key U.S. market. Bacardi remained far ahead, but a significant commercial rivalry was developing.

. . .

The Havana Club trial opened in New York before Judge Scheindlin in January 1999. Cuban officials of the state-owned Corporación CubaRon, which produced the Havana Club rum, were called from Havana to testify. Bacardi executives flew in from Miami and Nassau, and Pernod Ricard executives came from Paris. Lawyers for the French-Cuban partnership argued that their enterprise had established its rights to the Havana Club trademark and that Bacardi was attempting to take the trademark away because it feared commercial competition. The joint venture lawyers wanted to keep the trial focused narrowly on trademark law, as opposed to the highly charged politics of U.S.-Cuban relations. They reminded the judge that the Arechabala heirs had allowed their Havana Club trademark registration to lapse in 1973, even though they could have renewed it by paying a small fee and filing a "certificate of non-use" stating that they had abandoned the rum business only because Fidel Castro had taken it over. U.S. courts had consistently ruled that the owners of firms expropriated by the Castro regime were entitled to maintain their trademark registrations in the United States, as long as they made an effort to do so. The Cuban government had waited until the Arechabalas' registration expired before attempting to claim the Havana Club trademark for itself. Those were the essential facts, in the French-Cuban view.

For their part, the Bacardi lawyers set out from the beginning to steer the case away from trademark law issues and toward Castro's 1960 expropriation of the Arechabalas' business. They contended that the Cuban government stole the Havana Club trademark from the Arechabala family and therefore could not claim ownership. Bacardi's lead lawyer in the trial, William Golden, made his position clear in his opening statement. "Your honor," he said, "although this case has come to be called the Havana Club case, *it's really not about trademarks.* What this case is really all about is the right to private property." It was a point the Bacardi team would emphasize again and again. "Don't start with the premise that Cuba is a legitimate regime," lawyer Ignacio Sánchez advised a reporter. "Start with the premise that Castro's confiscations were illegal."

The problem for the Bacardi team was that U.S. and international trademark laws and agreements did not establish different rules for "legitimate" and "illegitimate" governments. If the Havana Club litigation were to be decided purely on the basis of preexisting law and case precedent, an outcome favorable to Bacardi was far from certain. Sánchez himself recognized what he later called the "vulnerabilities" in Bacardi's legal position: Existing U.S. legislation might well allow the registration of a trademark acquired as a result of the Cuban government confiscating a firm, as long as the prior owner of the mark did not take the necessary steps to protect it. In order for Bacardi to prevail in this fight, the U.S. Congress might actually need to pass another trademark law that would specifically cover the Havana Club situation.

Ignacio Sánchez drafted the legislative language. Congress, he said, should prohibit the Cuban government from registering a trademark that it acquired as a result of a property confiscation, unless the prior trademark owner gave permission. The provision he had in mind would effectively instruct U.S. courts, under certain conditions, to disregard the 1928 Inter-American Convention for Trademark Protection, and it would have retroactive effect. He introduced his proposal at a May 1998 House Judiciary subcommittee hearing dedicated to "miscellaneous patent and trademark issues." In his testimony, Sánchez cited just one example of what should be disallowed: the Cuban government's 1976 registration of the Havana Club trademark.

The Sánchez proposal was just one of six issues the subcommittee reviewed that spring day, and in the following months it could easily have been lost in the flood of legislative ideas drawn up to favor specific individuals or firms. With the dispute between Bacardi and Pernod Ricard about to go to trial, however, the Bacardi team was determined to get the provision enacted, and quickly. The company got a Florida senator, Republican Connie Mack, to advocate the Sánchez suggestion, even though only a few members of Congress knew the issue had even been raised. For the first time in its history, Bacardi also hired a legislative lobbyist, Jonathan Slade, one of the many Capitol Hill operatives who know how to negotiate deals and deliver results. Slade had been the chief lobbyist for the Cuban American National Foundation, which under Jorge Mas Canosa's leadership was famous for treating adversaries harshly and allies generously.

In a few weeks, Slade worked with Senator Mack and his fellow Florida senator, Democrat Bob Graham, and with Lincoln Diaz-Balart and Ileana

Ros-Lehtinen, both Republicans, in the House of Representatives to get the pro-Bacardi trademark law changes inserted in the Omnibus Appropriations Act of 1999 during House-Senate consultations on the pending legislation. A provision prohibiting U.S. courts from upholding most trademarks "used in connection with a business or with assets that were confiscated" by the Cuban government became Section 211 of the spending bill, one of many such extraneous provisions inserted at the last minute. It was barely noticeable, a few paragraphs tucked into a piece of legislation so massive that the printed version was sixteen inches thick and weighed forty pounds. It passed without protest. The Section 211 provision had been informally approved by the Republican leaders of the relevant congressional committees, but with the exception of the May hearing, the legislation was not openly discussed or analyzed, and few members of Congress realized the full ramifications of its passage.

· · ·

The Section 211 legislation effectively trumped the major legal issues in the Havana Club trial. U.S. judicial doctrine was clear: When Congress deliberately acts to override a treaty, the congressional intention takes precedence. Judge Scheindlin's ruling in April 1999 therefore came as no surprise. Section 211, she wrote, "would appear to prevent Havana Club International from asserting its trade name claims." Because of the legislation's retroactive effect, Pernod Ricard and the Cuban government had lost their right to claim the Havana Club trademark. Scheindlin made clear, however, that her ruling did not address the issue of whether the Arechabalas were still in ownership of the brand at the time they sold it to Bacardi. While Judge Scheindlin had effectively taken the trademark away from the French-Cuban venture, she had not given it back to the Arechabalas, or to Bacardi as their successor in rights.

In the aftermath of Scheindlin's decision, the new legislation was suddenly the subject of feverish discussion. Fidel Castro was outraged, saying the rejection of the Cuban government's duly registered trademarks was a "bald-faced violation of international law." The general counsel for Pernod Ricard, Pierre-Marie Chateauneuf, said the legislative intervention unfairly affected his company's litigation effort against Bacardi. "It is exactly as if at the end of a soccer game the referee says, 'O.K. guys, I'm sorry, but the rules of this game changed while you were playing.'" The French company persuaded the European Union to challenge the new U.S. trademark law at the World Trade Organization (WTO) as an abrogation of international trade agreements.

Even some Bacardi allies had mixed feelings about the legislation. Daniel Fisk, the Jesse Helms aide who had worked with Ignacio Sánchez and other

Bacardi lawyers on the Helms-Burton Act, said later he understood why the company felt it had to push for the 211 provision, but he was not sure it was a good idea for Congress to pass legislation concerning legal issues that were in litigation at the time. "The question about 211," Fisk said in a 2000 interview, "is whether the judicial process should be interrupted by [Congress] telling the courts, 'We're going to take jurisdiction away from you.'" Fisk pointed out that whereas the 1996 Helms-Burton Act was intended to advance broad U.S. interests with respect to Cuba, Section 211 "was written with one entity in mind—Bacardi."

The legal and political fight over Havana Club had turned bitter. Bacardi and Pernod Ricard were both highly successful, professionally managed liquor empires, and in the past they had enjoyed amicable relations. But one company was Cuban and the other was French, and under the condition of conflict each reverted to a stubborn cultural type. As worldly and capitalist as Bacardi had become, down deep it still had a passionate Cuban temperament, and nothing burned its corporate soul like the thought of Fidel Castro laying claim to the Cuban rum tradition. For Cuba-born Bacardi executives and family members, the fight took on an emotional dimension that non-Cubans would never understand. As for Pernod Ricard, the trademark battle inevitably became a struggle to uphold French national honor. An American representative of the French firm tried in vain to convince the Paris-based management that the company should consider developing an entirely new Cuban rum brand with a trademark that Bacardi could not oppose. After all, only a tiny minority of American drinkers had ever heard of "Havana Club" rum anyway. Why fight so hard for a brand that hardly anyone recognized? But the Pernod Ricard management wouldn't budge. "It was a matter of French pride," the American executive said. "They just could not back down."

The third party in the dispute—the Cuban government—only made matters worse. To Fidel Castro, the Havana Club battle was a propaganda opportunity. Cuban accounts of the trademark dispute portrayed Bacardi as a thieving commercial predator and the leader of Cuba's exile "mafia." In European leftist circles, the Section 211 controversy spurred a "Boycott Bacardi" movement that also played to Castro's advantage. A retelling of the Bacardi story by one solidarity group began by saying the family's fortune "was accumulated in pre-Revolutionary Cuba through the exploitation of impoverished Cuban sugar workers," and it ended by declaring that Bacardi was so intent on destroying "the real Cuban Havana Club" that it "resorted to stealing its label." It made a powerful narrative, and keeping it alive apparently mattered more to Fidel Castro than any chance to resolve the trademark dispute quietly. Sources in both the Bacardi and Pernod Ricard managements said Castro personally blocked at least one proposal for an out-of-court settlement of the Havana Club case.

• • •

The big winners in the rum trademark war were lawyers and lobbyists. Litigation and representation fees rose well into the millions of dollars for both sides, and with appeals and unresolved issues, the end was not in sight. To Bacardi's dismay, the U.S. Patent and Trademark Office did not immediately cancel the Cuban government's registration of the Havana Club trademark in spite of the federal court ruling (the ruling barred only the enforcement of the trademark, not the trademark itself), nor did it give the Havana Club mark to Bacardi. The battle took yet another turn in January 2002, when the World Trade Organization dispute settlement board concluded that parts of the Section 211 legislation violated U.S. trade commitments and needed to be amended by Congress to conform to WTO rules. As enacted, the U.S. prohibition against registering confiscated trademarks appeared to apply only to Cuban petitioners, a feature the WTO considered discriminatory. Bacardi thus found itself needing help from both the executive and the legislative branches of the U.S. government in order to press its claim to the Havana Club brand. The stage was set for a massive lobbying push. It was time for Bacardi to get seriously into the money-and-politics game.

The company was a relative latecomer to the world of lobbyists and political fund-raising, but it quickly become a major player. In the 1996 election cycle, Bacardi-Martini made just ten thousand dollars in political contributions at the federal level. Two years later, with the company pushing for a change in U.S. trademark law, its contributions jumped to nearly $110,000, with Bacardi family members and employees contributing another $44,000, to Republicans and Democrats alike. For the 2000 election cycle, Bacardi political contributions soared again, with the company giving more than $400,000 to party organizations, political action committees, and advocacy groups. The company also became active in Florida state politics. From 1998 to 2002, Bacardi political contributions in Florida totaled about $240,000, with more than 90 percent of the total going to the Florida Republican Party, under the leadership of Governor Jeb Bush, a Bacardi friend.

The company's political activism was spearheaded by two individuals, lobbyist Jonathan Slade in Washington and in Miami by Jorge Rodríguez, the Bacardi vice president for corporate communications (and a Bacardi son-in-law). Like many lobbyists, Slade specialized in gathering individual and corporate contributions in "bundles" earmarked for particular candidates or groups with whom the company wanted to establish a friendly relationship. Rodríguez, meanwhile, worked the Florida political scene. His top priority was to get the Patent and Trademark Office in Washington to settle the Havana Club issue definitively in Bacardi's favor, and his plan was to get his ally Jeb Bush to intervene with the agency on Bacardi's behalf.

"We need your help," Rodríguez e-mailed Bush in January 2002.

Bush responded within twenty-four hours: "Jorge, I will see what I can do."

It was the first of dozens of e-mail exchanges over the next several months between Rodríguez, Bush, and the governor's staff in Florida and Washington, all focusing on Bacardi's effort to get the PTO and the Office of Foreign Assets Control (OFAC) to take the Havana Club mark away from the French-Cuban venture and give it to Bacardi. As the months went by, Rodríguez became increasingly demanding. By April, he was furious with the lack of action on the part of what he called the "bureaucrats" at the PTO and OFAC. "This application NEEDS to be denied," Rodríguez wrote to a D.C.-based aide to Governor Bush, referring to the French-Cuban request for a renewal of the Havana Club trademark registration.

On April 23, the governor's Washington office notified Jeb Bush that his brother, President George W. Bush, had appointed a former Republican congressman from California, James Rogan, to oversee the Patent and Trademark Office. The governor's staff—guided by Jorge Rodríguez—immediately began drafting a letter for the governor to send to Rogan, explaining the Bacardi case. On May 23, Rodríguez arranged a $50,000 Bacardi contribution to the Florida Republican Party. Two weeks later, a slightly revised version of the letter drafted by Rodríguez and others went out over the governor's signature, with Jeb Bush asking Rogan to take "quick, decisive action" in Bacardi's favor. Rodríguez and the governor both insisted later that there was no connection between the Bacardi contribution and the subsequent letter written on Bacardi's behalf.

Meanwhile, the company faced the challenge of arranging a legislative "fix" to bring the Section 211 law into conformity with the WTO requirements. Senator Connie Mack, who had been so helpful in getting Section 211 enacted, had retired in 2000, but Bacardi lobbyist Jonathan Slade had found a new ally in Republican Tom DeLay of Texas. DeLay was second to no one in the U.S. Congress in his hatred for Fidel Castro, and he was almost as famous for holding the French in contempt, so he was a natural Bacardi ally in this fight.

As the House majority whip, DeLay was so effective in lining up Republican votes for his favored initiatives that he was called The Hammer. He was also known, however, for his "pay to play" approach. Special-interest groups or corporations who wanted DeLay on their side were expected to contribute generously to Republican coffers, in ways designated by DeLay or his associates. DeLay created or oversaw a vast network of political action committees, state party organizations, and other advocacy organizations. Jonathan Slade and the other Bacardi lobbyists knew that if they wanted DeLay's help in protecting the Section 211 achievement, it would be a good idea to support his various fund-raising efforts.

Bacardi USA (as Bacardi-Martini had been renamed) was credited with a December 31, 2001, contribution of $20,000 to DeLay's "leadership committee," Americans for a Republican Majority. DeLay's top priority at the time was to help Republican candidates during the 2002 state legislative elections in Texas, where the Democrats had long ruled. If the Republicans took control, DeLay figured, the legislature could then redraw congressional district boundaries and produce more districts that leaned Republican. Business groups and lobbyists who wanted to gain influence with DeLay were instructed to contribute to the political action committees that had been set up to bring about Republican control in the state. In July 2002, Bacardi USA followed up with a second $20,000 contribution, this one to DeLay's Texans for a Republican Majority. With those contributions, Bacardi became one of DeLay's leading backers.

One year later, DeLay took up the Bacardi cause in Washington, agreeing to amend the Section 211 language to make it apply to all confiscated trademarks, not just those expropriated by the Cuban government. Such a change would presumably make the law acceptable to the WTO and thus preserve the protection it afforded Bacardi in the company's standoff with Pernod Ricard and its Cuban partner. DeLay's spokesman, Jonathan Grella, bristled at the suggestion that DeLay's action was a quid pro quo for the Bacardi donations, saying that his boss was only seeking "to protect American companies from predatory French companies that are conspiring with a murderous dictator." In truth, DeLay needed little encouragement to go after a French firm allied with Fidel Castro, but the Texas congressman customarily demanded contributions from all his corporate allies.

In October 2003, DeLay attempted to insert the Section 211 revision into the 2004 Defense Authorization Act. His intention was to move quietly, without hearings or debate, as Florida senator Connie Mack had done in promoting the original legislation five years earlier. This time, however, the maneuver encountered opposition, and it had to be dropped. A second attempt the following spring also failed, due at least in part to controversy over the Bacardi-DeLay connection.

Before the congressional session was concluded, three DeLay aides were indicted for their management of the Texans for a Republican Majority political action committee (TRMPAC). The indictment charged that the corporate contributions to the committee, including Bacardi's $20,000, had been directed to state legislative candidates, in violation of campaign finance laws. Bacardi USA and seven other corporations were also indicted, charged with violating Texas laws that prohibit corporate contributions to political campaigns. Four of the companies subsequently settled, but the charges against Bacardi and the other companies were still pending in early 2008. Bacardi spokespersons insisted that contributions were legal and that the company was innocent. DeLay, who had broken official ties with TRMPAC after the passage of campaign finance reform legislation in 2002, was not himself indicted at the time, although charges were brought against him three years later. The effort to revise the Section 211 legislation was put off indefinitely, WTO pressures notwithstanding.

Some of the Bacardi energy that had gone into the long Havana Club fight had meanwhile begun to dissipate. In the summer of 2000, Manuel Jorge Cutillas retired as Bacardi chairman, ending more than forty years of active service to his family company. He was replaced by Rubén Rodríguez, the company's former chief financial officer. Rodríguez simultaneously took on the functions of chief executive, replacing George "Chip" Reid, who had lost favor with family members and directors after unsuccessfully pushing an effort to take the company public. While Reid had been an enthusiastic advocate of the litigation against Pernod Ricard and the Cuban government, Rodríguez was less convinced it was a good use of Bacardi time and resources.

Though a native Cuban (and a cousin of Jorge Rodríguez), Rodríguez was the first company chairman from outside the Bacardi family, and he was less emotionally connected with the company's Cuba history than his predecessors had been. With his background in financial analysis, he was also mindful of bottom-line concerns. Between the lawyers' fees and the campaign contributions and the lobbying charges, the Havana Club fight had become quite costly, and Rodríguez was anxious to bring the expenditures under closer control. A few months after taking charge, he disbanded the company's so-called Cuba Group, which had been coordinating the Havana Club fight and other Cuba-related issues. Subsequent accounting showed that between 1998 and 2003 Bacardi had spent nearly three million dollars on lobbying expenses alone.

As part of its effort to press its Havana Club case, Bacardi exerted political pressure on U.S. government agencies, interrupted a judicial proceeding through special congressional action, and paid out millions of dollars to lobbyists and political action committees. The efforts inevitably tarnished Bacardi's achievements. The conservative *Washington Times* newspaper, editorializing on the passage of the pro-Bacardi Section 211 legislation, suggested that the members of Congress who approved it were "perhaps intoxicated by visions of campaign dollars."

More than a hundred years earlier, the patriot José Martí—a Cuban whose writings and friendship inspired Emilio Bacardi—observed while living in the United States that the U.S. House of Representatives "is chosen by such corrupt methods that every election is falsified by the use of vast sums of money." What, then, would Martí have thought of Bacardi's contributions to Tom DeLay's political action committees at the very time it was seeking his legislative help? In the process, Bacardi had been linked not only to DeLay himself, but to what *New York Times* columnist David Brooks called "DeLay-ism," by which he meant "the whole culture that merged K Street [the center of lobbying activity] with the Hill, and held that raising money is the most important way to contribute to the team."

In truth, all this was unfamiliar territory for Bacardi. According to Otto Reich, a Cuban-American who had served as U.S. ambassador to Venezuela and later became a Bacardi lobbyist, company executives were initially reluctant to get their company involved in the Washington game. "They had this corporate Latin American view that politics is dirty," Reich said in a 2007 interview. "They didn't want anything to do with lobbying or political activism." Reich, who subsequently became an anti-Castro hard-liner on George W. Bush's foreign policy team, pushed the Bacardi leadership to take a strong stand. "I kept saying to them, 'But you have a role!'"

What was perhaps most unfortunate for the Bacardi leadership was that the company's management of its fight with the Havana Club joint venture overshadowed, at least for a time, the company's established progressive ideals and long record of civic activism. From Cuba to Puerto Rico to Miami to Brazil, Bacardi had been known as a fair employer, a responsible corporate citizen, a patron of the arts, and a friend of the environment. In truth, it would be a mistake to read too much into the company's political activism during the decade from 1994 to 2004. Those were also years when the company distinguished itself by making wise investment decisions, acquiring prestigious brands, and increasing its capitalization beyond the predictions of many financial analysts.

Within the spirits industry generally, Bacardi's reputation was enhanced, not diminished, by its performance as a company in the late 1990s.

In fact, its promotion of special-interest legislation in the U.S. Congress hardly put Bacardi in a category all by itself. U.S. corporations, including U.S. subsidiaries of foreign corporations, had made similar efforts before. Bacardi was different only because its activism around the Havana Club dispute developed in the context of a long history of involvement in Cuban causes. It was a company with deep Cuban roots, still entirely owned by a Cuban family. It had reason to reclaim its heritage as the originator of Cuban rum, and family members had long assumed the company would return to the island once Fidel Castro was no longer an issue. That day was now approaching. But what the Havana Club episode showed was that Bacardi would reengage with Cuba on vastly changed terms, as a wealthy and sophisticated spirits empire, one more multinational firm accustomed to confronting global rivals and triumphing over them. On one level, Cuba would be just another battlefield.

Chapter 23

Who Gets Cuba

Fidel Castro was energetically addressing an outdoor rally one sunny afternoon in June 2001 when he suddenly faltered, his voice weakening and his face
quickly glistening with sweat. He reached up to wipe his brow, then slumped
silently forward onto the podium. In an instant, uniformed security officers
were at his side, gently leading him off the stage. Another officer, his hand on
his gun, scanned the hushed crowd. Never before had people seen Castro collapse. His most loyal aide, Foreign Minister Felipe Pérez Roque, looking terrified, moved to the microphones. "¡Calma y valor!" he shouted. "Stay calm
and be brave!" Many in the crowd responded by furiously waving the tiny
paper Cuban flags they had been given when they arrived. "Fidel! Fidel! Fidel!"
they chanted.

Castro's brief fainting spell reminded Cubans of the obvious but rarely acknowledged facts: that he was an old man, that his physical powers were diminishing, and that his command of the island would one day end. Within
hours, state security agents had appeared outside the homes of prominent dissidents in Havana. By then, everyone knew that Castro had recovered, but the
authorities could still show how the regime would deal with any political emergency that might arise. In Miami, where Cuban-Americans waited endlessly
for Castro to die, the news of his "illness" dominated Spanish-language radio
programs for hours.

In October 2004, Castro tripped as he stepped off a stage after a graduation
ceremony. Hitting the floor hard, he fractured both an arm and a knee. His
stumble was captured by a television camera, but the image of the old comandante falling clumsily on his face was not one his aides wanted broadcast in
Cuba. The footage was kept off the air. It did not matter; Castro's aging was
not a secret. Twenty-one months later, two weeks before his eightieth birthday,
his personal secretary appeared on Cuban television and announced that Castro had suffered "an acute intestinal crisis" and undergone "complicated" sur-
gery. Castro's presidential, military, and political functions were all delegated

to his brother, Raúl. For the first time in the memory of most living Cubans, Fidel was no longer in charge.

In Miami, some exile leaders encouraged Cubans on the island to seize the moment and launch a rebellion. "The time has come in Cuba for a campaign of civil resistance, civil disobedience," said Republican Congressman Lincoln Diaz-Balart, whose father Rafael was Castro's former brother-in-law. On previous occasions, Diaz-Balart had advocated the imposition of a naval blockade around Cuba, and he had been quoted as saying the U.S. government should consider assassinating Castro. Now he was boldly anticipating a confrontation between the Cuban people and the *fidelista* security forces. "It's time for the military not to shoot. They either stand with the Cuban people, or their names will be on a list of infamy," he said, as if he were in a position to know what lay ahead. He was not. In the months that followed Castro's disappearance from public view, there was no unrest, no violence, and no special security crackdown.

Over four decades, Cuban exile leaders in south Florida such as Diaz-Balart—not to mention Pepín Bosch and other Bacardi players—had repeatedly misjudged conditions in Cuba and made erroneous predictions. It was an indication of the power of wishful thinking, of how much more Cuba had changed than they realized, and of the vast gap between the experience of exile in south Florida and the reality of life on the island. On the other hand, a significant segment of the Cuban population had lost all faith in Castro's revolution, and the regime authorities could not be sure they would stay in power once Fidel was gone. The reaction among the population to Castro's disappearance from public view was almost impossible to measure. There was neither joy nor sadness. After forty-seven years under an authoritarian regime where political guidance was passed down from above and where taking the initiative often got one in trouble, Cubans had learned to be inscrutable. The prevailing national sentiment was just anxiety. Life was hard, and people lived so close to the edge that the prospect of dramatic change frightened even those who wanted it. Cuba was entering the post-Fidel era, and its future was a mystery—to its own people and especially to those Cubans who had left.

. . .

Amelia Comas Bacardi, a great-great-granddaughter of Don Facundo, returned to Cuba in April 2002, one of the first of the U.S.-based Bacardis to do so in more than forty years. She had always wanted her husband Robert to see the tiny island near Santiago where she had spent the enchanting summers of her Cuban girlhood. Vacationing year after year with him and their children at his old family place in Connecticut, she complained that all she could share of her own homeland were the stories, such as how she and her sisters and brothers and Bacardi cousins used to jump from the deck of their grandmother's summer house straight into the cool waters of Santiago Bay and dive for conch and starfish. Amelia had left Cuba when she was still a teenager, and she wasn't even sure it was really as lovely as she remembered it.

On a perfect April morning, she and Robert boarded a rusting ferry in Santiago for the slow trip out to Cayo Smith, the island where the Bacardis had once summered. The Cayo is a rounded hump of land set like a gem in the shimmering bay, about a mile from the old Morro fortress that has guarded the sea entrance to Santiago for more than three centuries. At the crest of the hump is a graceful little whitewashed church. Amelia got teary as soon as she caught sight of it. So much felt and looked familiar: the island's contour against the surrounding hills, the brilliant blueness of the sky, the stillness of the Cuban air, the boatmen oaring soundlessly in the distance.

Cayo Smith was in many ways unchanged from the days when the Bacardi family had vacationed there. There were no cars on the island in 1959, and the houses were built on piles over the water's edge so boats could berth alongside. The *fidelistas* later renamed it Cayo Granma after the yacht that carried Fidel and his fellow rebel fighters to Cuba from Mexico, but the narrow street encircling the island was still for pedestrians only, and many houses were still perched on posts. As the ferryboat approached, however, Amelia could see that the Cayo and its environs had not so much been preserved as simply neglected. The beach where she and her friends had held swimming parties was mostly deserted—untended, overgrown with weeds, and strewn with uncollected litter. When Amelia spotted her grandmother's house, she was horrified. The grand summer place of her childhood was now a teetering wreck. Many of the windowpanes were gone, and the rusty, corrugated tin roof was missing patches. The wood-frame siding still showed tinges of color, but the house appeared not to have been painted in years. The porch posts looked like they were rotting.

Leaving the ferry landing, Amelia and Robert took the stone walkway that led to her old house and on around the island. They passed young men idling in the shade of the banyan trees, and Amelia wondered if she had played with their parents. She now had a full head of gray hair, her gait had slowed, and she was worlds apart from this poor place. The family rum business founded in Santiago by her forebears had developed into the largest family-owned spirits firm in the world, worth at least five billion dollars. Amelia, a stockholder, was well off and well traveled, and when she came back to Cuba it was at the suggestion of the ranking U.S. diplomat in Havana.

The front door of the old summer house was locked. A sign identified the building as a handicrafts center, but no one was there, and the windows were shuttered. As they were investigating, a short, wiry man with curly gray hair suddenly approached, clearly perturbed by the nosy strangers. "What are you doing here?" he wanted to know. Dressed only in shorts and sandals, his deeply bronzed skin suggested a life around the water.

"I'm looking around," Amelia said. "This is my house."

"No, it's not," he said. "This house belonged to Cachita Bacardi."

"She was my grandmother."

The man's eyes widened. "Are you Marlena?" he asked excitedly. "Lucía?" Amelia had two older sisters. "Amelia?"

"Yes."

"I'm Priki!" he announced with a giggle, opening his arms to hug her. As a boy, he had lived across the street from the Bacardi house and played regularly with Amelia's twin brothers. It was Priki who had taught Amelia and the others how to dive for shellfish. He had lunched at Amelia's house and she and her brothers at his. He now had a slight paunch around the middle, but his arms and shoulders were as sinewy as ever. He and his wife and daughters still lived with his elderly mother in the house where he had grown up, and Priki considered himself the custodian of the Bacardi property. "I stop everyone who comes snooping around here," he declared proudly.

Priki had a key to the house and showed the visitors inside. After Amelia's family left, he explained, the house was assigned to the Federation of Cuban Women, an organization created by the Cuban authorities to mobilize women for the chores of the revolution. Later, a pharmacy operated there. For the past fifteen years, the house had been used as a marine taxidermy workshop by a group of twenty local women, including Priki's wife. They stuffed and mounted local exotic fish, lacquered seashells, and produced postcards and other souvenir items for sale to tourists. The interior walls of the house had been removed, leaving two large rooms filled by worktables and lined with shelves where the women kept their supplies. The house was even flimsier than it had appeared from afar. Several of the floorboards were rotten, and the water below was visible between the cracks. Walking through the house, Amelia reconstructed the layout as she remembered it. "The kitchen was over here," she said, pointing to a corner of the crafts work area near the front porch. Only the bathroom was in its original location.

The taxidermy collective was organized as a unit of the National Union of Light Industry Workers, under the control of the Cuban Communist Party. The walls were covered with signs and posters exhorting the women who worked there to maintain "high revolutionary values" and work for the "defense of socialism," but Priki ignored them. Many people on Cayo Smith, he said, remembered Caridad "Cachita" Bacardi fondly and still viewed this decaying structure as her house. The news that a Bacardi daughter was back on the island spread within minutes, and local residents were soon swarming around the visitors. "Do you want to see the church?" someone asked. "Run and get the key! We have to show her the church!"

• • •

The Bacardis were white, upper-class Cubans, and it is impossible to generalize from their lives to the experience of the whole Cuban people, a great many of whom were poor. They had once been slave owners on an island where nearly half the population had some African ancestry. But they did love their country and were generous citizens, and they played a progressive leadership role in Cuba as long as they were able to. Much of the national narrative in Cuba is about missed opportunities, and the Bacardis' story is intriguing partly because it raises what-if questions: The country would have evolved differently if the Bacardis were the rule rather than the exception among a generally irresponsible Cuban elite, or if they had been asked to stay and help and not been pushed away in the name of the country's "social transformation." In response to Fidel Castro's revolution, a million Cubans—a tenth of the country's population—went into exile. A broken thread in modern Cuban history was left to dangle, with its own cast of characters and a unique set of experiences, ideas, and possibilities. Part of the Cuban question now is whether and how its past and future can be reconnected. The Bacardi case is instructive.

Amelia returned to Santiago half expecting to find that her family had been forgotten—or worse, that they were now seen as enemies. A whole generation of the city's population had grown up without any contact with the Bacardis, and to the extent her family was still mentioned by the authorities, it was in a critical context. The name "Bacardi" was now associated with the counter-revolution and the U.S. embargo and the effort to "steal" Cuba's premier rum brand. Ricardo Alarcón, for years Castro's point man on U.S. relations, told a reporter in 2001 that he considered the Bacardis to be "key to the whole policy of economic warfare against Cuba. They are the group that opposes the Cuban revolution abroad." Knowing the Cuban government's sensitivity to the Bacardi connection, Amelia used her married name in filling out her visa application, but Castro's agents figured out who she was and followed her and her husband almost everywhere they went in Cuba, making little effort to hide their presence.

In the Bacardis' hometown, however, Amelia found that her family was still held in high regard. When she visited the Bacardi plot at Santiago's Santa Ifigenia cemetery, she found the graves all carefully tended. Emilio Bacardi's monument, an obelisk of polished black granite on a pedestal, was in perfect condition. The patch of grass surrounding it was neatly trimmed and bordered by a black wrought-iron fence. The tomb of Amelia's grandfather, Emilio's son Facundo Bacardi Lay, was in similar condition. The white marble column at the head of his grave was topped by a bust of Facundo as a man of about forty. (He died young.) Someone had removed the pair of steel spectacles that were once fastened to his stone face, but otherwise the monument was untouched.

Amelia was also pleased by her visit to the municipal museum that Emilio Bacardi had established in Santiago during his mayoralty, a grand neoclassical edifice with Corinthian columns. She knew that the Communists had kept it open and that it was still called the Museo Bacardi, but she did not expect to find it so well maintained. Showing up at the front door with Robert one afternoon, Amelia casually told the attendant who she was. Astonished, the attendant called the museum director, José Olmedo, at home, and he came running over to give the couple a personal tour. Amelia told him she only wanted to see "a few things" that she remembered from visiting the museum as a child.

Olmedo's father and grandfather had worked for the Bacardis in their rum and beer businesses before the revolution, and he told Amelia that they had always spoken highly of her family. A diligent student of Santiago history, he could recite Emilio's achievements as mayor and was delighted that he could show off his knowledge to someone who appreciated it. Though rules are not broken lightly in Cuba, Olmedo told Amelia and Robert they could see whatever they wanted in the museum and could disregard the posted signs against taking pictures. "That doesn't apply to you," he said.

◆ ◆ ◆

In his old age, Fidel Castro became more intransigent than ever. He may have been worrying that the reforms he had reluctantly supported after the collapse of the Soviet bloc could set the stage for a rollback of his revolution. In 1995 he had complained that "every opening has brought risks to us," and within the next few years he reversed many of the previous reforms. Opportunities for self-employment were once again restricted, and Castro made further foreign investment on the island so unattractive that by 2001 it totaled only about forty million dollars, less than in any year since 1993. At the same time, he moved to further limit any political activity that could potentially undermine his rule. When a human rights activist named Oswaldo Payá organized a petition drive in 2001 to pressure Cuba's National Assembly to expand civil liberties, Castro countered with an intimidating campaign of his own. Cubans across the country were pressured to sign a declaration that the one-party socialist system should be "untouchable," and the Assembly subsequently amended the constitution to say precisely that. A year later, Castro ordered the arrest of seventy-five prominent dissidents, human rights activists, and independent journalists, all of whom were put through summary trials and sentenced to long prison terms, allegedly for having collaborated with the U.S. government. It was the most sweeping repression of the opposition movement in Cuba in four decades. The dissident crackdown cost Castro important support in the West, but he dared go ahead with it because he had found a new strategic ally in Venezuela's oil-rich autocrat, Hugo Chávez. By 2005, Chávez was providing Cuba with more than ninety thousand barrels of oil per day, a subsidy worth nearly two billion dollars a year.

After the initial burst of enthusiasm in Cuban investment opportunities, foreign businesses became increasingly disillusioned about the prospect of making good money on the island. A major complaint was the unenforceability of laws and contracts. There was no independent judiciary in Cuba, so when businesses saw taxes unfairly imposed, contracts broken, or regulations misapplied, they had nowhere to turn for an appeal. The inescapable reality was that Cuba remained a dictatorship, where authorities were deeply suspicious of foreigners and determined to monitor their every move. One Spanish businessman, frustrated after years of dealing with the Cuban state, wrote an open letter advising other businessmen to stay away from the island. "Transactions and business dealings do not occur between genuine entrepreneurs," he wrote, "but rather in a dark universe of spies and police." By 2006, the London-based Economist Intelligence Unit was judging Cuba to be among the least attractive business environments in the world, ranked eightieth of eighty-two nations, trailed only by Iran and Angola.

At Castro's direction, the Cuban government by then had recentralized control over the economy, withdrawing much of the autonomy given to state enterprise managers and their foreign partners in the mid-1990s. Preserving the regime's hold on power was the single idea behind all economic, investment, and trade policies. In tourism, the government favored the development of huge, physically isolated complexes that could be closely controlled, and it promoted all-inclusive packages over less restrictive tourism that would allow foreigners to interact with ordinary Cubans. In other sectors, secret investment deals with Venezuela and China took precedence over transparent arrangements with Western firms. By the end of 2006, the number of Cuban businesses operating jointly with foreign partners had dropped by nearly 50 percent from the level of four years earlier. Those that survived were primarily large-scale ventures in high-profit areas: mining, energy, tourism, telecommunications, biotechnology. And rum.

. . .

There may be no bar on Earth where a mojito is quite so perfect as one sipped on the terrace of Havana's elegant Hotel Nacional. Under the portico, gray-haired guitarists in straw hats and white guayabera shirts sing old Cuban love songs and sway to the conga beat of the beaming young musicians at their side. The rocky bluff at the far end of the hotel gardens drops sharply to the sea and the blue sky beyond. The air is steamy, and when the waiter arrives with the iced drink, the napkin around the glass is damp. The sweetness of the rum and cane sugar and the fragrance of the crushed mint refresh instantly.

Rum is one of the precious elements—along with cigars—that keep a hallowed place in Cuba no matter which ideology rules. Julia Ward Howe, the Bostonian songstress and social reformer, was shocked to be offered a drink everywhere she went on a visit in 1859. "Rum is not a wicked word in Cuba," she noted with amazement in her diary. It still isn't and never will be. When Cuban men gather to play dominoes on a card table in a park or along a sidewalk, there is often a bottle at someone's elbow. When a new one is opened, it is first tipped; a splash of rum on the ground sanctifies the spot. The history of Cuba can be narrated around tales of rum; it has been a symbol of Cuban life from the days of sugar and slaves through the Castro era. Visiting tourists who rarely drink rum at home ask for it as soon as they arrive, just as they always have.

The Hotel Nacional was famous for its rum mojitos back when it was the favored accommodation of Miami gangsters and Hollywood stars, and in March 2004 the Havana Club venture celebrated its tenth anniversary at the same hotel. The highlight of the week-long celebration was the International Havana Club Grand Prix, a cocktail-mixing competition sponsored by the French-Cuban venture as a way of promoting its products. Some of the world's most flamboyant bartenders flew to Havana for the event, along with hundreds of invited guests. The contestants, representing twenty-three countries, assembled on the stage of the hotel ballroom to take turns preparing four cocktails with Havana Club rum—a mojito, a daiquiri, a Cuba libre, and a "Habanísima," basically a mojito without the soda water. They had five minutes to mix the drinks before a panel of judges and were rated on flair points as well as on the quality of the final product. The onlooking guests were continuously supplied with free samples.

Cuba was a police state, but it was becoming a playground again, as it had been in the golden age when beautiful people came to Havana and fell under a charm of sweet mambo rhythms and Caribbean romance. The authorities had concluded that their country had an economic interest in promoting tourism, rum, and cigars, even if it meant presenting an image of Cuba more reminiscent of the 1950s than of Che Guevara and leftist solidarity brigades. The collaboration with Pernod Ricard to promote and market Havana Club products was one of the government's few remaining alliances with a Western capitalist firm, but it had become a top priority. At the state-owned Hotel Nacional, the musicians' shirts were all emblazoned with the Havana Club logo, and every drink served in the hotel bar came in a Havana Club glass. The yellow scooter taxis parked outside the front gate all carried Havana Club decals, and the drivers all wore Havana Club T-shirts.

The French-Cuban operation made strategic as well as commercial sense. Marketing Havana Club rum meant marketing Cuba. The joint venture hired Cuban salsa musicians, dressed them in Havana Club outfits, and sent them on European tours to play at outdoor festivals and cultural events, advertising a Cuban lifestyle. Pernod Ricard had not simply joined with a state-owned company; the partnership was with the state itself. It had an inherently political aspect—not because it promoted revolutionary socialism or an anti-U.S. message, but because it presented Cuba in entirely positive tones.

The arrangement was good for both sides. In the first ten years after the establishment of the joint venture, global Havana Club rum sales increased fourfold, from 460,000 cases in 1994 to 1.9 million cases in 2003. The brand was still far behind Bacardi worldwide, but Bacardi sales were flat, whereas Havana Club had the top growth rate in the world among spirits. Its seven-year-old rum was doing especially well, drawing positive reviews from connoisseurs and comparing well to highly regarded rums from such countries as Haiti, Guatemala, Venezuela, Nicaragua, and Jamaica. As a premium product, a bottle of seven-year-old Havana Club rum sold for more than twenty dollars in Europe.

Cuban manufacturing was generally in a disastrous state, but rum production was a definite bright spot, and that was likely to be true whether Cuba remained socialist or evolved into a democratic, market-oriented state. One effect of foreign investment in the rum industry was to introduce principles of capitalism where they had previously been absent. Pernod Ricard's partnership with Corporación CubaRon exposed Cuban managers and executives to the importance of brands, marketing strategy, competitive pricing, intellectual property, and other concepts from the Western commercial world.

CubaRon was one of the first state-owned firms in Cuba to be integrated into the *perfeccionamiento empresarial* (enterprise improvement) program, set up by the Cuban government in 1998 to prepare Cuban enterprises for the challenge of competing in the market economy as separate firms, rather than as units within a government ministry. The program was intended to introduce state enterprises to such unfamiliar practices as cost accounting, budgeting, managerial decision making, and customer service. Most Cuban firms failed to satisfy the minimum criteria to complete the program, but CubaRon executives embraced it, inspired perhaps by contact with their Pernod Ricard counterparts.

The Cubans' exposure to capitalism gave them reasons to question their own economic system. They learned, for example, that in a market economy, enterprise managers who perform well are rewarded with good salaries. Not so in Cuba. Pernod Ricard compensated the Cuban state in hard currency for the services of its Cuban employees, but the Cubans received only a tiny fraction of that pay, with the government keeping the remainder. Under the circumstances, the Havana Club joint venture with Pernod Ricard produced a paradox in Fidel Castro's Cuba: The more money it made for Cuba, the more it undermined socialist ideology and fed the demand for economic reforms.

Speaking privately with their French colleagues, the Cuban professionals who worked for Havana Club International regularly hinted that they were looking forward to the post-Castro era in Cuba, in anticipation of the economic and political changes they expected it to bring. To be sure, some of them were members of the Cuban Communist Party, because the Cuban authorities selected the people who were allowed to work for joint ventures and chose only those considered politically reliable. The experience of the ex-socialist countries of the Soviet bloc, however, showed how common it was for well-connected Communist technocrats to become eager capitalists overnight when the firms they managed were about to be privatized.

The state-owned CubaRon side of the joint rum venture was clearly a prime candidate for capitalist transformation. By 2008, Havana Club sales had reached 2.6 million cases, with a growth rate still in the top ranks of the spirits industry. As part of the company's strategy to achieve annual sales of five million cases by 2013, the joint venture had inaugurated a new distillery, this one for the production of the premium dark rums that were popular in European markets. Havana Club was genuinely *El Ron de Cuba*, and it would not be easily dislodged.

During her visit to Santiago de Cuba in April 2002, Amelia Comas Bacardi took her husband Robert to see all the old Bacardi haunts, a tour that revealed how the city had changed after forty years and how it had simply aged. In addition to the Museo Bacardi and the Santa Ifigenia cemetery, they stopped by the former Bacardi administrative offices on Aguilera Street (formerly Marina Baja), the ancient brick building where the young Emilio Bacardi once passed his workdays writing stories on the backs of blank ledger sheets. The Bacardi bat logo was still visible on the concrete pillars at the curbside, but the ceramic tiles that spelled out B-A-C-A-R-D-I in the sidewalk had been ripped out. The building now housed a men's stocking factory, though for lack of materials and equipment problems it was rarely operating.

The old bottling facility and rum factory on Matadero Street was in better shape, operated by Corporación CubaRon and producing rum under the "Ron Santiago de Cuba" label. From the outside, the factory looked the same as it had in 1960, though the little grassy courtyard where the Bacardis' coconut palm once grew had been enclosed and incorporated into the building itself. Tourists had formerly been allowed to step inside, but the factory in recent years had been closed to all outsiders. The rum-aging warehouse, next door to the factory, was also off limits. Had Amelia and Robert been able to go inside, they would have seen thousands of oak barrels stacked from floor to ceiling, each barrel marked with a number to identify the age and batch, just as in the old days. The side of the warehouse facing the street was colorfully painted with Santiago scenes and a city motto, in bright red letters: *Santiago de Cuba: Rebelde Ayer, Hospitalaria Hoy, Heróica Siempre* (Rebellious Yesterday, Welcoming Today, Heroic Forever). The street traffic was light. Every few minutes a horse-drawn taxi carriage came clopping by, full of passengers who had paid a few pennies for a ride into town.

Villa Elvira, the luxurious country home where Emilio Bacardi had lived out his days with his wife Elvira Cape, had been turned into a school for children with disabilities. No effort had been made to maintain the sculpture garden that once graced the property, and statues made by Emilio and Elvira's daughter Mimín lay broken and covered by weeds. The house where Amelia's uncle, Daniel Bacardi, had once lived with his family was now the Russian consulate. The mansion Pepín Bosch had inherited from his father in the fashionable suburb of Vista Alegre had become the provincial headquarters of the Young Pioneers, the Communist youth group in Cuba. A Soviet-era MiG fighter jet sat on a pedestal in the front yard. Amelia also showed Robert the two-story house on Plaza Marte that had once belonged to her grandfather and where she had lived as a young girl in Santiago. It was now a budget hotel.

The two waitresses in the hotel dining room were dressed like aging flight attendants on a Soviet airliner, in navy blue polyester skirts with matching vests, light blue blouses, and red scarves around their necks. The women were perfectly pleasant, but having spent their entire adult lives in a socialist system where there was no reward for extra effort, they showed little interest in their work. One sat at a table, writing a letter. The other stood behind the cash register, sewing a button on a flowered blouse, singing softly to herself. *No quiero flores. No quiero estampas. Lo que quiero es la Virgen de la Caridad.* It was a traditional Cuban *son* tune, sung in praise of the patron saint of Cuba. She was still singing sweetly when she eventually sauntered over to attend to her customers. Her manner was so gentle that it was impossible to be perturbed by her inattentive service. In Cuba, visitors learn to be patient.

Amelia asked questions of the Cubans she met, though she was always polite. She carried herself with a quiet dignity, dressing conservatively and keeping her judgments to herself. Among her last memories of the island was a long, miserable night spent outside the U.S. embassy in Havana, waiting in line with her sisters for a visa. Pro-Castro Cubans had been sent to jeer at those who wanted to leave the island. It would have been natural for Amelia, back in Cuba for the first time since that awful experience, to feel some residual anger toward the Cubans who had said nothing when she and her family were publicly denounced, who had not spoken up against Castro when they had a chance, who had opted to stay on the island and make their peace with him. But she felt only sympathy.

In Santiago, Amelia tracked down the one relative still living there, a second cousin once removed named Marta María Cabrera, from a non-Bacardi branch of her family. Marta María's grandmother was a first cousin to Amelia's mother and had taken care of Amelia when she got sick with whooping cough as a child. Her grandfather had been a prosperous Santiago lawyer, but unlike the Bacardis and many other Cuban professionals, he had decided to remain in Cuba after the revolution. Over the coming years, his family's living standards had plummeted, and he had died a poor man. By the time Amelia returned to Cuba, her Bacardi wealth was unimaginable to her Santiago relatives.

On the morning after Amelia and Robert arrived, Marta María visited them in their room at the Hotel Casagranda on Santiago's main square. Though her own house was full of antique mahogany furniture, much of it left to her family by departing relatives, Marta María had never set foot inside a tourist hotel in Cuba, and she was overwhelmed by what she saw. "Oh my God, look at this beautiful bedspread," she said, running her hands lovingly across it. "And these towels they give you! And all these little soaps and shampoo bottles!" Amelia, somewhat embarrassed by her cousin's reaction to what was a quite ordinary hotel room by international standards, invited Marta María to join her and Robert for breakfast on the top floor of the hotel. "Oh, can I?" she pleaded.

At the breakfast buffet, Marta María was once again awestruck by what was available to visiting foreign tourists: fresh pineapple, mangoes, bananas, papaya, and grapefruit; pastries, eggs made to order, with bacon and ham. "I've never seen anything like this!" Marta María said, her eyes tearing. All her life, like other Cubans, she had seen eggs and meat as luxuries, scarcely rationed and affordable only on special occasions. Fresh fruit was rarely to be found, and pastries were unheard of. When Amelia and Robert met Marta María the following morning, they brought with them a bundle of sweet rolls from the buffet wrapped up in napkins for Marta María to take home to her son. They never made it. Over the next few hours, while accompanying Amelia and Robert around town, Marta María ate the pastries one by one. When she realized none were left, she began weeping. "I can't believe what I've done," she told Amelia. "But you don't understand what it is not to have these things."

Amelia and her husband returned to the United States thinking there was much they had not fully understood about Cuba. After meeting many ordinary Cubans, they were inclined to challenge facile assumptions back home about how Cubans really felt or what policies the United States should favor. Amelia's husband, Robert O'Brien, concluded on the basis of his observations on the island that the U.S. trade embargo was working to Castro's advantage by providing an excuse for his economic policy failures, though he was not yet prepared to advocate its suspension. Back in the United States, he began following Cuba issues much more closely and joined the board of the Center for a Free Cuba, an anti-Castro organization partly supported by Bacardi family money.

For her part, Amelia told friends and relatives that Cubans could not be characterized simply as active Castro supporters or as dissidents; there were too many in between. "If you're going to live there, you have to mold yourself to the regime," she said. She realized that former family friends in Santiago and Havana had helped themselves to the art, furniture, silver, and other treasures her parents and relatives had left behind, but that thought no longer upset her. "Some people say they're going to go back to Cuba to claim what they had there," she said. "Not me. These people who might be in your old house, you think maybe they're with the regime. I don't know if they are or not. But they're suffering. Look at the conditions under which they live."

• • •

For more than a hundred and fifty years, the Bacardi name had been associated with "the Cuban cause," but that idea had been redefined so often that its meaning was no longer clear. After Fidel Castro turned Cuba into a totalitarian Communist state, the Bacardis stood for liberating the nation from his rule, but even that aim had lost urgency. Though Fidel remained a tyrant, he became progressively less relevant. The rhetoric of revolution and struggle was hollow. It did not matter what Fidel Castro or Ricardo Alarcón said about the Bacardis; many Cubans paid no heed. On the other hand, this did not mean that the old rum family could expect to come back to Cuba and pick up where they had left off in 1960. Too much had changed. Many Cubans had adjusted to the system, enthusiastically or not. An enterprise like Havana Club, established on a combination of old and new power bases, seemed relatively secure.

A separate question was how much Bacardi had changed. Its long commitment to Cuba distinguished the company from its peers. Few, if any, firms have maintained a political identity as Bacardi has with its Cuba connection, either publicly or privately. The depth of the Bacardi attachment to Cuba could be taken as a measure of the company's uniqueness, and it might reveal how wholly owned family firms, even very big ones, remain a category unto themselves.

Since its 1862 founding, the company has been led by a Bacardi son or son-in-law throughout its history, except for the 2000–2005 period, when the directors went outside the family and chose Rubén Rodríguez as their new board chairman. When Rodríguez retired, the board turned back to the family, selecting Don Facundo's thirty-eight-year-old great-great-grandson, who also happened to be named Facundo Bacardi. The young Facundo was the seventh family member to chair the company since its establishment, though he was the first in the branch descending from Facundo Bacardi Moreau, the founder's second son. Young Facundo had inherited one of the largest blocks of Bacardi stock in the family, and his stockholdings gave him considerable clout within the company. Despite his relatively young age, he had been playing a prominent role on the Bacardi board for ten years already by the time he was named chairman.

Facundo's youth did mean that his connection to Cuba was a bit weak. He was born in Chicago, had never set foot in Cuba, and, in his own words, had an "American mind frame" that occasionally clashed with the "Cuban Bacardi" views of other family members. When he became chairman, however, Facundo noted that his predecessors had all felt a responsibility "to move both the family and the company forward in a way that preserved its Cuban heritage." He was taking over the company just as political change in Cuba appeared imminent, and he knew that as the Bacardi corporate leader he was expected to follow through on the family's long-standing plan to play a role in post-Castro Cuba. "The historical significance of my chairmanship is to be the one to reestablish the Bacardi company in its homeland," he said shortly after being chosen. "I feel a great obligation to devote every effort in leading the family, and the company, back to its birthplace and to help the people of Cuba in every way possible." No one named Facundo Bacardi could say any less.

But what exactly did it mean? There would be no family company to lead back to Cuba if Bacardi Limited did not survive as an independent firm. As chairman, Facundo needed to focus more on competitive business pressures than on the political situation in Cuba. For more than a decade, the global spirits industry had been in a period of feverish consolidation, propelled by significant economies of scale in the liquor business. In an effort to keep up with its rivals, Bacardi had bought Martini & Rossi vermouth in 1992, Dewar's whiskey and Bombay Sapphire gin in 1998, and Cazadores tequila in 2002. Those acquisitions nevertheless still left Bacardi trailing Diageo, the spirits industry giant, and in 2004 the company purchased Grey Goose vodka for more than two billion dollars. Archrival Pernod Ricard surged far ahead the following year, however, by acquiring all of Allied Domecq, a British firm whose brands included Beefeater gin, Kahlúa liqueur, and Perrier-Jouët champagne. By the time Facundo Bacardi became chairman, Bacardi Limited was struggling to maintain third place among the big spirits companies. Most of the available brands had already been acquired, and the few remaining buying opportunities were hotly contested. In the spring of 2007, when the Swedish government announced plans to sell its own Absolut vodka brand, Bacardi and Pernod Ricard jostled to be first in line to buy it. At the same time, Bacardi committed itself to the development of new markets, as the company had done successfully under the leadership of Enrique Schueg a century earlier. In 2006 the company moved its Asia headquarters from Hong Kong to Shanghai in order to be closer to the emerging Chinese market. A year later, the company announced plans to invest four million dollars promoting its brands in India.

It was not easy to say precisely where Cuba fit among all the concerns on the complex Bacardi agenda, in part because it was hard to separate commercial considerations from political and emotional ones. Bacardi advertising experts had long been prepared to exploit the new interest in Cuba by underscoring the company's own Cuban heritage, even while Bacardi lobbyists were urging the U.S. government to maintain an uncompromising line in dealing with the Castro regime. One notable ad appeared in *Cigar Aficionado* magazine in June 1999, a special issue titled "Cuba: Is It Time to End the Embargo?" The magazine that month included a travel guide for Americans who wanted to visit the island, along with reports on the best cigars and rums produced on the island and which hotels and resorts offered the best accommodations. At the time, the Bacardi political position was that U.S. travel to Cuba should still be restricted, but the company's marketing team concluded that if *Cigar Aficionado* was going to highlight Cuba's rum tradition, Bacardi needed to be represented. The company placed a two-page color ad near the front of the magazine, featuring a picture of three vintage Bacardi bottles from the days when the rum was still bottled in Santiago de Cuba, alongside a Cuban cigar burning in an ashtray. The caption read, "When the Great Cuban Cigars Were Born, They Were Enjoyed with the World's Great Rum."

As long as Fidel Castro still ruled the island, however, there was some sensitivity around the issue of how heavily the company should promote its Cuba connection. In some countries, Bacardi rum advertising and bottle labels included the statement Established Cuba 1862, but internal company guidelines called for the word "Cuba" to be dropped in those countries "where a Cuban heritage statement is not allowed, desired or relevant." The bigger questions, of course, were whether the company should return to Cuba, how soon, and under what conditions. The Bacardi name was still associated with rum in Cuba, and some company executives were eager to produce a young white rum on the island, oriented primarily to the domestic market. Another issue was whether the company should make much of an effort to reclaim any properties in Cuba, including the distillery, bottling plant, and aging warehouse in Santiago. The consensus among company executives was that it would be better to build a new operation from scratch. They had caught a glimpse of the inside of a Havana Club bottling plant in a BBC documentary film and concluded from what they saw that it was badly out of date. If the old Bacardi facility in Santiago was in similar condition, there would be little reason to redevelop it.

The other dimension to the Bacardi interest in Cuba was sentimental. In 2003 the company spent eight million dollars on a visitors' center in Puerto Rico that told the Bacardis' Cuba story in great detail, complete with replicas of the original Santiago distillery, the company offices on Aguilera Street, and the art deco executive bar at the Edificio Bacardi in Havana. The center was largely the work of Pepín Argamasilla, a trained historian who was the grandson of José Argamasilla, the company's last public relations chief in Santiago, and his wife Zenaida Bacardi, Emilio Bacardi's granddaughter. Upon becoming chairman in 2005, Facundo Bacardi threw his support behind such heritage efforts, even creating a foundation to support them. One of the first projects was to provide funding for Argamasilla and his cousin Mari Aixalá to produce a deluxe, limited-edition coffee-table book on the Bacardi history, largely for the family's own use.

Industry analysts had differing views on the company's investment in highlighting its history. Some saw it as an effective way to promote brand awareness and loyalty, while others saw it as a wasteful expense that the directors of a public company would never approve. Tom Pirko, the analyst who had followed Bacardi closely for a long time, scoffed at the Bacardi museum project, telling a *Miami Herald* reporter that such projects are "monuments to vanity."

The company's fierce determination to challenge Pernod Ricard over the use of the "Havana Club" trademark stemmed in part from its interest in post-Castro Cuba and its concern about who would benefit from Cuban rum sales to the United States. But the campaign also reflected the Bacardis' personal passions. Tom Pirko was intrigued when Bacardi executives rolled out their own "Havana Club" rum in August 2006, supposedly based on a formula the company had acquired from the Arechabalas when it purchased their trademark rights. "Following this company is like watching a long-running soap opera," he said at the time. "Only Bacardi behaves like this. It's a very macho culture, a very Latin culture, very emotional."

• • •

In the spring of 2007, an appeals court in Spain threw out Bacardi's claim that it owned the "Havana Club" trademark in that country, leaving the brand with Pernod Ricard and its Cuban government partner. The decision meant the French-Cuban venture was essentially free to sell its Havana Club rum all across Europe without interference from Bacardi. The United States, on the other hand, appeared to be Bacardi territory, barring the reversal of earlier rulings that took the "Havana Club" rights away from Pernod Ricard and CubaRon. Unanswered was who would ultimately prevail in Cuba, the country that mattered most. Contained in that question was the mystery of Cuba's future.

The alliance between the Cuban government and Pernod Ricard appeared solid, but it was impossible to say whether that might change in a post-Castro era. It depended on how much of Fidel Castro's regime would survive him and what character it would have. Would the technocrats and managers responsible for Cuba's economic activity maintain their positions after Castro was gone, and where would their loyalties lie? Would foreign firms that worked closely with Cuban authorities during the Castro era be rewarded for their role or be seen as having collaborated with an undemocratic regime? The joint venture with the totalitarian Cuban state was a classic example of crony capitalism. Pernod executives were complicit in the maintenance of a two-tier system under which Cuban professionals earned a tiny fraction of what their French counterparts made, served at the whim of Communist bureaucrats, and enjoyed no independent labor rights. It was not inconceivable that a future Cuban government, responding to popular pressure, might reconsider joint ventures established under the old regime. Pernod Ricard had only a 50 percent interest in Havana Club International. When asked during the 1999 Havana Club trial whether the Arechabalas might seek to reclaim their rum trademark under a new government, Pernod executive Thierry Jacquillat candidly responded, "Obviously there will be litigation."

Both sides were gambling that their positions would be strong. In his 1993 letter warning other liquor companies to stay away from former Bacardi assets, Manuel Jorge Cutillas said his company expected "that under a future democratic government, traditional constitutional guarantees will be restored and unlawful conveyances by the Castro regime will not be recognized by the courts as passing good title." Cutillas predicted the Cuban courts in the post-Castro era would "recognize and implement Bacardi's right to recover damages from anyone who has occupied and exploited Bacardi's properties at any time during the Castro regime." Such bold declarations surely amounted in part to bravado by company lawyers. It was hard to see how the company could be so confident its interests would be respected under a new Cuban government, even a democratic one.

Back when Bacardi Rum was the leading all-Cuban company on the island, its nationalism was beyond question. In the early twentieth century, many Cuban political and business leaders were accused of being overly subservient to the United States, but never the Bacardis. Since going into exile, however, Bacardi had pursued its interests in Cuba by working through the U.S. government. Indeed, to the extent the company would have clout in a new Cuba, it would largely be the consequence of U.S. legislation working in Bacardi's favor. Under the terms of the 1996 Helms-Burton Act, the restoration of trade relations with Cuba could depend on the Cuban government first returning confiscated properties to the original owners or their designated heirs. During the Havana Club trial in New York, a Bacardi lawyer interpreted this provision of the law to mean that "when the preconditions for the lifting of the embargo are satisfied, it will be Bacardi, not Havana Club, that has the rights to the [Havana Club] trademark in Cuba."

The Bacardi case against Pernod Ricard and its Cuban government partner was also reinforced by the 1998 Section 211 legislation, which effectively precluded the French-Cuban joint venture from registering the Havana Club trademark in the United States. Some Cuban nationalists might argue that by using the U.S. government to advance its interests in Cuba, the company had surrendered the patriotic high ground that Emilio Bacardi once held as a defender of Cuban sovereignty in the face of U.S. interventionist pressure. The country's epic myth had always featured Cubans fighting bravely for their freedoms against foreign enemies, and Fidel Castro drew regularly on this theme to give his revolution historical legitimacy. Such a representation could now be turned against the Bacardis.

But it was by no means clear that Cubans were still motivated by nationalist arguments. After fifty years of hardship and broken promises, there was significant cynicism in the population. One dissident Cuban, writing anonymously from Havana for the U.S.-based CubaNet Web site in 2004, argued angrily that the Castro regime "has destroyed any nationalist sentiment among the youth sector of the population.... Emigrating to the United States or waiting for Fidel Castro to die, those are the favored options in Cuba. If there were a referendum to choose between sovereignty and annexation to the colossus of the north, the independent Cuban nation would perish unnoticed, and *this is the crime that history will not pardon.*"

The relative stability of Cuba during the shift of leadership from Fidel to Raúl Castro, culminating in Fidel's resignation and Raúl's "election" as his successor in February 2008, suggested that change on the island was unlikely to come quickly or conform to any pattern seen elsewhere. For a decade or more, Cuba analysts had been studying the transitions from Communism to democracy in Eastern Europe for clues as to what might happen in Cuba, but the comparison was far from perfect. Among other factors, there was no Eastern European counterpart to the Cuban *exiliado*. The Cuban-Americans of south Florida promised to be an independent force in a Cuban transition, though it was unclear whether their effect would be to encourage Cubans on the island to embrace change hopefully or to resist it defensively.

The exile community had long been a source of financial support and inspiration for Cubans still in Cuba, but Fidel Castro had warned endlessly that the "Miami Cubans" might one day return and reclaim the houses they had abandoned, dislodging anyone who was living there. Some exiles opposed contact with Cuba so rigidly as to suggest they had no sympathy for the position of ordinary Cubans who could not afford to take morally pure stands against the Castro regime. Was there something about living long and comfortably in the United States over time that had narrowed the exiles' thinking, making them less Cuban and more American? José Martí, writing from New York in 1881, considered whether the "colossal nation" that was his adopted home contained "ferocious and terrible" elements. "Does the absence of the feminine spirit, source of artistic sensibility and complement to national identity, harden and corrupt the heart of this astonishing people?" he wondered.

The one certainty about a transition to a new era in Cuba was that it would not come easily. Nothing did in Cuba. One wise man who always counseled against despair was Emilio Bacardi. Writing from Santiago in 1907 to his American friend Leonard Wood, Emilio said it should not be so hard for Cubans to find the president they deserved. "We are neither as difficult nor as bad as we are said to be," he wrote. "We need tenderness and tolerance; we need someone who is just and who truly loves his nation." A century later, Cubans needed that leader more than ever.

Acknowledgments

꒦꒷꒦

My friends, family, and work colleagues all know how long it took me to produce this book, and I thank everyone for cheering me on or simply putting up with me through what seemed an interminable period. I did not realize when I began this project how heavily I would depend on others to help me finish it. I must first mention four Bacardi people whose assistance and cooperation was vital. Robert O'Brien, who happens to be a neighbor, agreed at the outset to support me and told his Bacardi in-laws and associates that I would tell their story fairly. Manuel Jorge Cutillas, the retired Bacardi chairman, opened doors for me throughout the family and the company and made himself available to me over and over in spite of his busy schedule. Guillermo G. Mármol, whose career and contacts at Bacardi date from the 1940s, patiently spent many hours with me and answered hundreds of my questions, especially concerning the life and work of Pepín Bosch, whom he served as an aide and attorney for nearly thirty years. Pepín Argamasilla, the Bacardi archivist and historian, generously shared his impressive knowledge (and photographs) and corrected as many of my errors along the way as he could catch. I may have spent five years immersed in the Bacardi story, but Pepín remains the expert.

Many others in the Bacardi world were similarly helpful, including Tito Argamasilla, Facundo Bacardi, Carlos and Jorge Bosch, José Bolivar, José Bolivar Jr., José R. Bou, Alicia Castroverde, Amelia Comas O'Brien, Clara María del Valle, Georgina García Lay, Richard Gardner, Juan Grau, Barbara Johnson, Raúl Mármol, Patricia Neal, Juan Prado, Rino and Ileana Puig, Rubén Rodríguez, and Elsie Williams MacMullin. In the broad community of Cuban Americans and Cuba experts, I thank Ramón Arechabala, Ernesto Betancourt, Frank Calzon, Tony Calatayud, Ramón Colas, Oscar Echeverría, Pamela Falk, Antonio Gayoso, Louis A. Pérez Jr., Marifeli Pérez-Stable, Berta Mexidor, José Antonio Roca, Mercedes Sandoval, Mary Speck, Jaime Suchlicki, and Julia Sweig.

In Santiago de Cuba, I spent many hours with Pepín Hernández, the former director of the Museo del Ron, and with José Olmedo, who directed the Museo

Emilio Bacardi and later the Museo del Ron. José's wife, Daimi Ruíz, also a Santiago historian, helped me, as did Sara Inés Fernández of the Biblioteca Elvira Cape and Rafael Duharte of the Casa del Caribe. In Havana, I was helped by Carmen Guerrero and Regla Jimenez at Havana Club International, María de los Angeles Meriño at the University of Havana, and Patria Cok at the Archivo Nacional, and by my friend and colleague Moisés Saab and his wife, Maite. The late great photographer of the Cuban revolution, Alberto Korda, steered me toward his remarkable pictures of Fidel at the Bacardi plant in Santiago. Korda's longtime colleague José Figueroa also helped me, as did Korda's daughter Diana Díaz. The Cuban government officials with whom I worked over the last several years will not be pleased by some of what they read in this book, but I must say that Roberto de Armas, Josefina Vidal, Luís Mariano Fernández, and Lázaro Herrera have been unfailingly courteous and professional in their dealings with me.

Marisabel Villagómez and Esther Gentile provided superb and invaluable research assistance to me through the course of this project. Esperanza de Varona made available the archival treasures of the Cuban Heritage Collection at the University of Miami's Richter Library, and Annie Sansone and Zoe Blanco-Rosa helped me explore them. I made use of Monica Klien's impressive language and literary expertise in translating some (to me) odd Spanish phrases and archaic epigrams. I also want to acknowledge the assistance, advice, and solidarity I received from Melissa Appleyard, Phil Bennett, John Boertlein, Don Bohning, Ray Bourgeois, Robert Chapman, Roger Cohen, David Corn, Georgie Anne Geyer, Dan Gjelten, Ed Hamilton, Rod Heller, Sylvio Heufelder and Jeanette Erazo Heufelder, Richard Hurst, Peter Kornbluh, John Lilly, Jay Mallin, Tom Miller, Robert Muse, Mark Orr, George Volsky, Elaine Walker, Abby Yochelson, and Gertraud Zangl. At NPR, many longtime colleagues were supportive of my book writing even though it meant my prolonged neglect of reporting duties. I owe special thanks to Ted Clark, Pam Duckett, Cheryl Hampton, Loren Jenkins, Jim Lesher, Kee Malesky, Bill Marimow, Peter Overby, Barbara Rehm, Didi Schanche, David Sweeney, and Ellen Weiss.

I have been blessed with the best professional support team an author could dream of having. Gail Ross of the Gail Ross Literary Agency has encouraged me, prodded me, and stood up for me for years and years, assisted by her talented associate Howard Yoon and her editor Kara Baskin. And words fail me in characterizing the guidance, insight, wisdom, and—yet again—*patience* of the wonderful Wendy Wolf of Viking, the best editor in the business. Wendy first asked for this book about a decade ago, never gave up on it, and helped me turn a thousand-page manuscript into something much more readable. In that thankless effort she and I were ably assisted by Ellen Garrison and the rest of the top-notch Viking staff. Finally, I am thankful for good friends who provide bottomless moral support and invigorating company: Dick, Judy, Kim, Joel, Nancy, Sunisa, George, Sheila, Pete, and Beth.

My wife, Martha Raddatz, is an awesome journalist, a deeply devoted mother, and a loving and supportive mate. In the time I have been working on this book, she has been around the world about a dozen times, reported and written a bestselling book of her own, and held down one of the most demanding jobs in the news business, but her belief in what I was doing all these years in my upstairs study never wavered. Jake made sure that I stayed focused on the important things and marked my weighty manuscript with cartoons just when I needed it most. Greta inspires me with her sparkle and energy and kindness. She and Jake and Martha are my foundation, and I dedicate this book to them.

My one regret is that my mother and father did not survive to see me finish this work, though they followed my progress closely and with enthusiasm. The two of them provided unconditional love and support throughout my life.

NOTES

Chapter 1. Santiago de Cuba

p. 6. **"Tell me," Hatuey:** This is Emilio Bacardi Moreau's version of the Hatuey story, related in his *Crónicas de Santiago de Cuba*, Vol. I, 99–100. Emilio's version of the Hatuey story is based on the contemporary account by Bartolomé de las Casas, who was with Velázquez in Cuba.

P. 8. **With turkeys and cakes:** Bacardi Moreau, *Crónicas*, 2:373.

P. 9. **There were also the developments:** Ibid., 344; also Speck, 58.

P. 10. **"A people's history can be seen:** Bacardi Moreau, *Crónicas*, 2:5.

P. 10. **"The deed with all its rawness:** Bacardi Moreau, *Crónicas*, 1:8.

Chapter 2. Entrepreneur

P. 11. **Facundo Bacardi Massó, Emilio's father:** Accounts of life in Sitges and the early years in Santiago come from Bacardi family histories, including Amalia Bacardi Cape, *Emilio Bacardi* and José Argamasilla Bacardi, *Las Crónicas de Bacardi*. Other sources for this chapter include Padura Fuentes and Aixalá and Argamasilla, as well as archival documents in Cuba.

P. 11. **As one American visitor:** Rev. Abiel Abbot, *Letters Written in the Interior of Cuba* (Boston, 1829), quoted in Atkins, 65.

P. 13. **Town records show:** Fondo Protocolos Notariales, Archivo Histórico Provincial, Santiago de Cuba. Notario: José Ramón Chacón. Libro 397, folios 397–98, August 9, 1851. Libro 398, folios 214–15, May 19, 1852.

P. 13. **The sky that morning:** The account of the earthquake is from Estorch.

P. 14. **"God does with us:** John Neumann, "A Very Special Patron: Saint Anthony María Claret," *From the Housetops*, no. 17 (1979).

P. 17. **By one estimate:** McCusker, 234.

P. 17. **The dean of Cuban sugar:** Moreno Fraginals, 1976, 122.

P. 19. **As early as 1816:** Marrero, 10: 260.

P. 19. **Given the high cost:** Moreno Fraginals, 1976, 122; Wurdemann, 152.

P. 19. **"able to satisfy:** Missen, et al., 15

P. 19. **Between 1851 and 1856:** Campoamor, 56 77.

P. 20. **A Bacardi company narrative:** Roig de Leuchsenring, *El libro de Cuba*, 838.

P. 21. **A distiller writing in 1757:** Quoted in Broom, 15.

P. 23. **"It was a light product:** Bonera, 76.

P. 24. **"It was the end-product:** H. Zumbado, *The Barman's Sixth Sense* (Havana: Cubaexport, 1980), quoted in Barty-King, 110.

Chapter 3. A Patriot Is Made

P. 26. **Upon his return:** Sources for the account of Emilio Bacardi's adolescent and early manhood years are Bacardi Moreau, *Crónicas*; Bacardi Moreau, *Florencio Villanova y Pío Rosado;* and Bacardi Cape, *Emilio Bacardi*.

P. 26. **"All nerves:** Bacardi Moreau, *Florencio Villanova*, 37–38.

P. 29. **The slightest transgression:** Goodman, 220.

P. 29. **In 1864 they invited:** Foner, *A History of Cuba* 2:166.

P. 29. **(fn) Juan's mother was:** Juan Bacardi Moreau to Elvira Cape, September 20, 1922, Bacardi archives. The June 16, 1947, memorandum was dictated by José M. Bosch to his secretary Bessie Story and is in the Bacardi archives.

P. 30. **"Ring the bell and call:** Emilio's version of the story is in Bacardi Moreau, *Crónicas*, 4: 32–34.

P. 30. **Clever as a fox:** This Rosado story is from Bacardi Moreau, *Florencio Villanova*, 39.

P. 31. **In a message to his governors:** Bacardi Moreau, *Crónicas*, 4:33–34.

P. 32. **Gas lanterns:** A typical *retreta* in Santiago is described in Goodman, 141–46. The uprising attempt is described in Bacardi Moreau, *Crónicas*, 4:46–47; Bacardi Cape, *Emilio Bacardi*, 48–49; and Alegría, 155–56.

P. 33. **Writing in retrospect:** Bacardi Moreau, *Crónicas*, 4:46.

P. 33. **To the astonishment:** Bacardi Moreau, *Crónicas*, 4:48–49; Bacardi Moreau, *Florencio Villanova*, 40–41.

P. 34. **When a group of local:** Bacardi Cape, *Emilio Bacardi*, 49.

P. 34. **A young slave:** Bacardi Moreau, *Crónicas*, 4:112; Buch López, 243.

P. 34. **"The Spanish authorities:** Buch López, 243.

P. 34. **The authorities officially defined:** Bacardi Moreau, *Crónicas*, 4:104.

P. 35. **He and his wife:** Bacardi Cape, *Emilio Bacardi*, 52; Alegría, 160.

P. 36. **"glorious and bloody:** Toledo Sante, 21.

P. 36. **El presidio político:** Martí, *Selected Writings*, 9–18.

P. 37. **As part of his research:** Bacardi Moreau, *Crónicas*, 5:54.

P. 37. **In October, an American:** The *Virginius* story is told in Foner, *A History of Cuba*, 2:244–47; Thomas, 262–63; Alegría, 163; Bacardi Moreau, *Crónicas* 5:363–66; and Bacardi Cape, ed., *Steamer "Virginius" Incident*.

P. 38. **Facundo Jr. was working:** Facundo Jr. recollects the execution in a February 28, 1915, letter to his brother Emilio, excerpted in "Fiel Vigia de Bacardi," *Bacardi Gráfico* 3, no. 8 (January 1958), 10–11.

P. 38. **In 1874, still in:** Reorganization details are from Bacardi Cape, *Emilio Bacardi*; Torres Hurtado; and archival documents.

P. 40. **José Martí famously described:** Martí, *Obras Completas* 1:675–76.

P. 41. **He cosponsored a measure:** Bacardi Moreau, *Crónicas* 6:259.

P. 41. **"No concrete charges:** Bacardi Cape, *Emilio Bacardi*, 74.

P. 42. **A clerk at the field headquarters:** Bacardi Moreau, *Florencio Villanova*, 46–49; Bacardi Moreau, *Crónicas*, 6:349–52.

Chapter 4. A Time of Transition

P. 43. **In October 1880:** Bacardi Cape, *Emilio Bacardi*, 83–84.

P. 46. **In 1879 the Bacardis:** Fondo Protocolos Notariales, Archivo Histórico Provincial, Santiago de Cuba. Notario: Rafael Ramírez, Libro 561, folio 604, November 9, 1879. See also, Aixalá and Argamasilla, 34.

P. 47. **Martí's idea:** Mañach, 243.

P. 48. **Emilio's first venture:** Bacardi Moreau, *Crónicas*, 7:155–67.

P. 49. **For the 1888 Barcelona fair:** Ibid., 7:194–95.

P. 50. **"A trifling increase:** A draft copy of the Bacardi response is in the company archives.

P. 50. **"At a time when:** Bacardi Moreau, *Crónicas*, 7:243–46

P. 50. **When El espíritu:** Ibid., 7:238

P. 51. **"the tranquility of:** Ibid., 7:232–33.

P. 51. **in Martí's words, the political:** Martí, "On: The Pan-American Congress."

P. 52. **In March 1889, a Philadelphia:** "Do We Want Cuba?" originally published in *The Manufacturer* and excerpted in the *New York Evening Post*, March 21, 1889. Martí's reply was published in the *Post* on March 25, 1889. Both articles are reprinted in Martí, *Selected Writings*, as "A Vindication of Cuba," 261–67.

P. 52. **"everyone looks like his own:** José Martí, "Impressions of America (by a very fresh Spaniard)," in *Selected Writings*, 32.

P. 52. "the excessive worship of wealth: Quoted in Mañach, 218.

P. 52. "to extend its dominions: Martí, "On: The Pan-American Congress."

P. 53. "They admire this nation: Martí, "A Vindication of Cuba," in *Selected Writings*, 263.

P. 53. to promote "war and the: Quoted in Foner, *A History of Cuba*, 2:313.

P. 53. A dinner party there: Bacardi Moreau, *Crónicas*, 7:285.

P. 53. Federico Pérez Carbó noted: Ibid., 7:347–53.

P. 54. The deputy mayor: Ibid., 7:349–50.

P. 54. "not so much a mere political: Foner, *History of Cuba*, 2:319.

P. 55. "And he stayed there: Bacardi Moreau, *Vía crucis*, 264.

P. 56. Using commercial matters: Bacardi Cape, *Emilio Bacardi*, 105; Aguilar, "Emilio Bacardi, en el tiempo y para el tiempo."

P. 56. Annual interest on the war: Thomas, 307.

P. 56. In a house just down: Ravelo, *La ciudad*, 48; Buch, 279.

P. 57. "a certain disdain and coldness: Quoted in Mañach, 342.

Chapter 5. Cuba Libre

P. 58. Seventeen-year-old Emilito: The account of Emilito joining the rebel army is from Martha Padilla, "Hasta algún día, coronel," *Diario Las Américas* (Miami), October 25, 1972; Mercedes García Tudurí, "El último coronel: Emilio Bacardi Lay," *Diario Las Américas*, November 8, 1972; Luis Varona, "Palestra: El centenario del Coronel Bacardi," *Miami Herald*, June 12, 1977; Luis Varona, "Coronel Emilio Bacardi Lay: El centenario de su nacimiento," *Diario Las Américas*, June 12, 1977; Tulio Díaz Rivera, "Sepamos quien fue el Coronel Emilio Bacardi," *Diario Las Américas*, August 6, 1976. See also Bacardi Cape, *Emilio Bacardi*; Buch López, 281; Ravelo, *La ciudad* (HAVANA: 1951), 195.

P. 59. "General, my son has gone: Quoted in Varona, "Coronel Emilio Bacardi Lay."

P. 59. "It was the most emotional: Varona, "Palestra."

P. 59. For a true revolutionary: See Ferrer, especially 157–69.

P. 60. Santiago was more militarized: Ravelo, *La ciudad*, 175–221; Buch López, 275–85.

P. 60. Martínez, who knew José: Cape, "Desde Céspedes."

P. 60. He oversaw the smuggling: Ibid.; Bacardi Cape.

P. 61. In July 1895, Gómez: Quoted in Foner, *The Spanish-Cuban-American War*. 1:22.

P. 61. beginning with his own mother-in-law: Cape.

P. 61. In some months, his collections: Bacardi Cape, *Emilio Bacardi*, 111.

P. 62. The owner, Andrés Brugal: Chez Checo, 1:224.

P. 63. On his first day in command: de Quesada, 90.

P. 63. One day in May: The incident at Emilio's house is described in Bacardi Cape, *Emilio Bacardi*, 112; Bacardi Moreau, *Crónicas*, 8:363, and 9:40; and in Cape.

P. 64. One Cuban officer: Forment, 20–21.

P. 65. Her sister Herminia later: Cape.

P. 65. A brown paper bag: The originals of the notes and typewritten transcriptions are in the archive of the Museo Emilio Bacardi in Santiago de Cuba.

P. 66. "Whatever our fate: Related in Bacardi Cape, ed., "De Cuba a Chafarinas," in *Epistolario*, 7.

P. 67. The mission was highly dangerous: The account of Maceo's death is from Bacardi Moreau, *Crónicas*, 9:48–54, and a letter from Emilio Bacardi Lay to Luis Varona, December 7, 1970, cited in Varona, "Palestra."

P. 67. In a letter to Maceo's: Bacardi Moreau, *Crónicas*, 9:65–66.

P. 67. On December 28, 1896: Foner, *Spanish-Cuban-American War*, 1:97.

P. 67. Morocco in front: Bacardi Cape, ed., "De Cuba a Chafarinas," in *Epistolario*, 28.

Chapter 6. The Colossus Intervenes

P. 68. Hanging prominently: "A Listless Opening," *New York Times*, June 17, 1896.

P. 68. "enlists the ardent: "The First Day's Work," *New York Times*, June 17, 1896.

P. 69. **Tomás Estrada Palma:** The smuggling work of Pérez Carbó is revealed in Federico Pérez Carbó, "Relación de las expediciones armadas para auxiliar a los revolucionarios cubanos, durante los años de 1895 a 1898," Archivo Nacional, Havana, caja 32, número 42.

P. 69. **"You're thinking:** The letters from Federico Pérez Carbó to Elvira Cape and Emilio Bacardi in Jamaica are reprinted in Bacardi Cape, ed., *Epistolario.*

P. 70. **"I don't expect anything:** Antonio Maceo to Federico Pérez Carbó, July 14, 1896, Archivo Nacional, Havana, caja 100, número 4186.

P. 71. **A Santiago writer described:** Ravelo, *La ciudad,* 229.

P. 71. **In May, police raided:** Bacardi Cape, *Emilio Bacardi,* 122.

P. 72. **In an essay he wrote:** Ibid., 119–20.

P. 73. **One top U.S. diplomat:** Pérez, Jr., *The War of 1898,* 19 and 82.

P. 74. **"We will oppose any:** Ibid., 20.

P. 74. **García's soldiers carried out:** Cosmas, 186.

P. 74. **"Landing at Daiquirí:** Pérez, *War of 1898,* 86.

P. 75. **214 U.S. soldiers:** Casualty figures are from Trask, 245.

P. 75. **Roosevelt reported:** Cosmas, 218.

P. 75. **The two men soberly reviewed:** Bacardi Cape, *Emilio Bacardi,* 127.

P. 76. **A Cuban resident described:** Ravelo, *La ciudad,* 253.

P. 76. **The surrender ceremony:** The scene is described in Goldstein, et al., 152–53.

P. 77. **"To be brief and:** "The Future of the 71st," *New York Times,* August 31, 1898.

P. 77. **General S. B. M.:** Foner, *The Spanish-Cuban-American War,* 2:394–95.

P. 77. **"Allow me, sir:** Bacardi Moreau, *Crónicas* 10:133–34.

P. 77. **"all [the undersigned]:** "The Petition to Mr. McKinley," *New York Times,* July 25, 1898.

P. 78. **"It does not make any:** "Admiral Sampson on Cuba," *New York Times,* December 24, 1898.

P. 78. **"The obligation of those:** "Carta abierta a Sr. Alcalde Municipal," July 27, 1898, Museo Emilio Bacardi archives, Santiago de Cuba.

P. 79. **Long lines of wan:** Leonard Wood, "Santiago Since the Surrender," 516–17.

P. 80. **On the job at the break:** Hagedorn, 189.

P. 80. **"The passion for:** Ibid., 196.

P. 80. **"With one or two:** Ibid., 198.

P. 80. **"If that man is as good:** Bacardi Cape, *Emilio Bacardi,* 135.

P. 80. **"I don't know what my:** Hagedorn, 217.

Chapter 7. A Public Servant in a Misgoverned Land

P. 81. **The U.S. military governor:** Archibald, 89.

P. 81. **"The Isle of Pines:** Leonard Wood to Elihu Root, April 4, 1901, Leonard Wood Collection, Library of Congress.

P. 82. **They despaired when:** Robinson, 134.

P. 82. **During the occupation:** Pérez, *On Becoming Cuban,* 117.

P. 82. **He wrote later that:** Bacardi Moreau, *Hacia tierras viejas,* 21–23.

P. 83. **On his first day:** Bacardi Moreau, *Crónicas* 10:191

P. 83. **"We have three parties:** Ibid., 10:194.

P. 84. **With no city council:** Meriño, 26 (sted 14).

P. 84. **General Calixto García:** Foner, *The Spanish-Cuban-American War* 2:390–94.

P. 84. **"I am surrounded:** Emilio Bacardi to his father, December 20, 1898, Emilio Bacardi Archive, Cuban Heritage Collection, University of Miami Richter Library.

P. 85. **After he discovered:.** "School Squabble in Santiago," *New York Times,* December 8, 1898.

P. 85. **As a result, he won:** Bacardi Cape, *Emilio Bacardi,* 141.

P. 86. **In an article he wrote:** Wood, "The Existing Conditions."

P. 86. **In a July 1899:** Hagedorn, 251.

P. 86. **Wood believes:** Hugh Thomas, 440.

P. 87. **"Without exception:** Wood, "The Present Situation."

P. 87. **Emilio wrote Wood:** Emilio Bacardi to Leonard Wood, June 1901, handwritten copy of letter in Archivo Histórico Provincial, Santiago de Cuba.

P. 87. **The *property-holding:*** "Gen. Wood on the Cubans," *New York Times,* June 24, 1899.

P. 88. **"ignorant and incompetent:** Pérez, *Cuba: Between Reform and Revolution,* 182.

P. 88. **"Giving the vote:** Foner, *Spanish-Cuban-American War,* 2:529.

P. 88. **"The possibility of negro:** Hagedorn, 267.

P. 88. **"to block the will:** Meriño, 36 (sted 24).

P. 88. **"some talk of universal:** Foner, *Spanish-Cuban-American War,* 2:529.

P. 88. **In an official:** Ibid., 531.

P. 89. **Faced with the prospect:** Hagedorn, 421.

P. 89. **Elihu Root warned:** Pérez, *Cuba: Between Reform and Revolution,* 188.

P. 90. **They exploit your:** Alejandro Gonzalez to Emilio Bacardi, October 8, 1900. Bacardi archives.

P. 90. **Before taking office:** Emilio Bacardi to Leonard Wood, June 1901, handwritten copy of letter in Archivo Histórico Provincial, Santiago de Cuba.

P. 91. **Emilio concluded:** Emilio Bacardi, Last Will and Testament dated January 25, 1902, Bacardi archives.

P. 92. **When Roosevelt was elected:** Forment, 127.

P. 93. **After greeting the candidate:** Bacardi Cape, *Emilio Bacardi,* 167.

P. 93. **"It would be a travesty:** Forment, 173.

P. 93. **He introduced legislation:** Bacardi Cape, *Emilio Bacardi,* 170–71.

P. 94. **"For winners and losers:** Forment, 85.

P. 94. **On September 8:** Ibid., 190.

P. 95. **Estrada Palma asked:** Thomas, 476.

P. 95. **"My increasingly firm:** Emilio Bacardi to Elvira Cape, September 27, 1906, Bacardi archives.

P. 96. **Emilio wrote back:** Emilio Bacardi to Leonard Wood, March 19, 1907, Leonard Wood Collection, Library of Congress.

P. 96. **To my people:** Forment, 261.

P. 97. **Emilio returned to the:** Emilio Bacardi to Carlos García Velez, December 25, 1908, Bacardi archives.

P. 97. **"My only affiliation:** Ramón Corona, "Don Emilio Bacardi," *Diario Las Américas,* August 11, 1970.

Chapter 8. *The One That Made Cuba Famous*

P. 98. **The Bacardi story:** Bacardi Cape, *Emilio Bacardi en su tiempo,* 147–52; Bacardi ad in *Life* magazine, 1966.

P. 99. **For the Pan-American:** Bacardi Moreau, *Crónicas,* 10: 257.

P. 99. **Their rum beat out:** Bonera, 156.

P. 99. **The historic event:** Forment, 410.

P. 100. **Unlike Emilio:** Bacardi Cape, *Emilio Bacardi,* 175.

P. 100. **A friend and admirer:** J. Aristegueta, "Crónicas del sentimiento: Don Facundo Bacardi," *El Periódico de la Mañana* (Santiago de Cuba?), November 28, 1926.

P. 101. **Emilio had arranged:** Manuel Johnson to Eudaldo Romagosa, February 24, 1901; memorandum from Tasker Bliss, Collector of Customs for Cuba and Port of Havana, July 1, 1901, Leonard Wood Collection, Library of Congress.

P. 101. **"He is an honest man:** Leonard Wood to Elihu Root, April 4, 1901, Leonard Wood Collection, Library of Congress.

P. 101. **He negotiated the opening:** Argamasilla Bacardi, 44.

P. 102. **Estrada's letters back:** Bacardi archives.

P. 103. **The pitch got its start:** Bacardi Cape, *Emilio Bacardi,* 98–99; see also company promotional literature.

P. 104. **An ad from about 1910:** Bacardi archives.

P. 104. **A British physician touted:** R. Fielding Ould to President, West Indies Committee, March 5, 1932, reprinted in Bacardi pamphlet, November 1932.

P. 104. **as late as 1934:** García López.

P. 104. **the American Medical Association:** Resolution on Alcohol Submitted by Council on Health and Public Instruction, Minutes of Sixty-Eighth Annual Session, American Medical Association House of Delegates, June 4–7, 1917, 68.

P. 104. **"It's a young woman:** Leyva, 176.

p. 105. **"to reduce the purely:** H. P. Blavatsky, *The Key to Theosophy* (1890; repr., Pasadena CA: Theosophical University Press, 1972), 270–71.

P. 105. **Years later, Mimín's daughter:** Grau, 14.

P. 105. **"The church that is said:** Bacardi Moreau, *Hacia tierras viejas*, 135.

P. 105. **One of his angriest:** Emilio Bacardi to Manuel Plana, August 26, 1910, Bacardi archives.

P. 106. **They declared it to be worth:** Manuel García Vidal (lawyer and notary public), "Transformación de Sociedad Mercantil Colectiva en Mercantil e Industría Anónima," May 2, 1919, Archivo Histórico Provincial, Santiago.

P. 107. **The new distillery was inaugurated:** *Luz de Oriente* magazine (February 1922).

P. 107. **"an uncountable number:** "La fiesta del Ron Bacardi," *El Cubano Libre* (Santiago), February 6, 1922.

P. 107. **On the last afternoon:** Ducazcal, "Vida ejemplar," *Luz de Oriente* 1, no. 6 (September 1922) (special issue dedicated to Emilio Bacardi), 7.

P. 107. **"the khaki uniforms:** Carlos E. Forment, "Hacia la tierra," *Luz de Oriente* 1, no. 6 (September 1922), 13.

P. 108. **One of his mourners:** Alberto Duboy, "El último criollo," *Luz de Oriente* 1, no. 6 (September 1922), 10.

P. 108. **"a great rebel:** Federico Pérez Carbó, letter to the editor, *Diario de Cuba*, reprinted in *Luz de Oriente* 1, no. 6 (September 1922), 22.

P. 108. **"a man of business without:** Fernando Ortiz, "La muerte de Bacardi," *Luz de Oriente* 1, no. 6 (September 1922), 9.

Chapter 9. The Next Generation

P. 109. **"Goodbye forever:** Ring Lardner, "Prohibition Blues," (New York and Detroit: Jerome Remick & Co., 1919).

P. 109. **Between 1916 and 1928:** Pérez, *On Becoming Cuban*, 167.

P. 109. **Some U.S. bar owners:** Ibid., 168; Woon, 42.

P. 110. **The favored Havana watering hole:** Woon, 4–7.

P. 110. **"the aristocrat of cocktails:** Ibid., 40–41.

P. 111. **by 1924 had surpassed:** Roig de Leuchsenring, *El libro de Cuba*, 840.

P. 111. **Some studies even suggested:** Jeffrey A. Miron, "The Effect of Alcohol Prohibition on Alcohol Consumption" (Working Paper 7130, National Bureau of Economic Research, Cambridge, MA, May 1999).

P. 111. **By 1925, it was said to be:** Roig de Leuchsenring, *El libro de Cuba*, 838.

P. 112. **"could not have been more:** Bacardi Cape, *Emilio Bacardi*, 211.

P. 114. **"the loveliest and:** Durand, "My Mad Romance," part 3, December 16, 1923.

P. 114. **"There was a great deal:** Ibid., part 2, December 9, 1923.

P. 114. **description of her honeymoon:** Ibid., part 6, January 6, 1924.

P. 114. **When Martha asked him:** Ibid., part 5, December 30, 1923.

P. 115. **Basil Woon reported:** Woon, 257.

P. 115. **"one of the most popular:** "Bacardi Near Death in Pistol Accident," *New York Times*, July 19, 1932.

P. 116. **We have seen the emergence:** Roig de Leuchsenring, *La colonia superviva*.

P. 116. **If we have taken:** Roig de Leuchsenring, *El libro de Cuba*, 718.

P. 116. **"This trademark:** Ibid., 838.

P. 117. **one of which had purchased:** Pérez, *On Becoming Cuban*, 169.

P. 118. **"there are more drinkers:** Woon, 259.

P. 118. **U.S. Department of Commerce:** Willoughby, 17.

P. 118. **New York newspapers took:** "Bacardi Near Death."

P. 118. **In 1928 his tax department:** "Lifts Bacardi Embargo: Machado Orders Inquiry into Tax Claim Against Rum Company," *New York Times*, July 13, 1928.

P. 118. **The Bacardis were already:** *Diario de La Marina* (Havana), July 12, 1928.

P. 120. **The jobs of two thousand:** "Lifts Bacardi Embargo."

P. 121. **When he heard that a friend:** Pepín Bosch, in videotaped interview by Miguel Gonzalez-Pando, September 1990, video recording in Cuban Living History Project, Florida International University.

P. 121. **More than half the buildings:** "$4,000,000 Damage in Santiago Quake," *New York Times*, February 4, 1932; "Recuerdo histórico del terremoto de 3 de febrero de 1932," in *Magazine Las Noticias* (Santiago de Cuba: Arroyo Hermanos, 1932).

P. 123. **"have seen the importance:** Flyer distributed by Comité Central de Huelga de la Federación Obrera de Santiago de Cuba, August 17, 1933.

P. 123. **He angrily wired:** Enrique Schueg to Pedro Lay, Western Union Cablegram, Havana to Santiago, August 18, 1933, Bacardi archives.

P. 123. **"for the purpose of:** Pedro E. Lay to Hipolito Garrido, August 21, 1933, Bacardi archives.

P. 123. **"In this critical hour:** Enrique Schueg, undated open letter, "Al sindicato en formación, obreros y empleados todos de la Compañía Ron Bacardi, S.A.," Bacardi archives.

P. 123. **"The Bacardi Company:** El Comité de Huelga, Sindicato de Obreros y Empleados de la Empresa Bacardi, Confederación Nacional Obrera de Cuba, open letter, "A los compañeros trabajadores y pueblo en general," August 31, 1933, Bacardi archives.

P. 124. **"coalition of convenience:** Louis A. Pérez Jr., "Cuba, c. 1930–1950," in *Cuba: A Short History*, ed. Leslie Bethell (London: Cambridge University Press, 1993), 68.

P. 124. **"frankly Communistic":** Ibid., 70.

P. 125. **Historians later viewed:** See, e.g., Aguilar, *1933*; Suchlicki.

P. 125. **Although we know:** "Estatutos del sindicato de empleados de oficinas de la Compañía Ron Bacardi, S.A., de Santiago de Cuba," October 20, 1933.

Chapter 10. *The Empire Builder*

P. 126. **The new Bacardi rum:** Company treasurer Frank L. Dorothy informed Bacardi stockholders in a letter dated March 12, 1958, that 1931 Bacardi sales from Mexico had totaled 102,499 Mexican pesos. The exchange rate in 1931 was 2.6 Mexican pesos to one U.S. dollar.

P. 126. **"You're not doing anything:** Pepín Bosch, in videotaped interview by Miguel Gonzalez-Pando, September 1990, video recording in Cuban Living History Project, Florida International University.

P. 127. **"I was a bum student:** "Dynamic Pepín Bosch," *Havana Post*, January 15, 1950.

P. 127. **He also figured that:** Gallo.

P. 127. **By December 1934:** Foster, 43.

P. 128. **industry analysts had:** "Rum Rush," *Time*, December 4, 1933; see also "Liquor in America: An Interim Audit," *Fortune*, October 1934, 104.

P. 128. **As many as forty thousand:** "Liquor Scramble," *Time*, October 9, 1953.

P. 128. **"For the plump:** "Downtown," *Time*, November 20, 1933.

P. 129. **As it was passed:** "Rum Rush."

P. 129. **Some liquor importers:** William J. Dorion, letter to the editor, *Time*, October 23, 1933.

P. 129. **Schenley contracted to import:** Barty-King and Massel, 145.

P. 129. **His first contribution:** Foster, 55.

P. 130. **"totally linked to this land:** Roig de Leuchsenring, *El libro de Cuba*, 839.

P. 130. **A 1935 article in the:** "Proper Names Give Us New Words," *New York Times Sunday Magazine*, December 8, 1935.

P. 130. **Enrique Schueg himself came:** Foster, 56.

P. 130. **(Other bartenders, called:** "Cocktails Must Live Up to Name," *New York Times*, April 29, 1936.

P. 131. **Bosch briefly considered Louisiana:** Foster, 57.

P. 131. **Bosch visited Puerto Rico:** Bosch, 20.

P. 131. **Many Puerto Ricans in 1936:** Monge, 88–98.

P. 132. **Members of Congress:** Monge, 95.

P. 132. **"from all competition:** "Rum Company Wins Case," *New York Times*, May 11, 1938.

P. 132. **At the same time, Pepín:** "New Liquor Tax Law Is Signed by Winship," *New York Times*, May 17, 1937.

P. 132. **"I shall consider my:** Gallo.

P. 132. **He also claimed:** "New Liquor Tax Law."

P. 133. **"to elevate the moral level:** Newspaper ad in *El Mundo* (San Juan, PR) (among others), February 4, 1937.

P. 134. **"more than 200 workers:** Flyer distributed by El Comité-Ejecutivo de la Unión de Obreros y Empleados de la Empresa "Bacardi," April 27, 1939, Bacardi archives.

P. 134. **The company quickly responded:** Bacardi legal department, "Informe, en relación a la carta cursada por la Sucursal Bacardi de la Ciudad de la Habana, el día 10 de Mayo del presente año 1939," Bacardi archives.

P. 134. **Union leaders labeled:** Union flyers in Bacardi archives.

P. 134. **"not only because of the:** Draft of Bacardi letter to Secretary of Labor, undated, Bacardi archives.

P. 135. **Tensions rose sharply:** Union charges and company responses quoted in "There Are Still Judges in Cuba!" paid Bacardi advertisement, *Havana Post*, October 6, 1943.

P. 135. **Management officials were:** "Government of Cuba Seizes Bacardi Plant," *Washington Post*, October 7, 1943.

P. 136. **A dinner held in his honor:** "Santiago de Cuba honra a Enrique Schueg," *Carteles*, February 6, 1944.

P. 136. **But Luis and Espín had both:** Foster, 62.

P. 137. **When Espín and Luis:** Ibid., 61–62.

P. 137. **In the midst of the 1943:** Text of speech by Guillermo G. Mármol in honor of Pepín Bosch, November 21, 1993, Miami, Florida.

P. 137. **With Schueg's support:** Foster, 62–63.

P. 137. **In the coming years, he showed up:** Guillermo G. Mármol, letter to author, faxed October 23, 2005.

P. 139. **"Dear Danielito:** Emilio Bacardi Lay to Daniel Bacardi, December 9, 1943, Bacardi archives.

P. 140. **Daniel said he was sure:** Daniel Bacardi to Emilio Bacardi Lay, February 9, 1944, Bacardi archives.

P. 141. **His lawyer and aide:** Mármol letter to author, October 23, 2005.

P. 141. **The business world:** Elbert Hubbard, *A Message to García* (New York: Roycrofters, 1899).

P. 142. **"an American imitation:** "Liquor in America: An Interim Audit," *Fortune*, October 1934, 108.

P. 142. **"It would be my suggestion:** Memorandum from José M. Bosch to Enrique Schueg, October 24, 1945, Bacardi archives.

P. 142. **The yacht captain was killed:** Foster, 64.

P. 142. **By the end of 1946:** *The U.S. Rum Market* (New York: Rums of Puerto Rico, 1953), 5.

P. 142. **By 1948, Bacardi rum sales:** "Beating the Yanqui at His Own Game . . . ," Liquor Survey, Research and Marketing Department, *New York Journal-American*, March 1948.

P. 143. **Company advertising in the early:** "Bacardi Bar Book," cocktail recipe booklet produced by Schenley Import Corporation, 1940.

Chapter 11. *Cuba Corrupted*

P. 144. **"When I got to the:** Gosch and Hammer, 305.

P. 144. **His longtime associate:** Ibid., 269.

P. 145. **For five days, the capos:** Cirules, 38.

P. 146. **"Lansky and Batista:** Gosch and Hammer, 284.

P. 147. **calling him *guajiro*:** Castro schoolmate Alfredo "Chino" Esquivel, interviewed by Adriana Bosch for 2004 PBS documentary film, *Fidel Castro*; see also Pardo Llada, 19.

P. 147. **"I arrived at the university:** Ramonet, 106.

P. 147. **"I never went to classes:** Ibid., 108.

P. 147. **He made his big public:** *El Mundo* (Havana), November 28, 1946.

P. 148. **"That was when my:** Ramonet, 109.

P. 148. **According to an eyewitness:** Alfredo Esquivel, PBS interview. The story is also reported in Geyer, 50–51; Bardach, 239; and Montaner, 14.

P. 149. **"It was difficult to dislike:** Thomas, 760.

P. 149. **"a scandalous bacchanalia:** Ibid., 767.

P. 150. **"I told him I was:** The Prío-Bosch discussion comes from Miguel Gonzalez-Pando's interview of Pepín Bosch, September 1990, video recording in Cuban Living History Project, Florida International University.

P. 150. **"the naming of the dynamic:** "Dynamic Pepín Bosch Hopes to Put Nation on 'Business Basis,' " *Havana Post*, January 15, 1950.

P. 151. **"no political ambitions:** Typewritten text of remarks, Bacardi archives.

P. 151. **So many friends, family:** "Será respetado quien cumpla con su deber." *El Mundo* (Havana), January 10, 1950.

P. 151. **"I was an aide:** Ibid.

P. 151. **"I'm a working businessman:** "Daré protección a todos los productores de Cuba," *Diario de la Marina* (Havana), January 5, 1950.

P. 151. **"Dodging taxes:** "J. P. McEvoy Observes," *Havana Post*, April 8, 1951.

P. 152. **"Everyone will pay:** "An Honest Man," *Time*, March 19, 1951.

P. 152. **"I don't want to be:** "Yo sólo aspiro a irme a mi casa," *Carteles*, October 22, 1950.

P. 153. **"realized that as the:** "An Honest Man," *Time*, March 19, 1951.

Chapter 12. Cha-Cha-Chá

P. 155. **(fn) A 1999 dictionary:** José Sánchez-Boudy, *Diccionario Mayor de Cubanismos* (Miami: Ediciones Universal, 1999), 637.

P. 156. **"The foreign visitor:** Herminio Portell Vilá, "Futilidad de la ley," *El Mundo* (Havana), June 20, 1952.

P. 157. **On the eightieth:** Foster, 72.

P. 157. **Titled "Bacardi:** "Bacardi, La Gran Industria Cubana," in Otero, ed., *Libro de Cuba*, 755–58.

P. 157. **The Cuban ballerina:** "The Imperious Vision of Cuba's Other Ruler-for-Life," *New York Times*, February 6, 2005.

P. 157. **The rum company had sponsored baseball:** González Echevarría, 101.

P. 158. **The most popular Cuban:** "Mensaje de Roberto Ortiz," *Bacardi Gráfico* 3, no. 11 (October 1958), 4.

P. 158. **a "danceable program:** Radio scripts in Bacardi archives.

P. 159. **Family members were fond of:** José "Tito" Argamasilla, interview by author, January 13, 2006, Miami.

P. 160. **The plan was to lead:** The account of the Moncada attack is from Szulc, 255–81; Thomas, 824–44; and Castro's own recollections in Ramonet, 117–46.

P. 161. **"We could hear and feel:** Vilma Espín, interview by Tad Szulc, May 15, 1985, Havana transcript, Tad Szulc Papers, John F. Kennedy Library, Boston, Massachusetts.

P. 162. **"If this was something:** Pepín Bosch, in videotaped interview by Miguel Gonzalez-Pando, September 1990, video recording in Cuban Living History Project, Florida International University; see also Pepín Bosch, interview by Georgie Anne Geyer, January 17, 1985, Miami, Florida, transcript, Georgie Anne Geyer Papers, Hoover Institution Archives, Stanford, CA.

P. 162. **One of Grau's most enduring:** The account of Grau and Fidel on Pan de Guajaibón is based on the author's interviews with Juan Grau, June 1, 2004, and Father Armando Llorente, June 30, 2005, both in Miami. Portions of the story are recounted in Latell, 70–72; Szulc, 120–21; and Blanco, 205–6.

P. 164. **"I do not fear prison:** Castro Ruz, "History Will Absolve Me."

P. 164. **(fn) Castro carefully studied:** See Geyer, 37–38.

P. 164. **quietly arranged to cover:** Bosch interview by Geyer; Bosch interview by Gonzalez-Pando.

P. 165. **On one occasion:** Guillermo Mármol, interview by the author, January 12, 2006, Miami.

P. 165. **Daniel Bacardi's chauffeur:** The kidnapping story is laid out in detail in Juan Amador Rodríguez, "Doce horas de angustía: El secuestro de Facundito Bacardi," *Bohemia* (Havana) 46, no. 9 (February 28, 1954) 74–81.

P. 167. **"Do you plan to stay:** Carlos Franqui, "Una entrevista con Fidel Castro," *Carteles* (Havana), May 22, 1955.

P. 167. **In 1965 he told:** Szulc, 207.

P. 167. **"Show much guile:** Thomas, 853–54.

Chapter 13. *A Brief Golden Age*

P. 168. **"He had drunk double frozen:** Ernest Hemingway, *Islands in the Stream* (New York: Charles Scribner's Sons, 1970), 211.

P. 168. **he mentioned Bacardi products:** Hemingway mentions Hatuey beer in *To Have and Have Not* (New York: Charles Scribner's Sons, 1937), 30, and in *The Old Man and the Sea* (New York: Charles Scribner's Sons, 1952), 22.

P. 169. **The event was held:** The Bacardi reception for Hemingway is described in detail by Guillermo Cabrera Infante in "El viejo y la marca," *Ciclón* 2, no. 5, (September 1956); in Fuentes, 28–30; Heufelder, 253–55; and in contemporary Havana newspapers.

P. 170. **At Lansky's urging:** Accounts of Mafia ties to gambling in Cuba are from Ernest Havemann, "U.S. Gambling Mob in Cuba," *Life*, March 10, 1958, 28–37; see also, Lowinger and Fox.

P. 170. **87 percent:** Louis A. Pérez Jr., *Cuba: Between Reform and Revolution*, 302.

P. 171. **Grau urged Vilma to:** Juan Grau, interview by the author, June 1, 2004, Miami.

P. 171. **"I couldn't put it down:** Vilma Espín, interview by Tad Szulc, May 15, 1985, Havana, Cuba. Tad Szulc Papers, Series 1, Box 1. John Fitzgerald Kennedy Library, Boston, MA.

P. 172. **"She had been somewhat:** Grau, interview by the author, June 1, 2004.

P. 172. **With U.S. funding:** Thomas, 855.

P. 172. **Vice President Richard Nixon:** Szulc, 319, Schlesinger, 173.

P. 172. **"I'm glad Ambassador:** Phillips, 325.

P. 173. **"With a Head Held:** Bacardi advertisement from company archives.

P. 174. **A World Bank team:** Truslow, 779–83.

P. 175. **"After detailed investigation:** Truslow, 979.

P. 175. **When a Bacardi executive:** Urbano Real to Compañía Ron Bacardi, December 31, 1949, Bacardi archives.

P. 175. **"With a little good fortune:** José Bosch to Manuel Andrial, June 17, 1949, Bacardi archives.

P. 175. **"Pepín Bosch never misses:** *Gente* (Havana), May 8, 1956.

P. 176. **"You know everybody:** José "Tito" Argamasilla, interview by the author, January 13, 2006, Miami.

P. 177. **"Juan, could you come:** Grau, interview by the author, June 1, 2004, MIAMI.

P. 178. **"He was a big believer:** Pepín Hernández, interview by the author, July 25, 2002, Santiago.

P. 178. **Cobo recalled Pepín:** Raimundo Cobo, interview by the author, September 24, 2004, Santiago de Cuba.

P. 179. **Hernández readily acknowledged:** Pepín Hernández, interview by the author, July 2, 2005, Santiago de Cuba.

P. 179. **remembered Rivas as:** Pepín Hernández, interview by the author, October 2004, Santiago de Cuba.

P. 180. **Guillermo Mármol, whose:** Guillermo Mármol, interview by the author, February 9, 2006, Miami.

P. 181. **The Matamoros boys were:** "Entrevista con Miguel Matamoros" (interview with Miguel Matamoros), date unknown, *Trabajos de Muguercía*, available at www.soncubano.com.

P. 181. **He asked Matamoros:** Manuel Jorge Cutillas, interview by the author, May 24, 2004, Miami.

P. 182. **As Grau waited:** Grau, interview with the author, June 1, 2004 MIAMI.

P. 183. **an architectural firm assessed:** Sáenz-Cancio-Martín Ingenieros, "Report on Bacardi Office Building," April 1954, Bacardi archives.

P. 184. **The final Mies:** Franz Schulze, *Mies van der Rohe: A Critical Biography* (Chicago: University of Chicago Press, 1985), 302.

Chapter 14. *Rising Up*

P. 185. **Suddenly, the tallest:** Juan Grau, interview by the author, June 1, 2004, Miami.

P. 186. **Recounting their meeting:** Alberto Bayo, *Mi aporte a la revolución cubana* (Havana: Ejército Rebelde, 1960), quoted in Szulc, 327.

P. 188. **"The one and only:** Anderson, 216.

P. 189. **she suggested that the:** Phillips, 298.

P. 189. **Che Guevara later:** Franqui, 139.

P. 189. **"Comandante, the liaison:** Szulc, 409.

P. 189. **Castro told Matthews:** "Cuban Rebel Is Visited in Hideout," *New York Times*, February 24, 1957.

P. 190. **whiled away his time:** Thomas, 791.

P. 190. **Police interrogators tortured:** Dubois, 150.

P. 191. **Bosch later said:** Pepín Bosch, interview with Georgie Anne Geyer, January 17, 1985, Hoover Institution Archives, G.A. Geyer Collection (Box Number 7, Folder ID 45), Stanford, CA.

P. 191. **Bosch told his assistant:** Guillermo Mármol, interview by author, February 9, 2006, Miami.

P. 191. **"Almost all of us here:** Speech reported in *Bacardi Gráfico* 2, no. 4 (January 1957), 3.

P. 191. **"We will collect the funds:** Rolando Masferrer to Pepín Bosch, March (date illegible), 1957, Bacardi archives.

P. 191. **These dictatorships have:** Pepín Bosch, undated, memorandum in Bacardi archives.

P. 192. **Pazos was at work:** Felipe Pazos, interview by Miguel Gonzalez-Pando, July 1991, Cuban Living History Project, Florida International University, Miami.

P. 193. **given Pazos two thousand:** Guillermo Mármol, interview by the author, January 12, 2006, MIAMI.

P. 193. **fifteen local civic:** The country club dinner is described in Dubois, 163–64.

P. 194. **"The wealthiest and most:** "Finds Revolt Spirit Aflame in Cuban City," *Chicago Tribune*, June 18, 1957.

P. 194. **Teofilo Babún:** Babún and Triay, ix.

P. 195. **Bacardi rival:** Dorschner and Fabricio, 89–90.

P. 195. **Roca later recalled:** José Antonio Roca, interview by the author, March 28, 2006, Falls Church, VA.

P. 195. **In interviews with a:** Bosch's Mexico City discussion of his contributions to Castro was reported in a State Department memorandum from R. G. Cushing and J. L. Montllor, American Embassy, Mexico, October 11, 1960, "Cuban Industrialist's Views on Cuba," Foreign Service Despatch no. 397. Department of State Cuba Series, 737.00/10-1160. Bosch also acknowledged his funding of Castro to a *New York Times* reporter in "From Sugar to Banking to Rum," *New York Times*, June 9, 1963.

P. 195. **"a mutually convenient:** Padula, "Financing Castro's Revolution," 234.

P. 195. **Bosch also helped:** Fursenko and Naftali, 6–7.

P. 196. **Frank País wrote:** Sweig, 29.

P. 197. **police arrested Pepín Bosch's son:** "Claim 2 Yanks Tortured in Santiago Jail," *Chicago Tribune*, August 8, 1957.

P. 197. **Lindy overheard one:** Carlos "Lindy" Bosch, interview by the author, March 16, 2006, Hamilton, Bermuda.

P. 198. **"We cannot stimulate:** Associated Press, "Cuban Strike Averted, Batista Forces Claim," *Washington Post*, August 5, 1957.

P. 198. **His aide Guillermo Mármol:** Guillermo Mármol, letter to the author, faxed March 1, 2006.

P. 198. **"In all Mexico:** Eduardo Mascareñas to Pepín Bosch, March 18, 1957, Bacardi archives.

P. 199. **In his private diary:** Guevara, "Pasajes de la Guerra Revolucionaria," *Escritos y Discursos,* vol. 2, 120.

P. 199. **Guevara wrote Ramos Latour:** Ernesto Che Guevara, "Letter to Daniel [René Ramos Latour]," December 14, 1957, reprinted in Franqui, 268–270.

P. 199. **Ramos Latour wasted no:** René Ramos Latour, "Letter to Che Guevara," December 19, 1957, reprinted in Franqui, *Diary,* 272–76.

P. 201. **Bacardi women, including:** Amelia Comas, interview by the author, January 15, 2004, Arlington, VA.

P. 201. **The brewery manager:** Padula, "Financing Castro's Revolution," 243, citing 1971 interview with Miranda.

P. 201. **Manuel Jorge Cutillas:** Manuel Jorge Cutillas, interview by the author, May 24, 2004, Miami.

P. 202. **On November 4, the:** José M. Bou to "Juanito," November 4, 1958, Bacardi archives.

P. 203. **By the fall of 1958:** Kirkpatrick, 192.

P. 204. **"the strongest bulwark:** "Fidel Castro Speaks to Citizens of Santiago," Foreign Broadcast Information Service (FBIS), January 3, 1959.

Chapter 15. *Giving Fidel a Chance*

P. 206. **Another sumptuous feast:** The account of the planned luncheon is from Dubois, 360–61; Dorschner and Fabricio, 490, and from interviews with family members and company officials.

P. 207. **Manolo Ortega:** "Noticiario de Hatuey," *Bacardi Gráfico* 1, no. 2 (July 1956), 16–17.

P. 207. **Manuel Jorge Cutillas:** Manuel Jorge Cutillas, interview by author, April 2, 2006, Washington, DC.

P. 208. **"We will show them:** Dubois, 369.

P. 208. **"The triumph of the revolution:** "Pepín Bosh [sic] regresó a Cuba," *La Tarde* (Havana), January 6, 1959.

P. 209. **Virtually the entire:** The account of the wedding is from "Raul Castro Is Captured," *Life,* February 9, 1959; Cape, 185; and author interview with Cutillas, April 2, 2006.

P. 209. **Bosch brought with him:** López-Fresquet, 75.

P. 209. **López-Fresquet's deputy:** Oscar Villar Fernández [Tesorero General de la República] to José Bosch Lamarque, January 22, 1959, Bacardi archives.

P. 209. **"It pleases me to:** José M. Bosch to Miguel Díaz, January 25, 1959, Bacardi archives.

P. 210. **"a bad thing happening:** "The Vengeful Visionary," *Time,* January 26, 1959.

P. 210. **"To judge Dr. Castro's:** José M. Bosch to Luis Muñoz Marín, February 19, 1959, Bacardi archives.

P. 210. **"Crusade of Freedom:** *Bacardi Gráfico* 3, no. 12 (January 1959).

P. 211. **"would not be in the:** Senate Committee on the Judiciary, testimony of Ambassador Earl E. T. Smith, *Hearing on Communist Threat to the United States through the Caribbean,* 86th Congress, 2nd Session, August 30, 1960.

P. 211. **Members of Congress were:** "Congressman Asks U.S. to Halt Castro Executions," *Chicago Tribune,* January 15, 1959, 2.

P. 211. **"The situation in Cuba:** José M. Bosch to F. L. Dorothy, January 23, 1959, Bacardi archives.

P. 211. **"Now it's your turn:** José M. Bosch to Alberto Parreño, January 27, 1959.

P. 212. **"Fidel Castro:** Charles O. Porter, "La Cuba de Castro: Un reto para cubanos y americanos" (remarks, Santiago de Cuba, February 21, 1959), published in *Bacardi Gráfico* 3, no. 12 (January 1959), 8–11.

P. 212. **"You Americans:** "Cuba's Balance Sheet," *Wall Street Journal,* February 13, 1959.

P. 213. **"the Americans are going:** Franqui, 338.

P. 214. **My dear Abel:** José M. Bosch to Abel Mestre, January 27, 1959, Bacardi archives.

P. 214. **"It seems that:** José M. Bosch to José Miró Cardona, February 9, 1959, Bacardi archives.

P. 214. **On February 13:** All quotes pertaining to Miró Cardona's resignation are from "Castro Step Held End to Confusion," *New York Times*, February 15, 1959.

P. 215. **Castro, however, was:** Thomas, 1202.

P. 215. **(at least 475 executions:** "Nye Goes on Trial as 'Plotter' in Cuba," *New York Times*, April 12, 1959.

P. 215. **He told Sánchez:** The account of Bosch accompanying Castro to Washington is from José M. Bosch, in videotaped interview by Miguel Gonzalez-Pando, September 1990, video recording in Cuban Living History Project, Florida International University; José M. Bosch, interview by Georgie Anne Geyer, Miami, January 17, 1985, transcript in Georgie Anne Geyer Papers, Hoover Institution Archives, Stanford, CA; author interview with Ernesto Betancourt, November 11, 2003, Bethesda, MD; Foster, 100; and López-Fresquet, 105–6.

P. 217. **The tall, bearded rebel:** The account of Castro's U.S. tour is from Dumont, *Cuba*, 23–24; Edwards, 11–16; and "Castro Visit Triumphant," *Harvard Law Record*, April 30, 1959, 3–4.

P. 218. **"that does not forget:** Dumont, *Cuba*, 24.

P. 218. **"In all candor:** *Diario de la Marina* (Havana), April 18, 1959

P. 218. **To Bosch's delight:** *El País* (Havana), May 27, 1959.

P. 219. **endorsed the land redistribution:** *Diario de la Marina* (Havana), May 27–30, 1959.

P. 219. **The Bacardi Rum:** *El Mundo* (Havana), May 5, 1959.

P. 219. **The law that emerged:** Padula, "The Fall of the Bourgeoisie," 278–82.

P. 219. **The change was not painless:** Pérez, *Cuba: Between Reform and Revolution*, 321.

P. 219. **"You had entrepreneurs:** Antonio Jorge, interview by the author, June 23, 2004, Miami.

P. 220. **"precisely because of:** Arturo Chabau to Raúl Gutierrez, February 13, 1959, Bacardi archives.

P. 220. **"Given the extraordinary:** Arnold Rodríguez (*Comité Central de la Concentración Campesina*) to José Argamasilla, July 7, 1959, Bacardi archives.

P. 220. **"excessive facility:** Aguilar, "The Revolution, the Economy, and the Counterrevolution," in *Cuba in Revolution*, 142, originally published as "La Revolución, La economía y la contrarevolución," in *Prensa Libre* (Havana), March 21, 1959.

P. 221. **On one side:** Aguilar, "A Mounting Dilemma," in *Cuba in Revolution*, 144, originally published as "El dilema" in *Prensa Libre* (Havana), June 27, 1959.

P. 221. **"Embrace for history:** "Abrazo Para La Historia," full-page Bacardi ad taken out in several Havana newspapers, July 26, 1959.

P. 221. **"I said to myself:** Padula, "Fall of the Bourgeoisie," 248.

P. 222. **When President Manuel:** The account of the Urrutia resignation is from Thomas, 1232–33, Quirk, 249–52, and Szulc, 504–5.

P. 222. **The Havana municipal:** Dumont, *Cuba*, 26.

P. 223. **"a school of thought:** "Growing Economic Woe May Play Bigger Role Than Castro's Politics," *Wall Street Journal*, July 24, 1959.

P. 223. **As Bosch explained later:** José M. Bosch to Daniel Bacardi, March 2, 1959, Bacardi archives.

Chapter 16. The Year Cuba Changed

P. 224. **Both events were lavish.** Described in *Bacardi Gráfico* 5, no. 17 (June 1960).

P. 225. **a parallel task force:** Szulc, 476.

P. 225. **"Maybe when the time:** López-Fresquet, 165.

P. 226. **Guevara said there were:** Padula, "The Fall of the Bourgeoisie," 291.

P. 226. **López-Fresquet told the businessmen:** López-Fresquet, 143.

P. 226. **Matos had summoned:** The Matos affair is related in Quirk, 264–79.

P. 227. **The ninety-eighth year:** "Mensaje de Navidad de José M. Bosch," *Bacardi Gráfico* 4, no. 15 (December 1959), 3.

P. 228. **a "capitalist enemy:** Padula, "Fall of the Bourgeoisie," 316.

P. 228. **Pepín Bosch had concluded:** Guillermo Mármol, interview by the author, January 12, 2006, Miami; Manuel Jorge Cutillas, interview by the author, April 2, 2006, Washington, DC.

P. 228. **"Now the time of:** Aguilar, "The Curtain Falls," in *Cuba in Revolution*, 150–52, originally published in *Prensa Libre*, May 13, 1960.

P. 229. **After its publication:** Luis Aguilar, interview by the author, February 12, 2004, Miami.

P. 231. **"The tyrant Batista:** Daniel Bacardi to Tomás Viña, November 5, 1959, Bacardi archives.

P. 231. **Emilio got involved:** José "Tito" Argamasilla and Clara María del Valle, interview by the author, Miami, September 27, 2004.

P. 231. **Miranda, having supported:** Padula "Fall of the Bourgeoisie," 316.

P. 231. **Puig, who had lived:** Rino Puig, interview by the author, April 14, 2006, Key Biscayne, FL.

P. 233. **Daniel immediately:** Daniel Bacardi to Jefe de la Delegación Municipal No. 1 del Departamento Provincial de Trabajo de Oriente, September 30, 1960, Bacardi archives.

P. 233. **Manuel Jorge Cutillas:** Manuel Jorge Cutillas, interview by the author, February 10, 2004, Miami.

P. 233. **"a policy contrary to:** "Nacionalizan los bancos y 382 grandes empresas," *Hoy* (Havana), October 14, 1960.

P. 234. **The senior officer clutched:** Juan Prado, interview by the author, March 12, 2004, Coral Gables, FL.

P. 236. **"Rino, how are you:** Rino Puig, interview by the author, April 14, 2006, Key Biscayne, FL.

P. 238. **Even worse for her:** Clara María del Valle, interview by the author, June 24, 2004, Coral Gables, FL.

P. 238. **Nationalization resulted:** Padula, "Fall of the Bourgeoisie," 600–602.

P. 238. **"We're having some:** Manuel Jorge Cutillas, interview by the author, May 21, 2004, Miami.

P. 239. **"Don't worry:** Richard Gardner, interview by the author, May 21, 2004, Miami.

P. 240. **Her teenage daughters:** Amelia Comas, interview by the author, January 15, 2004 Arlington, VA.

P. 242. **The first letters:** Felicita Lavigne, interview by the author, January 7, 2005, Santiago de Cuba.

P. 244. **"a Marxist-Leninist:** Szulc, 568.

P. 244. **"between capitalism:** Fidel Castro press conference, July 25, 1960, Havana. Transcript published in *Revolución* (Havana), July 26, 1960.

P. 244. **"a convinced Marxist-Leninist:** Ramonet Leninist, 116.

P. 244. **"Raúl was on the left:** Ibid., 123.

P. 245. **Carlos Franqui, a prominent:** Franqui, 105.

P. 245. **"I measure the depth:** Heikal, 344.

P. 245. **"What do the ones:** Fidel Castro speech at the inauguration of the Basic Science and Preclinical Institute, Havana, October 18, 1962.

Chapter 17. Exile

P. 247. **"to decompress:** Jorge Bosch, interview by the author, January 5, 2005, Miami.

P. 247. **an average of about 170:** Metro-Dade County Planning Department, Miami, FL, "Background Paper on Cuban Immigration into Dade County," January 6, 1985.

P. 250. **The court said:** *Compañía Ron Bacardi, S.A. v. Bank of Nova Scotia*, 193 F. Supp. 814, 815 (S.D.N.Y. 1961).

P. 250. **"We have to reestablish:** Juan Prado, interviews by the author, June 23, 2004, and April 12, 2006, Miami.

P. 253. **The Bacardi lawyers:** Foster, 139.

P. 253. **"That was a product:** Enrique Oltuski, interview by the author, September 23, 2004, Havana.

P. 254. **"Oh, it was to be:** Juan Grau, interview by the author, July 28, 2004, Miami.

P. 256. **"In the year that the:** Maran, 20.

P. 257. **"Fidel Castro:** Theodore A. Ediger (Associated Press), "Florida's Cuban Exile Colony Includes 40 Millionaires," *Washington Post*, January 3, 1965.

P. 257. **The company sold 1.7:** Foster, 152.

P. 258. **By 1976, annual global sales:** "Complex Bacardi Empire Tries Collective Leadership," *New York Times*, August 16, 1976.

P. 258. **"A lot of people think:** Juan Prado, interview by the author, June 23, 2004, Coral Gables, FL.

P. 258. **In the 1970s, marketing:** Dávila, 233.

P. 259. **"Because of Bacardi:** Manuel Jorge Cutillas, interview by the author, April 2, 2006, Washington, D.C.

P. 260. **In his affidavit:** Advertisement, *Life*, May 20, 1966, 133.

Chapter 18. Counterrevolution

P. 261. **"little good to say:** State Department memorandum from R. G. Cushing and J. L. Montllor, American Embassy, Mexico, October 11, 1960. "Cuban Industrialist's Views on Cuba," Foreign Service Despatch no. 397. Department of State Cuba Series, 737.00/10-1160.

P. 262. **One sees a ferocious-looking:** Taber, 339.

P. 263. **"To Fidel, you are:** Matthews, *The Cuba Story*, 298–99.

P. 263. **"to clarify some:** Paid advertisement, *New York Times*, March 24, 1961, 12.

P. 264. **A report filed by:** "Report from AMCLATTER-1," CIA memo to Chief, Western Hemisphere Division, June 17, 1960, CIA record number 104-10163-10457, JFK Assassination Archive, National Archives.

P. 264. **Among the volunteers:** Tony Calatayud, interview by the author, April 12, 2006, Coral Gables, FL.

P. 265. **"A revolution that was not:** Fidel Castro, *Obra revolucionaria*, January 25, 1961 (as quoted in Thomas, 1058fn).

P. 265. **(fn) "but on the contrary:** Karl Marx, "The Class Struggles in France, 1848 to 1850," in Karl Marx and Frederick Engels, *Selected Works in Two Volumes* (Moscow: Foreign Languages Publishing House, 1958), 1:139.

P. 266. **"Operation Mongoose:** The Operation Mongoose plan is laid out in *Foreign Relations of the United States (FRUS)*, vol. 10 (Cuba, 1961–1962), document 157, and elaborated in Bohning.

P. 266. **"silly and stupid:** Bohning, 115.

P. 267. **(fn) "I tell you this:** Reprinted in Blight, et al, 481–82.

P. 267. **"to obstruct or slow:** "Prospects for and Limitations of a Maximum Covert Action Program Against the Castro Communist Regime," attachment to memorandum from Sterling J. Cottrell to Mr. Johnson, April 18, 1963, CIA record number 178-10004-10202, JFK Assassination Archive, National Archives.

P. 268. **"Bacardi cannot turn:** "Bacardi ofrece de 50 a cien mil dólares para tractores," *Diario Las Américas*, December 31, 1961, 1.

P. 268. **"Hmmm," he said:** Carlos Bosch, interview by the author, March 16, 2006, Hamilton, Bermuda.

P. 268. **Bosch had a plan:** The Bosch bombing plan was described by his associate Jorge Mas Canosa in Vargas Llosa, 60–61.

P. 268. **Without informing anyone:** A detailed (though mostly unverified) account of Bosch's B-26 was published in "Saga of the Bacardi Bomber," *Air Classics*, October 2007. The registration history of the aircraft can be found at www.warbirdregistry.org/a26registry/a26-4435918.html and at http://home.att.net/~jbaugher/1944_3.html.

P. 269. **According to a CIA:** "Report from AMBUD-1," March 4, 1963, CIA record number 104-10236-10178, JFK Assassination Archive, National Archives.

P. 269. **"refineries and power:** "Minutes of the Meeting of the Special Group, 25 April 1963," DAVIS record number 178-10004-10203, JFK Assassination Archive, National Archives.

P. 270. **"a nationwide discussion:** "Declaration of Purpose of Citizens Committee for a Free Cuba," published in the *Congressional Record* 109 (May 1, 1963), 64.

P. 270. **"aid to the Cuban freedom:** "Minutes of Membership Meeting," Citizens Committee for a Free Cuba, June 20, 1963, Rev. John LaFarge SJ Papers, box 3, folder 15, Georgetown University Library, Special Collections Division, Washington, DC.

P. 270. **"frankly disappointed:** Senate Committee on the Judiciary, *Hearings on Cuban Refugee Problem*, 88th Congress, 1st Session. May 22, 1963.

P. 270. **"acts will be performed:** "Prospects for and Limitations of a Maximum Covert Action Program Against the Castro Communist Regime," attachment to memorandum from Sterling J. Cottrell to Mr. Johnson, April 18, 1963, CIA record number 178-10004-10202, JFK Assassination Archive, National Archives.

P. 271. **"believes that a quick:** "Plans of Cuban Exiles to Assassinate Selected Cuban Government Leaders," memorandum from Richard Helms to John McCone, June 10, 1964, DAVIS record number 178-10004-10207, JFK Assassination Archive, National Archives.

P. 271. **A memorandum on the findings:** Ibid.

P. 272. **White House aide:** "Assassination of Castro," memorandum from Gordon Chase to McGeorge Bundy, June 15, 1964, Papers of Gordon Chase, JFK Library, National Archives.

P. 272. **Within a week, the:** "Plans of Cuban Exiles . . .," State Department Memorandum from Thomas C. Mann to Mr. Johnson, June 17, 1964, DAVIS record number 178-10004-10206, JFK Assassination Archive, National Archives; see also "Plans of Cuban Exiles . . .," Justice Department Memorandum from W. C. Sullivan to D. J. Brennan Jr., June 24, 1964, CIA record number 104-10310-10166, JFK Assassination Archive, National Archives.

P. 272. **In July, FBI agents:** "Plans of Cuban Exiles to Assassinate Selected Cuban Government Leaders," July 14, 1964, FBI Document DBA 80042, CIA record number 104-10308-10305.

P. 272. **For his part, Shackley:** "Report on Plots to Assassinate Fidel Castro," CIA Inspector General, May 23, 1967, CIA record number 104-10213-10101, 115–117, JFK Assassination Archive, National Archives.

P. 273. **His idea was to convene:** Esteban M. Beruvides, *Cuba: Anuario histórico 1963* (Miami: 12th Ave. Graphics, 1995), 215; and Memorandum to Director, FBI, September 11, 1963, FBI record number 124-10290-10078. JFK Assassination Archive, National Archives.

P. 273. **Standing behind a table:** "Referéndum para seleccionar la representación de los cubanos exiliados," *Diario Las Américas*, November 7, 1963, 1.

P. 273. **After a nine-hour:** Esteban M. Beruvides, *Cuba: Anuario histórico 1964* (Miami: Colonial Press Internacional, 2000), 1:129.

P. 274. **"pseudo-referendum:** "Observaciones sobre el referendum organizado por el Sr. J. M. Bosch," mimeographed declaration issued by Consejo Revolucionario de Cuba, Miami, January 15, 1964.

P. 274. **"Pepín Bosch's referendum:** "Referendum Finish, Ganó 'Pepín' Bosch," *Patria* (Miami), May 22, 1964, 1.

P. 274. **The RECE directors:** "Exiles Seek Funds to Combat Castro," *Miami Herald*, May 28, 1964; "New Command for Anti-Castro Cubans?" *U.S. News and World Report*, June 8, 1964; "Exiles Look to Oliva for Hope," *Miami Herald*, June 21, 1964.

P. 274. **"What extra time there:** Don Bohning, "Bacardi Boss Leads 3 Lives: Rum, Refugees and Rebellion," *Miami Herald*, August 13, 1964.

P. 275. **In August 1964:** Don Bohning, "New Exile 'Action' Group To Make Progress Report," *Miami Herald*, August 5, 1964; see also untitled telegram from John Crimmins to Department of State, August 12, 1964, LBJ Library, National Archives.

P. 275. **"think it over:** "Talks of Leaders of the Cuban Representation in Exile (RECE) During Visit to Latin American Countries," CIA cable, TDCS no. DB-315/01135-64, October 23, 1964, LBJ Library, National Archives.

P. 275. **"Oliva and Freyre:** "Department of Justice Inquiry—Antonio Cuesta del Valle, Jorge Mas Canosa," CIA memorandum from Chief, Western Hemisphere Division to Assistant General Counsel, January 15, 1966, CIA record number 104-10244-10076, JFK Assassination Archive, National Archives.

P. 276. **According to a subsequent FBI:** "Cuban Representation in Exile (RECE); Internal Security—Cuba; Neutrality Matters," FBI memorandum, July 13, 1965, file no. 105-8280, LBJ Library, National Archives.

P. 276. **Posada had trained:** "Cuban Representation in Exile (RECE); Internal Security—Cuba; Neutrality Matters," FBI memorandum, July 13, 1965, file no. 105-8280, LBJ Library, National Archives; "Plan of Nestor Gonzalez (or Garcia) to Reenter Cuba to Sabotage a Cuban Train," memorandum from JMWAVE, July 9, 1965, CIA record number 104-10178-10059, JFK Assassination Archive, National Archives.

P. 276. **Unbeknownst to Mas:** Untitled memorandum from JMWAVE to Western Hemisphere Division, CIA headquarters, June 17, 1965, CIA record number 104-10178-10057, JFK Assassination Archive, National Archives.

P. 276. **When he reported:** "Plans of the Cuban Representation in Exile (RECE) to Blow up a Cuban or Soviet Vessel in Veracruz, Mexico," July 1, 1965, CIA record number 104-10178-10060, JFK Assassination Archive, National Archives.

P. 277. **"disengage:** Memorandum from JMWAVE, July 24, 1965, CIA record number 104-10178-10056, JFK Assassination Archive, National Archives.

P. 277. **According to one:** Memorandum from "Pete" [Posada] to "Chip," July 20, 1966, attached to CIA memorandum from Grover T. Lythcott to Chief of Training, July 21, 1966, CIA record number 104-10178-10050, JFK Assassination Archive, National Archives.

P. 277. **Working through his RECE:** The story of Mas Canosa's business development is from Celia W. Dugger, "Leader's Zeal Powers Exile Lobby," *Miami Herald,* April 10, 1988; Christopher Marquis, "Mas Canosa Dead at 58," *Miami Herald,* November 24, 1997; and Vargas Llosa, 63–65.

P. 277. **At Mas's personal:** Evaristo R. Savon, "Crean Comité de 17 Senadores de EE.UU. Para la Lucha Contra Cuba Comunista," *Diario Las Américas,* Miami, November 15, 1975, 1.

P. 277. **"La Batalla de:** Pérez Castellón, 47.

P. 277. **"We have used:** Vargas Llosa, 38.

P. 278. **less of a "warrior:** "Assume Maritime Administration Will Refuse to Approve Boat Purchase," CIA memorandum from JMWAVE, December 12, 1966, CIA record number 104-10178-10209, JFK Assassination Archive, National Archives.

P. 278. **CIA reestablished contact:** Untitled CIA teletype message, October 13, 1976; see "Luis Posada Carriles: The Declassified Record," National Security Archive Electronic Briefing Book No. 153, National Security Archive, George Washington University.

P. 278. **The two men were subsequently:** Extensive documentation supporting allegations that Luis Posada and Orlando Bosch were involved in the Cubana bombing and the Letelier assassination is available at the Web site of the National Security Archive (www.gwu.edu/~nsarchiv/index.html): "Luis Posada Carriles: The Declassified File" and "The Posada File: Part II." Bosch and Posada were founders of the Cuban exile organization known as Coordinación de Organizaciones Revolucionarias Unidas (CORU), Coordination of United Revolutionary Organization, an umbrella association that brought together several militantly anti-Castro groups. U.S. government reports later implicated CORU operatives in the Letelier bombing.

P. 278. **(fn) When the violently anti-Castro militant:** Memorandum from FBI Special Agent in Charge, San Juan, to FBI Director, July 9, 1975, FBI record number 124-10279-10050, JFK Assassination Archive, National Archives.

P. 279. **(fn) In a 1984 interview:** Cassette recording of interview with Pepín Bosch by José Ignacio Rasco on "La Universidad del Aire," Radio Martí, 1984 (broadcast date unknown).

P. 279. **"Memories of an Ex-Finance:** Pepín Bosch, "Recuerdos de un Ex-Ministro de Hacienda," *Diario Las Américas,* August 27, 1984.

Chapter 19. Socialist Rum

P. 280. **By the time Fidel:** "Fidel en Oriente: Examina obras de rente," *Noticias de Hoy* (Havana), July 6, 1963. The report included a full text of his remarks.

P. 282. **In spite of Soviet:** Dumont, 75.

P. 282. **"Compañeros:** Castro's visit to the former Bacardi factory is described in Gabriel Molina, "Entusiasmo en Santiago por la visita de Fidel Castro," *Noticias de Hoy* (Havana), July 7, 1963, and Gabriel Molina, "Los errores de la burocracia," *Noticias de Hoy,* July 12, 1963. Additional details from author interviews with eyewitnesses: Alberto "Korda" Díaz, February 2000, Washington, DC; Enrique Oltuski, October 2004, Havana; Gabriel Molina, July 2005, Havana; and Gilberto Cala, July 2005, Santiago de Cuba.

P. 285. **employing more than 150,000:** Thomas, 1334 and 1334n84.

P. 286. **"Fidel makes bad:** "Bacardi Boss Leads 3 Lives," *Miami Herald,* August 13, 1964.

P. 286. **"If [Cuban] Bacardi:** "La calidad de los productos de Bacardi," *Diario de la Tarde* (Havana), January 3, 1964.

P. 287. **"They pampered me:** Cabrera, "Marianito (Ron Caney) Lavigne."

P. 288. **Lavigne claimed later:** Manuel Pereira, "Ron del bueno," *Cuba Internacional,* July 1970, 58–63.

P. 288. **"So where do you make:** Lavigne told the story of the Che Guevara visit in Cabrera, "Marianito (Ron Caney) Lavigne." Other details are from Pepín Hernandez, interview by the author, July 25, 2002, Museum of Rum, Santiago, Cuba.

P. 289. **Lavigne's daughter:** Felicita Lavigne, interview by the author, January 7, 2005, Santiago de Cuba.

P. 290. **A labor regulation issued:** Nelson, 119–22.

P. 291. **All workers were required:** Karol, 517n22.

P. 291. **In 1961 Che Guevara:** Executive Committee of the Central Planning Board, decision no. 11, April 1961, cited in Castañeda, 212.

P. 291. **"what is scarce today:** Fidel Castro, speech before the National Sugar Cooperatives Congress, Havana, August 18, 1962.

P. 291. **"our production of milk:** Nelson, 100.

P. 291. **By 1970, with the labor:** Mesa-Lago, *Market, Socialist, and Mixed Economies,* 190–91; Nelson, 99–108.

P. 291. **The problems and inefficiencies:** The critique of economic management in Cuba under Castro's rule is drawn largely from Karol; Dumont, *Cuba;* and Dumont, *Is Cuba Socialist?;* Nelson; and Sergio G. Roca, "Managing State Enterprises in Cuba," in Horowitz and Suchlicki; and Mesa-Lago, *Market, Socialist, and Mixed Economies.*

P. 291. **"reeks too much of capitalism:** Fidel Castro, speech before meeting of the Confederation of Cuban Workers, Havana, August 29, 1966.

P. 292. **"I have seen the havoc:** Karol, 47.

P. 292. **"The failure of the non-autonomous:** Dumont, *Cuba,* 124.

P. 292. **Dumont condemned:** Dumont, *Is Cuba Socialist?,* 95.

P. 293. **"I thought they:** Lavigne's trip is described in Pereira, "Rondel Bueno."

P. 294. **"the engagement of the nation's:** Dumont, *Is Cuba Socialist?,* 73.

P. 294. **So many resources:** Suchlicki, 159.

P. 294. **"Learning to build the:** Fidel Castro, speech, July 26, 1970, as reported in *Granma* (Havana), July 27, 1970.

P. 295. **Some managers found they:** Sergio G. Roca, "Managing State Enterprises," in Horowitz and Suchlicki, 283–84.

P. 295. **"The man who opposes:** Dumont, *Is Cuba Socialist?,* 108.

P. 295. **"We have some difficulties:** Cabrera, "Marianito (Ron Caney) Lavigne."

P. 296. **"As a rum drinker:** Herbert L. Matthews, *Revolution in Cuba,* 372.

P. 296. **With all his might:** Padura Fuentes, 147.

P. 297. **"When the blending:** "Normas de Empresa," unpublished document, Combinado de Bebidas Santiago, 1982.

Chapter 20. Family Business

P. 298. **"Tío, it's too:** José Argamasilla and Clara María del Valle, interview by the author, September 27, 2004, Miami.

P. 298. **"If only the *mambises:*** Luis Varona, "Coronel Emilio Bacardi Lay," *Diario Las Américas,* June 12, 1977.

P. 300. **"You have a successor:** Zenaida Bacardi, essay dated June 5, 1974, Emilio Bacardi Archive, Cuban Heritage Collection, University of Miami Richter Library.

P. 301. **"I made every one:** George Volsky, interview by the author, April 11, 2006, Coral Gables, Florida.

P. 303. **"I'm looking now for:** "Complex Bacardi Empire Tries Collective Leadership," *New York Times,* August 16, 1976.

P. 303. **A year earlier:** Ibid.

P. 303. **Business school professors:** L. J. Bourgeois, interview by the author, Darden Graduate

School of Business, University of Virginia, July 7, 2004, telephone. See also, e.g., Nancy Bowman-Upton, *Transferring Management in the Family-Owned Business*, Emerging Business Series, EB-1 (U.S. Small Business Administration, 1991); Paul Karofsky, "A Conversation with Harry Levinson," *Family Business Review* 10, no. 4 (December 1997): 411–19; and Geraldine Fabrikant, "Do Families and Big Business Mix?" *New York Times*, April 24, 2005.

P. 304. **"by sheer strength:** "Complex Bacardi Empire Tries Collective Leadership," *New York Times*, August 16, 1976.

P. 306. **the *New York Times* had already:** Ibid.

P. 306. **From 1976 to 1979:** Foster, 176.

P. 306. **Consumers during those years:** Raúl Mármol, former marketing director, Bacardi USA, e-mail message to the author, September 4, 2007.

P. 306. **By 1983, about two thirds:** "How Bacardi Became The Best-Selling Rum This Side of Havana," *Wall Street Journal*, July 29, 1983.

P. 307. **Eddy Nielsen and his Nassau ally:** The story of the Bacardi diversification is well told by Foster, 181–94; I have also drawn from several interviews with Guillermo Mármol in Miami and Robert O'Brien in Arlington, Virginia.

P. 309. **The conflicts within the:** The account of the Bacardi privatization battle draws from Anne Swardson, "Bacardi Rum Faces Potent Family Revolt," *Washington Post*, May 10, 1987; Mimi Whitefield, "Bacardi Family Splits Over Firm Going Private," *Miami Herald*, May 25, 1987; and Gail DeGeorge, "Yo, Ho, Ho, and a Battle for Bacardi," *Business Week*, April 16, 1990; as well as Foster, 195–230.

P. 310. **"A picture is emerging:** Jason Nisse, "Citizen Cane," *Independent* (London), August 1, 1993.

P. 311. **"No one knows about:** Ricardo Blanco, interview by the author, February 20, 2004, telephone.

P. 311. **"Bacardi has a culture:** Juan Grau, interview by the author, June 1, 2004, Miami.

P. 311. **"When the company:** Richard Gardner, interview by the author, June 6, 2004, Nassau, Bahamas.

P. 311. **increasing worldwide:** 1960 figures are from Foster, 152; 1989 figures are from *Impact International* industry newsletter.

P. 312. **"One can't fault:** Gail DeGeorge, "Yo, Ho, Ho."

P. 313. **Rather than lower:** Carlos Bosch, interview by the author, March 16, 2006, Hamilton, Bermuda.

P. 313. **"the naïve segment:** Jon Nordheimer, "Bacardi's Glass Is Half Empty," *New York Times*, February 15, 1987.

P. 314. **Bacardi took on a company:** Bacardi CEO Rubén Rodríguez discussed the Martini & Rossi acquisition in "Strategies for a New Millennium," an audiotaped presentation before a spirits industry forum in New York City sponsored by *IMPACT* magazine in February 2001.

Chapter 21. Havana Club

P. 316. **"Within the revolution, everything:** Castro's 1961 "Words to the Intellectuals" speech is described by Guillermo Cabrera Infante, who was present at the meeting, in *Mea Cuba* 69–70.

P. 317. **In 1977 Fidel:** Larry Luxner, "Havana Pushes Rum Exports," *Journal of Commerce*, March 2, 1990; Barty-King and Massel, 115.

P. 318. **"Who's going to give:** trial and deposition transcripts, *Havana Club Holdings, S.A., et al. v. Bacardi-Martini USA, et al.*, docket no. 99–7582, U.S. Court of Appeals, Second Circuit, E 1556.

P. 318. **As a marketing man:** Juan Prado, interview by the author, January 12, 2007, CORAL GABLES, FLORIDA.

P. 318. **In 1973 Prado helped arrange:** Trial testimony, *Havana Club Holdings*, E342, E453.

P. 319. **A *Washington Post* travel:** Ronald Goldfarb, "Rum—Distilling Gold From the Sugar, Sun, and Politics of Cuba," *Washington Post*, April 13, 1978.

P. 319. **A rum reviewer:** Emanuel Greenberg, "The Cane Mutiny: Caribbean Rum Drinks," *Playboy*, December 1983, 129.

P. 319. **In 1978 the president:** Norman Heller to Carlos Rodríguez Benítez, October 10, 1978, cited in *Havana Club Holdings*, E 3499.

P. 319. **Between 1975 and 1984:** Export figures cited in "Convenio Asociativo" between Havana Rum and Liquors, S.A., Cuba Ron Corporación, S.A., and Pernod Ricard, S.A., November 22, 1993, reproduced in *Havana Club Holdings*, E 2592.

P. 319. **The Soviet Union shipped:** Figures on Soviet and East European aid and trade with Cuba are from Oppenheimer, 227.

P. 320. **In 1989 Cuba:** Carmelo Mesa-Lago, "The Economic Effects on Cuba of the Downfall of Socialism in the USSR and Eastern Europe," in *Cuba: After the Cold War*, 180.

P. 320. **Cuban economists:** Jorge F. Pérez-López, "Cuba's Socialist Economy: The Mid-1990s" in *Cuban Communism*, ed. Irving Horowitz and Jaime Suchlicki, 9th ed. (New Brunswick, NJ: Transaction Publishers, 1998). Other economic figures are from José F. Alonso, "Current Political and Economic Trends in Cuba," paper presented at Second Annual Meeting of the Association for the Study of the Cuban Economy (ASCE), Florida International University, Miami, August 15–17, 1992.

P. 321. **"True revolutionaries never:** Fidel Castro, speech before the closing session of the Sixth Congress of the Union of Communist Youth, April 4, 1992.

P. 321. **As of 1988, the only:** Philip Peters, "A Different Kind of Workplace: Foreign Investment in Cuba," paper published by Alexis de Tocqueville Institution, Arlington, Virginia, March 1999.

P. 321. **"Capital and capitalism:** Damian Fraser, "Cuban Revolutionary in an Army Green Business Suit," *Financial Times*, July 14, 1992.

P. 322. **In 1986 Cubaexport:** "Ventas de Ron Havana Club, 1985–1998," *Havana Club Holdings*, Plaintiff's Exhibit 381, E 2295.

P. 323. **"The idea was that the:** Jacquillat trial testimony, *Havana Club Holdings*, E 1281.

P. 323. **Bord told Jacquillat:** Ibid., E 1284.

P. 324. **"Bacardi has reason to:** Manuel Jorge Cutillas to Robert J. Maxwell, President, National Association of Beverage Importers, October 28, 1993, reproduced in Calvo Ospina, *Ron Bacardi: La guerra oculta* (Havana: Casa Editorial Abril, 2000).

P. 325. **The thirty-six-page:** "Convenio Asociativo," Defendant's Exhibit 186, *Havana Club Holdings*, E 2592.

P. 326. *Forbes* **magazine:** "Royals and Rulers," *Forbes* magazine, March 15, 2004.

P. 326. **Prado wrote to Jacquillat:** Juan Prado to Thierry Jacquillat, December 3, 1993, Defendant's Exhibit 497, *Havana Club Holdings*, E 3336.

P. 327. **"to recover possession:** Letter from Ramón Arechabala to Patrick Ricard, December 14, 1993, Defendant's Exhibit 488, *Havana Club Holdings*, E 3334.

P. 327. **Thierry Jacquillat said later:** Jacquillat trial testimony, *Havana Club Holdings*, E 1293.

P. 328. **Six months after the:** Faxed memorandum from Javier G. San Miguel, Distribuidora Bacardi, S.A., Madrid, to G. N. Bichard, Bacardi Imports, Miami, May 25, 1994, Plaintiff's Exhibit 58, *Havana Club Holdings*, E 1606.

Chapter 22. Rum Politics

P. 331. **In his introductory:** A. Armando Alejandre, "Habla Helms de la posibilidad de un bloqueo naval a Cuba," *Diario Las Américas*, April 19, 1995.

P. 331. **The luncheon at the:** Mark Matthews, "Helms Tapping a Fresh Source of Funds," *Baltimore Sun*, May 22, 1995; Christopher Marquis, "How Bacardi and Politics Mix: The Cuba Embargo Bill," *Miami Herald*, July 17, 1995.

P. 331. **A year earlier:** "Trade Briefs," *Journal of Commerce*, April 19, 1994. See also, Senate Committee on Foreign Relations, Western Hemisphere Subcommittee, *Cuban Liberty and Democratic Solidarity Act*, prepared statement of Otto Reich, President of the U.S. Cuba Business Council, 104th Congress, 1st Session, June 14, 1995.

P. 332. **"It is exactly because:** Roberto Fabricio, "Latest U.N. Vote Condemns Trade Embargo Against Cuba," *Fort Lauderdale Sun-Sentinel*, October 27, 1994.

P. 333. **the Bacardi Claims Act:** Wayne Smith, a former Havana-based U.S. diplomat, is said to have used this term first, while working at the Center for International Policy in Washington.

P. 335. **to goad its French-Cuban:** Ignacio Sánchez, interview by the author, February 9, 2007, Washington, DC.

P. 336. **"Your honor," he said:** Trial transcript, *Havana Club Holdings*, E 10.

P. 336. **"Don't start with the:** Campo-Flores, 63.

P. 337. **Sánchez himself recognized:** Ignacio Sánchez, interview by the author, February 9, 2007, WASHINGTON, DC.

P. 337. **He introduced his proposal:** House Judiciary Committee, Subcommittee on Courts and Intellectual Property, *Hearing on Miscellaneous Patent and Trademark Issues*, 105th Congress, 2nd Session, May 21, 1998.

P. 338. **Fidel Castro was outraged:** Ana Radelat, "Decision on Trademark Rights for a Rum Spurs a Global Dispute," *New York Times*, June 1, 1999.

P. 338. **"It is exactly as if:** Ibid.

P. 339. **"The question about 211:** Daniel Fisk, interview by the author, October 30, 2000, Washington, DC.

P. 339. **Cuban accounts of the:** For example, "De cómo el ladrón fue declarado inocente," *Granma* (Havana), April 27, 1999.

P. 339. **A retelling of the Bacardi:** "Rock Around the Blockade" leaflet available at www.rcgfrfi .easynet.co.uk/ratb/boycott/bacardi.pdf.

P. 340. **In the 1996 election:** Bacardi political contributions are identified in Federal Election Commission (FEC) records, as well as in such databases as the Congressional Quarterly's CQ Moneyline; the Center for Responsive Politics' www.opensecrets.org; and the National Institute on Money in State Politics's www.followthemoney.org.

P. 341. **"We need your:** The e-mails were later obtained by the Florida Democratic Party through a lawsuit and made publicly available.

P. 341. **On April 23:** Thomas B. Edsall, "Letter by Jeb Bush in Trademark Fight Followed Donation," *Washington Post*, September 14, 2002. A full chronology of the letters and e-mail exchanges is laid out in Dan Christensen, "Governor Worked to Help Company in Trademark Dispute Amid Barrage of Emails, Timely Political Contributions," *Miami Daily Business Review*, October 17, 2002, and in Thomas B. Edsall, "Gov. Bush Reveals Lobby Effort; Documents Show Intervention in Trademark Case of GOP Donor," *Washington Post*, October 18, 2002. The denials of a quid pro quo between the contribution and the Bush letter are cited in all three stories.

P. 342. **DeLay's spokesman, Jonathan:** Ana Radelat, "DeLay Aids Bacardi Rum Empire," *CubaNews*, October 1, 2003.

P. 344. **The conservative *Washington Times*:** "A Special Interest Cocktail," *Washington Times*, January 20, 2002.

P. 344. **"is chosen by such corrupt:** José Martí, *Political Parties and Elections in the United States*, 19.

P. 344. **"the whole culture:** David Brooks, "Saving the House," *New York Times*, January 5, 2006.

P. 344. **"They had this corporate:** Otto Reich, interview by the author, February 22, 2007, Washington, DC.

Chapter 23. Who Gets Cuba

P. 347. **"The time has come:** Associated Press, "Cuba Exile Joy over Castro's Illness Gives Way to Questions," August 2, 2006; "Speculation Swirls in Miami, Havana," *Miami Herald*, August 2, 2006.

P. 350. **"key to the whole policy:** Tom Gjelten, "Castro and Bacardi Battle over Cuban Rum," *All Things Considered*, National Public Radio, August 3, 2001.

P. 351. **In 1995 he had complained:** Quoted in Marifeli Pérez-Stable, "La victoria pírrica del comandante," *Foreign Affairs en Español*, April–June 2007.

P. 351. **totaled only about forty million dollars:** "Foreign Investment in Cuba Plummets," Reuters, July 8, 2002.

P. 352. **"Transactions and business:** José Fernández González, "Riesgo y miseria de invertir in Cuba," Association for the Study of the Cuban Economy (ASCE) News Service, February 22, 2004.

P. 352. **By 2006, the London-based:** Doreen Hemlock, "The Grim Outlook for Cuba," *South Florida Sun-Sentinel,* February 11, 2007.

P. 353. **By the end of 2006:** Doreen Hemlock, "Cuba Curbs Foreign Investment," *South Florida Sun-Sentinel,* August 10, 2004; and "Experts Predict Grim Outlook for Cuba," *South Florida Sun-Sentinel,* February 19, 2007.

P. 353. **"Rum is not a wicked:** Howe, 78.

P. 360. **and, in his own words:** Facundo Bacardi e-mail to author, March 3, 2004.

P. 360. **"to move both the family:** David Willison, "Bacardi: One Family's Exquisite Quest for Perfection," *Value Rich,* Winter 2006.

P. 362. **Tom Pirko, the analyst:** Elaine Walker, "Visitor Center Offers Window onto Bacardi Brand's History," *Miami Herald,* April 28, 2003.

P. 362. **"Following this company:** Tom Pirko, interview by the author, August 8, 2006, telephone.

P. 363. **"Obviously there will be:** Jacquillat trial testimony, *Havana Club Holdings,* E 1299.

P. 364. **"when the preconditions:** Trial transcript, *Havana Club Holdings,* E 14.

P. 364. **One dissident Cuban:** Anonymous, "Las dos caras de la esperanza," www.cubanet.org, February 3, 2004.

P. 365. **José Martí, writing:** José Martí, "Coney Island," in *Selected Writings* 89, originally published in *La Pluma,* Bogotá, Colombia, December 3, 1881.

P. 365. **"We are neither:** Emilio Bacardi to Leonard Wood, March 19, 1907, Leonard Wood Collection, Library of Congress.

SELECTED SOURCES

In addition to the following cited sources, I reviewed correspondence to and from Leonard Wood, Elihu Root, and Emilio Bacardi in the Leonard Wood Collection at the Library of Congress and the Emilio Bacardi Archive at the Cuban Heritage Collection of the University of Miami's Richter Library. I had limited access to materials from the Museo Emilio Bacardi (Fondo Emilio Bacardi), the Biblioteca Elvira Cape, the Museo del Ron, and the Archivo Histórico Provincial (Fondo Compañía Ron Bacardi, S.A.) in Santiago de Cuba and from the Archivo Nacional in Havana.

Aguilar, Luis E. *Cuba 1933: Prologue to Revolution*. Ithaca, NY: Cornell University Press, 1972.

———. "Emilio Bacardi, en el tiempo y para el tiempo." *Diario Las Américas* (Miami), March 25 and 26, 1988 (in two parts).

———. "Revolution and Counterrevolution." In *Cuba in Revolution*, edited by Rolando E. Bonachea and Nelson P. Valdés, 141–152, Garden City, NY: Anchor Books, 1972. Series of articles originally published in *Prensa Libre* (Havana), March 1959–May 1960.

Aixalá Dawson, Mari, and Pepín R. Argamasilla. *Bacardi: A Tale of Merchants, Family, and Company*. Miami: Facundo and Amalia Bacardi Foundation, 2006.

Alegría, Ciro. "De la reforma a la independencia." *Revista de la Biblioteca Nacional José Martí* 12, no. 2 (May/August 1970): 153–65.

Anderson, Jon Lee. *Che Guevara: A Revolutionary Life*. New York: Grove, 1997.

Arboleya, Jesús. *The Cuban Counter-Revolution*. Translated by Rafael Betancourt. Athens, OH: Ohio University Center for International Studies, 2000.

Archibald, James F. J. "Havana Since the Occupation." *Scribner's Magazine* 26, no. 1 (July 1899): 86–96.

Argamasilla Bacardi, José Emilio. *Las Crónicas de Bacardi*. Privately published, 1992. Available at the Cuban Heritage Collection of the University of Miami's Richter Library.

Atkins, Edwin F. *Sixty Years in Cuba*. Cambridge, MA: Riverside, 1926.

Ayala, Luis K. *The Rum Experience*. Round Rock, TX: Rum Runner Press, 2001.

Babún, Teo A., and Victor Andrés Triay. *The Cuban Revolution: Years of Promise*. Gainesville, FL: University Press of Florida, 2005.

Bacardi Cape, Amalia. *Emilio Bacardi en su tiempo*. Valladolid, Spain: Gráficas Andrés Martín, 1986.

———, ed. *Steamer "Virginius" Incident: November 1873*. Privately published, 1982. Available at the Cuban Heritage Collection, University of Miami's Richter Library.

———, ed. *Epistolario: De Cuba a Chafarinas; El denunciante de Pinto; Cartas de Don Federico Pérez Carbó; Cartas de José A. González Lanuza*. Madrid: Playor, 1973.

Bacardi Moreau, Emilio. *Crónicas de Santiago de Cuba*, vols. 1–10. Santiago de Cuba: Tipografía Arroyo Hermanos, 1925.

_____. *Florencio Villanova y Pío Rosado*. Edited by Amalia Bacardi Cape. Madrid: Playor, 1972.

_____. *Hacia tierras viejas*. Valencia, Spain: F. Sempere y Compañía, 1914.

_____. *Vía crucis*. Barcelona, Spain: Imprenta Viuda de Tasso, 1914.

Bacardi U.S.A. *An Enduring Legacy* (historical pamphlet). Miami, FL: Bacardi Museum, 2000.

Ballou, Maturin M. *History of Cuba, or Notes of a Traveller in the Tropics*. Boston: Phillips, Sampson and Company, 1854.

Bardach, Ann Louise. *Cuba Confidential*. New York: Random House, 2002.

Barty-King, Hugo, and Anton Massel. *Rum: Yesterday and Today*. London: Heinemann, 1983.

Bethell, Leslie, ed. *Cuba: A Short History*. London: Cambridge University Press, 1993.

Blanco, Katiuska. *Todo el tiempo de los cedros: Paisaje familiar de Fidel Castro Ruz*. Havana: Casa Editora Abril, 2003.

Blight, James G., Bruce J. Allyn, and David A. Welch. *Cuba on the Brink: Castro, the Missile Crisis, and the Soviet Collapse*. New York: Pantheon, 1993.

Bohning, Don. *The Castro Obsession: U.S. Covert Operations Against Cuba, 1959–1965*. Washington, DC: Potomac Books, 2005.

Bonera, Miguel. *Oro blanco: Una historia empresarial del ron cubano*, vol. 1. Toronto: Lupus Libros, 2000.

Bonsal, Philip W. *Cuba, Castro, and the United States*. Pittsburgh: University of Pittsburgh Press, 1971.

Bosch, José M. *Puerto Rico: Un pueblo en superación*. San Juan, PR: Bacardi Corporation, 1963.

Broom, Dave. *Rum*. San Francisco: Wine Appreciation Guild, 2003.

Buch López, Ernesto. *Historia de Santiago de Cuba*. Havana: Editorial Lex, 1947.

Cabrera, Guillermo. "Marianito (Ron Caney) Lavigne." *Juventud Rebelde* (Havana), April 30, 1970.

Cabrera Infante, Guillermo. "El viejo y la marca." *Ciclón* 2, no. 5 (September 1956).

_____. *Mea Cuba*. New York: Farrar, Straus and Giroux, 1994.

Calvo Ospina, Hernando. *Ron Bacardi: La guerra oculta*. Havana: Casa Editorial Abril, 2000.

Campoamor, Fernando G. *El hijo alegre de la caña de azúcar: Biografía del ron*. Havana: Editorial Científico-Técnica, 1993.

Campo-Flores, Arian. "Rum Warriors." *American Lawyer*, January 2000.

Cape, Herminia. "Desde Céspedes hasta Fidel." Interview in *El pueblo cuenta su historia*, edited by Antonio Núñez Jiménez, 183–225. Havana: Gente Nueva, 1980.

Castañeda, Jorge G. *Compañero: The Life and Death of Che Guevara*. New York: Vintage Books, 1998.

Castro Ruz, Fidel. "History Will Absolve Me." Translated by Pedro Álvarez Tabío and Andrew Paul Booth. Havana: Editorial de Ciencias Sociales, 1975.

Chez Checo, José. *El ron en la historia dominicana*, vol. 1. Santo Domingo: Ediciones Centenario de Brugal, 1988.

Cirules, Enrique. *The Mafia in Havana*. Translated by Douglas E. LaPrade. New York: Melbourne, 2004.

Cosmas, Graham A. *An Army for Empire: The United States Army in the Spanish-American War*. College Station, TX: Texas A&M University Press, 1998.

Coulombe, Charles A. *Rum: The Epic Story of the Drink That Conquered the World*. New York: Kensington, 2004.

Cruz, Celia. *Celia: My Life*. New York: HarperCollins, 2004.

Curtis, Wayne. *And a Bottle of Rum: A History of the New World in Ten Cocktails*. New York: Crown, 2006.

Dávila, Arlene. *Sponsored Identities: Cultural Politics in Puerto Rico*. Philadelphia: Temple University Press, 1977.

DePalma, Anthony. *The Man Who Invented Fidel*. New York: Public Affairs, 2006.

de Quesada, Gonzalo. *Cuba's Great Struggle for Freedom*. New York: J. R. Jones, 1898.

Dorschner, John, and Roberto Fabricio. *The Winds of December*. New York: Coward, McCann & Geoghegan, 1980.

Dubois, Jules. *Fidel Castro: Rebel, Liberator, or Dictator?* New York: Bobbs-Merrill, 1959.

Dumont, René. *Cuba: Socialism and Development*. Translated by Helen R. Lane. New York: Grove, 1970.

_____. *Is Cuba Socialist?* New York: Viking, 1974.

Durand, Martha. "My Mad Romance with Bacardi the Rich Rum King, Conqueror of Women." *St. Paul Daily News* (Minnesota) and other U.S. newspapers, December, 1923–January 1924 (series).

Edwards, Jorge. *Persona Non Grata: A Memoir of Disenchantment with the Cuban Revolution*. New York: Nation Books, 1993.

Estorch, Miguel. *Apuntes para la historia sobre el terremoto que tuvo lugar en Santiago de Cuba y otros puntos el 20 de agosto de 1852*. Havana: Loreto Espinal, 1852.

Falcoff, Mark. *Cuba: The Morning After*. Washington, DC: AEI Press, 2003.

Ferrer, Ada. *Insurgent Cuba: Race, Nation, and Revolution, 1868–1898*. Chapel Hill: University of North Carolina Press, 1999.

Fleites, José M. "El ron en Cuba." *Industria Alimenticia* I, no. 1 (March 1969): 2–12.

Foner, Philip S. *A History of Cuba and Its Relations with the United States*, vols. 1 and 2. New York: International Publishers, 1962–63.

_____. *The Spanish-Cuban-American War and the Birth of American Imperialism*, vols. 1 and 2. New York: Monthly Review, 1972.

Forment, Carlos E. *Crónicas de Santiago de Cuba: Continuación de la obra de Don Emilio Bacardi*, vol. 1. Santiago de Cuba: Editorial Arroyo, 1953.

Foster, Peter. *Family Spirits: The Bacardi Saga*. Toronto: Macfarlane Walter & Ross, 1990.

Franqui, Carlos. *Diary of the Cuban Revolution*. New York: Viking, 1980.

Fuentes, Norberto. *Hemingway in Cuba*. Translated by Consuelo E. Corwin. Secaucus, NJ: Lyle Stuart, 1984.

Fursenko, Aleksander, and Timothy Naftali. *One Hell of a Gamble: Khrushchev, Castro, and Kennedy, 1958–1964*. New York: W. W. Norton, 1998.

Gallo, Samuel. *Bacardi, 1862–1962*. Nassau: Bacardi and Company, 1962.

García López, Guillermo. *El ron Bacardi: en terapeútica yi diética*. Havana: Imprenta Molina, 1934.

Geyer, Georgie Anne. *Guerrilla Prince: The Untold Story of Fidel Castro*. Kansas City: Andrews McMeel, 2001.

Goldstein, Donald M., and Katherine V. Dillon. *The Spanish-American War: The Story and Photographs*. With J. Michael Wenger and Robert J. Cressman. Washington, DC: Brassey's, 2000.

González Echevarría, Roberto. *The Pride of Havana: A History of Cuban Baseball*. New York: Oxford University Press, 1999.

Gonzalez-Pando, Miguel. *The Cuban Americans*. Westport, CT: Greenwood, 1998.

Goodman, Walter. *The Pearl of the Antilles, or An Artist in Cuba*. London: Henry S. King, 1873.

Gosch, Martin A., and Richard Hammer. *The Last Testament of Lucky Luciano*. Boston: Little, Brown, 1975.

Gott, Richard. *Cuba: A New History*. New Haven, CT: Yale University Press, 2004.

Grau, Manon. *Lucía Bacardi: Escultora cubana*. Madrid: Ediciones Beramar, 1992.

Guevara, Ernesto Che. *Escritos y discursos*, vols. 1–9. Havana: Editorial de Ciencias Sociales, 1977.

Hagedorn, Hermann. *Leonard Wood: A Biography*, vol. 1. New York: Harper & Brothers, 1931.

Heikal, Mohamed. *The Cairo Documents*. New York: Doubleday, 1973.

Heufelder, Jeanette Erazo. *Havanna Feelings: Die Magie des alten Kuba*. Bergisch Gladbach, Germany: Lübbe, 2001.

"Homenaje Póstumo a Don Emilio Bacardi." *Luz de Oriente* (Santiago de Cuba) 1, no. 6, September 1922, special memorial issue devoted exclusively to Emilio Bacardi.

Horowitz, Irving, and Jaime Suchlicki, eds. *Cuban Communism*, 9th edition. New Brunswick, NJ: Transaction Publishers, 1998.

Howe, Julia Ward. *A Trip to Cuba*. New York: Ticknor and Fields, 1890.

Ibarra, Francisco. "Don Emilio Bacardi Moreau." *El Caserón*, June 1987.

Johnson, Haynes. *The Bay of Pigs*. New York: W. W. Norton, 1964.

Karol, K. S. *Guerrillas in Power: The Course of the Cuban Revolution*. Translated by Arnold Pomerans. New York: Hill & Wang, 1970.

Kiger, Patrick J. *Squeeze Play: The United States, Cuba, and the Helms-Burton Act*. Washington, DC: Center for Public Integrity, 1997.

Kirkpatrick, Lyman B., Jr. *The Real CIA*. New York: Macmillan, 1968.

Kornbluh, Peter, ed. *Bay of Pigs Declassified: The Secret CIA Report on the Invasion of Cuba*. New York: New Press, 1998.

Latell, Brian. *After Fidel: The Inside Story of Castro's Regime and Cuba's Next Leader*. New York: Palgrave Macmillan, 2005.

Lender, Mark Edward, and James Kirby Martin. *Drinking in America: A History*. New York: Free Press, 1982.

Leyva, Armando. *Museo*. Santiago de Cuba: Tipografía Arroyo Hermanos, 1922.

López-Fresquet, Rufo. *My Fourteen Months with Castro*. New York: World, 1966.

Lowinger, Rosa, and Ofelia Fox. *Tropicana Nights: The Life and Times of the Legendary Cuban Nightclub*. Orlando, FL: Harcourt, 2005.

Luz de Oriente 1, no. 6. (special issue of quarterly magazine in honor of Emilio Bacardi). Santiago de Cuba, September 1922.

McCusker, John J. *Rum and the American Revolution*. New York: Garland, 1989.

Maingot, Anthony P. "Rum: Revolution and Globalization." Cuban Research Institute, Florida International University. Lecture presented at Biltmore Hotel, Miami, March 25, 2004.

Mañach, Jorge. *Martí: Apostle of Freedom*. Translated by Coley Taylor. New York: Devin-Adair, 1950.

Maran, Sidney M. *The World of Bacardi-Martini*. Bermuda: Bacardi Limited, n.d.

Marrero, Leví. *Cuba: Economía y sociedad*, vols. 1–15. Madrid: Playor, 1975–92.

Martí, José. *Obras Completas*, vols. 1–2. Havana: Editorial Lex, 1946.

———. "On: The Pan-American Congress." *La Nación* (Buenos Aires), December 19–20, 1889.

———. *Our America: Writings on Latin America and the Struggle for Cuban Independence*. Edited by Philip S. Foner. New York: Monthly Review, 1977.

———. *Political Parties and Elections in the United States*. Edited by Philip S. Foner. Havana: Editorial José Martí, 1988.

———. *Selected Writings*. Edited and translated by Esther Allen. New York: Penguin Books, 2002.

Matthews, Franklin. *The New-Born Cuba*. New York: Harper & Brothers, 1899.

Matthews, Herbert L. *Revolution in Cuban*. New York: Charles Scribner's Sons, 1975.

———. *The Cuban Story*. New York: George Braziller, 1961.

Meriño, María de los Ángeles. *Gobierno Municipal y Partidos Políticos en Santiago de Cuba, 1898–1912*. Ediciones Santiago, Santiago de Cuba, 2001.

Mesa-Lago, Carmelo, ed. *Cuba After the Cold War*. Pittsburgh: University of Pittsburgh Press, 1993.

———. *Market, Socialist, and Mixed Economies: Comparative Policy and Performance: Chile, Cuba, and Costa Rica*. Baltimore: Johns Hopkins University Press, 2000.

Miro, José. *Cuba: Crónicas de la guerra*, vol. 1. Havana: Editorial Lex, 1946.

Missen, François, Frane Nichele, Thierry Merle, and Jcan Baudot. *Cuba: The Legend of Rum*. Toulouse, France: Editions Bahia Presse (Havana Club Collection), n.d.

Monge, José Trías. *Puerto Rico: The Trials of the Oldest Colony in the World*. New Haven, CT: Yale University Press, 1997.

Montaner, Carlos Alberto. *Journey to the Heart of Cuba: Life as Fidel Castro*. New York: Algora, 2001.

Moreno Fraginals, Manuel. *El ingenio*, vols. 1–3. Havana: Editorial de Ciencias Sociales, 1978.

———. *The Sugarmill*. Translated by Cedric Belfrage. New York: Monthly Review, 1976.

Nelson, Lowry. *Cuba: The Measure of a Revolution*. Minneapolis: University of Minnesota Press, 1972.

Oppenheimer, Andres. *Castro's Final Hour*. New York: Simon & Schuster, 1992.

Otero, Juan Joaquín, ed. *Libro de Cuba: Una enciclopedia ilustrada*. Havana: Artes Gráficas, 1954.

Padula, Alfred. "Financing Castro's Revolution." *Revista/Review Interamericana* 8, no. 2 (summer 1978): 234–46.

———. "The Fall of the Bourgeoisie: Cuba, 1959–1961." Unpublished doctoral dissertation, University of New Mexico, 1974.

Padura Fuentes, Leonardo. "La larga vida secreta de una fórmula secreta," In *El viaje más largo*. San Juan, PR: Editorial Plaza Mayor, 2002, 136–50. Originally published in *Juventud Rebelde* (Havana), 1988.

Paquette, Robert L. *Sugar Is Made with Blood*. Middletown, CT: Wesleyan University Press, 1988.

Pardo Llada, José. *Fidel*. Bogotá: Plaza y Janés, 1976.

Paterson, Thomas G. *Contesting Cuba: The United States and the Triumph of the Cuban Revolution*. New York: Oxford University Press, 1994.

Pereira, Manuel. "Ron del bueno" (interview with Mariano Lavigne). *Cuba Internacional*, July 1970, 58–63.

Pérez, Louis A., Jr. *Cuba and the United States: Ties of Singular Intimacy*. Athens: University of Georgia Press, 1990.

———. *Cuba: Between Reform and Revolution*. New York: Oxford University Press, 1988.

———. *On Becoming Cuban: Identity, Nationality, and Culture*. New York: HarperCollins, 2001.

———, ed. *Slaves, Sugar, and Colonial Society: Travel Accounts of Cuba, 1801–1899*. Wilmington, DE: Scholarly Resources, 1992.

———. *The War of 1898: The United States and Cuba in History and Historiography*. Chapel Hill: University of North Carolina Press, 1998.

Pérez Castellón, Ninoska. *Un hombre y su tiempo: El pensamiento político de Jorge Mas Cunosa*. Miami: Cuban American National Foundation, 1998.

Pérez-Stable, Marifeli. *The Cuban Revolution: Origins, Course, and Legacy*. New York: Oxford University Press, 1994.

Phillips, R. Hart. *Cuba: Island of Paradox*. New York: McDowell, Obolensky, 1960.

Quirk, Robert E. *Fidel Castro*. New York: W. W. Norton, 1993.

Ramonet, Ignacio. *Fidel Castro: Biografía a dos voces*. Barcelona: Random House Mondadori, 2006.

Ravelo, Juan María. *La ciudad de la historia y la guerra del 95*. Havana: Ucar García, 1951.

———. *Páginas de ayer: Narraciones de Santiago de Cuba*. Manzanillo, Cuba: Editorial el Arte, 1943.

Rawson, Rev. James. *Cuba*. New York: Lane & Tippett, 1847.

Robinson, Alfred G. *Cuba and the Intervention*. New York: Longmans, Green, 1905.

Roca, José Antonio. *Recuerdos: Una autobiografía*. Oviedo, Spain: Columbres, 2000.

Roig de Leuchsenring, Emilio, ed. *El libro de Cuba: Historia, letras, artes, ciencias, agricultura, industria, comercio, bellezas naturales*. Havana: Artes Gráficas, 1925.

———. *La colonia superviva: Cuba a los veintidos años de la republica*. Havana: Siglo XX, 1925.

Schlesinger, Arthur. *A Thousand Days*. New York: Houghton Mifflin, 1965.

Speck, Mary. "Prosperity, Progress, and Wealth: Cuban Enterprise During the Early Republic, 1902–1927." *Cuban Studies* 36, 2005, 50–86.

Suchlicki, Jaime. *Cuba: From Columbus to Castro and Beyond*. Washington, DC: Brassey's, 2002.

Sweig, Julia. *Inside the Cuban Revolution: Fidel Castro and the Urban Underground.* Cambridge, MA: Harvard University Press, 2002.

Symmes, Patrick. *The Boys from Dolores: Fidel Castro's Classmates from Revolution to Exile.* New York: Pantheon Books, 2007.

Szulc, Tad. *Fidel: A Critical Portrait.* New York: William Morrow, 1986.

Taber, Robert. *M-26: The Biography of a Revolution.* New York: Lyle Stuart, 1961.

Thomas, Hugh. *Cuba: The Pursuit of Freedom.* New York: Harper & Row, 1971.

Toledo Sande, Luis. *Basket of Flames: A Biography of José Martí.* Havana: Editorial José Martí, 2002.

Torres Hurtado, Nicolás. *Orígenes de la Compañía Ron Bacardi.* Santiago de Cuba: Editorial Oriente, 1982.

Trask, David F. *The War with Spain in 1898.* Lincoln: University of Nebraska Press, 1996.

Truslow, Francis Adams (chief of Economic and Technical Mission). *Report on Cuba.* Washington, DC: International Bank for Reconstruction and Development, 1951.

Vargas Llosa, Alvaro. *El exilio indomable: Historia de la disidencia cubana en el destierro.* Madrid: Editorial Espasa Calpe, 1998.

Wallace, Caroline L. *Santiago de Cuba Before the War.* New York: F. Tennyson Neely, 1898.

Williams, Ian. *Rum: A Social and Sociable History of the Real Spirit of 1776.* New York: Nation Books, 2005.

Willoughby, Malcolm F. *Rum War at Sea.* Washington, DC: United States Coast Guard, 1964.

Wood, Eric Fisher. *Leonard Wood: Conservator of Americanism.* New York: G. H. Doran, 1928.

Wood, Leonard. "The Existing Conditions and Needs in Cuba." *North American Review* 168 (May 1899): 593–601.

_____. "The Present Situation in Cuba." *The Century Magazine* 58, no. 4 (August 1899): 639–40.

_____. "Santiago Since the Surrender." *Scribner's Magazine* 25, no. 5 (May 1899): 515–27.

Woon, Basil. *When It's Cocktail Time in Cuba.* New York: Horace Liveright, 1928.

Wurdemann, John G. F. *Notes on Cuba.* New York: Arno, 1971 (reprint of 1844 edition).

Zimmerman, Warren. *First Great Triumph: How Five Americans Made Their Country a World Power.* New York: Farrar, Straus and Giroux, 2002.

INDEX

PHOTOGRAPHIC SOURCES

Insert 1

page 1: Franklin Matthews, *The New-Born Cuba* (top); Bacardi Family Collection (bottom)

page 2: Compañía Ron Bacardi, S.A. (top); Bacardi Family Collection (bottom)

page 3: Gonzalo de Quesada and Henry Davenport Northrop, *Cuba's Great Struggle for Freedom*, 1898 (top); Valdes, Cuban Heritage Collection, University of Miami Libraries, Coral Gables, Florida (bottom)

page 4: F. D. Pagiliuchi, *Harper's Weekly*, February 19, 1898 (top); *El Libro de Cuba* (1925) (bottom)

page 5: Bacardi Family Collection (top); William Dinwiddie, Courtesy Library of Congress (bottom)

page 6: Bacardi Family Collection

page 7: *Scribner's Magazine*

page 8: Louis A. Perez, Jr., *On Becoming Cuban*, 1999

page 9: Library of Congress (top); Bacardi Family Collection (bottom)

pages 10–14: Bacardi Family Collection

page 15: Ernesto Ocaña (top); Compañía Ron Bacardi, S.A. (bottom)

page 16: Compañía Ron Bacardi, S.A.

Insert 2

page 1: Manuel R. Bustamante Photograph Collection, Cuban Heritage Collection, University of Miami Libraries, Coral Gables, Florida (top); Bacardi Family Collection (bottom)

pages 2–3: Compañía Ron Bacardi, S.A.

page 4: Author Collection (top); *El Libro de Cuba* (1953) (bottom)

page 5: Print courtesy Compañía Ron Bacardi, S.A. (top); Author Collection (bottom)

page 6: Print courtesy Compañía Ron Bacardi, S.A.

page 7: Print courtesy Compañía Ron Bacardi, S.A.

page 8. Compañía Ron Bacardi, S.A.

page 9: Vincent Muñiz, Cuban Heritage Collection, University of Miami Libraries, Coral Gables, Florida (top); Cuban Heritage Collection, University of Miami Libraries, Coral Gables, Florida (bottom)

page 10: Jose Trutie, Courtesy Teo Babún, *The Cuban Revolution* (top); Joseph Scherschel, Time & Life Pictures/Getty Images (bottom)

page 11: Copyright Robert Salas

page 12: Alberto Korda

page 13: Alberto Korda (top); *BusinessWeek* (bottom)

page 14: Bacardi Family Collection (top); Enrique Muñoz Studio (bottom)

pages 15–16: Author Collection